C2 000 0

D0270014

Where to Live in

LONDON

BIRMINGHAM LIBRARIES
DISCARD

● A Survival Handbook ●

David Hampshire & Graeme Chesters

Survival Books ● London ● England

First published 2010

All rights reserved. No part of this publication
may be reproduced, stored in a retrieval system or
recorded by any means, without prior written
permission from the author.

Copyright © Survival Books 2010
Cover photographs © Douglas_fr, Gofer & Grauzikas (🖥 www.dreamstime.com)
Illustrations and maps © Jim Watson

Survival Books Limited
9 Bentinck Street, London W1U 2EL, United Kingdom
☎ +44 (0)20-7788 7644, 🖷 +44 (0)870-762 3212
✉ info@survivalbooks.net
🖥 www.survivalbooks.net

British Library Cataloguing in Publication Data
A CIP record for this book is available
from the British Library.
ISBN: 978-1-907339-13-4

Printed and bound in India by Ajanta Offset

Acknowledgements

The authors would like to offer their sincere thanks to those who contributed to the successful publication of Where to Live in London, in particular all the London boroughs who provided information and photographs, plus Lilac Johnston (editing, research & proofreading); Peter Read and Grania Rogers (research & proofreading); and Di Tolland (research & DTP). We would like to offer a special thank you to Jim Watson for the cover design, illustrations and maps, and to the many photographers (listed on page 462), whose beautiful images add colour and bring London to life.

What Readers and Reviewers Have Said About Survival Books:

"If I were to move to France, I would like David Hampshire to be with me, holding my hand every step of the way. This being impractical, I would have to settle for second best and take his books with me instead!"

Living France

"We would like to congratulate you on this work: it is really super! We hand it out to our expatriates and they read it with great interest and pleasure."

ICI (Switzerland) AG

"I found this a wonderful book crammed with facts and figures, with a straightforward approach to the problems and pitfalls you are likely to encounter. The whole laced with humour and a thorough understanding of what's involved. Gets my vote!"

Reader (Amazon)

"Get hold of David Hampshire's book for its sheer knowledge, straightforwardness and insights to the Spanish character and do yourself a favour!"

Living Spain

"Rarely has a 'survival guide' contained such useful advice – This book dispels doubts for first time travellers, yet is also useful for seasoned globetrotters – In a word, if you're planning to move to the US or go there for a long term stay, then buy this book both for general reading and as a ready reference."

American Citizens Abroad

"It's everything you always wanted to ask but didn't for fear of the contemptuous put down – The best English language guide – Its pages are stuffed with practical information on everyday subjects and are designed to complement the traditional guidebook."

Swiss News

"A must for all future expats. I invested in several books but this is the only one you need. Every issue and concern is covered, every daft question you have but are frightened to ask is answered honestly without pulling any punches. Highly recommended."

Reader (Amazon)

"Let's say it at once. David Hampshire's Living and Working in France is the best handbook ever produced for visitors and foreign residents in this country; indeed, my discussion with locals showed that it has much to teach even those born and bred in l'Hexagone. It is Hampshire's meticulous detail which lifts his work way beyond the range of other books with similar titles. This book is absolutely indispensable."

The Riviera Reporter

"Covers every conceivable question that might be asked concerning everyday life – I know of no other book that could take the place of this one."

France in Print

"It was definitely money well spent."

Reader (Amazon)

"The ultimate reference book – Every conceivable subject imaginable is exhaustively explained in simple terms – An excellent introduction to fully enjoy all that this fine country has to offer and save time and money in the process."

American Club of Zurich

Important Note

L ondon is a huge city with many faces, numerous ethnic groups, religions and customs, added to which the UK has continuously changing rules, regulations, interest rates and prices - particularly after a change of government which the UK had in May 2010 as this book went to press. We cannot recommend too strongly that you check with an official and reliable source (not always the same) before making any major decisions or taking an irreversible course of action. However, don't believe everything you're told or read – even, dare I say it, herein!

Useful addresses, websites and references to other sources of information have been included in all chapters and in **Appendices A, B** and **C** to help you obtain further information and verify details with official sources. Important points have been emphasised **in bold print**, some of which it would be expensive, or even dangerous, to disregard. **Ignore them at your peril or cost.**

Note

Unless specifically stated, the reference to any company, organisation or product in this book doesn't constitute an endorsement or recommendation. None of the businesses, products or individuals mentioned in this book have paid to be mentioned.

Contents

7. BOROUGH SURVEYS

Authors' Notes

◆ Times are shown using am for before noon and pm for after noon. All times are local – you should check the time difference when making international telephone calls.

◆ Unless otherwise stated, prices shown usually include VAT and should be taken as estimates only, although they were mostly correct at the time of publication.

◆ His/he/him also means her/she/her (please forgive us ladies). This is done to make life easier for both the reader and the authors, and isn't intended to be sexist.

◆ All spelling is (or should be) British English and not American English. American English equivalents are sometimes shown in brackets where these differ significantly from British English words.

◆ Warnings and important points are shown in **bold** type or in 'Warning' boxes.

◆ The following symbols are used in this book: ☎ (telephone), 🖹 (fax), 💻 (Internet) and ✉ (email).

◆ Lists of **Useful Addresses, Further Reading** and **Useful Websites** are contained in **Appendices A, B** and **C** respectively.

◆ For those unfamiliar with the imperial system of **Weights and Measures**, conversion tables (imperial/metric) are included in **Appendix D**.

◆ Useful tables are included in **Appendix E**.

◆ A map of London's 32 boroughs and the City of London is shown inside the front cover and a map of the London underground network inside the back cover.

London Eye & River Thames

Introduction

L ondon is Europe's largest city and one of the most densely populated cities in the world. Greater London, the area covered by this book, is divided into 32 boroughs and the City of London, covering an area of 609mi² (1,579km²). London is Europe's most racially and culturally diverse city, and the most cosmopolitan city in the world, with residents from around the globe; a third of Londoners (some 2.5m people) were born outside Britain and between them speak over 300 languages. It's a melting pot of foreign culture and multiculturalism and almost anyone can feel at home there. In fact, London is not only what you make it, but you can make it anything your want it to be – and be anyone your heart desires. Yes, it's expensive and the weather is often lousy, but there's so much that's free and you'll enjoy the rare sunny days so much more when you know it'll be raining tomorrow…

London is one of the world's great cities, but it can be a confusing and daunting place for newcomers looking for somewhere to call home. It isn't just vast and labyrinthine, but is also chaotic. Many people are, not surprisingly, confused about where to live. North or south of the river? Is it safe in east London? What about south London? And where the hell is west London exactly? There is, of course, no perfect place for everyone, and all areas have their good and bad parts – and the 'shady' bits are often full of character (and characters). Don't worry if you can't afford to live in Chelsea, Hampstead or St Johns Wood; there are many more affordable areas, which for sheer joie de vivre, leave the more salubrious places for dead.

Whether you're already living in another part of the UK or moving from the other side óf the world (or even a different planet!), you have the key to London in your hands. Forget about those glossy guide books, excellent though they are for tourists; **Where to Live in London** (and its sister publication, **Living and Working in London**) was written especially with you in mind and is worth its weight in jellied eels. Inside is the lowdown about the best (and worst) places to live and, just as importantly, what you'll be able to afford and where!

In addition to essential information about rents and property prices, **Where to Live in London** contains a detailed survey of every borough (and the City of London) with information about the best areas to live, property and rental costs, health services, schools, crime rates, public transport, parking, shopping, entertainment, sports facilities and green spaces. In fact, everything you need to know to decide which area will suit your lifestyle and pocket. **Most importantly, it will help save you time, trouble and money, and repay your investment many times over.**

A period spent in London is a wonderful way to enrich your life, broaden your horizons, make friends and, with any luck (and some hard work), even make your fortune. We trust this book will help you find your dream home and smooth your way to a happy and rewarding stay in London, whether it's for a few months or a lifetime – enjoy!

Good luck!   *David Hampshire & Graeme Chesters*

May 2010

Houses of Parliament

1.
WELCOME TO LONDON

London is the capital city of England and the United Kingdom (it has also been dubbed 'the capital of Europe'), and is one of the world's four major global cities along with New York, Paris and Tokyo. It's the seat of the UK government and home of the British Royal Family; the UK's commercial, cultural and sports centre (it will host the 2012 Olympics); Europe's leading financial market (some would argue the world's); the 'capital' of the English-speaking world; and a world leader in advertising, architecture, the arts, fashion, film, food, music, publishing, theatre and television.

For many multinational companies and organisations, London is the only logical European base, with excellent air links to all corners of the globe; the city was built on commerce and trade. It's also a magnet for the rich and a favourite home location for the world's mega-wealthy – the international world village – and a safe place to invest with a favourable tax regime for non UK residents (so-called 'nondoms').

> 'London is not so much a city, as the world's biggest village.'
>
> G.K. Chesterton (English writer)

London is Europe's most racially and culturally diverse city, and one of the most cosmopolitan cities in the world, with residents from around the globe; one in every three Londoners (some 2.5mn people) was born outside the UK and between them they speak over 300 languages. Greater London is home to almost half the ethnic minority population of the UK – not surprisingly, it's a melting pot of foreign culture and multiculturalism, and almost anyone can feel at home there. To add to this cultural potpourri, London's resident population is swelled by some 25mn visitors a year, not to mention the hundreds of thousands of commuters from other parts of the country who flock there daily to work.

London is the UK's main employment centre, with a huge variety of career opportunities and relatively low unemployment. It's the UK's most appealing city culturally and historically with a wealth of attractions; its most racially tolerant region, where many locals don't care what you do or how you dress; has good public transport and taxi drivers who actually know where they're going; and has some of Europe's best private schools. However, in common with most capital cities, the cost of living is high and prices (particularly property) are among the highest in the world, although better salaries compensate to some extent. Like all large cities, London displays stark contrasts of wealth and poverty – it has the biggest wealth divide of any city in the western world – although few places offer such endless opportunities to make your fortune.

London's failings include rising air pollution, an ageing and over-burdened public transport system (although improving), traffic congestion (now eased by the congestion charge, and no worse than most other major cities),

substandard housing and homelessness, and over-crowding and high crime in some areas. It's a city that exhilarates and intimidates, stimulates and irritates in equal measure, a grubby metropolis studded with stellar sights; a cosmopolitan mix of First and Third Worlds, chauffeurs and beggars, the stubbornly traditional and the proudly avant-garde. However, it's the people – the good, the bad and the ugly – who make London what it is and give the city its unique character.

London is Europe's largest city and one of the most populous on earth. Greater London is made up of 32 boroughs and the City of London, covering an area of 609mi^2 (1,579km^2) with a population of around 7.5m, which is the definition of London used in this book. Historically 'London' referred to the City of London (or 'square mile'), from which the city grew, and between 1889 and 1965 was the former County of London.

London has a constantly changing population and in the last ten years has had the fastest-growing population in the UK, gaining some 300,000 more people in the last few years alone. This is despite the fact that hundreds of thousands people leave the city annually and over 2mn have left in the last ten years. However, despite the numbers who leave London each year, inward migration (mostly from abroad) helps sustain continued overall growth. The population of London is expected to increase by 700,000 by the year 2016 (source: office of the mayor of London).

ORIENTATION

The sheer size of London can be daunting to newcomers. It isn't only vast and labyrinthine, but also chaotic. Central London was originally an assortment of villages and some 250 years ago there were vast spaces between them, while the outer boroughs were largely rural farming areas just 100 years ago. Today, they've merged into an almost seamless metropolis. The growth of the surrounding parts of London accelerated in the Victorian period, when the 'suburbs' were at least partly planned. Here there's more open space and the population density is generally below 2,750 people per mi^2 (7,000 per km^2), compared with up to twice as many in central London.

Any attempt to divide London into manageable and comprehensible pieces can only be partially successful. The task is complicated by the overlap between the different artificial divisions that have been created over the years – geographical, cultural, historical, administrative and postal. The customary division of the city is marked by the River Thames, which flows from west to east through its centre, and divides it into northern and southern 'halves'. There's a widespread notion that the areas north of the river are more pleasant than those to the south, just as it's generally believed that the West End is superior to the East End. However, such generalisations often fail to stand up when you start looking at areas in detail.

'Central London' is a much-used but unofficial and vaguely defined term for the most inner part of London, for which there are many definitions, each with its own notional boundaries. All definitions share the idea that central London is smaller than, and a subset of, 'Inner London'. One of the most common (and that used in this book) is that central London includes the boroughs of Camden, the City of London, Hackney, Islington, Kensington & Chelsea, Lambeth, Southwark, Tower Hamlets and the City of Westminster.

The central area and the most important sights, theatres and restaurants are within the Underground's Circle Line on the north bank of the river. The trendy and tourist-ridden West End lies within the western portion of the loop and includes Soho, Covent Garden, Trafalgar Square, Piccadilly Circus, Leicester Square, Oxford Street and Regent Street. The East End, so beloved of Ealing comedies, lies east of the Circle Line; it used to be the exclusive preserve of the Cockney but is now a cultural melting pot. There are also interesting inner-city suburbs in North London, including Islington and Camden Town, while South London includes a mess of relatively poor suburbs, such as Brixton and Peckham, with vibrant subcultures of their own and where, in many ways, the real vitality of the city lies.

Other definitions of London used for particular purposes include the London postal districts (see below); the region within the 020 telephone area code (see page 22); the area accessible by public transport using a Transport for London Travelcard (see **Chapter 2**); the region within the M25 orbital motorway; and the London commuter belt. All of these have an influence on property prices and the attraction of an area or particular property.

> ☑ **SURVIVAL TIP**
>
> One of your first acts after arriving in London should be to buy a good street map, such as those published by the Geographers' A-Z Map Company.

Boroughs

Created in 1965, Greater London is divided into 32 boroughs and the City of London (see map) – which are the administrative areas of Greater London, which in turn is one of the 45 administrative regions (or counties) of England. Boroughs are the local authorities that raise taxes (through the council tax) and administer local services. The only exception is the City of London, which isn't run by a local authority but by the historical Corporation of London, and has certain peculiarities such as its own police force. The so-called City of Westminster, on the other hand, is a borough like any other. Two London boroughs, Kensington & Chelsea and Kingston, carry the purely honorary title of 'Royal Borough' due to their links with the monarchy.

The City of London (the 'square mile') has its own police force, and, since the Magna Carta in 1215, the monarch (i.e. HM the Queen) must still request permission to enter.

Unofficially, the boroughs are divided between 'inner London' (Camden, City of London, Greenwich, Hackney, Hammersmith & Fulham, Haringey, Islington, Kensington & Chelsea, Lambeth, Lewisham, Newham, Southwark, Tower Hamlets and Wandsworth) and 'outer London' (the remaining 19 boroughs). Inner London boroughs tend to be characterised by a huge gulf between rich and poor, and a wide racial and cultural mix. Outer London boroughs are more suburban, with swathes of green belt (areas in which building is restricted) and a predominantly white (and 'white-collar') population.

Many people still consider only the central areas to be 'proper' London, the outer areas belonging to the surrounding ('home') counties – e.g. Kingston was previously part of Surrey and Bromley was in Kent, although both towns have since given their names to London boroughs. The boroughs vary considerably in size but each has a population of between 150,000 and 350,000, with the exception of the City of London, which has just 7,800 residents.

Each borough has its own website containing a wealth of information, which can be accessed via 🖥 www.london.gov.uk. The addresses of individual sites are www.[borough name].gov.uk (e.g. 🖥 www.brent.gov.uk or www.barking-dagenham.gov.uk), with the exception of Hammersmith & Fulham (🖥 www.lbhf.gov.uk), Kensington & Chelsea (🖥 www.rbkc.gov.uk) and Waltham Forest (🖥 www.lbwf.gov.uk).

A comprehensive survey and map of each of London's 32 boroughs (plus the City of London) is contained in **Chapter 7**.

Greater London Authority

The Greater London Authority (GLA) was formed in 2000 to govern London and replaced the Greater London Council (GLC), which was abolished in 1986. It's the London-wide body responsible for co-ordinating the boroughs, strategic planning, and operating some of Greater London's services such as the Metropolitan Police Service, the London Fire Service and transport. The GLA consists of the Mayor of London (Boris Johnson, elected in 2008 – not to be confused with the Lord Mayor of the City of London, which is an honorary position for one year only) and the London Assembly, who are elected by Londoners every four years (the next elections are in 2012).

When the GLC was abolished, most of its functions were taken over by the London boroughs, while others became the responsibility of joint-boards and other unelected bodies. The boroughs thus enjoyed a high degree of autonomy when the GLC was abolished, and although they lost some of their powers when the GLA was formed, they still retain many responsibilities which they didn't have under the GLC.

The GLA is twinned and has sister city agreements with Beijing, Berlin, Moscow, New York, Paris and Tokyo.

Constituencies

The creation of the Greater London Authority grouped the boroughs into 14 constituencies (listed below). (There are other more or less arbitrary divisions: 16 health authority areas, five police regions, four ambulance service zones and three fire brigade sectors.)

Officially, each borough is also divided into 'wards' (an administrative district of a parliamentary constituency), although most residents don't know their names. Most people refer instead to districts, which in some cases don't appear on maps, but which are either named after places long since swallowed by the outward sprawl of the city or derive from contemporary 'estate agent speak' (e.g. 'Blythe Village' and 'Brackenbury Village' in the borough of Hammersmith & Fulham and 'Limehouse Village' in Docklands). In many cases, these districts straddle borough or county boundaries.

POSTCODES

The most perplexing of London's various partitions is its division into postal areas, each

Constituencies

Constituency	Boroughs
Barnet and Camden	Barnet, Camden
Bexley and Bromley	Bexley, Bromley
Brent and Harrow	Brent, Harrow
City and East London	Barking and Dagenham, City of London, Newham, Tower Hamlets
Croydon and Sutton	Croydon, Sutton
Ealing and Hillingdon	Ealing, Hillingdon
Enfield and Haringey	Enfield, Haringey
Greenwich and Lewisham	Greenwich, Lewisham
Havering and Redbridge	Havering, Redbridge
Lambeth and Southwark	Lambeth, Southwark
Merton and Wandsworth	Merton, Wandsworth
North East	Hackney, Islington, Waltham Forest
South West	Hounslow, Kingston-upon-Thames, Richmond-upon-Thames
West Central	Hammersmith and Fulham, Kensington and Chelsea, Westminster

London Postcode Areas

Included	Boroughs
Entirely	City of London, Camden, Hackney, Hammersmith & Fulham, Haringey, Islington, Kensington & Chelsea, Lambeth, Southwark, Tower Hamlets, Wandsworth, Westminster
Mostly	Greenwich, Lewisham, Newham, Waltham Forest
Partly	Barnet, Bexley, Brent, Bromley, Croydon, Ealing, Enfield, Harrow, Hounslow, Kingston-upon-Thames, Merton, Redbridge, Richmond-upon-Thames
Excluded	Barking & Dagenham, Havering, Hillingdon, Sutton

with a different 'postcode' (the equivalent of US zip codes), which seldom bear any relationship to counties, boroughs or districts.

The postcode is the most important part of any address when sending post, which, together with the house number, uniquely identifies an individual building or dwelling.

The system was designed at a time when the official London boundary was restricted to the square mile of the City of London. The area has continually expanded over the centuries and in 1965, when Greater London was created, the boundaries of Greater London extended far beyond the London postal districts. The boroughs with a London postal district are shown in the table below.

Areas in central London (an area stretching in some cases to the borders of Greater London) have postcodes beginning with W (for west), NW (north-west), N (north), E (east), SE (south-east) and SW (south-west) – there are no NE or S postcodes, which were abolished between 1866 and 1868. Those in outer London have codes relating to the nearest town where there's a main sorting office, which is in some cases a 'borough' town (e.g. BR for Bromley, CR for Croydon, EN for Enfield, HA for Harrow, KT for Kingston and SM for Sutton – although there's no M in Sutton!) and in other cases isn't (e.g. IG for Ilford in Redbridge, RM for Romford in Havering, TW for Twickenham in Richmond and UB for Uxbridge in Hillingdon).

As if all this weren't confusing enough, the numbers following the initial letter or letters of postcodes can also be misleading. Originally, the system was based on the initial letter of

each sub-district in the alphabet; a district beginning with the letter 'A' was given the number 1 and so on. Many people erroneously believe that the numbers indicate the distance from the centre of London, whereby logically the lowest numbers would be nearest the centre and the highest furthest out, which isn't usually the case. The most central districts were allocated a '1' (W1, N1, SW1, etc.) but after that the numbers were allocated in alphabetical order, so SW2 is Brixton, SW3 Chelsea, SW4 Clapham, SW5 Earls Court, and so on.

To further complicate matters, between 1968 and 1971, some 'central' London postcodes were subdivided to create new, smaller postcode districts, and gained an extra letter, e.g. part of W1 become W1H. These letters have changed in recent years – no doubt making life easier for the Post Office but (like the constant telephone number changes) costing London residents and businesses millions of pounds without improving their lives one iota. Postcodes have also been 'extended' with an additional digit and two letters (separated from the first 3 or 4 'digit' postcode by a space) – which are all unique and together with the house number uniquely identify an individual address.

You can find the postcode for any UK address via the Royal Mail website (🖳 www.postcode.royalmail.com), which also displays a map showing the location (you can also display and print a map by entering the postcode into the Multimap website – 🖳 www.multimap.com). To find property for sale by postcode,

Outer London Postcodes

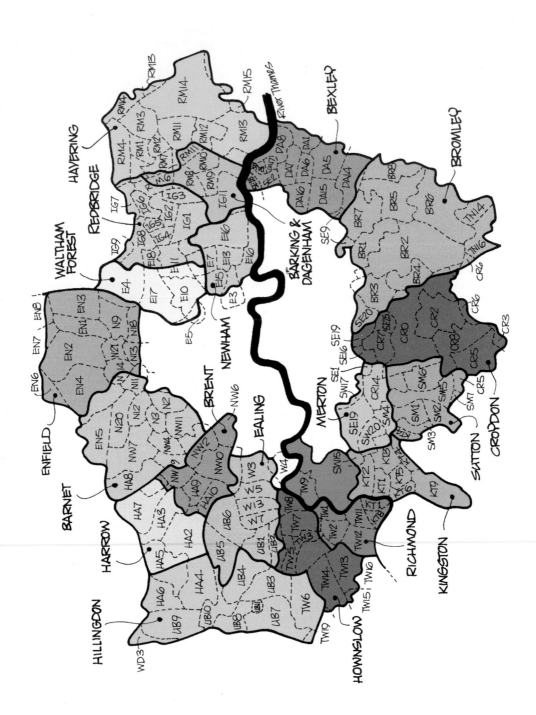

Inner London Postcodes

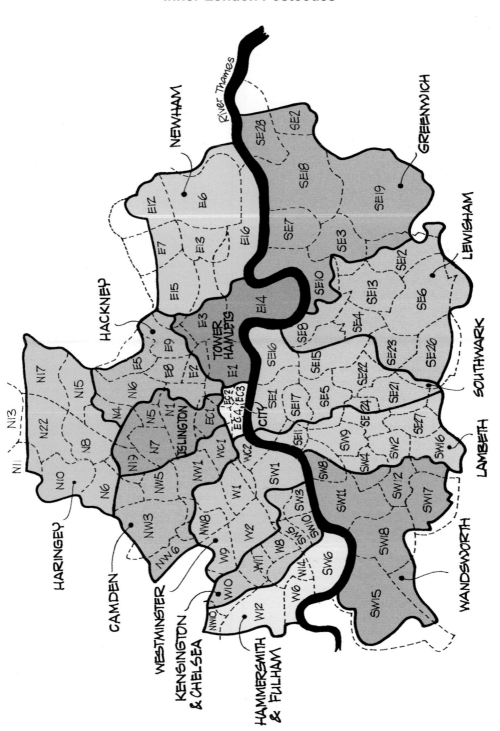

see 🖳 www.homesandproperty.co.uk/sale/london/postcode.html.

House prices in London are mainly defined by location and some people are willing to pay above the odds to acquire a home with a desirable postcode, which can inflate or reduce the value of a property. You can therefore sometimes save a great deal of money simply by buying a home on the other side of a street.

Significance

It's common to use postal districts as place names in London, particularly in the property market, where a property's location may be described as being 'in W11 or SW5'. This is especially common where a postal district is synonymous with a prestigious area but also covers other less desirable places.

Some postcodes convey a certain social status (particularly W1, SW1, SW3, NW3, W8, W11) and a 'desirable' postcode can add significantly to the value of a property, so much so that property developers and other groups sometimes lobby for postal districts to be altered. However, this is futile, as the Royal Mail only changes postcodes to facilitate the delivery of mail. (The postcode also affects insurance premiums, as insurers base their insurance rates for homes and cars on the postcode.)

A list of London postcodes and the town(s) or area(s) they cover is shown in the table below.

TELEPHONE NUMBERS

London telephone numbers were changed (unnecessarily) in 1995 and again in 1999 (to rectify the mistake made in 1995). All London numbers now have the code 020, followed by eight digits, the first of which is 7 for numbers in 'inner' London – an area which, needless to say, doesn't correspond with the geographical concept of inner London – and 8 for outer London. It's widely believed, even by Londoners, that the code for inner London is 0207 and for outer London 0208, but this isn't the case, and you can dial a number within the same area without using the 020 code, but not if the 7 or 8 is omitted.

Note that there's a certain snob appeal in having an 0207 number rather than an 0208 number.

Postcodes

E1	Whitechapel, Stepney, Mile End
E2	Bethnal Green, Shoreditch
E3	Bow, Bromley-by-Bow
E4	Chingford, Highams Park
E5	Clapton
E6	East Ham
E7	Forest Gate, Upton Park
E8	Hackney, Dalston
E9	Hackney, Homerton
E10	Leyton
E11	Leytonstone
E12	Manor Park
E13	Plaistow
E14	Poplar, Millwall, Isle of Dogs, Docklands
E15	Stratford, West Ham
E16	Canning Town, North Woolwich, Docklands
E17	Walthamstow
E18	South Woodford
EC1	Clerkenwell, Finsbury, Barbican
EC2	Moorgate, Liverpool Street
EC3	Monument, Tower Hill, Aldgate
EC4	Fleet Street, St. Paul's
N1	Islington, Barnsbury, Canonbury
N2	East Finchley
N3	Finchley Central
N4	Finsbury Park, Manor House
N5	Highbury
N6	Highgate
N7	Holloway
N8	Hornsey, Crouch End
N9	Lower Edmonton
N10	Muswell Hill
N11	Friern Barnet, New Southgate
N12	North Finchley, Woodside Park
N13	Palmers Green
N14	Southgate
N15	Seven Sisters
N16	Stoke Newington, Stamford Hill
N17	Tottenham
N18	Upper Edmonton
N19	Archway, Tufnell Park
N20	Whetstone, Totteridge
N21	Winchmore Hill
N22	Wood Green, Alexandra Palace

Postcodes (Cont.)

NW1	Regent's Park, Camden Town	SW1	Westminster, Belgravia, Pimlico
NW2	Cricklewood, Neasden	SW2	Brixton, Streatham Hill
NW3	Hampstead, Swiss Cottage	SW3	Chelsea, Brompton
NW4	Hendon, Brent Cross	SW4	Clapham
NW5	Kentish Town	SW5	Earl's Court
NW6	West Hampstead, Kilburn, Queens Park	SW6	Fulham, Parson's Green
		SW7	South Kensington
NW7	Mill Hill	SW8	South Lambeth, Nine Elms
NW8	St John's Wood	SW9	Stockwell, Brixton
NW9	Kinsbury, Colindale	SW10	West Brompton, World's End
NW10	Willesden, Harlesden, Kensal Green	SW11	Battersea, Clapham Junction
		SW12	Balham
NW11	Golders Green, Hampstead Garden Suburb	SW13	Barnes, Castelnau
		SW14	Mortlake, East Sheen
		SW15	Putney, Roehampton
SE1	Waterloo, Bermondsey, Southwark, Borough	SW16	Streatham, Norbury
		SW17	Tooting
SE2	Abbey Wood	SW18	Wandsworth, Earlsfield
SE3	Blackheath, Westcombe Park	SW19	Wimbledon, Merton
SE4	Brockley, Crofton Park, Honor Oak Park	SW20	South Wimbledon, Raynes Park
SE5	Camberwell		
SE6	Catford, Hither Green, Bellingham	W1	Mayfair, Marylebone, Soho
SE7	Charlton	W2	Bayswater, Paddington
SE8	Deptford	W3	Acton
SE9	Eltham, Mottingham	W4	Chiswick
SE10	Greenwich	W5	Ealing
SE11	Lambeth	W6	Hammersmith
SE12	Lee, Grove Park	W7	Hanwell
SE13	Lewisham, Hither Green	W8	Kensington
SE14	New Cross, New Cross Gate	W9	Maida Vale, Warwick Avenue
SE16	Rotherhithe, South Bermondsey, Surrey Docks	W10	Ladbroke Grove, North Kensington
		W11	Notting Hill, Holland Park
SE15	Peckham, Nunhead	W12	Shepherd's Bush
SE17	Walworth, Elephant & Castle	W13	West Ealing
SE18	Woolwich, Plumstead	W14	West Kensington
SE19	Upper Norwood, Crystal Palace		
SE20	Penge, Anerley	WC1	Bloomsbury, Gray's Inn
SE21	Dulwich	WC2	Covent Garden, Holborn, Strand
SE22	East Dulwich		
SE23	Forest Hill		
SE24	Herne Hill		
SE25	South Norwood		
SE26	Sydenham		
SE27	West Norwood, Tulse Hill		
SE28	Thamesmead		

London's iconic red Routemaster double-decker buses

2.

GETTING AROUND LONDON

O ne of the most important decisions regarding where to live in London is communications and being able to get around easily and relatively inexpensively. This is particularly important if you will be working in London, when you will want to be able to get from your home to your workplace as quickly and effortlessly as possible. For most people this means using public transport; owning and driving a car in London, as in most large cities, can be a liability and is expensive – and it's also usually unnecessary.

Greater London has a large and complicated transport system, with 8,451mi (13,600km) of roads, 2,317mi (3,730km) of bus routes, 204mi (329km) of tube lines, 15mi (28km) of tramways and 490mi (788km) of national rail lines. Every day over 27mn journeys are made on this transport network, of which 8.5m are made on public transport, 11mn by car or motorcycle, 7mn on foot and 300,000 by bicycle.

Transport is one of the four areas of policy administered by the Mayor of London, through Transport for London (TfL, 🖥 www.tfl.gov.uk). London's public transport network is the most expensive to use in the world (three times the cost of New York and Sydney, and six times that of Athens), and faces serious congestion and reliability issues as a result of decades of neglect by central government. However, it's currently undergoing a £10bn, five-year improvement programme, particularly London Underground and the Docklands Light Railway, which has taken on a further significance (and priority) with London hosting the 2012 Olympic Games. In the last few years London has seen a huge improvement in bus services and reduced traffic congestion (thanks in large part to the congestion charge – see page 39).

Public transport improvements – such as the East London Line rail extension (see page 27)

and Crossrail (see page 33) – can have a huge impact on property values. If you're planning to buy property in London as an investment, it's wise to check out the major planned or proposed schemes (see 🖥 www.tfl.gov.uk or 🖥 www.alwaystouchout.com).

☑ SURVIVAL TIP

One of the top tips when buying property is to follow the transport network, whether it's a new railway, tube or tramline (or a new station or intersection), or a new motorway or other fast road.

PUBLIC TRANSPORT

London has a comprehensive public transport system encompassing suburban trains, underground (tube) trains, trams, buses, river ferries and taxis. Most services are integrated and one ticket usually allows you to use the tube, buses and overground trains. The network is divided into concentric pricing zones, where zone 1 is the central area and zone 6 the outlying areas (there are also a few tube and overground stations in zones 7 to 9).

Getting around London by tube, train and tram (where it operates) is relatively fast and convenient, whereas travel by bus or car can be slow due to traffic congestion. However, although using public transport is usually a better option than attempting to get around by car, both from a convenience and environmental standpoint, services are often stretched to breaking point, particularly during peak hours and the summer tourist season. Tube users also have to put up with never-ending 'engineering works', which often shut down lines and curb travel, particularly at weekends.

It's also relatively easy to get around central London by bicycle (although you will need a smog mask) or moped/scooter or even on foot, particularly in the central area which is surprisingly compact. However, you will need a good street map, such as those published by the Geographers' A-Z Map Co.

The umbrella organisation for London transport is Transport for London (TFL), which has an excellent website (🖥 www.tfl.gov.uk), including a useful journey planner (🖥 www.journeyplanner.tfl.gov.uk). A wealth of information about public transport is also published by borough councils, local transport authorities and transport companies, many of which you will find mentioned in the relevant section in this chapter.

FARES

Despite more people using public transport in London than in any other European city – it has the world's largest rail and tube network – the city also has the most expensive public transport of any capital city in Europe, with basic (cash) fares two to four times higher than in most other major European cities. Public transport is, however, cheaper if you're able to take advantage of the wide range of discount, combination (e.g. rail, bus and underground), season and off-peak tickets available.

For the purposes of public transport, London is divided into six main concentric fare zones stretching 12mi (19km) from the centre (there are a few stations in outlying areas, mainly on the Metropolitan tube line, designated as zones 7 to 9). The central area is designated zone 1, while the outer suburbs are in zone 6, and ticket prices depend on how many zones you travel through. You can buy a ticket for a single

or day return trip, although a Travelcard provides better value if you're planning to use public transport extensively. Travelcards offer unlimited travel for one day, seven days, one month or one year, and are valid on the underground (tube), the Docklands Light Railway (DLR), buses and many suburban trains.

If you're travelling into central London by rail, your ticket can include a Travelcard supplement so that you can use it for onward travel on the tube and buses. If you want a Travelcard for seven days or more (called a Seasonal Travelcard) or a child rate ticket for a child aged under 17, you need a free 'photocard', for which a passport-size photograph and proof of age are required for children.

Oyster Card

If you don't need a season ticket, one of the most convenient and cheapest ways to use London's public transport is with an Oyster Card, which offers discounts of over 50 per cent compared with single-journey tickets, e.g. a zone 1 tube journey costs £1.80 with an Oyster Card, compared with £4 when you pay cash. Pre-pay Oyster Cards don't need to be registered (you pay a refundable £3 deposit) but can be used like a debit card (you can store up to £90) on the tube, DLR, buses and Tramlink services. There's no queuing for tickets or hunting for change for machines and you simply touch your card on the card readers at tube and DLR stations, on buses and at tram stops.

You can obtain an Oystercard at some 4,000 Oyster ticket stops; at tube and overground rail stations; at some National Rail stations; at London Travel Information Centres; and online at the TfL website (🖥 www.tfl.gov.uk). You can also buy an Oyster Card abroad via the Visit Britain Direct website (🖥 www.visitbritaindirect.com).

If you're aged 60 or over or have an eligible disability and are a permanent London resident, you can apply for a Freedom Pass from your borough council. This entitles you to **free** travel on all London's public transport, including buses, tube, trains, Docklands Light Railway and trams. Enquire at your borough council offices or visit the Freedom Pass website (💻 www.freedompass.org).

It pays to have auto top-up for your Oyster Card, which automatically tops up your card by £20 or £40 (you decide) when the credit balance falls below £5. This can be set up online at 💻 www.//oyster.tfl.gov.uk.

When using an Oyster Card, always ensure that your card has registered the payment, e.g. when using buses – a beep indicates that you have insufficient funds on your card and you must pay the driver or get off at the next stop and buy a ticket. Inspectors frequently board buses to check tickets and card payments, and if you're discovered not to have paid you must pay a penalty fare of of £50 (£25 if paid within 21 days) or face prosecution (the inspector decides).

UNDERGROUND RAIL (TUBE)

The London underground (tube) system is the oldest (parts of it have been around since the 1860s) and largest in the world, with some 500 trains and over 270 stations handling over 3mn passenger journeys a day. Given the congestion above ground, London without its tube would be unthinkable and it's easily the fastest and most convenient way to get around the city and its suburbs (provided stations and lines aren't closed for engineering work – an increasing occurrence in recent years, particularly at weekends). Outside the central areas (and even within some of them) trains actually run above ground – something which, not surprisingly, many first-time visitors to the city find confusing.

In most European countries, an underground rail system is called a metro system, while in the US it's the subway. In London the underground vernacular is the 'tube' – a term derived from the tube-shaped tunnels through which the trains run under the city.

Although most Londoners criticise the tube service, it's nowhere near as bad as some people would have you believe. Despite hot, sticky and airless conditions in some older parts of the network (most trains aren't air-conditioned, although it's planned), there are other areas, such as the recently opened Jubilee Line extension to Greenwich, which are clean, efficient and air-conditioned. After years of neglect, the entire tube network is currently undergoing a transformation, which involves rebuilding or updating the signals, tracks, stations and trains.

The East London Line was closed in December 2007 for a major extension and will become part of the London Overground network (see 💻 www.tfl.gov.uk/assets/downloads/london-overground-network-map.pdf), linking up with the North London Line (see page 32). The northern extension will run from a new Shoreditch High Street station as far as Dalston Junction (2010) and on to Highbury & Islington (2011), via Hoxton, Haggerston, Dalston Junction and Canonbury. The southern extension (south of the river) will link with existing overground lines to provide services to West Croydon (2010), with a further extension proposed from Surrey Quays via Peckham Rye to Clapham Junction. Further details of the scheme can be found at 💻 www.ellp.co.uk or www.tfl.gov.uk.

Tube Network

Free maps of the tube network are available at stations, Travel Information Centres and from Transport for London (☎ 020-7222 1234, 💻 www.tfl.gov.uk/tube). The award-winning tube map (see inside back cover) is a model of clarity and the system is easy to understand. The network has 11 separate lines (strictly speaking, the DLR – see above – is classed as part of the tube network), each of which is colour-coded on the tube map, e.g. yellow for the Circle Line, green for the District Line, red for the Central Line and so on. This makes it easy to follow your route and find your way to the correct platform (although you need to know whether you're travelling north, south, east or west in order not to catch a train going in the opposite direction!). Some larger stations have electronic route planners where you input the name of your destination station and the shortest route is displayed.

Although the tube is most widely used in the centre of the city, where it provides a useful alternative to fighting your way through London traffic, it also includes extensive coverage of the suburbs to the north, east and west of the city. There are fewer lines and stops south of the River Thames, where commuters tend to use the overground rail network. The tube operates for some 20 hours a day, from around 5am until 00.30 or 1am – it varies with the day of the week, the station and the line (there are proposals to extend this so that the last trains leave the West End at 1am).

▲ Caution

Smoking isn't permitted anywhere on the tube network (including stations) and drinking alcohol has been banned since June 2008 on the tube and all other forms of London public transport.

Stations & Tickets

A typical tube station has an entrance above ground, indicated by the Transport for London 'bull's eye' logo of a red circle with a horizontal line through the middle.

Unlike on some other systems (such as New York) you don't have to worry about which direction you're travelling when accessing a station, as all stations have access to trains travelling in all directions and to all connecting lines.

You can buy tickets from machines and from ticket windows at most stations. Most machines provide change and if a machine runs out of change it will display a message telling you to deposit the exact fare. It's wise to carry some

change when travelling on the tube, as queues at ticket windows in central London can be long (or preferably buy a multi-ride/season ticket or an Oyster Card and never have to queue for a ticket!).

Like all London's public transport, the tube network is divided into fare zones. The city centre is designated zone 1, while the outer suburbs are mostly in zone 6 (a few stations on the Metropolitan line are in zones 7 to 9). A basic adult single cash fare starts at £3.50 (excluding zone 1) and increases depending on the number of zones and whether the journey includes zone 1; a single journey that includes zone 1 (up to zone 4) costs £4. A one-day Travelcard for zones 1 and 2 costs £7.20 during peak times (Monday to Friday from 7am and before 7pm), £5.60 off-peak (all other times) and £16.20 for all 9 zones (£9.00 off-peak).

Three-day, seven-day, monthly and annual Travelcards are also available and offer better value if you're going to be using the system extensively. You can limit a Travelcard to specific zones if your journey won't cover the whole network and it can also be used on the DLR, buses and many overground trains (including National Rail).

Most central London stations have automatic ticket barriers that speed up the flow of passengers from the concourse to the platforms. Once you have your ticket, insert it into the slot on the front of the machine. It will pop out at the top and as you remove it the gates open to let you through. If you have an Oyster Card (see page 26) just touch it on the sensor and the barrier will open. If you have a problem, there's usually a member of staff nearby to help, who also operates special wide gates for wheelchair users and those with children in pushchairs and bulky baggage.

Don't risk travelling without a ticket or without using an Oyster Card, as prosecution for fare evasion can result in a large fine and possibly a criminal record.

Once through the barrier, access to platforms is via escalators or lifts, although some stations have stairs only. Escalators can be tricky if you have young children with you, so fold pushchairs before you start and take extra care. Stand on the right (this dates back to the design of the original escalators) – those in a hurry (half of London) like to stampede

Keep a tight hold on your valuables. The District Line is the busiest, although the shorter Victoria Line carries more passengers per mile, with Victoria and Oxford Circus the two busiest stations on the network.

At quiet times, tube travel can be moderately relaxing, provided you keep an eye on the frequent stops and don't miss your destination or interchange point. Each carriage has seats, although priority should be given to the elderly, pregnant, disabled or those laden with children or heavy bags. If you don't have a seat, it's wise to hang on tight, as trains can hurtle through twisting tunnels at an alarming rate and it's easy to find yourself tumbling into the lap of a surprised stranger. There are plenty of rails to hold on to, as well as handles or 'straps' that dangle from the ceiling for support.

If you have small children with you, keep a firm grip on them, as it's easy to become separated in the crush on a train or platform. You should also stand well back from the platform edge.

If you stand too close to the edge of the platform, it's possible to fall or be pushed onto the live rail or under the wheels of an approaching train (the wind in the stations can be surprisingly strong because trains force pockets of air along the tunnels). New lines, such as the Jubilee line, have protective barriers between passengers and tracks, although there are no plans to upgrade stations on older lines. When you arrive at your destination, follow the directions to the exit. In central London you will probably have to negotiate more escalators or lifts and another set of automatic barriers. If a single ticket has expired the machine will retain it.

past you on the left – and if necessary hold the moving handrail at the side. If you have young children, you may need to help them to jump on and off at the right moment. Note that stiletto heels and long skirts can be dangerous on escalators, so take care.

Once safely at the bottom of the lift or escalator, make sure that you're following the signs to the right line in the right direction, e.g. Northern Line south-bound or Piccadilly Line west-bound. There are electronic displays on platforms that indicate the time until the next train and its destination. Note that on many lines, trains can have more than one destination on the same line (i.e. a number of branches) and some trains terminate before the end of the line. Train doors usually open and shut automatically, although you may need to press a button near the door to open them.

Travelling by Tube

The tube system can be very crowded, particularly during peak hours (around 8 to 9.30am and 5 to 6.30pm, Mondays to Fridays). It's wise to avoid these times if possible. Standing in a train that's packed to the gills can be an uncomfortable and claustrophobic experience, and congested platforms and trains are a haven for pickpockets and gropers.

Tube Information

Transport for London (TFL) centres provide extensive information about the tube network (plus bus services and the DLR). TFL centres are located throughout central London at Euston, King's Cross, Liverpool Street, Oxford Circus, Piccadilly Circus, Victoria, and St James's Park rail/tube stations and Hammersmith Bus Station (plus Heathrow Airport). Business hours vary, but there's also a 24-hour hotline (☎ 020-7222 1234) and a recorded information line (☎ 020-7222 1200).

Transport for London publishes a booklet about facilities for disabled passengers called *Access to the Underground*, available free from ticket offices or from TFL's special Unit for Disabled Passengers (☎ 020-7941 4600, ✉ access&mobility@tfl.gov.uk). The book *Access in London* (Bloomsbury) provides details of the most accessible tube stations and step-free routes for wheelchairs.

The internet positively pulsates with tube-related websites, both official (e.g. 💻 www.tfl.gov.uk) and enthusiastically amateur; one of the best is Annie Mole's cult blog Going Underground (💻 www.goingunderground.net).

BUSES

When you mention London buses, most people immediately conjure up the image of the old Routemaster buses: bright red double-deckers with a roving conductor or 'clippie' and a rear platform where you could hop on and off. Sadly for many, the last Routemaster buses were taken out of service on 9th December 2005 and replaced with cheaper-to-operate, one-man buses. With conductor-less buses, you board at the front and pay the driver, so the new buses also tend to be slower – it's wise to have the correct change ready, which on some buses is mandatory. The new buses have step-free access, ramps, special areas for wheelchairs and space for unfolded pushchairs, making them the most accessible buses in the world.

Double-decker buses can be one of the most pleasurable and scenic ways to get around the capital (or out to the suburbs), provided you don't try to do it during the rush hour when progress can be painfully slow and it may be quicker to walk (seriously). Fares are reasonable, with a single cash fare costing £2 peak or £1.20 with an Oyster Card (see page 26). Most bus routes accept Travelcards (see page 26) or you can buy a daily, weekly or monthly pass that's valid for any number of travel zones. A one-day adult pass costs £3.90 and allows travel on buses and trams anywhere in London. Children aged under 16 travel free on buses and trams.

To catch a bus, first find a bus stop (a roadside concrete post with a red sign at the top) on the correct side of the road for the direction in which you want to travel. Many are

request stops, which means you need to put your arm out to hail the bus as it approaches, otherwise it won't stop. There are many different routes serving the same stops, so check the front of the bus for its destination or route number, or study the bus routes by picking up a free bus map and timetable from a Travel Information Centre. Alternatively, you can buy a bus map; the Greater London Bus Map series (💻 www.busmap.co.uk) is highly rated.

The regular red bus service operates from 6am until midnight, after which a restricted night bus service comes into operation on some routes. These buses have numbers prefixed with the letter 'N' (most routes radiate out from Trafalgar Square); they run approximately every hour and journeys cost the same as day buses: £2 cash or £1.20 with an Oyster Card. You can also use Travelcards (see above) on night buses. Night bus route maps are available on the Transport for London website (💻 www.tfl.gov.uk/gettingaround/1110.aspx - click on night bus maps).

The outer suburbs of London within a 40mi (64km) radius are served by Green Line buses (☎ 0844-801 7261, 💻 www.greenline.co.uk), most of which leave from Victoria Coach Station in Eccleston Street, SW1. Travelcards can be used on some Green Line bus services.

Further information about London's bus services can be obtained from Transport for London (☎ 020-7918 4300, 💻 www.tfl.gov.uk/buses).

OVERGROUND RAIL NETWORK

The British railway system is the world's oldest, but has been the subject of controversy, scandal and tragedy in recent decades. Privatised in 1996, the service went from boom (two years later) to bust when, in 2001, the operating company, Railtrack, went into liquidation with debts of £700m. It also suffered several fatal crashes as a result of poor maintenance and inept management. The new not-for-profit operator, Network Rail, has inherited something of a poisoned chalice, with unreliable services and an infrastructure badly in need of renovation. Network Rail owns the infrastructure but the trains are operated by a number of regional companies.

There isn't a clear distinction between 'mainline' rail services between major cities and local services, and a train company may offer either or both services on its routes. Suburban or local trains stop at most stations along their routes, while long-distance trains are express services that stop only at major towns and often include first or 'executive' class carriages.

While it's usually possible to buy a meal on long-distance trains, either in a restaurant car or from a buffet, suburban trains usually offer only a snack trolley service or nothing at all. Toilets are provided on trains on all but the shortest services and smoking is banned on all British trains.

Travel during peak periods is best avoided, when packed trains (often standing room only) can be a nightmare for those commuting into central London from the suburbs and provinces.

Suburban Trains

London's suburban rail network is largely concentrated to the south of the city, where the underground service terminates (or there are

Railway Network

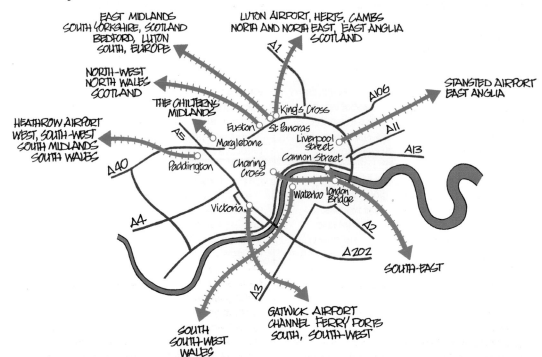

London Mainline Stations

Station	Region(s) Served	Train Operators	Information
Cannon St	south-east	South Eastern Trains	☎ 0871-200 4927
Charing Cross	south-east	South Eastern Trains	☎ 0871-200 4929
Euston	north-west, north Wales, Scotland	Silverlink, Virgin Trains	☎ 0871-200 4938
Kings Cross	Herts., Cambs., Luton airport, north and north-east, East Anglia, Scotland	Great North Eastern Railways (GNER), Wagn	☎ 0871-200 4959
Liverpool St	Stanstead airport, East Anglia	Anglia Railways, Wagn, First Great Eastern,	☎ 0871-200 4955
London Bridge	south-east	South Eastern Railway	☎ 0871-200 4952
Marylebone	the Chilterns	Chiltern Railways	☎ 0871-200 4969
Paddington	Heathrow airport, west, south-west, south Midlands, south Wales, Scotland	Arriva, First Great Western, Heathrow Express, Thames Trains	☎ 0871-200 4972
St Pancras	east Midlands, south Yorkshire	Eurostar, Midland Mainline	☎ 0871-200 4977
Victoria	Gatwick airport, Channel Ferry ports, south, south-west	Gatwick Express, South Eastern Trains,	☎ 0871-200 4984
Waterloo	south, south-west, Wales	South Central Trains, South Eastern Trains, South West Trains	☎ 0871-200 4992

no services), although there are also suburban services to the east, north and west of the city. Most lines are used by commuters in south-east England, from where hundreds of thousands of workers travel into London on weekdays.

The rail companies serving London stations (see map) are listed above.

Links to the websites of regional rail operators can be found on the Network Rail website (💻 www.networkrail.co.uk), which contains timetables for all mainline services nationwide.

Cross-London Trains

London is the hub of most long-distance rail travel in the UK, although there are only a few cross-London overground rail services; in most cases if you want to cross London by rail, you must make your way between stations by underground, bus or taxi. There are currently three cross-London train services connecting North and South London, which are listed below. A number of others are planned or have been proposed, including Crossrail (see below), City Tram and Cross River Transit (see page 36), and the East London Line Project (see page 27).

North London Line: the route of the North London Line runs from Richmond in South London to Stratford in East London, following a rough semicircle from the southwest to the northeast, avoiding central London. It serves the following stations: Richmond, Kew Gardens, Gunnersbury, South Acton, Acton Central, Willesden Junction, Kensal Rise, Brondesbury Park, Brondesbury, West Hampstead, Finchley Road & Frognal, Hampstead Heath, Gospel Oak, Kentish Town West, Camden Road, Caledonian Road

& Barnsbury, Highbury & Islington, Canonbury, Dalston Kingsland, Hackney Central, Homerton, Hackney Wick and Stratford.

The line was closed in February 2010 between Gospel Oak and Stratford for upgrading, with re-opening planned for 1st June 2010. After the re-opening work will continue until May 2011 with a reduced service and none on Sundays.

The line is planned to join up with the former East London Line (now closed for upgrading) at Highbury & Islington in February 2011 and become part of the London Overground network (🖳 www.tfl.gov.uk/assets/downloads/london-overground-network-map.pdf) operated by Transport for London. By joining together the North and East London Railways a new orbital rail artery around the city will be created, serving 20 boroughs. See also East London Line on page 33 (before Tube Network).

South Central Line: The South Central Line runs from Watford in Hertfordshire, just north of London, to Brighton and other towns in the south-east via Harrow & Wealdstone and Kensington north of the river, and Clapham Junction and Croydon south of the river. This line is now part of the London Overground network (see above).

Thameslink: This service, which dates from 1989 when the Snow Hill Tunnel under central London was re-opened, has two lines. One runs from Bedford (Bedfordshire) to Brighton on the south coast via Luton and Gatwick airports and serves King's Cross, Farringdon, City, Blackfriars and London Bridge in central London, and East Croydon in the borough of Croydon. The other line runs from Luton and Luton Airport to Sutton, serving the same London stations listed above (except London Bridge) plus Mill Hill, Hendon, Cricklewood, West Hampstead and Kentish Town north of the river, and numerous stations south of the river including Elephant & Castle, Streatham, Wimbledon, South Merton, Morden, Sutton and Mitcham. For train information, see (🖳 www.firstcapitalconnect.co.uk).

A major (and much delayed) upgrade to Thameslink, the north-south rail link through London, started in 2007 but isn't expected to be completed until 2015. Luton Airport Parkway station is being extended and will link up with a new station at St Pancras (St Pancras Midland Road) and Eurostar services to Europe. The upgrade will benefit rail passengers across the south-east and result in a doubling of capacity.

Crossrail: London's biggest project, Crossrail, will have a new railway tunnel between Paddington & Whitechapel, enabling suburban trains to travel from Heathrow and Maidenhead in the west to Canary Wharf, Shenfield and Abbey Wood in the east. The scheme has a budget of £16bn and has been approved; preliminary work started in 2009 and the line is scheduled for completion in 2017 (but don't hold your breath). The core of the Crossrail scheme is the tunnel connecting the line into Paddington in the west to the lines out of Liverpool St in the east. Central London stations are proposed at Bond Street, Tottenham Court Road and Farringdon. The main towns that will benefit from Crossrail include Abbey Wood, Hanwell, Hayes, Southall, Stratford and West Drayton. For more information, see 🖳 www.crossrail.co.uk.

Tickets

Although a number of companies may be involved, you can buy 'through' tickets to stations on a different company's network; the price shouldn't vary, irrespective of where you purchase your ticket, although individual train companies sometimes offer reduced fares on their own routes. Depending on the special offers available, you may obtain a better deal by purchasing separate tickets for different 'legs' of a long journey.

A 1,700-mile (2,736km) first class return train journey from Newquay (Cornwall) to the remote Scottish fishing village of Kyle of Lochalsh cost £1,002 in 2009 when purchased on the day of travel (£561 when bought in advance).

There's a bewildering array of discount tickets available, including child and youth discounts (up to 25 years of age), family and group tickets, and discounts for the over-60s (known as 'seniors') and the disabled, as well as special holiday and advance purchase excursion (Apex) tickets. Some tickets require the purchase of an annual 'railcard', which entitles you to discounts each time you buy a ticket. If you're a regular train traveller, you can buy a weekly, monthly or annual (point-to-point) season ticket, for which you need a passport-size photo.

Travelcards (see page 26) are valid on London suburban trains and you can purchase a Network Railcard for £25 a year that provides discounts on most fares in London and the south-east of England. You may also be eligible for a Family & Friends, Senior or 16-25 Railcard (all £26 per year), which provide a discount of one-third off normal adult fares (see www.railcard.co.uk). There's also a Disabled Persons Railcard costing £18 per year (one-third discount).

Information about tickets is available from information and ticket offices at stations. To check timetables, book tickets and obtain other information, you can consult the Network Rail website (www.networkrail.co.uk) or go to www.nationalrail.co.uk, 'the gateway to the UK's national rail network', operated by the Association of Train Operating Companies. Alternatively you can visit www.thetrainline.com, run by the Trainline Rail Enquiry Service and Trainline.com – wholly owned subsidiaries of Trainline Holdings, which is owned by travel groups Virgin Group Investments and Stagecoach Group.

If you're planning a long journey by train, bear in mind that buying a ticket doesn't guarantee you a seat on any particular train unless it's specifically reserved. If you know what time you plan to travel, it's recommended to reserve a seat, particularly during holiday periods and at weekends.

Station Facilities

Most main railway stations have restaurants, buffets and snack bars, although the quality of food may leave a lot to be desired and can also be expensive. Smaller stations sometimes have vending machines for snacks, sweets and drinks. A majority of train stations have toilet facilities (sometimes for a fee – usually 20p) and many have baby changing facilities. All stations have payphones, most of which accept credit/debit cards and coins, and most larger stations provide photo booths. Some larger stations have a First Class Lounge for passengers with first-class tickets, which usually have internet terminals, televisions and lounge and shower facilities.

▲ Caution

Car parking is provided at most country and suburban stations, although there's a high level of theft of (and from) cars parked at railway stations, so don't leave your belongings on the back seat.

Many stations and airports have luggage lockers or 'left luggage' offices and you can usually find a trolley to wheel your bags around; porters are rare these days and lifts aren't provided at many stations.

There are shops at most central London stations, and some have extensive shopping centres with banking facilities; Liverpool Street station is particularly well supplied with shops and other services, as is the new St Pancras International station.

Disabled Passengers

Wheelchairs are available at major railway stations and most trains have facilities for their storage. Special arrangements can be made for disabled or mobility-impaired passengers when travelling by train, e.g. station staff can usually help passengers on and off trains, but cannot lift disabled passengers or heavy items such as mobility scooters.

DLR

When booking a journey, disabled passengers should provide as much information as possible regarding their needs. On services with seat reservations, you can reserve a seat or wheelchair space without charge (ramps are provided at stations). Most trains can accommodate wheelchair users and new trains also have facilities to assist sensory impaired people, for example public information systems that are both visual and audible. Ramps for disabled access are provided at train stations, but you must ensure that you give staff sufficient time to help you.

Transport for London operates an 'Assisted Travel' scheme – see their website for information (🖳 www.tfl.gov.uk/modalpages/2669.aspx).

TRAMS & LIGHT RAIL SYSTEMS

The most recent development in London's transport system has been the introduction of 'light rail' systems, sometimes comprising trams, which are making a comeback in the UK after the original pre-war systems were abandoned in the 20th century. Familiar to Americans as 'transits' or 'streetcars', these systems are different from traditional railways. Short trains or 'trams' run as single or articulated units on tracks laid along streets, in cuttings or on elevated platforms. They usually stop more frequently than conventional trains, even where there's no driver. Fuel-efficient (they're electrically powered), quiet and non-polluting, they also help to reduce traffic congestion on London's busy roads.

London's two main light rail systems are the DLR, serving East London, and Tramlink, serving South London (see below).

Docklands Light Railway (DLR)

The DLR was one of the first success stories of the light rail revival. Treated as part of the underground network (see below) with regard to fares, the DLR covers the whole Docklands area and beyond, from Tower Gateway to Beckton, Stratford to the Isle of Dogs, Greenwich and Lewisham. It's also an excellent way to see some of the most interesting parts of London, where old meets new in a redeveloped and regenerated landscape. London's docks were once the busiest port in the world, but now they're home to many of London's workers and to industries such as the UK's major newspapers, which moved from Fleet Street to Canary Wharf in the '80s.

The DLR has three lines: the Red line running from north to south, the Green line running from east to west, and the Beckton line starting at Poplar station and running 5mi (8km) to the east. Unusually for light rail systems, the DLR uses modern station designs with high level platforms. The trains are driver-less and remotely operated from the permanently-staffed control centre situated at Poplar. Facilities for disabled passengers are excellent, with all stations having wheelchair access. Most stations are also unmanned, although they're equipped with closed-circuit TV for security purposes. Like underground stations, all DLR platforms are equipped with screens that display trains' destinations and their arrival times.

The DLR network links with both the main overground railway system and the tube, and a number of extensions are under construction or proposed. The Woolwich Arsenal extension in 2009 linked Woolwich Arsenal, to the south of the river, with the King George V station in North Woolwich. A new Stratford International (a Eurostar station) DLR extension is due to open in summer 2010 with new stations at Star Lane, Abbey Road, Stratford High Street and Stratford International. There's also a proposed extension to Dagenham Dock.

Information about the DLR is available from DLR Customer Service (☎ 020-7363 9700 and via the internet (💻 www.tfl.gov.uk/dlr), where there's a map of the network.

Tramlink

Tramlink (formerly called Croydon Tramlink) is a light rail system in South London which began operating in 2000. It connects New Addington and Addington Village on one line and Beckenham Junction, Birbeck and Elmers End on another – situated in the east of the borough of Croydon – with Wimbledon in the borough of Merton (via East and West Croydon and Mitcham Junction). New stops and extensions are planned or under proposal, including Hattington Road to Crystal Palace (proposed completion date 2013); Sutton to Wimbledon; Sutton to Tooting; Streatham to Purley; and Crystal Palace to Beckenham Junction/Croydon.

Tramlink has been incredibly successful in one of London's most congested regions, so much so that trams are often packed and passengers waiting at stops are unable to board! True to form, a number of planned and much-needed extensions have been delayed or cancelled. However, TFL did make one important decision: to repaint the trams in a fetching combination of lurid lime green, white and blue.

Further details and a map of the system (now operated by Transport for London) can be found on 💻 www.tfl.gov.uk.

Other Proposed Light Rail Systems

A number of other light rail systems are in the pipeline or have been proposed and are in various stages of planning, including the following:

♦ **City Tram:** A proposed light rail system running from Battersea to Hackney via Vauxhall, Elephant & Castle, Borough High Street, Bishopsgate and Shoreditch (💻 www.lrta.org/london-citytram.html).

♦ **Cross River Transit:** A proposed light rail system expected to operate from King's Cross and Camden via Euston, Holborn and Waterloo to Peckham and Brixton; the scheme is still being planned but is expected to be completed by 2016 (💻 www. lrta.org/london-Xriver.html).

♦ **Hounslow Tram Project:** A proposed tram system aimed at relieving increased traffic congestion caused by Heathrow airport's Terminal 5 (see page 46), running from the airport to Hammersmith and possibly to Kingston (see 💻 www.lrta.org/london-Hounslow.html).

For further information see the Light Rail Transit Association website (💻 www.lrta.org), which provides everything you could ever want to know about light rail systems.

RIVER FERRIES

One method of getting around London that's often overlooked is river transport. If your daily route to and from work follows the line of the River Thames, it's a pleasant (but relatively expensive) way to travel, although most services don't operate in winter. However, in order to have broader appeal and be a real alternative to other forms of public transport, the service needs to be more extensive, operate more frequently, be cheaper and operate all year round.

London River Transport Services

London River Services/LRS (☎ 020-7941 4500, 🖳 www.tfl.gov.uk/modalpages/2648.aspx) is a subsidiary of Transport for London, which aims to develop river passenger transport by providing new river piers and boat services. To this end, LRS has recently acquired seven piers: Bankside, Embankment, Greenwich, Temple, Tower, Waterloo (formerly Festival) and Westminster. It's also building a new pier at Blackfriars. Other piers on the river are in private or local government ownership. Its river taxi services include those listed below. Travelcard (see page 26) holders qualify for a one-third discount off most fares and Freedom Pass holders (see page 27) receive a 50 per cent discount.

The following commuter river services operate all year round:

◆ **Embankment-Woolwich:** Daily service stopping at most piers between the Embankment and Woolwich Arsenal. An adult single ticket costs between £3.20 and £5.30.

◆ **Hilton Docklands-Canary Wharf direct service:** Daily service across the River Thames operating from 6.20am-23.55pm. An adult single ticket costs £3.20.

◆ **Putney-Blackfriars**: A Monday to Friday service stopping at Wandsworth, Chelsea Harbour, Cadogan and Embankment. An adult single costs £8.25 and £15.00 return (Putney-Chelsea costs £4.50 single and £7.50 return). For further details and bookings, contact Thames Executive Charters (☎ 01342-82000, 🖳 www.thamesexecutivecharters.com).

◆ **Woolwich Ferry:** Daily free ferry (five minutes) across the Thames, operated by the borough of Greenwich (☎ 020-8853 9400) from Woolwich and North Woolwich, linking the north and south circular roads across the Thames. It operates from 6.10am-8pm, Mondays to Saturdays, and from 11.30am-7.30pm on Sundays.

For further details and to download timetables see 🖳 www.tfl.gov.uk/gettingaround/1131/aspx.

Leisure River Services

Leisure river services operated by independent companies include those listed below.

◆ **Bankside-Millbank (Tate to Tate):** From the Tate Modern (Bankside) to the Tate Britain (Millbank). An adult single ticket costs £5 and a Roamer £12 (Thames Clippers, ☎ 020-7001 2222).

◆ **Richmond-Hampton Court:** A daily service between mid-April and late September (Mondays only late July to late August), stopping at Kingston. An adult return ticket for the whole route costs £8.20 and a single £6.70. For further details and bookings, contact Turks Launches (☎ 020-8546 2434, 🖳 www.turks.co.uk).

◆ **Westminster-Greenwich:** Daily service stopping at the London Eye and Tower or St Katharine's. An adult single costs £9 and a return £12. There are two operators: City Cruises (☎ 020-7740 0400, 🖳 www.citycruises.com), stopping at the London Eye and Tower, and Thames River Services (☎ 020-7930 4097), stopping at St Katharine's.

◆ **Westminster-St Katharine's:** Daily service stopping at the Embankment. An adult single ticket costs £7.50 and a return £10 (Crown River Cruises, ☎ 020-7936 2033, 🖳 www.crownriver.com).

TAXIS

London's 'black' cabs (which now come in around 12 colours!) are officially called Hackney Carriages, a term that has no connection with the name of the London borough but derives from an old French word *haquenée*, meaning a type of horse that could be hired.

London is famous for its purpose-built taxis or 'black cabs', although other taxi services are also provided (see **Minicabs** below). They cover a vast area of around 610mi^2 (1,580km^2), stretching well into the outer suburbs, and are obliged to undertake journeys of up to 12mi (19km) from anywhere in Greater London (or 20mi/32km from Heathrow Airport).

Although most of London's purpose-built cabs are black, hence the name 'black cabs', they also come in other colours (usually thanks to advertisers), including *Financial Times* pink

to £8.20 for 1 mile (5 to 12 minutes), £7.20 to £11.20 for 2 miles (8 to 15mins), £11 to £19 for 4 miles (15 to 30mins) and £17 to £28 for 6 miles (20 to 40 mins.). The fare from London-Heathrow airport to central London costs between £43 and £75 and takes 30 to 60 mins. There are extra charges for journeys between 8-10pm Mondays to Fridays and at weekends, at night (between 10pm and 6am) and on public holidays.

The London boroughs and the Mayor of London finance a subsidised taxi service, called Taxicard, for Londoners with serious mobility impairments for whom public transport isn't usually accessible. The scheme varies slightly depending on the borough where you live, but generally members pay a flat fare of £1.50 per trip. For more information or an application form, ☎ 020-7484 2929 or visit ⌨ www.taxicard.org.uk. Most drivers are pleased to help disabled passengers and wheelchairs can usually be stored inside the cab along with any luggage.

If you want to book a black cab, call Radio Taxicabs (☎ 020-7272 0272) or Dial-a-Cab (☎ 020-7253 5000), email the Licensed London Taxi Booking Service (✉ sttaxi@aol.com) or visit the London Black Taxis website (⌨ www.londonblacktaxis.net). Further information about London taxis is available from the Transport for London website (⌨ www.tfl.gov.uk/pco). If you have a complaint about a taxi driver, contact the Public Carriage Office (☎ 0845-602 7000, ✉ coms@pco.org.uk) with the cab's licence number and the driver's badge number.

and *Evening Standard* 'newsprint' pattern. All taxis have a yellow 'For Hire' sign at the front and a white numbered licence plate on the back. In addition to 'standard' cabs, there are also 'business-class' cabs with luxurious seats, soundproofing and a telephone (and higher fares than standard cabs). Cabs are licensed by the Metropolitan Police and bear a licence number plate, and the driver (known as a cabby) wears a badge bearing his driver number.

Although they're an expensive way to get around (unless three or four people share the fare), a licensed cab driver won't usually take anything but the shortest route between two points (unless he does so to avoid traffic congestion, when he should tell you). Before obtaining his licence, a cab driver must undergo a long training period and pass a stiff exam on what's known as 'The Knowledge' – an encyclopaedic test of London's streets and landmarks. They almost always know where a destination is without referring to a map or using a GPS. You can also be pretty sure that you won't be cheated by a London cabbie (unlike taxi drivers in many other countries).

Taxis are very expensive in London (particularly as you spend most of your time in jams) and have a strictly regulated scale of fares and charges (see ⌨ www.tfl.gov.uk/gettingaround/taxisandminicabs/taxis/1140.aspx), to which it's customary to add a tip of around 10 per cent (although it isn't obligatory). Fares vary depending on the day and time, with a minimum charge of £2.20. Approximate fares (Monday to Friday, 6am-8pm) are £4.60

Minicabs

As an alternative to a black cab, you can take a minicab, which, unlike a black cab, cannot be hailed in the street and must be booked by phone. It's illegal for minicabs to ply for hire in the street like licensed taxis, although some do. Minicabs are cheaper than licensed taxis, but you have no guarantee that the driver will be reliable, honest or know his way around. There's no official training scheme for minicab drivers and there are dozens of companies, so the best way to find a good one is to ask someone for a recommendation.

You must phone for a minicab in advance (although they often hang around hot spots at night) and agree the price to your destination before starting your journey, as they don't usually have meters. If you're female and worried about your safety late at night, you might wish to consider Ladycabs (☎ 020-7272 3300, 🖥 www.ladyminicabs.co.uk), which employs women only.

In addition to taxi services, many taxi and minicab companies operate private hire (e.g. for weddings or sightseeing), chauffeur and courier services, and provide contract and account services, e.g. to take children to and from school.

Transport for London provide a taxi text service called Cabwise; simply text CAB to 60835 and TfL will use GPS to text you the two nearest minicab numbers and one taxi (black cab) number.

DRIVING IN LONDON

You need nerves of steel and the patience of Job to drive in central London – and it also helps to be a little crazy. Not only will it cost you dearly in terms of time, petrol (the most expensive in Europe), insurance and headache pills, it's also virtually impossible to find affordable parking (see below) in central London. However, it isn't essential to own a car if you live in central London – in fact a car is a liability. If you commute into London from one of the outer boroughs, using public transport will almost certainly be faster than travelling by car.

In common with most major cities, London is plagued by traffic congestion and many roads are permanently jammed with traffic, making travel by car slow and frustrating. Parking in central London is at best difficult (and expensive) and at worst impossible. During rush hours, from around 7 to 9.30am and 4.30 to 6.30pm, Mondays to Fridays, traffic flow is painfully slow, particularly in central London, where the average traffic speed is around 10mph – it takes as long to get around by car today as it did 200 years ago in a horse and cart!

An additional hazard of driving in London is having your car stolen. The number of cars stolen in London is among the highest (per capita) in Western Europe and if you live or work in central London and park your car there, there's a high risk of it being stolen or broken into.

Congestion on London's roads and the resulting air pollution have reached nightmare proportions in recent years. Getting anywhere by private car takes eons, and an accident at a busy intersection can cause long tailbacks or even gridlock for miles around. There's been a widespread debate about traffic congestion in recent years and various measures have been introduced to limit its effects, including the congestion charge (see below), special bus and cycle lanes, and punitive parking fees to discourage driving in the city.

There are a number of ways to reduce the cost of motoring, including car-sharing and short-term rentals via a car club. There are numerous car-sharing schemes in London, including Liftshare (🖥 www.liftshare.org) and Car Share (🖥 www.carshare.com) which has a directory of London car-share schemes. Another option is to join a car club, such as City Car Club (🖥 www.citycarclub.co.uk), Streetcar (🖥 www.streetcar.co.uk), Whizgo (🖥 www.whizgo.co.uk) or Zip Car (🖥 www.zipcar.com), where members can hire a car for an hour, a day or as long as they like. Some borough councils such as Westminster (🖥 http://westminster.zipcar.co.uk/westminster) have partnered with car clubs, which allow cars to be picked up from reserved on-street spaces in the borough.

Speed Limits

UK speed limits are 30mph (48kph) in urban areas, 60mph (96kph) on unrestricted single-carriageway roads (outside towns) and 70mph (113kph) on motorways and dual-carriageways, unless otherwise indicated.

Congestion Charge

In an effort to reduce traffic and improve the traffic flow in central London, a 'congestion charge' was introduced in February 2003, which has proved successful, although unpopular with those unable or unwilling to forsake their cars, who must pay £8 per day to enter the restricted area. Transport for London claims that the congestion charge has reduced the number of cars entering

Congestion Charge Zone

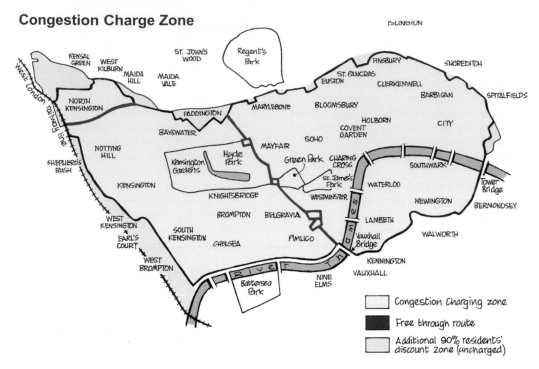

central London by some 70,000 a day. Most vehicles (motorcycles, scooters and mopeds are exempt) must pay the fee to enter the congestion charge zone between 7am and 6pm, Mondays to Fridays. There's no charge at weekends, on local public holidays, designated non-charging days (e.g. between 25th December and January 1st) and between the hours of 6pm and 7am.

The charge zone (see map) is indicated by signs (signposts and road markings) showing a white C in a red circle. You can pay the charge by phone (☎ 0845-900 1234), text message (residents only), post (Congestion Charging, PO Box 2985, Coventry CV7 8ZR), online (💻 www. ttl.gov.uk/roadusers/congestioncharging), at selected retail outlets and petrol stations, and at self-service machines.

You can pay up to 90 days in advance; for example, you could pay for one day, three days, a week, two weeks, a month or a year. If you pay monthly or annually there are discounts available and you can claim refunds in certain circumstances. You can pay the charge before or after the journey on the day of travel, but you must pay by midnight. You can also pay the charge on the following day, but it increases to £10 and can only be paid via the

TFL website or call centre. If you travel on a Friday, you have until midnight on the following Monday to pay. If you fail to pay the charge by midnight on the following charging day, you receive a Penalty Charge Notice of £120, which is reduced to £60 if paid within 14 days, but which increases to £180 if not paid within 28 days.

CCTV cameras check whether your car remains in the charging area for longer than the period paid for, in which case you're liable to be fined. Certain vehicles and drivers are exempt from the congestion charge, including the disabled, vehicles using 'alternative' fuel (including electrically-powered vehicles and hybrid vehicles such as the Toyota Prius) and those with nine or more seats. Residents living within the congestion charge zone can register one private vehicle each and receive a 90 per cent discount, for which there's an annual £10 registration fee.

Plans to increase the congestion charge to £25 for vehicles with high emissions have been shelved following the election of a new mayor (Boris Johnson) in May 2008.

For more information, see 💻 www.tfl.gov.uk/roadusers/congestioncharging or www.tfl.gov.uk/roadusers/congestioncharging/6722.aspx.

Parking

Parking in central London is at best difficult and expensive, and at worst impossible. Few central London properties have garages or off-road parking, although you may be fortunate to find a house or flat with a residents' parking scheme (see page 43). Very few employers provide workplace parking in central London, and when they do it's usually for an elite few employees only. Parking meters are for temporary stays of up to two hours and private car parks (see below) are only for the seriously rich.

On-road parking (waiting) restrictions in the UK are indicated by yellow or red lines at the edge of roads, usually accompanied by a sign indicating when parking is prohibited, e.g. 'Mon-Sat 8am-6.30pm' or 'At any time'. If no days are indicated on the sign, restrictions are in force every day, including public holidays and Sundays. Yellow signs indicate a continuous waiting prohibition and also show times when parking is illegal, while blue signs indicate limited waiting periods. Loading restrictions for loading and unloading goods may be shown by one, two or three short yellow lines marked diagonally on the kerb and a sign.

Red lines along the side of a road indicate that it's a red route, which means that you aren't permitted to stop between the hours

of 7am and 7pm (or as indicated by a sign) from Mondays to Fridays, except for loading or unloading. (Parking bays marked in red have similar restrictions.) **A double red line indicates no stopping, loading or parking at any time!** If you park illegally on a red route, your car will be towed away in the blink of an eye. For more information consult the *Highway Code*.

A summary of the road markings used to indicate parking and waiting restrictions in London and its suburbs is shown in the table below.

In most towns there are public and private off-road car parks, indicated by signs showing

Road Marking Guide	
Road Marking	**Meaning**
White zigzag line (e.g. by zebra crossing)	No parking or stopping at any time
Single red line*	No stopping between 7am and 7pm (or as indicated by a sign) from Mondays to Fridays, except for loading or unloading
Double red line*	No stopping, loading/unloading or parking at any time
Single yellow line	No parking between around 7am and 7pm on four or more days a week
Double yellow lines	No parking at most or all times (as indicated by signs)
Broken yellow line	Restricted parking (see sign for details)
* known as 'red routes'	

a white 'P' on a blue background. Parking in local authority (council) car parks usually costs from around 50p an hour. Parking in short-term (local authority) car parks may become progressively more expensive the longer you stay, although parking is generally cheaper (per hour) the longer you park, up to a maximum of around nine hours.

Information about parking regulations throughout London (including how to appeal against parking tickets) is available from the Parking Committee for London (New Zealand House, 80 Haymarket, SW1Y 4TE, ☎ 020-7747 4700, ✉ admin@pcfl.gov.uk).

⚠ Caution

Note that, unlike many other European countries, the UK doesn't have a cavalier attitude towards illegal parking and the authorities never turn a blind eye to it. In most parts of London you will get a parking ticket (or even have your car clamped or towed away) in a flash if you park illegally.

Car Parks

Parking in a private central London car park costs over £7 an hour or over £50 per day, although monthly and annual season tickets are usually available for commuters. National Car Parks (NCP), the UK's largest car park operator, has a number of 24-hour car parks in central London. A free map of NCP car parks can be ordered by telephone (☎ 0845-050 7080) or an area can be searched using the Car Park Finder function on the NCP website (🖳 www.ncp.co.uk). You may be able to find cheaper parking at 123 Car Parking (🖳 www.123-car-parking.co.uk).

In many areas there are short- and long-stay car parks. Fees may be reasonable for short stays of up to two or three hours, beyond which rates at short-stay car parks are much more expensive. Some car parks, such those operated by Westminster City Council, have introduced a scheme which links fees to demand, with fees starting as low as 20p an hour, although a six-hour stay can cost £25.

If you commute into London, it's cheaper to drive to a convenient railway station (where parking usually costs around £3 to £4 a day) and take a train into central London. Weekly, monthly and annual parking season tickets are usually available at rail and underground stations. Parking in car parks and at meters may be free on Sundays and public holidays, so check the notice before buying a ticket.

London's most expensive car park is the NCP multi-storey car park in Pavilion Road, Knightsbridge, SW1, where up to two hours costs £16 and a seven-hour stay £44!

Parking Meters

The maximum permitted parking period at meters varies from 30 minutes to two hours. Meter-feeding (i.e. returning to a meter to insert more money) is illegal, although many people do it. You're supposed to vacate a parking space when the meter time expires, even if it was under the maximum time permitted, and you shouldn't move to another meter in the same group. Meters usually accept a combination of coins and are usually in operation from 7am until 7pm, Mondays to Fridays, and from 7am to 6pm on Saturdays (check the notice on meters). Sundays are usually free, although meters at railway stations and airports may be in operation 24-hours a day.

Don't park at meters that are suspended or out of service (as indicated), or your car can be clamped or towed away. If you remain at a meter beyond the excess charge period, you're liable for a fixed penalty (fine) from a police officer or one of London's infamous and much reviled traffic wardens. Parking meters are being phased out in many areas and replaced by pay-and-display parking areas.

Pay-and-display

Parking areas where you buy a ticket from a machine and display it behind your windscreen are called pay-and-display. It may have an adhesive backing which you peel off and use to stick the ticket to the inside of your windscreen or a car window. Parking costs £4 an hour in most central London areas and machines usually accept only £1 coins. When you've inserted sufficient coins for the period required, press the button to obtain your ticket. Pay-and-display parking areas usually operate from

7am until 7pm, excluding Sundays and public holidays.

Pay-and-display parking areas and tariffs for individual boroughs are shown on a map on borough websites (see 🖥 www.cityoflondon. gov.uk/Corporation/LGNL_Services/Transport_ and_streets/Parking/).

Parking Fines & Penalties

The fine for illegal parking depends on where you park. There's usually a fixed penalty ticket, e.g. £80 to £120 in the City of Westminster, for overstaying your parking period or parking illegally on a yellow line. Parking in a dangerous position or near a pedestrian crossing (i.e. on the zigzag lines or studded area) results in a higher fine, plus three penalty points on your driving licence. Penalties for non-payment or overstaying your time in a permitted parking area, e.g. at a parking meter or in a pay-and-display area, are set by the local authorities who issue parking tickets.

You shouldn't even think about parking illegally, e.g. in a residents' only area, on a double yellow line or at an expired meter. Illegal parking can result in your car being 'clamped', where a large metal device (a clamp) is fixed to one of its wheels, thus preventing you from driving it away. Thousands of cars are clamped each week in London and many more are towed away. If your car is towed away and you don't collect it within a certain time, it can be sold at auction to pay the fine and is likely to be sold for well below its market value – so don't park illegally before you go on a long holiday!

If your car is clamped, there will be a sticker on the windscreen – to prevent you inadvertently attempting to drive off and damaging your car and to tell you how to get the clamp removed. You will need to pay a substantial fee (e.g. up to £250) before your car is released, plus the parking fine (if applicable). If you've been clamped, you will have a lengthy wait even after you've paid the fine (some boroughs allow you to pay over the phone by credit card, while others insist that you pay in person).

Clamping companies say they will unclamp your car within four hours of receiving your payment, but they won't give you a precise time. If they do unclamp it and you don't remove the car quickly, e.g. within an hour, they're within their rights to clamp it again and the process starts all over again. If you don't arrange for release of the clamp within a certain period (e.g. four hours), it may be towed away.

If you find that your car is missing, it has either been stolen or, more likely, towed away; call Trace Information (☎ 020-7747 4747) who will tell you whether it has been towed away and what to do to recover it. You must pay around £200 to get it released and a car pound won't release it until you've paid (in cash or by debit or credit card) and they charge a daily storage fee (e.g. £25-50) after the first 24 hours. You cannot be towed away from a pay-and-display area or a parking meter, unless the parking bay has been suspended.

If you believe that you've been treated unfairly, there's a Parking Appeals Service (PO Box 279, Chertsey, Surrey KT16 6BU, ☎ 020-7520 7200, 🖥 www.parkingandtrafficappeals.gov.uk) or contact AppealNow (🖥 www.appealnow.com), who may also be able to help. If you're in the habit of parking illegally, you can join the London Motoring Club (☎ 0845-601 8843, 🖥 www.londonmotoringclub.com), which will recover your car for you for an annual charge of £245 for up to two cars – plus any fines!

Note that the owners of private car parks or private land can clamp a car parked illegally and can set their own fees to remove clamps, which can run into hundreds of pounds.

It's unwise to park on private land, particularly where there's a 'clamping' sign, as private clamping is widespread throughout the UK. However, since May 2005 it has been a criminal offence to clamp a vehicle without a licence from the Security Industry Authority (SIA), which has at least done away with some of the cowboys; now we have licensed cowboys!

Residents' Parking

Most central London residents – those whose postcode lies within a Controlled Parking Zone (CPZ) – can obtain a residents' parking permit which provides inexpensive local (on-street) parking in designated spaces. Any resident whose postcode lies within a CPZ can apply for a permit from his local council by providing proof of identity and residence (usually a Council Tax bill).

Charges are set by local borough councils and vary considerably, costing from nothing (Hillingdon, first vehicle only) up to £140 (Kensington & Chelsea, highest band) per year for the first car. Around a quarter of borough councils calculate parking charges on a car's CO_2 emissions, which on average doubles the cost of parking for many people

The number of permits issued for a dwelling (usually up to three or four) also varies, as does the cost (a permit for a second car in Hammersmith & Fulham costs a whopping £450 per year). There are also special permits for disabled drivers, who can park in reserved spaces, free at meters and in car parks, and ignore many on-road parking restrictions.

If you have a parking space, garage or even a plot of land which isn't being used, you can rent it out on a daily, weekly or monthly basis (from around £100 per month). There are a number of websites that put space providers and users together, including 🖳 www.parkatmyhouse.com, 🖳 www.parklet.co.uk and 🖳 www.yourparkingspace.co.uk/london-parking-spaces-and-garages-to-rent.html.

Car Hire

To hire (rent) a car you need at least a year's driving experience and must be aged at least 21 (or 25 with some hire companies). The major car hire (rental) companies in London include Avis (☎ 0844-581 0147, 🖳 www.avis.co.uk), Europcar

BCR (🖳 www.europcar.co.uk) and Hertz (🖳 www.hertz.co.uk). Shop around, as charges vary considerably – you may get a better deal from a small local company. You can shop around using a comparison website, such as 🖳 www.carrentals.co.uk or www.travelsupermarket.com.

Disabled drivers can hire vehicles with hand controls from Hertz and other national car hire companies, and specialist companies such as Wheelchair Travel (☎ 01483-233 640, 🖳 www.wheelchair-travel.co.uk) based in Guildford, Surrey, 32mi (51km) south of London.

Breakdown Assistance

If you break down anywhere in the UK, you can obtain emergency roadside assistance from a garage or motoring organisation (all car hire companies are members). However, to reduce the cost it's recommended to a join a motoring organisation such as the Automobile Association/AA (☎ 0800-085 2721, 🖳 www.theaa.com), the Royal Automobile Club/RAC (☎ 08705-722 722, (🖳 www.rac.co.uk) or Green Flag National Breakdown (☎ 0845-246 1557, 🖳 www.greenflag.com). Membership costs between around £33 and £150 per year, depending on the level of cover required.

CYCLING

Short of walking, cycling is the cheapest way to get around central London and one of the fastest. It's also the most dangerous! If the traffic doesn't flatten you first, any positive effect on your physical fitness may be offset by the adverse effects of air pollution.

When cycling in London, always wear a smog mask with a proper air filter as well as a safety helmet, and don't let your children loose on London's roads unless they're capable and experienced cyclists.

Carrying children on the back of a bike in London's heavy traffic isn't wise, but if you must do it, ensure that they're also fitted with a helmet and mask and are securely strapped into an approved child seat.

When you park your bicycle, make sure that you lock the frame to an immovable object or it's unlikely to be there when you return, although bicycles may be removed if you attach them to railings or street 'furniture'. There are a few cycle parking stands near

Whitehall and Parliament Square, and some multi-storey car parks in the City of London provide free cycle parking, which can potentially offer greater security than on-street parking. The London cycle guides (see below) list cycle parking facilities at stations.

The above information is discouraging for cycling enthusiasts, who need to head out to the suburbs to enjoy cycling in relative safety. Unfortunately, many modes of public transport won't carry bicycles. Restrictions on suburban railways vary, so phone to check before attempting to take your bike on a train. The DLR has a blanket ban on bikes and only four tube lines (the District, Circle, Metropolitan and Hammersmith & City) allow them, and then only outside peak hours. Other tube lines allow them on overground sections only, i.e. those in the outer suburbs.

However, things may be about to change. For over 25 years the London Cycling Campaign/ LCC (2 Newhams Row, SE1 3UZ, ☎ 020-7234 9310, ⬛ www.lcc.org.uk) has been attempting to promote the rights of cyclists in London. The crisis in London's transport system is widely acknowledged and the London boroughs are setting up a network of 1,200mi (1,931km) of cycle routes throughout the capital, with the help of government funding. Routes (marked by blue signs showing a bicycle) bypass the major thoroughfares, usually taking fairly direct routes through residential areas that are unsuitable for heavy traffic. Companies are beginning to encourage employees to cycle to work and there are increased facilities for cycle parking at workplaces and elsewhere.

Annual membership of the LCC costs £32 (£14 for students, youths, the unemployed and senior citizens, £55 for families) and includes a subscription to the bi-monthly magazine, *London Cyclist*. The LCC publishes a number of information booklets, most of which can be downloaded from its website.

If you want to get a taste of what cycling in London is like, you can hire a bike for around £18 per day or £48 per week from a number of sites in central London (a deposit is necessary). Try the London Bicycle Tour Company on the South Bank (1a Gabriel's Wharf, 56 Upper Ground, London SE1 9PP, ☎ 020-7928 6838, ⬛ www.londonbicycle. com), which also organises cycle tours.

A series of 14 free cycle guides covering the whole of Greater London is produced by TFL using route information provided by the London Cycling Campaign. They're designed to help Londoners to choose cycling as their mode of transport and are available from TFL (☎ 020-7222 1234, ⬛ www. tfl.gov.uk/modalpages/2663.aspx - and click on 'Cycle guides').

> Lorry drivers in London are being given free safety mirrors (with Fresnel lenses) to help them spot cyclists in their 'blind spot', especially when turning left. Collisions with goods vehicles account for over half of all cycle deaths on London roads.

MOPEDS, SCOOTERS & MOTORCYCLES

You can also use a moped, scooter or motorbike to get around London, which are exempt from the congestion charge (see page 39) and certainly quicker than using a car and most public transport. However, unlike most other major European cities, mopeds and scooters aren't very popular with Londoners, even among those who are too young to drive a car. A proposal by the mayor in 2008 to allow motorcycles to use bus lanes was strongly opposed by cyclists, who believe it would put lives at risk.

There are designated motorcycle and bicycle parking bays throughout London, where parking bays may be marked 'Solo Motorcycles' with the area delimited by broken white lines. Motorcycle parking in council-owned, multi-storey car parks is often free of charge, provided motorcycles are parked within the designated parking bays. You should, however, read the notice on the ticket machines to check whether payment is necessary.

The Motorcycle Parking website (⬛ www. motorcycleparking.com) provides comprehensive information about parking in London.

AIRPORTS

An important consideration to many people living in London is the proximity and access to international airports. London is one of the world's busiest air transport hubs and you can fly there from practically any country, whether you're travelling from San Francisco, Shanghai or Shannon. The city is served by five designated London airports: Heathrow, Gatwick, Stansted, Luton and City Airport, listed in order of size and passenger numbers below. With the exception of Heathrow and the small City Airport, all are some distance outside the city and entail a 30- to 60-minute journey into the centre (see the map of Major Roads & Airports below).

Heathrow Airport

Heathrow airport (☎ 0844-335 1801, 💻 www.heathrowairport.com) is 15mi (24km) south-west of the city centre and is one of the world's busiest airports, handling over 60mn passengers a year. Over 90 airlines are based there, spread among its five sprawling terminals. Demands from the airlines for a third runway (take-off and landing slots at Heathrow cost up to £10mn) have been met with vociferous objections on the grounds of pollution, which would exceed European Union limits.

Access

Train: The high-speed Heathrow Express (💻 www.heathrowexpress.co.uk) rail service is by far the quickest and easiest way to get to and from central London – or at least as far as Paddington Station (not exactly central!).

Major Airports & Roads

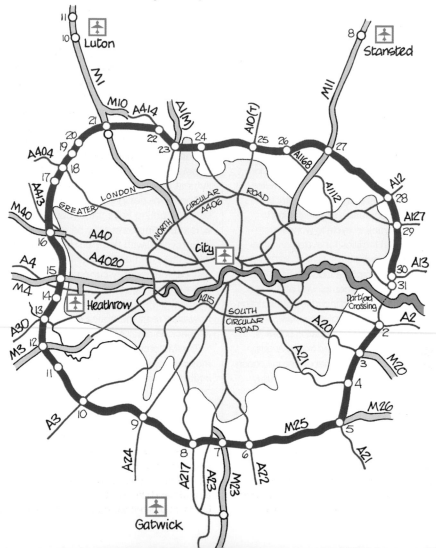

The airport has two stations (terminals 1-3 and terminal 4), operating direct trains to Paddington taking between 15 (terminals 1-3) and 25 minutes (terminal 4). Trains run every 15 minutes between 5am and midnight, and the fare is £18 (online £16.50) single or £30 return (online).

A cheaper way to get from Paddington to Heathrow is via Heathrow Connect (🖳 www.heathrowconnect.com), calling at Ealing Broadway, West Ealing, Hanwell, Southall, Hayes and Heathrow terminals 1-3 and 4. The journey time from Paddington is 25 minutes to terminals 1-3 and 35 minutes to terminal 4, from where there's a free inter-terminal transfer on the Heathrow Express to terminal 5. Heathrow Connect trains run every 30 minutes and the fare is £6.90 single or £13.80 return. For more information, ☎ 0845-678 6975 or book online (see website above).

Tube: Alternatively, you can take the cheaper and much slower Piccadilly Line underground service, e.g. 50 to 60 minutes to Piccadilly Circus, for £4 cash (adult single), £3.80 with an Oyster Card and £2.20 off-peak (outside 6.30-9.30am and 4-7pm); trains operate between 5.30am and 11.30pm. Information is available from Travel Information Centres at Heathrow's tube stations, by phone (☎ 0845-600 1515) or via the TFL website (🖳 www.tfl.gov.uk).

Bus: Bus services at Heathrow operate from the Central Bus Station above the underground station. The A2 service runs frequently between the five terminals and central London, but the journey takes over an hour and a half, with an adult single ticket costing £6 (£10 return), therefore the tube is preferable. If you arrive in the dead of night, you can catch the hourly night bus (N9) to Trafalgar Square – a leisurely trip of around 75 minutes and a bargain at just £2 single (90p with an Oyster Card – see page 26).

Taxi: The journey from Heathrow to the city centre by taxi costs between £50 and £70, and takes from 45 minutes to well over an hour, depending on traffic congestion.

Gatwick Airport

Gatwick airport (☎ 0844-335 1802, 🖳 www.gatwickairport.com) is 30mi (50km) south of London and is the UK's second-busiest airport – and the busiest single-runway airport in the world. It has two terminals (North and South), linked

by a driver-less monorail system. International flights are handled by both terminals, while most domestic flights use the South terminal.

Access

Train: Gatwick Express (☎ 0845-850 1530, 🖳 www.gatwickexpress.com) operates a regular train service from 5.20am to 1.35am between the airport's South terminal and Victoria station (trains usually run every 15 minutes, but every hour before 6.50am and after 8.50pm). The journey takes 30 minutes and tickets, which you can buy on the train, cost £16.90 single or £28.80 return. South Central's slower trains cover the same route for a slightly lower fare and run every 15 minutes during the day and every hour at night. There are also Thameslink trains running every 15 minutes from Gatwick to other London stations, including London Bridge, Blackfriars, City, Farringdon and King's Cross.

Bus: A cheaper but much slower option – the journey takes at least 80 minutes – is Shuttle bus 25, operated by National Express (☎ 0871-781 8181, 🖳 www.nationalexpress.com), which runs approximately every hour between 5.15am and 9.15pm to London's Victoria Coach Station (near the railway station). Single tickets cost £8.60 for adults (£15.00 return).

Taxi: A taxi from Gatwick to central London costs at least £70 and takes as long as the bus.

Stansted Airport

Stansted airport (☎ 0844-335 1803, 🖳 www.stanstedairport.com) is 34mi (60km) north-east of the capital. It's the newest of London's airports and the fourth-largest in the UK in terms of passenger numbers, serving over 60 destinations. It has two terminals and handles a range of flights within the UK and to most European countries.

Access

Train: The fastest way to get to central London from Stansted by public transport is via the Stansted Express (☎ 0845-600 7245, 🖳 www.stanstedexpress.com) to Liverpool Street station in the City of London, which takes 45 minutes (single £19, return £28.80 or £18/£26.80 when booked online). Trains depart every 15 or 30 minutes between 8am and 8pm, and hourly from 8pm to midnight and between 6 and 8am. Trains also stop at Tottenham Hale on the Victoria tube line. A slower, stopping service is also available.

Bus: Three bus services link Stansted airport with London. The A6 to Victoria Coach Station (stopping at Golders Green and Finchley Road underground stations) operates 24 hours a day (every 20 minutes at peak times), and takes around an hour and 40 minutes (£10.50 single, £17 return). The Terravision Express Shuttle to Victoria Coach Station operates from 9am until 00.30am (every 45 minutes at peak times) and costs £9 single (£14 return), while the National Express A7 to Liverpool Street and Victoria stations is a night service operating every half an hour between midnight and 4.30am (£10 single, £17 return).

> Further information about bus services is available from National Express (☎ 0871-781 8181, 🖳 www.nationalexpress.com) and Terravision (☎ 01279-680 028, 🖳 www.terravision.eu).

Taxi: A taxi to central London costs over £60 and the journey takes around an hour.

Luton Airport

Luton airport (☎ 01582-405 100, 🖳 www.london-luton.co.uk), around 30mi (50km) north-west of central London, handles scheduled (around two-thirds of the total) and charter flights to a wide range of destinations in the UK and Europe. It opened a second terminal in October 1999.

Access

Luton airport's promotional motto is 'We're easier to get to than you think', which suggests (incorrectly) that transport links are poor.

Train: Trains operated by First Capital Connect (🖳 www.firstcapitalconnect.co.uk for information, 🖳 www.flybytrain.co.uk for bookings) from Luton Airport Parkway station offer a direct link (the 'Luton Express') with King's Cross station in Camden. Trains run every half hour or so, 24 hours a day, take between 25 and 50 minutes, depending on the number of stops, and cost around £12 single. There are also trains to and from other London stations, including Hendon, Cricklewood, West Hampstead, Kentish Town, Farringdon, City, Blackfriars, London Bridge and East Croydon. A free shuttle bus operates between the airport and Luton station.

Bus: For a cheaper (£13.50 for an adult single, £14.50 return) and slower (70 minutes) journey, you can take a Green Line 757 coach (see page 30) to the Green Line Coach station near Victoria Coach Station. Coaches run approximately every half an hour throughout the day and night.

Taxi: A taxi to central London from Luton isn't recommended, as it takes over an hour and costs at least £90.

City Airport

City airport (☎ 020-7646 0088, 🖳 www.londoncityairport.com) is the smallest of London's five airports and is just 9mi (14km) east of London's centre in Docklands. It operates mostly domestic and European flights; destinations include Amsterdam, Antwerp, Basle, Belfast, Billund (Denmark), Copenhagen, Dublin, Dundee, Edinburgh, Eindhoven, Frankfurt, Geneva, Glasgow, Isle of Man, Jersey, Luxembourg, Madrid, Milan, Munich, Nantes, New York, Newquay, Nice, Paris, Plymouth, Rotterdam, Strasbourg and Zurich. British Airways started a business only service to New York's JFK airport in September 2009. The airport courts its largely business clientele by offering (allegedly) the fastest check-in and arrival times in Europe.

Access

Train: Silvertown & City Airport railway station (DLR – see page 35) is ten minutes' walk from the airport, and trains to the centre of London (linking with the tube system) run every 20 minutes.

Bus: Shuttle bus services operate every ten minutes between 7am and 9pm on weekdays, from 7.30am to 1pm on Saturdays and 11am to 9pm on Sundays between the airport and Canning Town (£4 adult single), Canary Wharf (£3) and Liverpool Street (£8) underground stations.

Taxi: Taxis to the City take up to 40 minutes (depending on the traffic) and cost around £25.

3.
CHOOSING WHERE TO LIVE

There are some 3mn dwellings in London and around 20,000 new homes are built most years, which makes choosing where to live a difficult task. The most important consideration when buying or renting a home in London is usually the location – or as the old adage goes, the three most important points are location, location and location! The wrong decision regarding location is one of the main causes of disenchantment among property buyers and, to a lesser extent, renters in London.

Bear in mind that the costs of property and rents are astronomical in central London and finding property at an affordable price can be difficult. Unless you're wealthy, you will probably find that you need to make compromises in order to find a home that you like in an area where you wish to live. For example, you may need to pay more than you had planned, buy or rent a smaller home than you would like, or live in a less desirable area. You may also need to live further from the centre and possibly further away from public transport and other amenities than you would wish. However, don't despair – although you may not be able to afford to live in Kensington & Chelsea or Hampstead, there are many other desirable areas and enough variety to suit everyone's taste and pocket.

Most Londoners don't live in central London but in the numerous suburbs, where life's still largely community based. Most people who work in central London commute into the city from the surrounding boroughs and (home) counties, with thousands travelling from even further afield. Wherever you are in the suburbs, you're never far from a traditional 'high street' selling the essentials of life, and most areas provide a wide range of amenities such as schools, health and leisure facilities.

Much of London's suburbia is characterised by rows of brick terraced houses, mainly built in Victorian times to provide housing for the rapidly growing population, or tree-lined avenues of semi-detached properties dating from the '20s and '30s. The price of this kind of typical suburban architecture varies considerably depending on the area, although prices in London are generally much higher than in other parts of the UK

ACCESSIBILITY

Before choosing somewhere to live, it's wise to check the present and planned public transport services (see **Chapter 2**), particularly if you will be commuting to a job in central London or one of the suburbs. If you're buying, you will find that a planned improvement in local public transport – such as a new tube or rail extension – providing a fast journey into central London could have a dramatic, positive influence on property values.

If you're an employee, the location of your home is likely to be determined by the proximity to your place of employment or good public transport links. However, if you intend to look for employment or start a business in London, you must live in an area that allows you the maximum scope (unless you work from home). If you will be commuting, you should obtain a map of the area and decide the maximum distance (or commuting time) you wish to travel to work, e.g. by drawing a circle with your workplace in the middle, taking into account local traffic congestion and public transport. If you're prepared to commute, you can save a fortune by buying in one of London's outer boroughs. You will also have the benefit of the countryside on your doorstep, but you need to take into account the extra travelling time and the cost of commuting.

LIFESTYLE

The 'best' area in which to live depends on your lifestyle and (not least) your bank balance. For example, a family with a moderate income, school-age children and animals (dogs, cats, etc.) has a very different lifestyle from a young, professional couple with no children or pets who enjoy shopping, clubbing and 'weekending' abroad. When looking for a home, bear in mind the travelling time and cost to your place of work, shops and local amenities such as restaurants and pubs – don't believe the times and distances stated in advertisements or by estate agents, but check for yourself. What are the neighbourhood and the quality of shops, restaurants and other amenities like? Is it an up and coming area or down at heel? What are the neighbouring properties like and do the street and local town centre look well cared for?

> ### ☑ SURVIVAL TIP
>
> Some areas are said to be 'up and coming', which is estate agent speak for a poor area that may be worth more in future (but don't take their word for it).

Trying to find the next boom area or hotspot is a lottery and a national pastime. Hotspots are generally expensive, but if you get in while an area is still only lukewarm you may make a killing. Hotspots generally have an attractive environment, such as a pretty square or a conservation area in a town. Usually there must be easy access to public transport and no road, rail or air traffic noise. New public transport links (such as the east-west Crossrail railway link) and access to fast roads (such as motorways and dual carriageways) and other quality infrastructure can dramatically increase property values – but can also reduce them if they're within earshot. A Local Authority Search will tell you all you need to know about planned developments.

If you plan to live in or move to an unfamiliar area, read as much as you can about it and spend some time looking around the towns and areas of interest. Before looking at properties, it's important to have a good idea of the kind of property you're looking for and the price you wish to pay, and to draw up a shortlist of the areas or towns of interest. If you don't do this, you're likely to be overwhelmed by the number of properties to be viewed. It's recommended to make a list of what you absolutely **must** have in an area or town, and what you definitely **won't** consider, which will help narrow the search area.

If possible, you should visit an area a number of times over a period of a few weeks or months, both on weekdays and at weekends, in order to get a feel for the neighbourhood (walk – don't just drive around). A property seen on a balmy spring day after a delicious pub lunch and a few glasses of your favourite tipple won't be nearly so attractive on a subsequent visit in a downpour, lacking the warm inner glow. If you're planning to buy a home and are unfamiliar with an area, most experts recommend that you rent (see **Chapter 7**) for a period before deciding to buy.

LOCATION CHECKLIST

There are many things to consider regarding the location of a home in London, which can roughly be divided into the local vicinity, i.e. the immediate surroundings and neighbourhood, and the general area or region. When choosing the location for a home you should take into account the following:

♦ The most important consideration for most people when choosing the location for a

home in London is the local property prices or rents, which vary considerably and can be astronomical. To get an idea of property prices and rents in different boroughs, see the tables in **Appendix D**. If you wish to let a property (i.e. you're a prospective landlord), you should also check the rental potential and occupancy rates of local properties in your price range.

♦ Check for signs of urban blight. Some once desirable suburbs are in a crisis of neglect, with increasing crime and a breakdown of the community. Indications of this are unkempt homes, gardens and streets; dumped cars and rubbish; broken streetlights and signs; boarded-up shops and a profusion of second-hand shops; few local services; high crime rates; and stagnating property prices.

Information about residential areas is shown in the **Borough Surveys** in **Chapter 7**.

♦ What about your children's present and future schooling? What is the quality of local schools? Do they have any vacant places? (You may find that they're full and you have to enrol your children in schools miles away.) Even if your family has no need or plans to use local schools, the value of a home is often influenced by their quality and proximity. The quality of local state schools is one of the most important considerations for parents. Many people pay dearly to live within the catchment area of a good state school, which is a huge selling point that can add tens of thousands of pounds to the value of a property. If your children are planning to go on to higher education, could they commute to a local university from home?

Information about Schools is shown in the **Borough Surveys** in **Chapter 7**. See also **Schools** on page 61.

♦ Is the proximity to public transport, e.g. an international airport, railway or tube station, or access to a motorway important? If you will be commuting to work in another part of London, it's essential to check the local public transport (e.g. rail and tube) links and travel times. Don't believe what you're told about the distance and travelling times to the nearest motorway, airport, tube or railway station, but check for yourself.

Good transport links can increase the value of a property considerably, although a home within earshot of a busy railway line, airport or main road will be devalued.

Information about public transport is shown in the **Borough Surveys** in **Chapter 7**. See also **Chapter 2**.

♦ If you're planning to buy in central London, is there adequate safe parking? Failing that, is there a resident's parking scheme and what does it cost (see the **Borough Surveys** in **Chapter 7**). How far is the nearest parking area from the property? If you need to park a long way away, how do you feel about carrying shopping hundreds of yards to your home and possibly up several flights of stairs? You may also wish to check whether a property has wheelchair access and whether it has been designed with the elderly or disabled in mind.

Parking is a nightmare in central London, where private garages and parking spaces are rare and astronomically expensive – a single lock-up garage in Chelsea sold for £650,000! Chronic traffic congestion is also a problem in many areas. On the other hand, it's possible to cope quite well in central London without owning a car (like half of all Londoners), using public transport and taxis (see **Chapter 2**). Information about roads and parking is shown in the **Borough Surveys** in **Chapter 7**.

⚠ Caution

Some tradesmen may refuse to visit or work in areas where there's nowhere to park, which includes most of central London.

◆ What's the quality of local hospitals and other health services? Do local doctors and dentists have waiting lists for new NHS patients, and if so, can you afford to pay for private (e.g. dental) treatment? How far is the nearest hospital with an accident and emergency (A&E) department? For a full list of NHS doctors, dentists and clinics in a particular area, see 💻 www.nhs.uk.

Information about health facilities is shown in the **Borough Surveys** in **Chapter 7**. See also **Health** on page 58 and the **NHS League Tables** in **Appendix D**.

◆ What shopping facilities are provided in the local neighbourhood? How far is it to the nearest town with good shopping facilities, e.g. a major supermarket (or your favourite supermarket)? How would you get there if your car was off the road, you couldn't drive for health reasons or you lost your licence?

Information about shopping is shown in the **Borough Surveys** in **Chapter 7**.

◆ What's the local crime rate? A high incidence of burglaries, housebreaking, stolen cars, muggings, prostitution, drug dealing and crimes of violence will drastically reduce property values. Crime rates tend to be higher in areas where property is less expensive, and most experts warn against buying in a crime spot, no matter how inexpensive a property is. However, areas change and today's high crime area could become a property hotspot in future.

Information regarding the local crime rate is shown in the **Borough Surveys** in **Chapter 7** and you can also compare the crime rate in London boroughs using the table in **Appendix D**. However, bear in mind that the overall crime rate in a particular borough may be distorted by crime in a particular town or area, and you will probably find that many areas have little crime. See also **Crime** on page 56.

Home contents insurance premiums – which are usually based on postcodes – are a good indication of the local crime rate; insurance is prohibitively expensive in high-crime areas.

◆ What's the range and quality of local leisure, sports, community and cultural facilities? What's the proximity to sports facilities such as a gym, tennis court, golf course or waterway? Is there a local leisure centre, health club or swimming pool and will you be able to use it (at some clubs the membership is full and you may need to travel miles to the nearest one). Are there public parks and green spaces close by where you can get some exercise, walk your dog, take the children and have family picnics?

Information about leisure and sports facilities and green spaces is shown in the **Borough Surveys** in **Chapter 7**.

◆ What's the local council tax (see below), how much has it increased in recent years and is it more than in neighbouring boroughs? If it's high, it may be that the local borough council is profligate or it could mean that they provide residents with a lot of services. You can compare the council tax levied by boroughs using the table in **Appendix D**.

◆ How well is the local borough council run and what standard of services does it provide? The Audit Commission provides a Comprehensive Performance Assessment (CPA) for all London boroughs based on the following criteria: education, social care U16, social care 16+, environment, housing, leisure, benefits, use of resources and council ability. The rating is based on service performance, use of resources and council ability. To view the assessment for a particular borough, go to 💻 www.audit-commission.gov.uk/cpa and enter the borough council name at the bottom of the page. The CPA score for all boroughs is shown in the **Borough Surveys** in **Chapter 7**.

◆ Noise is a problem in all cities and London is no exception. Millions of people are affected by it (around 40 per cent of the population). It can be a disaster in flats (particularly conversions) and terraced and semi-detached (duplex) houses. Disputes have increased in recent years and have led to violence and even murder in a few cases. Much of the problem in cities arises from poor building techniques and the fact that new buildings often don't have the same levels of noise insulation as old ones. To check the noise level, you should view a property in the evening when everyone is at home.

♦ Although you cannot choose your neighbours, you can at least ensure that a property isn't situated next to a busy road, railway line, church (with a bell that 'dongs' often), airport, industrial plant, commercial area, discotheque, night club, bar or restaurant, or an area with a seedy nightlife and kerb crawlers. Look out for objectionable properties that may be too close to one you're considering and check whether nearby vacant land has been 'zoned' for commercial activities or tower blocks. Be wary of homes near airports (even small private airports).

The Department for the Environment, Food and Rural Affairs (DEFRA) has carried out a survey of noise ('noise mapping') in major urban areas in England, including London. To check the level of noise in a particular area go to 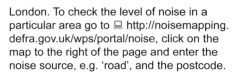 http://noisemapping. defra.gov.uk/wps/portal/noise, click on the map to the right of the page and enter the noise source, e.g. 'road', and the postcode.

♦ The orientation or aspect of a building is crucial (unless you have a revolving house – they do exist!); if you want morning or afternoon sun (or both) you must ensure that rooms, balconies, patios, terraces and gardens face the right direction. A north-facing house will be cool in summer, but may be damp and chilly in winter, while a south-facing conservatory could be unbearably hot in summer (unless it has air-conditioning).

♦ Does a flat have cable or satellite TV (many buildings have a communal dish on the roof) or can you install a satellite dish? If you want to receive satellite TV and live in a conservation area or a listed building, you may be prohibited from installing a satellite dish, so you need to check whether a property has cable TV.

COUNCIL TAX

Council tax is a local tax levied by councils on residents to pay for such things as education, police, roads, waste disposal, libraries and community services. The tax includes payments for the local borough council; the local police, fire and civil defence authorities; and possibly a 'special expenses' payment in certain areas. Each council sets its own tax rate, based on the number of residents and how much money it needs to finance its services, and rates vary considerably from borough to borough. Affluent boroughs don't necessarily charge higher taxes than relatively poor boroughs; in fact the opposite is often the case, although boroughs with low council tax rates may provide fewer services.

Generally you can expect to pay between £2,000 and £3,000 per year for a property in band H valued at over £320,000 (the main exceptions are Wandsworth and Westminster, which charge £1,364 and £1,375 respectively) and £400-500 less for a property valued between £160,000 and £320,000 (band G).

The council tax rates for 2010/11 for each London borough are shown in the Borough

Surveys in Chapter 7 and in the table on page 447. The amount payable depends on the value of your home, as rated by your local council (not necessarily the market value). Properties in England are divided into the following eight bands:

Council Tax Bands	
Band	**Property Value (£)**
A	Up to 40,000
B	40,001 – 52,000
C	52,001 – 68,000
D	68,001 – 88,000
E	88,001 – 120,000
F	20,001 – 160,000
G	160,001 – 320,000
H	Over 320,000

The government hasn't changed the bands since the introduction of council tax in 1993, so almost all London properties now fall into the top two bands. A much delayed review of property values was planned for 2007, but was postponed because it's political dynamite. Politicians fear it will result in a further sharp increase in bills, which many people are already struggling to pay.

In recent years, council tax has increased at well above the rate of inflation and bills in most areas have doubled in less than ten years, despite the fact that councils which increase their tax rate above a government-fixed threshold risk having their spending capped.

Council tax can usually be paid by direct debit from a bank or building society account, online, by phone, by post with a personal cheque, and by cash, cheque or credit/debit card at council offices. Payment can be made in a lump sum or in ten instalments from April to January.

The full council tax assumes that two adults are living permanently in a dwelling. If only one adult lives in a dwelling (as their main home), the bill is reduced by 25 per cent. If a dwelling isn't a main home, e.g. it's unoccupied or is a second home, there's usually a discount (e.g. 10 to 25 per cent) depending on your local borough

council. Exempt dwellings include those that are unfurnished (usually exempt for up to six months) or undergoing structural alteration or major repair (usually exempt for up to six months after completion), and those that are left empty for specific reasons (e.g. the occupier is in hospital, a nursing home or prison, or is a student) or are occupied only by people aged under 18. Always confirm a discount or exemption with your local borough council.

Certain people aren't counted when calculating the number of adults resident in a dwelling, e.g. full-time students and 18 and 19-year-olds who have just left school. If you or someone who lives with you has special needs arising from a disability, you may be entitled to a reduction in your council tax bill. Those receiving Income Support usually pay no council tax and others on low incomes have their bills reduced. You can appeal against the assessed value of your property and any errors due to exemption, benefits or discounts.

Anyone who's liable for council tax must register with his local council when they take up residence in a new area, and are liable to pay council tax from their first day of residence. A register is maintained by councils, containing the names and addresses of all people registered for council tax, and is open to public examination. If you don't want your name and address to appear on the register, you can apply for anonymous registration. New arrivals must register with their local council after taking up residence or after moving house. When moving to a new borough you may be entitled to a refund of a portion of the council tax paid to your previous council.

You can find out the council tax rate for any property from the Valuation Office Agency's website (🖳 www.voa.gov.uk).

CRIME

The total number of reported crimes in London fell to its lowest level in ten years in 2009-10, although some sceptics believe that it's due to under-reporting, because many victims of crime consider it a waste of time. There were 117 murders in the 12 months to March 2010 (38 less than in the previous 12 months and fewer than in most other major European cities); you're more likely to choke to death on your food than you are to meet a violent death in London. However, the use of knives among youths in London (and the UK as whole) is a cause for concern, although despite a slight rise of 2.2 per cent since 2008-09, knife crime (in 2009-10) was down by 11 per cent on 2007-08 levels.

Many crimes are drug-related and due to the huge quantity of drugs flooding into the UK in recent years. The use of hard drugs (particularly crack cocaine) is a major problem in London, where gangs increasingly use guns and knives to settle their differences. Around half of all London street crime is committed by cocaine addicts, although the level has also fallen and muggings and crimes of violence are rare in most areas. You can safely walk the streets in most places day or night, although the police warn people (particularly young women) against walking alone in dark and deserted areas late at night.

Crime is, however, a major concern for residents of some London suburbs, where the elderly are often afraid to leave the relative safety of their homes. The increase in crime is attributed by psychologists to poverty; the breakdown of traditional family life; the loss of community and social values in society; and a growing lack of parental responsibility and skills. The failure to deal with juvenile crime is one of the most serious problems facing the UK, particularly London, and many children are totally out of control by the age of ten or even younger.

Crimes against property (e.g. homes and vehicles) are a problem in London, although burglary rates are at their lowest since the '70s, thanks largely to better home security. Around 20 per cent of all UK crime takes place in London, where professional thieves even steal antique paving stones, railings, doors and casings. Garden 'furniture' such as statues is also a popular target, therefore you need to ensure that it's secure and insured.

Although the above may paint a somewhat depressing picture, London is generally a very safe place to live. In comparison with many other cities, including most European cities, the crime rate is relatively low, as is the incidence of violent crime. If you secure your home and take precautions against crime, your chances of becoming a victim are relatively low.

The crime rate varies considerably from area to area, and anyone planning to live in London should avoid high crime areas whenever possible.

The authorities have successfully reduced crime in recent years by putting more police officers and Police Community Support Officers (PCSOs) on the beat and with the extensive use of CCTV cameras. PCSOs are civilian police officers, described as the eyes and ears of the Metropolitan Police. They have special powers to deal with matters ranging from issuing fixed penalties for anti-social behaviour to carrying out vehicle checks. Their main purpose, however, is to maintain a highly visible street presence, deterring crime and reassuring the community, while leaving police officers free to deal with more serious crime.

The Metropolitan Police publishes monthly and annual crime figures for each borough, except the City of London, which has its own police force. The figures indicate the number of crimes of various types committed and can be viewed as interactive web pages at 💻 www.met.police.uk/crimefigures.

The table in Appendix D shows the total number of crimes committed in each borough between Jan 2009 and Jan 2010, as well as figures for the main four categories: violence, burglary, robbery and vehicle related crimes.

Note, however, that the figures for some boroughs, e.g. Westminster, are distorted by non-resident visitors, e.g. temporary workers and tourists. You should also bear in mind that the overall crime rate in a borough may be distorted by the crime rate in a particular town or area, and that many areas have little crime.

Information regarding borough crime rates is also shown in the **Borough Surveys** in **Chapter 7**. Neighbourhood statistics (by postcode) regarding crime, health and housing are available at 🖳 www.neighbourhood.statistics.gov.uk.

You can find the telephone number of your local police station in the yellow or white pages of telephone books or by visiting 🖳 www.met.police.uk/local and clicking on your borough.

HEALTH SERVICES

One of the most important aspects of living in London (or anywhere else for that matter) is maintaining good health. The UK is noted for its National Health Service (NHS), which celebrated its 60th birthday in 2008, that provides 'free' healthcare to all British citizens and most foreign residents. If you don't qualify for healthcare under the public health service, it's essential to have private health insurance. This is recommended in any case if you can afford it, owing to the inadequacy of public health services in many areas and long waiting lists for specialist appointments and non-urgent operations.

In 2009, the NHS was dragged into the US healthcare reform debate and was cited by the Republicans and vested interests as an excellent reason **NOT** to have a 'public' healthcare system. While the NHS is far from perfect (a number of horrors have been exposed in recent years) – there are many better public health systems in Europe – its faults pale into insignificance compared to the US healthcare 'system', where the wealthy and the *very* expensively insured get the best healthcare in the world on demand, while millions of others receive little or no healthcare at all and are forced to rely on charity. **And, what the debate failed to mention is that anyone in Britain can – and millions do – bypass the NHS waiting lists and 'rationing' and opt for private health treatment, which costs only a fraction of what it does in the US.**

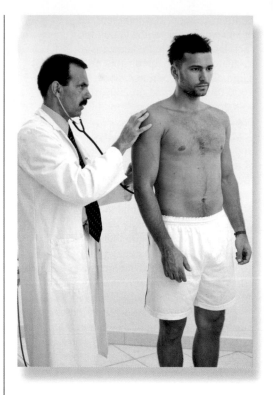

The NHS publishes league tables for around 400 NHS trusts in England. Each trust is measured against a wide range of criteria, which feed into two overall performance ratings: the quality of services and financial management. Services assessed include hygiene, safety and patient access, and the assessment includes whether they've met national targets on waiting times. With regard to financial management, trusts are assessed on their level of debt and whether they provide value. The overall performance rating for trusts is on a four-point scale: excellent, good, fair or weak. The rating for individual boroughs is shown in the **Borough Surveys** in **Chapter 7** and a table of London borough primary care trust ratings is shown in **Appendix D**.

Emergencies

If you have an accident or suffer a sudden serious illness, you can visit a hospital Accident & Emergency (A&E) department, many of which provide a 24-hour service. If you cannot get there under your own steam you can call for an ambulance by dialling 999 (calls are free) and asking for the ambulance service.

ACCIDENT & EMERGENCY

Hospitals in Central London

◆ **Central:** St Mary's Hospital (Praed Street, W2, ☎ 020-7886 6666, 💻 www.imperial.nhs.uk/stmarys/index.htm, Paddington tube) and University College Hospital (Cecil Flemming House, Grafton Way, WC1, ☎ 0845-155 5000, 💻 www.uclh.org, Euston Square/Warren Street tube).

◆ **East:** Hackney & Homerton Hospital (Homerton Row, E0, ☎ 020 8510 5555, 💻 www.homerton.nhs.uk, Homerton rail) and the Royal London Hospital (Whitechapel Road, E1, ☎ 020-7377 7000, 💻 www.bartsandthelondon.org.uk, Whitechapel tube/Liverpool Street rail).

◆ **North:** Royal Free Hospital (Pond Street, NW3, ☎ 020-7794 0500, 💻 www.royalfree.org.uk, Belsize Park tube) and Whittington Hospital (St Mary's Wing, Highgate Hill, N19, ☎ 020-7272 3070, 💻 www.whittington.nhs.uk, Archway tube).

◆ **South:** St Thomas's Hospital (Westminster Bridge Road, SE1, ☎ 020-7188 7188, 💻 www.guysandstthomas.nhs.uk, Waterloo/Westminster tube), Guy's Hospital (Great Maze Pond, SE1, ☎ 020-7188 7188, 💻 www.guysandstthomas.nhs.uk, London Bridge tube) and St George's Hospital (Blackshaw Road, SW17, ☎ 020-8672 1255, 💻 www.stgeorges.nhs.uk, Tooting Broadway tube).

◆ **West:** Charing Cross Hospital (Fulham Palace Road, W6, ☎ 020-8846 1234/1799, 💻 www.imperial.nhs.uk/charingcross/index.htm, Barons Court/Hammersmith tube) and Chelsea & Westminster Hospital (369 Fulham Road, SW10, ☎ 020-8746 8000/, 💻 www.chelwest.nhs.uk, buses 14, 73 or 211).

State your name and location, and describe your injuries or symptoms (or those of the patient) and an ambulance with paramedics will be despatched to take you to hospital (the response time depends on your location and how busy the ambulance service is at that time). The UK doesn't have a national air ambulance service, although there are emergency helicopter services in London for critical cases.

It's wise to check in advance which local hospitals are equipped to deal with emergencies and the fastest route from your home, which could be critical in the event of an emergency, when a delay could mean the difference between life and death. Not all London hospitals have A&E departments and, of those that do, not all are open 24 hours a day. Hospitals in central London (there are more in the outer suburbs) with 24-hour emergency facilities include those shown in the box above.

Hospitals with an Accident & Emergency department and other major local hospitals are listed in the **Borough Surveys** in **Chapter 7.** To find the nearest hospital to your home with an A&E department, see 💻 www.nhs.uk/Pages/homepage.aspx.

It's wise to keep a record of the telephone numbers of your doctor, local hospitals and clinics, ambulance service, first aid, poison control, dentist and other emergency services next to your telephone. You should also note the **NHS Direct** telephone number (☎ **0845-4647), where you can obtain fast and free medical advice.**

For a full list of NHS doctors, dentists, clinics and hospitals in your area, see 💻 www.nhs.uk; for private medical services, see 💻 www.privatehealth.co.uk.

Minor Injuries

Many people go to a hospital Accident & Emergency department (see above) when they could be treated just as professionally and usually more quickly at a **Minor Injuries Unit.** Minor Injuries Units are for patients with less serious injuries, such as sprains, cuts and grazes. The waiting times are usually much shorter than those in A&E, where staff must give priority to serious and life-threatening conditions. You don't need an appointment to visit a Minor Injuries Unit, which are staffed by highly-qualified nurse practitioners with more experience and expertise than many doctors in this kind of treatment.

NHS Walk-in Centres

NHS Walk-in Centres offer fast and convenient access to a range of NHS services, including health information, advice and treatment for a range of minor illnesses (coughs, colds, infections) and injuries (strains, sprains, cuts). Most centres are open from early morning until late evening, seven days a week and you don't need to make an appointment, but check opening times, as they may vary. The centres are run by experienced NHS nurses and provide thousands of patients with immediate treatment for troublesome minor health problems or injuries. To find the nearest NHS Walk-in Centre to your home, visit ⌨ www.nhs.uk/Pages/homepage.aspx and enter your postcode.

If you're unsure whether your injury is minor and can be treated at a Minor Injuries Unit or an NHS Walk-in Centre, you can call **NHS Direct** (☎ **0845-4647**) who will tell you the most appropriate place for treatment. You could also phone your family doctor for advice or use a service such as 247 GP (⌨ www.247gp.co.uk), a private online medical advice service (see below under **Doctors**).

> Police stations keep a list of doctors' and chemists' private telephone numbers in the event of minor emergencies.

Private Medicentres

A fairly recent innovation has been the introduction of private 'Medicentres' (☎ 08456-808 999, ⌨ www.medicentre.co.uk), where doctors and nurses provide consultations and perform tests, screenings, health checks, vaccinations and minor treatment. A Medicentre offers a walk-in service – there's no need to be registered and you don't require an appointment. Patients pay around £65 for a 30

minute appointment with a doctor, £39 for a nurse consultation and £20 for repeat prescriptions. A full list of treatments and fees is shown on the Medicentre website.

Medicentres are located in the 'high street', main railway stations and shopping centres. Centres in London include: Victoria Station, Waterloo Station, Euston Station, Bank (City), Fenchurch Street (City), the Plaza Shopping Centre (Oxford Street), Paddington Station, Eldon Street (City) and Lower Marsh Road (near Waterloo Station).

Doctors

NHS doctors are contracted by their local Family Health Services Authority (FHSA) to look after a number of patients (average around 2,000) who make up their 'list'. Doctors are paid by the NHS according to the number of NHS-registered patients on their list and can refuse to register you as a patient if they have no vacancies. To register with an NHS doctor you must live within his catchment area, although if you're resident in a district for less than three months or have no permanent home, you can register with a local doctor as a temporary resident. After three months, you must register with the doctor as a permanent patient or you may register with another doctor.

If you have trouble finding an NHS doctor, you should contact your local FHSA, which has a duty to find you one. An NHS doctor must give 'immediate necessary treatment' for up to 14 days to anyone without a doctor in his area until the patient has been accepted by a doctor as a permanent or temporary resident.

The best way to find a doctor is to ask your work colleagues, friends or neighbours if they can recommend someone in your area. Alternatively you can consult a list of GPs for your Strategic Health Authority (StHA) in your Community Health Council (CHC) office or contact your local Family Health Services Authority (FHSA). FHSAs publish lists of doctors, dentists, chemists and opticians in their area, which are available at libraries, post offices, tourist information offices, police stations and Citizens' Advice Bureaux. GPs or family doctors are listed under Doctors (Medical Practitioners) in the *Yellow Pages*.

NHS London

NHS London, the Strategic Health Authority for London (105 Victoria Street, London

SW1E, ☎ 020-7932 3700, 🖳 www.london.nhs.uk), was established on 1st July 2006. It has overall responsibility for the performance of 31 primary care trusts (PCTs) – one for each borough (the City of London and Hackney, and Sutton and Merton, are combined) – 24 acute trusts, three mental health trusts and the London Ambulance Service.

Private doctors

There are private, 24-hour doctors' services in London (such as Doctor Call, ☎ 0844-257 0345, 🖳 www.doctorcall.co.uk) which make house calls, but you should check the cost before using them. You can also find a private GP online at 🖳 www.privatehealth.co.uk. Private telephone GP consultations are available from 247 GP (🖳 www.247gp.co.uk), where you can talk in confidence to a qualified doctor – without the worry and inconvenience of time constraints and remembering appointments – 24 hours a day, seven days a week. Membership costs £78 per year for a single person, £156 for a couple or single parent (with up to 4 dependent children) and £234 for a family.

Dentists

There are excellent dentists in all areas of London, although the number that provide free or subsidised NHS treatment has reduced considerably in recent years and those that treat NHS patients often have no vacancies. Ask your colleagues, friends or neighbours (particularly those with perfect teeth) if they can recommend a dentist in your area. Dentists are listed under Dental Surgeons in the *Yellow Pages*, where they may advertise any special services they provide, such as an emergency or 24-hour answering service, dental hygienist and evening or weekend surgeries. The British Dental Association (64 Wimpole Street, W1M 8AL, ☎ 020-7935 0875, 🖳 www.bda.org.uk) can also provide a list of dentists in your area.

In some areas, community dental clinics or health centres provide a dental service for children, expectant and nursing mothers, and disabled adults. Around half of dentists hold a surgery one evening a week or on Saturday mornings. Some hospitals provide a free emergency service, e.g. on Sundays and public holidays, and dental hospitals in London provide a free emergency service on most days. There are also private emergency dental services on call 24 hours a day, seven days a week, such as Baker Street Dental (☎ 020-7486 1047, 🖳 www.bakerstreetdental.com) and Crystal Dental Care (☎ 020-8245 7575, 🖳 www.crystaldentalcare.co.uk).

SCHOOLS

The quality of London schools varies considerably, from world-class to among the worst in the developed world – and everything in between. The quality and proximity of local state and private schools can have a huge influence on property values and the performance (i.e. exam pass rates) of local state schools is one of the most important considerations for parents. Some parents will do almost anything to buy a home within the catchment area of a good primary school and there's an increasingly frantic market for homes in the catchment areas of the best state schools. Schools are one of the most common reasons for moving house in London and some people even buy or rent a home in an area just so they can get an address there – but don't actually move house!

Many families pay dearly to live within the catchment area of a good state school, which can add tens of thousands of pounds (even as much as £100,000) to the value of a property. A study by the London School of Economics put the average price differential between homes within and outside the catchment area of a top primary school at 33 per cent, while properties in the catchment area of a top secondary school cost around 20 per cent more.

Bear in mind that paying more to live near a popular state school might not be the best option, and you may be better off spending the money on private education.

Even if your family has no need or plans to use local schools, the value of a home will be influenced by their quality and proximity, and a home near a good school will command a premium and be a good investment (provided the school continues to rate highly). A local school with top grades can double the rate of increase in the value of property within its catchment area.

Foxton, London's largest chain of estate agents, has a useful facility on its website (💻 www.foxtons.co.uk/education/kensington-and-chelsea - click on the borough at the right of the screen) which shows the percentage of pupils attaining level 4 or above in the Key Stage 2 examination (English, Maths and Science) at primary schools, the percentage of pupils gaining five or more GCSEs with Grades A* to C at secondary schools, plus a list of sixth form colleges. You can then search for properties for sale and rent in the vicinity of a particular school.

League Tables

The ranking of state primary and secondary schools compared to all other London Education Authorities (150 in total) is shown in the **Borough Surveys** (**Chapter 7**) along with the percentage of pupils gaining five or more GCSEs at grades A* to C. Note, however, that an increasing number of schools are shunning traditional 'tough' subjects such as English, geography, history, languages, maths and science in order to do well in official league tables, opting for 'easy' vocational subjects such as intermediate General National Vocational Qualifications (GNVQs). These are generally the softer option and aren't valued by employers.

Bear in mind that test results aren't necessarily the best indicator of how children are progressing and the quality of the teachers and a school's reputation are often just as important, if not more so. You can compare the performance of schools in different boroughs using the table in **Appendix D**. (A boycott of SATs tests - the results of which are used to create the league tables - by some schools in Spring 2010 has thrown the future of league tables into doubt.)

To help you choose an appropriate independent school in London, see *Which London School?* (John Catt Educational). Updated every two years, it contains surveys of nursery, day, boarding and International schools in Greater London, plus colleges of further education.

☑ **SURVIVAL TIP**

If you're interested in how good a school really is and have high ambitions for your child, check the subjects that pupils are taking and how the GCSE league table results are calculated. From 2007, league tables have automatically included results for English and maths.

Added Value

Some schools are designated as having 'added value', which is a measure of how pupils perform in certain Key Stage (KS) tests. Added value measures the progress of pupils at the end of KS4, i.e. in year 11 (aged 15/16), since taking their KS2 tests in year 6 (generally aged 11). In other words, the measure looks at the progress that pupils have made during their entire secondary period of education. Like league tables, many analysts believe that the added value measure is of little or no value, but it may help you to decide on the quality of a particular school.

Specialist Schools

Certain schools are classified as having 'specialist' status by the Department for Education and Skills (💻 www.specialistschools.org.uk). The Specialist Schools Programme (SSP) helps schools, in partnership with private sector sponsors and supported by additional government funding, to establish distinct identities through their chosen specialist subjects and achieve their targets to raise standards. Specialist schools focus on their chosen specialist subjects, but must also meet the National Curriculum requirements and deliver a broad and balanced education for all pupils.

All maintained secondary schools in England can apply for specialist status in one of ten specialist subjects: arts, business & enterprise, engineering, humanities, languages, mathematics & computing, music, science, sports and technology. In practice, a school must raise a certain amount of money and demonstrate excellence in its chosen area. Specialist schools aren't to be confused with 'special' schools, which cater for students with physical disabilities and learning difficulties.

If applicable, before committing yourself to buying a property you should ensure that it's actually within a school's catchment area and that there are no plans to change the boundaries (it happens). Many schools operate a loose 'proximity test' when it comes to admissions and the nearer to a school you live, the more likely your child is to get a place. This leads to incomers with school-age children buying up homes next door to their favoured educational establishment and squeezing out locals living on the margins of the catchment area (a practice which many think is immoral).

A voluntary aided school is a school that's supported financially, usually by a religious organisation, and pupils may need to be of a particular faith in order to obtain a place, particularly if the school is over-subscribed. Entry to selective schools, which are among the best state schools available, is decided by examination and interview. There is, however, no catchment area.

You must ensure that there are places vacant at the school of your choice, otherwise you may find that it's full and you need to enrol your children in a school miles away. If you have young children or are planning a family, you may also wish to consider the proximity and quality of local nursery schools or kindergartens before buying a home. Another consideration for parents may be the distance to local universities or other higher education establishments, particularly if your children plan to commute to university from home.

4.
PROPERTY MARKET

It's virtually impossible to discuss the London property market as a single entity, because the city covers such a vast area with an infinite variety of property in every price range. Many people make a division between central London and the outer boroughs (or inner and outer London), or north and south of the River Thames, although these are arbitrary and fairly meaningless unless you're intimate with the actual towns, neighbourhoods and even the streets concerned. Even within a particular borough or town, there's invariably a huge difference in the type and quality of housing, the character and reputation of neighbourhoods, local services and facilities, and – not least – house prices and their investment potential.

The London property market is quite different from the rest of the UK; not only are prices much higher but price rises (and falls) don't correspond to the national average.

According to a report from the London Housing Federation, high property costs are leaving Londoners hard up, run down and stressed out. Many Londoners move to the country in search of a better quality of life; better and cheaper housing, slower pace of life, lower cost of living, shorter commutes, more space and a healthier lifestyle are cited as the main reasons. However, some 40 per cent move back to London within a few years after finding that rural life doesn't agree with them and that they miss the more stimulating city lifestyle (the grass isn't always greener in the country!).

BOOM & BUST

The UK property market is prone to boom and bust cycles, particularly in the last few decades. For example, the boom years of the late '80s (when property values were doubling every few years in some areas) ended in a disastrous collapse during the recession of the early '90s, when property investment was anything but as safe as houses! Thousands of people lost their homes when interest rates

soared to over 15 per cent, leaving almost 2mn owners with negative equity (where the amount owed on the mortgage exceeds the value of a property). The shock of falling home values hit the British particularly hard, as they traditionally view buying a house as an investment rather than a home for life (as is common in most of the rest of Europe).

It took almost ten years for UK house prices to return to what they were at the end of the '80s, although there was a strong recovery at the end of the '90s which sparked a decade of growth. Between 2002 and 2007 alone, prices in many areas doubled and in some parts of central London they rose by up to 150 per cent (particularly 'prime' properties). However, a downturn was under way in Summer 2007 and was exacerbated in 2008 by the credit crunch (following the sub-prime lending scandal in the US) and spiralling oil prices. Prices fell at their fastest rate for 50 years in 2008 and between between August 2007 and March 2009 they had fallen by around 25 per cent. However, by Spring 2010, house values (particularly prime properties) were close to their 2007 peak.

Despite the sometimes bumpy ride, buying a home in London is an excellent long-term investment – in 2010 property prices were around five times what they had been 20 years previously. As a rough rule of thumb, property values in the UK double every seven years, although in recent years prices in many areas have doubled in as little as three or four years. Property prices in the UK have risen in 36 out of the past 40 years by an average of over 10 per cent per annum.

> Thanks largely to the sharp rise in property values in recent years, one in 20 householders in London is a millionaire.

Most people still find buying preferable to renting, depending, of course, on how long you're planning to stay in London. If you're staying for a short period only, say less than two years, then you may be better off renting (see **Chapter 6**). If you're planning to stay for longer than two years, have a secure job and can afford to buy, then you should probably do so, particularly as buying is generally no more expensive than renting and you could make a sizeable profit.

Renting isn't as common in the UK as it is in many other European countries, and some 70 per cent of Britons own their own homes – one of the highest figures in Europe – and even in London over half of all homes are owner-occupied. However, the average age of first-time buyers has increased to over 30, largely due to the escalation in house prices over the last ten years which has priced a vast number of people out of the market (in 2009, the number of first-time buyers fell to its lowest since records began).

AFFORDABLE HOUSING

In recent years the shortage of housing, particularly affordable housing, in London has been widely debated and is one of the most important issues facing those responsible for planning the city's future. The supply of new housing has averaged around 20,000 units per annum over the last 20 years. However, it has been estimated that over 30,000 new homes are required annually, half of which need to be affordable to London's essential staff. The quantity, quality and cost of housing are of crucial importance to the social and economic wellbeing of London and Londoners.

Many of London's employers (who must also contend with among the world's highest office costs) experience recruitment problems, mainly due to the high cost and scarcity of housing, which has led some companies to leave London for the provinces or even go abroad. High housing costs force Londoners to live further and further from their work, friends and family, and they spend more time travelling than people in other areas of the UK.

The problem is most acute at the lower end of the market, making it even harder for first-time buyers to get a foot on the property ladder. London's housing crisis affects not just low-income workers, but mid-range earners engaged in occupations that are vital to the smooth functioning of the city, such as teachers, NHS staff, fire-fighters, police officers, prison warders, probation officers, council staff and social workers – all of whom find their salaries insufficient to cover the cost of buying a home in London.

There are a number of schemes to help first-time buyers and key workers get on the housing ladder in London, and many developments must now include a percentage of 'affordable' properties. For information see 🖳 www.london.gov.uk/mayor/housing or contact your local borough council.

PROPERTY PRICES

Property prices in London are the highest in the UK and among the highest in the world. For the price of a two-bedroom flat in London you can buy a substantial three or four-bedroom detached house in most of the rest of the country. In April 2010 the average value of a house in London was £336,409, compared with just £164,288 for the UK as a whole. (A walk-in wardrobe in London can cost more than a three-bedroom house in Scotland and the north of England!)

However, average prices don't give an accurate picture, as not only do prices vary considerably according to the borough (from an average of £860,838 in Kensington & Chelsea to £216,271 in Barking & Dagenham), but prices in central London are distorted by the runaway prices at the top end of the prime (i.e. houses selling for £2mn plus) market.

The prime (and super-prime) property market in central London has a life of its own and is largely unaffected by what the rest of the market is doing. There's an increasing and unsatisfied demand for prime properties in central London. Large houses and flats in excess of 3,000ft^2 (278m^2) are in high demand and can command a premium of 50 per cent, with exceptional properties attracting competitive bidding and gazumping, sometimes even on the day of the exchange of contracts!

In 2007, high-end property in London bucked the trend and prices soared by 30 per cent (compared with 10 per cent overall), and the sale of properties costing over £10mn more than doubled between 2007 and 2008. However, the prime market began to be affected by the downturn in 2008, although buyers were still fighting over super-prime properties costing as much as £6,000 per ft^2 (£65,000 per m^2). Although the prime market fell between 2008 and 2009, by Spring 2010 properties costing £5mn plus were reaching prices equal or surpassing their 2008 peaks.

Half of London's prime £3mn-plus houses are purchased by nondoms (non-domiciles who don't pay UK tax and pay far less stamp duty by using offshore trusts) and over two-thirds of sales above £5mn.

A flat in St James's Square SW1 was sold off-plan for an estimated £115mn in March 2008, making it the most expensive home in the world.

In Spring 2010, the cheapest property in London (i.e. a studio flat in a poor area) cost from around £100,000 and a large house (four bedrooms or more) cost anything between £500,000 and £10mn depending on the property and the area. The price of flats varied from between £125,000 for a one-bedroom flat in an outer borough to over £1mn for a two-bedroom flat in Kensington & Chelsea. In central London, properties cost anything from £500 to £5,000 per ft^2 (£5,000 to £50,000 per m^2) or more for super-prime properties.

The less expensive properties tend to be found in unfashionable 'working class' suburbs mainly situated south of the Thames in districts such as Clapham and Streatham, or in the East End away from Docklands, although even there prices have risen dramatically in the last decade. Note, however, that the cheaper areas generally have poor housing stock and are subject to the typical inner city problems of neglect, poor health services and schools, poverty, unemployment and high crime rates.

After more than a decade of continual double-digit growth, property prices starting falling in London in late 2007 – when the average rate of annual increase was over 20 per cent - and by mid-2008 were falling in most boroughs. The number of sales (the best market indicator) in 2008, which was already down on the previous year, fell by over a third. Many market analysts were expecting prices to fall by up to 30 per cent by 2011, although this has proved pessimistic. The market started recovering in 2009 and by spring 2010 the annual price increase was around 10 per cent compared with a year earlier, with prices above their peak of 2007 in many areas. The growth in prices in the last year – to Spring 2010 – has largely been fuelled by a dramatic shortage of supply, with recorded sales some 40 per cent below the peak in 2007.

The increasing prices are bad news for many people, as property prices are around seven times average earnings in London and have never been more unaffordable for the average worker. According to the International Monetary Fund, UK property in general is over-valued by some 40 per cent, although London is a law unto itself, where demand exceeds supply, particularly of prime properties, and is exacerbated by a high percentage of foreign investors.

Nobody knows what will happen to house prices, either in the short or long term, and it's a brave (or foolish) person who's prepared to make predictions.

The table in **Appendix D** gives an indication of house prices in Spring 2010 in all 32 London boroughs and the City of London (prices are also shown in the **Borough Surveys** in **Chapter 7**). Note, however, that these are intended only as a guide and prices vary considerably in some boroughs – the cost per square foot can vary by up to 1,000 per cent, depending on the location and the particular property.

When buying a home in London, don't forget to take into account stamp duty and other expenses such as a survey, legal fees and removal costs.

Price Indices

A number of companies and organisations provide monthly or quarterly house price indices, although none agree entirely and figures should be taken only as a guide. These include the Halifax Bank of Scotland (⌨ www.hbosplc.com), Nationwide (⌨ www.nationwide.co.uk/hpi/review.htm), Right Move (⌨ www.rightmove.co.uk), Hometrack (⌨ www.hometrack.co.uk) and the Land Registry (⌨ www.landregistry.gov.uk) – the latter is the most accurate and authoritative, as it's based on actual sale prices, but it isn't the most up-to-date (the figures are already out of date by the time they're published).

To obtain up-to-date property prices (and other information) in a particular region or town in England and Wales you can also visit websites such as Up My Street (⌨ www.upmystreet.com), Proviser (⌨ www.proviser.com) and Hometrack (⌨ www.hometrack.co.uk). And you can check the actual price that properties have sold for online at ⌨ www.landregisteronline.gov.uk (where you can obtain the price paid/value stated information of any property sold since April 2000 for £4) and ⌨ www.rightmove.co.uk/soldprices.rsp.

If you want to know whether prices are rising or falling in an area, visit Property Snake (⌨ www.propertysnake.co.uk).

LONDON HOMES

Four out of five people in the UK live in houses rather than flats (apartments) and most Britons aren't keen on flats or townhouses and want their own detached or semi-detached (duplex) house with a garden and garage. Nevertheless, many Londoners live in flats, as there's usually no alternative, particularly if you wish to live in central London, and the young have taken to apartment living with a passion.

There's a wealth of different types and styles of home in London, which encompass everything from cottages and mansions to terraced houses, 17th to 19th century period houses to ultra modern houses and luxury apartments with the latest cutting-edge design. Many people prefer older period houses with an abundance of 'charm and character' to 'sterile' modern homes, although you often find pseudo period features such as beams and open fireplaces in new homes. Some new luxury homes are built to modern standards using reclaimed materials, thus combining the best of both worlds.

As with most things, higher-priced houses generally provide much better value than cheaper houses, with a proportionately larger built area and plot of land, better build quality, and superior fixtures and fittings. Many semi-detached and detached houses

have a single or double garage included in the price. When property is advertised, the number of bedrooms and bathrooms is given and possibly other rooms such as a dining room, lounge (living/sitting room), study, breakfast room, drawing room, library, playroom, utility room, pantry, cloakroom, cellar and conservatory. With more expensive properties, often only the number of bedrooms and reception rooms (e.g. lounge, dining room, study, drawing room, etc.) is listed.

The total living area in square feet or square metres is almost never stated in advertisements, although knowing the size of house you want can save a lot of wasted time when house-hunting. For many people the size (total area) is more important than the number of bedrooms or reception rooms. The average size of new homes in inner London is: one-bedroom flat (650ft²/60m²), two-bedroom flat (850ft²/80m²), three-bedroom flat (1,300ft²/120m²), four-bedroom house (2,000-2,500ft²/185-230m²) and five-bedroom house (3,000-3,500ft²/280-325m²).

☑ SURVIVAL TIP

When comparing the price of properties, always take into account their overall size (in square feet or square metres) and check the measurements yourself if they don't seem correct.

Although new properties can be small and lacking in character, they're usually well endowed with all mod cons and services, which certainly cannot be taken for granted in older properties. Plumbing, electrical installations and heating systems in modern houses are more comprehensive and generally of better quality than those in old houses. Central heating, double glazing and good insulation are standard in new houses and are considered essential by many buyers.

In the last few decades, flats have become more popular in London, many of which are tasteful developments of old buildings that have been converted into luxury loft and penthouse apartments. These often come with stainless-steel kitchens, designer bathrooms and other features such as ducted air-conditioning/heating, multi-room audio systems and broadband internet connections in all rooms.

TYPES OF PROPERTY

London property includes the following:

♦ **Bungalow:** A single-storey detached or semi-detached house that's popular with the elderly because they don't have stairs.

♦ **Cottage:** Traditionally a pretty, quaint house in the country, possibly with a thatched roof, although the name is often stretched nowadays to encompass almost anything except a flat. May be detached or terraced.

♦ **Detached House**: A house that stands alone, usually with its own garden (possibly both front and rear) and garage.

♦ **Duplex:** A flat that's on two floors connected by a staircase – similar to a maisonette but without its own external entrance.

♦ **Flat:** A flat or apartment (the same as an American condominium or a 'unit' in Australia) usually on one floor, although it can be spread over a number of floors (when it's generally called a duplex or maisonette). A block of flats is an apartment building, high-rise tower block, a converted building (such as a warehouse or factory) or a large period house that has been converted into flats – called conversions and common throughout London. In central London there are blocks of mansion flats with ornate façades containing stylish and spacious Victorian and Edwardian flats built in the late 19th and early 20th century. Loft flats are generally in converted industrial buildings and often have double or triple height 'cathedral' ceilings.

♦ **Houseboat:** Modern houseboats are luxurious and spacious, limited only by your budget, and much cheaper than the equivalent size house or flat. There is, however, one huge drawback: finding a mooring, which is expensive and practically impossible, with hundreds of people on waiting lists.

♦ **Maisonette:** Part of a house or apartment block with separate living accommodation, usually spread over two floors with its own external entrance.

◆ **Mews House:** A house that's converted from old stables, carriage houses or servants' lodgings (usually 17th to 19th century), which is the town equivalent of a genuine cottage. They're fairly common in central London, although expensive.

◆ **Penthouse:** A penthouse has traditionally been a large luxury flat on the top floor of a high building, although the term is often used nowadays to mean any large (or even not so large) luxury flat, which may or may not be on the top floor of a building (or it may be the top floor of a relatively low-rise building).

◆ **Period Property:** A property built before 1911 and named after the period in which it was built, e.g. Georgian (1714-1830), William & Mary (1830-1837), Victorian (1837-1901) or Edwardian (1901-1910).

◆ **Semi-detached House:** A detached building containing two separate homes joined in the middle by a common wall (US: duplex). They usually have front and rear gardens and off-road parking and/or a lock-up garage.

◆ **Studio or bedsit:** There's a fine line between a studio and bedsit, and in the UK a 'studio' is often just a posh name for a bedsit. In general, a bedsit consists of one room, usually in an old house, which may have a separate bath/shower room and a small kitchenette or mini kitchen area (or shared facilities). A studio flat may be purpose built and should always have its own bathroom and kitchen facilities (the latter may be a separate room or part of the main living area).

◆ **Terraced House:** Houses built in a row of three or more, usually two to five storeys high.

◆ **Townhouse:** A modern building similar to a terraced house, but often with an integral garage.

RESEARCH

Don't be in too much of a hurry when buying a home in London, as the buying process has been accurately described as 'sluggish as a snail under sedation'. Have a good look around your chosen area and obtain an accurate overview of the kinds of property available, the

Mews Houses, Notting Hill, W11

relative prices and what you can expect to get for your money. However, before doing so you should make a comprehensive list of what you want (and don't want) from a home, in order to narrow the field and save time on wild goose chases.

It's sometimes difficult to compare homes in different areas of London, as they often vary considerably and few houses are exactly comparable. Properties range from period terraced, semi-detached and detached houses, to modern townhouses and flats with all modern conveniences; from rambling, dilapidated period homes requiring complete renovation to luxury modern executive homes and vast penthouses in converted buildings.

Although property in London is expensive compared with most other European cities, the fees associated with the purchase of property are among the lowest in Europe and add around 3 to 5 per cent to the cost (depending on the purchase price).

To reduce the chances of making an expensive error when buying in an unfamiliar area, it's often prudent to rent a home for a period (see **Chapter 6**). This allows you to become familiar with the area and gives you plenty of time to look for a permanent home at your leisure.

Wait until you find something you fall head over heels in love with and then think about it for another week or two before rushing headlong to the altar. However, don't dally too long, as good properties at the right price don't remain on the market for long.

☑ SURVIVAL TIP

It's sometimes better to miss the 'opportunity of a lifetime' than end up with an expensive pile of bricks around your neck.

The more research (due diligence) you do before buying a property the better, which should include advice from those who already own a house locally, from whom you can often obtain invaluable information (possibly based on their own mistakes). A huge number of magazines and newspapers (see **Appendix A**) are published for homebuyers, and property exhibitions are also staged throughout the year in London. Property is advertised for sale in all major newspapers (many of which contain property supplements on certain days) and local free newspapers. Information about properties for sale is also available on the internet and most estate agents have their own website. Numerous books are published for homebuyers in the UK (see **Appendix B**) and building societies and banks publish free booklets, most of which contain excellent (often) unbiased advice.

Research Methods

♦ **Estate agents:** There are estate agents (see below) in every town and area in London, where you can register and receive regular information about properties for sale matching your requirements. See **Estate Agents** below and **Appendix C**.

♦ **Internet:** Millions of people a year or some 75 per cent of all house hunters use the internet to find a home or at least do their initial research. There are numerous websites (see **Appendix C**) where you can enter the name of an area or town and the kind of property you're seeking and do a search online. You can also register with agents and receive details of properties

matching your requirements by email. See also **The Internet** below. Knowledge is power when you're house hunting and the best place to get it is online.

♦ **Search agencies:** Relocation agents (see page 73) – also called home search consultants or buying agents – can find you a dream home and are particularly useful for overseas buyers or when you're buying a luxury home and have special requirements. For information, contact the Association of Relocation Professionals (ARP, PO Box 189, Diss, Norfolk IP22 1PE, ☎ 08700-737 475, 🖳 www.arp-relocation.com).

♦ **Newspapers and magazines:** Local weekly newspapers are a good source of information about property prices, the types of property for sale and local agents. Most have a property section and free property newspapers are also published in most areas. Property magazines (see **Appendix A**) are good for new homes and usually contain a list of new developments throughout London. Major daily and Sunday newspapers, such as the London *Evening Standard* (Wednesday edition), *The Times* (Friday edition), *The Daily Telegraph* (Saturday edition) and *The Sunday Times*, contain property or home supplements, and are particularly good for up-market and prime properties.

The *London Property News* (☎ 020-7388 1744, 🖳 www.zoopla.co.uk) contains details of hundreds of properties for sale and rent in four regional monthly editions. Central, South and West; Northwest and Central; City, Islington and Docklands; and South of the River. You can peruse back issues on their website.

♦ **Property shows:** A number of annual property shows are staged in London each year, including the *Ideal Home Show* in March and the *Autumn Ideal Home Show* (🖳 www.idealhomeshow.co.uk) in October, both held at the Earls Court Exhibition Centre (SW5), and *Grand Designs Live* in May and the *Property Investor Show* (🖳 www.propertyinvestor.co.uk) in October, both staged at the ExCel Centre (E16). Property shows are a good source of information for anyone planning to buy property, while home shows are a useful resource for those seeking inspiration for design, décor, furniture and furnishings.

- **Auctions:** Auction sales are popular in London, where they account for an increasing number of sales. For information about auctions see Property Auctions (www.propertyauctions.com), UK Auction List (www.ukauctionlist.com), UK Property Auctions Guide (www.uk-property-auctions-guide.co.uk), Auction Property for Sale (www.auctionpropertyforsale.co.uk) and the Essential Information Group (www.eigroup.co.uk). A good book for anyone planning to buy property at auction is *Buying Bargains at Property Auctions* by Howard R. Gooddie (Lawpack Publishing Ltd.).

- **Private sales in newspapers and on websites:** Private sales are becoming more popular in the UK through websites and newspapers such as *Loot* (www.loot.com), although the vast majority of properties are still sold by estate agents.

- **'For Sale' boards:** Drive around the areas in which you're interested, looking for 'For Sale' boards.

Estate Agents

Most property in the UK is bought and sold through estate agents (they aren't called real estate agents, realtors or brokers in the UK) who sell property on commission for owners. Property sold by estate agents is said to be sold by private treaty, a method of selling a property by agreement between the vendor and the buyer, either directly or through an estate agent. Although there are nationwide chains of estate agents in the UK, e.g. covering England and Wales, most agents are local and don't have a nationwide listing of properties in other regions.

Thousands of estate agents' offices closed or went bust in 2007 and 2008, during which even the major chains were under pressure from their creditors.

There's no multi-listing system in the UK, as there is, for example, in North America, and agents jealously guard their property lists from competitors. There's a plethora of estate agents in London boroughs; so many in fact, that in some areas high streets are sorely lacking in shops – one street in Lavender Hill, SW11 had 26 estate agents in 2007!

If you wish to find an agent in a particular town or area, look under estate agents in the local *Yellow Pages*, check the internet (see below) or hire a relocation consultant (see page 73) to find you a home. Many estate agents are also letting and management agents.

The major estate agents in London are listed in **Appendix C**.

The Internet

You can search for an estate agent or property on the internet, which has come a long way in recent years and is expected to dominate the market in the future. It's particularly useful when you're looking for a property in London and don't live there, as it allows you to peruse property lists at your leisure and even take a guided virtual tour around a property on your computer. A directory of UK agents' websites (there are hundreds of them) can be found on the 'Find a Property' website (www.findaproperty.com) and a list of the major London estate agents is contained in **Appendix C**. Many estate agents produce free newspapers and magazines containing details of old and new houses, and colour prospectuses for new property developments.

It's recommended that you choose an estate agent who's a member of a professional organisation, such as the National Association of Estate Agents (NAEA, ☎ 01926-496 800, 💻 www.naea.co.uk). You may also wish to check whether an agent is a member of the Ombudsman Scheme for Estate Agents (☎ 01722-333 306, 💻 www.oea.co.uk), whose members must abide by a code of practice and to whom you can complain if you have a problem.

Relocation Agents

If you know what sort of property you want, how much you wish to pay and where you want to buy, but don't have the time to spend looking (or you live in another region of the UK or overseas), you can engage a relocation agent – also called home search consultants or buying agents – to find a home for you. This can save you considerable time, trouble and money, particularly if you have special or unusual requirements. Many relocation consultants act as buying agents, particularly for overseas buyers, and claim they can negotiate a better deal than private buyers (which could easily save you the cost of their fees) and they may also have access to properties before they come on the open market. Some specialise in finding 'exceptional' residences costing upwards of £500,000 (which buys only a modest flat in central London).

Relocation agents can usually help and advise with all aspects of house purchase and may conduct negotiations on your behalf; organise finance (including bridging loans); arrange surveys and insurance; and even organise your move. Most agents can also provide a comprehensive information package for a chosen area, including information about employment prospects, health services (e.g. doctors and hospitals), local schools (state and private), shopping facilities, public transport, local amenities and services, sports and social facilities, and communications.

Agents generally charge a fee of between 1 and 3 per cent of the purchase price and a retainer of between £1,000 to £2,500, typically covering a three- or six-month search period. The retainer is deducted from the fee when a property is purchased, but if no deal is done it's usually non-refundable; always check the conditions carefully before paying a retainer. To find a relocation agent, contact the Association of Relocation Professionals (ARP), PO Box 189, Diss, Norfolk IP22 1PE (☎ 08700-737 475, 💻 www.arp-relocation.com) or look in the *Yellow Pages* under 'Relocation Agents' (💻 www.yell.com).

BUYING FOR INVESTMENT

Property has traditionally been an excellent investment in London, where many buyers purchase new homes off-plan without even seeing them (particularly overseas buyers). In fact, in recent years many people have bought off-plan (early buyers typically get a 5 to 10 per cent discount) and sold on before completion, termed 'flipping', where it's possible to make a profit in a fast-rising market without actually ever paying for a property (you can also get your fingers burnt).

In the last decade UK property has far out-performed the stock market and all forms of savings, and provides both capital growth and income (if you let a property). Prices in many areas have been fuelled by investors – some two-thirds of all new homes in London have been purchased purely for investment in recent years.

Your Mortgage magazine provides a handy five-year price history (past five years) and prediction (next five years) service on its website (💻 www.propertyprices.co.uk), and the Global Property Guide (💻 www.globalpropertyguide.com/europe/united-kingdom) shows rental yields for London property and also comparisons with other countries.

> ☑ **SURVIVAL TIP**
>
> Although rents in London are very high compared with other European countries, rental yields are relatively modest at around 5 per cent per annum, although rents have been rising in recent years.

A property investment should usually be considered over the medium to long term, say a minimum of five and preferably ten or more years. Bear in mind that property isn't always 'as safe as houses' and property investments can be risky over the short to medium term – unless you get an absolute bargain or add value. When buying a new property off-plan – particularly a flat – you ideally need to get a good discount which will (hopefully) allow you to recoup your investment if you need to sell quickly. You also need to take into account income tax if a property is let and capital gains tax when you sell a second home or an investment property.

There are various kinds of property investment. Your principal family home is an investment (and should be regarded as a **business** investment) in that it provides you with rent-free accommodation and hopefully will make a profit when you sell it. In the last 10 to 20 years, climbing the property ladder has made hundreds of thousands of Britons property millionaires, simply by trading up every five or ten years.

Think about how easy it will be to sell when buying, i.e. you need to have an exit strategy – if it will be easy to sell, it will also be a good investment. Bear in mind that although you may make a hefty profit on your home, it may be difficult to realise unless you trade down or move to another area (or country) where property is less expensive. Of course, if you buy property other than for your own regular use, i.e. a property that isn't your principal home, you will be in a position to benefit from a more tangible return on your investment.

☑ SURVIVAL TIP

For those who plan to live in a property for a long time, it's best to buy a home, not simply a good investment. Nevertheless, it pays to have an eye on the investment potential of a property, as you never know when you may need to sell.

Types of Investment

There are essentially six main categories of investment property:

♦ **A holiday home**, which can provide a return in a number of ways. It can provide your family and friends with rent-free accommodation and you may also be able to let it to generate income. It may also produce a capital gain if property values rise faster than inflation (as they have done in recent years).

♦ **A pied-à-terre** for when you're in London, which can be for business, pleasure or both. It can be a studio, a one-bedroom flat or something grander; somewhere to crash (sleep) while working, shopping or having a night out on the town; a place to stay from Monday to Thursday when working in town; or even a bachelor pad for guys (or girls) who are no longer bachelors (when a few friends can buy a place together).

♦ **A purpose-built retirement home**, provided you or your partner are aged over 55. Retirement homes are a good investment, as the demand far outstrips the supply. You can buy a retirement home before you retire, although it must usually be your principal residence.

♦ **A property purchased purely for investment**, which could be a capital investment, provide a regular income from letting, or both. In recent years many people have invested in property to provide an income in retirement. See also **Buy-to-Let** below.

♦ **A home for a student child**, which may also realise a capital gain. In recent years an increasing number of parents have purchased homes for their children while they're attending university, which they generally share with fellow students (who pay rent which can go towards the mortgage). It's also a good investment because property in top university cities (e.g. London) has doubled in value in the last decade. The property can be retained and rented after your child has graduated or sold (usually for a tidy profit).

♦ **A commercial property**, which can be anything from bed and breakfast accommodation to a hotel, shop, office or industrial premises (or even farmland). This is a more specialised market sector and not generally something for the novice investor.

Where to Buy

Trying to determine the next hotspot is a national sport among property investors, although you should bear in mind that an 'emerging area' is another term for a 'fringe area'. A desirable address (postcode) can upgrade a property from an ordinary house to a desirable residence – just one street (or even the opposite side of a street) can make all the difference in value. Property within a mile or two of a fashionable area may be much better value, simply due to a different postcode, and it will often have better investment potential.

It may be more profitable to look for an up-and-coming area for maximum profit – for example Hackney and Tower Hamlets will benefit hugely from the Olympics in 2012 and the improved infrastructure (not least excellent public transport links), and the Elephant & Castle is undergoing a huge redevelopment – rather than an area that's already well-established with fashionable restaurants, pubs and shops.

The most recession proof boroughs in London are (from 1 to 10): Richmond-upon-Thames, Kingston-upon-Thames, Bromley, Kensington & Chelsea, Wandsworth, Southwark, Ealing, Lambeth, Greenwich and Bexley, all of which are south of the river apart from Ealing and Kensington & Chelsea.

The key to spotting an up-and-coming area is improved transport links, e.g. a new motorway, railway station or tube/tram/metro link, which is more important than private parking. These include anywhere on the East London line (see page 33) scheduled for completion in 2010 and areas on the Crossrail (see page 33) project planned for 2017. It also pays to buy in an area where there are lots of jobs and insufficient homes, rather than a region where property is cheaper but in less demand due to falling employment. Any area where property costs much less than the surrounding areas is likely to be a good long-term investment, provided it isn't in terminal decline due to crime and urban blight. In general, buy-to-let property must have 'sex appeal', i.e. a high specification and luxury finishes.

You can use websites such Up My Street (🖥 www.upmystreet.com), Proviser (🖥 www.proviser.com) or House Prices (🖥 www.houseprices.co.uk) to check the facilities and property prices in a particular town or suburb.

Buy-to-let

When buying property that you plan to let, you must ensure that the rental income will cover the mortgage, outgoings and vacant (void) periods. Bear in mind that being a landlord can be stressful and the rewards aren't as attractive as they may appear. Market analysts stress that it shouldn't be seen as a way to get rich quick and that investors should view it as a long-term investment (at least ten years).

Average gross rental yields (the annual rent as a percentage of a property's value) have fluctuated wildly in recent years and vary considerably depending on the area and the

Limehouse, Tower Hamlets

type of property. In 2010, average yields for Greater London were around 5 per cent gross per annum.

The best way to ensure a high yield is to cut out the middlemen and find your own tenants, do your own contracts and maintenance, and collect the rent yourself. You can also let a property as shared accommodation (see page 99), which – when done properly – can increase your yield and prevent void periods.

In recent years, there's been a glut of new-build flats on the market in some parts of London and many more were being built. The over-supply of properties for rent has led to a shortage of tenants in some regions, making buy-to-let a risky proposition. One way to test the waters before buying a buy-to-let property is to place an ad in a local newspaper or *Loot* (🖳 www.loot.com). If you get a huge response you know that you're on to a winner.

Bear in mind that there may be a huge difference in what a developer or agent says you should be able to get in rent (high), and the actual market rent (much lower).

Student Homes

If you have a spare 'few hundred thousand' pounds you may wish to buy a home for a child studying at college or university. Not only do they get to live in better accommodation and save on rent, but it's also an excellent investment because good rental property in university towns (e.g. London) is always in demand. When your child finishes university you can sell at a profit or continue to let it. An ideal property should be close to a university or college, have good transport links and lots of bedrooms, but it doesn't need to be in tip-top decorative condition. The sharing of bills must also be carefully considered and controlled, and the payment of rent is best made through an agent if you cannot handle it yourself.

Buying property to let to students in a university city is a lucrative market, with 100 per cent occupancy virtually guaranteed.

GARAGES & PARKING

A garage or off-road private parking space isn't usually included in the price when you buy a flat or townhouse, although a private parking space may be available at an additional cost, possibly in an underground garage. Modern semi-detached and detached homes usually have a garage or car port. Smaller homes usually have a single garage, while larger 'executive' homes often have integral double garages. Period homes (such as Georgian townhouses and Victorian cottages) rarely have a garage, but may have a parking area or space.

When buying a flat or townhouse in a new development, a garage or parking space may be available for an extra cost. You should think carefully before deciding not to buy a garage or parking space (even if you haven't got a car), as it will be worth its weight in gold when you sell and could clinch a sale. In suburban and rural areas, a garage is essential. The cost of parking is an important consideration when buying in London, where on-road parking (even with a resident's parking permit – see page 43) can be difficult to find. Note that in some areas, the local borough may not even issue resident parking permits, therefore check before buying. It may be possible to rent a garage or parking space, although this is difficult and can be expensive.

Bear in mind that in a large development, the nearest resident parking area may be some distance from your home. This may be an important factor, particularly if you aren't up to carrying shopping hundreds of yards to your home and possibly up several flights of stairs. Without a private garage or parking space, parking can be a nightmare.

In London, tradesmen may even refuse work when there's nowhere to park. You can usually get the council to suspend a parking bay for a period, but it costs around £20 per day and you need to apply around a week in advance (not much use in an emergency!). Free on-street parking is non-existent in central London and difficult or impossible to find in most towns, even in outer boroughs. A lock-up garage is important if you have a valuable car, particularly in areas with a high incidence of car theft, and is also useful to protect your car from climatic extremes.

Garages and parking spaces are in huge demand in central London, where single garages sell for £500,000 or more and a space in an underground car park easily sells for £100,000-plus in Westminster – if you can find one! It's possible to rent a space in a garage, which costs as much as £10,000 a year in central London. A garage can add as much as 15 per cent (e.g. £150,000 to £500,000) to the value of a property in central London, and in new developments in areas such as Docklands a parking space in an underground garage costs up to £30,000.

The acute shortage of private parking and garages in central London has led many owners to build garages beneath their houses and some developers even build underground and multi-storey garages on vacant lots, rather than housing.

When buying a flat or townhouse where a garage or parking space is optional, you should **always** buy one (or two if possible) if you can afford to, even if you don't own a car and have no plans to buy one. Parking will be much appreciated by your visitors and guests, and having a garage makes a home **much** easier to sell and is likely to be an excellent investment. Alternatively, you can rent it out and earn a regular income.

HOME INFORMATION PACKS

Important Note

In May 2010, the new government announced that they were scrapping HIPs but keeping energy performance certificates. However, although HIPs are suspended, the information in this section remains valid until the legislation is enacted.

Controversial Home Information Packs (HIPs) were introduced on 14th December 2007 in England and Wales, ostensibly to improve and speed up the process of buying and selling homes and reduce the number of failed home sales. Before the introduction of HIPs, much of the information required by buyers was only available after the offer to purchase had been tendered, which meant that any problems regarding the condition of a property or its documentation wasn't revealed until costs had already been incurred. This often led to the need to renegotiate the terms of the sale, lengthy delays in the exchange of contracts and the failure of many transactions.

By far the most common reason so many sales fail is that prospective buyers in the UK – unlike buyers in most other countries – aren't required to pay a deposit when they agree to buy a property. Therefore a 'buyer' can pull out of a deal anytime before the exchange of contracts without any penalty.

HIPs have done nothing to reduce or eradicate gazumping (where the vendor agrees a price with a buyer and then sells to another buyer for a higher price) and gazundering (where the buyer drives down the agreed price by threatening to pull out of an agreed purchase at the last minute), both of which are rife in the UK.

For buyers, a HIP provides essential information about properties they're considering buying and reduces the chance of unwelcome surprises later in the process, while for sellers it reduces the likelihood of any nasty surprises in the selling process that could delay the sale, as buyers will be able to make more informed decisions about purchasing a home.

A key component of the HIP is the Energy Performance Certificate (EPC – see ⌨ http://epc.direct.gov.uk), which rates a home's energy efficiency, using graphs like those on fridges and washing machines, and includes recommendations about how to cut fuel bills and reduce carbon emissions, encouraging people to make improvements to the energy efficiency of their homes.

A HIP must be provided by the vendor or the agent selling a property and must contain the following compulsory documents for freehold properties:

♦ Home Information Pack Index;

♦ Property Information Questionnaire (PIQ) – see below;

♦ Energy Performance Certificate (EPC) or Predicted Energy Assessment (PEA);

♦ sustainability information (required for newly built homes);

♦ sale statement;

♦ evidence of title;

♦ standard searches (local authority and drainage and water).

Leasehold properties require all the compulsory documents listed above plus a copy of the lease.

The Property Information Questionnaire (PIQ) was introduced on 6th April 2009 for those selling homes in England and provides supplementary relevant information of interest to prospective buyers, such as:

♦ when a property was purchased;

♦ the council tax band;

♦ parking facilities;

♦ insurance and claims associated with the property (fire, flood, storm);

♦ supply of utilities;

♦ alterations to the property and permissions gained;

♦ access;

♦ leasehold information (if relevant).

The HIP can also include additional optional information that's of interest to buyers, such as a home condition report, other searches, guarantees and warranties on the property,

details of any relevant planning or listed building regulations, and a legal summary. The regulations prohibit the inclusion of marketing or advertising material in the pack, and sellers must ensure it includes only official material.

> A HIP must be commissioned by the seller or his agent and costs a buyer nothing. The cost varies considerably, from £95 on the internet (if the ads are to be believed) to a more typical £300-350.

The jury is still out on HIPs, but the general consensus is that they have done nothing to speed up sales – on the contrary, they have actually slowed the sales procedure – and have even deterred prospective sellers from putting their houses on the market.

For further information, see 💻 www. homeinformationpacks.gov.uk.

City Hall, Southwark

5.
BUYING PROPERTY

The vast majority (over 80 per cent) of people in the UK live in houses rather than flats, although these are less common (and more expensive) the closer you get to central London. Houses encompass any dwellings other than flats (apartments) and include detached and semi-detached houses, bungalows, terraced houses and townhouses – in fact any building with its own plot of land.

Most property in the UK is owned freehold, where the owner acquires complete legal ownership of the property and land and his rights over it, which can be modified only by the law or specific conditions in the contract of sale. However, most flats are 'owned' under a system called leasehold (see page 84). Houses are generally better value than flats and may also be a better investment. If you decide to buy a house, your first decision is whether to buy a new or an old house.

NEW HOMES

The quality of new buildings in the UK is strictly regulated and they must conform to stringent building regulations and energy efficiency standards. However, in practice, quality varies and some new developments in London suffer from poor standards and tiny proportions (dubbed Noddy houses), being built primarily for the investment (letting) market and not for owner-occupiers. A recent housing audit carried out by the Commission for Architecture and the Built Environment (CABE, 🖥 www.cabe.org.uk) found that only 18 per cent of new housing qualified as 'good' or 'very good', the rest being poor (29 per cent) or average (53 per cent).

The British preoccupation with the number of bedrooms rather than the total area of a property has led developers to build ever smaller homes; a typical house built today is 55 per cent smaller than one built in 1920.

New houses may contain a high level of 'luxury' features, depending on individual developments and (of course) the price. You can also have a range of 'custom' extras included for an additional cost. An added advantage is that the cost of options can be included in your mortgage, although it's important to check that they provide good value (many developers overcharge on extras, which is a common cause of complaints). The cost of land is usually included when buying a detached house on its own plot, unless you sign separate contracts for the land and house.

Most new homes are made of brick but some employ steel-framed panels, a fairly recent introduction to the UK, which are pre-fabricated with foam insulation board ready for bolting together; this increases fuel efficiency and sound insulation. Although rare and relatively expensive, stone (usually from a local source) is once again in vogue as a building material for luxury homes.

In some areas, new homes must be styled to blend in with existing homes and many builders offer a variety of 'mock' period styles, possibly using recycled materials (e.g. bricks, tiles, oak timber beams, fireplaces, doors, etc.) from old properties, thus offering the best of both worlds for those who cannot decide between a period home and a maintenance-free new home. Some developers even create new houses in the style of barn conversions. Homes with thatched roofs have always been popular and specialist builders offer thatched homes of almost any size – at a price (there's also been a shortage of the special roofing reeds in recent years).

Most new properties are covered by the National House Building Council's (NHBC, ☎ 0844-633 1000, 💻 www.nhbc.co.uk) Buildmark ten-year warranty or the Zurich Municipal Building Guarantee (💻 http://www.zurich.co.uk/buildingguarantee/home/introduction.htm, ☎ 01252-387 535). Most lenders refuse to lend against a new house without a warranty. The NHBC warranty covers the owner for claims of up to £10,000 or 10 per cent of the original purchase price (whichever is greater) against the builder's failure to complete a house, loss of a deposit or any expenses incurred in completing building work.

Home and property magazines (see **Appendix B**) contain a wealth of information about new homes, including a list of new developments throughout London, plus numerous advertisements from developers. Daily newspapers are a good source of information, particularly the broadsheet Saturday and Sunday newspapers such as *The Times* and *The Daily Telegraph* (Saturday editions), *The Sunday Times* and *The Sunday Telegraph*. You can also search for a new home on the internet on numerous websites, including New Homes (💻 www.new-homes.co.uk), Smart New Homes (💻 www.smartnewhomes.co.uk) and Your New Home (💻 www.yournewhome.co.uk). See also **Appendix C**.

Many home and property exhibitions are held in London throughout the year, including the *Daily Mail Ideal Home Show* (💻 www.idealhomeshow.co.uk) staged in March at the Earls Court Exhibition Centre, the *House & Garden Fair* (💻 www.houseandgardenfair.co.uk) held in June at the Olympia Exhibition Centre and the *Homebuyer Show* (💻 www.homebuyer.co.uk) staged in March at the ExCel Centre.

OLD HOUSES

In the UK, the term 'old houses' generally refers to buildings that are pre-1940, while homes built before 1911 are referred to as 'period homes'. The age of period homes is identified by reference to the monarch(s) reigning at the time they were built, e.g. Georgian (1714-1830), William & Mary (1830-1837), Victorian (1837-1901) or Edwardian (1901-1910). In the case of Victorian properties, these are sometimes qualified as 'early', 'mid-' or 'late Victorian'.

If you want a property with abundant charm and character, a building for renovation or conversion, outbuildings or a large plot, you must usually buy an old property. When buying an old building, you aren't just buying a home, but a piece of history, part of the UK's cultural heritage, and a unique building that represents the architects' and artisans' skills of a bygone age.

Old houses can provide better value than new houses, although you must check their quality and condition carefully. As with most things, you generally get what you pay for, so you shouldn't expect a fully modernised period property for a knock-down price. If a house needs extensive renovation or modernisation, it's important thoroughly to investigate the costs, which are invariably higher than you imagined or planned.

If you're planning to buy a property that needs major renovation, you should have a full structural survey carried out and obtain an accurate estimate of the costs before buying it. While you may get more for your money when buying an old home, the downside is that they require more maintenance and upkeep than new homes, and heating costs can be high if a property doesn't have good insulation.

Listed Buildings

Listed buildings are those of special architectural or historic interest, that are protected throughout the UK. Buildings can be listed because of their age, rarity, architectural merit or method of construction, or a combination of these. Occasionally a building is listed because it has played a part in the life of a famous person or was the scene of an important event. An interesting group of buildings, such as a model village or a square, may also be listed.

☑ SURVIVAL TIP

There are also conservation areas in many historic towns and cities, where there are strict rules governing new developments and the changes that can be made to existing houses.

The older a building is, the more likely it is to be listed. There are over half a million listed buildings in the UK – around 350,000 Grade I and II listed buildings in England and Wales, plus a further 175,000 in Scotland and Northern Ireland – most of which were built before 1840. They include all buildings built before 1700 that survive in anything like their original condition and most built between 1700 and 1840. After that date, the criteria becomes tighter with time and post-1945 buildings need to be exceptionally important to be listed.

In England and Wales, buildings are graded to show their relative architectural or historic interest as follows:

♦ **Grade I** – buildings of exceptional interest (only some 2 per cent of listed buildings are in this grade).

♦ **Grade II*** – particularly important buildings of more than special interest (some 4 per cent of listed buildings).

♦ **Grade II** – buildings of special interest warranting every effort to preserve them (over 90 per cent of listed buildings).

The task of identifying and protecting buildings in England and Wales is under the control of English Heritage (1 Waterhouse Square, 138-142 Holborn, London, EC1N 2ST, ☎ 0870-333 1181, 💻 www.english-heritage.org.uk).

Making Alterations to Listed Buildings

You must obtain listed planning consent to make alterations to a listed building and may also need planning permission; you can obtain advice from the local planning department or English Heritage about any changes you wish to make. All building work must also comply with building regulations – your local library should have a copy of the 'Planning Policy Guidance. Note 15', which contains (in annexe C) a detailed guide to what you can and cannot do to a listed building and the materials to use.

With a listed building, you cannot even change the colour of your front door without permission.

No structural changes are permitted with Grade I (mostly churches and public buildings) and Grade II* (star) buildings of outstanding interest, but usually in a local context. Grade I and II* buildings may be eligible for English

Heritage grants for urgent major repairs, although you're unlikely to get any sort of grant for a Grade II listed building. Restoration costs are exempt from VAT when the work has been granted listed building consent, although it mustn't consist of repairs or maintenance (which means that it's often more economical to replace something than repair it). Grants are also available from English Heritage and the Heritage Lottery Fund to restore derelict Grade I and Grade II* properties (or install indoor sanitation), and to repair items such as old iron railings or sash windows in conservation areas.

Bear in mind when restoring a listed building that costs can spiral dramatically (adapting or converting a listed building can add 25 per cent to your budget) and you will invariably face battles with English Heritage at every turn with a major restoration. It doesn't matter if a listed building was trashed by the previous tenants/owners – YOU must do everything by the book if you wish to return a property to its former glory, irrespective of the cost. If a listed building is in a conservation area it must comply with the borough's Unitary Development Plan (UDP).

Organisations of interest to owners of listed building include the Listed Buildings Information Service (☏ 020-7208 8221, 💻 www.heritage.co.uk/apavilions/glstb.html), the Listed Property Owners Club (☏ 01795-844 939, 💻 www.lpoc.co.uk), Save Britain's Heritage (☏ 020-7253 3500, 💻 www.savebritainsheritage.org), the Society for the Protection of Ancient Buildings (☏ 020-7377 1644, 💻 www.spab.org.uk), the Georgian Group (☏ 0871-750 2936, 💻 www.georgiangroup.org.uk) and the Victorian Society (☏ 020-8747 5899, 💻 www.victoriansociety.org.uk).

⚠ Caution

Make sure (as far as possible) that what you want to do with a property, such as extend it, will be permitted BEFORE buying it.

Private Gardens

Many London squares and developments have private communal gardens for the exclusive use of residents, which can add considerably to the cost of a property. London's shared gardens date back to the 19th century when the landed gentry came up to town for the 'season'. Gardens often have strict rules and regulations, such as no animals, ball games, barbecues, large parties or unsupervised children – their peace and tranquillity add to their charm. Residents pay an annual fee and receive a key.

BUYING A FLAT

Nearly half of all new homes built in the UK are flats (also called apartments) or maisonettes (a flat on two or more floors), compared with less than a quarter five years ago, while in London over 90 per cent of planning permissions are for flats. If you're planning to buy a property in central London – where houses are prohibitively expensive for most people – the chances are that you will be buying a flat rather than a house. Flats are generally a good investment and have excellent letting potential (always assuming that the rental market isn't saturated) – those with two bedrooms and good views are the most popular.

Flat Ownership

Most property in the UK is owned freehold, where the owner acquires complete legal ownership of the property and land and his rights over the property. This includes most houses, whether detached, semi-detached, terraced or townhouses, with their own plot of land. However, most flats in England and Wales are sold leasehold (see below), which includes some 3mn homes in the UK. However, it's possible for leaseholders to buy the freehold, manage their own flats and even own flats under a system of commonhold (which is similar to the system in most other countries), all of which are explained below.

Leasehold

Under leasehold property 'ownership', the freeholder owns the site and charges the leaseholder an annual ground rent; the leaseholder must also pay an annual service charge to the freeholder to cover the maintenance and repairs of the building and its common parts. Ownership is limited to the life of the lease, for example, 80 to 100 years for an old building and up to 999 years for a new building, after which ownership reverts to the freeholder.

Leasehold is a medieval form of 'ownership' ('property serfdom'), whereby you agree to rent a property for at least 100 years, most of which is paid in advance, and you must pay service fees and maintenance costs which are decided by your landlord (who decides what work needs doing, when and by whom). Leasehold law means that you can pay a fortune for a property and technically still not be able to call it your own. At best, leaseholders pay only ground rent on their homes, but there can be restrictive rules whereby they can be prohibited from changing their curtains, wallpaper or even keeping pets. Abuse by landlords such as charging high 'administration' costs, presenting leaseholders with bogus bills and harassment is widespread.

A property can change hands many times during the life of a lease and when the lease expires the property reverts to the original

Buying the Freehold

Since 1993, when the Leasehold Reform, Housing and Urban Development Act became law, leaseholders have had the right to buy the freehold between them, called a joint freehold. At least half the qualifying leaseholders in a building must want to buy the freehold and there's no longer a residency test (previously leaseholders had to have lived in their home for at least one year). Many flats are now sold with a share of the freehold rather than a lease. In 2005, a ruling by the Lands Tribunal changed the way the value of the freehold is calculated, which means that in future leaseholders may have to pay more to buy a property's freehold. When landlords and leaseholders cannot agree on the value, the case is decided by a leasehold valuation tribunal.

owner (the freeholder). However, a leaseholder with a long lease doesn't automatically lose all rights to possession upon the expiry of the lease, but instead becomes entitled to an assured tenancy paying a rent to be agreed between the parties or, in default of such an agreement, a rent determined by the leasehold valuation tribunal.

When buying a leasehold flat, the most important consideration is the length of the lease, particularly if it has less than 50 years to run, in which case you will have difficulty obtaining a mortgage. Most experts consider 75 years to be the minimum lease you should consider. It is, of course, possible to extend a lease and some speculators buy a flat with a relatively small number of years left on the lease in expectation of being able to extend it, after which the property is worth much more. Bear in mind that the cost of extending a lease (or buying the freehold – see below) can run into hundreds of thousands of pounds, although this is usually more than reflected in the property's increased market value.

For advice or information about leases, contact the leasehold advisory service (☎ 020-7374 5380, 🖳 www.lease-advice. org), which can also provide an application form for a leasehold valuation tribunal. There are numerous other websites offering advice for leaseholders, including the Leasehold Advice Centre (☎ 01483-889 922, 🖳 www. leaseholdadvicecentre.co.uk).

Owners of a joint freehold can choose to manage the building themselves or appoint a managing agent, which is generally preferable because it avoids the disagreements that inevitably arise when owners manage a building themselves (and ensures that it's done properly). The 1993 act also made it possible for some leaseholders to extend their lease by 90 years, and if the freeholder decides to sell the freehold he must give the present tenant(s) the right of first refusal to buy it. Under a new 'commonhold' (see below) form of ownership of flats introduced in 2004, leaseholders have the right to buy the freehold and establish a commonhold association to manage the common parts of a property.

If you employ a managing agent, make sure that they obtain three quotations for all work to be done (and that you see the quotes and approve the contractor) and check the annual accounts thoroughly. It isn't unknown for agents to double or treble the cost of work and pocket the difference.

For information, contact the Leasehold Advisory Service (☎ 020-7374 5380, 🖳 www. lease-advice.org), which provides free advice and maintains lists of valuers and solicitors who specialise in leasehold properties. If you sell a lease that was drawn up before 1996, you must ensure that your solicitor includes an indemnity in the contract that allows you to pass liability for any debts on to the new leaseholder, otherwise you could be held liable. This anomaly was abolished in the Landlord and Tenants (Covenants) Act of 1995.

Right to Manage

Another option for leaseholders who don't want to buy the freehold is the 'right to manage' (RTM). This allows leaseholders who're dissatisfied with the way their flats are managed to set up an RTM company and take over the management of their building. The building must meet certain conditions and a minimum number of leaseholders is required to take part. For example, qualifying buildings must include at least two flats and at least two-thirds must be let to 'qualifying tenants' whose lease was originally granted for a term of over 21 years. The number of qualifying tenants must be equal to at least half the number of flats in a building.

For more information, see 🖳 www.right-to-manage.org or www.lease-advice.org/rtmframe.htm.

Commonhold

Under the Commonhold and Leasehold Act 2002, a new kind of property ownership was established (the first since 1925), called commonhold. This is similar to strata title in Australia – a type of home ownership which has existed there for over 50 years – and condominiums in the US (and the system employed throughout Europe). Commonhold allows freehold ownership of individual flats, houses and non-resident units (such as shops) within a building or an estate, and is an alternative to the leasehold system.

Under commonhold, there's no landlord and every resident or 'unit holder' in a multi-unit property has equal rights, with each owner owning his own flat as a freehold and a share in the common structure. All unit-holders take joint responsibility for the maintenance and repair of the commonly-owned areas and their obligations are formally laid down. The common parts are owned and managed by a limited company, know as a Commonhold Association (CA).

It was hoped that commonhold would be adopted in new developments, although most developers prefer to stick with leasehold which is more profitable. A group of flat owners cannot force the landlord of an existing leasehold building to convert to commonhold, although they can buy the freehold (see above). Once leaseholders have the freehold they can apply to convert it into a commonhold, provided the necessary requirements are met, which includes the unanimous consent of all parties concerned.

Property investors can decide whether to make a new development either commonhold or leasehold, and those who are currently leaseholders can also switch to the commonhold system. However, developers can decide to stick with the freehold/leasehold system until they're confident that commonhold properties will hold their value, and leaseholders may be deterred by the complexity of the process.

Types of Flat

Flats are common in central London and in new developments in East London, but rarer elsewhere, particularly in towns in the outer boroughs. In central London, they generally consist of purpose-built

Victorian and Edwardian mansion blocks of luxury flats (with porters) and conversions of large period houses, although there are also many modern high-rise apartment blocks. In the last few decades a wealth of old industrial sites and buildings have been transformed into chic urban flats and loft penthouses, with stainless-steel kitchens and designer bathrooms, plus there's been redevelopment of stately homes, hospitals, schools, warehouses, mills, offices and factories.

So called 'mega-apartments', i.e. huge open plan flats, and loft apartments with double or triple height 'cathedral' ceilings are popular in London, as are penthouses, some of which sell for £5mn or more (or up to £5,000 per ft²/£50,000 per m²). They're often an emotive purchase, where you pay dearly for the panoramic views. You can also buy a 'shell' flat – which is literally a shell with no internal walls or fixtures and fittings – which needs to be fitted out. With this type of flat you can usually obtain a maximum 75 per cent mortgage and, if necessary, you will need to take out another loan to fit it out. Fitting out costs between £25,000 and £75,000 for a 1,000ft² (92.9m²) flat, depending on the number of rooms and the quality of fixtures and fittings.

Modern Flats

New flats are invariably lavishly appointed, which is essential if they're to sell well or have good letting potential. Flats in London are increasingly being bought by middle-aged buyers and retirees, who want an ultra-modern contemporary look: sleek lines, wooden floors and lots of glass. The best flats are beautifully designed and finished, with developers vying with one another to design the most alluring interiors. These include designer kitchens complete with top quality appliances; however, bear in mind that although kitchens full of gleaming stainless steel and gadgets may look great, they aren't always practical, well-designed or good for cooking. Other features may include balconies, en suite bathrooms to all bedrooms, with separate showers, and designer fittings; built-in (or walk-in) wardrobes; under-floor heating, telephone, TV and internet points (including cable) in all

rooms; fitted carpets; and ceramic floors in kitchens and bathrooms.

Luxury flats usually come with a menu of high-tech options, including discrete, multi-room audio systems; home cinemas; ducted air-conditioning/heating; state-of-the-art security; and broadband connections in all rooms.

They may also have air-conditioning or what may be termed comfort cooling, air-cooling or a climate-controlled, refrigerated-air system. Security is a key feature of most developments, which may have a 24-hour caretaker/concierge, CCTV surveillance and a security entry system with entry phones – some even have a video entry system that takes a picture of callers who press your bell when you aren't at home.

Some developments – so-called 'lifestyle' flats – also have a leisure complex with a swimming pool and gymnasium, sauna, Jacuzzi and tennis courts, plus secure parking and landscaped courtyards or gardens. Sports facilities are often the sale clincher in an inner-city development. Some developments also have other amenities, such as an in-house medical centre, business centre, private meeting rooms for the exclusive use of residents and a restaurant, café or bar.

Size

The size of flats varies considerably, although new flats are getting smaller, particularly in London – it isn't uncommon to find purpose-built student studios (or micro-flats) of less the 250ft² (23m²) and one-bedroom flats of 425ft² (40m²). When comparing the price of flats, always take into account their size (in square feet or square meters) which is a huge factor. Most experts recommend that you avoid studios, which are invariably tiny, cramped and difficult to sell – for a bit more money you can buy a one-bedroom flat (most people want a separate bedroom).

However, studios and small one-bedroom flats are popular among commuters who stay in London during the week and return to their country homes at the weekend. They're more comfortable and cheaper than staying in a hotel, you can prepare your own meals, and you also save money and time on travelling.

Research

Before buying a resale flat (rather than a new flat off plan – see page 89) it's wise to investigate the market and particular developments thoroughly. For example, is a development popular and do people like living there; what are the charges and restrictions; how noisy are other residents; are the recreational facilities easy to access; and, most importantly, is the development well managed? Some small apartment blocks are run by resident 'dictators', while larger developments may be managed by developers who increase the service charges at the drop of a hat – needless to say, both are best avoided. You may also wish to check on your prospective neighbours. A flat that has others above and below it is generally noisier than a ground or top floor flat. If you're planning to buy a flat above the ground floor, ensure that the building has a lift (unless you enjoy lugging shopping and everything else up stairs).

☑ SURVIVAL TIP

Note that ground or garden level flats (along with penthouses) are more prone to theft and an insurance company may insist on extra security before they will insure a property.

Cost of Flats

The cost of flats in London varies considerably, from £100,000 for a studio or one-bedroom flat in an outer borough to well over £300,000 for a one-bedroom flat in central London. Many flats in London are purchased by investors and prices have risen considerably in the last decade; in Spring 2010 prices were generally between £500 and £1,000 per ft² (£5,380 to £10,760 per m²) in central London, but prime properties cost £1,000 to £1,500 per ft² (£10,760 to £16,140 per m²) and, at the top end of the market, 'super-prime' properties were as much as £5,000 per ft² (over £50,000 per m²)!

Cheaper flats are available in Docklands and south of the river, although even there new flats cost from between £250 and £500 per ft² (£2,690 to £5,380 per m²). Note that the cost per ft² of small flats is usually much higher than the cost per ft² of spacious flats. The price may include a year's free membership of a health club or gymnasium, but bear in mind that amenities such as this don't come cheap (see **Service Charges** below).

The price you pay for a flat is also influenced by the state of the property market and the vendor's personal circumstances. There's a glut of new-build flats on the market in some areas (exacerbated by the slow down in buy-to-let purchases), most of which are small, with one or two bedrooms. Some developers offer discounts of 10 to 20 per cent (but they may not advertise them), although this depends on the actual development and the price of the flat – the highest discounts are offered on slow-selling expensive flats. Discounts may be in the form of the deposit or stamp duty paid by the developer, rather than a reduction in the price (but amounts to the same thing). Bear in mind that the market for flats is more buoyant in London than in other parts of the UK, and you may not get any reduction at all on a flat in a popular development that's selling well off-plan (see below).

Buying from a broker can save you 10 to 20 per cent, depending on the cost of the flat – the broker buys flats in bulk, e.g. ten or more, and sells them to individual buyers for a premium of say £10,000 plus a £5,000 fee. The broker may have bought them for a 20 per cent discount, 10 to 15 per cent of which he passes on to buyers.

In an older development, you should check whether access to private grounds and a parking space are included in the cost. In new developments, you must usually pay extra for a garage or a space in an underground car park.

If you're buying a resale property, check the price paid for similar properties in the same area or development in recent months, but bear in mind that the price you pay may have more to do with the seller's circumstances than the price fetched by other properties. Find out how many properties are for sale in a development; if there are many on offer you should investigate why, as there could be management or other problems. If you're still keen to buy, you can use any negative aspects to drive a hard bargain.

Note that in popular developments, you must usually buy off-plan (see below) long before a development is completed.

Buying Off-plan

When buying a new property in a development, you're usually obliged to buy it 'off-plan', i.e. before it's built. In fact, if a development is finished and largely unsold, particularly in a popular area, you should be wary because it probably means that there's something wrong with it. In recent years people have queued overnight to buy properties in many new developments. In a rising market, it's possible to make a profit buying off-plan, between the period when you pay the deposit and when the property is completed a year or two later, and sell it without completing (a practice known as 'flipping').

However, in a stagnant or falling market, some analysts advise buyers against buying off-plan. It may be better to wait until a property is almost complete before buying, or you could

end up paying more than a property is worth or the developer could even go bust. You must pay a deposit of at least 10 per cent of the price and over £500 in legal fees to exchange contracts, which legally obliges you to go through with a purchase. If the developer goes bust, you may have to wait years for a property to be completed and there's no guarantee that it will be finished to the original specifications. Added to which, you could lose your mortgage if bad publicity has an adverse effect on the market value of the property.

In the last few years, many buyers have pulled out of off-plan purchases (and lost their deposits – some have even been sued by developers and been forced to complete purchases), amid fears that the property wouldn't be worth what they had agreed to pay and that the rent (assuming they could find a tenant) wouldn't cover their mortgage payments. When buying off-plan, choose a large developer or one who's selling different types of property in different areas, as he will be better placed to weather a downturn.

Service Charges

Flat owners pay service charges for the upkeep of communal areas and for shared services, with charges calculated according to each owner's share of the development. A proportion of the common elements is usually assigned to each flat owner depending on the number and size of flats in a development. Service charges may include the following:

- Garden maintenance;
- Cleaning (including roads and pathways), decoration and maintenance of communal areas and buildings;
- Caretaker, concierge or porter;
- Lift maintenance, entry phone and security;
- Lighting in communal areas and grounds;
- Water supply (e.g. for gardens);
- Pest control;
- Buildings insurance;
- Administration;
- General maintenance;

- Membership and upkeep of communal facilities, such as a health club, gymnasium or swimming pool;
- Sink (reserve) fund for major repairs.

Buildings insurance is provided by the freeholder, but you're usually required to have third party insurance to cover damage you may cause to other flats, e.g. due to a burst pipe or fire.

> **☑ SURVIVAL TIP**
>
> Always check the level of service charges and any special charges before buying a flat.

Fees are usually billed monthly or biannually and adjusted at the end of the year (which can be a nasty shock), when the actual expenditure is known and the annual accounts have been finalised. If you're buying a flat from a previous owner, ask to see a copy of the service charges for previous years, as owners may be 'economical with the truth' when stating service charges, particularly if they're high.

Service charges vary considerably and can run into thousands of pounds (£10,000 or more a year) in luxury developments with a high level of amenities such as a gymnasium, fitness room and spa. Charges may include hot water and heating, but not extraordinary repairs (although they may be covered by the sink fund). An apartment block with a resident caretaker will have higher charges than one without a caretaker, although it's preferable to buy in a block with a caretaker.

If a management company is employed to manage and maintain an apartment block, the service fees are usually higher, but the building is also likely to be better managed. High fees aren't necessarily a negative point (assuming you can afford them), provided you receive value and the development is well managed and maintained. The value of a flat depends to a large extent on how well the development is maintained and managed.

In the past, landlords have used threats of expensive court action to intimidate owners into paying higher fees. Many landlords have increased their service charges significantly in recent years, which often bear little or no relationship to their actual costs, and many leaseholders have been hit by high charges for major repairs (see below). The 2002 Commonhold and Leasehold Act was supposed to put an end to the bitter disputes between freeholders and leaseholders. It gave leaseholders new powers to challenge excessive service charges and maintenance fees before an independent body (replacing county courts), known as a Leasehold Valuation Tribunal (LVT), with a panel comprising a solicitor, a valuer and a third experienced person.

However, according to the Campaign for the Abolition of Residential Leasehold (🖳 www.carl.org.uk), landlords are still overcharging for service charges and repairs, and getting away with it. Although LVTs have made it easier to resolve disputes, this hasn't made the outcome any fairer for leaseholders, who are often opposed by high-powered legal firms and barristers, resulting in astronomical legal costs. Landlords can also still have cases transferred to the high court, in the almost certain knowledge that leaseholders won't have the financial muscle to oppose them. A website that may be of interest to prospective flat owners is 🖳 www.service-charge.co.uk.

Maintenance & Repairs

If necessary, owners can be assessed an additional service charge to make up for any shortfall of funds for maintenance or repairs. You should check the condition of the common areas (including all amenities) in an old development and whether any major maintenance or capital expense is planned for which you could be assessed. Beware of bargain flats in buildings requiring a lot of maintenance work or refurbishment. All major developments have a sink or reserve fund to pay for one-off major repairs, which is funded from general service charges.

Ground Rent

Ground rent is a nominal rent for the land on which an apartment block is built and is usually around £100 to £200 per year. The lease should indicate whether the ground rent is fixed or can be reviewed after a certain period.

Covenants & Restrictions

Covenants are legally binding obligations of the freeholder and leaseholder to do or refrain from doing certain things. Restrictions are regulations governing how leaseholders are required to behave. They usually include such things as noise levels; the keeping of pets; renting; exterior decoration and plants (e.g. the placement of shrubs); waste disposal; the use of gymnasiums or fitness rooms and other recreational facilities; parking; business or professional use; and the hanging of laundry.

Check the regulations and discuss any restrictions you're unsure about with management and residents. Permanent residents should avoid buying in a development with a high proportion of rental flats, i.e. flats that aren't owner-occupied, although you may have little choice in London.

Household Cavalry (Life Guards)

6.
RENTING PROPERTY

Some 70 per cent of Britons own their own homes – one of the highest figures in Europe – therefore renting isn't as common in the UK as in many other European countries, where many people are happy to rent for their entire lifetimes (or simply cannot afford to buy). Traditionally there hasn't been a particularly strong rental market in the UK, although this has changed dramatically in the last few decades with new laws regarding renting and the introduction of buy-to-let mortgages. Nowadays renters get a better deal and can afford to be choosy, with the booming buy-to-let market creating a wealth of rental properties, particularly in London where the cost of property is prohibitively expensive for many people.

If you need to rent a property for a short period while looking for a long-term home, you can rent a serviced apartment. This is a fully furnished and equipped self-catering flat with a kitchen, television, video, broadband and maid service. These are generally intended for short lets of a few weeks or months and cost around twice as much as a similar apartment with a long-term tenancy (or around the same as a hotel room). They are, however, ideal for a short period while you look for a long-term rental.

To find a serviced apartment in London, simple enter 'serviced apartments, London' into a search engine such as Google.

WHY RENT?

Some people prefer to rent (rather than buy) a home, which certainly isn't just for the young, the insecure and the desperate – which is how it has customarily been portrayed in the UK (although many homeowners still look down on renters as an inferior species). Although most Britons prefer to buy, and it certainly pays to buy a home in the long term, there are a number of advantages to renting:

◆ renting allows you to live in a size or style of property that's out of your price range, or in an area where you couldn't possibly afford to buy a home;

◆ it can save you money and leave you better placed to buy a home at a later date, as you

can move quickly to buy when the market is favourable;

◆ renting gives you time to save a deposit so that you can afford a mortgage and/or can obtain a better mortgage deal;

◆ it can be a more sensible financial option, as there are hidden costs with owning a home (owning property is a liability as well as an asset);

◆ renting allows you to use your capital for a more lucrative venture, such as starting a business or buying a home abroad, where property may be a better investment;

◆ you can rent a furnished property, which saves you having to spend money on furniture and furnishings;

◆ renting gives you freedom from DIY and maintenance costs;

◆ it allows increased flexibility, particularly if you don't expect to remain in London long-term – renting a home is generally the best option for those who plan to stay less than two years.

It's often wise for prospective buyers to rent for a period, e.g. six months, which allows you time to become familiar with an area, the type of housing available and the cost, before committing yourself to a purchase.

RENTAL AGREEMENTS

The 1988 Housing Act caused something of a revolution in the rental market in London by deregulating new lettings in the private sector. From 15th January 1989, new lettings were either an assured tenancy, with long-term security of tenure, or an assured shorthold tenancy (see below) for a fixed period of at least six months. These changes encouraged greater choice and competition in the rental market and made it much easier for landlords to evict unwanted tenants. Previously the law (the Rent Acts) had kept a stranglehold on rent levels and the general freedom of landlords, and was heavily weighted in favour of tenants.

However, from 1989 the private rental market was turned on its head and now favoured landlords, and the privately-rented housing stock improved considerably as a consequence. The law was amended again under the Housing Act (1996) and from 28th February 1997 all new lettings have automatically been assured shorthold tenancies unless otherwise agreed. Exceptions include when the rent's over £25,000 per annum or for other arrangements such as company lets, which are generally known as 'common law' or 'contractual' tenancies. You must be over 18 to hold a tenancy agreement.

If you deal directly with the landlord of a property, rather than an agent, he may try to

avoid having a tenancy agreement and suggest an informal arrangement whereby you pay him weekly or monthly (possibly in cash). Don't be tempted by this kind of arrangement, which provides neither party with security or protection under the law.

There are a number of useful books detailing the legal rights and duties of both landlords and tenants, including the *Which? Guide to Renting and Letting* (Which?). A Citizens' Advice Bureau (💻 www.citizensadvice.org.uk) can offer advice regarding the legal aspects of renting and your rights.

Assured Shorthold Tenancy

All new tenancies since 28th February 1997 have automatically been assured shorthold tenancies, unless the landlord serves notice to say it isn't or it's written into the agreement that it isn't an assured shorthold tenancy. A shorthold tenancy provides a landlord with a guaranteed right to repossess his property at the end of the term, doesn't provide long-term security for tenants and isn't regulated by any rent controls.

A shorthold tenancy has a fixed time limit, which was previously for an initial minimum period of six months, although it can now be for any term agreed between the landlord and tenant. A tenancy is usually for a set period, known as a 'fixed-term tenancy', but it can also be on a week to week or month to month roll-over basis, known as a 'periodic tenancy', although this is unusual. New agreements are usually for six or 12 months, although some landlords are reluctant to agree an initial period longer than six months (they want to make sure that you're a good tenant before committing to a longer term and may also wish to increase the rent).

You cannot terminate your agreement (or be evicted) during the initial period and, thereafter, you or your landlord must give two months' notice in writing to terminate the agreement. The landlord is legally entitled to repossess the property at the end of the fixed period, provided he gives you notice in writing two months before the expiry of the fixed term. If the landlord wishes to gain repossession of the property before the end of the fixed term, he must give you 14 days notice in writing, and, if you don't agree to leave, he must get a court order requiring you to leave. A court will only order you to leave before the end of your tenancy agreement if the landlord can prove grounds for repossession, such as your poor treatment of the property or not paying the rent. If you have done nothing wrong, the landlord will usually only be able to evict you before the end of your agreement if he can offer you reasonable alternative accommodation. It's a criminal offence for a landlord to harass you in any way in an attempt to drive you out.

If you have any questions regarding your rental agreement or problems with your landlord, you can ask a Citizens Advice Bureau (💻 www.citizensadvice.org.uk) for advice. They will also check your rental agreement and advise you of your rights under the law.

DEPOSITS

After signing an assured shorthold tenancy you must usually pay one month's rent in advance, depending on the type of property and the rental agreement, plus a deposit against damages equal to one to three months' rent. A deposit equal to one or two months' rent (the maximum permitted by law) must be paid when renting an unfurnished property and up to three months' rent for a furnished property.

Your deposit should be repaid when you leave, provided there are no outstanding claims for rent, unpaid bills, damages or cleaning. Note that in the past some agents and landlords have gone to almost any length to avoid repaying deposits, and tenants (particularly students) have historically been defrauded out of millions of pounds by unscrupulous landlords and agents who refused to repay deposits. Often a landlord will make a claim for 'professional' cleaning running into hundreds of pounds, even when you leave a property spotless.

> Around one in five tenants believes that all or part of his deposit is withheld unreasonably and deposit disputes are commonplace.

However, from 6th April 2007, all deposits (for rent up to £25,000 per annum) taken by landlords and agents for assured shorthold tenancies (AST) in England and Wales **must** be protected by an authorised Tenancy Deposit Scheme (TDS). Nevertheless, although it's mandatory, not all landlords have signed up to it, despite the fact that if a landlord doesn't protect a tenant's deposit he must repay three times the amount received to the tenant.

The scheme is intended to implement a speedy and efficient settlement of deposit disputes and the rapid return of disputed deposit monies. It removes much of the mutual suspicion that builds up towards the end of a tenancy, which frequently leads to the last month's rent being withheld for fear of the landlord refusing to return a deposit. The TDS guarantees the return of tenants' deposits, less any legitimate expenses owed to the landlord, and removes the burden from letting agents of having to resolve irreconcilable differences of opinion between landlords and tenants.

There are two types of tenancy deposit protection scheme: custodial schemes and insurance-based schemes. Under both schemes the tenant pays the deposit to the landlord, who either pays the deposit into the scheme (custodial scheme) or retains the deposit and pays a premium to the insurer (insurance-based scheme). Within 14 days of receiving a deposit, the landlord or agent must provide the tenant with details about how their deposit is protected, including the contact details of the tenancy deposit scheme selected. The interest accrued on deposits in the scheme is used to pay for the scheme's operation, but any surplus will be used to pay interest to the tenant (or the landlord if the tenant isn't entitled to it).

At the end of the tenancy – provided an agreement is reached between the parties about how the deposit is to be divided – the scheme will return the deposit as agreed. If there's a dispute, the scheme holds the deposit until the alternative dispute resolution (ADR) service – the aim of which is to make disputes faster and cheaper to resolve than going to court – decides a fair outcome. The ADR, which acts like an ombudsman, makes its decision within ten working days and the deposit is distributed around five days later. The decision of the ADR may be legally binding, but if it isn't either party can still take the dispute to court.

For further information, see 💻 www.tenantdepositscheme.com or 💻 www.tds.gb.com.

An alternative to the tenancy deposit protection scheme is the Paragon Smart Deposit Solution (💻 http://paragonadvance.com/index.cfm?action=smart_

deposit_solution), whereby tenants pay a one-off 'insurance' fee of £145 plus VAT without having to find a large, often unaffordable, deposit.

FINDING A RENTAL PROPERTY

Rental property can usually be found within two to four weeks in most areas, with the possible exception of large houses (four or more bedrooms) and prime properties in central London. Family accommodation is in short supply in central London, with the exception of luxury homes with astronomical rents, and most families settle for something in the outer boroughs and commute to work in central London (if applicable). You can rent a furnished or unfurnished property, both of which are common in London and have similar rents.

> ### ☑ SURVIVAL TIP
>
> If you need to travel into central London each day from an outer borough, you should be prepared to spend at least an hour travelling each way, which adds two or more hours to your working day.

Most properties are let through letting agents or estate agents (often one and the same), who carry out credit and reference checks, and draw up tenancy agreements and an inventory. A fee is payable for these services, which can be anything up to £200. When you agree to rent a property, you may also need to pay a holding deposit (of around £100 or a maximum of two weeks' rent) to reserve the property until the tenancy agreement is signed. Some letting agents may ask for a registration fee or a fee for providing a list of addresses and details of accommodation. You should refuse, as any requests for payments are illegal until an agent has found you a home.

Agents usually have properties available for immediate occupancy and lists are normally updated weekly. You should have no problem finding something suitable in most areas if you start looking around four weeks before you wish to take up occupancy. However, in central London many properties are snapped up within days, therefore you need to allow longer to find somewhere suitable and do some research well in advance.

Most letting agents require a reference from your employer (or previous employer, if you've been with your current employer less than one year), previous landlord or letting agent (if applicable), bank and possibly a personal referee.

Young people usually find it more difficult to find a rental property than more mature people, due to the usual arguments that the young are unreliable, noisy, poor, itinerant, untidy and so on. If you're seeking inexpensive accommodation such as a bedsit or studio flat (see page 98), you may find it more difficult in September when the new term starts and students are looking for accommodation.

There are numerous websites for property rentals in London, including 💻 www.easylondonaccommodation.com, www.findaproperty.com, www.gumtree.com/london/2548_1.html, www.homesandproperty.co.uk and www.net-lettings.co.uk (with a useful link to letting agents), plus hundreds of letting agents with their own websites (see **Appendix C**).

Local Housing Aid or Advice Centres provide advice regarding finding somewhere to live, and usually deal with both private and council house problems. Contact your local borough council for information.

RENTS

Rents in London have increased by around a third since 2002, albeit at a much slower pace in real terms than the increase in property prices (up to 150 per cent). However, in the last year or so (mid-2009 to mid-2010) rents in prime areas have risen by around 15 per cent. Rents for one- to three-bedroom properties have been fairly static for the last few years (except for prime areas), while those for four-bedroom properties have increased. The demand for rental property outstrips supply in some areas – particularly central London – and has increased in recent years due to the effects of the credit crunch which has reduced sales (which have fallen dramatically in the last few years).

Demand from would-be, first-time buyers and foreign executives, particularly for good quality one-bedroom flats in central London, is particularly high and can lead to a bidding war, with offers often made above the asking price. Young professionals are caught between a rock and a hard place, being unable to afford to buy while also being priced out of the rental market (see **Shared Accommodation** on page 99).

Rents in London vary considerably, depending on the size (number of bedrooms and area) and quality of a property, its age, the facilities provided and whether it's furnished or unfurnished (although generally an unfurnished property is no cheaper than a furnished property). The major factor determining the rent is the neighbourhood and borough. For example, £2,000 per month in central London (e.g. Kensington) will get you a small two-bedroom flat (twice the cost in most other European cities), while in an outer borough it will pay for a spacious, four-bedroom, detached house in most areas.

Rents range from under £500 per month for a tiny bedsit or studio flat outside central London to over £10,000 per month for a four-bedroom townhouse or luxury apartment (e.g. 2,000ft²/200m²) in a desirable area of central London. The rent for a one-bedroom flat ranges from around £600 per month in an outer borough to well over £2,000 per month in a desirable central location, while a two-bedroom property varies from around £800 per month in an outer borough to as much as £4,000 or more per month in a prime area, e.g. Kensington & Chelsea. The table in **Appendix D** shows the range of monthly rents in Spring 2010 that you can expect to pay in each London borough (listed in alphabetical order).

If you like a property but think the rent is too high, you could try negotiating a reduction or ask an agent to put an offer to the landlord. Many owners are flexible regarding the rent, particularly if the market is flooded with rental properties and you can provide good references and have a reliable source of income. In addition to the rent, tenants must pay for utilities such as gas, electricity and possibly water (water rates are usually paid by the landlord, although the tenancy agreement may make the tenant liable).

> ☑ **SURVIVAL TIP**
>
> Note that most rental agreements ban the keeping of pets, prohibit smoking and may also exclude young children.

Letting agents usually expect your income to be around 30 times the monthly rent. For example, if the rent is £1,000 per month your annual income should be around £30,000. If you don't meet the criteria or cannot prove your income, you may need to pay six months rent in advance or obtain a guarantor. A landlord and tenant can freely agree the rent but the tenant can (in certain circumstances) refer the rent to a Rent Assessment Committee during the first six months of the term, although the rent won't be reduced below the open market rent for the property. If there's no provision for a rent increase in the agreement, it must be agreed between the landlord and tenant, and the landlord must give notice in writing. With a long fixed-term agreement, e.g. longer than 12 months, there's usually a provision for rent increases.

Rent can be paid weekly, fortnightly, monthly, quarterly or annually. If you pay your rent weekly, you should have a rent book in which payments are recorded. Most tenants pay their rent monthly by standing order from a bank account. Note that agents usually quote weekly rents, although almost nobody pays their rent weekly, therefore monthly rents are shown throughout this book.

STANDARDS

The standard of rental properties varies considerably and (not surprisingly) depends on the rent and the area. A furnished property may include some or all of the following: bed linen; a fully-equipped kitchen (dishwasher,

microwave, etc.); television and DVD; cutlery, crockery, glassware and cookware; stereo system; cable or satellite TV; broadband internet; bath and power shower; off-road parking; and a resident concierge (caretaker or porter). Furniture and furnishings should be of decent quality (not second-hand tat) and in good condition.

Kitchens should be fully equipped, even in an unfurnished property, with an oven/grill, hob, fridge/freezer, fitted kitchen units and possibly a dishwasher and microwave. A washing machine is usually provided and possibly a dryer, which will be located in the kitchen or a bathroom if a property doesn't have a utility room or basement. Family bathrooms may contain a bath and separate shower, and there's often an en suite shower room or bathroom to the master bedroom (or to all bedrooms in a luxury property). In modest properties there may be only a feeble shower (without a pump) operated from a bath; bathrooms rarely contain a bidet. In general, British plumbing is better than in many other countries, although Americans won't be impressed (particularly with the showers). All modern properties have central heating, usually gas-fired, and continuous hot water.

Unfurnished properties usually have light fittings in all rooms, although there may be no bulbs or lampshades. Fitted wardrobes in bedrooms are rare in older homes and curtain rails may not be provided unless they're built-in, although many unfurnished properties have curtains. Most properties, whether furnished or unfurnished, are fully or partly carpeted. Many flats are conversions of old houses which have been modernised and converted into flats. These are often as good as (or better than) purpose-built flats and many have been expertly converted with a high specification and luxury finishes. A house in an outer borough may have a garage or private parking space, although off-road parking is extremely rare in central London.

One of the most important tasks after moving into a furnished home is to check the inventory of furniture and furnishings. An inventory should be provided by the landlord or letting agent and (after it has been agreed) a copy should be appended to the tenancy agreement. There's usually a fee for an inventory when it's drawn up by an agent. You should note the reading on your utility meters (e.g. electricity, gas and water) and check that you

aren't overcharged on your first bill. The meters should be read by utility companies before or soon after you move into a property, although you may need to arrange this yourself.

STUDIOS & BEDSITS

If you prefer to live on your own but don't want to pay a lot of rent (who does?), the solution may be a studio or bedsit (short for 'bedsitter', which is itself an abbreviation of 'bed-sitting room'). There's a fine line between a studio and bedsit, and in the UK a 'studio' is often just a posh name for a bedsit.

A bedsit usually consists of a furnished room, often in an old house, where you live, eat, sleep and cook. It may have a separate bathroom or shower room and a small kitchenette or mini kitchen area, although in some bedsits you must share a communal bathroom and kitchen with one or more other bedsits.

A studio flat should always have its own bathroom and kitchen facilities, which may be a separate room or part of the main living area. There should be no shared facilities and you should have your own lockable front door. Studios are more spacious than bedsits and are expensive. A single bedsit costs from around

£100 per week (doubles start at around £150 per week), while studios start at around £150 per week, but can be much more expensive in central London, particularly for 'luxury' studios.

SHARED ACCOMMODATION

Finding accommodation in London that doesn't break the bank is a huge problem for young people and students (and anyone who isn't earning a fortune). For many the solution is sharing accommodation, officially termed 'houses in multiple occupation' (HMOs). Houses or flats defined as HMOs have been subject to inspections and regulations (under a Housing Health and Safety Rating System) since July 2006 and may need official licensing if the local authority deems it necessary (usually for HMOs with three or more storeys or five or more tenants).

The law regarding renting is more complicated with regard to flat-sharing and it's simpler if one person is the tenant and sub-lets to others, which must be permitted by the rental agreement. It's possible for all sharers to be joint tenants with one tenancy agreement (in which case they're jointly and severally responsible) or to be individual tenants with individual tenancy agreements. Whatever the agreement, you should have just one rent book (if you pay your rent weekly) and pay the rent in a lump sum.

The main benefit of flat-sharing is that you can afford to live in a bigger and better property in a better area than you could afford on your own, and you will have a larger choice. Good small one- or two-bedroom properties are usually snapped up quickly, whereas larger properties are often offer better value and may be easier to find. However, you need to find a landlord who's willing to let to sharers. Sharing a property means either sharing with friends, renting a property yourself and advertising for flatmates, or responding to a 'room to let' advertisement.

Sharing usually involves sharing a kitchen, bathroom, living room and dining room, but not usually a bedroom. It also involves sharing all bills (in addition to the rent), including electricity, gas and telephone, and may also include sharing food bills and cooking (by mutual agreement). Some landlords include electricity and gas (plus heating) in the rent. The cleaning and general upkeep of a house or flat is also usually shared (although it's better to employ a cleaner). As always when living with others, there are advantages and disadvantages, and its success depends on the participants' ability to live together in harmony.

The cost of sharing a furnished flat varies considerably, depending on the size, location and amenities. Rents start from around £75 per week for a single room and £100 per week for a double room (which may be rented to one person or a couple) or £300 to £400 per month. At the other extreme, sharing a luxury property in central London can run to £1,000 or more per month.

In recent years a new breed of landlord (e.g. 🖥 www.fulhamrooms.com) has emerged, who convert spacious houses into excellent 'communal living' with all mod cons (including personal satellite TV, Wii), no bills to pay (included in the rent) and reasonable rents. However, such accommodation is still rare and those offering it tend to have a waiting list.

☑ SURVIVAL TIP

If you rent a property with the intention of sharing with others, you should ensure that it's permitted in your rental agreement.

Many newspapers and magazines contain advertisements for flat-sharers, such as the *Evening Standard* (🖥 www.homesandproperty. co.uk), *Loot* (🖥 www.loot.com), *Time Out* (🖥 http://flatshare.timeout.com) and the free daily *Metro* newspaper, available from tube stations, plus a number of free expatriate publications such as *TNT Magazine* (🖥 www.tntmagazine.com/uk). There are numerous flat-share websites covering London, including 🖥 www.spareroom.co.uk, 🖥 www.net-lettings.co.uk, http:// uk.easyroommate.com, www.flatmates.net, www1.flatmateclick.co.uk, www.net-lettings.co.uk and www.gumtree.com/london-flatshare.html.

There are a number of book for flatsharers including *The Essential Guide to Flatsharing* by Rupert Hunt and Matt Hutchinson (How To Books).

BOROUGH SURVEYS

This chapter contains a comprehensive survey of each borough to help you decide where you can afford to live and whether a borough offers the kind of lifestyle and facilities you're seeking. Each borough survey contains a map; council contact details and statistics; development plans and an overview of the primary residential areas; housing and rental costs; crime, health and school statistics; public transport and road information; the main shopping facilities; entertainment amenities, including theatres, cinemas, museums, libraries, clubs, live music, pubs and restaurants; and sports facilities and green spaces. Also included are snippets of local information and famous past and present residents.

A more detailed description of what's contained in each section is shown below:

♦ **At a Glance:** shows key points for prospective residents of a borough, including the good and bad aspects, who lives there, and housing stock and costs.

♦ **General Information:** Council contact details and statistics, including a link to the Comprehensive Area Assessment (CAA) website, which provides an assessment of local services, such as hospitals, schools and the police (which are monitored by separate watchdogs). The CAA brings the work of these watchdogs together so that you can see the whole picture of a borough in one place.

> The CAA Assessment is an annual independent assessment of all public services in a borough, from rubbish collection to fighting crime, which provides an invaluable picture of how well a borough is managed and run (see 🖥 http://oneplace.direct.gov.uk).

♦ **Overview:** A general description of the borough and its history.

♦ **Development Plans:** Major plans for renewal and developments in the borough, including public transport.

♦ **Residential Areas:** The main residential areas of the borough and general housing stock.

♦ **Property Costs:** Average property prices and rental costs in the borough. The average house and rental prices for each borough are also shown in **Appendix E**, where you can compare costs across all London boroughs.

♦ **Crime:** The crime rate in the borough and police contact details. A borough's crime rate can be compared with other boroughs in the table on page 443.

♦ **Health:** Medical facilities and major hospitals (public and private) in the borough. The performance of a borough's Primary Care Trust (the body that provides public health services) compared with other boroughs is shown in the table on page 446.

♦ **Schools:** An overview of the public and private schools in the borough, including pre-school, secondary, special schools, further and higher education. School league tables (based on the results of SAT National Curriculum tests and GCSE examinations) are shown on page 444.

♦ **Public Transport:** Underground (tube), rail, bus and river transport within a borough, and the proximity to the five international airports serving London.

- **Roads:** The major roads serving a borough, the proximity to motorways, local parking facilities and the cost of residents' parking permits.

- **Waste & Recycling:** Collection and recycling services and facilities in the borough.

- **Shopping:** The main shopping areas, streets, centres and towns in the borough, including markets and major supermarkets.

- **Entertainment:** The borough's major entertainment amenities, including theatres, cinemas, museums and galleries, libraries, and a selection of clubs, live music venues, pubs and restaurants.

- **Sports Facilities:** A borough's major sports and leisure centres and facilities, including swimming pools, golf courses, tennis centres and water sports.

- **Green Spaces:** Overview of a borough's main green spaces, including public parks, commons, woods, canals/rivers, gardens and private parks open to the public.

Barking & Dagenham

IG11, RM6 (part), RM8, RM9, RM10

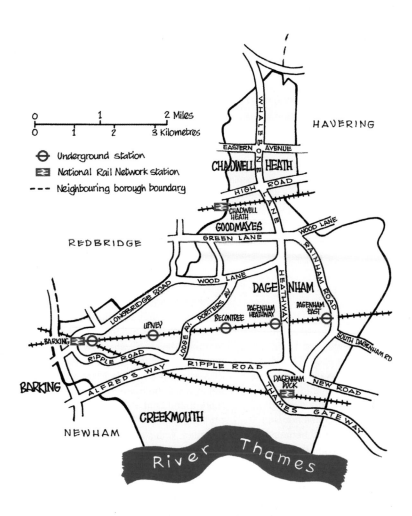

At a Glance

Best for: affordable housing, public transport, shopping, open spaces
Not so good for: schools, deprivation, culture/entertainment, nightlife
Who lives there: working class, first time buyers, singles/single parents
Housing stock: low quality public housing, mostly terraced houses and flats
Housing costs: inexpensive

General Information

Council Offices: Civic Centre, Dagenham, RM10 7BN (☎ 020-8592 4500)

CAA Assessment: (see ⌨ http://oneplace.direct.gov.uk > Search by area > London > Barking and Dagenham)

Controlling Party: Labour

Website: ⌨ www.barking-dagenham.gov.uk

Council Tax 2010/11: £2,210 (Band G), £2,652 (Band H)

Main Areas/towns: Barking, Becontree, Chadwell Heath, Dagenham

Postcodes: IG11, RM6 (part), RM8, RM9, RM10

Population & Ethnicity: 168,900, with the majority of people aged between 25 and 45. There's a high number of single-parent families in the area. The borough has a predominantly white population, with just 13.9 per cent belonging to Afro-Caribbean and Asian ethnic groups.

Unemployment: 9.7 per cent (the London average is 8.2 per cent)

Overview

The borough of Barking & Dagenham was formed in 1965 as the London Borough of Barking and was renamed Barking & Dagenham in 1980. It's a working class suburb to the east of London and was one of the earliest Saxon settlements in Essex, once an area of marshland. Most of the area was developed in the '20s and '30s when Becontree, the largest council housing estate in the country – with 27,000 homes – was built to re-house families from the East End slums. Much of the vast housing estate, which stretches from Dagenham to Chadwell Heath in the north, is still publicly owned.

For years, employment in the borough was dominated by the Ford Motor Company and other light industries, including chemicals, paint and pharmaceuticals. Since the decline of these industries (e.g. Ford downsized from full car production to gearboxes and engines in 2002) employment has shifted to the service sector, but the borough is generally deprived. On the upside, reliable transport into central London and the presence of large brown-field sites ripe for redevelopment have placed southern areas of the borough at the heart of the Thames Gateway regeneration scheme.

The Barking Barrage (a flood barrier that regulates the water flow within the old town quay in Barking) has already enabled development along the River Roding in the south-west and there are plans to reclaim more marshland at Barking Riverside along the north bank of the Thames over the next two decades, with plans for some 4,000 new homes. Improvements to the transport infrastructure are being considered and Barking town centre will be redeveloped to provide more facilities and jobs.

From the 14th century until the second half of the 19th century, the most important industry in the Barking area was fishing; England's largest fishing fleet, the Short Blue Fleet, was once based there. Many of Henry VIII's royal ships were also repaired and maintained in the area.

Development Plans

Major changes are planned for the borough, many as a result of the 2012 Olympic Games. The government is to spend £800mn on infrastructure improvements in the Lower Lea Valley, which will be the main location for the 2012 Olympic and Paralympic Park. It's one of the most challenging urban regeneration schemes in the UK, with the potential to accommodate up to 40,000 new homes and provide 50,000 new jobs. Public transport will also undergo major expansion and improvements in preparation for the 2012 Olympic Games.

Barking Town Centre is being regenerated under a number of schemes, which include new quality retail outlets and a business centre. Plans for the new Town Square, part of the Mayor of London's '100 Public Spaces' plan, were unveiled in September 2007. By 2016, the London Riverside development aims to provide 25,000 new jobs and 20,000 new homes. In 2010 plans were announced to build the first council houses in the borough for 25 years.

Residential Areas

The relatively small amount of private housing available is among the cheapest in London and consists of new properties, Victorian and Edwardian houses around Barking, and ex-council houses on the Becontree Estate. Over 64 per cent of properties in the borough are terraces (the highest proportion in London) and a further 26 per cent are flats, mostly purpose-built. There are a few semi-detached houses around Chadwell Heath.

Barking (IG11)

Barking is the commercial and retail heart of the borough, where the town centre is a conservation area and offers streets of small Victorian terraced houses, many unsympathetically modernised. Larger Edwardian and inter-war properties can be found on the outskirts and along the main Longbridge Road, with the most sought-after overlooking Mayesbrook Park to the east. Some council tower blocks from the '50s and '60s are scheduled for demolition and will be replaced with new homes. New property on Barking Reach is popular.

Becontree & Dagenham (RM8, RM9, RM19)

The Becontree Estate consists of thousands of two- and three-bedroom terraced red brick houses, mostly built between 1920 and 1934. Many of the houses share arched entrances and buildings are laid out in small squares and

Barking Abbey

cul-de-sacs; the overall effect is featureless and dull. Most of Dagenham's housing dates from the '30s, although there are also some post-war homes. Good transport into central London and low property prices maintain the area's popularity, particularly with local families and first-time buyers.

Chadwell Heath (RM6)

Part of the town lies in the borough of Redbridge, including the station, which causes some conflict over whose responsibility it is for keeping the area clean and tidy. There are more privately-owned homes in Chadwell Heath than in other parts of the borough, with mid-war semis adding to the rows of uniform terraces and some new properties on the Redbridge side of town.

LOCAL INFORMATION

Dagenham is known for the Ford Motor Company factory – Europe's largest car production plant from 1931-2002 – which, although much smaller nowadays, remains the town's largest employer.

Property Costs

Property Prices

The table below shows average property prices in the borough:

Detached: £263,799

Semi-detached: £205,157

Terraced: £176,826

Flat: £117,003

Rental Costs

The table below shows average monthly rents in the borough:

5+ bed: £1,750

4-5 bed: £1,500

3-4 bed: £1,000

2-3 bed: £900

Flat 2-bed: £850

Flat 1-bed: £700

Crime

Barking & Dagenham has the eighth-lowest overall crime rate of all London boroughs, with low rates of burglary, drugs offences and thefts from cars. The most common crimes are violence against the person and stolen cars. Priorities for the next three years include targeting antisocial behaviour, violent crime and drug abuse.

The police station HQ is in Dagenham (561 Rainham Road South, RM10, ☎ 0300-123 1212), with other stations in Barking and Marks Gate in Chadwell Heath.

To compare crime rates throughout London, see the table in **Appendix D**.

 FAMOUS RESIDENTS

Famous people born in Barking & Dagenham include Billy Bragg (singer/songwriter), Dudley Moore (actor), Alf Ramsay (England football manager), Sandie Shaw (singer) and Ross Kemp (actor). Captain James Cook was married in Barking.

Health

NHS services in the borough are provided by the Barking & Dagenham Primary Care Trust. For a full list of doctors, dentists and clinics, visit 🖥 www.nhs.uk.

To see how the Primary Care Trust compares with others in London, see the table in **Appendix D**.

Doctors & Dentists

◆ There are 51 NHS GP surgeries, providing a range of clinics and health services.

◆ The borough has 37 dental and orthodontic practices, although few accept new NHS patients.

Hospitals

Barking Hospital (Upney Lane, IG11, ☎ 020-8983 8000, 🖥 www.bhrhospitals.nhs.uk) has A&E facilities and an NHS walk-in centre. The Hedgecock Centre provides mental health care on the same site.

Private Medical Facilities

There are no private hospitals in the borough. The nearest private hospital is the BUPA Roding Hospital in Ilford (see **Redbridge**) and there's the Belvedere Private Clinic in Abbey Wood (see **Greenwich**). To find a private GP, visit 🖥 www.privatehealth.co.uk.

Schools

Educational standards are generally below the national average, although the council is working hard to improve its schools and in 2005 received an award for its work in 'transforming secondary education' There are no private schools in the borough. In the 2009 school league tables, primary schools were placed 16th out of the 33 London boroughs (75th out of 150 UK local authorities) and secondary schools 30th (123rd in the UK).

To compare schools throughout London, see the table in **Appendix D**.

Pre-school

A wide choice of nursery schools, playgroups and day nurseries is provided by the private and public sectors. There are also nursery classes attached to most infant and primary schools.

State Schools

First schools: 48 infant, junior and primary schools, of which seven are voluntary aided. In 2009, Manor Junior School and Thames View Junior School were the top schools in the borough for Key Stage 2 results.

Secondary schools: Nine comprehensive schools, one of which is voluntary aided (All Saints Catholic School in Dagenham). All schools have sixth forms and four have specialist status. The best performers in 2009 were Barking Abbey and the All Saints and Robert Clack schools in Dagenham.

Special schools: Trinity School in Dagenham is a special school catering for students aged 3-19 with physical disabilities and learning difficulties. There are additional special needs units at the Dorothy Barley Junior School and the Richard Alibon Primary School, both in Dagenham.

Further Education

Barking College (🖳 www.barkingcollege.ac.uk) offers a wide range of courses leading to recognised qualifications for students aged 16+. Adult education is also available through the Adult College in Dagenham (🖳 www.adult-college.bardaglea.org.uk) and the City Learning Centre (☎ 020-8270 6814) based at the Robert Clack and Eastbrook secondary schools in Dagenham.

LOCAL INFORMATION

Famous alumni of the University of East London include Garry Bushell (TV critic and presenter), Jake Chapman (artist and Turner prize winner), Mark Frith (editor of *Heat* magazine), Ken Russell (film director) and Sir Alexander Trotman (Lord Trotman of Osmotherley, Ford Motor Company CEO).

Higher Education

The Barking Campus of the University of East London (🖳 www.uel.ac.uk) is in Dagenham. Barking College (see above) also offers degree courses.

Public Transport

Public transport is decent in most areas, particularly for commuting into central London. Buses are the best option for travelling from north to south in the borough.

New public transport plans include the Stratford International (Eurostar) Station (opened in 2009); the upgrading of the Docklands Light Railway (see below); the London Overground line (formerly the North London Line) extension; and the new Javelin high-speed rail service, using Hitachi 'bullet' trains. A new Stratford International DLR extension is due to open in 2010, with new stations at Star Lane, Abbey Road, Stratford High Street and Stratford International, in time for the 2012 Olympics (there's also a proposed extension to Dagenham Dock).

Other proposals include a new Thames Gateway Bridge, connecting Beckton to Thamesmead, and a new East London Transit bus service. In November 2007, the mayor of London announced £3.3mn for transport improvements in the borough, to include funds for new 20mph zones, cycle lanes, better road-crossing facilities and street lighting.

Underground

The district line runs through Barking, Becontree and Dagenham, and the Hammersmith & City line terminates at Barking (all are located in zone 4). A typical journey to Cannon Street or Kings Cross on either line takes around 35 minutes.

Rail

Three Overground lines provide services within the borough:

♦ c2c trains go to Fenchurch Street from Dagenham Dock and Barking in 15 minutes.

- 'one' trains go to Liverpool Street from Chadwell Heath in 25 minutes.

- London Overground services go from Barking to Gospel Oak in 35 minutes, for connections to Richmond in south-west London.

Buses

There are many bus routes serving the main towns and neighbouring boroughs, but no daytime buses go to central London. Useful routes include the number 5 to Canning Town and the number 173 to Beckton, from where there are connections to the Docklands Light Railway and the Jubilee underground line respectively. Two night buses serve the borough: the N15 from Oxford circus and the N86 from Stratford.

Airports

Below are approximate distances and times from Barking to the five London airports using public transport.

- **City** – 5 miles; 40 minutes via Plaistow.

- **Gatwick** – 30 miles; 70 minutes via Victoria.

- **Heathrow** – 26 miles; 95 minutes via Paddington.

- **Luton** – 32 miles; 110 minutes via Farringdon.

- **Stansted** – 25 miles; 70 minutes via Liverpool Street.

Roads

Barking & Dagenham is within easy reach of the M25 and M11 motorways, the A406 North Circular Road and the A13 to Essex and the east coast. The A13 has undergone a complete overhaul in recent years, including landscaping, to improve traffic flow and the appearance of the road.

There are good cycle routes throughout the borough.

Parking

Barking and Dagenham's streets have been getting busier in recent years. There are several car parks in the main towns and limited on-street, short-stay parking bays. The borough has six Controlled Parking Zones, where a resident's parking permit costs £22.50 (for the first vehicle) per year.

Waste & Recycling

General household rubbish is collected weekly on the same day as recyclable materials, which include cans, paper and plastic bottles. Other recyclable materials may be taken to 'bring banks' (such as bottle banks and paper receptacles) throughout the borough. Garden waste can be taken to mobile collection points on Sundays during the spring and summer, while bulky items such as furniture and kitchen appliances are collected free of charge by arrangement. The borough's civic amenity site (recycling centre) is situated in Dagenham.

Shopping

Barking is the best town for shopping, with an indoor mall and a pedestrianised area featuring a mix of high street names (including Argos) and independent retailers. Dagenham and Chadwell Heath have smaller shopping districts, with several cheaper chains (e.g. Wilkinson's in Dagenham, and Peacocks and Primark in Chadwell Heath) and useful shops for everyday essentials.

LOCAL INFORMATION

For the widest choice of shops (over 300 plus free parking), the Lakeside Shopping Centre at Thurrock (Essex) is just 15 miles away.

Shopping Centres

- The Mall (Heathway, RM10) – 32 shops, including Iceland.

- Vicarage Field Shopping Centre (Ripple Road, IG11) – 55 shops, including Adams, Game, WH Smith and the cheaper fashion chains.

Supermarkets

- Asda in Barking (Vicarage Field Shopping Centre) and Dagenham.

- Morrisons in Dagenham.

- Sainsbury's in Chadwell Heath.

- Tesco in Barking (open 24 hours).

Markets

- Barking Town Centre Market (East Street, IG11) – general household goods; Tuesday, Thursday and Saturday.

♦ Dagenham Sunday Market (River Road, IG11) – assorted household goods in a huge market area; Sunday.

♦ The nearest Farmers' markets are at Blackheath SE3 (Sundays 10am-2pm) and Walthamstow E17 (Sunday 10am-2pm).

Entertainment

There are two cinemas, one theatre and one museum in the borough. Several major cultural events take place throughout the year, including the Molten Arts Festival, a programme of arts activities celebrating cultural diversity; the Dagenham Town Show in the summer, with a funfair, concerts and craft market; and the Barking Classical Concert event in May, which culminates in a firework display in the ruins of Barking Abbey.

Restaurants tend to be of the 'takeaway' variety and pubs are fairly ordinary, usually crammed with hordes of young adults looking for a night out not too far from home.

Theatres

The Broadway Theatre (Broadway, IG11, ☎ 020-8507 5601, 💻 www.thebroadwaybarking. com) has a modern, comfortable auditorium (refurbished in 2004) presenting a wide programme of repertory shows, live music, comedy and shows performed by local community groups. It's one of the few venues in which you can still see a traditional East End variety show.

Cinemas

♦ Showcase Cinema (Jenkins Lane, Barking, IG11, ☎ 0871-220 1000).

♦ Vue Dagenham (Cook Road, RM9, ☎ 020-8592 2211, 💻 www.myvue.co.uk).

Museums & Galleries

♦ Eastbury Manor House (Eastbury Square, IG11, ☎ 020-8724 1000, 💻 www. nationaltrust.org.uk) – Elizabethan manor house with a walled garden, currently being developed as an arts, heritage and community centre.

♦ Valence House (Becontree Avenue, RM8, ☎ 020-8270 6745) – 17th century manor house with a local history and heritage (museum) collection and O'Leary Art Gallery.

Libraries

There are eleven local authority libraries in the borough, with one mobile service. None of the libraries are open on Sundays. The main library is the Barking Library (Barking Learning Centre, 2 Town Square, Barking IG11 ☎ 020-8724 8725).

Clubs

There's one night-club in Barking – Club Luca (formerly Legends) Restaurant & Night-club (20-30 London Road, IG11, ☎ 020-8594 3051) – offering an eclectic musical mix along with theme nights. Otherwise you need to head closer to central London. There are regular comedy nights at the Broadway Theatre (see above).

Live Music

The Broadway Theatre is the main venue for live music and there are sometimes open-air classical concerts in Barking Park. Occasionally a local pub will host live gigs, including the Barking (2 Linton Road, IG11, ☎ 020-8591 1415) and the Coopers Arms in Chadwell Heath (2 High Road, RM6, ☎ 020-8590 1216).

Pubs

Pubs tend to be fairly ordinary – this isn't a borough for style bars or gastropubs. However, one or two are worthy of mention, such as the Britannia in Barking (1 Church Road, IG11, ☎ 020-8594 1305), a cosy back street boozer and winner of several CAMRA certificates, and the Captain Cook (Axe Street, IG11, ☎ 020-8594 2539), which has regular Karaoke evenings. In Dagenham, the Cross Keys (Crown Street, RM10, ☎ 0871-258 6403) is small and welcoming, while Becontree's Matapan (945 Green Lane, RM8, ☎ 020-8596 9641) is friendly.

Restaurants

Takeaways and fast food outlets predominate in the borough, which isn't the place to go for gourmet food. Dagenham offers a wider choice and there's a decent selection of ethnic restaurants in Dagenham and Barking, including China Square (640 Ripple Road, IG11, ☎ 020-8592 1188). Pizza restaurants are popular, such as Estressa Pizza in Dagenham (673 Green Lane, RM8, ☎ 020-8599 9695).

Sports Facilities

There are four council-funded sports and leisure centres in the borough: the Abbey in Barking, the Goresbrook in Dagenham, Dagenham swimming pool in Althorne Way and the Wood Lane sports centre in Dagenham (with no swimming pool). There are also several other public amenities: at Barking Abbey School leisure centre in Woodbridge Road, the Warren Sports Centre in Chadwell Heath, and at Castle Green, Dagenham Park, the Robert Clack School and the Sydney Russell leisure centre, all in Dagenham.

The amenities include:

♦ Four swimming pools – Abbey centre in Barking, Dagenham Pool (which has two pools) and the Goresbrook leisure centre in Dagenham.

♦ Six indoor sports halls available for a variety of sports, including exercise classes, badminton, five-a-side soccer and martial arts.

♦ Three squash courts.

♦ Outdoor sports pitches.

Sports pitches and tennis courts are provided in several parks and there are additional indoor facilities at the YMCA Sports Centre in nearby Romford. Horse riding is available in Eastbrookend Country Park, the Chase Local Nature Reserve and Beam Valley. All leisure centres have decent gymnasiums and fitness suites, and there are also a few privately-operated gyms. For the less energetic, there's tenpin bowling at the Dagenham Leisure Park (Ripple Road, Cook Road, RM9, ☎ 020-8593 2888).

Green Spaces

The borough boasts 25 parks and open spaces, each with a range of sporting facilities or wildlife havens, although they're all rather flat. The largest space is Eastbrookend Country Park, a beautiful reclaimed area of green belt countryside to the east of Dagenham. A triple Green Flag award (🖳 www.greenflagaward. org.uk) winner, the park was once an area of gravel pits that provided the raw materials for the Becontree Estate and much of Dagenham. After WWII, it became a dumping ground for rubble and was reclaimed as a park during the '70s. Another popular area is Parsloes Park, with a boating lake and several sports pitches, including a skateboarding and BMX area.

Barking Abbey Ruins, now a significant archaeological site, is situated in Barking town centre behind the Curfew Tower and hosts a firework display in May during the Classical Concert. Recent archaeological excavations have revealed ancient jewellery, carved bone, pottery, gold thread and evidence of glassmaking.

Around Becontree, attractive Valence Park forms the grounds to Valence House and features a tree-lined fishing lake, while Mayesbrook Park near Barking is a varied sporting venue with impressive lake views. The Ripple Nature Reserve is set in Barking Reach and is a tapestry of woodland, scrub and grassland, established on a former industrial dumping ground.

LOCAL INFORMATION

Barking Abbey is the second-oldest Saxon Abbey in the country (dating back to AD 666) and was the headquarters of William the Conqueror while he was waiting for the Tower of London to be built.

Barnet

EN4 (part), EN5, HA8 (part), N2, N3, N11, N14 (part), N20,
NW2 (part), NW4, NW7, NW9 (part), NW11

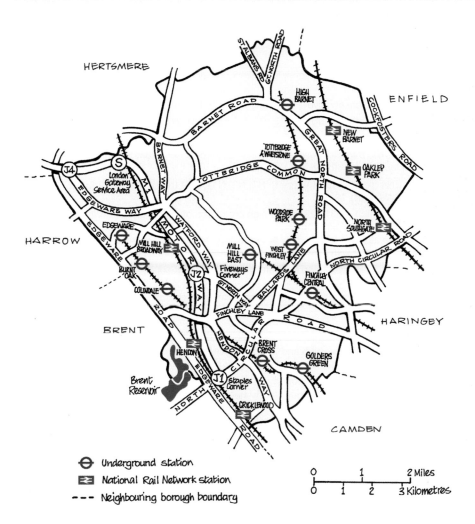

⊖ Underground station

🚉 National Rail Network station

- - - Neighbouring borough boundary

At a Glance

Best for: education, restaurants/pubs, open spaces, tranquillity

Not so good for: nightlife (apart from pubs), car crime

Who lives there: middle-class families, young professionals, wealthy ethnic minorities

Housing stock: detached/semi-detached family homes, Georgian mansion blocks, townhouses, flats/apartments

Housing costs: moderate

General Information

Council Offices: Hendon Town Hall, The Burroughs, Hendon, NW4 4BG (☎ 020-8359 2000)

CAA Assessment: (see 🖳 http://oneplace.direct.gov.uk > Search by area > London > Barnet)

Controlling Party: Conservative

Website: 🖳 www.barnet.gov.uk

Council Tax 2010/11: £2,372 (band G), £2,846 (Band H)

Main Areas/towns: Barnet, Edgware, Finchley, Golders Green, Hampstead Garden Suburb, Hendon, Mill Hill, Totteridge, Whetstone

Postcodes: EN4 (part), EN5, HA8 (part), N2, N3, N11, N14 (part), N20, NW2 (part), NW4, NW7, NW9 (part), NW11

Population & Ethnicity: 331,522, with a high proportion of middle-class families. Almost 25 per cent of residents belong to ethnic minorities, including London's largest Jewish and Gujerati communities, plus sizeable Japanese and Chinese communities. The borough is popular with middle-class families and young professionals.

Unemployment: 7.7 per cent (the London average is 8.2 per cent)

Overview

The borough of Barnet was created in 1965 and combines several urban areas from the old county of Middlesex and from Hertfordshire. It developed around the building of the Northern underground line during the early 20th century and the borough stretches from the top of Hampstead Heath to the Hertfordshire border. Barnet offers open spaces, safe streets, good transport links and excellent shopping.

London's most established Jewish settlement is around Finchley, Golders Green and Hendon. In 2003, an 11-square mile *eruv* was established there, consisting of distinctive tall poles linked by thin wires, inside which the Sabbath laws may be relaxed. The borough is also home to some of the capital's wealthiest residents, particularly around Hampstead Garden Suburb. Totteridge, with its vast common and few roads, is a favourite with media and sporting celebrities.

To the west, Edgware and Hendon are more down-to-earth in character. Hendon's claim to fame is as the birthplace of British aviation and part of the former aerodrome is now home to the RAF museum. The shabbier districts around Cricklewood and West Hendon are due for an overhaul by 2020, with a multi-million pound housing development and the creation of a new 'mini town' encompassing the Brent Cross Shopping Centre.

LOCAL INFORMATION

Barnet was first made famous in 1471 by the Battle of Barnet, a decisive battle of the War of the Roses between the Yorkists under Edward IV and the Lancastrians led by the rebel Richard Neville, Earl of Warwick ('the Kingmaker', who was killed in the battle).

Development Plans

Barnet's planning objectives include providing more housing and improving transport

Barnet High St

infrastructure to maximise movement in and around the borough. April 2008 saw the completion of the first phase of the shared ownership housing project at Beaufort Park.

In March 2008, plans for one of the largest regeneration schemes London has ever seen were submitted to Barnet Council. The £4.5bn regeneration is designed to provide a new gateway to London and a vibrant new urban quarter in Barnet. The plans, for a whole new town centre based around Cricklewood, Brent Cross and West Hendon, would create 27,000 jobs, 7,500 homes, three schools, new health facilities, high quality parks and open spaces, and investment of over £400mn in improving transport. If the project is approved, development is expected to start in 2010.

Residential Areas

Family homes are plentiful in Barnet, where property is evenly divided between flats, terraces and semi-detached houses, and there are also a number of expensive detached homes. Victorian and Edwardian properties tend to be clustered around the underground stations, while elsewhere architecture ranges from Georgian mansion blocks to '30s semis to new-build apartments and townhouses. The *eruv* has boosted prices within its boundaries. The grandest houses are found in Totteridge, Hampstead Garden Suburb and along London's 'Millionaire's Row', The Bishops Avenue (north of Hampstead Heath), where one mansion was recently on the market for £50mn.

Barnet (EN4, EN5)

High Barnet feels more like the country market town it once was rather than part of a London borough, with its pleasant high street and surrounding green spaces. There's a good supply of four- and five-bedroom homes costing between £450,000 and £600,000. Some of the most sought-after properties are the elegant Georgian townhouses overlooking Hadley Common. New apartment blocks are springing up in (appropriately) New Barnet. Friern Barnet is made up of 1930s semis, maisonettes and purpose-built flats, while there's a decent selection of Late Victorian and Edwardian properties to the north of the area just off the main road.

LOCAL INFORMATION

In recent years, class-conscious graffiti artists have taken it upon themselves to improve the borough's image by adding an acute accent to the 'e' in Barnet – making it Barnét – on scores of road signs.

Edgware (HA8)

Half an hour from central London at the end of the Northern line, Edgware has an attractive, bustling high street, a cosmopolitan atmosphere and reasonably priced family properties (typically £300,000 for a three-bedroom semi). Burnt Oak is good for first-time buyers.

Finchley (N2, N3, N11, N12, N14)

Formerly home to household names such as Spike Milligan and Mick Jagger, Finchley is less suburban than Barnet's other towns, with decent leisure facilities, making it popular with young couples. East Finchley has a village-like atmosphere and is home to several actors and musicians, while North Finchley is more family-oriented. There's a good stock of flats (conversions and new blocks) and family-sized terraces in all areas. Some of the most sought-after roads are close to Fortis Green and Church End. In nearby Friern Barnet, smart new flats and townhouses have been built on the site of a former lunatic asylum.

Golders Green (NW11)

This peaceful neighbourhood has a large number of synagogues and Jewish shops and restaurants, plus the world's only kosher ice cream van! There's a good choice of flats and apartment blocks, many built alongside the busy main roads, although semi-detached family houses predominate.

Hampstead Garden Suburb (NW11)

Quiet and picturesque, 'the Suburb' was built in the early 20th century as a social experiment to enable the rich and poor to live side by side in a harmonious environment. Modest cottages, carefully designed apartment blocks and substantial houses are arranged around neat squares and along tree-lined streets. Strict rules govern the appearance of the properties and all but the wealthy have long been priced out of the area.

Hendon & Colindale (NW4, NW9)

Three major roads (the M1, A41 Watford Way and A406 North Circular) are lined with rows of uninspiring inter-war semis, creating a poor impression of these areas. However, there are pockets of attractive, quieter streets and a mix of properties to suit the families, young professionals and students who live there. The average price for a three-bedroom home is £325,000. The former RAF station is being turned into 2,800 studios and flats in a parkland setting (prices start at around £150,000), and the tatty Grahame Park council estate is to be replaced with a mix of private and social housing.

Mill Hill, Totteridge & Whetstone (NW7, N20)

With plenty of parks and golf courses, Mill Hill begins to feel like the country. Semis from the '30s are common and there are some attractive areas with larger, more prestigious homes, as well as new developments. Even more rural is pretty Totteridge, where substantial mansions set in generous grounds have gated entrances, private gyms and swimming pools. Whetstone, with shops and restaurants along the main road, has smaller, more modestly priced homes.

LOCAL INFORMATION

The Bishops Avenue (north of Hampstead Heath) is London's most exclusive address, dubbed 'Billionaires Row' and the 'richest street in the world'. Here houses change hands for anything up to £50mn and are often left empty by their mega-rich owners – the Saudi royal family owns ten mansions here which are unoccupied.

Property Costs

Property Prices

The table below shows average property prices in the borough:

Detached: £821,975
Semi-detached: £454,124
Terraced: £332,493
Flat: £273,641

Rental Costs

The table below shows average monthly rents in the borough:

House 5+ bed: £4,000
House 4-5 bed: £2,200
House 3-4 bed: £1,550
House 2-3 bed: £1,250
Flat 2-bed: £1,000
Flat 1-bed: £750

Crime

Barnet has the 16th-highest overall crime rate of all London boroughs and the sixth-highest rate for car theft. The Metropolitan Police training college is located in Colindale, as is the NW London police headquarters (Grahame Park Way, NW9, ☎ 0300-123 1212), with other police stations in Barnet, Finchley, Golders Green and Whetstone.

To compare crime rates throughout London, see the table in **Appendix D**.

Health

NHS services in the borough are provided by the Barnet Primary Care Trust. For a full list of doctors, dentists and clinics, visit 💻 www.nhs.uk.

To see how the Primary Care Trust compares with others in London, see the table in **Appendix D**.

Doctors & Dentists

◆ There are 126 NHS GP surgeries, providing a range of clinics and health services.

◆ Barnet has 113 dental and orthodontic practices, although only some 25 per cent accept new NHS patients.

Hospitals

◆ Barnet General Hospital (Wellhouse Lane, EN5, ☎ 0845-111 4000, 💻 www.bcf.nhs.uk) – A&E.

◆ Edgware Community Hospital (Burnt Oak Broadway, HA8, ☎ 020-8952 2381, 💻 www.bcf.nhs.uk) – NHS walk-in centre.

◆ Finchley Memorial Hospital (Granville Road, N12, ☎ 020-8349 7500, 💻 www.royalfree.nhs.uk) – minor injuries unit.

Private Medical Facilities

◆ The Garden Hospital (46/50 Sunny Gardens Road, NW4, ☎ 020-8457 4500, www.bmihealthcare.co.uk).

To find a private GP, you can also visit 💻 www.privatehealth.co.uk.

👤 FAMOUS RESIDENTS

Famous people with links to the borough include Tony Blackburn (DJ), Trevor Howard (actor), Humphrey Lyttelton (jazz musician), Samuel Pepys (diarist), Roger Moore (actor) and Cliff Richard (singer).

Schools

Educational standards in Barnet are good. In the 2009 school league tables, primary schools were placed fourth out of the 33 London boroughs (18th out of 150 UK local authorities) and secondary schools seventh (tenth in the UK).

To compare schools throughout London, see the table in **Appendix D**.

Pre-school

First schools: There are four nursery schools and 49 nursery classes attached to primary schools.

State Schools

First schools: 91 infant, junior and primary schools, of which 34 are voluntary aided, including several Jewish schools. Four schools were among the top primaries in the UK in 2009 – St Paul's C of E Primary School at Mill Hill, Brookland Junior School at Hill Top, St. Andrew's C of E Voluntary Aided Primary School at Totteridge, and Garden Suburb Junior School at Childs Way.

Secondary schools: Three selective schools and 19 comprehensives, of which eight are voluntary aided, including a City Academy in Edgware. All but three schools have sixth forms and 14 have specialist status. In 2009, the top performers were three selective schools: St Michael's Catholic Grammar School in North Finchley, the Queen Elizabeth's School for Boys in Barnet and the Henrietta Barnett School in Hampstead Garden Suburb. The Hasmonean High School in Hendon scored highly for added value.

Special schools: There are four schools catering for pupils with physical disabilities and learning difficulties.

Private Schools

There are 22 private schools in the borough, catering for all age groups. Several are selective, five are for Jewish pupils and one is a special school for Jewish children with physical or learning difficulties. St Martha's Senior School at Hadley, the London Jewish Girls' High School and the King Alfred School in Golders Green had excellent results in 2009, while the Mount School (Mill Hill) was one of the top UK schools for added value.

The Woodside Park International School (💻 www. wpis.org) has pre-preparatory, preparatory and senior departments located at different sites. There's also one specialist school, the Susi Earnshaw Theatre School in Barnet (💻 www.susiearnshaw. co.uk), which provides a full national curriculum timetable alongside classes in performing arts.

 FAMOUS RESIDENTS

Famous former residents of the Georgian houses around Hadley Green (Barnet) have included Kingsley Amis (novelist, 1922-1995), David Livingstone (explorer, 1813-1873) and William Thackeray (novelist, 1811-1863).

Further Education

Barnet College (💻 www.barnet.ac.uk) is one of the largest colleges in the UK and offers a wide choice of courses for students and adults. There are also three sixth form centres:

♦ Brampton College in Hendon (💻 www. bramptoncollege.com) – independent.

Golders Green

♦ Wentworth Tutorial College in Hendon (💻 www. wentworthcollege.co.uk) – independent.

♦ Woodhouse College in Finchley (💻 www. woodhouse.ac.uk) – comprehensive.

Hampstead Garden Suburb Institute (💻 www.hgsi. ac.uk) offers adult learning courses at several sites.

Higher Education

Middlesex University has a campus in Hendon (💻 www.mdx.ac.uk).

Public Transport

The Northern Line is the main public transport artery, although trains can be infrequent, slow and crowded. Barnet isn't well served by mainline trains, but local bus services are good and some routes run into central London.

Underground

All areas are served by the Edgware and High Barnet branches of the Northern Line, except Friern Barnet and Hampstead Garden Suburb, which are a 30-minute walk from the nearest stations. Typical journey times are:

♦ High Barnet (Northern line, zone 5) to Leicester Square, 35 minutes.

♦ Hendon Central (Northern line, zone 4) to Kings Cross, 20 minutes.

Rail

Mill Hill, Hendon and Cricklewood are all served by the Thameslink line, with a journey time of 20 minutes from Mill Hill to Kings Cross and 64 minutes to Wimbledon. Eventually the service will take passengers to Paris with just one change at St Pancras. Improvements to Hendon and Mill Hill stations are planned as part of the Thameslink 2000 project.

Buses

A few services go to the West End, including the number 82 (North Finchley to Victoria) and the 113 (Edgware to Oxford Circus). Late night clubbers can choose from the N5, N13 and N20 routes, which all serve Barnet. Local services are generally good, although Totteridge is poorly served and only the 251 travels east to west across Totteridge Common.

Airports

Below are approximate distances and times from Mill Hill Broadway to the five London airports using public transport.

◆ **City** (15 miles; 70 minutes via Bank).

◆ **Gatwick** (32 miles; 75 minutes via Blackfriars, or 85 minutes via Victoria).

◆ **Heathrow** (14 miles; 88 minutes via Paddington).

◆ **Luton** (19 miles; 34 minutes from Mill Hill Broadway).

◆ **Stansted** (28 miles; 110 minutes via Liverpool Street).

Roads

The UK's first motorway, the M1, originates in the borough and other main roads, including the A1 and A41, cut through the borough from north to south. The North Circular Road (A406) joins the M1 at the busy Brent Cross intersection, where there are often long tailbacks. The A5 runs along the boundary between Barnet and Brent. The A1000 often has queues in both directions through High Barnet as drivers try to avoid coming into London on the A1 and commuters head towards the A1M or M25 at South Mimms.

Parking

Most areas have Controlled Parking Zones, where parking costs residents £40 per year for one car and an additional £70 per year for each second and third cars.

Waste & Recycling

The council provides wheelie bins for non-recyclable waste, which is collected weekly. There's a kerbside collection scheme for recyclable materials, including cans, glass, paper, textiles and tinfoil. In some areas garden waste is also collected. Other types of rubbish can be taken to the Civic Amenity and Recycling Centre in Finchley.

LOCAL INFORMATION

Hampstead Garden Suburb, founded in 1907 by Dame Henrietta Barnett and designed by Raymond Unwin and Sir Edward Lutyens, is internationally recognised as one of the finest examples of early 20th century domestic architecture and town planning.

Shopping

Barnet is second only to Westminster in terms of the number of retailers within its boundaries. Shops range from specialist Jewish shops in Golders Green to London's only Oriental shopping centre in West Hendon to the shopping 'mall' at Brent Cross. Town centres at Chipping Barnet, Edgware, Hendon, Mill Hill and North Finchley all have a decent selection of shops, while High Barnet was recently listed as one of the top ten high streets for everyday essentials in a *Yellow Pages* survey.

Shopping Centres

◆ Brent Cross Shopping Centre (Hendon Way, NW4, ☎ 020-8202 8095, ▭ www.brentcross.co.uk) – houses over 100 shops, including most of the major high street retailers such as Fenwick, John Lewis, M&S and WH Smith.

◆ **Broadwalk Shopping Centre** (Station Road, HA8, ☎ 020-8905 6303, ▭ www.themall.co.uk) – Argos, Boots, M&S, etc.

◆ Oriental City (399 Edgware Road, NW4, ☎ 020-8200 0009) – shopping centre for Chinese and Japanese goods.

◆ The Spires Shopping Centre (111 High Street, EN5, ☎ 020-8449 7505) – high street outlets, including Monsoon, WH Smith and Waterstones.

Retail parks in Friern Barnet, Mill Hill and Whetstone provide branches of DIY, furniture and electrical goods stores.

Supermarkets

Asda in Colindale (open 24 hours).

◆ Marks & Spencer in Mill Hill, Temple Fortune and Whetstone.

◆ Sainsbury's in Edgware (Broadwalk Centre), Hendon, Golders Green, New Barnet and North Finchley.

◆ Tesco Superstores at Brent Cross, Ballards Lane in Finchley and on the North Circular at Colney Hatch (all open 24 hours); Express and Metro stores at Burnt Oak, Edgware, Golders Green and Hendon.

◆ Waitrose in the Brent Cross Shopping Centre, Ballards Lane in Finchley, Mill Hill, Temple Fortune and Whetstone.

Markets

Barnet Market (St Albans Road and Chipping Close, EN5) – fresh produce, fish, meat and household goods; Wednesday and Saturday.

◆ North Finchley Market (Lodge Lane car park, N12) – general food and household goods; Friday.

◆ Watling Market (car park off Barnfield Road, behind Burnt Oak underground station, HA8) – fresh produce, household goods, clothes, books, second-hand goods, etc.; Saturday.

The nearest Farmers' Market is in Ealing (Leeland Road, West Ealing W13); Saturday from 9am-1pm.

There's also a regular car boot sale on Sunday afternoons opposite the Colney Hatch Tesco on the North Circular Road.

Entertainment

Local theatre, cinema and museums are well catered for in Barnet. Artsdepot is the borough's major new arts and leisure centre, providing two theatres, a gallery, dance and drama studios, and a range of courses to suit the creatively minded. As well as an abundance of restaurants, there are plenty of pubs, although for night-clubs you're better off heading to central London.

Theatres

◆ Allsaints Arts Centre (122 Oakleigh Road North, N20, ☎ 020-8445 8388) – plays, concerts, dance and other events.

◆ Artsdepot (5 Nether Street, Tally Ho Corner, N12, ☎ 020-8369 5454, 🖥 www.artsdepot.co.uk).

◆ The Bothy Garden Theatre (Avenue House Grounds, East End Road, N3, ☎ 020-8455 4640, 🖥 www.bothyartsfinchley. org.uk) – theatre space for community productions in a Grade II concrete building.

◆ The Bull Theatre (68 High Street, EN5, ☎ 020-8441 5010) – showcases productions by the Susi Earnshaw Theatre School.

Cinemas

◆ Odeon High Barnet (Great North Road, EN5, ☎ 0871-224 4007, 🖥 www.odeon.co.uk).

◆ Phoenix Cinema (52 High Road, N2, ☎ 020-8444 6789, 🖥 www.phoenixcinema.co.uk) – believed to be the oldest purpose-built cinema in the UK.

◆ Vue Cinema (Great North Leisure Park, Finchley High Road, N12, ☎ 0871-224 0240, 🖥 www.myvue.com).

Museums & Galleries

◆ Avenue House (East End Road, N3, ☎ 020-8346 7812) – former home of 'Inky Stephens', the inventor of blue/black ink.

◆ Church Farmhouse Museum (Greyhound Hill, NW4, ☎ 020-8359 3942) – local history and decorative arts.

◆ Golders Green crematorium (Hoop Lane, NW11, ☎ 020-8455 2374) – not strictly a museum, but interesting as the final resting place for many famous names, including Marc Bolan and Enid Blyton.

◆ London Museum of Jewish Life (Sternberg Centre, 80 East End Road, N3, ☎ 020-8349 1143, 🖥 www.jewishmuseum.org.uk) – Jewish social history.

◆ **RAF Museum (**Grahame Park Way, Hendon, NW9, ☎ 020-8205 2266, 🖥 www.rafmuseum. org) – over 100 aircraft, aviation artefacts and memorabilia.

Libraries

Barnet has a network of 16 libraries and two mobile services, with varying opening hours, including evenings and Sundays. The borough's flagship library is Hendon Library (**The Burroughs, NW4, ☎ 020-8359 2628**).

Clubs

Night-clubs are thin on the ground, with the exception of Volante (618a Finchley Road, NW11, ☎ 020-8201 8968) and Ashtons (194 Cricklewood Broadway, NW2, ☎ 020-8452 0176).

Live Music

Although there are no dedicated music venues (the Torrington Arms, once legendary on the North London music scene, has now closed) a few pubs offer live music, including:

♦ The Crown (142 Cricklewood Broadway, NW2, ☎ 020-8452 4175).

♦ The Claddagh Ring (10, Church Road, NW4, ☎ 020-8203 2600).

♦ The Galtymore (194 Cricklewood Broadway, NW2, ☎ 020-8452 8652).

♦ The Wishing Well (686 High Road, N12, ☎ 020-8445 8881).

Pubs

Barnet has plenty of pubs, ranging from the traditional to modern gastropubs, with the widest choice in Cricklewood and Finchley, including numerous Irish pubs. Students tend to frequent pubs in Hendon. There are fewer pubs in other areas – Totteridge has only one, the popular and secluded Orange Tree (7 Totteridge Village, Totteridge Lane, N20, ☎ 020-8343 7031), while there are no pubs in Hampstead Garden Suburb (posh people don't frequent pubs).

Restaurants

All the main towns have well-known restaurants, including Ask!, Pizza Express and Starbucks. Mill Hill's Pentavia retail park has a Thank God It's Friday restaurant, while there's a Café Rouge in Finchley. Finchley also has one of the best fish 'n' chips establishments in London, the Two Brothers (297-303 Regent's Park Road, N3, ☎ 020-8343 1209).

Excellent Jewish cuisine is available in Golders Green and surrounding districts, and Hendon even has a kosher Chinese restaurant, Kaifeng (51 Church Road, NW4, ☎ 020-8203 7888). Golders Green also has some more unusual restaurants, such as Just Around the Corner (466 Finchley Road, NW3, ☎ 020-7431 3300), where there's no price list – you decide how much you want to pay! Ethnic restaurants of many different cuisines are popular in Cricklewood and Finchley, such as the lively Turkish eatery Izgara (11 Hendon Lane, Finchley, N3, ☎ 020-8371 8282).

LOCAL INFORMATION

Barnet is the site of an ancient horse fair, hence the Cockney rhyming slang of 'Barnet (fair)' for 'hair'. The fair dates back to 1588, when Queen Elizabeth I granted a charter to the Lord of the Manor of Barnet to hold a biannual fair.

Sports Facilities

The new state-of-the-art sports complex at Burnt Oak has added to the range of council-funded sports centres in the borough. Other centres are located in Barnet, East Barnet, Hendon and Finchley. Amenities include:

♦ Swimming pools at East Barnet, Finchley Lido and Hendon.

♦ A climbing wall at Burnt Oak.

♦ Indoor sports halls in Burnt Oak and Hendon.

♦ Outdoor sports pitches at Burnt Oak and Finchley.

Sports such as bowls, cricket, football, rugby, skateboarding and tennis can be played in several of the borough's parks. Other 'sports' available include horse riding in Barnet, Mill Hill and North Finchley, and tenpin bowling at the Hollywood Bowl in Finchley. Golfers have a choice of three public golf courses and several private clubs.

Branches of leading health centres are dotted throughout the borough, including a David Lloyd Centre in Finchley, and there are health suites (spa, sauna, etc.) at all the sports centres.

Green Spaces

Barnet boasts over 200 green spaces, ranging from community parks and golf courses to wooded areas and commons such as the Hampstead Heath Extension (created out of farmland). Many open spaces lie towards the Hertfordshire border, notably the Welsh Harp Reservoir (Cool Oak Lane, NW9 – see box). The borough has a working farm, in Totteridge, and five nature reserves, including a bog on Rowley Green Common in Arkley. Many walks and nature trails can be followed through woods and other open spaces, such as the Dollis Valley Greenwalk from ancient woodlands in Mill Hill to Hampstead.

LOCAL INFORMATION

The Welsh Harp or Brent Reservoir covers 420 acres (170 hectares) of open water, marshes, trees and grassland, and straddles the border between the boroughs of Barnet and Brent. It's designated a Site of Special Scientific Interest (SSI) – it provides a valuable habitat for wildlife, particularly its abundant wildfowl and wetland plants – and has an attractive recreational centre.

Bexley

DA1, DA5, DA6, DA7, DA8, DA14, DA15, DA16, DA17, DA18, SE2 (part), SE28 (part)

At a Glance

Best for: green spaces, affordable property, grammar schools, low crime, transport connections

Not so good for: bland suburbia, nightlife, culture, restaurants, no tube

Who lives there: mix of working and middle-class families, mainly white

Housing stock: a high proportion of semis and terraces

Housing costs: inexpensive

General Information

Council Offices: Bexley Civic Offices, Broadway, Bexleyheath, Kent (☎ 020-8303 7777)

CAA Assessment: (see 🖳 http://oneplace.direct.gov.uk > Search by area > London > Bexley)

Controlling Party: Conservative

Website: 🖳 www.bexley.gov.uk

Council Tax 2010/11: £2,397 (Band G), £2,877 (Band H)

Main Areas/towns: Bexley, Bexleyheath, Blackfen, Crayford, Erith, Sidcup, Thamesmead, Welling

Postcodes: DA1, DA5, DA6, DA7, DA8, DA14, DA15, DA16, DA17, DA18, SE2 (part), SE28 (part)

Population & Ethnicity: 223,300, with a high proportion aged between 25 and 45. Around 7 per cent belong to ethnic minorities, mostly South Asian and Afro-Caribbean, centred around Belvedere, just outside Erith. The borough is popular with middle income families, with a fair number of commuters, while young professionals are beginning to move into Thamesmead.

Unemployment: 6.8 per cent (the London average is 8.2 per cent)

Overview

Formed in 1965, the borough of Bexley is 12 miles from central London and follows the course of the River Thames from Greenwich in the west to Dartford (Kent) in the east. Little more than a series of small villages in the 19th century, the borough was largely developed in the '30s. Modern Bexley is characterised by streets of suburban housing fanning out from five town centres which provide local employment, although many residents take advantage of good transport connections and commute into the City or West End (around 30 minutes by train). The main A2 to Kent cuts through the middle of the borough, providing easy access to the Channel ports and the coast. Towards the outskirts, the urban sprawl gives way to green belt countryside.

The name Bexley first appeared in records in 814 when King Kenulph, the King of the Mercians, granted lands at Bexley to Wulfred, Archbishop of Canterbury, and it was a rural district (the name literally means 'clearing in the box wood') until the early 20th century.

Development Plans

The main focus of regeneration in Bexley is at Thamesmead, which it shares with Greenwich, where the Thames Gateway scheme is providing thousands of new homes, jobs and improved transport on the flat marshland section. Erith, the shabbiest area, is beginning to benefit from new housing and recreational facilities, and more residential and commercial schemes are planned. Bexley council is continuing the development of Bexleyheath as a successful commercial, leisure and civic centre. The present civic offices site is being developed to provide improved accommodation for council staff and further improvements to pedestrian facilities and public transport links. Plans also include the provision of more shops, restaurants, health centres and education facilities.

FAMOUS RESIDENTS

Famous residents of Bexley have included Kate Bush (singer), Michael Crawford (actor), Roald Dahl (writer), Bernie Ecclestone (Formula One boss), Sheila Hancock (actress), Sir Edward Heath (Prime Minister), Lennox Lewis (boxer), Sir Roger Moore (actor) and Neville Shute (novelist).

Residential Areas

Most housing dates from the '30s, although there are pockets of Victorian and Edwardian buildings as well as modern tower blocks around Thamesmead. The smartest areas are around Sidcup and the scruffiest around Erith. Overall prices are among the cheapest in London.

A large proportion of property is semi-detached (44 per cent – the highest in London), with 30 per cent terraced, 21 per cent flats (almost all purpose-built) and 6 per cent detached.

Bexley, Bexleyheath, Crayford & Welling (DA1, DA5, DA6, DA7, DA16)

Green space, fresh air and good schools characterise these areas, with the bustling town centre of Bexleyheath providing the main shopping and recreational centre. Uniform, tidy, but slightly dull streets of inter-war semis and terraces predominate. Welling to the west is slightly cheaper, with more council properties. The area around Danson Park, which has a recently refurbished 18th century mansion, has some of the best properties, many of them large detached houses dating from the '20s.

Bexley (sometimes called Old Bexley or Bexley Village) is prettier, older and more village-like, with small Victorian cottages and larger terraces near the River Cray. The wide roads of the Parkhurst Estate have sought-after semi-detached and detached Victorian houses with large gardens. Crayford to the east is more industrial, where many of the semi-detached houses to the north-east of the town centre were built for workers at the Vickers Aircraft Factory.

Erith & Thamesmead (DA8, DA17, DA18, SE28)

Over the years, industrial Erith has become neglected and run-down, although since the late '90s the town has attracted new housing and recreational and retail developments, which are beginning to improve the area. Victorian terraces and '30s semis make up much of the housing stock and attract first-time buyers, along with tower blocks in the town centre. New homes by the river are attractive. Thamesmead is seeing a lot of redevelopment (see **Greenwich**) and there are some Victorian terraces and modern houses among the existing tower blocks. More new housing is planned as part of the Thames Gateway scheme.

Sidcup & Blackfen (DA14, DA15)

In the south of the borough, Sidcup is regarded as the smartest area, providing easy access to the Kent countryside and a fast journey into central London for commuters. Chalet-style houses with four bedrooms (costing around £400,000) from the '30s are popular with families. Some of the best streets are wide and tree-lined, featuring larger and more expensive Victorian homes. The Hollies Estate in North Sidcup includes some original Victorian buildings alongside '80s homes set in parkland with a striking water tower. Blackfen to the north is slightly cheaper.

Bexley Church

Property Costs

Property Prices

House prices are generally relatively low, with the most expensive areas around Sidcup.

The table below shows average property prices in the borough:

> Detached: £388,214
> Semi-detached: £239,182
> Terraced: £194,501
> Flat: £147,063

Rental Costs

The table below shows average monthly rents in the borough:

> House 5+ bed: £2,000
> House 4-5 bed: £1,500
> House 3-4 bed: £1,300
> House 2-3 bed: £900
> Flat 2-bed: £800
> Flat 1-bed: £650

Crime

Overall, Bexley is the sixth-safest London borough, with the seventh-lowest crime rate for burglary and the eighth-lowest rate for thefts from cars and for violent crime. One-third of all recorded crime in Bexley occurs in Slade Green to the east of Erith, and current priorities include tackling this.

The police station HQ is in Bexleyheath (2 Arnsberg Way, DA7, ☎ 020-8301 1212), with other stations in Belvedere and Sidcup.

To compare crime rates throughout London, see the table in **Appendix D**.

Health

NHS services in the borough are provided by the Bexley Primary Care Trust. For a full list of doctors, dentists and clinics, visit ⌨ www.nhs.uk.

To see how the Primary Care Trust compares with others in London, see the table in **Appendix D**.

Doctors & Dentists

◆ There are 66 NHS GP surgeries, providing a range of clinics and health services.

◆ Bexley has 46 dental and orthodontic practices, most of which accept new NHS patients.

Hospitals

◆ North House Hospital (237 Erith Road, DA7, ☎ 020-8304 5819) – mental health care.

◆ Oakwood House Hospital (42 Oakwood Drive, DA7, ☎ 01322-556 497) – community residential hospital.

◆ Queen Mary's Hospital (Frognal Avenue, DA14, ☎ 020-8302 2678) – A&E.

There's a minor injuries unit at the Northumberland Heath Medical Centre in Bexley (Hind Crescent, DA8, ☎ 01322-336 556).

Private Medical Facilities

There are no private hospitals in the borough. The nearest are the Blackheath Hospital (see **Lewisham**) and the Fawkham Manor Hospital in Dartford (Kent). To find a private GP, visit ⌨ www.privatehealth.co.uk.

Schools

Educational standards in Bexley are above the UK average. In the 2009 school league tables, primary schools were placed 11th out of the 33 London boroughs (47th out of 150 UK local authorities) and secondary schools tenth (25th in the UK).

To compare schools throughout London, see the table in **Appendix D**.

Pre-school

Bexley council provides nursery classes at 41 primary schools, although there are no council-funded nursery facilities. There are additional playgroups and nursery schools in the private sector.

State Schools

First schools: 58 primary schools, of which 14 are voluntary aided.

Secondary schools: Four selective grammar schools and 14 comprehensive schools. A second academy, Haberdashers' Aske's Crayford Academy in Bexley, was opened in 2009. Three schools are voluntary aided, all have sixth forms and nine have specialist status. St Luke's Catholic Sixth Form College in Sidcup provides sixth form facilities for three schools and shares a site with St Mary and St Joseph's Catholic School.

In 2009, the best overall 5+ A*-C results were those of selective schools: Beths Grammar School in Bexley, Bexley Grammar School in Welling and Chislehurst and Sidcup Grammar School in Sidcup.

Special schools: Five special schools cater for students with physical disabilities and learning difficulties.

Private Schools

There are a handful of private schools in the borough, although none cater for secondary age pupils. West Lodge School in Sidcup focuses on children with special educational needs, including dyslexia.

Further & Higher Education

- Bexley College in Belvedere (🖥 www.bexley. ac.uk) offers a wide range of full-and part-time courses leading to recognised qualifications, including degrees.

- The Doreen Bird College of Performing Arts in Sidcup (🖥 www.birdcollege.co.uk) is an independent college offering degree-level courses in dance and theatre performance.

- Rose Bruford College in Sidcup (🖥 www.bruford. ac.uk) provides degree-level courses in theatre studies and related arts.

Public Transport

The underground doesn't extend as far as Bexley, but overground rail services into central London and Kent are good, with trains stopping at Greenwich and Lewisham for connections to the Docklands Light Railway. Bus services are frequent.

Rail

South Eastern Trains runs fast and direct rail services from Bexley's main towns to several central London destinations:

- Services to Blackfriars, Cannon Street, and London Bridge provide connections to the City, with a typical journey time of 20 minutes (Sidcup to London Bridge).

- Services to Charing Cross and Waterloo provide connections to the West End (37 minutes from Bexleyheath).

Buses

Daytime buses are frequent and operate every 15 minutes on most local routes. Several services connect to Greenwich, Lewisham and Woolwich for the Docklands, the City or the West End, but in common with other outer London boroughs, there aren't any direct daytime buses from Bexley to central London. Useful routes include the number 51 to Woolwich, 89 to Lewisham, 269 to Bromley and the 422 to Greenwich. Routes 428 and 492 go to the Bluewater shopping Centre. Two night buses provide services from Trafalgar Square – the N21 to Sidcup and the N89 to Erith.

Airports

Below are approximate distances and times from Bexleyheath to the five London airports using public transport.

- **City** – 5 miles; 70 minutes via Canary Wharf.

- **Gatwick** – 25 miles; 70 minutes via London Bridge.

- **Heathrow** – 26 miles; 100 minutes via Paddington.

- **Luton** – 37 miles; 90 minutes via London Bridge.

- **Stansted** – 31 miles; 110 minutes via London Bridge.

Roads

The main A2 and A20 roads linking London with Kent and the Channel ports slice through the borough and are invariably choked with traffic,

despite being red routes (no stopping) for much of their length. Local roads have been getting busier in recent years and the council is looking at proposals to improve the main dual carriageways around town centres to improve traffic flow.

Parking

As the borough's streets get busier, more Controlled Parking Zones (CPZs) have been introduced, particularly around railway stations. CPZs also operate in Bexleyheath and Sidcup town centres. An annual resident's permit costs £35 for one car in most areas, increasing by 25 per cent for each additional car in a household up to a maximum of four cars. Resident's permits are more expensive in Bexleyheath town centre (£70 per year, rising to £140) and Sidcup town centre (£60 per year, rising to £120).

Waste & Recycling

Recyclable materials are collected weekly and include aerosols, cans, cardboard and paper, glass, plastic bottles and tinfoil. All Bexley libraries sell caddy bags and garden waste sacks, and their staff can also deal with general waste queries and complaints. General household rubbish is collected fortnightly, and bulky items such as furniture and kitchen appliances are collected for a small charge. Bexley's two largest amenity (recycling) centres are located in Crayford, and there are also over 60 mini recycling sites throughout the borough.

Shopping

Bexleyheath is the borough's largest shopping district, with a shopping mall featuring most well-known high street names and a pedestrianised area of smaller shops, including a smattering of the now ubiquitous charity shops. More traditional high streets in Sidcup and Welling (the latter almost a mile long) are good for everyday essentials, with food stores and some general-purpose shops and DIY outlets, plus a number of small independent shops selling various items, including computer games, sports goods, toys and flowers.

The shopping precinct in Erith has recently been renovated and now includes some of the cheaper chains, such as Wilkinsons, while Crayford has a large retail park containing large branches of shops such as Comet, Hobbycraft, Homebase, Matalan and Next.

LOCAL INFORMATION

Although it isn't in Bexley, the massive Bluewater retail and leisure destination – Europe's largest, with over 330 shops and restaurants plus three leisure villages – is just 8mi (13km) away at Greenhithe, Kent (two miles from the M25 Junction 2, on the A2 London to Canterbury Road).

Shopping Centres

The Mall Broadway Shopping Centre (Broadway, DA6, ☎ 020-8301 2956, 🖳 www.themall.co.uk/broadway) – high street names, including Argos, M&S, Next and WH Smith.

Supermarkets

◆ Asda in Bexleyheath.

◆ Marks & Spencer in Bexleyheath.

◆ Morrisons in Erith, Sidcup and Thamesmead.

◆ Sainsbury's in Bexleyheath and Crayford, plus Local stores in Sidcup and Welling.

◆ Tesco in Sidcup (open 24 hours), with a Metro store in Welling, and there's a controversial proposal to build a Tesco in Bexleyheath.

Markets

◆ Erith Market (Market Square, DA8) – general household goods, Wednesday and Saturday; bric-a-brac, Thursday; plus an occasional farmer's market.

◆ Bexley Village Country Market (Freemantle Hall, High Street, DA5) – locally grown produce, arts and crafts; Friday.

◆ Bexleyheath Farmers' Market (Market Place, Kidbrooke, SE9) – first Thursday of the month, 9am-3pm.

Entertainment

There are three theatres in the borough but only one cinema, located in Bexleyheath. Museums concentrate on local history and there are several interesting houses to visit. In the summer the council hosts an annual arts festival in Bexleyheath

Broadway, showcasing the work of local arts groups, with live music and family-oriented events. There are a few night-clubs and bars for the younger set; most restaurants are fairly ordinary.

Theatres

♦ The Edward Alderton Theatre (5 Brampton Road, Bexleyheath, DA7, ☎ 020-8301 5584, 🖥 www.edward-alderton.ukf.net) – amateur repertory theatre.

♦ Erith Playhouse (38-40 High Street, DA8, ☎ 01322-350 345, 🖥 www.playhouse.org.uk) – amateur repertory theatre.

♦ Geoffrey Whitworth Theatre (Beech Walk, DA1, ☎ 01322-526 390, 🖥 www.thegwt.org.uk) – amateur club theatre.

♦ Old Barn Theatre & Theatre in the Round (Rose Bruford College, Burnt Oak Lane, DA15, ☎ 020-8308 2616) – student theatre.

Cinemas

Cineworld Bexleyheath (28 The Broadway, DA6, ☎ 0871-220 8000, 🖥 www.cineworld.co.uk) – multi-screen cinema.

Museums & Galleries

♦ Crossness Pumping Station (Belvedere Road, SE28, ☎ 020-8311 3711) – Victorian sewage works, open by appointment.

♦ Danson House (Danson Park, DA16, ☎ 020-8303 6699) – Palladian villa recently opened to the public.

♦ Hall Place and Gardens (Bourne Road, DA5, ☎ 01322-526 574) – Grade I listed country house with great hall, local history collection, galleries and award-winning gardens.

♦ Red House (13 Red House Lane, DA6, ☎ 020-8304 9878) – former home of Victorian artist, designer and poet, William Morris (see box).

LOCAL INFORMATION

One of Bexley's most famous buildings is the Red House in Bexleyheath, designed by Philip Webb in 1860 for designer William Morris. It was purchased by the National Trust in 2003 and is now open to the public.

Libraries

There are 12 local authority libraries in the borough, with adult and children's mobile services. The main library is the Bexley Central Library (Townley Road, DA6, ☎ 020-8303 7777, option 4), which has recently been refurbished and opens seven days a week. Erith Library (100 Erith High Street, Erith, DA8, ☎ as Bexley Library, above) moved to its new location in a development opposite Morrison's Supermarket in March 2009.

Clubs

The best night-clubs are outside the borough in New Cross, although there are a few bar/clubs in the main towns, targeted predominantly at the young, with mixed reputations. These include:

♦ Club Xtreme (28 Pier Road, DA8, ☎ 01322-347632);

♦ OHM Bar (Albion Road, DA6, ☎ 020-8301 3336);

♦ Plastic Red (101 Station Road, DA14, ☎ 020-8300 0855).

Live Music

There are no purpose-built music venues in the borough, although the theatres present a variety of musical performances. Some pubs host live cover bands, such as the Bear and Ragged Staff in Crayford (2 London Road, DA1, ☎ 01322-522 906). There's live music at the annual arts festival in Bexleyheath and occasional open air concerts in Danson Park. The Sidcup Symphony Orchestra performs regularly in local halls.

Pubs

Pubs in the borough are a mixture of traditional boozers, family-friendly pubs with gardens, plus modern music bars in the town centres. The widest choice of modern bars is in Bexleyheath, including Affinity (247 Broadway, DA6, ☎ 020-8304 0011) and the Zero Bar (295 Broadway, DA6, ☎ 020-8303 0219).

In Erith, the Ship is a gay-friendly bar with cabaret on Fridays (110 West Street, DA8, ☎ 01322-439 673). Regular entertainment is also provided at the traditional Leather Bottle in Belvedere (131, Heron Hill, DA17, ☎ 01322-432 066). For an olde worlde atmosphere, there's the George in Bexley (74 High Street, DA5, ☎ 01322-523 843), while Sidcup has a wide range of hostelries, including the Hogshead (47 High Street, DA14, ☎ 020-8308 9490) and the Portrait (7 Main Road, DA14, ☎ 020-8302 8757).

Restaurants

The best choice of restaurants is in Bexleyheath and Sidcup, with plenty of Chinese, Greek, Indian and Italian eateries interspersed with fast food chains such as McDonalds, Pizza Hut and Southern Fried Chicken. Bexleyheath and Sidcup have branches of Pizza Express. Many local pubs serve good food.

Sports Facilities

There are new council-funded leisure centres in Bexleyheath, Erith and Sidcup, with swimming pools and indoor sports halls. The Lamborley Swim Centre provides an additional swimming pool in Sidcup. The David Ives Stadium in Erith has a floodlit, all-weather track and athletics facilities, and councillors hope that this and the other leisure centres will be used as training grounds during the 2012 London Olympics.

As well as sports pitches and courts in many of the boroughs' parks, the lake in Bexleyheath's Danson Park is home to the Danson Watersports Centre, a council-supported organisation providing sailing, canoeing and windsurfing courses. There are a number of outlets of well-known sports and health clubs in the borough, including a David Lloyd Tennis Centre in Sidcup. For golfers, there's a public nine-hole course in Bexleyheath (Barnehurst Golf Course) as well as an 18-hole private course in Sidcup. There are several local riding stables and tenpin bowling is possible at the Megabowl in Bexleyheath.

Green Spaces

Bexley boasts over 1,500 acres (600ha) of open spaces, spread over 100 parks and areas, ranging from small gardens and large urban parks to river and woodland areas. Four parks have Green Flag Awards (🖳 www.greenflagaward.org.uk), the highest number consistently held in the country, and there are several sites of Special Scientific Interest. Green Flag parks include Hall Place Gardens on the banks of the River Cray, featuring rose gardens, a topiary lawn and a working nursery, and Lesnes Abbey Woods, a local nature reserve. There are some lovely walking trails in the borough, notably through Lesnes Abbey Woods and along the riverside at Thamesmead and Erith.

LOCAL INFORMATION

Danson Park (another Green Flag park) is believed to have been landscaped by Capability Brown. It's one of Bexley's most popular parks, hosting many annual events, including circuses, concerts, festivals and motor shows.

Brent

NW2 (part), NW6 (part), NW9 (part), NW10, HA0,
HA3 (part), HA9

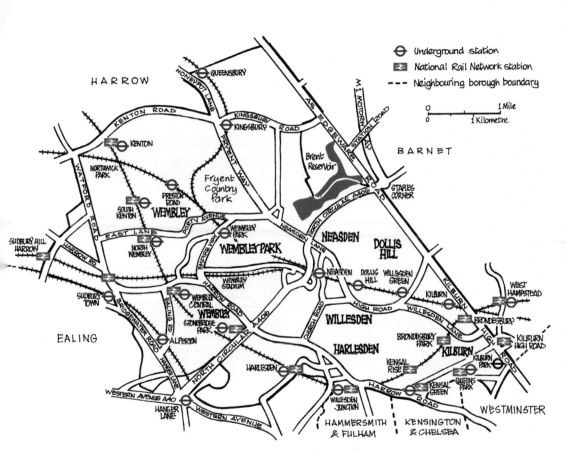

At a Glance

Best for: affordable housing, transport links, parking, gastropubs

Not so good for: poor housing stock, deprivation, crime, nightlife

Who lives there: multicultural, working class families, first-time buyers, young professionals

Housing stock: mostly flats (one-third conversions) with terraces and semis

Housing costs: moderate

General Information

Council Offices: Town Hall, Forty Lane, Wembley, HA9 9HD (☎ 020-8937 1234)

CAA Assessment: (see 💻 http://oneplace.direct.gov.uk > Search by area > London > Brent)

Controlling Party: Labour

Website: 💻 www.brent.gov.uk

Council Tax 2010/11: £2,281 (Band G), £2,738 (Band H)

Main Areas/towns: Brondesbury, Harlesden, Kenton, Kilburn, Kingsbury, Neasden, Queens Park, Wembley, Willesden, Willesden Green

Postcodes: NW2 (part), NW6 (part), NW9 (part), NW10, HA0, HA3 (part), HA9

Population & Ethnicity: 270,600, with the largest group aged between 20 and 44. Over half of Brent's residents are from ethnic minorities, mainly Asian and Afro-Caribbean. The borough also has the largest Irish community in London and is particularly popular with families.

Unemployment: 8.4 per cent (the London average is 8.2 per cent)

Overview

The borough of Brent was formed in 1965 and takes its name from the river that runs through it. Brent is one of the UK's most multicultural areas, with equally diverse economic and social characteristics. Having shed its '80s 'loony left' image, today the borough is neither typically 'inner' nor 'outer' London. Some areas suffer from inner city levels of social deprivation (around Harlesden, South Kilburn and Stonebridge, for example), while other places – such as Brondesbury, Dollis Hill and Kingsbury – present a more genteel and suburban air, with tree-lined streets and well-maintained houses.

Wembley – dominated by its Stadium (the national stadium and home of English football), Arena and Conference Centre – is set to become one of London's showcase centres for the 2012 Olympic Games. Further east, Neasden has an unfortunate reputation for dullness, although one claim to fame is the largest Hindu temple (Shiri Swaminarayam Mandir) outside India. In the south-east corner, Kilburn and Queen's Park, once considered rather down-at-heel, are among the capital's upwardly mobile areas, increasingly popular with those priced out of Hampstead and Maida Vale.

LOCAL INFORMATION

The new Wembley Stadium and the regeneration of the surrounding area and transport infrastructure cost a staggering £750mn.

Development Plans

In June 2008, plans were approved for the provision of a 10-screen cinema, a designer outlet store and homes with underground parking and open spaces, to be built on land surrounding Wembley Stadium. These are the first of many new housing, retail and leisure facilities planned for the local community, and for the thousands of visitors who attend events at Wembley Stadium and Arena. The development should be completed towards the end of 2010.

Residential Areas

Nearly half of all property in Brent is flats, over a third of which are conversions. The flats around Queens Park are particularly attractive, being spacious and close to central London. Terraces and semis make up a large part of the remaining housing stock, with a mere 4 per cent being detached houses.

Brondesbury & Willesden Green (NW2, NW10)

These once solidly Jewish areas have become more cosmopolitan as newcomers have arrived in search of large Victorian and '30s houses with gardens front and back. Brondesbury Park is Brent's most expensive area, where it isn't unusual to find foreign diplomats rubbing shoulders with celebrities, and grand detached houses sell for £millions. Willesden Green is cheaper, with an attractive mix of Victorian houses and conversions in wide tree-lined streets and plenty of parking. A three-bedroom flat in the desirable Mapesbury conservation area costs around £400,000.

Cricklewood, Dollis Hill & Neasden (NW2, NW10)

Cricklewood is a mix of houses and conversions (attracting people priced out of West Hampstead), plus period terraces and inter-war semis, sandwiched between the railway lines that dissect the area. Already a good location for first-time buyers, Cricklewood will benefit from the current redevelopment around Brent Cross in neighbouring Barnet, with new homes, shops and public transport set to increase its potential as an up-and-coming area.

Families look to Dollis Hill and Neasden for the large number of Edwardian and '30s semis set in peaceful streets. There are also a number of modern blocks of flats that are increasingly popular with

young couples. The nearby Brent Cross shopping centre (in the borough of Barnet) is an attraction.

Harlesden & Willesden (NW10)

Dominated by its Afro-Caribbean community, Harlesden has some great Jamaican food and ethnic shops. On the downside, it's also the most deprived part of the borough, overshadowed by large council tower blocks and high crime rates. However, better low-rise flats are now replacing some of the blocks, and newcomers are moving into the area in search of properties ripe for gentrification. Willesden has a reputation as a friendly community and is a good choice for first-time buyers and young families, with plenty of flats and small Victorian terraces, and a range of social amenities.

Kingsbury & Kenton (NW9, HA3)

Leafy streets and abundant green spaces characterise this corner of the borough. Handsome detached houses overlooking Fryent Park, as well as '30s semis, make these towns popular with families. There are also some '20s thatched cottages in Kingsbury and distinctive 'mock Tudor' estates in Kenton.

Queen's Park & Kilburn (NW6)

The benefits of excellent transport links and a location surprisingly close to Paddington and Maida Vale have made these areas extremely popular in the last few years. Queen's Park in particular has seen property prices soar, thanks to young professionals and families moving in and renovating the once shabby Victorian and Edwardian houses. A typical three-bedroom terrace (with a loft conversion creating a fourth bedroom) can cost around £750,000. Kilburn, known for its large Irish community, is a mixture of scruffy and smart areas, and is slightly cheaper than Queen's Park. Terraced houses are common, interspersed with larger houses (now mostly converted into flats), council blocks and the occasional new-build.

Wembley (HA0, HA9)

Wembley is full of inter-war terraces and semis, starting at £370,000 for three bedrooms. Modern apartment blocks and ex-council properties are also available, and the area is being further developed. The most sought-after area is the Sudbury Estate, which is quiet and within walking distance of two stations. Hugely multicultural in character, this is a predominantly family area, with little in the way of nightlife. In addition to the Stadium and Arena, Wembley is also home to a large television studio.

FAMOUS RESIDENTS

Brent's famous residents have included John Logie Baird, who received the first television signals from Berlin and first combined sound and sight transmission in 1930, Peter O'Toole (Irish actor), Keith Moon (drummer with *The Who*), Louis Theroux (British broadcaster) and Shane Ritchie (actor/singer).

Property Costs

Property Prices

The table below shows average property prices in the borough:

Detached: £840,521
Semi-detached: £ 390,695
Terraced: £402,610
Flat: £243,144

Rental Costs

The table below shows the average monthly rents in the borough:

House 5+bed: £7,000
House 4-5 bed: £4,800
House 3-4 bed: £3,600
House 2-3 bed: £2,500
Flat 2-bed: £2,200
Flat 1-bed: £1,500

Crime

Brent has the tenth-highest crime rate of all London boroughs, with violent crime, burglary and drugs-related offences the most common.

The police station HQ is in Wembley (603 Harrow Road, HA0, ☎ 0300-123 1212) and there are other stations in Chalkhill, Harlesden, Kilburn, Kingsbury and Willesden Green.

To compare crime rates throughout London, see the table in **Appendix D**.

Health

NHS services in the borough are provided by the Brent Primary Care Trust. For a full list of doctors, dentists and clinics, visit 💻 www.nhs.uk.

To see how the Primary Care Trust compares with others in London, see the table in **Appendix D**.

Doctors & Dentists

♦ There are over 85 NHS GP surgeries, providing a range of clinics and health services.

♦ Brent has 66 dental and orthodontic practices, roughly half of which accept new NHS patients.

Hospitals

♦ Central Middlesex Hospital (Acton Lane, NW10, ☎ 020-8965 5733) – A&E.

♦ Northwick Park Hospital (Watford Road, HA1, ☎ 020-8864 3232) – A&E.

♦ Wembley Centre for Health & Care (116 Chaplin Road, HA0, ☎ 020-8795 6001) – Minor Accidents and Treatment Service (MATS).

Wembley Hospital and Willesden Community Hospital provide a range of clinics.

Private Medical Facilities

There are no private hospitals in the borough. The nearest one is the Garden Hospital in Hendon (see **Barnet**). To find a private GP, visit 💻 www.privatehealth.co.uk.

Schools

Despite the culturally diverse population (over 100 different languages are spoken in Brent's schools), educational standards are around the national average. In the 2009 school league tables, primary schools were placed 25th out of the 33 London boroughs (106th out of 150 UK local authorities) and secondary schools 11th (27th in the UK).

To compare schools throughout London, see the table in **Appendix D**.

Wembley Stadium

School in Neasden was one of the top UK schools for GCSE results and added value, while the Brondesbury College for Boys and the Islamia Girls' High School also performed well.

Further Education

The College of North West London in Willesden (🖥 www.cnwl.ac.uk) offers a variety of courses for students aged 16+.

Higher Education

The Harrow Campus of the University of Westminster is just inside Brent's borders, in Northwick Park (🖥 www.wmin.ac.uk).

Public Transport

Public transport in Brent is generally good, with three underground lines serving most areas and an overground service stopping at several stations. A number of buses serve central London.

Underground

The Bakerloo, Hammersmith & City and Jubilee lines provide frequent services. Typical journey times are as follows:

◆ Harlesden (Bakerloo line, zone 3) to Charing Cross, 27 minutes.

◆ Kilburn (Jubilee line, zone 2) to Bond Street, 13 minutes.

◆ Wembley Park (Hammersmith & City line, zone 4) to Kings Cross, 21 minutes.

Rail

Four rail lines run through the borough, with three stopping at busy Willesden Junction. One of London's trans-Thames rail services usefully links Wembley to Clapham Junction and places south.

◆ London Overground services stop in Wembley, Harlesden, Willesden and Queen's Park en route to Euston from the north (Willesden Junction to Euston, 20 minutes).

◆ Chiltern Railways stop at Wembley Stadium en route to Marylebone (journey time, 13 minutes).

◆ Southern Railways go from Watford to the south coast via Wembley Central.

◆ The North London line travels east-west through Brent, stopping at Willesden Junction,

Pre-school

As well as four community nursery schools, there are nursery classes attached to many infant and primary schools, and a wide choice of privately-run nurseries and playgroups.

State Schools

First schools: 59 infant, junior and primary schools, of which 20 are voluntary aided, including one Muslim school.

Secondary schools: 13 comprehensives, including one City Academy in Harlesden. Four schools are voluntary aided, all have sixth forms and 12 have specialist status. The top performer in 2009 was the JFS School in Kenton. (same)

Special schools: Five schools and four specialised units cater for students with physical disabilities and learning difficulties.

Private Schools

There are nine private schools in the borough, of which three are Muslim schools and one is for Hindu students. The TCS Tutorial College in Kingsbury is a selective school for students aged between 14 and 16. In 2009, the Swaminarayan

Kensal Rise and Brondesbury, en route to Richmond and Barking.

LOCAL INFORMATION

Brent was transformed from a collection of country villages in a setting of fields and hedgerow trees over a period of eighty years from 1858, mainly as a result of the development of the railways (especially the Metropolitan line) and the British Empire exhibition in 1924-5.

Buses

Several routes serve central London, including the number 16 from Kilburn to Victoria, the 18 from Wembley to Euston and the 52 from Willesden to Victoria. Otherwise, there are routes to Brent Cross Shopping Centre and the Central Middlesex hospital, as well as to neighbouring boroughs. Brent is also served by the N16, N18 and N98 night buses from central London.

Airports

Below are approximate distances and times from Willesden Junction to the five London airports using public transport:

♦ **City** (14 miles; 60 minutes via Canning Town).

♦ **Gatwick** (28 miles; 62 minutes via Clapham Junction).

♦ **Heathrow** (10 miles; 50 minutes via Paddington).

♦ **Luton** (23 miles; 80 minutes via West Hampstead).

♦ **Stansted** (32 miles; 105 minutes via Liverpool Street).

Roads

The A406 North Circular Road, which cuts the borough in half, has been widened, but still tends to jam at peak times, with the junctions at Neasden and Stonebridge Park particularly busy. The A5 runs along the boundary with Barnet.

Parking

Apart from Wembley Stadium, where parking is always a problem and is strictly controlled, the majority of the Controlled Parking Zones are in the south-eastern corner of the borough, around Kilburn,

Brondesbury Park and Kensal Rise. Residents' parking permits in these areas costs £50 per year for one car, £75 per year for a second car and £100 per year for a third.

Waste & Recycling

The council provides wheelie bins for general household rubbish, which are emptied weekly. There's also a kerbside collection service for recyclable materials, including cans, engine oil, glass, newspapers and magazines, shoes, textiles and tinfoil. Bulky household items such as computers, furniture and kitchen appliances are collected free of charge. The new Brent Re-use and Recycling Centre is in Park Royal.

Shopping

Shopping in Brent tends to be functional or specialist. For example, Wembley High Road has a selection of chain stores, including Boots, M&S and Primark, while nearby Ealing Road is a haven for Asian shops and features some of the great jewellery houses of India, selling handcrafted gold and diamond creations. An extensively updated shopping mall is nearing completion close to the new stadium and should be finished by the summer of 2010.

Kilburn High Road has another M&S, several fashion shops and a number of food shops, while Queen's Park has a few independent delicatessens and clothes shops. Kenton is a biker's paradise, with two motorbike shops.

Shopping Centres

The Wembley Central Square Shopping Centre, adjacent to the station, is due for completion in 2010 and there are several retail parks offering DIY, furniture and carpet superstore outlets. Staples Corner Retail Park on the North Circular Road has a number of electrical goods shops, while nearby Brent Park is one of the capital's major shopping areas and has a branch of Ikea.

Supermarkets

♦ Asda in Wembley Park.

♦ Marks & Spencer in Kilburn.

♦ Morrisons in Queensbury.

♦ Sainsbury's in Wembley, Kenton, Kilburn and Willesden Green.

♦ Tesco at Brent Park (open 24 hours).

Markets

◆ Wembley Sunday Market (behind Wembley Stadium in Olympic Way, HA9) is a popular market for bargains in household goods, toys and clothes.

◆ The nearest Farmers' Market is at Ealing (Leeland Road, West Ealing W13); Saturday from 9am-1pm.

Entertainment

Although the area is best known for the new Wembley Stadium and Wembley Arena (which has recently been renovated at a cost of £35mn), there are a number of local venues for plays, concerts and films, notably the Tricycle in Kilburn (see below), which comprises a theatre, cinema, rehearsal and visual arts studios, and a gallery. Two festivals take place during the summer – the Respect Festival in Roundwood Park, which celebrates the borough's cultural diversity, and the Kilburn Festival in Kilburn Grange Park, which is a fun-packed family day with plenty of live music. Wembley is noted for its numerous Indian restaurants and there are a couple of night-clubs in Kilburn.

Theatres

◆ St Gabriel's Church (Walm Lane, NW2, ☎ 020-8830 6626) – small theatre for local productions.

◆ Tricycle Theatre (269 Kilburn High Road, NW6, ☎ 020-7328 1000, 🖥 www.tricycle.co.uk) – 230-seat theatre.

Cinemas

◆ UGC Staples Corner (Geron Way, NW2, ☎ 0871-200 2000, 🖥 www.ugccinemas.co.uk).

◆ The Tricycle Cinema (see above).

◆ Willesden Belle-Vue Cinema (95 High Road, NW10, ☎ 020-8830 0822).

Museums & Galleries

Brent's sole museum, the Grange Museum of Community History, has been moved to new premises at Willesden Green Library (see below). Not strictly a museum, but worth visiting, is Fountain Studios (128 Wembley Park Drive, HA9, ☎ 020-8900 5800), which is the largest purpose-built television studio in the country (*Who Wants to be a Millionaire?* is made there). The Swaminayaran Temple in Neasden is a marvellous building, with ornate, intricate carvings and ceilings – it was carved in India and assembled in situ.

There are several galleries showcasing modern art in the borough, including:

◆ The Stables Gallery and Arts Centre (Gladstone Park, NW2, ☎ 020-8452 8655).

◆ Tricycle Gallery (see above).

◆ Willesden Green Library Centre (95 High Road, NW10, ☎ 020-8937 3417).

Libraries

There are 12 local authority libraries in the borough, with one mobile service. The largest is the Willesden Green Library Centre (95 High Road, NW10, ☎ 020-8937 3400), which opens seven days a week, as do the Ealing Road and Kingsbury Library Plus libraries in Wembley.

Clubs

Clubs and late bars are mostly around Wembley and Kilburn, including:

◆ Diceys (295 Neasden Lane, Wembley, NW10, ☎ 020-8208 3539) – night-club.

◆ ZD Bar (289 Kilburn High Road, NW6, ☎ 020-7372 2544) – popular bar with dance floor and late licence.

You can watch comedy at the Lately Night Club (176 West End Lane, NW6, ☎ 020-7625 6474).

Live Music

Wembley Arena (Arena Square, Engineers Way, HA9, ☎ 020-8782 5500) is one of London's largest entertainment venues, with a capacity of 12,500. It was refurbished in 2006 at a cost of £35mn, which included new lifts, more entrances and toilets, better access to the restaurant and more space for wheelchair users.

Smaller venues include:

♦ Ace Café (North Circular Road, Alperton, NW10, ☎ 020-8961 1000, 🖳 www.ace-cafe-london.com) – famous former biker's haunt reinvented for live rock 'n roll gigs.

♦ The Crown (142-152 Cricklewood Broadway, NW2, ☎ 020-8452 4175) – animated pub with live music.

♦ The Luminaire (311 High Road, NW6, ☎ 020-7372 7123, 🖳 www.theluminaire.co.uk) – live gigs.

Pubs

Brent has long had a reputation for excellent Irish pubs (particularly in Cricklewood, Kilburn and Wembley) and there are still plenty around, such as the Corrib Rest in Harlesden (Salusbury Road, NW6, ☎ 020-7625 9585), which has live music at weekends.

Increasingly, modern gastropubs are springing up, particularly in places where gentrification is rife. The Black Lion in Kilburn (274 Kilburn High Road, NW6, ☎ 020-7625 1635) is a good example, noted for its decent food, while the Salusbury in Queen's Park (50 Salusbury Road, NW6, ☎ 020-7328 3286) is popular. There's also the inevitable selection of chain pubs, such as JJ Moons (553 Kingsbury Road, NW9, ☎ 020-8204 9675). Good pubs are rather thin on the ground around Neasden and Queensbury.

Restaurants

Some of the capital's best ethnic cuisine can be found in Brent, with Asian, Chinese and Mediterranean restaurants. Wembley's restaurants serve some of the more unusual 'Indian' cuisines, including Bangladeshi, Gujerati and Pakistani, as well as Sri Lankan vegetarian food. Kilburn also has some excellent Asian cuisine, for example Southern Indian food at the eccentric Vijay's (49 Willesden Lane, NW6, ☎ 020-7328 1087).

Elsewhere there are other interesting restaurants, including Japanese food at Sushi Say in Willesden Green (33B Walm Lane, NW2, ☎ 020-8459 2971) and Portuguese at O'Galinheiro Piri Piri Restaurant (414 High Road, HA9,

☎ 020-8903 0811). Hugo's Café/Bar has live Jazz on Sundays as a backdrop to its excellent organic food (25 Lonsdale Road, NW6, ☎ 020-7372 1232). The borough also has its fair share of fast food joints, takeaways and greasy spoons.

Sports Facilities

As well as sports pitches and courts in many of the borough's parks, there are currently four council-funded sports centres, in Kensal Rise, Kilburn, Stonebridge and Wembley. Facilities include:

♦ A swimming pool, squash courts and an all-weather pitch at the largest centre in Wembley.

♦ Indoor sports halls at all centres.

♦ Tennis courts at the Kensal Rise Centre.

A fifth centre, at Donnington Road in Willesden, has been redeveloped and reopened in November 2006. This new multi-million pound complex has a swimming pool, floodlit athletics track and indoor sports facilities, including a 'running tube'. It offers award-winning 'learning to swim' courses and the opportunity to learn martial arts.

Other sports facilities in the borough include horse riding in Fryent Country Park, tennis at the South Hampstead Tennis Club (Milverton Road, NW6, ☎ 020-8459 2348), as well as fitness centres operated by Cannons, Energie, Fitness First and Living Well. Part of Northwick Park in Kenton is being redeveloped as a state-of-the-art golf course.

Green Spaces

Brent has over 1,000 acres of open space, including Fryent Country Park in Kingsbury and the Welsh Harp Reservoir, which it shares with neighbouring Barnet. There are also numerous recreation grounds, open spaces and formal parks and gardens. Queen's Park is a 30-acre urban park complete with a children's farm, bandstand, assorted sports facilities and a woodland walk. Barham Park in Sudbury has a pretty walled garden, many mature trees and is the third most visited open space in the borough. Gladstone Park in Dollis Hill is another pretty park, with an arboretum, wildlife area and formal gardens. For walkers, there are plenty of trails along the Grand Union Canal and the River Brent.

Bromley

SE20, SE26, BR1 (part), BR2, BR3, BR4, BR5, BR6, BR7, BR8, CR6 (part), TN14 (part), TN16 (part)

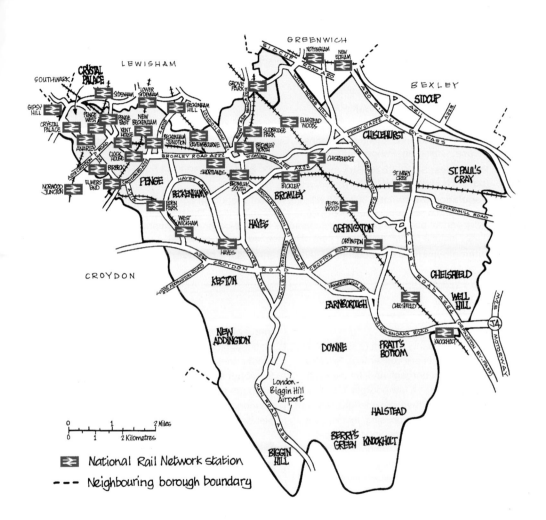

National Rail Network station

- - - Neighbouring borough boundary

At a Glance

Best for: transport connections, shopping, schools, leisure facilities, open spaces

Not so good for: crime, nightlife, no tube

Who lives there: middle-class families, business people, first-time buyers, commuters

Housing stock: detached houses (almost 20% – the most in London), the rest a mix of semis, terraces and flats

Housing costs: relatively inexpensive

General Information

Council Offices: Civic Centre, Stockwell Close, Bromley, BR1 (☎ 020-8464 3333)

CAA Assessment: (see 🖳 http://oneplace.direct.gov.uk > Search by area > London > Bromley)

Controlling Party: Conservative

Website: 🖳 www.bromley.gov.uk

Council Tax 2010/11: £2,169 (Band G), £2,602 (Band H)

Main Areas/towns: Anerley, Beckenham, Biggin Hill, Bromley, Chislehurst, Crystal Palace, Orpington, Penge, Petts Wood

Postcodes: SE20, SE26, BR1 (part), BR2, BR3, BR4, BR5, BR6, BR7, BR8, CR6 (part), TN14 (part), TN16 (part)

Population & Ethnicity: 302,600, with the highest proportion aged between 30 and 40. Around 6 per cent of people belong to ethnic minorities. The borough attracts independent business people and commuters in white-collar employment. The average family income is high and 86 per cent of homes are owner-occupied.

Unemployment: 6.0 per cent (the London average is 8.2 per cent)

Overview

Formerly within the county of Kent (it still is as far as most of its residents are concerned), Bromley is the capital's largest borough and, for the most part, typically suburban. A few pockets of Victorian development in the north-west corner give way to vast areas of '20s and '30s housing, thinning out to green belt woods, commons and the almost rural villages of Keston and Farnborough on the borough's outskirts.

Bromley's principal attraction was originally Crystal Palace, moved from Hyde Park to the top of Sydenham Hill after the Great Exhibition in the 1850s, but destroyed by fire in 1936. Several attempts have been made to redevelop the site and the park remains a popular recreation spot adjacent to the slightly faded national sports centre. Other attractions in the borough include Chislehurst Caves, the annual air fair at Biggin Hill airport and a Roman villa in Crofton.

The main town is Bromley, with its excellent shopping centre. Transport connections from there and other towns are good, with fast and frequent rail services to several central London stations, plus access to the East London Line (under construction) at Crystal Palace. Towns in the south are within easy reach of motorways. Although many residents commute into central London, there's a thriving local economy providing plenty of jobs closer to home.

LOCAL INFORMATION

The origin of the town's name is the old English brōme-hlæwe (broom hill), shown in records as Bramelewe in 1272.

Development Plans

Bromley is aiming to develop and improve its town centre in an ambitious fifteen-year plan that will ensure that the town maintains its position as a vibrant and thriving part of the borough. Plans include leisure, community and health facilities, shops and housing, while protecting the town's character and heritage. In addition to stimulating regeneration, the improvements should make the town a safer and a more attractive place to visit.

As the second-largest town in the borough, Orpington also intends to update and improve the appearance of its High Street, as well as a longer-term similar development plan (to Bromley) for the town centre.

Residential Areas

Bromley's north-west corner (bordering Croydon, Lewisham and Southwark) has the feel of inner London, with 19th century houses around Penge, Anerley and Crystal Palace. The borough's other main towns, once villages, were largely developed after WWI. Bromley has the highest percentage of detached houses in London (18 per cent), reflecting its large number of affluent residents. The remainder of properties are fairly evenly divided between semi-detached houses (29 per cent), terraces (25 per cent) and flats (29 per cent).

Beckenham (BR3)

Once the largest town in Kent, Beckenham is a pleasant suburb surrounded by parkland, although somewhat overshadowed by Bromley. Its two railway stations serve Victoria and London Bridge, and the town is also on the Tramlink service from Croydon and Wimbledon. Popular with City commuters, families and comfortably-off, first-time buyers, the town has a busy high street and a wide choice of properties, including Victorian terraced and semi-detached houses, a few older buildings, large detached inter-war homes and some newer apartment blocks in the centre. There's an attractive development of '60s Span houses to the north.

Biggin Hill (TN16)

In the south of the borough close to the M25, Biggin Hill (with no rail station) has a rural feel despite the increased traffic using the airport. Property consists mostly of '60s and '70s developments, and there are a number of interesting '30s properties originally built for RAF personnel.

Bromley (BR1, BR2)

Bromley is a popular commuter town, with two railway stations and a friendly town centre (it was recently honoured with a prestigious Safer Shopping Award). Families like the combination of good local leisure facilities and schools. Property ranges from Victorian cottages and larger homes near the centre

to mock Tudor '30s detached and semi-detached houses further out. New flats have been built in the town centre.

The leafy town of Hayes to the south is slightly more expensive, while West Wickham has a good stock of flats.

Petts Wood & Chislehurst (BR5, BR7)

Picturesque and village-like, Chislehurst is surrounded by commons and is one of the most desirable areas in the borough. Grand detached houses dating from the 19th century (and later) line wide, leafy roads in conservation areas, with some '60s and '70s estates to the west around Bickley. Petts Wood to the south is a classic '30s garden suburb, with a large number of 'mock Tudor' detached and plainer three-bedroom, semi-detached homes (prices range from £300,000 to £600,000, depending on size). One of the most desirable areas is the Chenies development of detached houses. There are few flats and maisonettes.

Crystal Palace, Penge & Anerley (SE20, SE26)

With a hilly vantage point and largely Victorian homes (a mixture of terraces and semis of varying sizes), these areas are gaining in popularity among families and first-time buyers, who can find something to suit their needs regarding size and price. Many of

the larger Victorian homes have been converted into flats. In Penge, a number of old almshouses, once the equivalent of affordable housing, are now highly sought-after, while Anerley has a few modern infill developments, including '60s townhouses and post-war council blocks. Crystal Palace remains one of the best areas for shopping and nightlife.

Orpington (BR6)

The borough's second-largest town, Orpington is a prosperous commercial and residential area within easy reach of motorways, Gatwick Airport and the Channel Tunnel. Convenient for commuters, the town has a thriving shopping district and a good supply of inter-war semis, as well as Victorian property closer to the centre. To the north-east, St Mary Cray and St Paul's Cray feature '50s council properties, many of which are now privately owned. To the south, the villages of Farnborough and Keston have local retail and leisure amenities, and are popular with families looking for a sense of space. Semi-detached and detached houses of different styles and ages are also found, with the most expensive properties on the edge of green spaces.

Property Costs

Property Prices

The table below shows average property prices in the borough:

Detached: £636,596
Semi-detached: £323,701
Terraced: £262,210
Flat: £186,952

Rental Costs

The table below shows average monthly rents in the borough:

House 5+ bed: £2,100
House 4-5 bed: £1,800
House 3-4 bed: £1,600
House 2-3 bed: £1,300
Flat 2-bed: £1,050
Flat 1-bed: £750

Crime

Overall, crime rates are slightly better than average for London, with burglary the most common offence. Crime hotspots are around the centres of Bromley, Beckenham, Crystal Palace, Orpington and Penge, plus east of the Cray Valley, where shoplifting and anti-social behaviour are the main offences. Current priorities include tackling youth violence and drugs, and an increased police presence on the streets is helping reduce crime.

The police station HQ is in Bromley (High Street, BR1, ☎ 01689-891 212) with other stations in Biggin Hill, Orpington, Penge and West Wickham. There are community police offices in Beckenham, Bickley, Burnt Ash Lane, Chislehurst, Petts Wood and St Mary Cray.

To compare crime rates throughout London, see the table in **Appendix D**.

Health

NHS services in the borough are provided by the Bromley Primary Care Trust. For a full list of doctors, dentists and clinics, visit 🖥 www.nhs.uk.

To see how the Primary Care Trust compares with others in London, see the table in **Appendix D**.

Doctors & Dentists

♦ There are over 110 NHS GP surgeries, providing a range of clinics and health services.

♦ Bromley has 85 dental and orthodontic practices, although few accept new NHS patients.

Hospitals

♦ Beckenham Hospital (379 Croydon Road, BR3, ☎ 01689-863 000, 🖥 www.bromleyhospitals. nhs.uk) – minor injuries unit and outpatients clinics.

♦ Orpington Hospital (Sevenoaks Road, BR6, ☎ 01689-863 000, 🖥 www.bromleyhospitals. nhs.uk) – rehabilitation and therapy services; planned surgery.

♦ Princess Royal University Hospital (Farnborough Common, BR6, ☎ 01689-863 000, 🖥 www. bromleyhospitals.nhs.uk) – A&E; minor injuries unit.

Private Medical Facilities

♦ The Priory Hospital Hayes Grove (Prestons Road, BR2, ☎ 020-8462 7722, 🖥 www. prioryhealthcare.co.uk) provides independent mental health care.

♦ The Sloane Hospital (125 Albemarle Road, BR3, ☏ 020-8466 4000, 💻 www.bmihealthcare.co.uk/Sloane).

To find a private GP, visit 💻 www.privatehealth.co.uk.

Schools

Education standards in Bromley are high and the borough has a significant number of independent schools. In the 2009 school league tables, primary schools were placed tenth out of the 33 London boroughs (39th out of 150 UK local authorities) and secondary schools sixth (ninth in the UK).

To compare schools throughout London, see the table in **Appendix D**.

Pre-school

The best provision for early years education is in the private sector, with a good choice of playgroups and nursery schools. Only ten primary schools provide nursery classes and there are no council-funded nursery schools, although in 2006 the council opened two children's centres to provide integrated childcare and education at Anerley and Orpington.

State Schools

First schools: There are 76 primary and junior schools, of which 17 are voluntary aided or controlled. In the 2009 Key Stage 2 attainment tables, the St James RC Primary School, Keston C of E Primary School, Highfield Junior School and the Chislehurst Church of England Primary School obtained excellent results, with the Holy Innocents Catholic Primary School and Clare House Primary School also doing well.

Secondary schools: Two selective schools and 17 comprehensives. Three schools are voluntary aided and the remainder are foundation schools; all have sixth forms and 13 have specialist status. The top performers in 2009 included the two selective schools in Orpington: Newstead (girls), which is one of the top UK schools for GCSE and A level results, and St Olave's and St Saviour's Grammar (boys).

Specialist schools: The borough has four special schools for students with physical disabilities and learning difficulties.

FAMOUS RESIDENTS

Famous former residents include David Bowie (rock star), Charles Darwin (naturalist), Enid Blyton (children's author), Peter Frampton (musician), W.G. Grace (cricketer), Napoleon III (who was exiled there), Camille Pissarro (French impressionist painter), H.G. Wells (writer) and Michael York (actor).

Private Schools

There are 15 private schools in the borough, with seven catering for secondary age pupils, three of which are selective. The Darul Uloom School in Chislehurst is an independent Islamic school. The

top performers in 2009 were Bromley High School (girls) and The Bishop Challoner School in Bromley, both of which are among the top UK schools for GCSE results, including English and maths. The Bishop Challoner School in Bromley was also one of the top UK schools for added value.

Further Education

Orpington College (💻 www.orpington.ac.uk) offers a wide range of courses leading to recognised qualifications. There are also two colleges for students with special needs: the Marjorie McClure School in Chislehurst and the Nash College of Further Education in Hayes.

Higher Education

Ravensbourne College of Design and Communication in Chislehurst (💻 www.rave.ac.uk) offers graduate and post-graduate degree courses, as well as services for business.

Public Transport

Bromley isn't currently served by the underground, although the East London Line extension should reach Crystal Palace by 2012. Overground rail services are comprehensive and provide regular services into central London and to the south and south-east coasts, while Beckenham and Elmers End are on the tram service from Croydon. Bus services are comprehensive.

Rail

There are Southern and South Eastern train services from Blackfriars, Cannon Street, Charing Cross, London Bridge, Victoria and Waterloo to stations throughout the borough. Bromley South also provides a regular service to Ashford for Eurostar connections. Typical travel times are:

- Express services from Bromley South to Victoria: 16 minutes.
- Chislehurst to London Bridge: 20 minutes.
- Orpington to Charing Cross: 26 minutes.

Buses

There's a comprehensive local network of buses serving all areas of the borough, including several circular routes. Two routes go to Oxford Circus – number 3 from Crystal Palace and 176 from Penge – although they're slow. Other useful routes include the 432 (Anerley to Brixton) and the 477 (Orpington to the Bluewater Shopping Centre). The N3, N47 and N137 night buses all serve the borough.

Trams

Beckenham and Elmers End are both stops on the Tram Link service, which runs from East Croydon and Wimbledon (16 minutes from Beckenham to East Croydon).

Airports

Below are the approximate distances and times from Bromley to the five London airports using public transport:

- **City** – 7 miles; 75 minutes via New Cross and Canary Wharf.

- **Gatwick** – 19 miles; 50 minutes via East Croydon.
- **Heathrow** – 21 miles; 95 minutes via Paddington.
- **Luton** – 38 miles; 90 minutes via Herne Hill.
- **Stansted** – 36 miles; 100 minutes via Victoria Station.

Roads

Bromley has one of the highest car ownership levels in London, with the result that traffic congestion is a problem on many main roads, particularly during peak periods. The only primary road to run through the borough is the A232, which becomes the A21 around Orpington, before joining the M25. Bromley is within easy reach of the M25, M20, M26 and M2, for routes around the perimeter of London and to the south-east coast.

The council is trying to encourage more people to cycle – there are now over 50 miles of dedicated cycle routes in the borough.

> ### LOCAL INFORMATION
>
> Biggin Hill Airport
>
> **Bromley is home to Biggin Hill airport, which during the Second World War was a key airfield during the Battle of Britain. Today it provides a fast-growing business and executive service to domestic and European destinations.**

Parking

Despite the borough's large numbers of cars, there's only one Controlled Parking Zone, in the centre of Bromley town, where an annual resident's permit costs £55 and visitor vouchers are £30 throughout the borough.

Waste & Recycling

As well as a weekly collection for general household rubbish, the council provides a fortnightly doorstep collection scheme for recyclable materials, including cans, garden waste, glass bottles and jars, paper and cardboard, and plastic bottles. Bulky items are collected by arrangement and for a small charge. The borough has two Refuse and Recycling centres, in Beckenham and Bromley.

Shopping

Bromley town centre is the most popular shopping district, with a pedestrianised high street and the Glades covered shopping mall (one of the largest in the south-east) for high street names, plus a good selection of specialist independent shops. In a survey carried out for the *Yellow Pages* in 2005, Bromley scored well for the variety of its shops.

Orpington and Beckenham are reasonable shopping destinations, with a good selection of high street stalwarts. Elsewhere, shopping facilities consist of useful small parades of shops for daily essentials. Penge has a fairly new shopping centre, while Chislehurst's high street is a much more up-market affair, with antique shops and designer boutiques.

Shopping Centres

♦ Blenheim Shopping Centre (High Street, SE20) – selection of chains.

♦ The Glades Shopping Centre (High Street, BR1) – over 120 shops, including high street names such as Debenhams, the Disney and M&S, plus bars and restaurants.

♦ The Walnut Shopping Centre (High Street, BR6) – high street names plus a lively food and clothes market in its main square.

A mile outside Orpington town centre there's a large retail park with branches of Comet, Halfords, Homebase and Magnet, among others.

Supermarkets

♦ Morrisons in Biggin Hill and Petts Wood.

♦ Marks and Spencer in Bromley.

♦ Sainsbury's in Beckenham, Bromley and Chislehurst, with a Local store in Hayes.

♦ Tesco in Elmers End (open 24 hours).

♦ Waitrose in Beckenham and Bromley.

Markets

♦ Bromley Charter Market (car park, Station Road, BR1) – general household goods; Thursday, 9am-2pm.

♦ Bromley Market (High Street, BR1) – fresh produce; arts and crafts; occasionally a

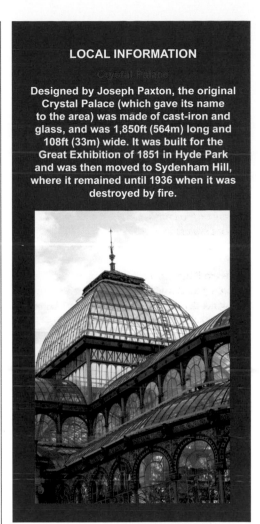

LOCAL INFORMATION

Crystal Palace

Designed by Joseph Paxton, the original Crystal Palace (which gave its name to the area) was made of cast-iron and glass, and was 1,850ft (564m) long and 108ft (33m) wide. It was built for the Great Exhibition of 1851 in Hyde Park and was then moved to Sydenham Hill, where it remained until 1936 when it was destroyed by fire.

traditional French market; Friday and Saturday, 9am-5pm.

♦ Penge Market (Maple Road, SE20) – general household goods; Tuesday to Saturday. Also a Penge Farmers Market on Saturdays from 10am-3pm.

♦ Bromley Farmers' Market (Pedestrian High Street, Bromley); every Friday and Saturday, 9am-5.30pm.

Entertainment

As well as one theatre, two cinemas and a few museums, Bromley has an arts centre which hosts various musical events and runs a number of courses (Ripley Arts Centre, 24 Sundridge Avenue, BR1, ☎ 020-8464 5816). Popular annual events include the Biggin Hill International Air Fair (💻 www.airdisplaysint.co.uk) and the Bromley Pageant of Motoring, a one-day classic car show held in Norman Park (💻 www.bromleypageant. co.uk). There's a reasonable selection of clubs, pubs and restaurants in most of the larger towns.

Theatres

The borough has one mainstream theatre and two small private theatre clubs with their own auditoria (members only):

◆ Beckenham Theatre Centre (46 Bromley Road, BR3, ☎ 0790-574 4991) – private theatre club producing a full programme of productions.

◆ Bromley Little Theatre (North Street, BR1, ☎ 020-8460 3047) – private theatre club producing a cross-section of productions.

◆ Churchill Theatre (High Street, BR1, ☎ 020-8464 7131, 💻 www.theambassadors.com/churchill) – comfortable mainstream theatre staging national and local productions.

Cinemas

◆ Odeon Beckenham (High Street, BR3, ☎ 0871-224 4007, 💻 www.odeon.co.uk).

◆ Odeon Bromley (High Street, BR1, ☎/💻 as above).

Museums & Galleries

◆ Bromley Museum (The Priory, Church Hill, BR6, ☎ 01689-873 826) – local history collections.

◆ Crofton Roman Villa (Crofton Road, BR6, ☎ 020-8460 1442) – the remains of ten rooms inside a public viewing gallery.

◆ Crystal Palace Museum (Anerley Hill, SE19, ☎ 020-8676 0700) – exhibition about the famous palace in the only building to have survived the spectacular 1936 fire.

◆ Down House (Luxted Road, BR6, ☎ 01689-859 119, 💻 www.english-heritage.org.uk) – former home of Charles Darwin.

Libraries

There are 15 local authority libraries in the borough, with one mobile service. The largest is the Central Library in Bromley

(High Street, BR1, ☎ 020-8460 9955), which includes the local archives. No libraries open on Sundays.

Clubs

Although the borough isn't known for its vibrant clubbing scene, there are a few night-clubs in the Bromley and Beckenham areas:

◆ Bar Flux (1 Southend Road, BR3, ☎ 020-8650 6262).

◆ Biba's (29 Widmore Road, BR1, ☎ 020-8464 0513).

◆ Delano's (30 East Street, BR1, ☎ 020-8464 7777).

◆ Jazzmins Music & Dance Bar (6 Elmfield Road, BR1, ☎ 020-8464 0901).

◆ Langtry's Night-club (2-4 High Street, BR3, ☎ 020-8650 1250).

◆ Phantoms (239 High Street, BR1, ☎ 020-8466 1101).

There's live comedy at the Clink Bar (Court Street, BR1, ☎ 020-8466 0558).

Live Music

Large concerts are held in Crystal Palace Park, while smaller events are regularly presented at the Ripley Arts Centre (see **Entertainment** above) and the Underground Bar at the Churchill Theatre (see above). Several pubs also present live music, notably the Hop House in Penge (Maple Road, SE20, ☎ 020-8659 9674).

Pubs

There are plenty of pubs in the borough, although most are fairly ordinary. Chains include O'Neills (Bromley and Beckenham), JD Wetherspoons (Bromley), Jack Beards (Crystal Palace and Penge), Slug and Lettuce (Bromley) and Jim Thompson's (Chislehurst). The Oakhill in Beckenham is a noted real ale pub (90 Bromley Road, BR3, ☎ 020-8650 1279) and the Bo Peep in Chelsfield is a lovely country-style pub in a Grade I listed building (Hewitts Road, BR6, ☎ 01959-534 457). Another pub with rural overtones is the Rambler's Rest in Chislehurst (Mill Place, BR7, ☎ 020-8467 1734).

Restaurants

There's a huge variety of eateries in Bromley, ranging from cheap cafes to gourmet restaurants (although the latter are rather thin on the ground). Many local restaurants have a good reputation for quality food, while café/restaurant chains include the ubiquitous Ask!, Café Uno, Café Rouge and Pizza Express, to name but a few. For fine dining in a one-star Michelin restaurant, there's Chapter One (Farnborough Common, Locksbottom, BR6, ☎ 01689-854 848).

Sports Facilities

Sport is well catered for within the borough, with five leisure centres, sports facilities available to the public in three schools, and outdoor sports pitches in several parks. The National Sports Centre at Crystal Palace also has a wide range of competition-standard facilities.

Sports facilities include:

◆ Swimming pools in Beckenham, Bromley, Crystal Palace, Orpington and West Wickham (the Spa in Beckenham has been voted the best UK swimming pool by the *Independent* newspaper).

◆ Indoor sports halls in Biggin Hill, Crystal Palace and Orpington.

◆ Outdoor sports pitches in Beckenham, Biggin Hill, Crystal Palace and Orpington.

◆ Squash courts in Beckenham, Bromley and Orpington.

◆ A climbing wall at Crystal Palace.

Tennis courts are available throughout the borough and there's also a new, purpose-built Bromley tennis centre in Orpington. There are public golf courses at Bromley and Downe, as well as several private clubs, and horse riding is also well catered for, with many bridle-paths and stables, particularly in the south of the borough. For winter sports fans, there's an open-air ice rink at Crystal Palace at Christmas and the Bromley Ski Centre provides excellent facilities for skiing and snowboarding.

Green Spaces

With over 100 parks, commons and open spaces, Bromley is one of the greenest London boroughs. The best known park is at Crystal Palace, with its children's farm and boating lake (both currently being refurbished), the largest maze in the south-east and life-size model dinosaurs built in the 1850s. One of the prettiest and largest parks is Kelsey Park in Beckenham, which has ornamental pleasure grounds, natural woodlands and lakes that are home to a variety of waterfowl.

LOCAL INFORMATION

Chislehurst, bounded to the east by the 300-acre Scadbury Park Nature Reserve and ancient woodlands, is also home to Chislehurst Caves – 22 miles of man-made caverns dating back 8,000 years. Fossils, Druid altars and Roman mines are just some of the features there, as well as the remains of Britain's largest public air raid shelter, used during WWII, and affectionately known as the 'Chislehurst Hotel'.

Queen Victoria Memorial, The Mall, SW1

Camden

N6 (part), NW1 (part), NW3, NW5, NW6 (part), WC1

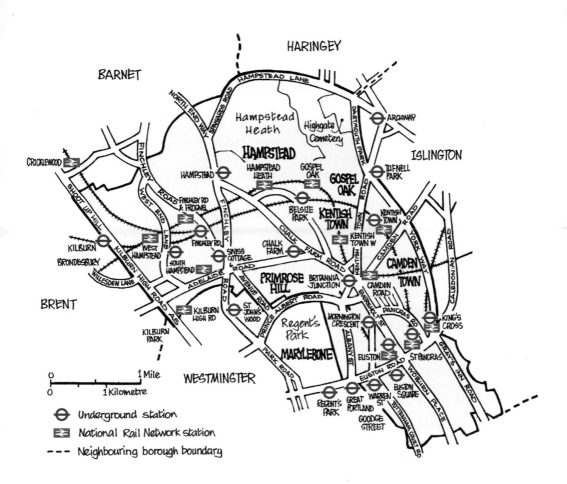

At a Glance

Best for: education, health services, public transport, open spaces, shopping

Not so good for: road congestion, crime, affordable housing, parking

Who lives there: wealthy families, young professionals, singles, celebrities

Housing stock: mostly purpose-built flats and conversions

Housing costs: expensive

General Information

Council Offices: Camden Town Hall, Judd Street, WC1H 9JE (☎ 020-7278 4444)

CAA Assessment: (see 🖥 http://oneplace.direct.gov.uk > Search by area > London > Camden)

Controlling Party: Labour

Website: 🖥 www.camden.gov.uk

Council Tax 2010/11: £2,219 (Band G), £2,663 (Band H)

Main Areas/towns: Belsize Park, Bloomsbury, Camden Town, Hampstead, Holborn, Kentish Town, King's Cross, Primrose Hill, Regent's Park, West Hampstead

Postcodes: N6 (part), NW1 (part), NW3, NW5, NW6 (part), WC1

Population & Ethnicity: 235,700, with a high proportion aged between 20 and 35. Over 20 per cent of the population comes from an ethnic minority and there are large Irish, Jewish and Turkish communities. The borough attracts the super-rich and successful professionals, although some of the country's poorest also live there.

Unemployment: 6.9 per cent (London average is 8.2 per cent)

Overview

The borough of Camden encompasses some of London's smartest areas – around Regent's Park to the south-west and Hampstead to the north-east – as well as some of its seediest, around King's Cross, one of the capital's unofficial red light districts. The latter area is due for a major facelift (see **Development Plans** below).

The jewel in Camden's crown is Hampstead, with its medieval street plan and exclusive, village atmosphere. Hampstead Heath is a popular destination, particularly in summer, when the open-air bathing ponds and the outdoor concerts at Kenwood House are big attractions. Originally a summer retreat for writers and artists, Hampstead has become one of London's most expensive and fashionable districts.

Camden Town is a bustling, cosmopolitan area with an energetic atmosphere, thanks largely to the famous markets and the town's vibrant nightlife. In a *Yellow Pages* survey in 2005, it emerged as the best place to live for young, professional singletons.

The British Museum, British Library, University of London and numerous other institutions dominate Bloomsbury and Holborn. Among famous former residents were the Bloomsbury Set, a mix of influential writers, artists and critics in the early 20th century.

LOCAL INFORMATION

The borough was named after Camden Town, which gained its name from Charles Pratt, 1st Earl of Camden in 1795.

Development Plans

The Kings Cross Central development scheme is one of the largest in Europe and involves regenerating an area of some 65 acres (25ha) between King's Cross and St Pancras stations, which will provide almost 2,000 new homes and 5,234,000ft² (486,280m²) of offices and new roads, creating 30,000 jobs. In addition there will be retail (shops, cafés, bars and restaurants), leisure, health, education, community and cultural facilities, twenty major new public routes and ten new public spaces, covering around 25 acres (10ha) or almost 40 per cent of the whole site. The first offices, homes and a university are due to be completed in 2012.

Kenwood House

At the heart of the area's regeneration has been the restoration and redevelopment of St Pancras railway station – which opened in November 2007 – as the new London terminus (St Pancras International) for Eurostar high-speed trains to Lille, Paris and Brussels.

Residential Areas

Property types and prices vary enormously, from reasonably-priced ex-local authority flats to multi-million pound mansions. In between are the Georgian terraces of Camden, Italianate villas of Primrose Hill and new flats springing up at King's Cross. The majority of properties are flats (86 per cent), of which over a third are conversions of large houses. A further 10 per cent are terraces and just 4 per cent are detached and semi-detached houses.

Belsize Park, Primrose Hill & Regent's Park (NW1)

Attractive stucco-fronted houses, quiet streets and chic cafes make this a popular area with celebrities and wealthy families. A four-storey house overlooking Primrose Hill costs well over £2mn, but there's no shortage of spacious flats and maisonettes, plus some pretty mews cottages at more reasonable prices. At Swiss Cottage there are several swanky new apartment blocks. Some of the most expensive property in the borough is to be found on Crown Estate land bordering Regent's Park, where spectacularly large mansions and grand terraces can cost £20mn or more.

Bloomsbury & Holborn (WC1)

Among the offices and institutions occupying many of the Georgian terraces there, converted flats and the odd single house are snapped up by professionals who can afford to live within walking distance of the West End and the City. Inter-war mansion blocks, once used as offices, are being converted back into flats, and a crop of smart developments has appeared around Hatton Garden. There's a brisk rental market for ex-local authority properties and flats above shops among hospital workers, students and academics.

Camden Town & Kentish Town (NW1, NW5)

The mixture of large and carefully-restored houses, post-war council blocks and varied flats suits the trendy families and young professionals attracted to Camden Town. The most desirable areas are the quieter roads away from the busy high street, which becomes frantic at weekends when crowds descend on the markets. Kentish Town is more down-at-heel, but is only a short journey to the West End; with a good stock of early Victorian terraces and ex-council houses, it remains a good choice for the bargain hunter.

Hampstead (NW3)

Hampstead owes much of its grandeur to one of London's greatest disasters, the 1665 Great Plague, when many of the district's imposing streets, such as Judge's Walk and King's Bench Avenue, were created when the Courts of Law were transferred to Hampstead. Zealously protected by local organisations determined to preserve the town from unsympathetic builders, Hampstead offers a wealth of period properties with seriously high price tags – £5mn or more for a family-sized house. As well as handsome Georgian and Victorian houses, there are some interesting and individual properties, including smart flats in converted hospitals; the Bauhaus-style Isokon building, built as an experiment in communal living; and the exclusive Holly Lodge Estate, a Tudor-style blend of houses and flats dating from the '20s.

King's Cross & St Pancras (N1)

This entire area is poised for transformation, thanks to the massive investment in the St Pancras Central redevelopment scheme (see **Development Plans** above). A smaller (6-acre/2.4-hectare) development, Regent Quarter, to the east of King's Cross, is already completed, with cobbled courtyards and apartments from £315,000, plus offices, a hotel, shops and restaurants. Away from the stations there are lots of ex-council Victorian properties, mostly converted into flats, which are slowly being bought up and refurbished.

West Hampstead (NW3, NW6)

Once regarded as being too close to Kilburn for those aspiring to Hampstead, nowadays the area is being dubbed the 'new Notting Hill'. Its Victorian mansion blocks and family houses are reasonably priced (a one-bedroom flat costs around £300,000) and attract young families and professionals. There's a healthy rental market.

Property Costs

Property Prices

The table below shows average property prices in the borough:

Detached: £2,521,903
Semi-detached: £1,566,760
Terraced: £988,539
Flat: £471,685

Rental Costs

The table below shows average monthly rents in the borough:

House 5+ bed: £8,500
House 4-5 bed: £5,850
House 3-4 bed: £3,750
House 2-3 bed: £2,750
Flat 2-bed: £2,400
Flat 1-bed: £1,600

Crime

Camden has the fourth-highest overall crime rate of all London boroughs and the 15th-highest rate for burglary. CCTV surveillance in key trouble spots at King's Cross and Camden Town is helping bring crime under control.

The police station HQ is in Holborn (10 Lambs Conduit Street, WC1, ☎ 020-7404 1212), with other stations in Albany Street, Camden, Hampstead, Kentish Town and West Hampstead.

To compare crime rates throughout London, see the table in **Appendix D**.

Health

NHS services in the borough are provided by the Camden Primary Care Trust. For a full list of doctors, dentists and clinics, visit 🖥 www.nhs.uk.

To see how the Primary Care Trust compares with others in London, see the table in **Appendix D**.

Doctors & Dentists

♦ There are 108 NHS GP surgeries, providing a range of clinics and health services.

♦ Camden has 71 dental and orthodontic practices, fewer than half of which accept new NHS patients.

Hospitals

♦ The Royal Free Hospital (Pond Street, NW3, ☎ 020-7794 0500, 🖥 www.royalfree.org.uk) – A&E.

♦ University College Hospital (235, Euston Road, NW1 ☎ 0845-155 5000, 🖥 www.uclh.org) – A&E.

Specialist hospitals include Great Ormond Street Hospital for Children, the Royal National Throat Nose and Ear Hospital, and the Hospital for Tropical Diseases.

Private Medical Facilities

♦ BUPA Wellness Centre (Battle Bridge House, 300 Gray's Inn Road, WC1, ☎ 0800-616 029) – general medical assessments.

♦ Doctor Today (182 Finchley Road, NW3, ☎ 020-7433 1444, 🖥 www.doctortoday.co.uk) – private walk-in centre.

♦ Ocean Park Private Clinic (2 Bloomsbury Place, WC1, ☎ 020-7580 4848, 🖥 www. oceanparkclinic.co.uk) – general medical clinic.

To find a private GP you can also visit 🖥 www. privatehealth.co.uk.

Schools

Educational standards in Camden are above the UK average. In the 2009 school league tables, primary schools were placed ninth out of the 33 London boroughs (37th out of 150 UK local authorities) and secondary schools 21st (68th in the UK).

Gray's Inn

To compare schools throughout London, see the table in **Appendix D**.

Pre-school

LEA and privately-operated nursery schools and playgroups include 36 nursery classes attached to infant, primary and independent schools, and eight early years centres.

State Schools

First schools: 41 infant, junior and primary schools, of which 21 are voluntary aided. In 2009, the Hampstead Parochial C of E Primary School obtained the best Key Stage 2 results.

Secondary schools: Nine comprehensive schools, four of which are voluntary aided. All schools have sixth forms, with four providing the largest sixth form consortium in London (La Swap). Seven schools have specialist status. The Camden School for Girls and Hampstead School were the top performers in 2009.

Special schools: Six schools cater for students with physical disabilities and learning difficulties.

♟ FAMOUS RESIDENTS

Famous Camden figures have included Charles Dickens (novelist), Noel Gallagher (singer), Bob Hoskins (actor), John Keats (poet), George Michael (singer), J.B. Priestley (writer), Willie Rushton (comic and actor), George Bernard Shaw (playwright), Kenneth Williams (actor) and Virginia Woolf (novelist).

Private Schools

There are 31 private schools in the borough, including the Hampstead campus of the Southbank International School (💻 www.southbank.org). In 2009, top scorers were the North Bridge House Senior School in Camden, the Royal School in Hampstead and South Hampstead High School.

Further Education

♦ The City Literary Institute in Holborn (💻 www.citylit.ac.uk) provides a broad range of courses for students aged 16+.

♦ Westminster Kingsway College (💻 www.westking.ac.uk) has sites in Kentish Town and Regent's Park.

The Mary Ward Centre in Bloomsbury (💻 www.marywardcentre.ac.uk) and the Working Men's College at King's Cross (💻 www.wmcollege.ac.uk) offer vocational and recreational courses for adults.

Higher Education

Many colleges of the University of London are located in the borough (💻 www.lon.ac.uk), including the Royal Veterinary College in Camden and the School of Pharmacy in Brunswick Square. Camden has three famous drama schools:

♦ Central School of Speech and Drama (💻 www.cssd.ac.uk).

♦ Conservatoire for Dance and Drama (💻 www.cdd.ac.uk).

♦ Royal Academy of Dramatic Art (💻 www.rada.org).

Public Transport

There are excellent connections to neighbouring boroughs from all parts of Camden, with a good choice of buses, tubes and trains. This is just as well, because the council is waging war against the use of cars and parking is difficult. By 2013, the planned Cross River Tram will provide a long-awaited new link between Camden, Brixton and Peckham, with a spur providing services to King's Cross.

Underground

King's Cross is an underground 'hub,' where five lines intersect (Circle, Metropolitan &

LOCAL INFORMATION

St Pancras

St Pancras station was designed by W.H. Barlow and built by the Midland Railway; when it opened in 1868 the train shed was an engineering marvel and the world's largest enclosed space. However, it's the station's stunning red-brick Gothic façade – originally the Midland Great Hotel, designed by Sir Gilbert Scott and built between 1868 and 1876 – that makes the station one of London's most striking buildings. In 2007, the station was renamed St Pancras International when it became the London terminus for Eurostar trains to the continent.

Hammersmith, Northern, Piccadilly and Victoria). The Northern Line splits at Camden to serve stations to Hampstead or Kentish Town, while the Jubilee line serves stations in the west of the borough. Typical journey times are as follows:

♦ Camden Town (Northern line, zone 2) to Tottenham Court Road, 8 minutes.

♦ Hampstead (Northern line, zone 2) to Oxford Circus, 18 minutes via Euston.

♦ West Hampstead (Jubilee line, zone 2) to Bond Street, 10 minutes.

There are proposals to revamp Camden's grubby station, although a time-scale hasn't been set.

Rail

♦ West Hampstead and Kentish Town are on the Thameslink line, which runs across the river to Sutton (journey time to King's Cross is 11-22 minutes). Eventually this service will connect to Paris, with just one change at St Pancras.

The London Overground line operates two services crossing North London: one to North Woolwich (45 minutes from Hampstead Heath) and another to Barking (36 minutes from Gospel Oak).

Buses

There are several bus routes from all parts of the borough to the West End and neighbouring boroughs, with Camden Town offering the widest choice. Night buses from Trafalgar Square include the N5, N20 and N28.

Airports

Below are approximate distances and times from Camden Town to the five London airports using public transport.

♦ **City** – 10 miles; 40 minutes via Bank.

♦ **Gatwick** – 26 miles; 80 minutes via Victoria.

♦ **Heathrow** – 14 miles; 75 minutes via Paddington.

♦ **Luton** 26 miles; 60 minutes via West Hampstead.

♦ **Stansted** – 30 miles; 90 minutes via Liverpool Street.

Roads

Congestion is a problem in much of the borough, particularly along the A501 Euston Road, which is a main east to west thoroughfare and always jammed with traffic, particularly by King's Cross station. Holborn and Bloomsbury are busy during office hours, but quieter in the evenings and at weekends. Other trouble spots include the one-way high street in Camden and along Chalk

Farm Road at weekends. The high streets in Hampstead and West Hampstead are also busy.

Parking

Most of the borough is a Controlled Parking Zone, with a resident's permit costing from £82 to £159 per year, in four bands – among the highest in London.

Waste & Recycling

The council provides a twice-weekly collection service for household rubbish and recyclable materials, including cans, electrical 'white' goods, glass, paper and textiles. Plastic bottles and aerosols are collected from households south of the Euston Road. The council also collects furniture for a fee. The borough's main waste and recycling centre is in Kentish Town.

Shopping

For shoppers Camden offers everything, from interesting local shops and designer clothes in Hampstead to the sprawling markets of Camden Town and the high-tech wonderland of Tottenham Court Road. Camden Town high street has a range of well-known names, including M&S, and scored well for basics in a recent *Yellow Pages* survey. West Hampstead also has good high street shopping. There's a clutch of chic individual shops in Primrose Hill, while stores in Kentish Town tend to be cut-price and shabby. South of Euston Road, London's jewellery quarter is in Hatton Garden and there are some specialist bookshops around King's Cross.

Shopping Centres

The 02 centre (south-west of Hampstead at 255 Finchley Road, NW3, ☎ 020-7794 7716, 🖥 www.02centre.co.uk) has the largest Sainsbury's in London, plus Homebase, Books Etc, a cinema, gym and numerous restaurants.

Supermarkets

Marks & Spencer in Camden Town, plus Simply Food outlets in Euston Station, Swiss Cottage and Tottenham Court Road.

♦ Morrisons in Chalk Farm.

♦ Sainsbury's in Camden High Street and the 02 Centre; Local stores in Euston, Gospel Oak, Holborn and Mornington Crescent.

♦ Tesco Express stores in Belsize Park and Hampstead.

♦ Waitrose in South Hampstead.

Markets

Camden Farmers' Market (opposite the Hampstead Theatre, Eton Avenue, NW3); Wednesday, 10am-4pm.

♦ Chalton Street Market (between Euston Road and Churchway, NW1) – household goods, fabrics and cheap clothes; Friday.

♦ Leather Lane Market (behind Hatton Garden, WC1) – fresh produce, clothes and accessories, CDs and DVDs; Monday to Friday.

♦ Queen's Crescent Market (between Maiden Road and Grafton Road, Kentish Town, NW5) – household essentials and fresh produce; Thursday and Saturday.

Swiss Cottage Market (between Avenue Road and Winchester Road, NW3) – second-hand books, DVDs, clothes, bric-a-brac; Friday and Saturday. Farmers Market on Wednesday.

LOCAL INFORMATION

Camden Market (Camden High Street, Camden Lock and Chalk Farm Road, NW1) is actually six separate markets, although it's impossible to tell them apart on the ground. Goods range from retro clothes to trendy street wear, furniture, jewellery, arts and crafts, computer accessories, books and bric-a-brac – in short, something for everyone. The market was partly destroyed by fire in February 2008, but most stalls were in business again just a week later.

Entertainment

Camden offers plenty of local entertainment, as well as close proximity to London's theatre land, the British Museum in Bloomsbury and the British Library at St Pancras. There's a huge choice of restaurants, pubs and clubs. The Camden Guide (🖥 www.camdenguide.co.uk) is a comprehensive guide to everything that happens in Camden and Camden Market.

Theatres

Apart from the host of venues in the West End and the open air theatre in Regent's Park (☎ 0844-826 4242, 24 hours), 🖳 http://openairtheatre.org), there are several smaller theatres in Camden, including:

◆ Camden People's Theatre (58-60 Hampstead Road, NW1, ☎ 020-7916 5878, 🖳 www.cpt.dircon.co.uk) – innovative and contemporary productions.

◆ Courtyard Theatre (10-14 York Way, N1, ☎ 020-7833 0876, 🖳 www.thecourtyard.org.uk) – drama school productions.

◆ Etcetera Theatre (265 Camden High Street, NW1, ☎ 020-7482 4857, 🖳 www.etceteratheatre.com) – fringe theatre.

◆ Hampstead Theatre (Eton Avenue, NW3, ☎ 020-7722 9301, 🖳 www.hampsteadtheatre.com) – provocative work by new talent.

◆ New End Theatre (27 New End, NW3, ☎ 0870-033 2733, 🖳 www.newendtheatre.co.uk) – off-West End productions.

◆ The Roundhouse (Chalk Farm Road, NW1, ☎ 0844-482 8008, 🖳 www.roundhouse.org.uk) – former rock venue reinvented as an arts, rock and theatre venue.

◆ The Shaw Theatre (100-110 Euston Road, NW1, ☎ 020-7666 9037, 🖳 www.shawtheatre.com) – small theatre attached to a Novotel hotel.

LOCAL INFORMATION

The iconic Roundhouse was originally a railway building constructed in 1847 for the London and Birmingham Railway. It became derelict and was converted into a theatre in the '60s, and is now one of London's leading music venues.

Cinemas

◆ Odeon Camden (14 Parkway, NW1) and Odeon Tottenham Court Road (WC1, ☎ 0871-224 4007, 🖳 www.odeon.co.uk).

◆ The Screen on the Hill (203 Haverstock Hill, NW3, ☎ 020-7435 3366, 🖳 www.screencinemas.co.uk).

◆ The Everyman (1 Hollybush Vale, NW3, ☎ 0870-066 4777, 🖳 www.everymancinema.com).

◆ Vue Cinema (02 Centre, 255 Finchley Road, ☎ 0871-224 0240, 🖳 www.myvue.com).

Museums & Galleries

The borough is home to London's most popular museum, the British Museum in Bloomsbury (🖳 www.thebritishmuseum.ac.uk), and the British Library at St Pancras (🖳 www.bl.uk). Camden also has numerous smaller museums, several in Hampstead, including:

◆ The Freud Museum (20 Maresfield Gardens, NW3, ☎ 020-7435 2002, 🖳 www.freud.org.uk).

◆ The Jewish Museum (Raymond Burton House, 129 Albert Street, NW1, ☎ 020-7284 7384, 🖳 www.jewishmuseum.org.uk).

◆ Keats House (Keats Grove, NW3, ☎ 020-7332 3868, 🖳 www.keatshouse.cityoflondon.gov.uk).

For a full list of places to visit in the borough, see the council's website (🖳 www.camden.gov.uk).

Libraries

In addition to the British Library (see above), there are 13 local authority libraries in Camden, with one mobile service. The largest is the Swiss Cottage Central Library (88 Avenue Road, NW3, ☎ 020-7974 4001). Two libraries open on Sundays, the Heath Library, situated in the grounds of Keats House in Hampstead, and the West Hampstead Library, while several have restricted opening hours.

Clubs

One of the most vibrant clubbing spots in London is at King's Cross Goods Yard (behind the station off York Way, N1), where young crowds flock to Bagleys (☎ 020-7278 2777), Canvas (☎ 0845-371 4489), Cross (☎ 0871-971 6511), Key (☎ 020-7837 1027) or nearby EGG (☎ 020-7609 8364). The best of the rest are around Camden Town:

◆ Barfly (49 Chalk Farm Road, NW1, ☎ 020-7482 1268, 🖳 www.barflyclub.com).

◆ Dingwalls (Middle Yard, Camden Lock, NW1, ☎ 020-7428 5929, 🖳 www.dingwalls.com).

◆ The End (18 West Central Street, WC1, ☎ 020-7419 9199, 🖳 www.endclub.com).

◆ Koko, formerly the Camden Palace (1A Camden High Street, NW1, ☎ 0870-4325 527, 🖳 www.koko.uk.com).

◆ Underworld (174 Camden High Street, NW1, ☎ 020-7482 1932, 🖳 www. theunderworldcamden.co.uk).

Comedy clubs include the leading comedy chain Jongleurs @ Camden Lock, (Middle Yard, Camden Lock, NW1, ☎ 0870-0111 890, 🖳 www. jongleurs.com) and the smaller Hampstead Clinic at the White Horse (154 Fleet Road, NW3, ☎ 0871-223 9109).

Live Music

Choices range from open air classical concerts at Kenwood House (Hampstead Heath, ☎ 020-8348 1286) to obscure live rock bands in local pubs. Venues include:
◆ The Bull and Gate (389 Kentish Town Road, NW5, ☎ 020-8826 5000, 🖳 www.bullandgate. co.uk) – well known pub gig.

◆ The Dublin Castle (94 Parkway, NW1, ☎ 020-7485 1773) – live Britpop.

◆ Electric Ballroom (184 Camden High Street, NW1, ☎ 020-7485 9006, 🖳 www. electricballroom.co.uk) – Camden fixture no longer threatened with closure.

◆ Jazz Café (5 Parkway, NW1, ☎ 020-7688 8899, 🖳 www.jazzcafe.co.uk) – renowned jazz restaurant.

◆ Kentish Town Forum (9 Highgate Road, NW5, ☎ 020-7344 0044) – mid-sized rock venue.

◆ St Pancras Parish Church Euston Road, N1, ☎ 020-7388 1461) – lunchtime recitals.

Pubs

Camden offers plenty of pubs to cater for every taste. Some of the prettiest are in Hampstead, where the 16th century Spaniards Inn (☎ 020-8731 6571) on Hampstead Heath is so well-known it even appears in the London A-Z! You will also find the King William IV (☎ 0871- 223 7582) there, which claims to be the oldest gay pub in Britain. In Camden Town the pubs tend to be lively and noisy, although chains dominate. For Irish pubs, try Kentish Town. Bloomsbury has hip bars and traditional English pubs packed with tourists, while Holborn has several 'proper' pubs as well as a Polish bar serving over 60 types of vodka (Na Zdrowie, ☎ 0871-223 1047).

For details of pubs around the borough, see Time Out's *Eating and Drinking Guide*.

Restaurants

There's a vast choice of excellent restaurants in Camden in every price bracket. King's Cross has mainly fast food places, although just behind Euston Station in Drummond Street there are several restaurants serving south Indian food. Bloomsbury has a number of inexpensive establishments around the museum and some

Camden Town

up-market restaurants off Tottenham Court Road, for example the Michelin-starred Pied-a-Terre (34 Charlotte Street, W1, ☎ 020-7636 1178).

Hampstead has a number of chains, as well as a few trendy and ethnic restaurants, such as Al Casbah (42 Hampstead High Street, NW3, ☎ 020-7435 7632), complete with belly dancing and Shisha pipes. Around Camden Town and Primrose Hill there's a wide choice of lively restaurants that are particularly busy at weekends, including the Camden Brasserie (216 Camden High Street, NW1, ☎ 020-7482 2114).

Sports Facilities

Camden has five council-funded sports centres, in Mornington Crescent, Covent Garden, Kentish Town (two centres) and Swiss Cottage, which was refurbished in 2006. Facilities include:

♦ Swimming pools at Covent Garden, Kentish Town and Swiss Cottage.

♦ A climbing wall at Swiss Cottage.

♦ Indoor sports halls at Kentish Town, Mornington Crescent and Swiss Cottage.

♦ An Astroturf pitch in Kentish Town.

As well as indoor pools, Camden is the place for outdoor bathing, with a Lido in Parliament Hill Fields and three famous outdoor bathing ponds – men's, women's and mixed – on Hampstead Heath. Health clubs and gyms are well represented in the borough, and there's an adult go-karting circuit at King's Cross (Central Warehouse, York Way, N1, ☎ 020-7833 1000).

Green Spaces

Camden is rich in open spaces, ranging from the grandeur of Hampstead Heath and Regent's Park, to small neighbourhood playgrounds and residents-only 'garden' squares. The 800 acres of Hampstead Heath offer walks and woodlands, the formal gardens of Kenwood House and the fields of Parliament Hill, a favourite haunt for kite flyers (expect to see lots of politicians). Regent's Park highlights include a boating lake and London Zoo (☎ 020-7722 3333, 🖳 www.londonzoo.co.uk).

The Camley Street Natural Park in Camden Town (☎ 020-7833 2311) features 2 acres (0.8ha) of wild nature reserve on the banks of the Regent's Canal. The canal is also a favourite for waterside walks and river tours. For children,

Kentish Town City Farm is a popular attraction (1 Cressfield Close, NW5, ☎ 020-7916 5421, 🖳 www.aapi.co.uk/cityfarm/home.htm).

LOCAL INFORMATION

The Regent's Canal runs through the north end of Camden Town and has an 8.5mi (14km) towpath, which passes through London Zoo and is a popular trail. If you take a boat trip along the canal (from Camden Lock) you may notice that many of the handrails by the bridges show deep indentations made by the towropes with which horses pulled canal barges until the '50s – you can also still see the underwater ramps built to assist horses that bolted (usually frightened by trains on the overrunning railway bridges) and fell into the canal.

City of London

EC1 (part), EC2, EC3, EC4

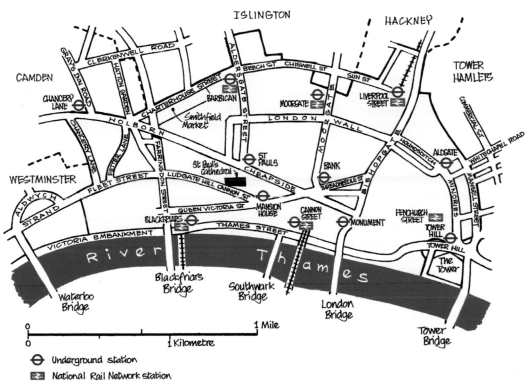

- ⊖ Underground station
- ☰ National Rail Network station
- - - - Neighbouring borough boundary

At a Glance

Best for: public transport, gyms, culture, restaurants, low crime
Not so good for: expensive property, schools, parking, open spaces
Who lives there: singles, City professionals
Housing stock: mostly flats/studios, a few period houses
Housing costs: very expensive

General Information

Council Offices: Corporation of London, Guildhall, P O Box 270, EC2P 2EJ (☎ 020-7606 3030)

CAA Assessment: (see 💻 http://oneplace.direct.gov.uk > Search by area > London > City of London)

Controlling Party: apolitical

Website: 💻 www.cityoflondon.gov.uk

Council Tax 2010/11: £1,584 (Band G), £1,901 (Band H)

Main Areas/towns: Barbican, Broadgate, Smithfield, St Paul's, Whitechapel

Postcodes: EC1 (part), EC2, EC3, EC4

Population & Ethnicity: 7,900, with a high proportion aged between 25 and 34. Around 15 per cent of the population belong to an ethnic minority, mostly Asian, although there are also significant Afro-Caribbean and Chinese communities. Around 14 per cent of residents live in council homes, the majority being professionals working in the City.

Overview

The City of London's boundaries have remained almost constant since Roman times, when it was a walled city, and hence it's now only a tiny part of the much larger London metropolis. It's usually referred to as simply 'the City' or 'the Square Mile', as it's almost exactly one square mile (2.6km²) in area. The City stretches from Chancery Lane in the west to Aldgate in the east, and from the Barbican and Broadgate in the north to the River Thames in the south. At its heart lies the imposing odifioo of St Paul's Cathedral and the bastions of the UK's financial markets, the London Stock Exchange and the Bank of England.

This tiny area (only 20 minutes walk from side to side) is quite separate administratively from the rest of London and is controlled by the City of London Corporation, an apolitical body with its own police force. It isn't one of London's 32 boroughs and isn't administered by the mayor of London. While some 350,000 people work in the City, there are less than 8,000 residents and even fewer homes – it becomes a ghost town at weekends. Most homes are concentrated around the Barbican and Liverpool Street, although there are a few pockets of new-build flats, converted offices and flats above shops dotted around the fringes. The Corporation frowns on homes in the banking district, which makes up much of the EC3 postcode.

If the downside of city living is a lack of schools, open space and NHS facilities, the upside is that residents can walk to work (provided you work in the City!), the West End is a short bus, tube or taxi ride away and the City boasts the renowned arts and sports complex at the Barbican Centre, plus a few attractions providing local entertainment.

LOCAL INFORMATION

The City of London has been administered separately since 886, when Alfred the Great appointed his son-in-law, Earl Æthelred of Mercia, as Governor of London. The monarch of England has traditionally had to request permission from the Lord Mayor to enter the City.

Development Plans

While the resident population isn't expected to exceed 10,000 in the coming years, office development is gradually giving way to residential projects, with new accommodation being created from smaller commercial buildings which aren't suitable for the large companies now providing much of the local employment. In recent years several hotels have opened, as has the City's first department store, and a shopping mall is being built near St. Paul's Cathedral.

The City skyline is expected to change dramatically in the coming years, with a number of major buildings approved or under construction, including the Bishopsgate Tower or 'The Pinnacle' (22-24 Bishopsgate, 945ft/288m), the Broadgate Tower (201 Bishopsgate, 541ft/165m), the Heron Tower (110 Bishopsgate, 600ft/183m), the Leadenhall Building or 'Cheese Grater' (122 Leadenhall Street, 736ft/224m) and the London Bridge Tower or 'Shard of Glass' (21 London Bridge Street, 1,016ft/310m); many more mid-rise buildings are also under construction or planned.

Residential Areas

Virtually all property (99 per cent) consists of purpose-built flats – the largest single development is the Barbican – while new flats have been built around Fleet Street and St Paul's. All properties are expensive, both to buy and rent, and service charges can be high. Period houses do exist, although they rarely come on the market and are very expensive.

The Barbican (EC2)

A grey and unattractive concrete fortress from the exterior, the Barbican houses over 2,000 flats (a quarter of the residential units in the City) of varying styles, built in the '70s. This 'city within a city', originally intended as council flats (although most are now privately owned), consists of residential blocks linked by confusing raised walkways. Flats range from studios (around £200,000) to 5-bedroom luxury penthouses (£2mn). Next door is the renowned arts centre, a music school and an independent secondary school (see **Schools** below). Adjacent to the arts centre is the Grade II listed Golden Lane Estate,

Lloyd's Building

council-built in the '60s, with about half of its one-, two- and three-bedroom flats now privately owned. Nearby, although actually in Islington, are Peabody Trust and council homes.

Fleet Street & St Paul's (EC4)

While legal institutions dominate the Temple in the far west of the borough, the area around Fleet Street and New Fetter Lane is where most of the residential property can be found. Once the newspaper industry left for the Docklands, several old press offices were converted into smart flats, which are highly popular among City workers (roughly £495,000 for two bedrooms and considerably more for a penthouse). There are further pockets of apartments around Blackfriars and Cannon Street stations, some with river views.

Smithfield (EC1)

Chiefly associated with the wholesale meat market and St Bartholomew's Hospital, and close to buzzing Clerkenwell (see **Islington**), Smithfield has a surprisingly good supply of fashionable new flats and a few of the borough's rare Georgian houses. This is also the best area for bars, restaurants and clubs, and is becoming extremely sought-after among wealthy young City bankers and investors, who foresee a healthy rental market.

Property Costs

Property Prices

The table below shows average property prices in the City:

> Detached: £0
> Semi-detached: £0
> Terraced: £0
> Flat: £472,553

Rental Costs

The table below shows average monthly rents in the City (and in the immediate area):

> House 5+ bed: £6,500
> House 4-5 bed: £3,900
> House 3-4 bed: £3,250
> House 2-3 bed: £2,600
> Flat 2-bed: £1,750
> Flat 1-bed: £1,650

Crime

The City has its own police force, the City of London Police, which was established in 1839 and publishes its own crime statistics. In 2009, crime in the City was generally declining, with property theft accounting for the highest number of reported incidents. However, crimes of violence increased. The use of 'stop and search' is proving helpful in preventing and detecting crime. For more information, visit 🖥 www.cityoflondon.police.uk. The City is divided into two territorial divisions, each with its own police station:

◆ Snow Hill (5 Snow Hill, EC1, ☎ 020-7601 2406).

◆ Bishopsgate (182 Bishopsgate, EC2, ☎ 020-7601 2606).

To compare crime rates throughout London, see the table in **Appendix D**.

Health

NHS services in the borough are provided by the London NHS Trust. For details of doctors, dentists and clinics, visit 🖥 www.cityoflondon.gov.uk.

To see how the Trust compares with others in London, see the table in **Appendix D**.

Doctors & Dentists

◆ There's one NHS GP surgery: Dr. G M Neaman (15 Half Moon Court, EC1A, ☎ 020-7600 9740).

◆ Three dental practices accept NHS patients.

Hospitals

◆ St Bartholomew's Hospital (Smithfield, EC1, ☎ 020-7601 8888, 🖥 www.bartsandthelondon.nhs.uk) has a minor injuries unit. The nearest A&E departments are just outside the City.

◆ The Royal London Hospital (Whitechapel Road, E1, ☎ 020-7377 7000, 🖥 www.bartsandthelondon.nhs.uk), where there's also an NHS walk-in centre.

◆ University College Hospital (Grafton Way, WC1, ☎ 020-7837 9300, 🖥 www.uclh.org).

◆ Moorfields Eye Hospital (City Road, EC1, ☎ 020-7253 3411, 🖥 www.moorfields.org.uk) – eye treatment and emergencies only.

Private Medical Facilities

There are a several private facilities, largely catering for the City's working population, including:

◆ BUPA Wellness Centres in the Barbican Centre and Moorgate (☎ 020-7200 2700, 🖥 www.bupa.co.uk/wellness).

◆ The Fleet Street Clinic (29 Fleet Street, EC4, ☎ 020-7353 5678).

◆ General Medical Clinics in Broadgate, Fleet Street and Tower Hill (🖥 www.genmed.org.uk).

To find a private GP, visit 🖥 www.privatehealth.co.uk.

Schools

There's one state primary school in the City, whose Key Stage 2 results placed the borough first out of the 33 London boroughs in the 2009 school league tables (and first out of 150 UK local authorities). There are no state secondary schools and pupils transferring to state secondary education at age 11 attend schools in Southwark or Tower Hamlets. There are three independent schools.

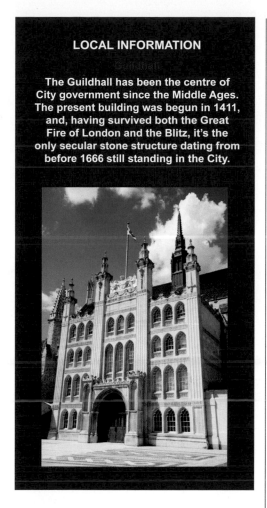

LOCAL INFORMATION

The Guildhall has been the centre of City government since the Middle Ages. The present building was begun in 1411, and, having survived both the Great Fire of London and the Blitz, it's the only secular stone structure dating from before 1666 still standing in the City.

To compare schools throughout London, see the table in **Appendix D**.

Pre-school

The local primary school (see below) has a nursery centre and children may also attend the Fortune Park Early Years Centre in Islington (Moreland Street, EC1, ☎ 020-7253 3823). In the private sector, there's a playgroup near the Barbican and a day nursery in Bridgewater Square. Just across the boundary in Islington, the independent Charterhouse Square School has a pre-preparatory department (see below).

State Schools

Sir John Cass's Foundation Primary School in Whitechapel is a voluntary-aided school.

Private Schools

◆ Charterhouse Square School is a mixed preparatory school for three to 11-year-olds.

◆ City of London School is a selective day school for boys aged 10-18, which was rated as one of the top UK schools in 2009 for GCSE results (including English and maths) and A levels.

◆ City of London School for Girls is a selective day school for girls aged 7-18, rated in 2009 as one of the top UK schools for GCSE and A level results.

◆ St Paul's Cathedral Choir School is a day school for girls and boys aged 4-13, with boarding facilities for boy choristers.

Further Education

The City of London Community Education Centre in the Barbican runs day and evening courses for adults.

Higher Education

◆ The Guildhall School of Music and Drama (💻 www.gsmd.ac.uk) is a leading *conservatoire* of the performing arts and is located in the Barbican Centre.

◆ Queen Mary, University of London (💻 www.qmul. ac.uk) has campuses in Charterhouse Square and West Smithfield.

Public Transport

The City is well served by tube, rail and bus services, which permit easy travel to the rest of London and beyond.

Underground

No fewer than 11 stations provide access to eight underground lines: Central, Circle, District, Docklands Light Railway, Hammersmith & City, Metropolitan, Northern and the Waterloo & City (also known as 'the drain'). A typical journey to the West End takes just 8 minutes.

Rail

There are five railway terminals:

◆ Blackfriars – Thameslink services to Luton and the north, and Gatwick and the South coast; South Eastern Trains to Kent.

◆ Liverpool Street – 'one' Railway services to north-east London, Essex and East Anglia.

◆ Fenchurch Street – South West Trains to the East End and the East coast.

◆ Cannon Street – South Eastern Trains to south-east London and Kent.

◆ Moorgate – WAGN trains to North London, Hertfordshire and the North East.

Buses

There are regular bus services to the West End, East End and other areas of inner London. Night buses serving the City include the N8, N11, N15, N26, N50 and N113. For details see 🖥 www.tfl.gov.uk.

River Transport

Commuter river services run mornings and evenings between the following piers, with several stops en route:

◆ Blackfriars and Chelsea Harbour or Greenwich.

◆ Tower Millennium Pier and Embankment, Westminster or Greenwich.

Airports

Below are the approximate distances and travel times from St Paul's to the five London airports using public transport.

◆ **City** – 7 miles; 22 minutes via the Docklands Light Railway.

◆ **Gatwick** – 25 miles; 45 minutes via London Bridge.

◆ **Heathrow** – 16 miles; 50 minutes via Paddington.

◆ **Luton** – 28 miles; 70 minutes via Moorgate.

◆ **Stansted** – 31 miles; 60 minutes via Liverpool Street.

Roads

All of the City is within the Congestion Charge Zone, which costs £8 per day. This has eased traffic density on the City's roads a little, but drivers still have to contend with one-way systems, bus lanes and a high density of speed cameras. There's a useful network of cycle lanes.

Parking

Parking is difficult in the City, with most roads having yellow or double yellow lines and few residences include garages or driveways. The

LOCAL INFORMATION

All routes around the City are subject to a 'ring of steel' security cordon, where vehicles can be stopped at police check points. Access to certain streets in the centre is restricted to vehicles not exceeding 7.5 tonnes.

Corporation provides seven car parks and almost 900 on-street parking bays, although these are intended for short stays only. A resident's permit for on-street parking costs £185 for 13 weeks, pay and display meters cost £4 per hour and car park fees are from £22 per day.

Waste & Recycling

The Corporation collects rubbish daily from all the city's households and workplaces, including large estates such as the Barbican, which have their own waste management facilities. The British Cleansing Council has voted the City's streets the cleanest in the UK. Recyclable materials are collected five days a week. Bulky items such as furniture and kitchen appliances are collected by arrangement. There's no civic amenity site (recycling/waste centre) in the City, although residents can use those in neighbouring boroughs.

Shopping

City shops have improved greatly in the last decade and although the majority of shoppers are the working population, it's possible to obtain most items locally, from luxury goods to daily essentials. The downside is that many shops are only open during the working week. There are a handful of shops on Fleet Street and around St Paul's; Moorgate has some useful stores, including an M&S; Cheapside is stocked with a good choice of shops, with several fashion outlets in the pedestrianised Bow Lane; Leadenhall Market (which is really more of a pedestrianised shopping centre than a market) has shops selling fresh produce, books and clothes; and the Broadgate Centre and Liverpool Street station both have decent shopping facilities. The Royal Exchange, opposite the Bank of England, has been converted into a fashion mall.

Shopping Centres

The Royal Exchange (between Cornhill and Threadneedle Street, EC3, 🖥 www. theroyalexchange.com) – over 30 up-market designer fashion shops, including Agent Provocateur, Lulu Guinness, Paul Smith and Prada (just the place to splash your City bonus).

Supermarkets

There are no large supermarkets in the Square Mile, although there are branches of M&S's Simply Food in Cannon Street, Liverpool Street Station, Moorgate and Paternoster Square, a Sainsbury's Local in Fenchurch Street, and Tesco Metro stores in Bishopsgate, Cheapside and Eastcheap.

Markets

♦ Leadenhall Market (off Gracechurch Street, EC3) – fresh produce, clothing and books in permanent shop sites within a Grade II listed Victorian market hall; Monday to Friday.

♦ Petticoat Lane Market (on the border with Tower Hamlets in Middlesex Street and nearby roads, E1) – famous cheap fashion market, with a few stalls selling toys, linens and textiles; Sundays, although the Wentworth Street section is also open Monday to Friday.

♦ Smithfield market (Charterhouse Street, EC1) – the last wholesale market in London, selling meat to businesses, although it's sometimes possible to make a small individual purchase later in the morning; Monday to Friday.

Entertainment

The Barbican Centre (Silk Street, EC2, ☎ 020-7638 4141, 🖥 www.barbican.org.uk) is the main entertainment venue in the City, funded by the Corporation of London, with theatres, cinemas, art galleries, a concert hall and a library. It's also home to the London Symphony Orchestra. Each November the City's history is celebrated in the pomp of the Lord Mayor's Show, with a procession that winds through the streets from the Guildhall to Temple. Another annual event is the London Maze, a free local history fair devoted to London that takes place in the Guildhall Building (Aldermanbury, EC2).

Theatres

♦ Barbican Theatre (contact details as above), with the smaller Pit Studio Theatre.

♦ Bridewell Theatre (Bride Lane, Fleet Street, EC4, ☎ 020-7353 3331, 🖥 www. stbrideinstitute.org).

Cinemas

Three cinemas in the Barbican Centre (see above) show a mixture of arthouse and blockbuster releases.

Museums & Galleries

There are art galleries within the Barbican Centre, and the historic Tower of London is just over the City boundary in Tower Hamlets. Otherwise the City offers:

- The Clock Museum (Guildhall Building, Aldermanbury, EC2, ☎ 020-7332 1868/1870) – history of London's clockmakers, with a collection of 600 watches and clocks.

- Guildhall Art Gallery (Guildhall Building, as above) – temporary art exhibitions exploring different themes.

- Museum of London (150 London Wall, EC2, ☎ 020-7001 9844) – free exhibition exploring 2,000 years of London's history.

Libraries

Three lending libraries, two reference libraries and the largest collection of local authority archives in the UK are available to residents and workers. The largest is the Barbican Library (Barbican Centre, as above, ☎ 020-7638 0569), while the Guildhall Library (Guildhall Building, as above, ☎ 020-7332 1868) includes a collection of manuscripts, prints and maps. None of the libraries open on Sundays and only the Barbican and Guildhall open on Saturdays.

Clubs

One of London's more popular clubs, Fabric, is on the fringe of the City in Smithfield (77A Charterhouse Street, EC1, ☎ 020-7336 8898, 🖳 www.fabriclondon. com) – open only at weekends, it has a capacity of 1,500 and a regular line up of popular DJs and live acts. Plastic People (147 Curtain Road, EC2, ☎ 020-7739 6471, 🖳 www.plasticpeople.co.uk) is

a small venue featuring rock 'n' roll, sleazy electro and a whole host of one-off events.

Live Music

The concert hall at the Barbican Centre (see above) presents an eclectic programme of classical and contemporary music.

Pubs

There are a large number of pubs in all parts of the City, with some of London's most historic in the Fleet Street and Blackfriars district, such as Ye Olde Cheshire Cheese (145 Fleet Street, EC4, ☎ 020-7353 6170) and Tipperary (66 Fleet Street, EC4, ☎ 020-7583 6470), London's first Irish pub. Around Liverpool Street station, pubs are often open Mondays to Fridays only – although when they *are* open, they're packed! Along with the chains (All Bar One, Jamie's and O'Neill's, among others) there are some interesting venues such as the George (Great Eastern Hotel, 40 Liverpool Street, EC2, ☎ 020-7618 7400), a Conran outfit serving good food, and Vertigo 42 (Tower 42, 25 Old Broad Street, EC2, ☎ 020-7877 7842), with its fantastic views from the tallest building in the City.

In the financial quarter there are plenty more chains, including a DJ/bar from the Harvey Nichols group, Prism (147 Leadenhall Street, EC3, ☎ 020-7256 3888), in a building that once housed the Bank of New York. For a classy

atmosphere, there's 1 Lombard Street (1 Lombard Street, EC3, ☎ 020-7929 6611). These are just a few of the many venues in the Square Mile – for more choice, consult a guide such as Time Out's *Eating and Drinking Guide*.

Restaurants

Cheap and cheerful, lively and trendy, expensive and award-winning, the Square Mile offers every type of restaurant in every price range, plus sandwich bars and coffee shops galore. Use a guide book to make exploring easier. At the top end, there's 1 Lombard Street (see above), where expensive French cuisine, caviar and champagne do justice to City bonuses. Another French eatery is Club Gascon (57 West Smithfield, EC1, ☎ 020-7796 0600), which boasts a Michelin star and serves fine food tapas-style.

For an unusual dining experience, there's Spaghetti Opera (109 Fleet Street, EC4, ☎ 020-7353 1282), where traditional Italian cuisine is accompanied by live performances of great opera moments. In the Barbican, Searcy's (Level 2, Barbican Centre, Silk Street, EC2, ☎ 020-7638 4141) is a relaxed restaurant with a fine view.

Sports Facilities

The one publicly-funded leisure centre in the City is Golden Lane, close to the Barbican, which has a 20-metre swimming pool, tennis courts and a multi-purpose indoor sports hall. There are also plenty of private gyms and health clubs catering for stressed workers, including branches of well-known chains Cannon's, Fitness First, Holmes Place and LA Fitness. Lambs Health and Fitness (1 Lambs Passage, Chiswell Street, EC1, ☎ 020-7638 3811) offers a gymnasium, aerobics classes and squash courts. In winter, the Broadgate Centre by Liverpool Street station has an open air ice rink.

Green Spaces

Space within the City is at a premium, although there are still some 150 gardens, churchyards, piazzas and landscaped areas to break up the concrete sprawl. The City's largest public garden is Finsbury Circus, London's oldest park, which dates back to 1606 and is on the English Heritage Register of Historic Parks and Gardens. Formed in an unusual oval shape, the park has as its centrepieces the immaculate lawn of the City of London bowls club and a bandstand, surrounded

by public lawns which are popular with office workers in fine weather.

LOCAL INFORMATION

Walking tours of the city, led by City of London Guides, take in 'secret' gardens, full of charm and character and planted to create oases of calm. One, Postman's Park in Aldersgate, is situated behind the old General Post Office building in a former churchyard and features 34 plaques commemorating people who lost their lives while trying to save others.

Tower of London

Croydon

SE19 (part), SE25, SW16 (part), CR0, CR2, CR5, CR7, CR8

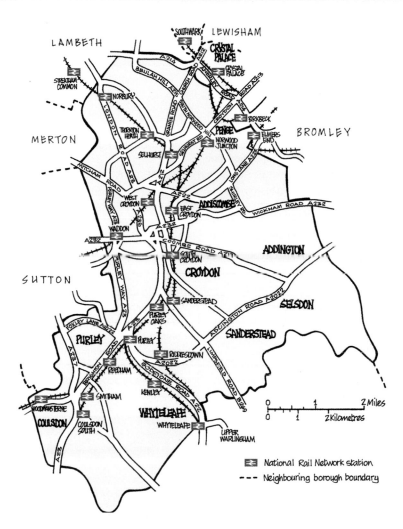

National Rail Network station
--- Neighbouring borough boundary

At a Glance

Best for: rail links, education, shopping, entertainment, affordable housing

Not so good for: traffic congestion, crime, culture, no tube

Who lives there: middle-class families, business people, young professionals

Housing stock: Almost equally divided between semi-detached, terraces (many Victorian) and flats.

Housing costs: average

General Information

Council Offices: The Town Hall, Katharine St., Croydon CR0 1NX (☎ 020-8686 4433)

CAA Assessment: (see 🖥 http://oneplace.direct.gov.uk > Search by area > London > Croydon)

Controlling Party: Conservative

Website: 🖥 www.croydon.gov.uk

Council Tax 2010/11: £2,433 (Band G), £2,920 (Band H)

Main Areas/towns: Addington, Coulsdon, Croydon, Norbury, Purley, Sanderstead, Selsden, Thornton Heath, Upper Norwood

Postcodes: SE19 (part), SE25, SW16 (part), CR0, CR2, CR5, CR7, CR8

Population & Ethnicity: 341,800, London's most populous borough. Around 25 per cent of residents are from Asian and Afro-Caribbean ethnic backgrounds. The borough attracts largely middle-class, white-collar families and young professionals.

Unemployment: 8.2 per cent (London average is 8.2 per cent)

Overview

Just ten miles south of London, Croydon was once regarded as the most fashionable, desirable and aspirational place to live, which reached a peak in the '20s and '30s, when families desperate for their own home away from the grime of London flocked to the fresh air and space outside the capital. Flat-roofed, modernist homes vied with neo-Georgian designs and mock-Tudor mini-mansions in a borough which proudly sold itself as London's greenest and most attractive.

Today, Croydon is a popular commuter borough, stretching from the outskirts of Crystal Palace at Upper Norwood to the Surrey border at Coulsdon. The main town is Croydon, which provides excellent rail links to the West End, London's first modern tram system and extensive shopping, commercial and recreational facilities. Although dominated by some ugly '60s concrete towers, recent re-developments have rejuvenated the town and the council is keen to promote it as a dynamic and modern centre.

The grandest parts of the borough are the expensive suburbs of Shirley to the east, home to the wealthy and the occasional celebrity, and Purley to the south, true stockbroker territory, with large houses set in private roads. Elsewhere the borough ranges from densely packed inner London suburbia in the north, to the more spacious, if unremarkable, towns in the south, which are fringed with green belt land and provide easy access to the M25 and Gatwick Airport.

LOCAL INFORMATION

The origin of the name Croydon is unknown, but one theory is that it derives from the old French *croie dune*, meaning 'chalk hill', as Croydon stands at the northern edge of the chalk hills called the North Downs.

Development Plans

Croydon Vision 2020 is a regeneration programme which spearheads Croydon's bid to become 'London's Third City' and the hub of living, retailing, culture and business in south London. Currently £3.5bn has been committed to the project with much more in the pipeline. One of the first developments has been Altitude 25, a 25-storey tower of 196 apartments on Fairfield Road close to East Croydon station, which was completed in 2008 and is currently Croydon's highest skyscraper, at 307ft (94m).

Another Vision 2020 project is the Croydon Gateway development on a 12.5-acre (5ha) site alongside East Croydon railway station. It will include a 12,500 seat Arena for international sporting events, business conferences and community activities; shops, restaurants, café and bars; 739 new flats in a 44-storey residential tower, combining affordable and private units; health and fitness, and community health centres; a new public square; and over 500,000ft² (46,000m²) of office space. The scheme was granted planning permission in June 2008.

There's also proposed redevelopment of Park Place, which would create over 130 shops and restaurants and a new department store, as well as revitalise the town centre and create a new focus for central Croydon.

Croydon Town Hall & Gardens

Residential Areas

While Victorian properties dominate the northern parts of the borough, southern districts were mostly developed during the 20th century. There's a fairly even mix of property styles, with 31 per cent flats (many of which are conversions), 34 per cent terraces and 35 per cent semi-detached or detached houses.

Coulsdon (CR5)

Coulsdon has all the ingredients of a popular commuter town: three railway stations into Croydon and central London, fast access to the M23 and M25, practical shops in the high street and plenty of green belt countryside. The majority of the housing dates from the '20s and '30s, and consists of three- and four-bedroom family semis, with a few larger detached properties, plus a new housing estate of 400 homes. Old Coulsdon is more village-like, with some attractive cottages and 15th century farmhouses fetching high prices on the rare occasions when they come up for sale.

Croydon (CR0, CR2)

The focal point of the borough, sprawling Croydon isn't particularly fashionable but is nonetheless popular with families and commuters. As well as family-sized houses, there's a good supply of smaller terraces and flats that are ideal for first-time buyers. Rented accommodation is readily available in South Croydon, where there are also some new apartments. To the west is a large '60s council estate. Along the Purley Way from Waddon to West Croydon are a series of major retail parks, which have the cheapest housing in the area. The most sought-after houses lie in wide, tree-lined roads by Lloyds Park and in Shirley, a village-like suburb to the east featuring '30s and more modern properties. Shirley Hills has huge houses on private roads and is home to the seriously wealthy.

Purley (CR8)

This well-established residential suburb has a bustling town centre for day-to-day shopping, plus two railway stations for convenient commuting. There are a few Edwardian detached and semi-detached properties, although most housing consists of inter-war semis, with some modern purpose-built flats. The most expensive areas are in Woodcote, where substantial detached properties have large gardens. The private Webb Estate is also located there, a pioneering garden village with some desirable half-timbered houses commanding prices of £1mn-plus.

Sanderstead, Selsden & Addington (CR2, CR0)

Only 8 miles by car from the M25, Sanderstead is a pleasant, leafy town bordered by three golf courses (Purley, Selsdon Park and Croham Hurst). Popular with comfortable middle-class families, the town's housing consists of inter-war semi-detached and detached houses in wide, tree-lined roads. Peaceful Selsden has predominantly '60s and '70s houses and flats, attractively laid out in small cul-de-sacs. The nearby Tram service compensates for the lack of a station. Neighbouring Addington Village is set in the grounds of a mansion, while New Addington is a large, purpose-built '60s estate, mostly council-owned, with its own swimming pool, library and local shops.

Thornton Heath (CR7)

Multicultural Thornton Heath is more urban in character than the borough's southern towns and has few open spaces – although Mitcham Common is nearby. Much of the property consists of Victorian semis, although there are some newer '60s townhouses and '30s 'mock Tudor' houses towards Croydon. Flats are plentiful (many are conversions) and it's a good area for renting.

Upper Norwood (SE19)

Upper Norwood is perched on the hill next to Crystal Palace (see **Bromley**). Shops, restaurants and bars lie in the shadow of the television mast, and spacious Victorian properties, many converted into flats, dominate the housing. Some modern, purpose-built flats have been slipped in here and there. At the bottom of the hill, South Norwood is rather downmarket, although cheaper, with a good number of houses and flats.

Property Costs

Property Prices

Costs vary widely in the borough; the cheapest areas are West Croydon and New Addington, and the most expensive are Shirley and Purley. The table below shows average property prices:

> Detached: £458,685
> Semi-detached: £283,152
> Terraced: £212,789
> Flat: £161,667

Rental Costs

The table below shows average monthly rents in the borough:

> House 5+ bed: £2,300
> House 4-5 bed: £1,500
> House 3-4 bed: £1,200
> House 2-3 bed: £1,100
> Flat 2-bed: £950
> Flat 1-bed: £750

Crime

Croydon has higher crime rates than its outer London neighbours, with the seventh-highest rate of all the boroughs for violent crime and the fourth-highest rate for stolen cars. Croydon's town centre is a particular trouble spot, followed by Thornton Heath and Norbury. The current police priority is to tackle street crime, including muggings, criminal damage and harassment. Street lighting is being improved and police officers are maintaining a greater presence on the streets.

The main police station is in Croydon (71 Park Lane, CR9, ☎ 020-8667 1212), with other stations in Kenley, New Addington, Norbury and South Norwood.

To compare crime rates throughout London, see the table in **Appendix D**.

Health

NHS services in the borough are provided by the Croydon Primary Care Trust. For a full list of doctors, dentists and clinics, visit ▣ www.nhs.uk.

To see how the Primary Care Trust compares with others in London, see the table in **Appendix D**.

Doctors & Dentists

♦ There are over 140 NHS GP surgeries, providing a range of clinics and health services.

♦ Croydon has 62 dental and orthodontic practices, around half of which accept new NHS patients.

 FAMOUS RESIDENTS

Notable people associated with Croydon include Dame Peggy Ashcroft (actress), Jeff Beck (musician), Samuel Coleridge-Taylor (composer), Sir Arthur Conan Doyle (author), D.H. Lawrence (writer), David Lean (film director), Kate Moss (model), John Ruskin (art critic) and Emile Zola (writer).

Hospitals

♦ Mayday University Hospital (530 Woodcroft Road, CR7, ☎ 020-8401 3000, ▣ www.maydayhospital.nhs.uk) – A&E.

♦ Parkway Health Centre (Parkway, CR0, ☎ 020-8714 2950) – minor injuries unit.

♦ Purley War Memorial Hospital (856 Brighton Road, CR8, ☎ as Mayday Hospital above).

There's an NHS walk-in centre in Croydon town centre (45 High Street, CR0, ☎ 020-8666 0555).

Private Medical Facilities

Shirley Oaks Hospital (Poppy Lane, CR9, ☎ 020-8655 5500, ▣ www.bmihealthcare.co.uk). To find a private GP, visit ▣ www.privatehealth.co.uk.

Schools

Croydon has a variety of state secondary schools, including community, foundation, voluntary aided and controlled, as well as a large number of private schools. There's also a school of performing arts. Standards are slightly below the UK average, although they vary widely between individual schools. In the 2009 school league tables, primary schools were placed 20th out of the 33 London boroughs (85th out of 150 UK local authorities) and secondary schools 20th (62nd in the UK).

To compare schools throughout London, see the table in **Appendix D**.

Pre-school

There's a large choice of playgroups and nurseries, particularly in the north of the borough, including four state nursery schools and two early years centres. Nursery classes are attached to many infant and primary schools.

State Schools

First schools: 88 infant, junior and primary schools, of which 20 are voluntary aided or controlled.

Secondary schools: 18 comprehensive schools, of which nine are voluntary aided. Seven schools have sixth forms and 11 have specialist status. A new City Academy was completed in November 2007 in South Norwood. The BRIT School in Croydon is a performing arts and technology centre, and achieved excellent results in 2009. Other top performers were the Coloma Convent Girls' School in Croydon and the Harris City Technology College in Upper Norwood.

Special schools: Six special schools cater for students with physical disabilities and learning difficulties, plus two units attached to mainstream schools. The Rutherford School in South Croydon and the Tudor Lodge School in Purley are independent special schools.

LOCAL INFORMATION

Croydon Palace, built in the 15th century, was the summer residence of the Archbishop of Canterbury for over 500 years, where regular visitors included Henry III and Queen Elizabeth I. The buildings are still in use as the Old Palace School (▣ www.oldpalace. croydon.sch.uk), an independent girls' school of the Whitgift Foundation and a multiple winner of the Independent School of the Year Award.

Central Croydon

Private Schools

There are 26 private schools in the borough, with seven catering for pupils up to the age of 18. In 2009, Croydon High School and the Old Palace School (see box) were among the top UK schools for GCSE results, with the Whitgift School in Croydon one of the top schools for A levels.

Further Education

♦ Cambridge Tutors College (💻 www.ctc.ac.uk) – independent selective college for students studying GCSEs and A levels.

♦ Coulsdon College (💻 www.coulsdon.ac.uk).

♦ Croydon College (💻 www.croydon.ao.uk).

♦ John Ruskin College (💻 www.johnruskin. ac.uk).

Higher Education

Croydon College (💻 see above) offers a comprehensive range of undergraduate degree courses.

Public Transport

East Croydon is a transport 'hub', with several rail services serving central London and the south coast, as well as local buses and trams. The underground doesn't extend as far as Croydon –

the nearest stations are Morden and Colliers Wood (see **Merton**).

If it gets the go-ahead, a proposed extension of the East London line to West Croydon would provide easy access to stations on the underground and Docklands Light Railway networks.

Rail

The borough is served by several rail services, all stopping at East Croydon:

♦ Southern trains runs extensive services into Charing Cross, London Bridge, Victoria and Waterloo, with branch lines serving all the borough's stations. Typical journey time from East Croydon to Victoria, 20 minutes.

♦ South Eastern trains stop at East Croydon and Norwood Junction en route to London Bridge (non-stop journey time is 15 minutes).

♦ The Thameslink service serves East Croydon on the way to Blackfriars and King's Cross.

Buses

Like other outer London boroughs, most buses stop short of central London, with the exception of the number X68, which runs from West

Croydon to Waterloo and then non-stop to Russell Square. Otherwise buses serve local areas and neighbouring boroughs – useful routes include the X26 (Heathrow to West Croydon), 60 (Old Coulsdon to Streatham) and 407 (Croydon to Sutton). The N159 and N68 night buses run to Croydon.

Trams

London's only tram system is in Croydon, with services between East Croydon and Beckenham, New Addington and Wimbledon. The trams are frequent and fast (23 minutes to Wimbledon and 16 minutes to Beckenham), and a welcome alternative to buses in the Addington area, where there's no railway station.

Airports

Below are approximate distances and times from East Croydon to the five London airports using public transport.

♦ **City** – 11 miles; 55 minutes via Bank.

♦ **Gatwick** – 15 miles; 16 minutes via Victoria.

♦ **Heathrow** – 17 miles; 90 minutes via either Paddington or X26 bus from West Croydon.

♦ **Luton** – 37 miles; 63 minutes on the Thameslink service.

♦ **Stansted** – 38 miles; 95 minutes via Liverpool Street.

LOCAL INFORMATION

Croydon Airport was London's major international airport between the wars (long before Gatwick and Heathrow came to dominate) and was the first airport in the world to introduce air traffic control, in 1921. The last scheduled flight was on 30th September 1959.

Roads

The A23 into Surrey can be slow south of Croydon, where it runs through the retail parks. The centre of Croydon is often congested during rush hours and at weekends when shoppers descend. A new bypass around Coulsden is improving traffic flow to and from the M25, although not by as much as hoped.

Parking

Controlled Parking Zones operate around much of Croydon town centre, as well as Coulsdon, Norbury, Purley, Sanderstead, South Norwood and Thornton Heath. A resident's parking permit costs £44 per year for one car, an additional £72 for a second car and £175 for a third car.

Waste & Recycling

Household rubbish and recyclable waste are collected every two weeks. Recyclable materials include cans, glass, paper, shoes and textiles. Various third party organisations collect bulky items such as furniture and kitchen appliances, by arrangement. There are amenity sites in West Croydon and New Addington, and a dedicated recycling centre in Purley Oaks.

Shopping

Croydon is one of the main shopping areas outside central London, with two indoor shopping malls and a pedestrianised shopping street offering branches of most major chains. Just out of the town centre major retail parks line the A23 Purley Way, with superstores for well-known chains, including B&Q, Comet, Ikea, Mothercare, PC World, TK Maxx and Toys 'R Us. Elsewhere in the borough, shopping is fairly unexciting, with high streets in Purley, Norwood and Thornton Heath providing daily essentials, Building Societies, estate agents and charity shops.

Shopping Centres

♦ Centrale (North End, CR0, ☎ 020-8681 5841, 🖳 www.centrale.co.uk) – Debenhams, House of Fraser, Next and Zara.

♦ The Whitgift Centre (North End, CR0, ☎ 020-8686 0297, 🖳 www.whitgiftshopping.co.uk), formerly the largest town shopping centre in Europe – BHS, M&S and other leading chains.

Supermarkets

♦ Asda in Wallington and a George clothing store in the Whitgift centre.

♦ Sainsbury's in Croydon (Whitgift Centre and Purley Way), Selsden and South Norwood.

♦ Tesco in Purley and Thornton Heath (both open 24 hours), plus a Metro store just into Surrey at Caterham.

♦ Waitrose in Coulsdon and Sanderstead.

Markets

♦ Croydon Market (Surrey Street, CR0) – fruit and veg, flowers and general goods; Monday to Saturday, 7am-6pm.

♦ Croydon Farmers' Market (Central Parade, CR0) – twenty stallholders; every Tuesday and Friday and the third Saturday monthly.

Entertainment

The borough's main entertainment venues are in and around Croydon town centre, where there's the award-winning Clocktower Arts Centre and Fairfield Halls, a major concert hall and theatre. In the summer the borough hosts a two-day festival in Lloyd Park (see **Green Spaces** below), with music, dance, theatre, a funfair and a market. Croydon also has the best choice of night-spots, although eating out is a fairly predictable experience.

Theatres

♦ Ashcroft Theatre (Fairfield Hall, Park Lane, CR9, ☎ 020-8688 9291, 🖥 www.fairfield.co.uk).

♦ Warehouse Theatre (Dingwall Road, CR0, ☎ 020-8680 4060, 🖥 www.warehousetheatre. co.uk).

Cinemas

♦ David Lean Cinema (Croydon Clocktower, Katherine Street, CR9, ☎ 020-8253 1030).

♦ Fairfield Halls Cinema (Park Lane, CR9, ☎ 020-8688 9291, 🖥 www.fairfield.co.uk).

♦ Vue Grants (14 High Street, CR0) and Vue Purley Way (Valley Park Leisure Complex, Hasterman Way, CR0, ☎ 08712-240 240, 🖥 www.myvue. co.uk).

Museums & Galleries

The Clocktower has three galleries, housing a ceramics collection, work by local artists and an art gallery. Croydon also has the following attractions open on certain days throughout the year:

♦ Croydon Airport Visitor Centre (Airport House, Purley Way, CR0, ☎ 020-8669 1196, 🖥 www.croydonairport. org.uk) – exhibition about the world's first purpose-built international airport.

♦ Croydon Palace (Old Palace Road, CR0, ☎ 01883-742 969, 🖥 www. friendsofoldpalace.org) – former residence of the Archbishops of Canterbury.

♦ Shirley Windmill (Postmill Close, CR0) – Croydon's only surviving windmill.

Libraries

There are 14 local authority libraries in the borough, with one mobile service. None open on Sundays. The largest library is in Croydon's Clocktower complex (address as above, ☎ 020-8760 5400), which also has a gay and lesbian section. The Upper Norwood Joint Library (39 Westow Hill, SE19, ☎ 020-8670 2551) is an independent library service, funded by Croydon and Lambeth councils, although not part of either borough's library services.

Clubs

There are enough clubs in Croydon to provide a good night out without venturing as far as the West End, including:

♦ Blue Orchid (22-24 Park Lane, CR0, ☎ 020-8667 0592).

♦ Edwards (18 High Street, CR0, ☎ 020-8686 3580).

♦ Medusa (32-34 High Street, CR0, ☎ 020-8686 3367, 🖥 www.medusa.co.uk).

♦ Tiger Tiger (16 Grant's Building, High Street, CR0, ☎ 020-8662 4949, 🖥 www.tigertiger-croydon.co.uk).

Centrale Shopping Centre

For comedy, Up the Creek (3 Brighton Road, CR2, ☎ 020-8293 4077, 💻 www.up-the-creek.com) is one of a small chain of comedy clubs.

Live Music

The concert hall at Fairfield is the main music venue, featuring a year-round programme of musical events. Other venues include:

◆ Black Sheep Bar (68 High Street, CR0, ☎ 020-8680 2233, 💻 www.blacksheepbar.com) – alternative music gigs every week, catering for a wide range of tastes.

◆ The Cartoon (179-183 London Road, CR0, ☎ 020-8239 1616) – rock music venue.

◆ The Ship (47 High Street, CR0, ☎ 020-8688 2810) – alternative pub with live music six nights a week.

Pubs

There are plenty of pubs and bars around the borough, with the widest choice in central Croydon, including style bars, gastropubs, traditional boozers and a large number of establishments with karaoke, TV screens and music. One of the most praised is the Beer Circus (282 High Street, CR0, ☎ 020-8680 3030), a freehouse with an enormous selection of beers. Another is the friendly Oval Tavern (131 Oval Road, CR0, ☎ 020-8686 6023).

Croydon also has a gay-friendly pub – the Bird in Hand (291 Sydenham Road, CR0, ☎ 020-8683 3104, 💻 www.birdinhand.uk.com). In the south of the borough pubs are fewer and further apart, including one or two with beer gardens and good food such as the Fox (Coulsdon Common, CR3, ☎ 01883-330 737).

North of Croydon town centre, South Norwood has little in the way of decent pubs, with the exception of Oceans Apart (152 Portland Road, SE25, ☎ 020-8663 8881, 💻 www.oceansapart-bars.com), a new style bar. Thornton Heath has a better choice, including the Fountain Head (114 Parchmore Road, CR7, ☎ 020-8653 4025), which has a pleasant garden.

Restaurants

Eating out is a mixed experience in the borough, with a few good restaurants such as the Rayon D'Or in Airport House (Purley Way, CR0, ☎ 020-8781 1933, 💻 www.rayondor.co.uk) set amid a lot of predictable or uninteresting ones. Chains tend to be of the cheap and cheerful variety (Pizza Hut and Nando's, for example) and there are a few Berni and Harvester Inns around the southern areas. There's a branch of Thank God It's Friday on the Purley Way by Airport House and there are branches of the up-market chain Il Ponte in Upper Norwood and Croydon centre. Ethnic cuisine dominates much of the restaurant choice in all areas, with the award-winning Mauritius Bar and Restaurant in Norbury one of the best (113 London Road, SE16, ☎ 020-8764 9879).

Sports Facilities

Croydon has six sports and leisure centres, providing a range of facilities, including:

◆ Swimming pools at New Addington, Purley, South Norwood and Thornton Heath.

◆ An eight-lane athletics track at the Croydon Arena in South Norwood.

◆ Indoor sports halls, a climbing wall and outdoor sports pitches at the Monks Hill centre in South Croydon.

There are sports facilities in 32 of the borough's parks, including areas for basketball, cricket, football, tennis and BMX cycling or skateboarding. Fishing and sailing take place on South Norwood Lake. Horse riding can be enjoyed in the Addington Hills, Lloyd Park and Shirley Heath, where there are many public bridlepaths. Golfers are also well served, with more golf courses than any other borough. All the borough's sports centres have fitness suites and there are branches of Cannons, Fitness First and LA Fitness. For the less active, there's a tenpin bowling alley at the Colonnades Leisure Complex on the Purley Way.

Green Spaces

There are 120 parks and open spaces, providing ornamental gardens, recreation grounds, sports facilities and heathland away from the bustle of the town centres. Much of the area to the east of the borough is open countryside. The largest space in the north of the borough is South Norwood Country Park, which has mature trees and a wetland area, with a nature reserve opposite its southern tip. To the west, there's a fine house and garden at Norwood Grove near Upper Norwood, with splendid views. Lloyd Park is an attractive area close to central Croydon, with mature trees and bridlepaths. The park merges into the vast open spaces of the Addington Hills to the east, from where there are extensive views over Croydon. There are several walking trails. In the far south around Old Coulsdon is the large Happy Valley Park, an important wildlife reserve, with bridlepaths, woodland and meadows.

LOCAL INFORMATION

Addington Palace

A Palladian-style mansion situated between Addington Village and Shirley, built in the 1770s with gardens designed by Capability Brown, Addington Palace was the home of the Archbishops of Canterbury between 1805 and 1897. Today it houses a health and country club, while the gardens and parkland, although still largely the original design, are home to a number of golf clubs.

Ealing

W3, W5, W7, W13, UB1, UB2, UB5, UB6

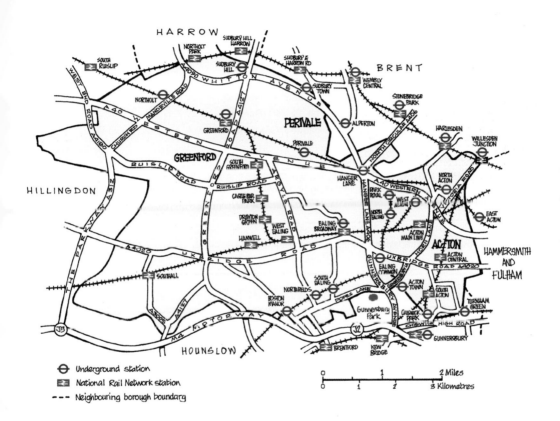

Underground station
National Rail Network station
Neighbouring borough boundary

0   1   2 Miles
0   1   2   3 Kilometres

At a Glance

Best for: public transport, shopping, leisure facilities

Not so good for: crime, deprivation, nightlife

Who lives there: middle-class families, young professionals, first-time buyers

Housing stock: flats (40%), terraces (35%), semi-detached, Victorian/Edwardian houses (20%)

Housing costs: moderate

General Information

Council Offices: Perceval House, 14/16 Uxbridge Road, Ealing, W5 2HL (☎ 020-8825 5000)

CAA Assessment: (see 🖳 http://oneplace.direct.gov.uk > Search by area > London > Ealing)

Controlling Party: Labour

Website: 🖳 www.ealing.gov.uk

Council Tax 2010/11: £2,283 (Band G), £2,740 (Band H)

Main Areas/towns: Acton, Ealing Broadway, Greenford, Hanwell, Northolt, Southall, West Ealing.

Postcodes: W3, W5, W7, W13, UB1, UB2, UB5, UB6

Population & Ethnicity: 309,000, with a high proportion aged between 20 and 44. Over a third of residents are Asian, including London's largest Sikh community, in Southall, and there's also a significant Afro-Caribbean population. There are also smaller Polish, Irish, French, Jewish, Armenian and Japanese communities. The borough attracts middle-class families and young professionals.

Unemployment: 9.0 per cent (London average is 8.2 per cent)

Overview

Ealing borough (the fourth-largest) is regarded as the 'Queen of the Suburbs' by its residents. It offers the best of inner and outer London living, including excellent transport links, interesting buildings, plenty of entertainment and lots of green space. The most sought-after area is Ealing Broadway, a lively, self-contained neighbourhood with the best shopping, nightlife and recreational amenities. People tend to stay put once they've moved in and the town is a favourite with families and young singles.

In the south-east, Bedford Park is the most expensive part of the borough, while in the east, multicultural Acton – once one of Ealing's most deprived areas – is now up-and-coming as new residents priced out of Hammersmith and Chiswick are gentrifying period properties. Southall, in the west, is colourful and crowded, home to a predominantly Asian community and boasting an exotic shopping district with London's only live animal market.

LOCAL INFORMATION

The name Ealing was recorded around 700AD as 'Gillingas', meaning 'place of the people associated with Gilla'. Over the centuries the name has changed and it has been known as Yealing, Zelling and Eling, until Ealing became the standard spelling in the 19th century.

Development Plans

The council has set aside over £15mn for an extensive programme to revamp every town centre in the borough: Acton, Ealing (including West Ealing), Greenford, Hanwell, Northolt, Perivale and Southall. In 2007, Ealing Council commissioned a number of town centre and key site studies (Acton, Southern Gateway, Ealing and Southall) for regenerating the borough. A major redevelopment of Greenford town centre is already underway, which is part of a ten-year improvement plan.

Plans were submitted in September 2007 for a new retail, residential and commercial development consisting of six new buildings in the centre of Ealing, on a 4.2-acre (1.7-hectare) site to be known as the 'Leaf Development'. A particular feature will be a tall residential tower block, which will be known as 'The Leaf', containing 700 flats, some 15 per cent of which will be affordable housing units. Car and cycle parking facilities will be provided, together with retail and office space, a health and fitness club, and a civic piazza. The expected completion date is 2014, if the plan goes ahead – certain objections to it have yet to be overcome.

Residential Areas

Property in Ealing and Acton is largely Victorian, with a good stock of grand semis and some attractive converted flats. North Ealing is more Edwardian, while Southall, Greenford and Northolt consist mainly of '30s semis. Some 40 per cent of properties in the borough are flats, 35 per cent are terraces, 20 per cent are semi-detached and just 5 per cent are detached houses.

Acton (W3)

Busy Acton is popular with young professionals, thanks to its copious supply of flats. Much property consists of conversions, although there are several new developments, with two-bedroom flats costing around £335,000. Terraced houses are good value (£455,000 for three bedrooms) and popular among BBC employees, as well as Japanese families keen to use the nearby Japanese School (see below). Many council blocks are due for refurbishment and the miserable South Acton Estate has been demolished and is to be replaced by new homes.

Bedford Park (W4)

Partly in Hounslow, this is Ealing's most prestigious area, a prototype garden suburb developed in the 19th century. Tree-lined roads feature a variety of homes in the 'Queen Anne style': red brick facades, Dutch gables and the occasional balcony. Most houses sell through word of mouth and they aren't cheap – around £2mn for five bedrooms – with residents predominantly wealthy professionals.

Ealing Town Hall

Ealing Broadway & North Ealing (W5)

Very central, with rail and underground trains accessible from one station (eventually to be joined by Crossrail trains), Ealing Broadway has a good range of houses and flats, including new developments close to Ealing Common. A three-bedroom house costs around £495,000. Grander properties lie to the north, where favoured locations include the '30s Hanger Hill Garden Estate, with a mix of 'mock Tudor' and modernist flat-roofed homes. Some of the most expensive property lies in Brentham Garden Suburb (or Pitshanger Village as estate agents like to call it) just south of the A40 Western Avenue.

Hanwell & West Ealing (W13, W7)

Cheaper than Ealing Broadway, these areas are a mix of Victorian terraces and larger homes, as well as some '30s properties. Hanwell has some pretty corners, particularly around the Grand Union Canal. Much of the property is ex-council, for example on the Cuckoo Estate, where a small flat costs under £170,000. There are new family townhouses near Greenford Park. West Ealing has languished in the Broadway's shadow for years, although this is beginning to change thanks to new apartment developments, notably the Iconica scheme along the Uxbridge Road, as well as others near Northfields underground station.

Northolt & Greenford (UB5, UB6)

Geographically divided from the rest of the borough by the A40 Western Avenue and the Greenford Road, these areas feature stretches of inter-war semis in quiet but unexciting streets, where there are lots of council properties. Homes are reasonably priced, attracting young families and first-time buyers. 'Grand Union Village' is a new urban village of flats and houses along the banks of the canal, where a two-bedroom flat costs around £180,000.

Southall (UB1)

Famed for its exotic culture, Southall is a popular residential area among Asian families. Property consists of large areas of '30s semis and terraces, although much of the housing stock is shabby and run-down, and a large proportion is rented, providing good opportunities for bargain hunters.

Property Costs

Property Prices

House prices and rents are comparable with neighbouring Hounslow, although those at the lower end of the scale are much cheaper. The table below shows average property prices in the borough:

Detached: £823,580
Semi-detached: £418,368
Terraced: £358,517
Flat: £228,220

Rental Costs

The table below shows average monthly rents in the borough:

House 5+ bed: £5,200
House 4-5 bed: £3,500
House 3-4 bed: £2,500
House 2-3 bed: £2,100
Flat 2-bed: £1,800
Flat 1-bed: £975

Crime

Ealing has the seventh-highest overall crime rate of all the London boroughs and the second-highest rate of thefts from motor vehicles. Burglary is also rife and there are incidents of violence on the streets and in pubs. Southall is a particular problem area, with incidents spilling over into Hanwell and West Ealing.

The police station HQ is in Ealing (67 Uxbridge Road, W5, ☎ 0300-123 1212), with other stations in Acton, Greenford and Southall, and with police offices at Norwood Green and Hanwell.

To compare crime rates throughout London, see the table in **Appendix D**.

Health

NHS services in the borough are provided by the borough Primary Care Trust. For a full list of doctors, dentists and clinics, visit 🖳 www.nhs.uk.

To see how the Primary Care Trust compares with others in London, see the table in **Appendix D**.

Doctors & Dentists

♦ There are 90 NHS GP surgeries, providing a range of clinics and health services.

♦ Ealing has 48 dental and orthodontic practices, of which some two-thirds accept new NHS patients.

Hospitals

♦ Ambulatory Care and Diagnostics Centre (Acton Lane, NW10, ☎ 020-8963 8857) – minor surgery.

♦ Ealing Hospital (Uxbridge Road, UB1, ☎ 020-8967 5000, 🖳 www.ealinghospital.org.uk) – A&E.

Elsewhere, the Clayponds Hospital in Ealing provides rehabilitation services, while the Penny Sangam Hospital in Southall provides specialised care for dementia patients.

Private Medical Facilities

There are no private hospitals in Ealing – the nearest are the Clementine Churchill (see **Harrow**) or the Cromwell in Earl's Court (see **Kensington & Chelsea**). To find a private GP, visit 🖳 www. privatehealth.co.uk.

Schools

Educational standards in Ealing are slightly above the UK average. In the 2009 school league tables, primary schools were placed 21st out of the 33 London boroughs (86th out of 150 UK local authorities) and secondary schools 14th (40th in the UK).

To compare schools throughout London, see the table in **Appendix D**.

Pre-school

There are a number of playgroups and nursery schools in both the private and public sectors,

👤 FAMOUS RESIDENTS

Famous residents of Ealing have included Lillian Board (athlete), Charlie Chaplin (comic actor), Henry Fielding (novelist), Sid James (actor and comedian), Matt Munro (singer), Fred Perry (tennis player), Dusty Springfield (singer) and Pete Townsend (musician).

including nursery classes in all but four infant and primary schools.

State Schools

First schools: 64 infant, junior and primary schools, of which ten are voluntary aided.

Secondary schools: 12 comprehensive schools, including one City Academy in Northolt. Two schools are voluntary aided, eight have sixth forms and eight have specialist status. The top performers in 2009 were the Twyford C of E High School in Acton and the Cardinal Wiseman RC School in Greenford (which also scored highly for added value).

Special schools: Six special schools cater for students with physical disabilities and learning difficulties.

Private Schools

There are a number of private schools catering for all age groups. The top performers in 2009 were St Augustine's Priory and St Benedict's School, both in Ealing, which achieved some of the best GCSE results in the UK. There are four specialist schools, all based in Acton:

◆ The Barbara Speake Stage School offers courses in the performing arts.

◆ The International School of London follows a curriculum based on the International Baccalaureate.

◆ The Japanese School adheres to the Japanese national curriculum.

◆ The King Fahad Academy follows the Saudi Arabian national curriculum.

Further Education

The Ealing, Hammersmith and West London College (💻 www.wlc.ac.uk) offers a range of courses for students aged 16+ in Acton, Ealing, Hammersmith and Southall.

Higher Education

Thames Valley University has several sites in Ealing offering a variety of degree courses (💻 www.tvu.ac.uk).

Public Transport

One of Ealing's attractions is its excellent train and underground links. Local bus routes are comprehensive, although congestion on main roads results in a slow journey into central London. Heathrow airport is 6mi (10km) away.

Underground

The Central line runs east-west across the middle of the borough, the Piccadilly line north-south, and the slower District line serves southern and central areas It's a long trek to the nearest station from Hanwell and West Ealing, and the underground doesn't extend as far as Southall. Typical journey times are as follows:

◆ Acton Town (District line, zone 3) to Paddington, 30 minutes.

◆ Ealing Broadway (Central line, zone 3) to Oxford Circus, 25 minutes.

◆ South Ealing (Piccadilly line, zone 3) to Leicester Square, 27 minutes.

Ealing Civic Centre

Rail

First Great Western operates a service into Paddington and out to Slough, serving all the main towns in the borough (Southall to Paddington takes 15 minutes). Ealing Broadway, West Ealing, Hanwell and Southall are also served by trains to Heathrow, while South Acton and Acton Central are also on the London Overground service from Richmond to North Woolwich, which provides an overground route to City Airport.

Buses

There are plenty cf local bus services covering all areas of the borough. Useful routes include the number 105 (Greenford to Heathrow Airport) and the 112 (Ealing Common to the Brent Cross Shopping Centre in Barnet). The 607 goes to Shepherd's Bush. Night buses include the N207 and N11.

Airports

Below are approximate distances and travel times from Ealing Broadway to the five London airports using public transport.

- ◆ **City** – 17 miles; 60 minutes via Bank.
- ◆ **Gatwick** – 26 miles; 60 minutes via Victoria.
- ◆ **Heathrow** – 6 miles; 20 minutes by rail from Ealing Broadway, or 55 minutes on the Piccadilly Line from South Acton.
- ◆ **Luton** – 25 miles; 80 minutes via Farringdon.
- ◆ **Stansted** – 36 miles; 105 minutes via Liverpool Street.

Roads

The A40 Western Avenue runs across the north of the borough, linking it to central London and Birmingham, but like all London's arterial routes it's often clogged. The A406 North Circular Road, which cuts through Ealing from north to south, is a particular bottleneck where it intersects with the A40 at Hanger Lane. The A4020 Uxbridge Road is the main east-west route and is painfully slow most of the time.

Parking

Controlled Parking Zones (CPZs) operate throughout much of Acton and Ealing, particularly near the stations. There are additional CPZs in Bedford Park, Southall, Greenford and Perivale. The council is proposing to introduce another around Gypsy Corner, where the A40 meets the A400. Resident's parking permits cost either £25 or £45, depending on the zone.

Waste & Recycling

General household rubbish is collected weekly, as are recyclable materials, including aerosols, batteries, cans, glass, newspapers, shoes, telephone directories, textiles and tinfoil. Garden waste is collected fortnightly during the spring and summer. The council has recently introduced a weekly food waste collection scheme for cooked and uncooked food scraps, which are composted. Bulky items such as furniture and kitchen appliances are collected for a fee and there are reuse and recycling centres in Acton, Southall and Greenford Road, Greenford.

> ### LOCAL INFORMATION
>
> **One of the borough's landmarks is Ealing Film Studios, the oldest in the world still in use, and famous for the Ealing comedies and for catapulting actors such as Peter Sellers and Alec Guinness to stardom. It's one of the largest film studios in the UK and is currently being redeveloped with state-of-the-art production facilities.**

Shopping

Ealing Broadway is the borough's shopping capital, with all the main high street names, as well as more specialised shops in two shopping centres and a pedestrianised street with Victorian shop fronts. Shops in West Ealing are concentrated along the Uxbridge Road, where there's a crop of specialist ethnic stores, while Southall boasts the largest Asian shopping centre in London, selling an array of exotic merchandise, from spices to saris, in a bazaar-like environment. Elsewhere, Acton's long high street provides everyday essentials and is gradually attracting more retailers, while Greenford and Hanwell have useful local parades of shops.

Shopping Centres

- ◆ Arcadia Shopping Centre (The Broadway, W5) – high street chains such as Argos and Boots.
- ◆ The Broadway Shopping Mall (The Broadway, W5) – high street chains, including Cargo Homeshops, Mothercare and TK Maxx.

- The Oaks Shopping Centre (High Street, W3) – predominantly discount chains such as Poundstretcher and Savers.

Supermarkets

- Asda in Park Royal.

- Morrisons in Acton.

- Sainsbury's in West Ealing and local stores in South Ealing and Ealing Broadway.

- Tesco in Greenford and at the Bull's Bridge Industrial Estate in Southall (open 24 hours). Express stores in Acton, Ealing, Haven Green, Northfields and Northolt.

- Waitrose in West Ealing.

Markets

- Southall Market (Cattle Market, High Street, UB1) – second-hand goods (Friday, 4am-1pm); general goods (Saturday, 9am-3pm).

- Western International Market (near the Bull's Bridge Tesco, Hayes Road, UB2) – horticultural produce; Monday-Saturday from 2.30am, Sunday 7am-3.30pm.

- Ealing Farmers' Market (Leeland Road, W13); Saturday 9am-1pm.

Entertainment

Ealing excels at festivals, with several taking place in summer, including the Ealing Comedy Festival and two music festivals in Walpole Park during July. Nightlife and restaurants tend to be concentrated in Ealing Broadway, where there's also a choice of night-clubs.

Theatres

- The Questors Theatre (Mattock Lane, W5, ☎ 020-8567 5184, ☐ www.questors.org.uk) is the largest amateur community theatre in Europe.

Cinemas

- Himalaya Palace Cinema (14 South Road, UB1, ☎ 020-8813 8844) – Asian films.

- UGC Ealing (59-61 Uxbridge Road, W5, ☎ 0870-907 0719, ☐ www.ugccinemas.co.uk).

- Vue Cinema (Royale Leisure Park, Western Avenue, W3, ☎ 08712-240 240, ☐ www.myvue. com).

Museums & Galleries

The borough's local history collection is held at the Gunnersbury Park Museum (see **Hounslow**). Other museums include:

- London Motorcycle Museum (Ravenor Farm, Oldfield Lane South, UB6, ☎ 020-8575 6644, ☐ www.london-motorcycle-museum.org) – London's only collection of motorbikes.

- Pitzhanger Manor Gallery & House (Walpole Park, Mattock Lane, W5, ☎ 020-8567 1227) – flagship cultural venue comprising a Grade I listed manor house and a contemporary art gallery.

Libraries

There are 13 local authority libraries in the borough, with one mobile service. Several libraries have restricted opening times, although two are open on Sundays: Southall library and the main library in Ealing Broadway (The Broadway Centre, W5, ☎ 020-8567 3670).

Clubs

Ealing Broadway has a choice of clubs, including:

- Club Boulevard (10 High Street, W5, ☎ 020-8840 0616).

- LA Confidential (1 High Street, W5, ☎ 020-8567 6733).

- The Red Room (42a The Broadway, W5, ☎ 020-8840 3613).

The rest of the borough isn't known for its nightlife, with the exception of Club Missions in Southall (49 High Street, UB1, ☎ 020-8574 5744), although there's plenty of choice in neighbouring boroughs.

Live Music

The largest live music events in the borough are the annual Ealing Blues and Roots Festival and the JVC Ealing Jazz Festival, which take place in Walpole Park on consecutive days during July. Both are free festivals and the largest of their kind in the UK. A few pubs present regular music nights, such as:

◆ Baroque (94 Uxbridge Road, W13, ☎ 020-8567 7346, 🖳 www.baroque-ealing.co.uk) – live jazz Thursday and Friday.

◆ The Redback (264 High Street, W3, ☎ 020-8896 1458) – popular Aussie hangout.

◆ The Spinning Wheel (227 Northfield Avenue, W13, ☎ 020-8567 8348) – Irish music.

Pubs

The widest choice of pubs and bars is along the Uxbridge Road. Chains include All Bar One and O'Neill's in Ealing Broadway and there's a JD Wetherspoon in Acton. There are also several Irish pubs such as Lavin's in Hanwell (97 Uxbridge Road, W7), known for its Karaoke evenings. Southall isn't renowned for good bars, although there's the infamous Glassy Junction (97 South Road, UB1, ☎ 020-8574 1626), which claims to be the first pub in the UK to accept rupees and is decorated in Bollywood style. Pubs of note include the Ealing Park Tavern (222 South Ealing Road, W5, ☎ 020-8758 1879), an elegant gastropub, and the Red Lion (13 St Mary's Road, W5, ☎ 020-8567 2541), popular with TV crews from the nearby studios.

Restaurants

Not surprisingly, Southall is where you can find some of the best and most authentic Asian cuisine in London. Among over 20 Indian restaurants, a number are exceptional, including the award-winning Gifto's Lahore Karahi Restaurant (162 Southall Broadway, UB1, ☎ 020-8813 8669), which is always packed and a worthy competitor for the more prestigious curry houses in central London.

Ealing Broadway offers the best choice of eateries, including branches of upmarket Carluccio's (5 The Green, W5, ☎ 020-8566 4458) and Café Rouge (17 The Green, W5, ☎ 020-8579 2788). Ethnic cooking includes Polish, Caribbean and Japanese, as well as the usual Thai, Chinese and Indian. Of particular note is Sushi-Hiro (1 Station Parade, Uxbridge Road, W5, ☎ 020-8896 3175), which is listed in the *Good Food Guide*.

Sports Facilities

There are eleven council-funded sports centres in Ealing's main towns, where the facilities include:

◆ Swimming pools at Acton, Dormers Wells, Gurnell Leisure Centre and Northolt

◆ Indoor sports halls at Acton, Greenford, Hanwell and Southall.

◆ Running and athletics tracks in Perivale.

◆ Multi-use sports facilities at Southall.

There's an all-weather Astroturf pitch at the new sports centre on the site of the West London Academy in Northolt and the Reynolds Sports Centre at Acton High School, both of which are open to the general public. Many sports can be played in the borough's parks, and there are golf courses in Greenford, Hanwell, Horsenden Hill (Perivale), Northolt and North Ealing. Horse riding is possible in Ealing and canoeing on the Grand Union Canal. There are branches of the main health clubs in Acton, Ealing and Greenford, and tenpin bowing at the Acton Mega Bowl.

Green Spaces

Ealing has a varied landscape, including woods, meadows, farms, parks and several golf courses. Much of the open space is in the north, where there are fine views from Horsenden Hill. The new Northolt and Greenford Country Park, created from 270 acres (110ha) of largely derelict land, includes water features, play areas, wildlife habitats and a network of footpaths. Other attractive walking areas are along the banks of the River Brent from Brentham to Brentford, and along the Grand Union Canal in the south-west.

The borough's parks range from small recreation grounds to lush Victorian gardens and offer a range of facilities for all the family. Hanwell's Brent Lodge Park, for example, is a haven for children, with its animal centre and Millennium Maze, Perivale Park is devoted to sports pitches, and the Glade Lane Canal Side Park in Southall has conservation habitats, a turf maze and a BMX moonscape. Ealing's premier park is pretty Walpole Park, with rose and water gardens and the Pitzhanger Manor Museum (see above).

Enfield

EN1, EN2, EN3, EN4 (part), N9, N11 (part), N13,
N14 (part), N18, N21

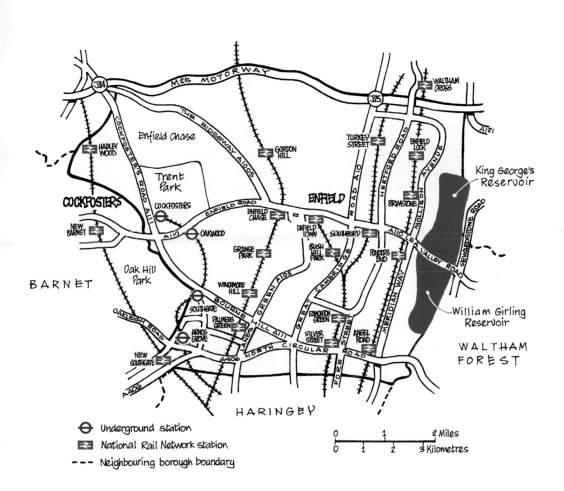

Underground station
National Rail Network station
- - - Neighbouring borough boundary

0   1   2 Miles
0 1 2 3 Kilometres

At a Glance

Best for: schools, open spaces, public transport

Not so good for: deprivation, culture, nightlife, few tube stations

Who lives there: middle-class couples, first-time buyers, singles

Housing stock: mostly terraces, some Victorian/Edwardian, public housing

Housing costs: relatively inexpensive

General Information

Council Offices: Civic Centre, Silver Street, Enfield, EN1 3XY (☎ 020-8366 6565)

CAA Assessment: (see 🖥 http://oneplace.direct.gov.uk > Search by area > London > Enfield)

Controlling Party: Labour

Website: 🖥 www.enfield.gov.uk

Council Tax 2010/11: £2,350 (Band G), £2,820 (Band H)

Main Areas/towns: Edmonton, Enfield Town, Hadley Wood, Oakwood, Palmers Green, Ponders End, Southgate, Winchmore Hill

Postcodes: EN1, EN2, EN3, EN4 (part), N9, N11 (part), N13, N14 (part), N18, N21

Population & Ethnicity: 287,600, one of London's most populous boroughs. Some 20 per cent of residents belong to an ethnic minority, mostly Indian and Afro-Caribbean, many of whom live in and around Enfield Town. The borough is popular with middle-class families and young professionals.

Unemployment: 9.7 per cent (London average is 8.2 per cent)

Overview

London's most northerly borough, Enfield stretches from just south of the North Circular Road to the M25, and from Hadley Wood in the west to Edmonton in the east. Around a third of the borough is green belt land, with country parks, gardens, farmland, golf courses and playing fields making an attractive backdrop in the northern and western districts. The Lea Valley area has traditionally been industrial land.

The borough is a mixture of salubrious suburbs in the west and grim council estates in the east, divided by the busy A10. The smarter parts are Palmers Green, Oakwood and Winchmore Hill, while the most expensive and sought-after is Hadley Wood, home to several wealthy celebrities. Enfield Town is more like a county town than a London suburb, and has many mature residents. In a 2005 *Yellow Pages* survey, the town emerged as the best place to live for 'empty nesters' thanks to its range of shopping and leisure facilities.

In the east of the borough, Edmonton and Ponders End are rundown industrial areas, with large tracts of council housing, which are currently being regenerated.

LOCAL INFORMATION

After the Norman Conquest, Enfield and Edmonton were mentioned in the Domesday Book (1086), both having churches and 400 and 300 inhabitants respectively. Enfield is also described as having a 'parc' (Enfield Old Park), a heavily forested area for hunting, which was key to Enfield's existence in the Middle Ages.

Development Plans

In 2007, Enfield Town centre completed a major redevelopment project under the name PalaceXchange, which updated the Palace Gardens Shopping Centre, while adding to the existing retail area and providing a second multi-storey car park and new road layout. Current developments include a new shopping centre in Edmonton Green, plus adjacent housing and communal facilities, which include health and leisure centres, a supermarket and new civic features.

Development of the Upper Lea Valley industrial districts (in Enfield and Haringey) is underway and more investment will be forthcoming over the next decade, with plans to encourage new businesses and shops and demolish some of the council estates.

Residential Areas

Terraced houses comprise over 40 per cent of properties in the borough, most of which are Victorian. A further one-third of the housing stock is flats, predominantly purpose-built, with Victorian, Edwardian and inter-war semi-detached houses making up another 20 per cent. Detached properties, some very large, tend to be situated around Hadley Wood, Winchmore Hill and Enfield Town.

Edmonton and Ponders End (N9)

This is the cheapest part of the borough and property includes Victorian former railway workers' cottages, '30s semis and flats in tower blocks. With a typical one-bedroom flat costing around £125,000, this is a good area for first-time buyers (and they can equip their homes

inexpensively from a new local Ikea). Ponders End is slightly more expensive than Edmonton. Most inhabitants are local families.

Enfield (EN1, EN2)

Solidly middle class and respectable, this is a pleasant town surrounded by parkland. Around the town centre are mostly Victorian terraces, Edwardian semis and purpose-built blocks of flats. A three-bedroom semi costs around £275,000. The most desirable areas border the town park, where there are larger houses (including some Georgian homes) set in generous gardens. Property becomes less expensive in the eastern districts of the town, close to the A10. Enfield Island Village at Enfield Lock (site of the former Royal Small Arms Factory) is being redeveloped for housing.

Hadley Wood (EN4)

Perched on the edge of green belt land, this exclusive area is popular with wealthy families and members of the Arsenal and Tottenham Hotspur football teams, who enjoy the attractive surroundings and relatively short commute to work. Large, inter-war detached houses predominate, with some Georgian houses bordering Monken Hadley Common.

Oakwood, Southgate and Winchmore Hill (N14, N21)

Much of the property in these areas dates from the inter-war period, so there's a mix of half-timbered 'mock Tudor' houses, some modernist flat-roofed blocks of flats and lots of '30s semis. Some large parks and open spaces, all with excellent leisure facilities, make Oakwood and Southgate particularly popular with middle-class families and professional couples. To the east of Southgate, Winchmore Hill is equally prosperous and quiet, with some large, upmarket Edwardian houses, Victorian terraces, inter-war semis and conversion flats.

Palmers Green (N13, N14)

A rich choice of flats in converted Edwardian houses, as well as new purpose-built, low-rise developments, make this a good area for first-time buyers. Cheaper than Southgate and Winchmore Hill, with some lovely well-maintained parks and sports facilities, this is a popular location for families. There are also plenty of '30s semis, some with sizeable gardens, away from the centre.

Property Costs

Property Prices

House prices are around the London average. The table below shows average prices in the borough:

Detached: £732,282
Semi-detached: £351,075
Terraced: £250,988
Flat: £186,287

Rental Costs

The table below shows average monthly rents in the borough:

House 5+ bed: £2,900
House 4-5 bed: £1,600
House 3-4 bed: £1,250
House 2-3 bed: £1,150
Flat 2-bed: £900
Flat 1-bed: £700

Crime

Enfield has a fairly low crime rate – it's ranked 19th out of 33 boroughs for overall crime – although it has the ninth-highest rate of vehicle crime in London. The police station HQ is in Edmonton (462 Fore Street, N9, ☎ 0300-123 1212), with other stations in Enfield, Ponders End, Southgate and Winchmore Hill.

To compare crime rates throughout London, see the table in **Appendix D**.

Health

NHS services in the borough are provided by the Enfield Primary Care Trust. For a full list of doctors, dentists and clinics, visit ⌨ www.nhs.uk.

To see how the Primary Care Trust compares with others in London, see the table in **Appendix D**.

Doctors & Dentists

◆ There are 72 NHS GP surgeries, providing a range of clinics and health services.

◆ Enfield has 65 dental and orthodontic practices, around half of which accept new NHS patients.

Hospitals

◆ Chase Farm Hospital (127 The Ridgeway, EN2, (☎ 0845-111 4000, ⌨ www.bcf.nhs.uk) – A&E.
◆ North Middlesex Hospital (Sterling Way, N18, ☎ 020-8887 2000, ⌨ www.northmid.nhs.uk) – NHS walk-in centre.

Private Medical Facilities

◆ The Priory Hospital North London (Grovelands House, The Bourne, N14, ☎ 020-8882 8191, ⌨ www.prioryhealthcare.co.uk).

◆ The North London Nuffield Hospital (Cavell Drive, Uplands Park Road, EN2, ☎ 020-8366 2122, ⌨ www.nuffieldhospitals.org.uk).

◆ The Kings Oak Hospital (Chase Farm North Side, The Ridgeway, EN2, ☎ 020-8370 9500, ⌨ www.bmihealthcare.co.uk).

To find a private GP, visit ⌨ www.privatehealth.co.uk.

Schools

Education standards in the borough are variable. In the 2009 school league tables, primary schools were placed 23rd out of the 33 London boroughs (98th out of 150 UK local authorities) and secondary schools 22nd (73rd in the UK).

To compare schools throughout London, see the table in **Appendix D**.

Pre-school

There's a wide choice of nurseries and playgroups operated by private organisations, plus 33 nursery classes in local schools.

State Schools

First schools: 65 infant, junior and primary schools, of which 17 are voluntary aided. In 2009, the Our Lady of Lourdes RC Primary School, St. Andrew's C of E Primary School and the Hadley Wood Primary School had excellent results in the UK Key Stage 2 exam.

Secondary schools: One selective school and 17 comprehensives. Four schools are voluntary aided, all have sixth forms and six have specialist status. The top performer in 2009 was the selective Latymer School in Edmonton, which was one of the top schools in the country for GCSE and A level results, as well as added value. A new City Academy (the Oasis) in Enfield Lock opened in September 2007.

Special schools: Six schools cater for students with physical disabilities and learning difficulties.

Private Schools

There are eight private schools in the borough, including a Muslim school for pupils aged up to 18, and Essential Achievers, a special school for pupils aged 11-16 in Winchmore Hill. Two schools cater for secondary pupils: St John's Preparatory and Senior School in Enfield and Palmers Green High School in Winchmore Hill, which had excellent GCSE results in 2009.

Further Education

◆ Enfield College (🖥 www.enfield.ac.uk).

◆ Southgate College (🖥 www.southgate.ac.uk).

Higher Education

◆ Capel Manor College (🖥 www.capel.ac.uk) is a specialist horticultural college.

◆ Middlesex University (🖥 www.mdx.ac.uk) has campuses in Enfield and Trent Park.

Public Transport

The west of the borough is served by the Piccadilly underground line and there are overground rail services from Moorgate and Liverpool Street stations to most areas. Few buses make the slow journey to central London.

Underground

The Piccadilly line terminates at Cockfosters and serves Oakwood, Southgate (with its famous '30s circular station) and Arnos Grove. The nearest

station to Palmers Green is Bounds Green. Typical journey times are as follows:

◆ Cockfosters (Piccadilly line, zone 5) to Heathrow, 84 minutes.

◆ Southgate (Piccadilly line, zone 4) to Piccadilly Circus, 32 minutes.

Rail

Two train lines run through the borough:

◆ WAGN railway operates services from Hertfordshire, Cambridgeshire and the north-east into Moorgate and Kings Cross, stopping at several stations (Winchmore Hill to Moorgate, 68 minutes).

◆ 'One' railway provides services from Essex, Hertfordshire and Cambridgeshire (Enfield Town to Liverpool Street, 27 minutes).

 FAMOUS RESIDENTS

Famous former and current residents of Winchmore Hill include singers Frank Ifield, Cliff Richard, Rod Stewart and Paul Young; Keith Moon (musician); Ted Ray (actor); Sir Roy Strong (historian & writer); and Ross & Norris McWhirter, founder editors of the *Guinness Book of Records***.**

Buses

The number 259 bus runs from Edmonton Green to Kings Cross, while the 341 travels from Upper Edmonton to Waterloo. There are no services to central London from western districts. The borough is served by three night buses: the N29, N91 and N279. Local bus services include routes into Hertfordshire and the 102 to the Brent Cross Shopping Centre.

Airports

Below are distances and travel times from Enfield Town to the five London airports using public transport.

◆ **City** – 12 miles; 70 minutes via Bank.

◆ **Gatwick** – 35 miles; 96 minutes via Victoria.

♦ **Heathrow** – 21 miles; 95 minutes via Paddington.

♦ **Luton** – 21 miles; 91 minutes via Kings Cross.

♦ **Stansted** – 21 miles; 70 minutes via Edmonton Green.

Roads

The main A10 bisects Enfield from north to south and provides easy access to the M25 at junction 25. The A406 North Circular Road cuts across the southern end of the borough. Traffic hotspots include a one-way system in Enfield Town.

The council promotes cycling with 15mi (24km) of dedicated cycle routes.

Parking

Controlled Parking Zones operate in Arnos Grove, Bush Hill Park, Enfield Town, Gordon Hill, Grange Park, Oakwood and Palmers Green. Residents parking permits cost £30 per annum in most areas, rising to £70 in Enfield Town and Palmers Green.

Waste & Recycling

General household rubbish is collected weekly, together with recyclable materials and compost material. Recyclables include bags, cans, clothes, paper and cardboard, plastic bottles, shoes and tinfoil. The council collects bulky items, such as furniture, for a small fee. There are two household amenity sites: Barrowell Green Recycling Centre in Winchmore Hill and Carterhatch Lane Recycling Centre in Enfield Town.

Shopping

The high street in Enfield Town has a good range of shops, including many well-known chains in the Palace Gardens Centre (see below), as well as traditional and specialist shops. In a 2005 *Yellow Pages* survey, Enfield was one of the top ten high streets for variety and choice. The other main shopping areas are at Angel Edmonton, Edmonton Green, Palmers Green and Southgate, offering sensible but uninspiring shops mostly selling daily essentials. There are several retail parks offering DIY and electrical/electronics shops and a new branch of Ikea. Winchmore Hill has an attractive high street with a few antique shops.

Shopping Centres

♦ Edmonton Green Shopping Centre (Market Square, N9, ☎ 020-8803 4414) – '60s shopping mall with chains, including Boots and Woolworths, and a range of cheap and cut price shops; currently being expanded.

♦ Palace Gardens Shopping Centre (Cecil Road, EN1, ☎ 020-8367 1210) – a selection of big-name retailers and a department store.

There are retail parks in Brimsdown, Enfield, Edmonton and New Southgate.

Supermarkets

♦ Asda in Southgate.

♦ Marks & Spencer in Southgate.

♦ Morrisons in Enfield and Palmers Green.

♦ Sainsbury's in Enfield and Winchmore Hill.

♦ Tesco in Enfield and Lea Valley (both open 24 hours). There's a smaller Tesco store in Ponders End, a Metro store in Edmonton and Express stores in Enfield, Enfield Lock, Oakwood and Winchmore Hill.

Markets

♦ Edmonton Market (Edmonton Shopping Centre, N9) – fresh produce, general household goods; Monday to Saturday.

♦ Enfield Market (Market Square, Church Street, EN1) – variety of household and crafts goods, including clothing, fabrics, flowers, fruit and vegetables, jewellery, luggage and meat; Mondays, and Thursday to Saturday.

There's a weekly farmers' market in Palmers Green (in the car park by Palmers Green station, N13); Sunday 10am-2pm.

LOCAL INFORMATION

Enfield has been a bustling market town since 1303, when the market charter was granted by Edward I. Today, with its cobbled market square, St Andrews Church, and the New River wending its way through the centre, it retains the feel of a traditional country town.

Entertainment

Enfield has a reasonable selection of entertainment options, including several cinemas and museums. The Millfield Arts Centre in Edmonton has a theatre

◆ Gallery Fore (107 Fore Street, N18, ☎ 020-8350 6653) – art gallery showcasing the work of local artists.

◆ MoDA – Museum of Domestic Design and Architecture (Middlesex University Cat Hill Campus, Cat Hill, EN4, ☎ 020-8411 4394, 💻 www.moda.mdx.ac.uk).

◆ Platform Gallery (Platform 1, Palmers Green Station, N13, ☎ 020-8350 6653, 💻 www. enfieldartspartnership.org) – unusual space for art exhibitions.

◆ RSA Island Centre (Enfield Island Village, 3 Island Centre Way, EN3, ☎ 01992-854 321, 💻 www. rsaiv.co.uk) – exhibition about the Royal Small Arms Factory and 18th century clock tower.

(see below) and exhibition space, and offers a range of arts courses for all age groups. In summer, the New River Festival (💻 www.enfield.gov.uk/ newriverfestival) takes place on the banks of the river and features live music, dance, mazes and circus skills workshops. There are plenty of pubs and restaurants in the borough, but few night-clubs.

Theatres

◆ Chicken Shed Theatre (Chase Side, N14, ☎ 020-8351 6161, 💻 www.chickenshed.org.uk) – award-winning children's and youth theatre.

◆ Millfield Theatre (Millfield Arts Centre, Silver Street, N18, ☎ 020-8807 6680, 💻 www. millfieldtheatre.co.uk) – popular theatre presenting concerts, dance shows, pantomimes, plays and talks.

Cinemas

◆ UCI Cinemas (Picketts Lock Lane, N9, ☎ 0871-224 4007, 💻 www.uci.co.uk).

◆ UGC Enfield (Southbury Leisure Park, 208 Southbury Road, EN1, ☎ 0871-200 2000, 💻 www.ugccinemas.co.uk).

Museums & Galleries

Enfield's Museum Service organises a number of temporary exhibitions in different venues around the borough. Permanent museums and galleries include:

◆ Forty Hall (Forty Hill, EN2, ☎ 020-8363 4774) – 17th and 18th century furniture and pictures, ceramics, glass, maps, local history displays and a walled rose garden.

LOCAL INFORMATION

Among the borough's claims to fame are that Barclays Bank in Enfield was the first place in the world to have an ATM, officially opened by actor Reg Varney in June 1967 (marked by a plaque).

Libraries

There are 16 local authority libraries in the borough, some with restricted opening times, and one mobile library. The largest is the Enfield Town Library (39, London Road, Enfield, EN2, ☎ 020-8379 8341), which opens seven days per week.

Clubs

Although Enfield isn't noted for its club scene, there's garage and hip hop at ClubVolts (formerly Club Xenon) in Edmonton (169-171 Fore Street, N18, ☎ 020-8884 0421) and various sounds at the Townhouse in Enfield (48 London Road, EN2, ☎ 020-8367 1920). Tottenham's clubs are within easy reach (see **Haringey**).

Live Music

Large concerts take place at the Millfield Theatre (see above) and several pubs provide smaller venues, including:

◆ The Fox (413 Green Lanes, N13, ☎ 020-8886 9674) – previously home to a comedy club, now concentrating on live gigs.

◆ The Hop Poles (320 Baker Street, EN1, ☎ 020-8363 0381) – good weekend entertainment.

◆ The Starlight Suite (The Stadium, Southbury Road, EN1, ☎ 020-8292 0665) – evening cabaret.

◆ The Waggon (Southgate, 107 Chase Side, N14, ☎ 020-8882 8242) – live jazz on Sundays.

Pubs

The best choice of pubs is around Enfield, Palmers Green, Southgate and Winchmore Hill, with a mixture of chains and independents. Ye Old Cherry Tree (The Green, N14, ☎ 020-8886 1808) is something of a landmark in the area and claimed by locals as the best pub for miles around, while the Woodman (128 Bourne Hill, N13, ☎ 020-8882 0294) is popular and crowded. The Kings Head in Winchmore Hill (The Green, N21, ☎ 020-8886 1988) is a modern-style bar. Edmonton has few good pubs.

Restaurants

There's a wide range of restaurants in the borough, notably around Enfield, Palmers Green and Winchmore Hill; Edmonton, however, has few restaurants. Some of the better restaurants include the award-winning Café Anjou (394 Green Lanes, N13, ☎ 020-8886 7267) and Taste of Raj (76 Aldermans Hill, N13, ☎ 020-8886 8773), which is listed in the Gourmet Guide. The Beautiful South restaurant in Enfield (25A Windmill Hill, EN2, ☎ 020-8367 1414) is also highly commended. Among several restaurants around Southgate, La Paella offers a fun night out, with flamenco dancing once a month (9 The Broadway, N14, ☎ 020-8882 7868), while Romna Gate (14 The Broadway, N14, ☎ 020-8882 6700) has been recommended by the Good Food Guide and the Curry Guide magazine.

All the usual chains are present in the area, including Café Rouge in Southgate, Café Uno and Enzos in Enfield, and Jim Thompson's in Winchmore Hill. There are plenty of ethnic restaurants, including Chinese, Greek, Indian, Polish, Thai and Turkish, and there's an unusual 'fusion' dining room in Ponders End, Oriental Fusion (252a High Street, EN3, ☎ 020-8804 5433), where you can eat Indian, Chinese and Thai food under one roof.

Sports Facilities

There are seven council-funded leisure centres in Enfield: the Albany, Arnos Grove, the Aspire Sport and Fitness Centre, Cockfosters, Edmonton, Southgate and Southbury, providing a wide range of sporting activities, including:

◆ Swimming pools at the Albany, Arnos Grove, Edmonton, Southbury and Southgate.

◆ Indoor sports halls at Edmonton, Cockfosters and Southbury.

◆ Squash courts at Edmonton and Cockfosters.

◆ An all-weather Astroturf pitch at Southbury.

Many sports can be played in the borough's parks, and activities include horse riding in Trent Park and Forty Hill Park, several public and private golf courses, a David Lloyd Leisure Centre in Enfield and branches of several well-known gym chains.

Green Spaces

Enfield has some lovely countryside within its borders, as well as over 120 parks and recreation grounds, and walking trails across farmland and along the New River Loop. Trent Country Park in Oakwood is the largest open space and incorporates the wooded remnants of the former royal hunting grounds at Enfield Chase. It provides several sporting facilities and nature trails. Nearby, Whitewebbs Park and Forty Hall Park provide acres of parkland, woodland and formal gardens, including rare and exotic plants at Myddelton House Gardens (Bulls Cross, EN2, ☎ 01992-702 200).

LOCAL INFORMATION

Broomfield Park

One of the prettiest parks in the borough, Broomfield Park in Palmers Green dates back to the 16th century when it was a royal hunting ground used by James I. It spans 500 acres (200ha) and includes playing fields, wooded areas, formal gardens, lakes and ponds (used by model boat enthusiasts), and a crazy golf course. Sadly, the fine Elizabethan Broomfield House at the centre of the park still awaits restoration, after being ravaged by fires in 1984 and the 1990s.

Greenwich

SE2 (part), SE3, SE7, SE9 (part), SE10, SE18, SE28 (part)

At a Glance

Best for: affordable housing, open spaces, riverside homes

Not so good for: deprivation, education, traffic congestion, parking, crime, no tube

Who lives there: working class, young families, singles, middle-class families

Housing stock: Period properties, council housing, new flats, terraces

Housing costs: moderate

General Information

Council Offices: 29-37 Wellington Street, Woolwich, London SE18 6PS (☎ 020-8854 8888)

CAA Assessment: (see 💻 http://oneplace.direct.gov.uk > Search by area > London > Greenwich)

Controlling Party: Labour

Website: 💻 www.greenwich.gov.uk

Council Tax 2010/11: £2,151 (Band G), £2,581 (Band H)

Main Areas/towns: Abbey Wood, Blackheath Park, Charlton, Eltham, Greenwich, Kidbrooke, Plumstead, Woolwich, Thamesmead

Postcodes: SE2 (part), SE3, SE7, SE9 (part), SE10, SE18, SE28 (part)

Population & Ethnicity: 222,900, with around 18 per cent of residents from an ethnic minority, principally Afro-Caribbean and Asian. The largest Asian community is in Woolwich. While Greenwich town attracts the affluent middle classes, the borough's population is mostly working class families.

Unemployment: 10.3 per cent (London average is 8.2 per cent)

Overview

Greenwich is a curious mixture of the historic and the futuristic, the grand and the derelict. While affluent Greenwich town is one of London's principal tourist attractions, home to a World Heritage Site that encompasses the Royal Observatory, National Maritime Museum and Royal Naval College, much of the borough is one of England's most deprived areas.

Stretching eastwards along the River Thames to Thamesmead, and southwards to suburban Eltham, the borough languished during the latter half of the 20th century as its major armaments and manufacturing industries declined. Now its fortunes are on the turn, as it begins to benefit from massive regeneration projects. One of these is bringing new homes and jobs to the Greenwich Peninsula, site of the Millennium Dome, which has been reinvented as a 20,000-seat sports and entertainment arena.

New housing schemes and improvements (see below) are transforming Woolwich, which has also benefited from new links across the river and the DLR in recent years.

LOCAL INFORMATION

Greenwich is one of five host boroughs for the 2012 London Olympics and will stage events at the Royal Artillery Barracks (Shooting), Greenwich Park (Equestrianism) and the O2-former Millennium Dome (Gymnastics; Basketball).

Development Plans

There's a considerable amount of new development in Greenwich, including up to 1,500 homes in the Millennium Village on Greenwich's so-called Peninsula (its north-west corner, which protrudes into a bend in the River Thames) near the O2 Arena (formerly the Millennium Dome). The development began in 2000 (over 1,000 homes had been built by 2010) and is expected to be completed by 2015.

Greenwich Peninsula extends to 300 acres (121ha) with 1.6mi (2.6km) of river frontage, equivalent to the distance from Waterloo to London Bridge. Around £5bn will be invested to create a real community, with schools, health and childcare facilities, and almost 50 acres (20ha) of green space and parkland. The project is expected to create some 30,000 jobs (including 5,000 during the construction phase) and buildings will eventually include 10,000 homes (including 3,800 for key workers and those on a range of incomes), 3.5mnft² (325,000m²) of office space and over 150 shops and restaurants.

There are plans for 2,500 more homes along Gallions Reach to add to the recently built 'starter' homes at Thamesmead North. Several of the more architecturally interesting buildings in and around Woolwich are also being renovated and converted into housing.

Residential Areas

Grand Georgian and Victorian houses in West Greenwich give way to small Victorian terraces as you move east, particularly around Woolwich and Plumstead. Much of Thamesmead and Abbey Wood consists of council estates, while Eltham in the south was largely developed between the wars. The majority of new developments are along the riverside stretches, from the Millennium Village on the Greenwich Peninsula to the Thames Gateway housing scheme at Thamesmead. Some 42 per cent of properties in the borough are flats (mostly purpose-built), 39 per cent are terraced houses, 16 per cent are semi-detached houses and just 3 per cent are detached houses.

Abbey Wood & Thamesmead (SE2, SE28)

Streets of small terraces and large council estates characterise Abbey Wood, with the most popular properties the few larger homes around Bostall Heath. Thamesmead was first developed 30 years ago as a riverside 'urban village'. Originally, it was isolated and unpopular, but new transport links have encouraged developers to re-examine its potential, and stylish new housing schemes are being built, attracting investors, young families and couples. Prices are low for London, with two-bedroom flats costing around £135,000.

Blackheath Park & Kidbrooke (SE3)

Although Blackheath Village is in Lewisham, the area around Blackheath Park is in Greenwich. Dotted with sports grounds, this district features some of the area's smartest homes on the gated Cator Estate, with a mixture of early 19th century villas, '30s detached houses and a collection of highly praised Span developments. To the south is the '70s Ferrier council estate, its tower blocks due for a much needed overhaul. On the other side of the A2, Kidbrooke is more suburban, featuring '30s family semis with large gardens. Council estates border Eltham.

Charlton (SE7)

Situated on high ground overlooking the Thames, central Charlton's pretty Victorian streets give way to '30s family houses in the south, some of which are detached. Council estates can be found near Charlton Park, while New Charlton to the north is largely commercial and industrial.

Eltham (SE9)

This family suburb features mostly '30s houses, with a few large Edwardian homes near Oxleas Wood. Busy roads carve up the area, although there's plenty of green space and even a Jacobean Palace south of the high street, where some of the most desirable houses are. Large council estates lie towards Kidbrooke, although many properties are now privately owned.

Greenwich (SE10)

Pretty, historic and colourful, the main drawback of living in Greenwich town is the number of tourists that regularly pack its streets. However, away from the main attractions, impressive Georgian and Victorian terraces to the west of Greenwich Park remain highly desirable, particularly among wealthy middle-class families. East Greenwich is less grand, but more affordable, with numerous Victorian terraces as well as low-rise council estates. The low-energy housing of the Millennium Village is proving popular, and thousands more new homes are planned for the Greenwich Peninsula.

Woolwich & Plumstead (SE18, SE28)

Once a thriving industrial town, hilly Woolwich has been depressed since the late '60s when munitions manufacturing at the Royal Arsenal shrank and unemployment soared. The closure of the factory in 1994 paved the way for 3,000 new homes and leisure facilities, which, together with improved transport across the Thames has made the area seriously worth considering for Docklands workers. A modern three-bedroom townhouse starts at £235,000 and older terraces and ex-council homes cost around £185,000 for three bedrooms. Overshadowed by Belmarsh Prison, Plumstead is a down-at-heel area, where the best homes lie in roads on Shooters Hill and near Plumstead Common.

Property Costs

Property Prices

Greenwich town and Blackheath Park are the most expensive districts, while Abbey Wood and Thamesmead are the cheapest.

The table below shows average property prices in the borough:

Detached: £606,033
Semi-detached: £309,538
Terraced: £250,474
Flat: £228,681

Rental Costs

The table below shows average monthly rents in the borough:

House 5+ bed: £2,600
House 4-5 bed: £2,150
House 3-4 bed: £1,750
House 2- bed: £1,400
Flat 2-bed: £1,300
Flat 1-bed: £950

Crime

Greenwich's crime rates are around average for London, although it has the tenth-highest rate for stolen cars and for violent crime. Woolwich town centre and surrounding council estates are crime hot spots, where an increasing number of street wardens are helping to keep incidents under control.

The main police station is in Greenwich (31 Royal Hill, SE10, ☎ 020-8855 1212), with other stations in Eltham, Plumstead, Thamesmead and Woolwich.

To compare crime rates throughout London, see the table in **Appendix D**.

Health

NHS services in the borough are provided by the Greenwich Primary Care Trust. For a full list of doctors, dentists and clinics, visit 🖥 www.nhs.uk.

To see how the Primary Care Trust compares with others in London, see the table in **Appendix D**.

Doctors & Dentists

♦ There are 61 NHS GP surgeries, providing a range of clinics and health services.

♦ The borough has 40 dental and orthodontic practices, around half of which accept new NHS patients.

Hospitals

The Queen Elizabeth Hospital in Woolwich (Stadium Road, SE18, ☎ 020-8836 6000, 🖥 www.queenelizabeth.nhs.uk) has A&E facilities and a minor injuries unit.

Private Medical Facilities

For general hospital treatment, the nearest private facility is the Blackheath Hospital (see **Lewisham**). To find a private GP, visit 🖥 www. privatehealth.co.uk.

FAMOUS RESIDENTS

Famous people associated with Greenwich include Henry VIII and Elizabeth I (who were both born at Greenwich Palace), Cecil Day-Lewis (poet), Boy George (singer), Bob Hope (comedian), Dr Samuel Johnson (compiler of the first English dictionary), E Nesbit (novelist) and Sir John Vanbrugh (architect, designer of Blenheim Palace).

Schools

Educational standards in Greenwich are below the national average. In the 2009 school league tables, primary schools were placed 24th out of the 33 London boroughs (100th out of 150 UK local authorities) and secondary schools 32nd (133rd in the UK).

To compare schools throughout London, see the table in **Appendix D**.

Pre-school

There's a wide choice of private playgroups and nursery schools, with council-run nurseries and nursery classes attached to most primary schools.

State Schools

First schools: 65 primary schools, of which 17 are voluntary aided or controlled.

Secondary schools: 13 comprehensive schools, five of which are voluntary aided or controlled. Seven schools have sixth forms and eight have specialist status. The top performers in 2009 were Thomas More RC Comprehensive in Eltham and St Ursula's Convent School in Greenwich.

Special schools: Four special schools cater for students with physical disabilities and learning difficulties, and there are another eight specialist units attached to mainstream schools.

Private Schools

The borough has a handful of private schools, with four catering for secondary age pupils. The top performers in 2009 were Blackheath High School (noted for added value), Colfes School in Eltham (one of the top UK schools for A level results) and Plumstead Manor/Negus School.

Further Education

◆ Greenwich Community College in Plumstead (🖥 www.gcc.ac.uk).

◆ Shooters Hill Post-16 Campus (🖥 www.shootershill.ac.uk) is a sixth form centre.

Higher Education

◆ Greenwich University (🖥 www.gre.ac.uk).

◆ Trinity College of Music (🖥 www.tcm.ac.uk) is a renowned music college located in the Old Royal Naval College.

Public Transport

The Jubilee underground line serves North Greenwich and the Docklands Light Railway (DLR) serves central Greenwich, with an

O2 Arena

extension to Woolwich Arsenal being built that will provide a direct link to City Airport. Elsewhere, residents rely on rail and bus services, which are better in some areas than others. River buses are useful for trips to Westminster.

Underground

The Jubilee line touches the north-west corner of Greenwich, while the DLR makes two stops in Greenwich town. Typical journey times:

- North Greenwich (Jubilee line, zone 2) to Green Park, 20 minutes.
- Greenwich (DLR, zone 3) to Canary Wharf, 11 minutes.

Rail

South Eastern Trains runs services from London Bridge, Charing Cross and Victoria to the main towns in the borough, although some areas – such as Thamesmead – are a long way from a station. Typical journeys take 20 minutes to London Bridge and 35 minutes to Victoria.

Buses

As well as local services, several routes serve central London, East London and Bexleyheath. Useful buses include numbers 53 (Plumstead to Westminster), 108 (Greenwich to Stratford), 188 (Greenwich to Holborn) and 486 (Greenwich to Bexleyheath). Night buses include the N1, N21 and N89.

River Transport

The Woolwich Ferry for cars and foot passengers is a free service connecting Woolwich with North Woolwich across the river. Journey time is 15 minutes. Daily commuter river services run between Greenwich and Savoy Pier (Waterloo Bridge), while additional services run to Embankment and Westminster in the west, and to Barrier Gardens in the east. There's also a fast service between the Royal Arsenal Pier, Canary Wharf and central London. River cruises from Greenwich to Gravesend and Tilbury run during the summer.

Airports

Below are approximate distances and journey times from Greenwich to the five London airports using public transport.

- **City** – 2 miles; 30 minutes via Westferry.
- **Gatwick** – 24 miles; 65 minutes via London Bridge.
- **Heathrow** – 22 miles; 85 minutes via Paddington.
- **Luton** – 34 miles; 80 minutes on the Thameslink service from London Bridge.
- **Stansted** – 30 miles; 95 minutes via Liverpool Street.

LOCAL INFORMATION

Greenwich is best known for its maritime history and for giving its name to the Greenwich Meridian (0° longitude) and Greenwich Mean Time (GMT). The meridian passing through Greenwich was internationally adopted as the earth's zero of longitude in 1884. Greenwich Mean Time (GMT) refers to mean solar time at the Royal Observatory in Greenwich (commissioned in 1675 by King Charles II), which is used as the basis for calculating time throughout the world.

Roads

The River Thames is the main cause of congestion in Greenwich, with both of the main routes across it (the free Woolwich Ferry and the Blackwall Tunnel) infamous for creating bottlenecks. The A205 South Circular Road crosses the river by ferry to connect with the North Circular, while the A102 emerges from the Blackwall Tunnel to join the South Circular at the busy Kidbrooke Interchange. A new bridge from Thamesmead to Beckton has been provisionally approved, although it will be many years before it's built. The A2 to Kent enters the borough at Blackheath, while the A20 runs through Eltham on the way to Sidcup in Bexley. Greenwich town can be very busy, particularly at weekends.

Parking

Parking is virtually impossible around Greenwich town, which is now a Controlled Parking Zone (CPZ). CPZs operate throughout the borough, including Woolwich town centre and parts of

Abbey Wood, Blackheath, Charlton, Eltham and Plumstead. The cost of an annual resident's permit ranges from £15 to £50, depending on the area, with the most expensive being in Greenwich and Woolwich.

Waste & Recycling

Greenwich's waste collection service is regularly rated the best in London. Household rubbish is collected weekly and recyclable materials are collected every two weeks. These include cans, cardboard, glass, paper, plastic bottles, plastic carrier bags and tinfoil. Bulky items such as furniture and kitchen appliances are collected by arrangement. All types of household rubbish and recyclable materials can also be taken to the borough's amenity site in Plumstead.

Shopping

Greenwich town is full of tourist shops, selling antiques, second-hand books, crafts and maritime paraphernalia. There's also a popular market. The shopping district in Woolwich, once thriving, is now full of dreary budget shops and fast food outlets, although there's an M&S, a Clarks factory shop and covered and open-air markets. The promised town centre revamp may improve shopping in Woolwich, although it will always face stiff competition from the larger centres in Bromley and Bexley. A better bet is Eltham town centre, which has a good range of chain stores (M&S, MFI, Next, etc.) plus some interesting specialist shops. Elsewhere, small parades supply the daily essentials. There are no covered shopping centres in the borough, although there are retail parks in Charlton and Thamesmead, which feature DIY, electrical and furniture superstores.

Supermarkets

♦ Asda in Charlton.

♦ Marks & Spencer in Greenwich Cutty Sark (Simply Food).

♦ Morrisons in Thamesmead.

♦ Sainsbury's in Eltham, Greenwich and Woolwich.

Markets

♦ Blackheath Farmers' Market (Blackheath Rail Station Car Park, SE3) – Sunday 10am-2pm.

♦ Greenwich Market (Greenwich Church Street, Greenwich High Road, Stockwell Street, SE10) – arts and crafts, antiques, bric-a-brac, food, furniture, second-hand books and clothing; Thursday (collectables), Friday (arts and crafts), weekends (all sections).

♦ Woolwich Market (Beresford Square, SE18) – cheap clothing, fruit and veg, miscellaneous household goods; Monday-Wednesday, 9am-4pm, Thursday, 9am-1pm, Friday and Saturday, 9am-4.30pm. Not open on Sundays.

Entertainment

Most entertainment options are concentrated around Greenwich, with more limited facilities in Woolwich, Thamesmead and Abbey Wood, although development plans include new venues. Most bars and restaurants are in Eltham and Greenwich town.

Theatres

♦ Bob Hope Theatre (Wythfield Road, SE9, ☎ 020-8850 3702, ⌨ www.bobhopetheatre. co.uk) – community theatre.

Royal Observatory

◆ Greenwich Dance Agency (Borough Hall, Royal Hill, ☎ 020-8293 9741) – dance performances.

◆ Greenwich Playhouse (St Christopher's Inn, 189 Greenwich High Road, SE10, ☎ 020-8858 9256, 🖳 www.galleontheatre.co.uk) – fringe studio theatre.

◆ Greenwich Theatre (Crooms Hill, SE10, ☎ 020-8858 7755) – popular mainstream theatre.

Cinemas

◆ UCI Film Works (Bugsby's Way, SE10, ☎ 0871-224 4007, 🖳 www.uci-cinemas.co.uk).

◆ The Greenwich Picturehouse (180 Greenwich High Road, SE10, ☎ 0871-704 2059, 🖳 www.picturehouses.co.uk).

Museums & Galleries

Famous attractions include the Royal Observatory, the National Maritime Museum (🖳 www.nmm.ac.uk), the Old Royal Naval College, a favourite Tudor royal residence, and the Queen's House, which together comprise Maritime Greenwich, a World Heritage Site (see box). Other attractions include:

◆ Charlton House (Charlton Road SE7, ☎ 020-8856 3951) – one of the finest specimens of Jacobean domestic architecture in the country.

◆ Cutty Sark (King William Walk, SE10, ☎ 020-8858 2698) – the last of the great tea clippers, built in 1869. It was almost destroyed by fire in 2007, while undergoing preservation work in dry dock.

◆ Eltham Palace (Tilt Yard Approach, Court Yard, SE9, ☎ 020-8294 2548, 🖳 www.elthampalace.org.uk) – former royal home leading into a '30s mansion.

◆ The Fan Museum (12 Crooms Hill, SE10, ☎ 020-8305 1441, 🖳 www.fan-museum.org) – collection of fans housed in two Georgian houses, with a Japanese garden.

◆ Firepower – The Royal Artillery Museum (Royal Arsenal, SE18, ☎ 020-8855 7755, 🖳 www.firepower.org.uk) – interactive exhibits tracing the science and history of artillery.

◆ Gypsy Moth (King William Walk, SE10, ☎ 020-8858 2698) – 54ft ketch in which Sir Francis Chichester completed the first solo circumnavigation of the world, in 1966-67.

◆ Thames Barrier & Learning Centre (Unity Way, SE18, ☎ 020-8305 4188) – exhibition about the unique flood barrier (between Silvertown and New Charlton).

Libraries

There are 13 local authority libraries in the borough, with one mobile service. The three largest district libraries are in Blackheath, Eltham and Woolwich, which is also a reference library

Royal naval college and Queen's house

(Calderwood Street, SE18, ☎ 020-8921 5750). None of the libraries open on Sundays.

Clubs

The club scene is increasingly vibrant in Greenwich town, with a number of venues:

◆ Club Ryu (243 Trafalgar Road, SE10, ☎ 020-8858 4394).

◆ Dorrington's (338 Tunnel Avenue, SE10, ☎ 020-8293 1769).

◆ North Pole (131 Greenwich High Road, SE10, ☎ 020-8853 3020).

◆ The Polar Bar (13 Blackheath Road, SE10, ☎ 020-8691 1678).

Elsewhere, Woolwich has Flamingos (Wellington Street, SE18, ☎ 020-7854 3933), while Up the Creek in Greenwich is one of London's top comedy clubs, which also doubles as a night-club (302 Creek Road, SE10, ☎ 020-8858 4581, 🖳 www.up-the-creek.com).

Live Music

Blackheath Halls (see **Lewisham**) presents a regular programme of musical events, as does Woolwich Town Hall (Wellington Street, SE18, ☎ 020-8854 8888). Classical recitals are performed at the Trinity College of Music (King Charles Court, SE10, ☎ 020-8305 4444) and St Alfege Church (Greenwich Church Street, SE10). Otherwise, various bars and pubs have live music, particularly in Greenwich town.

Pubs

Greenwich town, particularly the riverside and market areas, is packed with pleasant pubs and bars, ranging from tourist haunts and family pubs to style bars. The former tend to have a maritime or royal theme, such as the Cutty Sark Tavern (4 Ballast Quay, ☎ 020-8858 3146) or Trafalgar Tavern (6 Park Row, SE10, ☎ 020-8858 2909), to name but two.

For cool, modern environments, the best include the Laurence Llewelyn-Bowen-designed Inc bar & restaurant (7 College Approach, SE10, ☎ 020-8858 6721), famed for its cocktails, and Oliver's (9 Nevada Street, SE10, ☎ 020-8858 5855).

Elsewhere choice is more limited, with chains dominating most areas. In Woolwich, the Prince Albert (49 Hare Street, SE18, ☎ 020-8854

1538) is a classic old-style boozer with a friendly atmosphere, as is Plumstead's the Rose Inn (292 Waverly Road, SE18, ☎ 020-8855 0954). The Tudor Barn in Eltham (Well Hall Pleasaunce, SE9, ☎ 020-8850 5145) is an attractive pub/restaurant in an old Tudor building, which is all that remains of a 16th century moated manor house.

LOCAL INFORMATION

Maritime Greenwich was declared a World Heritage Site by UNESCO in 1997. Sir Christopher Wren, Inigo Jones, Sir John Vanbrugh, Nicholas Hawksmoor and Joseph Kay all have important and beautiful examples of their work there.

Restaurants

Greenwich is the best town for eating out, with a wide choice of wine bars, family restaurants, ethnic eateries and chains such as Café Rouge and Pizza Express. Establishments worthy of mention include one of the first wine bars in London, the Bar de Musce (17 Nelson Road, SE10, ☎ 020-8858 4710), and the Green Village Restaurant (11 Greenwich Church Street, SE10, ☎ 020-8858 2348), a family-run restaurant serving Mediterranean cuisine. Eltham has a few reasonable ethnic restaurants, while Woolwich and Thamesmead have a number of fast food outlets and little else.

Sports Facilities

There are five leisure centres in the borough, in Greenwich, Eltham, Plumstead, Thamesmead and Woolwich, plus an athletics track and two health and fitness centres. Facilities include:

◆ Swimming pools in Greenwich, Thamesmead and Woolwich, with an outdoor lido in Charlton.

◆ Indoor sports halls in Eltham, Kidbrooke, Plumstead and Woolwich.

◆ An all-weather athletics track in Eltham.

◆ Roller skating surface in Kidbrooke.

The Southmere Boating Centre in Abbey Wood offers sailing and canoeing courses, and there's rowing at the Trafalgar Rowing Centre in Greenwich. Several of the borough's parks have sports pitches and courts, including a BMX and mountain bike track at Plumstead Gardens. There's golf on Shooters Hill and in Eltham, a David Lloyd leisure centre near Blackheath, and branches of several privately-run gyms and fitness centres, including Fitness First.

The London marathon starts where Blackheath meets Greenwich Park.

Green Spaces

Greenwich has over 50 parks, woods and open spaces. Hilly Greenwich Park is London's oldest park, where deer have lived since 1515. A favourite with visitors and locals, there are flower gardens, a children's playground and a bandstand. Charlton Park features specially-planted sensory gardens for visitors with visual or physical disabilities; it was awarded a Green Apple Gold Medal (🖳 www.thegreenorganisation. info) in 2004 for its contribution to the local community. Nearby there's a small farm in Maryon Wilson Park.

Areas of ancient forest include Oxleas Woods by Shooters Hill, which is a Site of Special Scientific Interest and at least 8,000 years old. Nearby in Castle Wood is Severndroog Castle, a Grade II listed folly built in 1784, from which you can enjoy fine views over London. The castle is currently closed, although there are plans to restore it.

LOCAL INFORMATION

Well Hall Pleasaunce (French: the part of a garden with the sole purpose of giving pleasure to the senses), which dates from the 13th century, is a haven of formal gardens, ponds and woodland, and has been awarded the prestigious Green Flag (🖳 www.greenflagaward.org. uk). It contained a manor house at the time of Henry VIII and more recently was the home of *Railway Children* author E Nesbit.

Greenwich Ferry

Hackney

E2 (part), E5, E8, E9, EC2 (part), N1 (part), N4 (part), N16

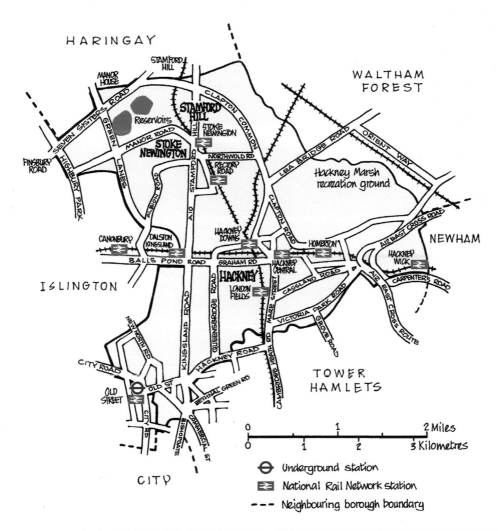

HARINGAY

WALTHAM FOREST

NEWHAM

ISLINGTON

TOWER HAMLETS

CITY

| 0 | | 1 | | 2 Miles |
| 0 | 1 | 2 | 3 Kilometres |

⊖ Underground station
⊠ National Rail Network station
‐ ‐ ‐ Neighbouring borough boundary

At a Glance

Best for: public transport, culture, nightlife, restaurants

Not so good for: education, deprivation, crime, tube services, parking

Who lives there: working class families, young professionals, first-time buyers, students

Housing stock: mostly flats/conversions (over 75 per cent) and terraces

Housing costs: moderate

General Information

Council Offices: Town Hall, Mare Street, E8 1EA (☎ 020-8356 3000)

CAA Assessment: (see 💻 http://oneplace.direct.gov.uk > Search by area > London > Hackney).

Controlling Party: Labour

Website: 💻 www.hackney.gov.uk

Council Tax 2010/11: £2,180 (Band G), £2,617 (Band H)

Main Areas/towns: Clapton, Dalston, De Beauvoir Town, Hackney Central, Hoxton, Shoreditch, Stamford Hill, Stoke Newington

Postcodes: E2 (part), E5, E8, E9, EC2 (part), N1 (part), N4 (part), N16

Population & Ethnicity: 212,200, with a high proportion of young adults and children. Traditionally working class, these days Hackney also attracts small business owners, middle-class homebuyers and artists (the borough claims to have the highest concentration of artists anywhere in Europe). Around 40 per cent are from an ethnic minority, mostly Afro-Caribbean and Asian. There are also significant Turkish and orthodox Jewish communities and a large number of students. Hackney is one of the most deprived areas in the UK.

Unemployment: 10.0 per cent (London average is 8.2 per cent)

Overview

Despite its reputation as one of London's poorest and most crime-ridden boroughs, Hackney is showing signs of being up-and-coming. The problems of high unemployment, inner city deprivation and failing schools haven't gone away, although with money pouring in from the government and private investors, improvements to the transport system underway and the 2012 Olympics on the horizon, the borough is seeing the beginnings of a welcome transformation.

The southern districts – Shoreditch and Hoxton – have seen the most changes to date. In the early '90s, young British artists discovered the disused warehouses and the area became the vibrant centre of the London art scene. Bars, clubs and restaurants followed, and developers spotted the desirability of an area within walking distance of the City.

The main commercial and retail centre of the borough is central Hackney, where around £100mn has been ploughed into regenerating the town and its council estates, and house prices have risen considerably. Fassett Square in nearby Dalston is the model for television's *Eastenders'* Albert Square, while in the north, Stoke Newington is more suburban and has found favour with trendy young professionals and families priced out of Islington. Multicultural Clapton, bordered to the east by the open spaces of Hackney Marshes, is in line for regeneration in the wake of the Olympics.

Development Plans

Hackney is one of the host boroughs for the London 2012 Olympic Games and will house a third of the Games area. Major improvements to public transport have already been made and there will be further progress with the opening of the East London Line in 2010, which will extend from a new Shoreditch High Street station as far as Dalston Junction (2010) and on to Highbury & Islington (2011), via Hoxton, Haggerston, Dalston Junction and Canonbury. Major investment in the North

London Line will also bring improved trains and services (see **Chapter 2**).

FAMOUS RESIDENTS

People with Hackney connections include Steven Berkoff (playwright and actor), Tony Blair (Prime Minister), Marc Bolan (musician), Michael Caine (actor), Daniel Defoe (novelist), Colin Firth (actor), Alfred Hitchcock (film director), Harold Pinter (playwright), Edgar Allan Poe (novelist) and Jessica Tandy (actress).

The media and broadcast centres for journalists reporting on the Games will be located in Hackney Wick, from where some 20,000 journalists will report to a global audience of up to three billion. After the games, the centres will be transformed into a major new employment hub for East London. When London's Para-Olympic Games close in September 2012, the legacy of the Olympic Park will begin to emerge, continuing the environmental improvements and regeneration of the Lower Lea Valley. It will be the largest urban park created in Europe for 150 years, offering local people and elite athletes access to facilities for sports including athletics, basketball, cycling, hockey, swimming and tennis, and East Marsh will be directly connected to the Park and all its facilities via a new land bridge, crossing existing roads.

Hackney Council is also working to create a new neighbourhood at Hackney Wick, including affordable homes, restaurants, shops and business areas, alongside indoor sports facilities and green spaces and parks.

Residential Areas

The borough has a lot of council property, much of which is being refurbished or replaced, with only just over half of all homes privately owned. Around 20 per cent of properties are terraces, many Victorian, with just 2 per cent semi-detached and less than 1 per cent detached, with most of these around Stoke Newington. Flats account for the remaining over 75 per cent of homes, either 20th century purpose-built blocks or conversions. Former warehouses and factories have been turned into smart 'lofts', particularly around Shoreditch and Hoxton.

Hackney & Dalston (E8, E9)

Home to the renowned Hackney Empire theatre, central Hackney is reinventing itself as the cultural heart of the borough, particularly now that young professionals and artists priced out of Shoreditch are settling in the area. Extensive tidying up of the council estates and demolishing the worst tower blocks is also bringing considerable improvements. There are numerous Victorian terraces and flats in converted buildings (grander houses, factories, even a synagogue), with the most sought-after overlooking Victoria Park. Nearby Dalston, due to be connected to the East London overground line in 2010, offers a similar property mix, plus new houses, live/work units and flats, some affordable. The odd six-bedroom Victorian terrace costs around £750,000.

Clapton (E5)

Pleasant stretches of open space coupled with some of Hackney's worst crime rates are the main characteristics of Clapton, one of the cheapest parts of the borough. There's a good choice of period terraces, a few Georgian examples overlooking Clapton Common, plus new developments of flats and houses on the banks of the River Lea. Council estates overlooking Hackney Marshes have been remodelled and some of these properties are now available at reasonable prices – around £235,000 for a two-bedroom flat.

Shoreditch & Hoxton (E1, EC2, N1)

Close to the City, this is East London's bohemian and artistic quarter, highly fashionable and packed with restaurants and bars. Former warehouses and factories have been converted to provide spacious and desirable 'lofts', which City professionals are queuing up to buy. Council flats are much in

Hackney Town Hall

evidence, many now in private hands, while Victorian houses and new flats in Hoxton are popular. To the north, De Beauvoir Town is more Islington than Hackney, one of the smarter parts of the borough, with quiet roads of Victorian houses and ornate neo-Jacobean villas in De Beauvoir Square. Modern apartment blocks are popular with professional couples.

Stoke Newington & Stamford Hill (N16)

Stoke Newington is one of the oldest recorded villages in London and where migrating Islington couples seek affordable family homes and the borough's better schools, while first-time buyers snap up attractive garden flats for around £315,000. Village-like and pleasant, property is diverse, with a good stock of Victorian terraces, the largest around Stamford Hill. The most sought-after properties overlook attractive Clissold Park. Contemporary developments include live/work units targeted at arty types, conversions of former business premises and some modern houses. The Peabody Trust is leading the way in providing tasteful apartments, which include shared ownership units for local people. Council estates tend to be low-rise.

Property Costs

Property Prices

The table below shows average property prices in the borough:

Detached: £0 (no recent sales recorded)
Semi-detached: £511,765
Terraced: £470,167
Flat: £269,577

Rental Costs

The table below shows average monthly rents in the borough:

House 5+ bed: £3,300
House 4-5 bed: £2,000
House 3-4 bed: £1,700
House 2-3 bed: £1,550
Flat 2-bed: £1,200
Flat 1-bed: £850

Crime

Hackney has the ninth-highest crime rate of London's boroughs, with the third-highest rate for drugs-related offences and the ninth-highest for violent crime. In the past, the Clapton area saw numerous shootings, as well as violent incidents between rival gangs of youths, although the number of violent incidents has reduced recently. Initiatives to combat these problems include targeting persistent offenders and CCTV surveillance.

The police station HQ is in Shoreditch (4-6 Shepherdess Walk, N1, ☎ 0300-123 1212), with other stations in Hackney and Stoke Newington.

To compare crime rates throughout London, see the table in **Appendix D**.

Health

NHS services in the borough are provided by the Hackney Primary Care Trust. For a full list of doctors, dentists and clinics, visit 🖥 www.nhs.uk.

To see how the Primary Care Trust compares with others in London, see the table in **Appendix D**.

Doctors & Dentists

♦ There are 49 NHS GP surgeries in Hackney, providing a range of clinics and health services.

♦ The borough has 26 dental and orthodontic practices, most of which accept new NHS patients.

Hospitals

♦ Homerton University Hospital (Homerton Row, E9, ☎ 020-8510 5555, 🖥 www.homerton.nhs. uk) – A&E; NHS walk-in centre; primary urgent care clinic.

♦ John Howard Centre (2 Crozier Terrace, E9, ☎ 020-8919 8314) – mental health care.

Private Medical Facilities

There are no private hospitals in Hackney, the nearest being the London Independent Hospital in Stepney Green (see **Tower Hamlets**). To find a private GP, visit 🖥 www.privatehealth.co.uk.

Schools

Hackney is dogged by persistently poor results from its state primary schools, which is often cited as a reason for people moving elsewhere.

In 2009, local authority primary schools were at the bottom of the school league tables for London and the UK. Secondary schools were placed 17th out of the London boroughs (56th in the UK). There are several private schools run by the local Jewish community.

To compare schools throughout London, see the table in **Appendix D**.

Pre-school

There are two local authority nursery schools and early years' centres, with nursery classes attached to most primary schools. There are private playgroups but few nursery schools.

State Schools

First schools: 53 primary schools, of which 13 are voluntary aided.

Secondary schools: Eight comprehensive schools, including one City Academy in central Hackney. Four schools are voluntary aided, four have sixth forms and seven have specialist status. The best performer in 2009 was Our Lady's Convent RC School in Stamford Hill.

Special schools: Four special schools cater for students with physical disabilities and learning difficulties.

Private Schools

Independent Jewish schools include the Tawhid Boys' School in Cazenove Road, the Tayyibah Girls' School in Stamford Hill and the high performing Yesodey Hatorah Senior Girls' School in Amhurst Park.

Further & Higher Education

◆ Brooke House Sixth Form College (💻 www. brookehouse.ac.uk).

◆ Hackney Community College (💻 www.tcch. ac.uk) – further and higher education college.

Public Transport

Hackney is well-served by overground rail and bus services, but the underground is only available at Old Street station, on the Islington border. The extension of the East London Overground line will provide stations at Dalston, Haggerston, Hoxton and Shoreditch by 2010. Dalston will also be a station on the proposed North-South Crossrail service.

Underground

Northern line trains from Old Street reach London Bridge in 5 minutes and Euston in 7 minutes.

Rail

◆ 'One' Railway trains from Liverpool Street stop at several stations en route to Enfield, Essex and Cambridge. A typical journey into central London from Hackney Downs takes 8 minutes.

◆ The east-west London Overground service between Richmond and North Woolwich stops at Dalston, Kingsland, Hackney Central, Homerton and Hackney Wick. This route will provide key services for the 2012 Olympic Games (11 minutes from Hackney Central to Stratford) and planned improvements will allow the running of eight trains an hour.

Buses

Buses into central London and out to neighbouring boroughs are frequent but overcrowded. Useful routes include number 30 (to Marble Arch), 38 (to Victoria), 55 (to Oxford Circus), 67 (to Aldgate), 243 (to Waterloo) and the 24-hour 242 service (to Tottenham Court Road). Night services include the N26, N38, N73, N76, N106, N243 and N253.

Airports

Below are approximate distances and journey times from Hackney Downs to the five London airports using public transport.

◆ **City** – 6 miles; 35-45 minutes via Canning Town.

◆ **Gatwick** – 28 miles; 60 minutes via Victoria.

♦ **Heathrow** – 18 miles; 45 minutes via Paddington.

♦ **Luton** – 26 miles; 55 minutes via Kings Cross.

♦ **Stansted** – 27 miles; 90 minutes via Liverpool Street.

Roads

Hackney's roads are continually clogged with traffic. The busy A10 cuts through the borough from north to south, providing access to the M25 at Waltham Cross, while the A12 from the Hackney Wick junction intersects with the M25 just outside Romford. The A104 Lee Bridge Road goes from Clapton to junction 4 of the M11.

A network of cycle routes criss-crosses the borough.

Parking

The entire western half of the borough is a Controlled Parking Zone – around Dalston, De Beauvoir Town, Hackney Central, Hoxton, Shoreditch and Stoke Newington. A resident's parking permit costs from £45 to £225 per year, depending on engine size.

Waste & Recycling

Household waste is collected weekly from most areas along with recyclable materials, which include cans, car batteries, cardboard/paper, engine oil, glass, shoes, textiles and tinfoil. A new service collects kitchen food waste from a limited number of households, which is gradually being extended throughout the borough, and there's also a fortnightly collection service for garden rubbish. Bulky items such as furniture and kitchen appliances are collected by arrangement. Residents can also take their rubbish to the Hornsey Street Recycling Centre in Islington.

Shopping

Central Hackney and Dalston are the main shopping areas, providing all the usual chain stores (Argos, M&S and many more) and independent retailers, including a Burberry factory shop for cut-price rainwear and up-market clothing. There are some interesting arts and crafts shops near Victoria Park, unusual fashion shops in Hoxton and a range of ethnic food shops in Clapton and Stamford Hill. Stoke Newington's trendy shopping street includes two garden centres, interior stores, independent clothing retailers and a toyshop.

Shopping Centres

Kingsland Shopping Centre (Kingsland High Street, E8, ☎ 020-7241 5455) – well-known chains.

Supermarkets

♦ Morrisons in Stamford Hill and Stoke Newington.

♦ Sainsbury's in Dalston (Kingsland Shopping Centre); local store in Clapton.

♦ Tesco in Hackney and nearby South Tottenham (both open 24 hours).

Markets

♦ Broadway Market (London Fields, E8) – organic foods, clothing and jewellery; Saturday.

♦ Hoxton Street Market (off Old Street, N1) – food, fashion and household goods; daily.

♦ Kingsland Waste Market (Kingsland Road, E8) – tools, car and bike accessories, second-hand goods; Saturday.

♦ Ridley Road Market (Ridley Road, E8) – fish, ethnic foods, general household goods, fashions; Monday to Friday.

♦ Well Street Market (between Morning Lane and Kenton Road, E9) – general household goods; daily.

♦ Hackney Farmers' Market (Broadway Market, Hackney, E8) – Saturday, 7.30am-6pm.

Entertainment

Facilities include the famous Hackney Empire theatre, an independent cinema, a state-of-the-art museum and library, plus a host of art galleries, particularly around Hoxton. Mare Street in central Hackney is a new 'cultural quarter', with numerous clubs and bars, and the best eateries are around Hoxton and Stoke Newington. Hackney hosts a number of annual festivals and public events, including the Hackney Spice Festival, which celebrates the 'spice of life' in the borough and showcases the work of local artists, and the colourful Hackney Mare de Gras, a Caribbean festival.

Theatres

♦ Arcola Theatre (27 Arcola Street, E8, ☎ 020-7503 1646, ⌨ www.arcolatheatre.com) – fringe theatre.

LOCAL INFORMATION

The Hackney Empire opened in 1901 and is still going strong. In its time it has hosted such legends as Harry Champion, Larry Adler, Marie Lloyd, Stan Laurel and George Formby, and among the greats who made their stage debuts there are Charlie Chaplin, Liberace and Maria Callas.

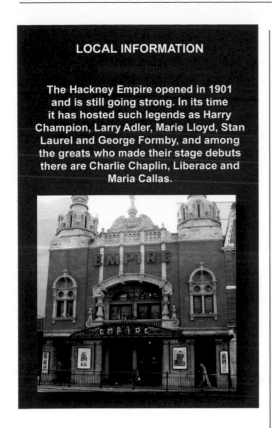

♦ Chat's Palace Arts Centre (42-44 Brooksby's Walk, E9, ☎ 020-8533 0227) – fringe theatre, comedy and live music.

♦ Hackney Empire (291 Mare Street, E8, ☎ 020-8985 2424, 🖳 www.hackneyempire. co.uk) – premier theatre with a reputation for comedy.

Cinemas

♦ Rio Cinema (103-107 Kingsland High Street, E8, ☎ 020-7241 9410, 🖳 www.riocinema.ndirect. co.uk) shows mainstream and arthouse films.

Museums & Galleries

Many resident artists open their studios to the public and there are lots of art galleries in the borough. One of the best known is the acclaimed White Cube (48 Hoxton Square, N1, ☎ 020-7930 5373, 🖳 www.whitecube.com), which presents imaginative exhibitions of contemporary Britart. Museums in Hackney include:

♦ Geffrye Museum (Kingsland Road, E2, ☎ 020-7739 9893, 🖳 www.geffrye-museum.org.uk)

– interior design collection housed in Georgian almshouses.

♦ Hackney Museum (Hackney Technology and Learning Centre, 1 Reading Lane, E8, ☎ 020-8356 3500) – local history collection.

♦ Sutton House (2 & 4 Homerton High Street, E9, ☎ 020-8986 2264, 🖳 www.nationaltrust. org.uk) – restored Tudor mansion.

Libraries

There are eight local authority libraries in the borough, with one mobile service. Shoreditch library opens on Sundays, from 1pm-5pm. The main lending and reference library is at the Hackney Technology and Learning Centre (☎ 020-8356 5239).

Clubs

♦ Aquarium (256 Old Street, EC1, ☎ 020-7253 3558, 🖳 www.clubaquarium.co.uk) – the only club in the UK with its own swimming pool!

♦ Herbal (10 Kingsland Road, E2, ☎ 020-7613 4462, 🖳 www.herbaluk.com).

♦ 333 (333 Old Street, EC1, ☎ 020-7739 1800, 🖳 www.333mothorbar.com).

As well as comedy events at Chat's Palace and the Hackney Empire (see above), there's a purpose-built comedy club in Shoreditch, the Comedy Café (66 Rivington Street, EC2, ☎ 020-7739 5706, 🖳 www. comedycafe.co.uk), with regular performances by fine comic talent.

Live Music

♦ Chat's Palace and the Hackney Empire (see above) both stage occasional musical events, although the best known venues are:

♦ The Vortex (Unit E1, 3 Bradbury Street, N16, ☎ 020-7254 4097, 🖳 www.vortexjazz.co.uk) – outstanding jazz club.

♦ Barden's Boudoir (38 Stoke Newington Road, N16, ☎ 020-7249 9557, 🖳 www.bardensboudoir. co.uk) – regular programme of live music.

Otherwise there's the occasional classical concert in one of the borough's churches, and several pubs and bars host live gigs featuring local bands.

Pubs

The stylish bars around Hoxton and Shoreditch have become so colonised by City types that the former regulars are beginning to look elsewhere.

Nonetheless, some of London's more interesting establishments are there, such as Dream Bags Jaguar Shoes (34 Kingsland Road, E2, ☎ 020-7729 5830) in a former fashion store. Central Hackney has a burgeoning selection of bars and pubs to satisfy the tastes of the new middle-class locals. The bar at the up-market 291 Gallery (291 Hackney Road, E2, ☎ 020-7613 5676) has some of the most stunning décor in the area, while the Cat & Mutton (76 Broadway Market, E8, ☎ 020-7254 5599) is a popular gastropub.

Stoke Newington is known for some decent watering holes, mostly on Church Street, such as the Fox Reformed (☎ 020-7254 5975), which has the feel of a French bistro. Slightly further afield, the Shakespeare (57 Allen Road, N16, ☎ 020-7254 4190) has a bohemian atmosphere. Most of the pubs in Clapton are nondescript affairs, although there are two down by the River Lea that buck the trend: the Anchor & Hope (15 High Hill Ferry, E5, ☎ 0871-258 5286) and the Princess of Wales (146 Lea Bridge Road, E5, ☎ 020-8533 3463).

Restaurants

Restaurants of all cuisines and price levels are available in the borough. Some of the best are around Hoxton and Shoreditch – this is where Jamie Oliver's Fifteen can be found (15 Westland Place, N1, ☎ 0871-330 1515), where tables must be booked weeks in advance, or there's Eyre Brothers (70 Leonard Street, EC2, ☎ 020-7613 5346), serving an adventurous fusion of Portuguese and Spanish cuisine.

Hackney itself has plenty of choice, with several fashionable eating venues such as the aptly named Hackney Central, housed in a former railway station building (Amherst Road, E8, ☎ 020-8986 5111), serving modern European dishes. Turkish cuisine is almost a borough speciality and there are several restaurants around Hackney and Stoke Newington, including the award-winning Istanbul Iskembecisi (9 Stoke Newington Road, N16, ☎ 020-7254 7291). Stoke Newington Church Street also has the excellent Yum Yum (☎ 020-7254 6751) for Thai food, and the Blue Legume (☎ 020-7923 1303) for big late breakfasts.

Sports Facilities

Six council-funded leisure centres (in Clapton, Dalston, Hoxton, London Fields Park, Shoreditch and Stoke Newington) provide swimming pools, indoor halls and outdoor sports pitches for a variety of sports. The Stoke Newington facility, the Clissold Leisure Centre, has been extensively refurbished, and the Queensbridge Sports & Community Centre in Dalston has facilities for a range of sports, including badminton, basketball, football, netball and short tennis.

Sports pitches and tennis courts are also provided in many parks, while to the east is the football Mecca of Hackney Marshes, as well as areas for other sports. Sailing, canoeing and kayaking are catered for at the Stoke Newington West Reservoir Centre, with additional opportunities at the River Lea Park in Waltham Forest, where there's also horse riding and golf. Private gyms and health centres include branches of Fitness First and Holmes Place.

Green Spaces

Hackney has the largest expanse of green space of all inner London boroughs, the biggest of which is Hackney Marshes (see box). Also to the east is Springfield Park in Upper Clapton, a traditional landscaped park with a dedicated Nature Conservation Site. Around Stoke Newington there's the lovely Clissold Park, with lakes, sporting facilities, an aviary and a large animal enclosure that includes deer, goats, rabbits and chickens. The park is used for a host of summer events, including fetes and circuses. The Victorian Abney Park Cemetery, with its magnificent memorials, is also situated there and is now a local nature reserve with attractive walks.

In the south-west of the borough, residential roads overlook the attractive expanse of Victoria Park (see **Tower Hamlets**), while London Fields, immortalised as the title of a book by Martin Amis, lies to the south of central Hackney. The Regent's Canal provides attractive waterside walks.

LOCAL INFORMATION

Hackney Marshes is an area of grassland on the western bank of the River Lee (also known as the River Lea) which was once a true marsh but was drained from medieval times. Today it's home to the largest single concentration of football pitches in Europe – almost 90 – as well as being a wildlife and conservation area.

Hammersmith & Fulham

NW10 (part), SW6, W6, W12, W14 (part)

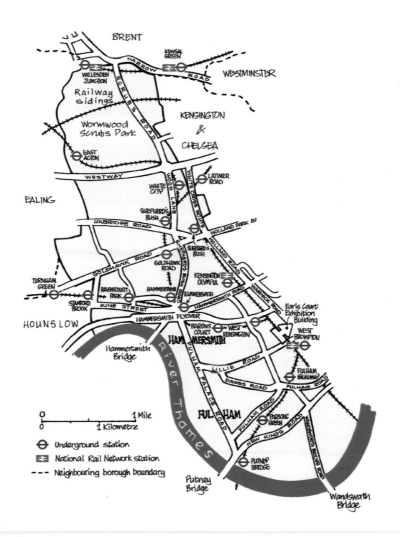

At a Glance

Best for: river location, education, shopping, entertainment, public transport

Not so good for: affordable housing, car crime, traffic congestion/pollution, parking

Who lives there: middle-class families, singles, young professionals

Housing stock: many Victorian, flat conversions, terraces, relatively few semis/detached houses

Housing costs: expensive

General Information

Council Offices: Town Hall, King Street, W6 9JU (☎ 020-8748 3020)

CAA Assessment: (see 🖳 http://oneplace.direct.gov.uk > Search by area > London > Hammersmith and Fulham)

Controlling Party: Conservative

Website: 🖳 www.lbhf.gov.uk

Council Tax: 2010/11: £1,869 (Band G), £2,243 (Band H)

Main Areas/towns: Chelsea Harbour, Fulham, Hammersmith, Shepherd's Bush, West Kensington.

Postcodes: NW10 (part), SW6, W6, W12, W14 (part)

Population & Ethnicity: 172,200, with around half the population aged between 17 and 39. There are significant Afro-Caribbean and Asian populations around Shepherd's Bush and White City, while 13 per cent of residents are asylum seekers. The borough attracts large numbers of young professionals (earning it the label 'Yuppie-land') and it's favoured by middle-class families.

Unemployment: 8.7 per cent (London average is 8.2 per cent)

Overview

Hammersmith & Fulham has been fashionable since the '80s, when young professionals discovered the advantages of its central location (only 20 minutes from the West End), good transport connections and abundant entertainment facilities. The River Thames forms the southern boundary and this is where some of the smartest areas are, including Hammersmith, Fulham and the exclusive Chelsea Harbour.

The further north you go, the scruffier and more deprived the borough becomes, through Shepherd's Bush to White City and Wormwood Scrubs, the latter dominated by council estates and the prison of the same name. However, these areas are at the centre of a multi-million pound regeneration scheme, which includes the BBC's new media village at White City and the huge Westfield shopping, commercial and residential development (see below). Ripples from these schemes have smartened up Shepherd's Bush, where new bars and restaurants are appearing.

Although there are lots of young couples and singles, it's also a popular borough with families and Fulham was recently described as 'nappy valley' due to its child-oriented shops and facilities.

 FAMOUS RESIDENTS

Famous residents (past and present) include A.P. Herbert (novelist and playwright), Joe Calzaghe (boxer), Sacha Baron Cohen (comedian/screenwriter), Linford Christie (athlete), Roger Daltrey (rock singer), Jill Dando (TV journalist), Robert Fripp (musician), Jemima Khan (socialite), William Morris (artist), Vanessa Redgrave (actress) and Alan Rickman (actor).

Development Plans

The vast Westfield shopping centre in Shepherd's Bush, which opened in October 2008, is having a

Hammersmith Town Hall

profound effect on the area, not least the property prices. The centre boasts a retail floor area of 1.615mnft² (150,000m²) and is the largest in-town shopping mall in Europe and the third-largest shopping centre in the UK, after the MetroCentre (Gateshead) and Bluewater (Kent). It features over 250 stores, including Debenhams, House of Fraser, Marks & Spencer, Next and Waitrose. The centre also includes over 40 cafés and restaurants, a state-of-the-art, 14-screen Cinema de Lux, a health and beauty retreat, and a gymnasium.

An unusual aspect of the development is a new high-end retail area called The Village, which features shops from designer names such as Armani, Hugo Boss, Calvin Klein, Gieves & Hawkes, Tommy Hilfiger, Mulberry, Thomas Pink, Tiffany & Co. and Louis Vuitton.

The Shepherd's Bush station on the Central Line has been extensively improved and enlarged to meet the increased flow of visitors, including creating step-free access from pavement to platforms. There's a new tube station on the Hammersmith & City line called Wood Lane, a new bus station and a new overground station on the West London line, providing a south to north link.

Westfield is expected to act as a catalyst for the redevelopment and regeneration of the area – creating 4,000 jobs – and future investment is expected to be in excess of £1bn over the next ten years. Further regeneration projects include affordable housing schemes, a new library, starter business units, provision for a town centre manager, a childcare trust fund, funding for street landscaping and grants for new retail shop fronts on Uxbridge Road.

Other developments in the borough include changes to Lyric Square in Hammersmith and proposals to redevelop the land next to Hammersmith Town Hall as part of the general improvements to the King Street area. Further regeneration projects are also planned in the North End Road area of north Fulham.

Residential Areas

Hammersmith & Fulham has only 3 per cent detached and semi-detached houses, 24 per cent terraces and 72 per cent flats, almost half of which are conversions. Most of the property is Victorian, although there are several modern developments around Chelsea Harbour. Council estates are mostly pre-war.

Chelsea Harbour (SW6)

Almost an extension of Chelsea, the exclusive harbour area is an '80s development of flats, townhouses and a five-star hotel, surrounding a small marina. The original shopping centre here failed and is now an interior design emporium, but there are plenty of shops and restaurants to satisfy the mostly professional residents. In nearby Sands End, modern flats have been built on the site of an old power station and a new overground rail station is under construction at Imperial Wharf (Chelsea, SW6), which will improve transport in the area.

Fulham (SW6)

Highly sought-after, particularly among wealthier couples, Fulham's two- and three-storey Victorian terraces command high prices, despite their uniform appearance (expect to pay around £650,000 for a three-bedroom terrace). Larger terraces and conversions can be found in the south-west corner by the river, and in Parsons Green to the east, one of the most popular areas.

Hammersmith (W6, W14)

With plenty of employment in the area (several companies have their headquarters there) there's a high demand for flats to rent and buy. Look beyond the council blocks and the congested town centre and you find pleasant streets of Victorian houses and conversions popular with first-time buyers and young families. Ravenscourt Park has family-sized houses.

Shepherd's Bush (W12)

Cosmopolitan and busy, Shepherd's Bush has a buoyant rental market, especially among young BBC staff. First-time buyers are increasingly drawn to the area, attracted by reasonable prices (a two-bedroom period flat costs around £300,000). Larger houses border Chiswick. White City and Wormwood Scrubs are fairly grim, although current regeneration schemes will improve these areas over the next few years.

West Kensington (W14)

This is part of London's 'bedsit land', where shabby, large stucco houses have been converted into small flats and studios, many on short lets and attracting a fairly transient population of short-term residents (particularly Aussies and Kiwis) and young professionals. Away from the busy A4, which cuts through the middle of the area, smaller terraces and mansion blocks can be found. The nicest are around Queen's Tennis Club.

Property Costs

Property Prices

There's a huge range of property prices and rents across Hammersmith & Fulham, with the cheapest areas in the north and the most expensive down by the Thames.

The table below shows average property prices in the borough:

Detached: £901,666
Semi-detached: £1,433,833
Terraced: £882,971
Flat: £372,908

Rental Costs

The table below shows average monthly rents in the borough:

House 5+ bed: £6,500
House 4-5 bed: £2,800
House 3-4 bed: £2,100
House 2-3 bed: £1,800
Flat 2-bed: £1,600
Flat 1-bed: £1,400

Crime

Crime rates are well below the London average for violence and burglary, with the 11th-lowest rate for stolen cars and for theft from cars. To tackle anti-social behaviour around Fulham Broadway, the council has introduced Controlled Drinking Zones (to deter drinking on the streets) and Dispersal Zones. CCTV in Hammersmith and Fulham shopping centres is targeting hooliganism.

The police station HQ is in Hammersmith (226 Shepherd's Bush Road, W6, ☎ 0300-123 1212), with other stations in Fulham and Shepherd's Bush.

Hammersmith Bridge

To compare crime rates throughout London, see the table in **Appendix D**.

Health

NHS services in the borough are provided by the Hammersmith & Fulham Primary Care Trust. For a full list of doctors, dentists and clinics, visit 🖥 www.nhs.uk.

To see how the Primary Care Trust compares with others in London, see the table in **Appendix D**.

Doctors & Dentists

◆ There are 38 NHS GP surgeries in Hammersmith & Fulham, providing a range of clinics and health services.

◆ The borough has 53 dental and orthodontic practices, some 60 per cent of which accept new NHS patients.

Hospitals

Hospitals are part of Hammersmith Hospitals NHS Trust (🖥 www.hhnt.org).

◆ Charing Cross Hospital (Fulham Palace Road, W6, ☎ 020-8846 1234) – A&E; minor injuries unit.

◆ Hammersmith Hospital (Du Cane Road, W12, ☎ 020-8383 1000) – A&E.

◆ Queen Charlotte's Hospital (Du Cane Road, W12, ☎ 020-8383 1111) – maternity care.

◆ Ravenscourt Park Hospital (Ravenscourt Park, W6, ☎ 020-8846 7777) – orthopaedic surgery.

There's an NHS walk-in centre in Parsons Green (5 Parsons Green, SW6, ☎ 020-8846 6758).

Private Medical Facilities

◆ Stamford Hospital (Ravenscourt Park, W6, ☎ 020-8742 6677) is a private hospital with a GP service. To find a private GP you can also visit 🖥 www.privatehealth.co.uk.

Schools

Standards in Hammersmith & Fulham's schools vary considerably. In the 2009 school league tables, primary schools were placed tenth out of the 33 London boroughs (74th out of 150 UK local authorities) and secondary schools eighth (ninth in the UK).

To compare schools throughout London, see the table in **Appendix D**.

Pre-school

There are numerous playgroups and nursery schools in the private sector. The Local Education Authority offers four community nursery schools, as well as nursery classes in most primary schools.

State Schools

First schools: 34 primary schools, of which 14 are voluntary aided. In 2009, St. Peter's Primary School and St. Augustine's RC Primary School, both in Hammersmith, were two of the top schools for Key Stage 2 results.

Secondary schools: Eight comprehensive schools, four of which are voluntary aided. Two schools have sixth forms and five have specialist status. The top performers in 2009 were the Phoenix High School in Shepherd's Bush and the London Oratory School in Fulham.

Special schools: Six special schools cater for students with physical disabilities and learning difficulties, with three additional units in mainstream schools.

Private Schools

Twenty one private schools cater for senior age students, including one stage school, The Ravenscourt Theatre School in Hammersmith. In 2009, two selective schools, both of which are in Hammersmith, had some of the best GCSE results in the UK:

◆ The Latymer Upper School (boys).

◆ St Paul's Girls School.

Further & Higher Education

◆ The Ealing, Hammersmith and West London College (🖥 www.wlc.ac.uk) – wide range of further education courses and undergraduate degrees.

◆ William Morris Academy (🖥 www.wma.ac.uk) – sixth form college in Hammersmith.

LOCAL INFORMATION

Shepherd's Bush derives its name from shepherds who, until 1900, used to graze their flocks on a triangular green in the north of the borough on their way to Smithfield Market in the City.

Public Transport

There have been recent improvements to the local public transport infrastructure, notably:

♦ A new underground station – Wood Lane – on the Hammersmith & City line near White City was opened in October 2008.

♦ New overground stations at Shepherd's Bush (opened September 2008) and Imperial Wharf (opened September 2009) on the West London line.

The aim is for Shepherd's Bush to become a transport hub for bus, train, tram and underground services.

Underground

Shepherd's Bush has three stations, one on the Central line and two on the Hammersmith & City line. The Central line station was modernised in 2008, as part of a swathe of improved transport facilities in the White City and Shepherd's Bush area, funded by Westfield and Transport for London. Tube (and bus) passengers now have much easier access to Shepherd's Bush overground station (which was also revamped in 2008) and can interchange easily to the overground service.

The Shepherd's Bush underground station on the Hammersmith & City line was renamed Shepherd's Bush Market, to avoid confusion with the above-mentioned stations in the new tube-overground interchange. The third tube station is Wood Lane, also on the Hammersmith & City line.

The District, Hammersmith & City and Piccadilly lines all stop at Hammersmith. Typical journey times are as follows:

♦ Fulham Broadway (District line, zone 2) to Leicester Square, 20 minutes via Earl's Court.

♦ Hammersmith (Piccadilly line, zone 2) to Piccadilly Circus, 22 minutes.

♦ Shepherd's Bush (Central line, zone 2) to Oxford Circus, 12 minutes.

Rail

Shepherd's Bush has three stations. West Brompton, on the borough border, is served by the Southern Railways service from Watford to the south coast, and the West London Line (operated by London Overground), which runs between Willesden and Clapham Junction. The new Shepherd's Bush station (see above) opened in 2008 and has direct London Overground and Southern Rail services to Willesden Junction, Watford Junction and Clapham Junction.

Imperial Wharf station is also new, opened in September 2009. Adjacent to Chelsea Harbour, it has London Overground and Southern services to Willesden Junction, Milton Keynes Central, Clapham Junction and East Croydon.

Buses

There's a decent choice of bus routes, although main roads are usually busy, so it can take a long time to travel a short distance. Hammersmith is a major terminus. Useful routes include the 74 (Putney to Marble Arch), 9 and 10 (Hammersmith to central London) and the 266 (Hammersmith to Brent Cross). Night buses include the N11, N22 and N207.

River Transport

A commuter river service runs mornings and evenings between Chelsea Harbour and Blackfriars, Monday to Friday only, with a journey time of 25-40 minutes.

Airports

Below are approximate distances and journey times from Hammersmith to the five London airports using public transport.

- **City** – 13 miles; 50 minutes via Canning Town.
- **Gatwick** – 24 miles; 60 minutes via Victoria.
- **Heathrow** – 10 miles; 44 minutes on the Piccadilly line.
- **Luton** – 27 miles; 70 minutes via Kings Cross.
- **Stansted** – 34 miles; 89 minutes via Liverpool Street.

Roads

The borough plays host to the two main routes in and out of central London from the west, the A4 and the A40 (M). Rush hour congestion continues to be a problem along these roads. Elsewhere, the one-way system in Hammersmith is often slow, grinding to a halt when the bridge across the Thames is closed. Shepherd's Bush is usually busy. And with three football clubs in the borough, congestion can be severe on match days.

Parking

Controlled Parking Zones (CPZs) operate in all areas, with the exception of White City. Zones in the north operate during the week only, while in the south this is extended to include Saturdays. Residents' parking permits are among the most expensive in London, with an annual permit for one car costing £99, leaping to £473 for a second car.

Waste & Recycling

Household rubbish and recyclable waste are collected weekly on the same day. Recyclable materials include aerosols, cans, glass, paper and cardboard, plastic bottles and tins. Garden waste collections have been stopped in favour of the greener solution of home composting, although non-compostable and large amounts of garden waste can be collected with ordinary household waste for a small charge. The council also collects bulky items such as furniture and kitchen appliances. The two civic amenity sites (recycling/waste) are at Smugglers Way in Wandsworth and at Cringle Dock in Battersea.

Shopping

Hammersmith has the best shopping in the borough, with indoor shopping centres and a pedestrianised square packed with high street names. Shepherd's Bush has plenty of local shops, including some excellent ethnic delis and a revamped shopping centre. Fulham's high street is good for everyday shopping and interesting antique, fabric and furniture shops in streets off the Broadway.

Shopping Centres

- Westfield Shopping Centre (Shepherd's Bush, W12, ☎ 020-3371 2300) – opened in October 2008 (see **Development Plans** above).
- Broadway Shopping Centre (Hammersmith Broadway, W6, ☎ 020-8563 0131) – over 40 shops, restaurants and bars.
- Fulham Broadway Retail Centre (Fulham Road, SW6, ☎ 020-7385 6965) – chain stores, restaurants, a cinema and a David Lloyd Leisure Centre.
- Kings Mall Shopping Centre (King Street, W6, ☎ 020-8741 2121) – high street names.
- West 12 Centre (Shepherd's Bush Green, W12, ☎ 020-8746 0038) – high street names, a cinema and a health club.

LOCAL INFORMATION

The 17th century Dove riverside pub in Fulham is the oldest surviving riverside pub in London with, reputedly, the smallest snug bar in the world, frequented in the past by Ernest Hemingway and Graham Greene. It's tucked away down a tiny alley, which is the only remaining remnant of the riverside village of Hammersmith.

Supermarkets

Marks & Spencer in Fulham and Shepherd's Bush (Westfield).

- Morrisons in Shepherd's Bush.
- Sainsbury's in Fulham (Townsmead Road) and in the Fulham Broadway Retail Centre, plus local stores in Shepherd's Bush and Hammersmith.
- Tesco in Hammersmith, plus a Metro store in the Broadway Shopping Centre.
- Waitrose in Fulham and Shepherd's Bush (Westfield).

Markets

♦ Hammersmith Market (Hammersmith Grove, W6) – tiny market selling fruit and vegetables, flowers and bread; Monday to Saturday.

♦ Hammersmith Farmer's Market (Lyric Square, King Street, W6) – Thursday, 10am-3pm; Lady Margaret Secondary School (Parsons Green, W6), Saturday 11am-3pm.

♦ North End Road Market (Fulham Broadway, SW6) – fresh produce, fish, specialist foods and clothing; Monday to Saturday, 8am-6pm.

♦ Shepherd's Bush Market (Goldhawk Road, W12) – exotic foods, clothing, shoes and luggage; Monday to Wednesday, Friday and Saturday, 9.30am-5pm, Thursday 9.30-1.30.

♦ Fulham Farmers' Market (Fulham Island); Sunday 10am-2pm.

Entertainment

The borough boasts several theatres and concert venues, some of national fame, such as the Apollo Hammersmith, Lyric and the Shepherd's Bush Empire. There isn't much in the way of museums, although London's 'museum borough', Hounslow, is next door. The Earl's Court and Olympia Exhibition Centres lie on the borough boundary in West Kensington (☎ 020-7385 1200, 🖳 www.eco.co.uk) and host a wide range of events and exhibitions throughout the year. Fulham, Parsons Green, Hammersmith and Shepherd's Bush all have a wide choice of restaurants, pubs and bars.

Theatres

♦ Barons Court Theatre (The Curtain's Up, 28a Comeragh Road, W14, ☎ 020-7386 7543, 🖳 www.thecurtainsup.co.uk) – fringe theatre specialising in classic plays.

♦ The Bush Theatre (Shepherd's Bush Green, W12, ☎ 020-8743 3584, 🖳 www.thebushtheatre.co.uk) – commissions and produces new work.

♦ Lyric Hammersmith (King Street, W6, ☎ 0871-221 1729, 🖳 www.lyric.co.uk) – unusual productions, concerts and children's theatre. The adjoining Lyric Studio presents smaller shows.

Westfield Shopping Centre, Shepherd's Bush

♦ Riverside Studios (Crisp Road, W6, ☎ 020-8237 1111, 🖳 www.riversidestudios.co.uk) – centre for TV production, theatre, films and special events.

Cinemas

♦ Riverside Studios Cinema (see above).

♦ Cineworld Hammersmith (207 King Street, W6, ☎ 0871-200 2000, 🖳 www.cineworld.co.uk).

♦ Vue Fulham Broadway (Fulham Broadway Retail Centre, Fulham Road, SW6) and Shepherd's Bush Green (W12, ☎ 0871-224 0240, 🖳 www.myvue.co.uk).

Museums & Galleries

♦ The BBC (Wood Lane, W12, ☎ 0870-603 0304, 🖳 www.bbc.co.uk/tours/televisioncentre. shtml) – backstage tours of the studios.

♦ Chelsea World of Sport (Chelsea Village, Fulham Road, SW6, ☎ 020-7915 2222, 🖳 www.chelseaworldofsport.com) – sports museum with interactive exhibits

♦ The Museum of Fulham Palace (Bishops Avenue, SW6, ☎ 020-7736 3233, 🖳 www. fulhampalace.org) – exhibition about the Bishops of London, set in riverside gardens.

♦ Kelmscott House (26 Upper Mall, W6, ☎ 020-8741 3735, 🖳 www.morrissociety. org/Kelmscott_House.html) – former home of William Morris, the celebrated poet and artist.

Libraries

There are six local authority libraries in the borough, with one mobile service. Three libraries open on Sundays: Fulham Library (598 Fulham

Road, SW6, ☎ 020-8753 3876), Hammersmith Library (Shepherd's Bush Road, W6, ☎ 020-8748 3020) and Shepherd's Bush Library, (6 Wood Lane, W12, ☎ 020-8753 3842).

LOCAL INFORMATION

The Bush Theatre is one of the UK's most celebrated new writing theatres and has a reputation for discovering, nurturing and producing the best new theatre writers. It's widely acclaimed as the seedbed for new playwrights, many of whom have gone on to become established names in the entertainment industry.

Clubs

There's a good choice of night-clubs in the borough, including:

◆ The Bluejay Jazz Lounge (184 Uxbridge Road, W12, ☎ 020-8222 6597).

◆ Po Na Na Hammersmith, formerly the iconic Hammersmith Palais (230-240 Shepherd's Bush Road, W6, ☎ 0870-444 0006) – weekend club nights.

◆ The Prospect (498 Fulham Road, SW6, ☎ 020-7386 7577) – weekend club nights.

◆ Ted's Place TV (305a North End Road, W14, ☎ 020-7385 9359) – private gay club.

◆ The Orange (The Fox Tavern, 3 North End Crescent, W14, ☎ 0872-148 2685).

Comedy can be found at the Well Hard Comedy Club in the Distillers Arms (64 Fulham Palace Road, W6, ☎ 020-8748 2834).

Live Music

Music venues range from vast concert halls to rooms in pubs and intimate corners in restaurants. The larger venues include:

◆ Bush Hall (310 Uxbridge Road, W12, ☎ 020-8222 6955, ⌨ www.bushhallmusic.co.uk) – concerts in an Edwardian ballroom.

◆ Carling Apollo Hammersmith (Queen Caroline Street, W6, ☎ 0870-606 3400, ⌨ www.london-apollo.com) – major venue in an old art deco cinema.

◆ Lyric Hammersmith (King Street, W6, ☎ 0870-050 0511, ⌨ www.lyric.co.uk).

◆ Shepherd's Bush Empire (Shepherd's Bush Green, W12, ☎ 020-8354 3300, ⌨ www.shepherds-bush-empire.co.uk) – major venue in a former music hall.

◆ Shebu (184 Uxbridge Road, W12, ☎ 020-8222 6597, ⌨ www.shebu.info) – stylish new venue.

Pubs

Pretty riverside pubs, historic boozers, modern bars and chains – all these and more can be found in Hammersmith & Fulham. Hammersmith has a huge choice, although it's best known for the clutch of lovely pubs down by the Thames, such as the Dove (19 Upper Mall, W6, ☎ 020-8748 9474 – see box) and the Old Ship (25 Upper Mall, W6, ☎ 020-8748 2593, ⌨ www.oldshipw6.co.uk). At the other extreme, the Penny Farthing (135 King Street, W6, ☎ 020-8748 7045) has nightly drag acts.

Fulham also has a good selection of pubs, with some more upmarket establishments in Parsons Green, including the White Horse (1 Parsons Green, SW6, ☎ 020-7736 2115), claimed to be one of the finest Victorian pubs in London, despite its nickname 'Sloaney Pony'. West Kensington has no noteworthy pubs and this was true of Shepherd's Bush, although modern places like the Detector's Weld (170 Uxbridge Road, W12, ☎ 020-8749 0008) are setting new standards for the area. For more examples of pubs in the borough, refer to guidebooks such as Time Out's *Eating and Drinking Guide*.

Restaurants

Typically for an inner London borough, there are plenty of restaurants, offering every kind of cuisine. In the end it comes down to personal taste, price and environment. The main restaurant chains crop up all over the borough, with branches of Ask!, Café Rouge, Pizza Express and Jim Thompson's Flaming Wok all present. The best known restaurant in Hammersmith is the River Café (Thames Wharf, Rainville Road, W6, ☎ 020-7386 4200), with an international reputation for gourmet Italian food.

Fulham has a number of quality restaurants, as well as some quirky ones – the Sugar Hut (374 North End Road, SW6, ☎ 020-7386 8950) is a good example, with décor reminiscent of a film set and excellent Thai food. Medea (561 Kings

Road, SW6, ☎ 020-7736 2333) is another exotic establishment, with belly dancers, floor cushions and hearty Moroccan food. Restaurants around Shepherd's Bush are at the cheaper end of the scale, with an emphasis on ethnic food.

Sports Facilities

The borough has five council-funded sports and leisure centres, in Fulham, Hammersmith, Hurlingham Park, White City and Wormwood Scrubs; the Phoenix Centre in White City is a new state-of-the-art gym and swimming pool complex. The borough's facilities include:

♦ Swimming pools in Fulham and White City.

♦ Squash courts in Hammersmith.

♦ Athletics stadiums at Hurlingham Park and at Wormwood Scrubs.

Sports pitches and tennis courts are available in many of the borough's parks, and there's horse riding for children and young people at Wormwood Scrubs Pony Centre. Canoeing clubs use the River Thames and there are several branches of private health clubs. Spectator sports are also popular and include:

♦ Queen's Tennis Club hosts the pre-Wimbledon Stella Artois Championships in June (Palliser Road, W14, ☎ 020-7386 3401, 🖥 www. queensclub.co.uk).

♦ Chelsea Football Club has its ground in Fulham (Fulham Road, SW6, ☎ 0871-984 1905, 🖥 www.chelseafc.com), Fulham Football Club play at Craven Cottage (Stevenage Road, SW6, ☎ 0870-442 1222, 🖥 www.fulhamfc. com) and Queen's Park Rangers play at Loftus Road Stadium (South Africa Road, W12, ☎ 08444-777 007, 🖥 www.qpr.co.uk).

♦ The annual Oxford and Cambridge Boat Race (held annually since 1856) – from Putney Bridge to Mortlake – takes place in March or April.

Green Spaces

There are few open spaces in Hammersmith & Fulham and the largest, Wormwood Scrubs Park, is a flat and uninteresting, overshadowed by the A40 Westway and the prison. However, it's an excellent sports facility (there's a stadium as well as sports pitches) and has been designated a nature reserve. Also in the borough is Brompton Cemetery, a huge Victorian burial ground with

lovely grounds. Riverside walks are popular and there are trails along the Thames from Hammersmith Bridge heading west, and also along the Grand Union Canal.

LOCAL INFORMATION

Fulham Palace

Fulham Palace was owned by the Bishops of Fulham for over 1,300 years (until 1973) and was their country home from the 11th century. Today it features a Tudor courtyard, an 18th century walled garden, a botanical collection and an intriguing museum (free), and stages a wide range of events.

Haringey

N4 (part), N6 (part), N8, N10, N15, N17, N22

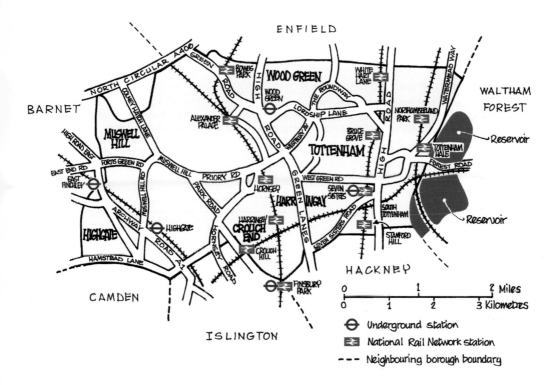

At a Glance

Best for: public transport, leisure facilities, open spaces, markets
Not so good for: crime, deprivation, traffic congestion, parking
Who lives there: middle-class families, young professional couples, singles
Housing stock: 50% flats, 40% terraces, good period homes
Housing costs: relatively expensive

General Information

Council Offices: Civic Centre, High Road, Wood Green, N22 8LE (☎ 020-8489 0000)

CAA Assessment: (see 💻 http://oneplace.direct.gov.uk > Search by area > London > Haringey)

Controlling Party: Labour

Website: 💻 www.haringey.gov.uk

Council Tax 2010/11: £2,490 (Band G), £2,988 (Band H)

Main Areas/towns: Crouch End, Finsbury Park, Harringay, Highgate, Hornsey, Muswell Hill, Tottenham, Wood Green.

Postcodes: N4 (part), N6 (part), N8, N10, N15, N17, N22

Population & Ethnicity: 226,200, with over 45 per cent aged between 20 and 44. Nearly 50 per cent of the population is from an ethnic minority, with the largest groups from Afro-Caribbean and Asian backgrounds, and significant Turkish, Kurdish and Eastern European communities. Some 11 per cent of London's asylum seekers live there. The borough is popular with wealthy families, young professionals, first-time buyers and key workers.

Unemployment: 10.4 per cent (London average is 8.2 per cent)

Overview

Despite having some lovely open spaces, Haringey has traditionally been less popular than Islington and Camden, with a longer commute into central London and a history of social tension. Some of London's wealthiest people live in Highgate in the south-west, while some of its poorest live in the north-east around Tottenham, scene of the Broadwater Farm riots in 1985.

Exclusive and expensive, Highgate commands magnificent views across London from its hilltop position and is home to one of London's most famous cemeteries (see box). More solidly middle class are Muswell Hill, Crouch End and Alexandra Palace, which are popular with families looking for good schools and professionals unconcerned by the lack of an underground station.

Huge injections of cash from the EU and the UK Government are regenerating the eastern areas around Wood Green, boosting the local economy and providing much-needed jobs. There's a vision to create a landmark 'urban centre' at Tottenham Hale to provide new shops, homes and leisure amenities.

LOCAL INFORMATION

The names Haringey, Harringay and Hornsey in use today are all different variations of the same old English phrase *Haeringes-hege*. Haering was a Saxon chief who probably lived in the area around Hornsey and *Haering's hege* meant Haering's enclosure, and evolved into Haringey, Harringay and Hornsey.

Development Plans

Current regeneration is aimed at bolstering the local economy, providing employment and making the borough more attractive to new residents and businesses. Plans proposed for the Tottenham Hale area and the Haringey heartlands will create new homes, a health centre, schools and business offices and retail units over the next 10 to 15 years. There will also be improvements to the road network and transport interchanges.

Residential Areas

Flats make up over 50 per cent of the property in Haringey and a further 41 per cent is terraced houses. There are less than 10 per cent semi-detached and detached homes. The larger properties lie in the western areas, with some lovely Georgian, Victorian and Edwardian buildings, while there are smaller homes as you move east to Wood Green. Many of the borough's council estates are in Tottenham.

Crouch End and Muswell Hill (N8, N10)

Close to Highgate Woods and Alexandra Park, but without an underground station, these are genteel, suburban areas with good shops and leisure facilities. Crouch End has a slightly arty feel and is popular with young professionals and first-time buyers, attracted by the many spacious flats in converted Victorian and Edwardian villas. Fashionable Muswell Hill offers panoramic views over London and is popular with families with school-age children. Large Edwardian redbrick houses, often with turrets or balconies, are set in leafy streets, and there are also a few private roads with Arts and Crafts-style houses built in the '20s.

Finsbury Park (N4)

Increasingly popular with young people priced out of Islington, this is good flat hunting territory, with plentiful conversions and purpose-built blocks. Although the area around the station is busy, noisy and dirty, with a major road junction as well as rail and underground lines, many of the surrounding streets are tree-lined and attractive. Transport links into central London are excellent.

Highgate (N6)

The most affluent part of the borough, this pretty village is highly sought-after, despite the traffic that creeps through the high street. Popular with wealthy families whose sons attend the private Highgate School, there are some elegant Georgian houses and attractive mews cottages, as well as a good stock of flats, including conversions.

Hornsey & Wood Green (N8, N22)

Cheaper than Muswell Hill and more cosmopolitan, Hornsey offers a mix of flats, terraced houses, post-war council blocks and the occasional new development of trendy apartments. This area attracts young couples taking a first step on the property ladder, while families prefer Wood Green with its rows of Victorian terraces and large shopping district. Noel Park is a conservation area with model housing built for railway workers in the late 19th century.

LOCAL INFORMATION

Highgate is famous for its cemetery, which is the final resting place of many notable people, including Douglas Adams (author), George Eliot (novelist), Michael Faraday (scientist), Radclyffe Hall (novelist and poet), Karl Marx (philosopher and revolutionary), Sir Ralph Richardson (actor), Christina Rossetti (poet) and Max Wall (comedian). The tomb of Karl Marx, the Egyptian Avenue and the Columbarium are all Grade I listed buildings.

Tottenham (N15, N17)

The cheapest and most run down part of the borough, with an abundance of two- and three-bedroom terraced houses, typically costing between £225,000 and £275,000, which are popular with families and key workers. Around Bruce Castle, a 16th century manor house in North Tottenham, there are a few Georgian properties set amid Edwardian terraces and pebble-dashed cottages. The council estates around White Hart Lane and Spurs football ground are gradually being refurbished and there are plans to regenerate the eastern areas.

Property Costs

Property Prices

The table below shows average property prices in the borough:

Detached: £769,241
Semi-detached: £816,923
Terraced: £427,868
Flat: £249,940

Rental Costs

The table below shows average monthly rents in the borough:

House 5+ bed: £5,850
House 4-5 bed: £4,200
House 3-4 bed: £3,900
House 2-3 bed: £2,900
Flat 2-bed: £ 1,600
Flat 1-bed: £ 1,350

Crime

Haringey has the 14th-highest crime rate of London's boroughs and the fourth-highest rate for drug related offences. Finsbury Park station has long been a trouble spot, although improved CCTV monitoring is beginning to make a difference. Tottenham's Broadwater Estate has a grim history, although community policing and other programmes have helped reduce problems. Much of the drug crime takes place in the Tottenham area.

The police station HQ is in Tottenham (398 High Road, N17, ☎ 020-8808 1212), with other stations in Hornsey, Muswell Hill and Wood Green.

To compare crime rates throughout London, see the table in **Appendix D**.

Health

The Haringey Primary Care Trust provides NHS services in the borough. For a full list of doctors, dentists and clinics, visit 🖥 www.nhs.uk.

To see how the Primary Care Trust compares with others in London, see the table in **Appendix D**.

Doctors & Dentists

◆ There are over 80 NHS GP surgeries in Haringey, providing a range of clinics and health services.

◆ The borough has 58 dental and orthodontic practices, around two-thirds of which accept new NHS patients.

Hospitals

There are three NHS hospitals, in Highgate, Muswell Hill and Tottenham, although these provide geriatric or psychiatric care only. The nearest general hospitals with A&E facilities are the Whittington Hospital near Highgate (see **Islington**) and the North Middlesex Hospital in Edmonton (see **Enfield**).

Private Medical Facilities

◆ Highgate Hospital (17-19 View Road, N6, ☎ 020-8341 4182, 🖥 www.highgatehospital.co.uk).

◆ Woolaston House Private Medical Chambers (25 Southwood Lane, N6, ☎ 020-8341 3422) – private GP practice.

To find a private GP you can also visit 🖥 www.privatehealth.co.uk.

Schools

Haringey's schools have varying standards, with some achieving excellent results, while others have some of the UK's poorest, at both primary and secondary levels. In the 2009 school league tables, primary schools were placed 31st out of the 33 London boroughs (146th out of 150 UK local authorities) and secondary schools 29th (117th in the UK).

To compare schools throughout London, see the table in **Appendix D**.

Pre-school

There are plenty of playgroups and nursery schools in Haringey, including three state nursery schools and four council-run Under Fives Centres. Nursery classes are attached to several primary schools.

State Schools

First schools: 63 primary schools, of which 17 are voluntary aided.

Secondary schools: 11 comprehensive schools, including a City Academy in Hornsey. Two schools are voluntary aided, one Roman Catholic and the other Seventh Day Adventist. All but one of the schools have sixth forms and eight have specialist status. The top performer in 2009 was Northumberland Park Community School in Tottenham.

Special schools: Five schools cater for students with physical disabilities and learning difficulties.

Private Schools

There are seven private schools in the borough, in Highgate, Muswell Hill and around Tottenham. The Greek Secondary School of London, a non-selective mixed school, is in Bounds Green. In 2009, the top-scoring school was the Channing School in Highgate, which is listed among the top UK schools for GCSE and A level results.

Further Education

♦ College of North East London (🖥 www.conel.ac.uk).

♦ North London College (🖥 www.northlondoncollege.co.uk).

Higher Education

♦ The Middlesex University (🖥 www.mdx.ac.uk) has several campuses in neighbouring Barnet, Enfield, and Hendon.

Public Transport

Two underground lines run through the borough, although Muswell Hill, Crouch End and parts of

Muswell Hill

Tottenham are a good walk from a station. There are plenty of trains running in and out of central London and bus services are good.

Underground

The Victoria and Piccadilly underground lines both stop at Finsbury Park, then diverge to serve the eastern and northern districts of the borough. Highgate is the nearest tube station to both Muswell Hill and Crouch End (30 minutes walk). Typical journey times are as follows:

◆ Finsbury Park (Victoria line, zone 2) to Oxford Circus, 11 minutes.

◆ Wood Green (Piccadilly line, zone 3) to Oxford Circus, 23 minutes.

◆ Highgate (Northern line, zone 3) to Leicester Square, 18 minutes.

Rail

◆ In the centre of the borough, WAGN trains stop at several stations en route to Moorgate (Alexandra Palace to Moorgate, 21 minutes).

◆ 'One' Railway provides services down the eastern side of Haringey, terminating at Liverpool Street (Seven Sisters to Liverpool Street, 24 minutes).

◆ London Overground operates an east-west service from Gospel Oak to Barking, stopping at Crouch Hill, Haringey and South Tottenham (Crouch Hill to Walthamstow, 12 minutes).

🎭 FAMOUS RESIDENTS

Notable current and former residents include Sir John Betjeman (poet laureate), Samuel Taylor Coleridge (poet, critic and philosopher), Jack Hawkins (actor), Boris Johnson (politician and London mayor), Yehudi Menuhin (violinist and conductor), George Michael (singer), George Orwell (novelist), J.B. Priestley (writer and broadcaster) and Alvin Stardust (pop singer).

Buses

There are buses to and from central London and the City from all parts of the borough, including the N279, N29 and N20 night buses. Connections are also good to neighbouring boroughs.

Airports

Below are approximate distances and journey times from Finsbury Park to the five London airports using public transport.

◆ **City** – 10 miles; 45 minutes via Bank.

◆ **Gatwick** – 36 miles; 45 minutes via Victoria.

◆ **Heathrow** – 17 miles; 40 minutes via Paddington.

◆ **Luton** – 23 miles; 41 minutes via Kings Cross.

◆ **Stansted** – 26 miles; 34 minutes via Tottenham Hale.

Roads

Haringey is well served by major roads in and out of central London. The A1 cuts across the south-west corner of the borough, the A10 makes its way up through the east side and the northern boundary sits just inside the A406 North Circular Road. All these roads are red routes (no stopping), as is the A503 Seven Sisters Road, although they're still slow during rush hours. A particular problem is rat running to avoid the North Circular, causing congestion around Bowes Park and Bounds Green. Routes between Muswell Hill, Highgate and Hampstead are particularly busy during the school runs.

Parking

Parking is difficult in some areas, particularly around Finsbury Park, Crouch End and Muswell Hill. Fortis Green suffers from commuters parking and using public transport (which leaves little parking for residents and visitors). Controlled Parking Zones operate in Finsbury Park, Harringay, Highgate, Seven Sisters, Tottenham Hale and Wood Green, where a resident's permit costs from £30 to £90 per year.

Waste & Recycling

The council provides a weekly collection service for household rubbish and recyclable materials, including cans, glass, paper, shoes, textiles and tinfoil. The service is gradually being extended to include plastic bottles, polythene bags, telephone directories, cardboard and garden waste. Residents in flats and council estates must take recyclable materials to bring banks. Kitchen appliances and furniture are collected by arrangement. The borough's Reuse and Recycling Centres are in Hornsey and Tottenham.

Shopping

The largest shopping area is in Wood Green (see below), although it's slightly down-at-heel. Muswell Hill and Crouch End have pleasant high streets with a good selection of interesting shops; Muswell Hill is the larger and includes M&S as well as specialist outlets selling toys, furniture and antiques.

Highgate offers small but individual shops, with several bookshops. Ethnic shops can be found in the Harringay Green Lanes area (mostly Greek and Turkish) and Tottenham (Afro-Caribbean), while Stroud Green has a number of delicatessens.

Shopping Centres

◆ The Wood Green Shopping City (High Road, N22, ☎ 020-8365 8631) houses a number of popular chain stores, including Boots, M&S and WH Smith. There's also a retail park at Tottenham Hale with outlets for DIY, electrical and furniture shops.

Supermarkets

◆ Marks & Spencer in Crouch End (Simply Food) and Muswell Hill.

◆ Morrisons in Wood Green.

◆ Sainsbury's in Harringay (open 24 hours), Muswell Hill, Tottenham and Wood Green, plus a local store in Hornsey.

◆ Tesco in Tottenham (open 24 hours), plus Express and Metro stores in Crouch End, Highgate, Stroud Green and Wood Green.

Markets

There's a wealth of markets (general markets unless noted otherwise) in Haringey, including the following:

◆ Seven Sisters Market (231-243 High Road, N15) – Monday 9am-6pm, Tuesday to Saturday 9am-7pm; 50-plus stalls.

◆ Tottenham Sports Centre (High Road, N17) – Thursday 8am-2pm.

◆ White Hart Lane Sports Centre (White Hart Lane, N22) – Friday 8am-2pm.

◆ Earlsmead School (Earlsmead Road, N15) – Saturday 8am-2pm.

◆ Coles Park Borough Football Club (White Hart Lane, N22) – Saturday and Sunday 8am-2pm.

◆ Brook Road Car Park (Mayes Road, N22) – Sunday 8am-2pm.

◆ The Irish Centre (Pretoria Road, N17) – Sunday 8am-2pm.

◆ Nightingale School (Bounds Green Road, N22) – Sunday 8am-2pm.

◆ All Hallows School Playground (High Road, N17) – Sunday 8am-2pm.

◆ Farmers' Market at Alexandra Palace (Hornsey Gate entrance, Wood Green, N22) – Sunday 10am-3pm.

Entertainment

Haringey is reasonably well provided with theatres, cinemas and museums, and boasts its own castle, Bruce Castle, a Grade I listed 16th century manor house in 20 acres (8ha) of parkland, which is said to be haunted. Other attractions include the recently rebuilt Alexandra Palace Exhibition Centre in Alexandra Park (see box). The borough also hosts several major music festivals in Finsbury Park.

Theatres

◆ Jackson's Lane Community Centre (269a Archway Road, N6, ☎ 020-8340 5226) – community productions.

◆ Mountview Conservatoire (104 Crouch Hill, N8, ☎ 020-8347 3602) – community productions.

- North London Performing Arts Centre (76 St James Lane, N10, ☎ 020-8444 4544) – performances by drama students.

- Two-Way Mirror Theatre Club (Starting Gate Pub, Station Road, N22, ☎ 020-8881 7977) – intimate pub theatre.

Cinemas

- Cineworld (Wood Green Shopping City, N22, ☎ 0871-220 8000, 🖵 www.cineworld.co.uk).

- Muswell Hill Odeon (Fortis Green Road, N10, ☎ 0871-224 4007, 🖵 www.odeon.co.uk).

- New Curzon Cinema (Frobisher Road, N8, ☎ 020-8347 6664).

- Showcase Cinema (Hollywood Green, 180 High Road, N22, ☎ 0871-971 6527, 🖵 www.showcasecinemas.co.uk).

Museums & Galleries

- Alexandra Palace (Alexandra Palace Way, N22, ☎ 020-8365 2121, 🖵 www.alexandrapalace.com) – exhibition centre and Gallery (see box).

- Bruce Castle Museum and Gallery (Lordship Lane, N17, ☎ 020-8808 8772) – local history collection.

- Markfield Beam Engine and Museum (Markfield Road, N15, ☎ 020-8800 7061, 🖵 www.mbeam.org) – 19th century sewage pump and works.

Libraries

There are nine local authority libraries in the borough, with one mobile service. The largest are the Wood Green Central Library (High Road, N22, ☎ 020-8489 2780) and the Alexandra Park Library (Alexandra Park Road, N22, ☎ 020-8489 8770), which both open on Sundays.

Clubs

The club scene attracts a predominantly young crowd, with a mix of drum 'n' bass, garage and hip-hop. Venues include:

- Bar Rocca (159 Tottenham Lane, N8, ☎ 020-8340 0101).

- Club N10 (Muswell Hill Broadway, N10, ☎ 020-8352 3860).

- Opera House Nightclub (2 Chesnut Road, N17, ☎ 020-8885 2200).

- Orleans (259-261 Seven Sisters Road, N4, ☎ 0871-971 3817).

- Rudolph's Night Club (750 High Road, N17, ☎ 020-8808 8751).

LOCAL INFORMATION

Alexandra Palace

In the Western half of the borough stands Alexandra Palace, which opened as 'The People's Palace' in 1873 and was the last great Victorian exhibition space in Europe (and the birthplace of television in 1936). Just 16 days after it opened, it was destroyed by fire but a new Palace opened less than two years later. Set in 196 acres (80ha), today it houses a gallery, theatre, bar and ice-rink, and is one of London's premier exhibition venues and a popular choice for corporate and private events.

Live Music

Live summer concerts in Finsbury Park include the Fleadh, at which major Irish artists perform for an enthusiastic audience. There's also Virgin's Party in the Park festival and the Big Gay Out concert. Several pubs present live music, including:

- Boogaloo (312 Archway Road, N6, ☎ 020-8340 2928).

- The Café on the Hill (46 Fortis Green Road, N10, ☎ 020-8444 4957).

- The King's Head (2 Crouch End Hill, N8, ☎ 020-8340 1028) – popular jazz venue.

- The World's End (23 Stroud Green Road, N4, ☎ 020-7281 8679).

For classical music, the Haringey Symphony Orchestra and the Young Musician's Symphony

Orchestra give regular concerts, as does the renowned Crouch End Festival Chorus.

Pubs

There are plenty of decent watering holes in Haringey. Classic village pubs are found in Highgate, such as the Flask, hidden away behind the high street (77 Highgate West Hill, N6, ☎ 020-8348 7346). Crouch End has a mix of trendy chains such as All Bar One (2 The Broadway, N8, ☎ 020-8342 7871) and traditional boozers, of which the best is the Harringay Arms (153 Crouch Hill, N8, ☎ 0871-258 7389). Elsewhere, there's the odd gastropub, including Victoria Stakes (1 Muswell Hill, N10, ☎ 020-8815 1793).

Moving east, Alexandra Palace has a few good pubs around the station, while Wood Green has seen modern bars spring up near the cinema complex. Pubs in Tottenham tend to be full of locals – those by the Spurs football ground are packed on match days – and the White Hart (51 The Hale, N17, ☎ 020-8808 5049) has a small gay bar with evening cabarets.

Restaurants

There are many fashionable eateries in Crouch End, Highgate and Muswell Hill. Choices range from well-known chains, such as Café Rouge and Pizza Express, to the individual Les Associes (172 Park Road, N8, ☎ 020-8348 8944). Finsbury Park and Hornsey are home to a number of popular European and ethnic restaurants, including Thai and Caribbean. There's Mediterranean cuisine at Viva (18 High Street, N8, ☎ 020-8341 0999) and South American food at Triangle (1 Ferme Park Road, N4, ☎ 020-8292 0516), while Greek and Turkish restaurants abound in the Harringay area.

Modern bars and restaurants serving European and ethnic food have sprung up around the cinema complex in Wood Green, such as Mosaica (The Chocolate Factory, Clarendon Road, N22, ☎ 020-8889 2400). Tottenham has several cheap restaurants, cafes and takeaways, such as Pizza Hut and Caribbean Express (116 Bruce Grove, N17, ☎ 020-8493 9000).

Sports Facilities

There are four council-funded sports centres, in Finsbury Park, Hornsey, Tottenham and Wood Green. Facilities include:

◆ Indoor Swimming pools in Hornsey and Tottenham.

◆ An outdoor pool at Hornsey's Park Road Swimming Pools complex.

◆ Athletics stadiums in Finsbury Park and Wood Green.

The College Road Sport Centre at the Haringey Sixth Form Centre in Tottenham has an outdoor all weather facility multi-use games area.

Many sports can be played in the borough's parks; for example, there's an ice rink at Alexandra Palace, a golf course in Muswell Hill and tenpin bowling in Finsbury Park. For climbing enthusiasts there's the Castle Climbing Centre (Green Lanes, N4, ☎ 020-8211 7000, 🖳 www.castle-climbing.co.uk) and there are also several health clubs. Haringey's top football club is premiership team Tottenham Hotspur (Bill Nicholson Way, 748 High Road, N17, ☎ 0870 420 5000, 🖳 www.tottenhamhotspur.com).

Green Spaces

Haringey has over 600 acres (242ha) of parks, recreation grounds and open spaces, including Alexandra Park, which provides fabulous views over London, and the River Lea on the border with Waltham Forest. Eight parks (the most of any borough) have achieved Green Flag (🖳 www.greenflagaward.org.uk) status for excellent park management, including Bruce Castle Park and the Railway Fields Local Nature Reserve in Finsbury Park (see box). In Highgate, Waterlow Park is one of the capital's most attractive open spaces, with wooded walks and ponds, and live performances in summer. To the west, the open space of Muswell Hill's golf course contrasts with the leafiness of Highgate and Queen's Woods, and there's a pleasant walk from Alexandra Palace to Highgate along a disused railway line.

LOCAL INFORMATION

Finsbury Park

In the south of the borough lies the Grade II listed 112-acre (45-hectare) Finsbury Park – one of London's first great parks designed in the Victorian period – with sports facilities, a children's play area, cafe, lake, gardens and an arboretum. It's been dubbed a 'people's park' and is a popular venue for festivals and large concerts.

Harrow

HA1, HA2, HA3, HA5 (part), HA7, HA8 (part)

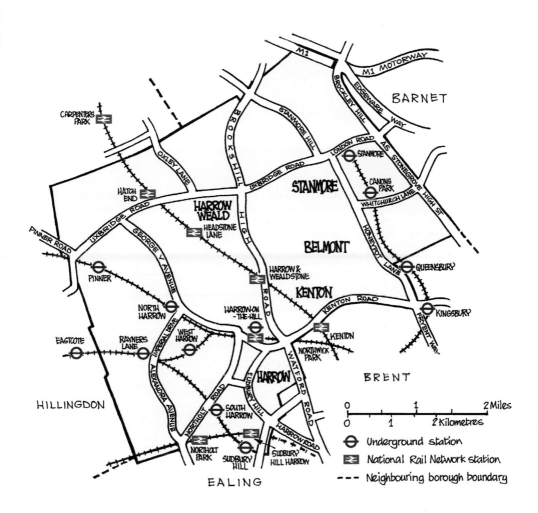

At a Glance

Best for: education, low crime, shopping, public transport, open spaces

Not so good for: traffic congestion, parking, nightlife, culture

Who lives there: wealthy middle classes, young professionals, commuters

Housing stock: mainly semis (40%), 50% terraces and flats, 10% detached

Housing costs: average

General Information

Council Offices: Civic Centre, Station Road, Harrow, HA1 2XF (☎ 020-8863 5611)

CAA Assessment: (see 💻 http://oneplace.direct.gov.uk > Search by area > London > Harrow)

Controlling Party: Labour

Website: 💻 www.harrow.gov.uk

Council Tax 2010/11: £2,494 (Band G), £2,993 (Band H)

Main Areas/towns: Harrow, Harrow-on-the-Hill, Hatch End, Pinner, Stanmore, Wealdstone

Postcodes: HA1, HA2, HA3, HA5 (part), HA7, HA8 (part)

Population & Ethnicity: 216,200, with 30 per cent of residents belonging to an ethnic minority, largely Indian (Harrow has the largest number of Hindu residents in London, centred around Harrow and Wealdstone). There are also long-established Jewish communities in Pinner and Stanmore. The borough is popular with families and white-collar commuters.

Unemployment: 6.7 per cent (London average is 8.2 per cent)

Overview

Harrow is an attractive outer London borough bordering the Home Counties and Hertfordshire, with traditional town centres surrounded by vast areas of commuter suburbs. Most people prefer to think they live in Middlesex, even though the county ceased to exist in 1965 and isn't marked on any current map! Prosperous and middle class (Harrow has the third-largest number of millionaires of all the London boroughs), a high proportion of residents work in the City or the civil service and travel into central London to work, taking advantage of excellent rail and underground links.

Harrow is famous for its public school, which has educated many politicians and men of letters. The school is actually in Harrow-on-the-Hill, the smartest part of the borough and also the highest. It has panoramic views over London, some lovely old buildings and the churchyard of St Mary's, where Byron composed some of his poems. Elsewhere, there's a village atmosphere in northern areas such as Pinner and Stanmore,

while Wealdstone and central Harrow are more urban and cosmopolitan in character.

 FAMOUS RESIDENTS

Famous people with connections to Harrow include Heath Robinson (cartoonist and illustrator), Sir Roger Bannister (athlete), Ronnie Barker (comic actor), Mrs. (Isabella) Beeton (the first celebrity cook), Lord Byron (poet), Sir Winston Churchill (Prime Minister), Sir Hugh Dowding (RAF Air Chief Marshall and Battle of Britain commander), Sir Elton John (singer), Patrick Moore (astronomer), David Suchet (actor) and Charlie Watts (member of the Rolling Stones).

Development Plans

Harrow council has recently replaced the old Petts Hill railway bridge on the boundary between

Harrow and Ealing. Ongoing improvements to the immediate area include creating a short section of bus lane, widening the carriageway to two lanes in each direction to ease traffic congestion, particularly for buses, improving conditions for pedestrians and cyclists, and ensuring better connections to nearby Northolt Park station.

The council is currently consulting on major proposals for Harrow's main town centre and the surrounding area, which aim to improve access and upgrade the environment.

Residential Areas

Harrow boasts one of the highest levels (some 89%) of owner occupancy in the UK. It has a high proportion of semi-detached houses (39 per cent), 11 per cent of properties are detached, while the remainder is made up of flats (27 per cent) and terraced houses (23 per cent). Many homes were built in the '20s and '30s, although there are pockets of Victorian and Edwardian houses, particularly in Harrow-on-the-Hill.

Harrow & Wealdstone (HA1, HA2, HA3)

Busy and culturally diverse, with a large Indian community, these districts provide good shopping and leisure facilities. Inter-war semis predominate, interspersed with smaller modern flats around Harrow, and Victorian and Edwardian terraces nearer Wealdstone. At the lower end of the market these are decent opportunities for first-time buyers – a one-bedroom flat costs around £165,000.

Harrow-on-the-Hill (HA1)

Harrow-on-the-Hill is a perfectly preserved Victorian village on a hill overlooking London, and although it's been linked to the Metropolitan Railway since 1880, development has left it largely untouched; it's still surrounded by parks, a golf course and playing fields. Dominated by Harrow School, many of the borough's most sought-after period properties are there, including some fine Georgian houses and 19th century detached Arts and Crafts houses. There are plenty of flats, some conversions, but also modern low-rise apartment blocks. Wealthy families and professional couples favour the area, which is the most expensive in the borough.

Hatch End & Pinner (HA5)

Semi-detached and detached '30s Tudor-style houses set in tree-lined roads mingle with '60s

townhouses and inter-war semis to create a pleasant, leafy environment. Good schools and shops, together with Pinner's attractive Tudor high street and nearby underground station, make these convenient districts for families and commuters. A three-bedroom semi costs around £385,000.

Stanmore (HA7)

Quiet and country like, with Stanmore Common on the doorstep, its own underground station and close to the M25, Stanmore is popular with families and retirees. It has some of Harrow's grandest properties, many on private roads, and there are also sizeable Edwardian and inter-war houses at affordable prices.

Property Costs

Property Prices

The table below shows average property prices in the borough:

Detached: £597,424
Semi-detached: £331,948
Terraced: £279,763
Flat: £200,865

Rental Costs

The table below shows average monthly rents in the borough:

House 5+ bed: £2,200
House 4-5 bed: £1,900
House 3-4 bed: £1,550
House 2-3 bed: £1,200
Flat 2 bed: £1,000
Flat 1 bed: £850

Crime

Harrow has a low crime rate – the fifth-lowest overall in London, the sixth-lowest for violent crime and the fourth-lowest for car theft and for drug-related offences. The borough has one of the most extensive CCTV networks in London and a large number of Police Community Support Officers on the streets.

The police station HQ is in South Harrow (74 Northolt Road, HA2 0DN, ☎ 0300-123 1212), with other stations in Pinner and Wealdstone.

To compare crime rates throughout London, see the table in **Appendix D**.

Health

NHS services in the borough are provided by the Harrow Primary Care Trust. For a full list of doctors, dentists and clinics, visit 🖳 www.nhs.uk.

To see how the Primary Care Trust compares with others in London, see the table in **Appendix D**.

Doctors & Dentists

◆ There are over 60 NHS GP surgeries, providing a range of clinics and health services.

◆ Harrow has 65 dental and orthodontic practices, around 50 per cent of which accept new NHS patients.

Hospitals

◆ The Royal National Orthopaedic Hospital (Brockley Hill, HA7, ☎ 020-8954 2300, 🖳 www.rnoh.nhs.uk) – specialist care for skeletal and muscular conditions.

◆ Roxbourne Hospital (Rayners Lane, HA2, ☎ 020-8423 8200) – psychiatric care.

The nearest hospitals with A&E departments are Hillingdon Hospital and Northwick Park in Brent. There's a minor injuries unit at Edgware Hospital (see **Barnet**).

Private Medical Facilities

◆ Bowden House Clinic (London Road, HA1, ☎ 020-8966 7000, 🖳 www.cygnethealth.co.uk) – psychiatric care.

◆ Clementine Churchill Hospital (Sudbury Hill, HA1, ☎ 020-8872 3872, 🖳 www. bmihealthcare.co.uk).

◆ Harrow Health Care Centre (84-88 Pinner Road, HA1, ☎ 020-8861 1221, 🖳 *www. harrowhealthcare.com*) – private GP practice.

To find a private GP you can also visit 🖳 www. privatehealth.co.uk.

Schools

Harrow's schools score well in the 'league' tables – the independent schools always come near the top and the state schools are also well above average. In the 2009 school league tables, primary schools were placed 12th out of the 33 London boroughs (46th out of 150 UK local authorities) and secondary schools eighth (11th in the UK).

To compare schools throughout London, see the table in **Appendix D**.

Pre-school

There are plenty of day nurseries, nursery schools and playgroups in both the private and public sector, including four council-funded nursery centres.

State Schools

Harrow has an unusual state school structure, with secondary schooling starting at the age of 12 instead of 11 and pupils moving to college at the age of 16. There's a proposal to build a new Hindu school in the borough.

First schools: 53 first and middle schools, of which nine are voluntary aided.

Secondary schools: Ten comprehensive schools, of which two are voluntary aided. No schools have sixth forms and eight have specialist status. The top performing schools in 2009 were The Sacred Heart Language College in Harrow, Canon High School in Edgware and Park High School in Stanmore.

Special schools: Four schools cater for students with physical disabilities and learning difficulties.

Private Schools

The famous Harrow School (see box) caters for boys whose parents are very wealthy; along with Eton, it's one of the UK's oldest and premier public schools, achieving consistently good exam results. There are several other private schools in the borough, a number of which (unlike the state sector) have sixth forms. The top achievers in 2009 were the Peterborough and St. Margaret's School in Stanmore and the John Lyon School in Harrow, which was also one of the top schools for added value. Both schools achieved some of the best GCSE results in the UK.

LOCAL INFORMATION

Harrow School

Harrow School for boys (all boarders) is one of England's most famous public schools, privately funded and independent, founded in 1572 under a Royal Charter granted by Queen Elizabeth I, although a school in some form has existed at Harrow-on-the-Hill since 1243. Old Harrovians include seven former British Prime Ministers (most notably Winston Churchill), the first Indian Prime Minister, Jawaharlal Nehru, and 19 winners of the Victoria Cross, the UK's highest award for bravery.

Further Education

◆ Harrow College has campuses in Harrow Weald and Harrow (🖥 www.harrow.ac.uk).

◆ St Dominic's Sixth Form College in Harrow is one of the top performing and most oversubscribed colleges in Greater London (🖥 www.stdoms.ac.uk).

◆ Stanmore College (🖥 www.stanmore.ac.uk).

Higher Education

The Harrow campus of the University of Westminster is just outside the borough boundary in Northwick Park (🖥 www.westminster.ac.uk › Business › Conference and Venues).

Public Transport

Harrow is only 10 miles from central London and is well connected by train and underground. Buses are good for local journeys but don't run as far as the West End.

Underground

The Bakerloo, Jubilee, Metropolitan and Piccadilly lines run through the western and eastern parts of the borough. Typical journey times are:

◆ Harrow & Wealdstone (Bakerloo line, zone 5) to Oxford Circus, 40 minutes.

◆ Harrow-on-the-Hill (Metropolitan line, zone 5) to Kings Cross, 25 minutes.

◆ Rayners Lane (Piccadilly line, zone 5) to Piccadilly Circus, 43 minutes.

◆ Stanmore (Jubilee line, zone 5) to Bond Street, 31 minutes.

Rail

◆ London Midland trains to Euston stop at Harrow & Wealdstone (journey time is 18 minutes).

◆ First Great Western trains stop at Harrow & Wealdstone en route to Clapham Junction and the south coast.

◆ Chiltern Railways services run into Marylebone, stopping at Harrow-on-the-Hill (journey time is 15 minutes)

Buses

The best choice of local buses is from Harrow and there are useful services to Heathrow (140) and Brent Cross (182 and 186). Travelling to central London by bus involves two or three changes. However, there are two useful night services: the

N18 from Great Portland Street to Sudbury and the N98 from Holborn to Stanmore.

Airports

Below are approximate distances and journey times from Harrow to the five London airports using public transport.

- **City** – 18 miles, 90 minutes via Canary Wharf.
- **Gatwick** – 30 miles, 65 minutes using the direct but infrequent service to Gatwick, or 80 minutes via Victoria.
- **Heathrow** – 9 miles, 40 minutes via the Piccadilly line, or 62 minutes via Paddington.
- **Luton** – 21 miles, 90 minutes via either West Hampstead or Kings Cross.
- **Stansted** – 33 miles, 95 minutes via Liverpool Street.

Roads

There are no major roads through Harrow, but plenty of traffic. Long-term congestion around Petts Hill Bridge in South Harrow has been addressed with the construction of a new bridge, and with work on new traffic lanes and cycle paths, which is expected to be completed in 2010.

LOCAL INFORMATION

Harrow was the scene of the UK's first fatal motor car accident involving a passenger, which occurred on Grove Hill in 1899.

Parking

There are Controlled Parking Zones in many areas, including most of Harrow, Pinner, Rayners Lane, Stanmore and Wealdstone. A resident's parking permit costs £46 per year for one car, £56 for a second car, £77 for a third and £122 per year for a fourth.

Waste & Recycling

The council provides wheelie bins for household rubbish, which are emptied weekly. There's also a fortnightly collection for recyclable materials and garden waste, including aerosols, cans, glass, newspapers and junk mail, telephone directories, textiles, tinfoil and small electrical appliances such as toasters. Cardboard, car batteries and bulky items such as fridges can be taken to

Harrow's Waste, Reuse and Recycling Centre in Wealdstone.

Shopping

Harrow's main shopping district is rated as one of London's top ten (according to market research company Experian). Two indoor malls include most of the well known chains and there's a pedestrianised main shopping street and a few specialised outlets (selling vintage clothes and collectible comics, for example). The low vacancy rate of shops reinforces a sense of prosperity.

Harrow-on-the-Hill has a pretty high street with school outfitters and antique shops nestled between useful local shops, while Pinner's picturesque shopping street features some original Tudor frontages and upmarket retailers, as well as chains such as M&S. Nearby Hatch End has Chaplin's Store, an amazing emporium for modern furniture. Elsewhere, Wealdstone's high street is budget-oriented, although it's also a good place to find music and arts supplies, while Rayners Lane and Stanmore have fairly ordinary, everyday shops.

Shopping Centres

- St Ann's Shopping Centre (St Ann's Road, HA1, ☎ 020-8861 2282) – high street chains.
- St George's Shopping Centre (St Ann's Road, HA1, ☎ 020-8424 2828) – high street chains and a cinema.

Supermarkets

- Marks & Spencer in Pinner.
- Morrisons in Hatch End.
- Sainsbury's in Pinner, South Harrow and Stanmore.
- Tesco in Pinner and a Metro store in Harrow.
- Waitrose in South Harrow and Harrow Weald.

Markets

- Harrow Market (Green Hill Car Park, Elmgrove Road, HA1) – general household goods, Thursday.
- South Harrow Market (opposite the station in Northolt Road, HA2) – flowers and jewellery in a tiny market, Monday to Saturday.
- Pinner Farmers' Market (Queen's Head pub car park, HA5) – Sunday 10am-2pm.

Entertainment

Harrow is especially well endowed with theatres, cinemas, museums and galleries, although the annual Arts Festival is well worth visiting; it showcases new and established talent from various disciplines, including comedy and visual arts. Festival events take place in assorted venues around the borough. There's a reasonable choice of restaurants in central Harrow, Harrow-on-the-Hill and Pinner.

Theatres

The borough's only theatre is at the Harrow Arts Centre (Uxbridge Road, HA5, ☎ 020-8416 8989, 🖥 www.harrowarts.com), which presents plays, music, dance and comedy shows all year round.

Cinemas

◆ Safari Cinema (Station Road, HA1, ☎ 020-8426 0303, 🖥 www.safaricinema.com).

◆ Vue Cinema (St George's Centre, HA1, ☎ 08712-240240, 🖥 www.myvue.com).

Museums & Galleries

◆ Harrow School Old Speech Room Gallery (Harrow School, 5 High Street, HA1, ☎ 020-8872 8205, 🖥 www.harrowschool.org.uk) – Egyptian, Greek and Roman antiquities, British paintings and Harroviana.

◆ Headstone Manor (Pinner View, HA2, ☎ 020 8861 2626, 🖥 www.harrowarts.com/museum) – local history and heritage centre.

◆ St Mary's Church (Church Hill, HA1, ☎ 020-8422 2652, 🖥 www.harrowhill.org) – dating back to the reign of William the Conqueror, this pretty church is most famous for the tombstone from which Byron used to look out over London and write poetry.

Libraries

There are 11 local authority libraries in the borough, with one mobile service. None are open on Sundays. The main reference collection is at the Civic Centre Library (Station Road, HA1, ☎ 020-8424 1055), while the lending collection is at the Gayton Road Library (Gayton Road, HA1, ☎ 020-8427 6012).

Clubs

Clubs aren't common and the few the borough has are in central Harrow:

◆ Club Mehfil (32 Railway Approach, HA3, ☎ 020-8863 2100).

◆ Time Night Club (314 Station Road, HA1, ☎ 020-8427 6690).

◆ Trinity Bar (378 Station Road, HA1, ☎ 020-8424 8558).

Live Music

The Harrow Arts Centre (see above) is the main venue for concerts in the borough, although there are occasional Gilbert and Sullivan evenings at the Grim's Dyke House Hotel (Old Redding, HA3, ☎ 020-8385 3100), which was W.S. Gilbert's former home. Headstone Manor (see above) holds Sunday lunchtime jazz concerts and there are a few pubs that host live gigs, including:

◆ The Malthouse (Stanmore Hill, HA7, ☎ 020-8420 7265).

◆ The Rayners Hotel (Village Way East, HA2, ☎ 020-8866 1666).

◆ The Star (Northolt Road, HA2, ☎ 020-8422 0505).

Pubs

There are a lot of pubs in the borough, many of which belong to chains such as JD Wetherspoons, O'Neills and Hennesseys. In central Harrow, pubs tend to be noisy and full of younger people, many with large TVs for sporting events. Elsewhere pubs range from the traditional to the gastropub, and attract a slightly older clientele. The Queen's Head in Pinner (31 High Street, HA5, ☎ 020-8868 4607) is a favourite for real ale and organises a famous annual wheelbarrow race through the town's streets. Also in Pinner, the Oddfellows Arms (2 Waxwell Lane, HA5, ☎ 020-8866 7372) is highly rated, while the Case is Altered (Eastcote High Road, HA5, ☎ 020-8866 0476) serves real ale and good food in olde worlde surroundings. The Sarsen Stone in Wealdstone (32 High Street, HA3, ☎ 020-8863 8533) is a friendly local.

Restaurants

From cheap takeaways to Michelin-commended haute cuisine, there are restaurants to suit all tastes and wallets in Harrow. The widest choice of eateries is in central Harrow, where there are several popular chains, including Ask! and Pizza Express, and a number of good ethnic restaurants. Sakonis (5 Dominion Parade, Station Road, HA1, ☎ 020-8863 3399) is noted for its vegetarian Indian food, while the Golden Palace (146 Station Road, HA1, ☎ 020-8424 8899) is reported to serve the best dim sum outside Chinatown. Also in central Harrow is award-winning Eden (395 Station Road, HA1, ☎ 020-8427 2001), known for excellent traditional English cuisine in stylish surroundings.

Harrow-on-the-Hill has one or two trendy restaurants, such as Incanto (41 High Street, HA1, ☎ 020-8426 6767), while Pinner has a mixture of chains (Pizza Express and Café Rouge) and some up-market independents, of which the best is Michelin- and AA-accredited Friends (11 High Street, HA5, ☎ 020-8866 0286), housed in a lovely 16th century building. Further afield, Hatch End has Sea Pebbles (352 Uxbridge Road HA5, ☎ 020-8428 0203), winner of several awards for its fish and chips. Restaurants in Wealdstone and Stanmore tend to be at the cheaper end of the market.

Sports Facilities

The council-funded Leisure Centre in central Harrow is one of the largest multi-sports centres in London, providing swimming pools, squash courts, a sports hall, a climbing wall and an outdoor stadium. Additional sports amenities in the borough include:

◆ A further swimming pool in Hatch End.

◆ The Roger Bannister Sports Centre in Harrow Weald, which has an eight-lane athletics track and outdoor sports pitches.

◆ Hatch End Tennis Club, with seven all-weather courts.

◆ The Aspire National Training Centre, a facility for disabled and able-bodied people.

Sports facilities in several schools are available for hire by clubs and other organisations, and there are outdoor sports pitches in many of the borough's parks. Members of the public can also join the Kodak-Eastman sports ground in Harrow. There are golf courses at Harrow-on-the-Hill, Grim's Dyke and Pinner Hill.

Green Spaces

Harrow has over 500 areas of open space, including parks, recreation grounds and green belt countryside. To the north there's an almost continuous belt of woodland, farmland and open space, stretching from Stanmore Common to Pinner. Closer to Hatch End is Grim's Dyke, an ancient Saxon earthwork that runs for 3 miles. For panoramic views over London, Harrow-on-the-hill cannot be beaten and is one of the highest points in the south of England.

Of the many parks in the borough, Stanmore Country Park is a popular picnic spot; Pinner Memorial Park has a duck pond, small aviary and an ornamental peace garden; and Canons Park in Stanmore has lovely memorial gardens. There are numerous walking and cycling trails. The London Loop (a circuit of paths around London) has recently been extended to include many areas in Harrow, while the Yeading Walk in Rayners Lane is an attractive path alongside Yeading Brook.

LOCAL INFORMATION

Bentley Priory

Bentley Priory was built in 1766 (it succeeded an original priory built in the 12th century) and was extended by Sir John Soane in 1788 for the First Marquis of Abercorn. During WWII it was the headquarters of Fighter Command (the RAF station closed in 2008). It's now home to the 215-acre (87-hectare) Bentley Priory Nature Reserve, an area of Special Scientific Interest, encompassing ancient woodland, scrub, grassland, Summerhouse Lake and Boot Pond.

Havering

RM1, RM2, RM3, RM4, RM7, RM9 (part), RM11, RM12, RM13, RM14, RM15 (part)

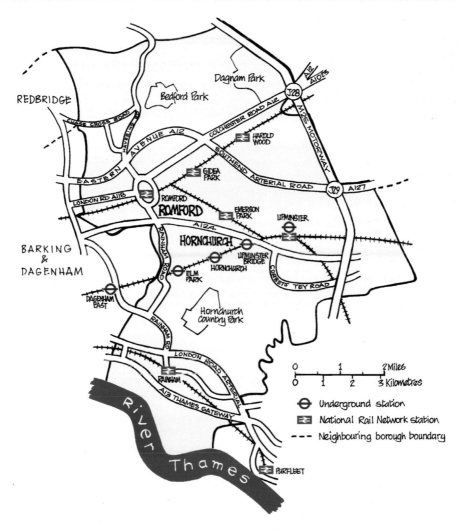

At a Glance

Best for: education, public transport, affordable housing, open spaces

Not so good for: traffic congestion, nightlife (except for Romford), parking, tube

Who lives there: families, commuters, first-time buyers, single parents, mostly white

Housing stock: 40% semi-detached, one-third terraces, lowest proportion of flats in London (less than 20%)

Housing costs: moderate

General Information

Council Offices: Town Hall, Main Road, Romford, RM1 3BD (☎ 01708-434 343)

CAA Assessment: (see 🖥 http://oneplace.direct.gov.uk > Search by area > London > Havering)

Controlling Party: Conservative

Website: 🖥 www.havering.gov.uk

Council Tax 2010/11: £2,518 (Band G), £3022 (Band H)

Main Areas/towns: Collier Row, Gidea Park, Harold Hill, Hornchurch, Romford, Upminster

Postcodes: RM1, RM2, RM3, RM4, RM7, RM9 (part), RM11, RM12, RM13, RM14, RM15 (part)

Population & Ethnicity: 230,100, with the highest percentage aged between 45 and 55. Havering has the lowest proportion of ethnic minority residents of any London borough (less than 5 per cent). Residents are split between high-income families, 'empty nesters' and low-income families, many of them single parents.

Unemployment: 6.3 per cent (London average is 8.2 per cent)

Overview

Lying on the easternmost edge of the capital and with half its land designated as green belt, Havering is more Essex than London. The main towns of Romford, Hornchurch and Upminster were built around the railway and then the District underground line as it moved eastwards, although even within these extensive developments there's more space between and surrounding the houses than in any other borough. Romford in the west is the main retail, commercial and recreational centre, the third-largest town centre in London and with a burgeoning economy. In the past few years new jobs and facilities have improved the area and the number of shops, homes and businesses is still growing.

In the north of the borough, the village of Havering-atte-Bower has largely escaped London's urban sprawl and is virtually in the country, while to the north-east lie the post-war council estates of Harold Hill and Collier Row, which were built to re-house families moved out of East End slums. In contrast, in the southern part of Havering is the semi-industrial marshland around Rainham, where over 200 acres of brownfield land is earmarked for redevelopment as part of the London riverside section of the Thames Gateway Scheme.

LOCAL INFORMATION

The name Havering is a reference to the Royal Liberty of Havering (1465 to 1892), an ancient manor – an area ruled by a lord or *seigneur* – and liberty (a local government unit). The manor was in the possession of the Crown from the 11th to the 19th centuries and was the location of Havering Palace from the 13th to the late 17th centuries.

Development Plans

With the 2012 Olympic Games being staged in the Lea Valley, Havering will greatly benefit from the economic regeneration that's planned locally. New jobs will be created and there will be more opportunities to take part in sports, the arts and in other cultural activities on a permanent basis. There will be improvements to public transport and also plenty of new business opportunities; and, after the Games, the welcome benefit of the nearby Olympic Park site's transformation into the largest urban park created in Europe for over 150 years.

The London Riverside development, part of the larger Thames Gateway redevelopment zone, encompasses parts of south Havering adjacent to the Thames. This is an area stretching from Barking Reach to Wennington Marshes, and encompassing Rainham Village, the areas of Ferry Lane and Coldharbour Lane, the former industrial areas once owned by the Ford Motor Company and the A1306. The Havering section of London Riverside could create 5,000 new homes and 10,000 jobs, and a conservation park. New transport links planned include further stations on the Rainham branch of the c2c line and the building of the East London transit line.

Residential Areas

Havering has seen two distinct phases of development, the first in the late 19th century when the 'garden-style' suburbs of Hornchurch, Upminster and Gidea Park were built. The second was in the '30s and '50s when new housing was constructed for workers in nearby Dagenham and the large Harold Hill estate was created to ease the housing shortages in central London. There are some modern developments in Romford. Havering has the lowest percentage of flats of any borough (18 per cent), with 32 per cent terraces, 40 per cent semi-detached houses and 10 per cent detached. The most exclusive area is Havering-atte-Bower, a small village surrounded by parkland, where the largest houses are found.

Gidea Park (RM2)

An early garden suburb (originally developed around 1910), with regular overground rail services to central London, Gidea Park is a popular middle-class commuter town. Elegant Edwardian three-bedroom cottages and four-bedroom detached houses, many featuring Tudor styling, sit on spacious plots along tree-lined streets. A later phase of building between the wars produced more modest semis and a few interesting modernist, flat-roofed, concrete houses. Just to the north, across the A13 Eastern Avenue, is Collier Row, an inter-war council estate, now largely privately owned.

Harold Hill (RM3)

Properties on this large '50s council estate are now over 50 per cent privately owned. Red brick terraces and prefabricated houses provide bargains for first-time buyers and young families. The nearest overground station is a short bus ride away at Harold Wood.

Hornchurch & Upminster (RM11, RM12, RM14)

These pleasant Essex suburbs offer good schools, regular train links to central London and easy access to the M25, attracting families and commuters. Designed along the principles of the garden suburb, they feature attractive houses in wide tree-lined roads, with a mixture of period and inter-war semis, and some more modern flats that appeal to first-time buyers. The largest and most sought-after properties are in Emerson Park, to the north of Hornchurch, and in the northern parts of Upminster.

Romford (RM1)

The most intensively developed part of the borough, Romford is a busy commuter town providing the main shopping, leisure and business facilities. New homes are part of a mixed-use redevelopment of former brewery land, while apartments under construction to the north of the town centre are likely to appeal to first-time buyers. Otherwise, the housing stock consists of Victorian and '30s terraces, converted and modern flats, plus some bungalows in the north of the town.

Property Costs

Property Prices

The table below shows average property prices in the borough:

Detached: £395,314

Semi-detached: £250,612

Terraced: £202,806

Flat: £155,838

Rental Costs

The table below shows average monthly rents in the borough:

House 5+ bed: £1,750

House 4-5 bed: £1,550

House 3-4 bed: £1,350

House 2-3 bed: £1,100

Flat 2-bed: £900

Flat 1-bed: £700

Crime

Havering is the seventh-safest borough in London, with low rates of violent crime, burglary and drugs-related offences, and also for stolen cars. Community police in the main towns work closely with residents' associations and other groups to provide help and advice on policing matters. Current priorities include tackling anti-social behaviour among young people; in the past year Havering has introduced a Restricted

Romford Town Hall

Alcohol Zone in Romford to deter drinking on the streets.

The main police station is in Romford (19 Main Road, RM1, ☎ 0300-123 1212), with other stations in Harold Hill, Hornchurch, Rainham and Upminster.

To compare crime rates throughout London, see the table in **Appendix D**.

Health

NHS services in the borough are provided by the Havering Primary Care Trust. For a full list of doctors, dentists and clinics, visit ▣ www.nhs.uk.

To see how the Primary Care Trust compares with others in London, see the table in **Appendix D**.

Doctors & Dentists

♦ There are over 80 NHS GP surgeries in Havering, providing a range of clinics and health services.

♦ The borough has 61 dental and orthodontic practices, few of which accept new NHS patients.

Hospitals

♦ Harold Wood Hospital (Gubbins Lane, RM3, ☎ 01708-345 533, ▣ www.bhrhospitals.nhs.uk) – A&E; minor injuries unit.

♦ Oldchurch Hospital (Waterloo Road, RM11, ☎ 01708-345 533, ▣ www.bhrhospitals.nhs.uk) – A&E.

Private Medical Facilities

There are no private hospitals in Havering. The nearest facilities are the BUPA Roding Hospital in Redbridge and the BUPA Hartswood and Essex Nuffield Hospitals, which are both in Brentwood,

Essex. To find a private GP, visit 🖥 www. privatehealth.co.uk.

Schools

Educational standards in Havering are well above the national average, with state schools performing particularly well. In the 2009 school league tables, primary schools were placed fifth out of the 33 London boroughs (22nd out of 150 UK local authorities) and secondary schools ninth (22nd in the UK).

To compare schools throughout London, see the table in **Appendix D**.

Pre-school

The borough offers good pre-school provision in both the state and independent sectors, with four local authority nurseries, 11 playgroups and six independent nursery schools. There are nursery classes attached to 15 of the borough's infant and primary schools.

State Schools

First schools: 62 infant, junior and primary schools, of which ten are voluntary aided.

Secondary schools: 18 comprehensive schools, of which two are voluntary aided. Five schools have sixth forms and 12 have specialist status. The majority of pupils transfer to a college of further education at the age 16. Two Upminster schools topped Havering's league tables in 2009: the Coopers' Company and Coborn School, and the Sacred Heart of Mary Girls' School, both of which gained some of the best A level results in the country.

Special schools: Three special schools cater for students with physical disabilities and learning difficulties, with additional SEN units in several mainstream schools.

LOCAL INFORMATION

The 13th century Havering Palace was one of many royal residences in England during the Middle Ages. It was located in the village of Havering-atte-Bower, just to the north and west of the existing parish church of St John the Divine. All of England's kings and queens from Edward the Confessor to Charles I resided at Havering Palace at some stage.

Private Schools

There are a handful of private schools, with three catering for secondary age pupils. The Immanuel School in Romford and the Raphael Independent School (selective) in Hornchurch were the best performers in 2009.

Further Education

♦ Havering College of Further and Higher Education (🖥 www.havering-college.ac.uk).

♦ Havering Sixth Form College (🖥 www. havering-sfc.ac.uk) – a high performing college attracting students from throughout Essex and East London.

Higher Education

♦ Havering College (see above) offers degree level courses as part of its broad curriculum.

♦ London South Bank University's Faculty of Health and Social Care (🖥 www.lsbu.ac.uk/health) has its Essex campus at Harold Wood Hospital.

Public Transport

Havering has good train links to central London and surrounding areas, and an extensive bus network. The Thames Gateway project (see **Development Plans**) is expected to provide new overground train stations to the south of the borough.

Underground

The District line runs roughly through the middle of the borough, with stations at Elm Park, Hornchurch and Upminster, where the line terminates. A typical journey from Hornchurch to Piccadilly Circus takes 30 minutes.

Rail

♦ c2c trains from Fenchurch Street pass through Upminster on the way to Tilbury and Southend, while a branch line serves Rainham. (Upminster to Fenchurch Street takes 25 minutes).

♦ 'One' Railway services from Liverpool Street pass through the north of the borough, serving Romford, Gidea Park and Harold Wood, with a branch line to Upminster. (Romford to Liverpool Street takes 17 minutes).

Buses

Plenty of local bus routes provide good links between the main towns and into neighbouring boroughs. Community buses cover main routes and travel to other areas, operating on a 'hail and ride' basis, although residents in outlying villages do better travelling by car. The best choice of buses is in Romford, where useful routes include the number 86 to Stratford and the 551 to Basildon. Several routes go to the Lakeside Shopping Centre at Thurrock. No daytime buses travel as far as central London, although the N15 night bus from Paddington goes as far as Romford. The N86 from Stratford also serves Havering.

Airports

Below are approximate distances and journey times from Romford to the five London airports using public transport.

♦ **City** – 10 miles; 40 minutes via Canning Town.

♦ **Gatwick** – 36 miles; 80 minutes via London Bridge.

♦ **Heathrow** – 30 miles; 90 minutes via Paddington.

♦ **Luton** – 33 miles; 110 minutes via Kings Cross.

♦ **Stansted** – 20 miles; 80 minutes via Liverpool Street.

Roads

The A12 cuts through the northern part of the borough and the A13 goes through the southern part. These are both Red Routes (no stopping), but nonetheless suffer from heavy congestion during rush hour. The M25 in the east of the borough is within easy reach of most towns.

Parking

As in all London boroughs, parking can be a problem in town centres and near stations, where commuters often park all day, preventing residents from parking near their homes. As a result the council has introduced six Controlled Parking Zones, in Gidea Park, Harold Wood, Hornchurch, Romford, Upminster and Upminster Bridge. An annual resident's parking permit costs just £13, rising to £17 for a second vehicle and £75 for a third.

Waste & Recycling

General household rubbish is collected weekly, together with recyclable materials and light garden waste, provided they're contained in special bags. Recyclable materials include cans, paper, plastic bottles and carrier bags, and tinfoil. The council also collects bulky items such as furniture or kitchen appliances, for a small fee. Residents can also take waste and other recyclable materials to the civic amenity (recycling) site at Gerpins Lane in Upminster.

Shopping

Romford is the borough's leading retail centre and has had a makeover in the past few years, with improvements to the large indoor malls (the Liberty and Liberty 2) and new shops in the Brewery development (on land formerly owned by Romford Brewery). The huge Romford Market attracts crowds of shoppers and is the only market in the area. Hornchurch and Upminster also have extensive high streets, with a selection of shops providing daily essentials. The largest branches of high street names and department stores are at the Lakeside Shopping Centre at Thurrock, only 15 miles away.

LOCAL INFORMATION

Romford has been a market town since 1247 and holds the exclusive right to hold markets over an area of radius 'six and two-thirds miles' centred on Romford. Although granted in medieval times, it was successfully used to prevent nearby Ilford from opening a market as recently as the '90s.

Shopping Centres

♦ The Brewery Centre (Waterloo Road, RM1) – Sainsbury's and other high street names.

♦ Liberty and Liberty 2 Shopping Centre (Mercury Gardens, RM1) – large retail space with covered and uncovered sections featuring a wide range of high street names, including BHS, Dixons and M&S.

♦ Romford Shopping Hall (Market Place, RM1) – independent retailers specialising in a range of goods, from jewellery to fashions.

Supermarkets

♦ Sainsbury's in Romford (The Brewery Centre) and Hornchurch.

♦ Tesco in Hornchurch and Romford (Gallows Corner, open 24 hours).

Markets

♦ Romford Market (Town Centre, RM1) – large traditional market with 300 stalls selling assorted household goods; Wednesday, Friday and Saturday.

♦ Romford Farmers' Market (near Market Place, South Street RM1); 2nd Sunday of the month, 10am-3pm.

Entertainment

Most of the borough's entertainment choices are in Romford, which is packed in the evenings with young adults and youths over-indulging in the highest concentration of clubs and bars outside the West End. Community arts are thriving in Havering, with several groups, clubs and workshops available. The Fairkytes Arts Centre, close to the theatre in Hornchurch (53 Billet Lane, RM11, ☎ 01708-456 308), offers a wide range of arts and crafts workshops for children and adults.

Theatres

The Queen's Theatre (Billet Lane, Hornchurch, RM11, ☎ 01708-443 333, 💻 www.queens-theatre.co.uk) presents a wide range of professional and amateur plays, children's shows, concerts and other events. There are also open-air theatrical shows during the summer in Raphael Park in Romford.

Cinemas

Ster Century Cinema (1 The Brewery, RM1, ☎ 01708-759 100, 💻 www.stercentury.co.uk).

Museums & Galleries

There are no art galleries in Havering, although other visitor attractions include:

♦ Rainham Hall (The Broadway, RM13, ☎ 020-7799 4552, 💻 www.nationaltrust.org.uk) – 18th century manor house owned by the National Trust.

♦ Upminster Windmill (St Mary's Lane, RM14, ☎ 01708-505 865) – smock mill dating from 1803 with intact machinery and fine views to Canary Wharf and Crystal Palace.

♦ Upminster Tithe Barn Agricultural and Folk Museum (Hall Lane, RM14, ☎ 07855-633 917 – Curator) – 14th century barn with agricultural artefacts.

Tythe Barn Museum, Upminster

Libraries

There are ten local authority libraries in the borough, with an additional service for housebound residents. No libraries open on Sundays. The main library, with the longest opening hours, is the Central Lending Library in Romford (St Edwards Way, RM1, ☎ 01708-432 389), while the newly refurbished library in Upminster (26 Corbets Tey Road, RM14, ☎ 01708-221 578) incorporates an extensive advice centre providing Citizen's Advice Bureau functions and information about council services.

Clubs

The borough's many clubs and DJ bars cater for a largely young crowd and most are located in South Street or Market Place in Romford, including:

- Bar Mango (72 South Street, RM1, ☎ 01708-775 160).
- Brannigans (South Street, RM1, ☎ 01708-732 211).
- Edwards (South Street, RM1, ☎ 01708-747 711).
- Onethreeone (131 South Street, RM1, ☎ 01708-734 392).
- Opium Lounge (36 North Street, RM1, ☎ 01708-730 355).
- Liquid and Envy (108 South Street, RM1, ☎ 01708-767 807).

Live Music

The Queen's Theatre presents assorted concerts, including regular jazz in the foyer on Sundays, and in summer there are occasional live music events at the bandstand in Romford's Raphael Park. Otherwise live music is occasionally presented at various venues, including:

- Ford Sports and Social Club (Rush Green Road, RM5, ☎ 020-8590 3797) – Sunday fortnightly jazz.
- The Golden Lion (2 High Street, RM1, ☎ 01708-740 081) – live bands in upstairs function room.
- New Windmill Hall (St Mary's Lane, RM14, ☎ 01708-220 242) – rock and blues nights.
- Pinewoods (St Johns Road, RM5, ☎ 01708-762 965) – various live music nights, rock, R&B and blues.

Pubs

Romford has the highest concentration of bars and nightclubs anywhere in Greater London outside the West End. The borough's pubs range from traditional boozers to wine bars, with those in Romford usually crowded and noisy – not places for a quiet drink. Out-of-town favourites with the young include the Farmhouse Tavern (Dagenham Road, RM7, ☎ 020-8592 0301), the Archers in Gidea Park (194 Main Road, RM2, ☎ 01708-727 770), an old Tudor inn, and the Spencers Arms (124 Ardleigh Green Road, RM11, ☎ 01708-442 550), which has regular quiz nights.

The JD Wetherspoon chain has several outlets, including the Moon and Stars (99 South Street, RM1, ☎ 01708-730 117) and JJ Moons in Hornchurch (46 High Street, RM12, ☎ 01708-478 410). Real ale lovers have a number of choices, such as the Orange Tree (Havering-atte-Bower, RM4, ☎ 01708-740 471), which is an old-fashioned country pub, and the Kings Head in Hornchurch (189 High Street, RM11, ☎ 01708-443 934).

LOCAL INFORMATION

Opposite the Queen's Theatre is a listed 18th century Georgian villa called Fairkytes, which was once the home of the family of Elizabeth Fry, the prison reformer. The house was later a public library before becoming Havering's Arts Centre, which it remains today.

Restaurants

Restaurants, fast food outlets and takeaways are all well represented in the borough, although again the widest choice is in Romford. Well-known chains include Brewers Fayre, Burger King, Cafe Uno, Frankie & Bennie's, Harvester, McDonalds, Pizza Express and Starbucks. Ethnic restaurants, mostly Chinese or Indian, feature heavily in all the main towns, with a large concentration along Victoria Road in Romford. Popular restaurants include the Coco Noodle Bar in Romford (91 South Street, RM1, ☎ 01708-757 888), Faraglioni Restaurant (142 Rush Green Road, RM7, ☎ 01708-748 652) and Bonaparte Restaurant in Hornchurch (179 High Street, RM11, ☎ 01708-445 533), a family-friendly eatery.

Sports Facilities

There are three council-funded sports centres, in Harold Hill, Hornchurch and Rainham. Each centre is equipped with a wide range of facilities and all have swimming pools. In addition there are:

◆ Indoor sports halls at Harold Hill and Hornchurch.

◆ Squash courts in Hornchurch.

◆ Five-a-side football pitches and a floodlit all-weather pitch at the Chafford Sports Complex in Rainham.

As well as outdoor sports pitches and tennis courts in various parks, other facilities in Havering include four private golf courses, horse riding in several parks and an ice rink in Romford. All the sports centres feature health and fitness suites equipped with a full range of gym facilities and there are also privately run gyms, including branches of Esporta Fitness Club and Fitness First.

Green Spaces

There are over 100 open spaces in the borough, ranging from small village greens to large country parks, of which there are three. Two miles north of Romford is Havering Country Park, an area of glades, mature woodland and meadows, with a huge variety of wildlife and a favourite spot for horse riding and hot-air ballooning. To the east, Hornchurch Country Park has many species of wild birds, while Bedfords Park is home to a herd of red deer.

Also in Hornchurch are Langtons Gardens – the grounds to a Grade II listed 18th century house that's now used as a registry office – which feature a lake, orangery and gazebo. Raphael Park in Romford is another popular spot, with a lake and sports facilities, and the venue for annual open-air theatre and music events.

LOCAL INFORMATION

Havering's largest urban park is Harrow Lodge Park in Hornchurch, with two mature lakes fed by the River Ravensbourne, which is also the borough's most popular park – it hosts the Havering Show, as well as fairgrounds throughout the year.

Bedford Park, Havering

Hillingdon

HA4, HA5 (part), HA6 (part), TW6, UB3, UB4, UB7, UB8,
UB9 (part), UB10, UB11, WD3 (part)

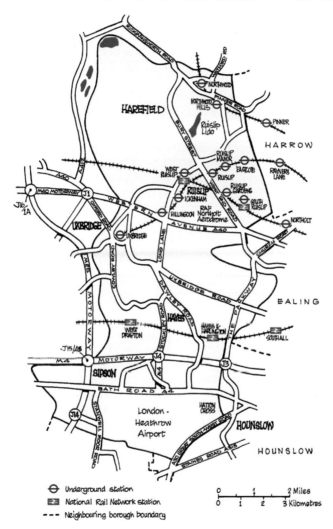

- ⊖ Underground station
- ⊡ National Rail Network station
- --- Neighbouring borough boundary

0   1   2 Miles
0   1   2   3 Kilometres

At a Glance

Best for: affordable housing, education, sports & facilities, open spaces

Not so good for: airport noise, traffic congestion, parking

Who lives there: middle-class families, commuters, singles, Asians

Housing stock: detached houses (over 40%), the rest an equal mix of semis, terraces and flats

Housing costs: inexpensive

General Information

Council Offices: Civic Centre, High Street, Uxbridge UB8 1UW, ☎ 01895-250 111)

CAA Assessment: (see 🖥 http://oneplace.direct.gov.uk > Search by area > London > Hillingdon)

Controlling Party: Conservative

Website: 🖥 www.hillingdon.gov.uk

Council Tax 2010/11: £2,371 (Band G), £2,846 (Band H)

Main Areas/towns: Eastcote, Harlington, Hayes, Hillingdon, Ickenham, Northwood, Northwood Hills, Ruislip, Uxbridge, West Drayton, Yeading, Yiewsley

Postcodes: HA4, HA5 (part), HA6 (part), TW6, UB3, UB4, UB7, UB8, UB9 (part), UB10, UB11, WD3 (part)

Population & Ethnicity: 253,200, with a high proportion aged between 16 and 44. Around 20 per cent of the population comes from an ethnic minority (predominantly Asian). The borough attracts middle-class, white-collar families.

Unemployment: 6.6 per cent (London average is 8.2 per cent)

Overview

Hillingdon is London's second-largest borough, lying to the west of Ealing and bordered by Hertfordshire, Buckinghamshire and Surrey. With swathes of unspoilt green belt land, yet only 40 minutes (14mi/23km) from central London, this is a comfortable suburb where many residents (as in Harrow) like to think they're living in Middlesex. The borough is home to Heathrow, the UK's and one of the world's largest airports, with five terminals, which covers a vast area and is a constant source of traffic congestion.

Hillingdon's smartest and most sought-after areas are in the north-east and include Eastcote, Ruislip, Northwood and Northwood Hills, where the inter-war building boom created large areas of suburban housing estates, satirised by Sir John Betjeman as 'Metroland' (taking its name from the Metropolitan underground line). Districts become less desirable in the south.

Uxbridge is the main shopping and commercial centre, dominated by glass-fronted office blocks and a retail and entertainment complex. Hillingdon is almost entirely residential, while nearby Hayes, traditionally an industrial area, became quite run-down as manufacturing industries shrank in the '70s and '80s. However, it's being revitalised by public and private investment, and new businesses, many in the hi-tech sector, have been established in the booming business park at Stockley.

Development Plans

In November 2007, the Mayor of London announced funding of £3.7mn for Hillingdon to be spent on improvements to local transport facilities. These include the provision of more cycle lanes, road safety projects, barriers to reduce traffic noise from the A4, A40 and A312 roads, and reconstruction work on Swakeleys Bridge Road, to strengthen it and to raise its present 25-tonne weight limit, and to improve its connecting route to the A40. Other priorities include reducing traffic congestion and journey times, providing alternatives to private cars for school runs and increasing safety around schools.

🗣 FAMOUS RESIDENTS

Famous people with a Hillingdon link include Linford Christie (athlete), Greg Dyke (Director-General of the BBC), Chris Finnigan (boxer), Russell Grant (astrologer), Glenn Hoddle (footballer), Bernard Miles (actor), George Orwell (novelist), Jane Seymour (actress) and Ronnie Wood (musician).

Residential Areas

Hillingdon boasts the second-highest percentage of detached houses (41 per cent) in London. The remaining property consists, in fairly equal proportions, of semi-detached houses, terraces and flats (mostly purpose-built). Much property is in the '30s 'suburban' style, although there are some Victorian terraces to the west of Uxbridge and in Hayes.

Hayes (UB3, UB4)

Dominated by endless streets of three-bedroom semis, this is a good area for affordable housing, with the benefit of an easy rail connection to central London (but no tube). The older part of the town is centred around a 13th century church, where there are a few Victorian terraces and cottages. Most of the residents are families and there's a large Asian community. Tucked away in nearby Yeading is Willow Tree Marina on the Grand Union Canal. Described by local estate agents as an 'oasis', the Scandinavian-style houses overlooking the canal are much more

expensive than in surrounding areas – for example, £370,000 for a three-bedroom house compared with £260,000 for a similar property in Hayes.

Ickenham (UB10)

The most village-like of all Hillingdon's towns, with a small number of shops clustered around a central pond, Ickenham sits in the middle of green belt land to the north of Uxbridge. Popular with commuters and families attracted by good local schools, the area offers a mixture of '30s semis and larger detached homes.

Northwood & Northwood Hills (HA6)

Easily Hillingdon's favourite area, with plenty of green spaces, good schools and large houses. Property includes inter-war 'mock' Tudor and neo-Georgian houses, as well as homes built in the '70s, and there are a few purpose-built flats. The area attracts wealthy families and international executives. Northwood Hills is less grand, although it boasts good views.

Ruislip & Eastcote (HA4, HA5)

Another area principally constructed in the '30s, this is pleasant rather than dull suburbia, thanks to the presence of Ruislip Common to the north and the large areas of green belt land to the north-west. Housing consists largely of detached houses, with areas of semis and smaller cottages; Eastcote has the most sought-after estates. Property becomes cheaper closer to Northolt airfield.

Uxbridge & Hillingdon (UB8, UB10)

Packed with shoppers at weekends, Uxbridge centre is dominated by retail and office

West Drayton

buildings, and surrounded by busy roads. The occasional older building still survives, there are pockets of period terraces and some new apartments are appearing on the banks of the Grand Union Canal. The rest of Uxbridge and most of Hillingdon is a mixture of semis and larger detached properties. A typical three-bedroom semi in Hillingdon costs £275,000.

Uxbridge Lido was built in 1935 and operated for 63 years until being closed in 1998. The council plans a £22mn refurbishment to restore the lido to its former glory, alongside a major new sports and leisure complex with an Olympic-sized pool, with completion expected to be in 2010.

Property Costs

Property Prices

The table below shows average property prices in the borough:

Detached: £499,922

Semi-detached: £268,428

Terraced: £239,311

Flat: £183,120

Rental Costs

The table below shows average monthly rents in the borough:

House 5+ bed: £2,500

House 4-5 bed: £2,000

House 3-4 bed: £1,550

House 2-3 bed: £1,350

Flat 2-bed: £1,050

Flat 1-bed: £750

Crime

Hillingdon is the 15th-safest borough in London, with slightly above average figures for violence and burglary, but much higher rates of vehicle-related crime. It has one of the highest car ownership rates of London's boroughs and initiatives to reduce vehicle crime are a priority. Others include tackling alcohol-related offences by introducing Controlled Drinking Zones to deter drinking on the streets and a 'bin a knife' scheme.

The police station HQ is in Uxbridge (1 Warwick Place, UB8, ☎ 0300-123 1212), with other stations in Harefield, Hayes, Ruislip and West Drayton, and a police office at Northwood.

To compare crime rates throughout London, see the table in **Appendix D**.

Health

NHS services in the borough are provided by the Hillingdon Primary Care Trust. For a full list of doctors, dentists and clinics, visit 🖥 www.nhs.uk.

To see how the Primary Care Trust compares with others in London, see the table in **Appendix D**.

Doctors & Dentists

♦ There are over 80 NHS GP surgeries, providing a range of clinics and health services.

♦ Hillingdon has 44 dental and orthodontic practices, two-thirds of which accept new adult NHS patients.

Hospitals

♦ Hillingdon Hospital (Pield Heath Road, UB8, ☎ 01895-238 282, 🖥 www.thh.nhs.uk) – A&E.

♦ Mount Vernon Hospital (Rickmansworth Road, HA6, ☎ 01923-826 111, 🖥 www.thh.nhs.uk) – minor injuries unit.

In addition, Harefield Hospital is a specialist heart and lung centre, while Northwood and Pinner Community Hospital has a range of clinics.

Private Medical Facilities

The Bishops Wood Hospital (Rickmansworth Road, HA6, ☎ 01932-835 814, 🖥 www.bmihealthcare.co.uk). To find a private GP, visit 🖥 www.privatehealth.co.uk.

Schools

Educational standards are above the national average at both primary and secondary level. In the 2009 school league tables, primary schools were placed 17th out of the 33 London boroughs (70th out of 150 UK local authorities) and secondary schools 19th (60th in the UK).

To compare schools throughout London, see the table in **Appendix D**.

LOCAL INFORMATION

The infamous highwayman and thief Dick Turpin used to hold people up in the 1700s on the roads of Uxbridge, which had an unsavoury reputation in the early 18th century. Judge William Arabin said of its residents "They will steal the very teeth out of your mouth as you walk through the streets. I know it from experience".

Pre-school

Hillingdon is well served with day care nurseries, nursery schools and playgroups in the private sector. A large number of primary schools have nursery classes.

State Schools

First schools: 65 infant, junior and primary schools, of which 13 are voluntary aided.

Secondary schools: 16 comprehensives, including one City Academy. Three schools are voluntary aided, one of which is a Sikh school. All schools have sixth forms and ten have specialist status. The top performers in 2009 were the Guru Nanak Sikh School in Hayes (which is also one of top schools for added value), the Queensmead School in Ruislip and the Haydon School in Eastcote. The John Penrose School in Harefield became the Harefield Academy in late 2006.

Special schools: Eight schools cater for students with physical disabilities and learning difficulties.

Private Schools

Most of the private schools in the borough are in Northwood, including two for girls up to the age of 18: Northwood College (which performed well in 2009) and St Helen's School. Just outside the borough boundary in Hertfordshire is Merchant Taylor's School (boys), another top UK school. Hillingdon also has an American Community School and the Hillingdon Chinese School, which is a Saturday school for children up to GCSE level, providing classes in the Chinese language, culture and arts.

Further Education

♦ Abbotsfield-Swakeleys Sixth Form Centre is a consortium sixth form for the two Uxbridge schools.

♦ Uxbridge College (🖳 www.uxbridge.ac.uk).

Higher Education

Brunel University is in Uxbridge (🖳 www.brunel.ac.uk).

Public Transport

Hillingdon is well served by both underground and overground trains, although some areas of Hayes and Yiewsley are quite a distance from the nearest station. Local bus services are good, but none go as far as central London. For those who want to get away from it all, there's Heathrow airport, which is served by bus, underground and the Heathrow Express rail link, although the easiest way to get there is by car.

Underground

The Central, Metropolitan and Piccadilly lines all terminate in the borough. A branch of the Piccadilly line goes to Heathrow airport. Typical journey times are as follows:

♦ Ickenham (Piccadilly line, zone 6) to Leicester Square, 54 minutes.

♦ Uxbridge (Metropolitan line, zone 6) to Kings Cross, 45 minutes.

♦ West Ruislip (Central line, zone 6) to Oxford Circus, 35 minutes.

Civic Centre, Uxbridge

Rail

♦ First Great Western runs a regular service into Paddington, stopping at West Drayton and Hayes (journey time is 20 minutes).

♦ Express services from Heathrow Airport to Paddington (15 minutes), with a stopping service for Hayes.

♦ Chiltern Railways trains to Marylebone stop at West and South Ruislip stations (journey time is 20 minutes).

Buses

Local bus services cover all areas in the borough, including several services to Heathrow Airport. Daytime services don't go as far as central London, but a couple of routes go to Shepherd's Bush – the number 607 goes along the A4020 Uxbridge Road and the 207's route is via the A312 Hayes by-pass. The N207 night bus runs from Holborn to Uxbridge.

Airports

Below are approximate distances and journey times from Uxbridge station to the five London airports using public transport.

♦ **City** – 21 miles; 100 minutes via Canary Wharf.

♦ **Gatwick** – 29 miles; 96 minutes via Victoria.

♦ **Heathrow** – 5 miles; 35 minutes on the A10 bus.

♦ **Luton** – 23 miles; 130 minutes via Kings Cross.

♦ **Stansted** – 38 miles; 125 minutes via Liverpool Street.

Roads

Three major roads cut across Hillingdon from east to west – the A4 and M4 in the south and the A40 in the centre – so it's a good place from which to escape urban life (except that all three roads are usually jammed with traffic!). The sheer number of cars in the borough means there are many other areas of congestion, particularly along the A312 Hayes by-pass and at the junction with the A4020 Uxbridge Road. Problems also occur along the A437 Long Lane around the junction with the A40 and on the High Road in Ickenham.

LOCAL INFORMATION

Heathrow airport in Hillingdon began life as a military airfield in World War I and after a period of private ownership was developed as an RAF base during the Second World War, but was never used. It was named after the hamlet of Heath Row which was demolished to make way for the airport. Today it's the world's third-busiest airport for passenger traffic and handles more international flights than any other airport in the world, with two parallel main runways (a third is planned) and five terminals.

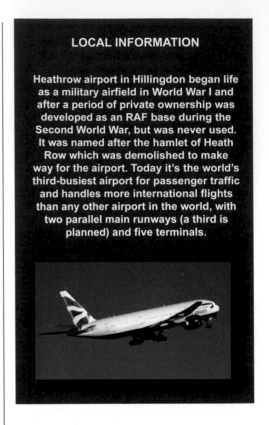

Parking

Commuter parking on local roads has long been a real headache in the borough, so the council has recently reduced all-day car parking charges (for up to 15 hours) to £2 per day at seven local car parks during the week, to reduce the number of people parking on the streets. At weekends, parking is a problem around Uxbridge, when huge numbers of people descend on the shops. There are Controlled Parking Zones in Eastcote, Northwood and Uxbridge, with another around Heathrow Airport. An annual resident's permit makes no charge for the first vehicle, then £40 per car up to a maximum of four per household.

Waste & Recycling

Household rubbish is collected weekly, as is recyclable material, which includes cans, cardboard, newspapers and plastic bottles. Garden waste is collected fortnightly in some areas. The council collects bulky items such as furniture and electrical appliances for a small fee. There are civic amenity (recycling/waste) sites in Harefield and South Ruislip, with the Hayes centre currently closed for site improvements.

Shopping

Uxbridge has two shopping centres providing outlets for most well-known chain stores, plus a few upmarket antique shops and jewellers off the main shopping street. Hayes is the second-largest location for shopping, with a pedestrianised town centre and a second string of shops along the Uxbridge Road. Shops in Hayes tend to be downmarket, with an abundance of cheap chains and burger bars. Hayes is also home to two retail parks. Further north, Ruislip and Northwood have a mixture of useful chains and local shops.

Uxbridge is among the top ten shopping destinations in London, with most leading stores represented in its Chimes and Pavilions shopping centres, while historic Windsor Street and the Market House have a number of independent shops.

Shopping Centres

♦ The Chimes Shopping Centre (High Street, Uxbridge, UB8) – BHS, Debenhams, Next and other high street chain stores.

♦ The Pavilions Shopping Centre (High Street, Uxbridge, UB8) – Argos, M&S and other chains, plus an indoor market.

♦ Terminals 1, 2, 3, 4 and 5 (Heathrow Airport, TW6) – an astonishing array of shops, including satellite stores for Harrods.

Retail parks in Hayes offer a number of out-of-town superstores.

Supermarkets

♦ Marks & Spencer at Heathrow Airport (Simply Food) and in Ruislip (Simply Food).

♦ Sainsbury's in Hayes, South Ruislip and Uxbridge.

♦ Tesco in Yeading, plus Metro stores in Uxbridge and Yiewsley, and Express stores in Cowley, Hayes, Northwood Hills and South Ruislip.

♦ Waitrose in Ruislip and Northwood.

Markets

♦ Hayes Giant Market (Blythe Road, UB3; Saturday 8.30-5pm) – general household goods.

♦ Uxbridge Market (in the Pavilions Shopping Centre; Friday and Saturday) – fashion, crafts, general household goods.

♦ West Drayton Market (Station Road, UB7; Thursday) – general household goods.

The nearest farmers' markets to Hillingdon are Ealing Farmers' Market (Leeland Road, West Ealing W13, Saturday 9am-1pm); and Pinner Farmers' Market (Queen's Head car park, Pinner High Street, HA5, Sunday 10am-2pm).

Occasional craft markets are held at the Southlands Arts Centre in West Drayton, and regular car boot sales are held in Eastcote and Hayes.

Entertainment

Although there's only one cinema, in Uxbridge, the borough is well endowed with arts centres. The Southlands Arts Centre in West Drayton offers a variety of classes, as well as exhibitions and other events, while Brunel University's Arts Centre is open to the public for concerts and exhibitions. The Nave in St Margaret's Church in Uxbridge is also an arts centre and Manor Farm in Ruislip offers a theatre, gallery and 16th century manor house. The majority of pubs in the borough are rather ordinary, night-clubs are virtually non-existent, and restaurants are dominated by fast food chains and takeaways.

Theatres

♦ The Beck Theatre (Grange Road, UB3, ☎ 020-8561 8371) – the borough's largest theatre presents a year-round programme of plays, films, concerts and dance.

◆ The Compass Theatre (Glebe Avenue, UB10, ☎ 01895-673 200) – community theatre.

◆ The Howell Theatre (Brunel University, Cleveland Road, UB8, ☎ 01895-266 074) – regular plays and concerts.

◆ Winston Churchill Hall (Manor Farm, Pinn Way, HA4, ☎ 01895-678 800) – community theatre.

Cinemas

◆ Odeon Uxbridge (Chimes Shopping Centre, Uxbridge, UB10, ☎ 0871-224 4007, 🖥 www.odeon.co.uk).

Museums & Galleries

The borough's local history museum is housed in Uxbridge Library (see below). Two other attractions are the Underground Operations Room at RAF Uxbridge (Hillingdon Road, UB10, ☎ 01895-237 144), which contains artefacts from World War II, and the free Visitor Centre at Heathrow Airport (Newall Road, TW6). Art exhibitions can be found at:

◆ The Atrium Gallery in Uxbridge Library (☎ 01895-277 798).

◆ The Bedlam Gallery at Brunel University (☎ 01895-266 074).

◆ The Cow Byre Gallery at Manor Farm (☎ 01895-678 800/450 300).

◆ Southlands Arts Centre (☎ 01895-442 784).

Libraries

There are 17 local authority libraries around the borough, with the Children and Youth Library, Home Library, Postal Talking Book and a Schools' Library Service available from the Uxbridge Central Library, the main borough library, at 14-15 High Street, UB8, ☎ 01895-250 600 (and the only one open on Sundays).

Clubs

The venues closest to being a night-club are in Uxbridge: Discotheque Royale (233 High Street, UB8, ☎ 01895-255 513) and Bar Nazdarovya (120 High Street, UB8, ☎ 01895-237 330). For a wider choice, you must head to Ealing, Harrow or central London.

Live Music

Regular concerts of contemporary, classical and world music are held at the Beck and Howell theatres (see above). Otherwise, live gigs take place at several pubs around Uxbridge and Ruislip, such as:

◆ The Crown and Treaty (90 Oxford Road, UB8, ☎ 01895-812 651).

◆ The Dolphin (1 Rockingham Road, UB8, ☎ 01895-232 656).

◆ Sweeney's (101 High Street, HA4, ☎ 01895-636 806).

Pubs

Although there are plenty of pubs in the borough, most are fairly ordinary. A notable exception is the Sky Bar in the Sheraton Skyline Hotel at Heathrow (Bath Road, UB3, ☎ 020-8759 2535), an exciting and upmarket venue that attracts trendy young people and celebrities. More down-to-earth pubs include:

◆ The Paddington Packet Boat in Cowley (High Road, UB8, ☎ 01895-442 392).

- The Prince of Wales in Uxbridge (1 Harlington Road, UB8, ☎ 01895-254 416).

- Tiger Cubs, just outside the borough in Denham (74 Oxford Road, UB9, ☎ 01895-239 503).

Restaurants

Hillingdon's restaurant scene is dominated by takeaways and fast food outlets; otherwise the choice is fairly restricted. Uxbridge has plenty of chains, including Nando's, Pizza Express and Starbucks, while the airport terminals at Heathrow have a wide choice of eateries, from McDonalds to Café Rouge, Carluccio's to Gordon Ramsay (terminal 5), although it's hardly the place to go for a romantic night out. Elsewhere, there's the occasional independent restaurant worth visiting, such as El Nomad in Ruislip (136 High Street, HA4, ☎ 01895-624 700) and the Quayside Bistro in Yeading (Willowtree Marina, West Quay Drive, UB4, ☎ 020-8841 2500), which serves modern European food in a tranquil setting.

Sports Facilities

There are five council-funded sports centres, in Hayes, Northwood and Ruislip. Facilities include:

- Swimming pools in Hayes and Ruislip.

- A Sports Wall at Hayes stadium.

- Indoor sports halls in Hayes, Northwood and Ruislip.

The newly refurbished Hillingdon Sports and Leisure Complex is due to open in 2010.

As well as sports facilities in many of the borough's parks (including tennis courts and football pitches) and outdoor bathing at Ruislip Lido in Ruislip Woods, a number of other sports centres are open to the general public. For example, there's an outdoor dry ski slope at the Hillingdon Ski Centre (Park Road, UB10, ☎ 01895-255 183) and an indoor climbing wall at Brunel University.

There are golf courses at Harefield, Hillingdon, Northwood, Ruislip, Stockley Park and West Drayton. Large areas of open space lend themselves to horse riding and there are several riding schools in the borough. Health and fitness centres are also popular and there are several independent gyms as well as branches of Holmes Place in Uxbridge and Virgin Active at Stockley Park.

Green Spaces

An astonishing 239 parks and green areas (comprising some 800 acres/324ha) lie within Hillingdon's borders, ranging from small open spaces in residential areas to woods and meadows. To the north is Ruislip Woods, the largest uninterrupted stretch of woodland in London, which is a nature reserve and also has a lido with a sandy beach, as well as a miniature steam railway. Ten Acre Woods is another nature reserve in Hillingdon. Also in the north of the borough are Bayhurst Wood and the adjacent Mad Bess Wood, both of which have facilities for picnics and barbecues.

Smaller open spaces include Ickenham Marsh; the Highgrove local nature reserve in Eastcote; Botwell Common, a new urban country park in Hayes; Stockley Country Park; and the traditional Fassnidge Park in the heart of Uxbridge. There are plenty of beautiful walks in the borough, such as the Hillingdon trail, a 20-mile path that runs from Cranford to Harefield. Sections of the London Outer Orbital Path (or London Loop – the M25 for walkers) also run through Hillingdon, and there are walks along the Grand Union Canal towpath heading out of the borough towards Denham.

LOCAL INFORMATION

Colne Valley Park, to the north-west of the borough, is a mosaic of farmland, woodland and water, with some 50mi (80km) of rivers and canals, and over 40 lakes. It's a haven for birds as well as offering leisure activities such as fishing, walking and cycling – large areas are open to the public or accessible via a network of paths.

The Gherkin, City of London

Hounslow

W4, TW3, TW4, TW5, TW7, TW8, TW13, TW14

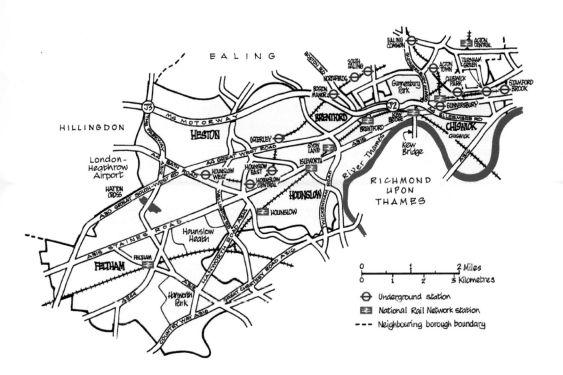

At a Glance

Best for: affordable housing, open spaces, riverside location

Not so good for: aircraft noise, crime, traffic congestion, culture, public transport

Who lives there: middle-class families, young professionals, first-time buyers

Housing stock: equally divided between detached/semis, terraces and flats, riverside homes

Housing costs: relatively inexpensive

General Information

Council Offices: The Civic Centre, Lampton Road, Hounslow, TW3 4DN (☎ 020-8583 2000)

CAA Assessment: (see 💻 http://oneplace.direct.gov.uk > Search by area > London > Hounslow)

Controlling Party: Labour

Website: 💻 www.hounslow.gov.uk

Council Tax 2010/11: £2,334 (Band G), £2,801 (Band H)

Main Areas/towns: Brentford, Chiswick, Feltham, Hanworth, Hounslow, Isleworth, Osterley

Postcodes: W4, TW3, TW4, TW5, TW7, TW8, TW13, TW14

Population & Ethnicity: 222,600. Over 25 per cent of residents are from an ethnic minority, mostly Indian, many of whom live around Hounslow. The borough is mostly white-collar, with many people employed at Heathrow Airport or in the media (Sky TV's headquarters is in Brentford and the BBC is in neighbouring Hammersmith & Fulham).

Unemployment: 7.6 per cent (London average is 8.2 per cent)

Overview

Dubbed 'the museum borough' owing to its wealth of historical buildings, Hounslow stretches from Hammersmith & Fulham to Surrey, and most residents still think it's part of Middlesex. Much of the borough lies directly beneath the Heathrow flight path, so there's a constant background roar from aircraft. Nevertheless, there are some highly desirable areas, particularly along the River Thames.

Trendy Chiswick, favoured by celebrities, is in Hounslow, as is part of the exclusive Bedford Park Estate (see **Ealing**), while further along the river is pretty Isleworth. Between the two is Brentford, once largely industrial, which has been reaping the benefits of massive investment in recent years as developers exploit Londoners' desire for riverside living.

The western districts of Feltham, Heston and Hounslow are typically suburban, with a plethora of '30s semis and rather down-at-heel high streets. However, things are changing there also: Feltham, infamous for its Young Offender's Institution, is getting new flats, shops and leisure facilities, and

Hounslow's high street is due a major face-lift over the next few years.

The town of Hounslow has existed since the 13th century and means 'Hund's mound' – the personal name Hund followed by the old English 'hlaew', meaning mound or barrow. The town was recorded in the Domesday Book as Honeslaw.

Development Plans

In November 2007, the borough was granted £4.3mn for local transport improvements, to include the provision of more cycle lanes, plans for less congested and safer school runs, and improvements to pedestrian crossings, road markings and signs. A footbridge has been built to allow pedestrians to cross the railway line at Bedfont Road; plus there have been major road renewals, modernisation of the Hounslow bus station, more bus stop accessibility, and the introduction of further controlled parking zones. Several railway stations have been completely renovated and all 75 District Line trains now include extra space for wheelchairs and have been refurbished with new seats and interiors.

Residential Areas

Hounslow has a mixture of property types, with 33 per cent detached and semi-detached houses, 31 per cent terraces and 36 per cent flats (mostly purpose-built). Victorian and Edwardian properties are clustered around Chiswick and Brentford, while Isleworth and Osterley have a mix of interesting properties, some dating back to the 16th century. The '30s semi predominates in western areas.

Chiswick House

Brentford (TW8)

An up-and-coming area, with lots of new apartment blocks along the river and around the marina, as well as on the site of former gasworks near the old docks. A riverside flat costs in the region of £350,000, while the '70s Brentford Dock estate is cheaper and a good choice for first-time buyers. Elsewhere there are streets of attractive Victorian terraces, and in the centre of the town around the Butts, some fine and quite large Georgian properties.

LOCAL INFORMATION

Standing at the confluence of the rivers Brent and Thames, Brentford is steeped in history. In 1016, Edmund Ironside defeated King Canute there, and in 1642 during the Civil War, Prince Rupert defeated two Parliamentarian cavalry regiments at the Battle of Brentford.

Chiswick (W4)

Ever popular with artists, actors and the middle classes, this is the most expensive part of the borough, benefiting from a riverside location and excellent connections to central London. Most of the property dates from the Victorian and Edwardian eras, although there are also some grand Georgian houses near the river and mansion blocks along the High Road. There are a few modern developments near the river at Corney Reach and further west at Strand-on-the-Green, which is one of the more sought-after areas, along with Bedford Park.

Feltham & Hanworth (TW13, TW14)

These are the cheapest areas of the borough, with depressing reputations and uniform housing, which consists mainly of inter-war semis and council estates. However, Feltham is on the way up, with new developments and improved recreational facilities adding to the attractions of nearby Bedfont Country Park. A further 930 new homes are planned over the next few years. Many residents work at Heathrow, although increasing numbers of central London commuters are moving in.

Hounslow (TW3, TW4)

With three underground stations as well as overground trains, multicultural Hounslow is well placed for easy access to central London. Property is fairly mixed, with a few Georgian houses and Victorian terraces in the centre, '60s blocks of flats and many plain '30s semis. New developments are appearing, particularly in the high street, where a two-bedroom flat costs around £200,000.

Isleworth & Osterley (TW7)

Village-like Isleworth has seen house prices rise in the past few years, although it's still cheaper than Richmond or Kew across the river. With some lovely riverside 18th century properties, smaller Victorian terraces towards the town centre and new developments of gated apartment blocks, this is fast becoming a fashionable area for well-heeled families and young professionals. Larger homes can be found around Osterley Park.

Property Costs

Property Prices

Feltham is at the cheaper end of the scale and Chiswick at the higher – and there's a vast difference between the two. The table below shows average property prices in the borough:

Detached: £732,961
Semi-detached: £388,249
Terraced: £335,536
Flat: £226,405

Rental Costs

The table below shows average monthly rents in the borough:

House 5+ bed: £2,400
House 4-5 bed: £1,850
House 3-4 bed: £1,350
House 2-3 bed: £1,250
Flat 2- bed: £1,050
Flat 1- bed: £850

Crime

Hounslow's crime rates are generally slightly below average for London, although violent crime is a problem. Feltham is a particular trouble spot and Hounslow has experienced problems on its streets, although this is being addressed by improved street lighting, CCTV and more street wardens.

The police station HQ is in Hounslow (3-5 Montague Road, TW3, ☎ 0300-123 1212), with other stations in Brentford, Chiswick and Feltham.

To compare crime rates throughout London, see the table in **Appendix D**.

Health

NHS services in the borough are provided by the Hounslow Primary Care Trust. For a full list of doctors, dentists and clinics, visit 🖳 www.nhs.uk.

To see how the Primary Care Trust compares with others in London, see the table in **Appendix D**.

Doctors & Dentists

◆ There are 70 NHS GP surgeries in the borough, providing a range of clinics and health services.

◆ Hounslow has 69 dental and orthodontic practices, around two-thirds of which accept new NHS patients.

Hospitals

◆ West Middlesex University Hospital (Twickenham Road, TW7, ☎ 020-8560 2121, 🖳 www.west-middlesex-hospital.nhs.uk) – A&E.

Private Medical Facilities

◆ Casualty Plus Ltd. (1010 Great West Road, TW8, ☎ 020-8380 6202) is a walk-in centre for minor injuries. To find a private GP, visit 🖳 www.privatehealth.co.uk.

Schools

Educational standards in Hounslow are well above the national average. In the 2009 school league tables, primary schools were 13th out of the 33 London boroughs (48th out of 150 UK local authorities) and secondary schools 12th (29th in the UK).

To compare schools throughout London, see the table in **Appendix D**.

Pre-school

There are plenty of nurseries and playgroups in the private sector, and nursery classes are attached to 15 of the borough's primary schools.

State Schools

First schools: 58 infant, junior and primary schools, of which nine are voluntary aided.

Secondary schools: 14 comprehensive schools, four of which are voluntary aided. All have sixth forms and ten have specialist status. In 2009, the Green School in Isleworth and the Cranford Community College in Hounslow were the top performers, with Gumley House RC Convent School in Isleworth also obtaining good results.

Special schools: Four special schools cater for students with physical disabilities and learning difficulties.

Private Schools

There are ten private schools in Hounslow, with four catering for students aged over 16, including the Arts Educational School in Chiswick, which specialises in dance, drama, music and art, and the International School of London in Isleworth.

Further Education

♦ West Thames College in Isleworth (www. thames.ac.uk).

Higher Education

♦ Brunel University has a campus at Osterley (☐ www.brunel.ac.uk).

♦ New London College is in Hounslow (☐ www. newlondoncollege.co.uk).

👤 FAMOUS RESIDENTS

Famous people associated with the borough of Hounslow include Phil Collins (singer), Vincent van Gogh (Dutch artist), William Hogarth (artist), Freddie Mercury (singer), Jimmy Page (musician), Katherine Parr (the last wife of Henry VIII), Alexander Pope (poet), William Thackeray (novelist), J.M.W. Turner (artist) and Captain Matthew Webb (the first man to swim the Channel).

Public Transport

Although the underground only covers the north-eastern and central districts, other parts of the borough are well served by the overground train network. Local bus services are frequent, although like other outer London boroughs none go as far as the West End. Heathrow Airport is close, although the easiest way to get there is by car. When Crossrail (see **Chapter 2**) is built, Gunnersbury will be on the north-south, high-speed, trans-London line.

Underground

Hounslow town has three underground stations, all served by the Piccadilly line, which also stops at Osterley. The District line only serves stations in the north of the borough. Typical journey times are as follows:

♦ Chiswick Park (District line, zone 3) to Oxford Circus, 38 minutes.

♦ Hounslow Central (Piccadilly line, zone 4) to Piccadilly Circus, 32 minutes.

Rail

The South West Trains service from Reading to Waterloo stops at Feltham, from where there's a bus link to Heathrow. After Feltham, some services stop at stations throughout Hounslow, while others go via Richmond. Typical journey time from Feltham to Waterloo is 30 minutes.

Buses

Although no routes go as far as the West End in the daytime, the borough is served by the N9 night bus from Aldwych. Otherwise, the number 237 goes from Hounslow to Shepherd's Bush and the H91 and 267 go to Hammersmith. Local services cover all areas and out to neighbouring districts, including the H98 to Hayes and the 120 to Southall. The 111 goes to Heathrow Airport.

Airports

Below are approximate distances and journey times from Hounslow to the five London airports using public transport.

♦ **City** – 20 miles; 95 minutes via Canning Town.

♦ **Gatwick** – 24 miles; 65 minutes via Clapham Junction.

♦ **Heathrow** – 3 miles; 21 minutes on the Piccadilly line, but 50 minutes by bus.

♦ **Luton** – 28 miles; 82 minutes via Kings Cross.

♦ **Stansted** – 40 miles; 97 minutes via Tottenham Hale.

Roads

The M4 starts at the end of the Chiswick High Road and thunders over parts of Brentford before skirting

the borough's northern border. The A4 divides Chiswick in two, with major congestion around the Hogarth Roundabout; traffic from both these main roads crawls along the Chiswick High Road during rush hour. The A30 starts at Hounslow, but isn't too troublesome. Bottlenecks can build up in Hounslow and Feltham.

LOCAL INFORMATION

Hounslow Heath was notorious for the highwaymen (on horseback) and footpads (who didn't have horses) who robbed travellers on the road to and from London during the 17th and 18th centuries. The Heath was so crime-ridden that gibbets, or gallows, were set up along the roadside as a warning.

Parking

Parking tends to be more difficult around Chiswick and Isleworth, although there are also problems in Hounslow. Controlled Parking Zones operate in Brentford, Chiswick, Feltham, Gunnersbury, Hounslow and Isleworth. The cost of an annual resident's parking permit varies depending on the area, ranging from £40 to £60 a year for one car, £55 to £80 for a second car and £80 to £130 for a third. Chiswick is the most expensive area and Gunnersbury the cheapest.

Waste & Recycling

General household rubbish is collected weekly, as are recyclable materials, which include aerosols, batteries, cans, cardboard, engine oil, glass, paper, shoes, telephone directories, textiles and tinfoil. Garden waste and bulky items such as fridges are collected separately. The borough's civic amenity site (recycling/waste) is at the Space Waye centre in Feltham.

Shopping

By far the best shopping area in terms of choice is Hounslow, with its shopping mall and pedestrianised high street offering many of the better-known chains (M&S, Debenhams, Dixons and more). However, for interesting and more upmarket shopping, Chiswick and Turnham Green are better, with designer clothes, antiques, delicatessens and Space NK available.

Isleworth has a good choice of shops and Brentford is beginning to attract more, but Feltham is currently in a state of flux: the dreadful '60s shopping centre has been demolished and shops in the high street are gradually being refurbished.

Shopping Centres

◆ Hounslow's Treaty Shopping Centre (High Street, TW3, ☎ 020-8572 3570) houses some 50 popular chain stores, including Debenhams and Wilkinsons, as well as the Paul Robeson Theatre, the library and the tourist information centre.

Supermarkets

◆ Marks & Spencer in Chiswick.

◆ Sainsbury's in Chiswick.

◆ Tesco at the Bull's Bridge Industrial Estate on the borough border at Southall (open 24 hours) and further branches in Feltham (open 24 hours) Hounslow, Isleworth and Osterley.

Markets

◆ The Western International Retail Market (near the Bull's Bridge Tesco, Hayes Road, UB2) has a wide choice of stalls selling general household goods; open weekends only.

◆ Hounslow Market (The West Station Market, Whitton Road, TW3; Saturday 7am-4pm) includes some fresh produce and has over 100 stalls.

◆ Chiswick Farmers' Market (The Pavilion, Market Drive, W4; Sunday 10am-2pm) has a wide selection of fresh produce, including Moroccan food. Plants are also for sale.

Entertainment

Hounslow was once where the rich and famous built their 'country' residences, leaving a legacy of five stately homes. These, together with several other visitor attractions, provide the borough with more museums than any other outside central London. Other entertainment includes Brentford's newly refurbished Watermans Arts Centre on the bank of the Thames, two cinemas and a summer festival in Gunnersbury Park, the London Mela, designed to celebrate the borough's diverse cultural heritage.

Theatres

◆ Paul Robeson Theatre (The Treaty Centre, High Street, TW3, ☎ 0845-456 2840) – regular and varied programme of productions.

- Watermans Arts Centre (High Street, TW8, ☎ 020-8232 1010, 🖳 www.watermans.org.uk) – interesting programme of children's events and Asian arts.

Cinemas

- Cineworld Multiplex Cinema (Leisure West, TW13, ☎ 020-8890 1985, 🖳 www.cineworld.co.uk).

- Watermans Arts Centre Cinema (see above).

Museums & Galleries

- Boston Manor House (Boston Manor Road, TW8, ☎ 0845-456 2800) – Jacobean house in attractive parkland.

- Chiswick House and Gardens (Burlington Lane, W4, ☎ 020-8742 3905, 🖳 www.english-heritage.org.uk) – splendid 18th century house now owned by English Heritage.

- Fuller's Brewery Shop (Chiswick Lane South, W4, ☎ 020-8996 2085, 🖳 www.fullers.co.uk/rte.asp) – tours of London's oldest brewery.

- Gunnersbury Park and Museum (Gunnersbury Park, Popes Lane, W3, ☎ 020-8992 1612) – local history collection housed in a former home of the Rothschild family.

- William Hogarth's House (Hogarth Lane, W4, ☎ 020-8994 6757) – former home of the British painter.

- Kew Bridge Steam Museum (Green Dragon Lane, TW8, ☎ 020-8568 4757, 🖳 www.kbsm.org) – steam-powered 19th century waterworks.

- Musical Museum (369 High Street, TW8, ☎ 020-8560 8108, 🖳 www.musicalmuseum.co.uk) – automated instruments.

- Osterley Park House (Jersey Road, TW7, ☎ 020-8232 5050, 🖳 www.nationaltrust.org.ul/osterley) – 18th century neo-classical villa in beautiful parkland.

- Syon House and Gardens (Syon Park, TW8, ☎ 020-8560 0882, 🖳 www.syonpark.co.uk) – spectacular house and gardens designed by Capability Brown, plus the London Butterfly House and Snakes & Ladders, a popular children's play area (see also box).

Libraries

There are 11 local authority libraries in the borough, with one mobile service. The largest is the Hounslow Library in the Treaty Centre, which includes Sunday opening, from 11.30am-4pm.

Clubs

With London's club scene on the doorstep, there are virtually no night-clubs, with the exception of Shannon's in Hounslow (32 High Street, TW3, ☎ 020-8572 8044). The Headliners chain of comedy clubs has a venue at the George IV Pub (Chiswick High Road, W4, ☎ 020-8566 4067, 🖳 www.headlinerscomedy.com/chiswick.html).

Live Music

There are no concert venues in the borough, although several pubs stage live gigs, including:

- The City Barge (27 Strand-on-the-Green, W4, ☎ 020-8994 2148).

- The Globe (104 Windmill Road, TW8, ☎ 020-8580 0086).

- The Red Lion (92 Linkfield Road, TW7, ☎ 020-8560 1457).

- The Rifleman (50 Hanworth Road, TW3, ☎ 020-8570 1487).

Pubs

The best choice of pubs is around Chiswick, home of Fuller's Brewery, whose ales are sold nearly everywhere. The High Road has a mixture of chains such as All Bar One and Pitcher & Piano, sitting alongside independents – the Old Pack Horse

(☎ 020-8894 2872) is one of the better ones. Down by the river are some attractive, family-oriented establishments, such as the Bell & Crown (11 Thames Road, Strand-on-the-Green, W4, ☎ 020-8994 4164).

Real ale lovers won't do better than the Red Lion in Isleworth (92 Linkfield Road, TW7, ☎ 020-8560 1457), winner of several CAMRA awards, with regular beer festivals. Hounslow has a few gastropubs as well as chains, although on the whole the pubs are fairly ordinary. The Sun (148 Hanworth Road, TW3, ☎ 020-8570 4675) is recommended for its food. Pubs in Feltham are generally nondescript.

Restaurants

Chiswick is the borough's food capital, with a plethora of restaurants displaying various degrees of trendiness. Chains such as Ask!, Café Rouge, Café Uno and Pizza Express mingle with the award-winning Fouberts Hotel (162 Chiswick High Road, W4, ☎ 020-8994 5202), Fishworks (6 Turnham Green Terrace, ☎ 020-8994 0086) and La Trompette (5 Devonshire Road, W4, ☎ 020-8747 1836).

There are plenty of ethnic restaurants in Isleworth, while Hounslow, which has a preponderance of competent-but-average restaurants, has recently had a lift with the Chapel Restaurant (82 Whitton Road, TW3, ☎ 020-8570 4503), serving excellent contemporary food at reasonable prices. More interesting eateries are likely to follow. Feltham lacks any decent eateries at present, but again this may well change once the much-needed improvements to the area are completed.

Sports Facilities

There are seven council-funded leisure centres, in Brentford, Chiswick, Feltham, Heston and Isleworth. The largest is the Fountain in Brentford, while the newest is the Feltham Airparcs. Facilities include:

♦ Swimming pools at Brentford (with a wave machine and slide), Chiswick, Feltham and Heston (both with water slides), and Isleworth.

♦ Indoor sports halls at Brentford and Heston.

♦ Outdoor sports pitches at Brentford, Feltham Arenas, Heston Sports Hall and Isleworth.

There are many private health centres, including branches of Esporta, Fitness First and Holmes Place. Tennis, football and cricket can be played in several parks and there are golf courses on Hounslow Heath

and in Gunnersbury and Osterley Parks. Feltham has a tenpin bowling facility at the Megabowl. Plans for an off-road motorcycling track at Bedfont Lakes Country Park are being considered by the council.

Green Spaces

Hounslow has the highest proportion of green spaces of all the London boroughs, ranging from open heathland to the gardens of stately homes and the more intimate surroundings of neighbourhood parks. Of the latter, Gunnersbury Park is the largest and has a range of attractions, including gardens, lakes and tree-lined paths. Hounslow Heath is a local nature reserve, with a diversity of natural habitats as well as walking trails. Another local nature reserve is at Pevensey Road in Feltham, which features scrubland, woodland and wetlands alongside the River Crane.

The gardens of Hounslow's stately homes are some of the loveliest in the capital and include some interesting sights, such as the replica rainforest in Syon Park (see box), which is a sanctuary for rare and endangered species. The Thames passes through the gardens, providing attractive riverside walks. Two country parks, Bedfont Lakes and Cranford, lie partly within the borough and have won Green Flag (🖥 www.greenflagaward.org.uk) awards for their facilities, while London's largest community farm is situated in Feltham (Hounslow Urban Farm, Faggs Road, TW14, ☎ 020-8751 0850).

LOCAL INFORMATION

Syon House was originally the site of a Syon Abbey (founded in 1415) and is the last surviving ducal residence – it's the London home of the Duke of Northumberland, whose family have lived there for over 400 years – complete with its country estate in Greater London. The house and its 200-acre (81-hectare) park is one of London's great houses, with an interior designed by Robert Adams and gardens by Capability Brown.

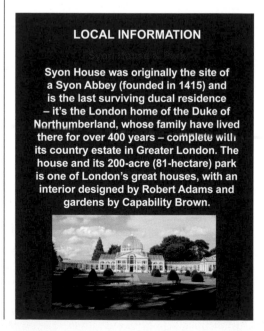

Islington

EC1 (part), N1 (part), N5, N7, N19

At a Glance

Best for: public transport, shopping, cycling paths, restaurants

Not so good for: crime, deprivation, open spaces, schools, parking

Who lives there: middle-class families, young professionals, artists, singles

Housing stock: period properties, flats (mostly period conversions), terraces

Housing Costs: expensive

General Information

Council Offices: Town Hall, Upper Street, Islington, N1 2UD (☏ 020-7527 2000)

CAA Assessment: (see 🖳 http://oneplace.direct.gov.uk > Search by area > London > Islington)

Controlling Party: Labour

Website: 🖳 www.islington.gov.uk

Council Tax 2010/11: £2,119 (Band G), £2,543 (Band H)

Main Areas/towns: Barnsbury, Canonbury, Clerkenwell, Finsbury, Highbury, Islington, Lower Holloway, St Luke's, Tufnell Park, Upper Holloway

Postcodes: EC1 (part), N1 (part), N5, N7, N19

Population & Ethnicity: 190,900, with a high proportion aged between 20 and 35. Over 25 per cent of residents belong to an ethnic minority and there's also an Italian community around Clerkenwell. The borough attracts young, well-off professionals, left-wing opinion formers, lawyers, artists and creative media types.

Unemployment: 9.7 per cent (London average is 8.2 per cent)

Overview

Islington has become one of the more fashionable London boroughs in recent years, thanks to its proximity to the City and West End, its vibrant nightlife and its abundance of interesting restaurants and shops. Straddling either side of the A1, Islington is London's smallest borough, stretching from Clerkenwell in the south to Upper Holloway in the north. Rundown and unfashionable in the first half of the last century, by the '80s central Islington had been rediscovered by the chattering classes, attracted by its charming Regency and Victorian squares, and numerous terraced houses ripe for refurbishment. Tony Blair was one of the borough's more famous residents before moving to Downing Street.

Islington has its problems and despite its reputation as a wealthy borough, over one-third of residents receive means-tested benefits. There are many large council estates badly in need of regeneration and as you travel north up the Holloway Road the area becomes increasingly shabby, although there are plans to revitalise Upper Holloway.

LOCAL INFORMATION

Islington was originally named Giseldone (1005) and later Gislandune (1062) by the Saxons, meaning 'Gīsla's hill' from the old English personal name Gīsla and dun ('hill' or 'down'). The name later mutated to Isledon, which remained in use until well into the 17th century when the modern form was adopted.

Development Plans

The council is working in partnership with housing associations and developers to build affordable housing. Over the next five to ten years, Islington will benefit from a number of regeneration projects throughout the borough, including the Archway area, the Old Street Roundabout and the Mount Pleasant post office site.

Recent upgrades in Islington have included major work on the London Cycle Network, resurfacing

St. John's Gate, Clerkenwell

carriageways, creating 20mph zones and improving pedestrian crossings. A road safety scheme is currently being implemented to reduce accidents on Highgate Hill, from Tollhouse Way to Hornsey Lane, and there are major improvements to Rosebery Avenue, Goswell Road, Hornsey Road and to the turning into Macdonald Road. Highbury & Islington station will be redeveloped for the extension of the East London Line, due to open in 2011.

Residential Areas

Islington has a wealth of Georgian, Regency and Victorian homes, both to rent and to buy, and property rarely stays on the market for long (unless there's a property crash!). Flats dominate the housing stock, a third of which are conversions of grand old houses. Plenty of family-sized terraces can be found in central Islington, Barnsbury and Canonbury; there are also a few cottages and semi-detached properties, but detached houses are rare.

Clerkenwell, Finsbury & St Luke's (EC1)

Here you will find a mixture of Georgian terraces, council blocks and classy new loft-style apartments created out of disused warehouses and factories. The advantages of the central location are matched by seriously high prices – a new two-bedroom 'loft' costs over £400,000.

Islington, Barnsbury & Canonbury (N1)

Either side of Upper Street are quiet residential streets of highly desirable (and expensive) Georgian and Victorian terraces. Expect to pay from around £950,000 to well over £1.75mn for a four-bedroom house. After Canonbury, property

tends to become less desirable the further east you go, with the exception of some attractive waterside homes that have recently been built around the City Road Basin. The Marquess Estate, a former council estate, is being refurbished in a partnership scheme between the council, housing corporations and private developers.

Highbury (N5)

Close to the nightlife of central Islington – but with quiet streets – and the open space of Highbury Fields, and with some spacious Victorian homes, this is a good bet for families priced out of the southern districts. There's also a good supply of one- and two-bedroom flats to rent and buy, making it popular with young professionals. There are also cheaper '30s semis and tower blocks of flats.

Lower Holloway & Tufnell Park (N7)

Post-war council properties (particularly around Holloway prison) sit side-by-side with Victorian terraces and grander homes, now mostly converted into flats. Tufnell Park tends to be the more expensive of the two areas. New development schemes – which include homes for key workers and underground parking – will provide over 2,000 apartments and do much to improve the desirability of the area.

Upper Holloway (N19)

This is the shabbier end of the borough, which makes property more affordable than elsewhere. There are a lot of flats in converted Victorian villas, particularly to the west, while the most sought-after properties are family-sized houses to the east of Archway Road, just south of affluent Highgate.

Property Costs

Property Prices

The table below shows average property prices in the borough:

Detached: £0 (no recent sales recorded)
Semi-detached: £772,652
Terraced: £726,097
Flat: £348,593

Rental Costs

The table below shows average monthly rents in the borough:

> House 5+ bed: £7,600
>
> House 4-5 bed: £3,900
>
> House 3-4 bed: £3,100
>
> House 2-3 bed: £2,700
>
> Flat 2-bed: £1,700
>
> Flat 1-bed: £1,250

Crime

Islington has the 11th-highest crime rate of London's boroughs, with violent crime and car theft well above the national average.

The police station HQ is in Islington (2 Tolpuddle Street, N1, ☎ 0303-123 1212), with another station in Holloway.

To compare crime rates throughout London, see the table in **Appendix D**.

Health

NHS services in the borough are provided by the Islington Primary Care Trust. For a full list of doctors, dentists and clinics, visit 💻 www.nhs.uk.

To see how the Primary Care Trust compares with others in London, see the table in **Appendix D**.

Doctors & Dentists

♦ There are 62 NHS GP surgeries in the borough, providing a range of clinics and health services.

♦ Islington has 31 dental and orthodontic practices, most of which accept new NHS patients.

Hospitals

♦ The Whittington Hospital (Highgate Hill, N19, ☎ 020-7272 3070, 💻 www.whittington.nhs.uk) – A&E and NHS walk-in centre.

♦ The Moorfields Eye Hospital (City Road, EC1, ☎ 020-7253 3411, 💻 www.moorfields.org.uk) – A&E for eye injuries only.

Private Medical Facilities

Symbiosis Healthcare has a private GP service at the Sobell Leisure Centre (1st Floor, Sobell Leisure Centre, Hornsey Road, N7, ☎ 020-7697

8982, 💻 www.symbiosishealthcare.co.uk). The nearest private hospital is the Highgate Hospital (see **Haringey**).

To find a private GP you can visit 💻 www.privatehealth.co.uk.

Schools

Standards in Islington's primary schools have begun to improve in recent years, although secondary schools remain near the bottom of the UK school league tables. In 2009, primary schools were placed 22nd out of the 33 London boroughs (96th out of 150 UK local authorities) and secondary schools 31st (124th in the UK).

To compare schools throughout London, see the table in **Appendix D**.

> **LOCAL INFORMATION**
>
> After a promising start in the 18th century, Islington deteriorated into a slum area during Victorian times. Even as recently as the late '60s, almost 60 per cent housing was in multi-occupation (shared by two or more families) – the highest in London – and many properties had only outside WCs and no baths. It's been transformed in the last few decades and is now one of London's most desirable addresses.

Pre-school

There are numerous private and council-run playgroups and nursery schools, including three state nursery schools and ten early years centres.

State Schools

First schools: There are 44 infant, junior and primary schools, of which 16 are voluntary aided.

Secondary schools: Islington has eight comprehensive schools, three of which are voluntary aided. Five schools have sixth forms and six have specialist status. The top performer in 2009 was St Aloysius RC College in Hornsey Lane, Highgate.

Special schools: Three schools cater for students with physical disabilities and learning difficulties.

Private Schools

The borough's only private secondary school is the selective Italia Conti Academy of Theatre Arts

(🖥 www.italia-conti.co.uk), the UK's first school for the performing arts. Charterhouse Square School is a preparatory school for 3-11 year olds on the border with the City (by Smithfield Market).

Further Education

♦ The City & Islington College in Islington (🖥 www.candi.ac.uk).

Higher Education

♦ City University is based around Finsbury (🖥 www.city.ac.uk).

♦ The London North Campus of the London Metropolitan University is in Holloway (🖥 www.londonmet.ac.uk).

♦ The American University in London is in Holloway (🖥 www.aul.edu).

Public Transport

Islington has good public transport links into the West End, the City and Docklands, as well as to other boroughs.

Underground

There are services to the West End from all parts of the borough on the Northern, Piccadilly and Victoria lines. The City branch of the Northern line provides access to the City from Angel, and on to Docklands via the Docklands Light Railway at Bank. Typical journey times are as follows:

♦ Angel (Northern line, zone 1) to Bank, 7 minutes.

♦ Highbury & Islington (Victoria line, zone 2) to Oxford Circus, 9 minutes.

♦ Holloway Road (Piccadilly line, zone 2) to Piccadilly Circus, 13 minutes.

♦ Archway (Northern line, zone 2) to Leicester Square, 15 minutes.

Rail

WAGN trains run to Moorgate from Highbury & Islington and Essex Road stations (journey time is 10 minutes, weekdays only). The North London line connects the borough to the East End at Highbury & Islington, and will link to the East London line in 2011.

Buses

There's a large number of routes into central London and out to neighbouring boroughs; the best choices are from Archway or Angel. Night buses include the N19, N20 and N29.

Airports

Below are approximate distances and journey times from Highbury & Islington station to the five London airports using public transport.

♦ **City** – 8 miles; 45 minutes via Canary Wharf.

♦ **Gatwick** – 27 miles; 60 minutes via Victoria.

♦ **Heathrow** – 6 miles; 65 minutes via Paddington.

♦ **Luton** – 26 miles; 53 minutes via Kings Cross.

♦ **Stansted** – 29 miles; 72 minutes via Tottenham Hale, or 80 minutes via Liverpool Street.

Roads

Islington has excellent road links north out of London via the A1, although this road is also the largest cause of congestion in the borough (despite being a red route), particularly by the Angel, along Upper Street and around the Archway roundabout. One-way schemes and traffic calming measures in Barnsbury and Canonbury have created much quieter residential streets.

👤 **FAMOUS RESIDENTS**

Islington is associated with many figures of English literature, including Douglas Adams (author of *The Hitchhikers' Guide to the Galaxy* **series), Kate Greenaway (children's writer & illustrator), Charles Lamb (writer), Edward Lear (writer and poet), George Orwell (novelist), Sir Walter Raleigh (writer and poet) and Evelyn Waugh (novelist). Other residents have included Tony Blair (Prime Minister), Benjamin Britten (composer), Edmund Halley (Astronomer Royal), William Hogarth (artist), Simon Rattle (conductor) and Charlie Watts (Rolling Stones drummer).**

Parking

Parking is a major problem in Islington, made worse by commuters trying to avoid the Congestion Charge Zone, which starts at the Pentonville and City roads. Much of the borough is a Controlled Parking Zone, where parking costs from £35 to £200 a year for a resident's parking permit for up to three cars, the cost depending on the CO_2 emissions or the engine size of your vehicle(s). Additional restricted parking measures operate on match days around the Emirates (Arsenal) football stadium. Since June 2005, the practice of clamping cars has largely stopped. The shortage of parking facilities means that private parking spaces are at a premium. Some new apartment blocks offer secure underground parking for an additional cost of £25,000 to £30,000.

Waste & Recycling

General household rubbish is collected weekly and there's a doorstep collection scheme for recyclable material, including cans, cardboard, garden refuse, glass and plastics. Residents can also take waste to the new £60mn, state-of-the-art, waste and recycling centre in Hornsey.

Shopping

Shopping in the borough is a mixture of average high street chains and pockets of interesting and quirky shops. For example, there are designer outlets along Islington's Upper, Cross and Theberton Streets, while some unusual retailers crop up on the Holloway Road (such as Fettered Pleasures, specialising in fetish gear). The main shopping areas are around the Angel and along Upper Street, plus the Nags Head in Lower Holloway, where there's a selection of high street names, including Argos, M&S and a Clarks factory shop for bargain shoes. Clerkenwell's Exmouth Market also has a few designer shops.

Shopping Centres

♦ N1 Shopping Mall (21 Parkfield Street, N1, ☎ 020-7359 2674, 🖳 www.n1islington.com) – upmarket fashion chains.

♦ Nags Head Shopping Centre (Holloway Road, Lower Holloway, N7, ☎ 020-7700 6344) – everyday essentials.

Supermarkets

♦ Morrisons in Lower Holloway.

♦ Sainsbury's in Liverpool Road (open until midnight) and local stores in Archway, Essex Road, Holloway and Upper Street.

♦ Waitrose in Lower Holloway.

♦ Tesco Metro in Islington Green.

Markets

♦ Archway Market (St. John's Grove/Holloway Road, Islington; Thursday 12pm-5pm and Saturday 10am-5pm).

♦ Camden Passage Market (opposite Islington Green by Essex Road, N1; antiques on Wednesday 10am-2pm and Saturday 10am-5pm; farmers' market on Sunday mornings). See also box.

♦ Chapel Market (between Liverpool Road and Penton Street, N1; Tuesday to Saturday 9am-6pm, and Sunday 8.30am-4pm) – fresh produce, clothes and speciality stalls selling cheese and olives, etc.

♦ Exmouth Market (Rosebery Avenue/Farringdon Road, Islington; Monday to Saturday 9am-6pm).

♦ Nags Head Market (Seven Sisters Road, N7; Monday to Saturday 8am-5pm) – indoor market selling household essentials and second-hand goods; with a flea market on Sunday (7am-2pm).

♦ Whitecross Market (Whitecross Street, EC1; Monday to Saturday 10am-5pm) – household goods and clothes; and a specialist food market, with over 50 producers, every Thursday and Friday.

♦ Islington Farmers' Market (William Tyndale School, behind the Town Hall, Upper Street, N1; Sunday 10am-2pm) has a huge selection of fresh produce.

For the past 40 years Camden Passage (Angel Tube, Wednesdays and Saturdays) has been one of London's most interesting venues for antique lovers. It's a fascinating hotch-potch of people and culture, and home to some 200 antiques dealers and stalls, plus a wealth of excellent eating places.

Entertainment

As well as proximity to the West End's theatres, cinemas, clubs and restaurants, Islington residents have several entertainment venues on their doorstep, including Sadler's Wells, London's premier theatre for ballet. Islington is also noted for fringe theatre. There are some excellent restaurants and pubs, particularly around Clerkenwell, Camden Passage and Upper Street.

LOCAL INFORMATION

Lower Holloway in Islington is home to Freightliners City Farm, which is one of the many city farms throughout London. The farm, which isn't like an industrial farm, contains a wide range of animals, including rabbits, cows, chickens and pigs, all free for the public to view.

Theatres

♦ Almeida Theatre (Almeida Street, N1, ☎ 020-7359 4404, 🖳 www.almeida.co.uk) – London's premier theatre for off-West End productions.

♦ Little Angel Puppet Theatre (Dagmar Passage, N1, ☎ 020-7226 1787, 🖳 www.littleangeltheatre.com) – children's puppet shows.

♦ Pleasance Theatre (Carpenters Mews, North Road, N7, ☎ 020-7609 1800, 🖳 www.pleasance.co.uk) – fringe events.

♦ Sadler's Wells and the adjoining Lillian Baylis Studio (Rosebery Avenue, EC1, ☎ 020-7863 8198, 🖳 www.sadlerswells.com) – ballet and contemporary dance.

♦ Tower Theatre (Canonbury Place, N1, ☎ 020-7226 3633, 🖳 www.towertheatre.org.uk) – fringe and community productions.

♦ Workhouse Theatre (242 Pentonville Road, N1, ☎ 020-7837 6030, 🖳 www.thepoorschool.com) – performances by the Poor School drama studio.

Pub theatres offer an intimate setting for many fringe productions. The best in Islington is the King's Head (115 Upper Street, N1, ☎ 020-7226 1916, 🖳 www.kingsheadtheatre.org).

Cinemas

♦ Odeon Holloway (419-427 Holloway Road, N7, ☎ 0871-224 4007, 🖳 www.odeon.co.uk).

♦ Screen on the Green (Upper Street, N1, ☎ 020-7226 3520, 🖳 www.screencinemas.co.uk).

♦ Vue Cinema (N1 Shopping Mall, 21 Parkfield Street, N1, ☎ 08712-240 240, 🖳 www.myvue.com).

Museums & Galleries

Islington has many interesting places to visit, including:

♦ Arsenal FC Museum (Highbury House, 75 Drayton Park, N5, ☎ 020-7704 4504, 🖳 www.arsenal.com) – club history and artefacts.

♦ Crafts Council Gallery (44a Pentonville Road, N1, ☎ 020-7806 2500, 🖳 www.craftscouncil.org.uk) – inspiring exhibitions of arts and crafts.

♦ Estorick Collection (39a Canonbury Square, N1, ☎ 020-7704 9522, 🖳 www.estorickcollection.com) – modern Italian art.

♦ Islington Arts Factory (2 Parkhurst Road, N7, ☎ 020-7607 0561, 🖳 www.islingtonartsfactory.org.uk) – three galleries of art, sculpture and photography.

♦ Islington Museum (Town Hall, Upper Street, N1, ☎ 020-7527 2837) – local history collection.

♦ London Canal Museum (New Wharf Road, N1, ☎ 020-7713 0836, 💻 www.canalmuseum.org. uk) – history of London's canals.

Libraries

There are ten local authority libraries in the borough, with one mobile service. The Central Library in Highbury opens seven days a week (Fieldway Crescent, N5, ☎ 020-7527 6900) and the local history centre is housed in Finsbury Library (245 St John Street, EC1, ☎ 020-7527 7960). The privately-run Marx Memorial Library is in Clerkenwell (37a Clerkenwell Green, EC1, ☎ 020-7251 4706).

Clubs

Islington's vibrant club scene offers numerous venues on the borough borders at Kings Cross Goods Yard (see **Camden**). Other clubs include:

♦ Central Station TV (37 Wharfdale Road, N1, ☎ 020-7278 3294).

♦ The Dome Club (1 Dartmouth Park Hill, N19, ☎ 020-7272 8153.

♦ Electrowerkz (7 Torrens Street, EC1, ☎ 020-7837 6419, 💻 www.electrowerkz.com.

♦ Turnmills (63B Clerkenwell Road, EC1, ☎ 020-7250 3409, 💻 www.turnmills.co.uk).

Comedy can be seen at the Comedy Brewhouse at the Camden Head (2 Camden Walk, N1, ☎ 020-7359 0851).

Live Music

Several pubs offer live music and there are a few dedicated music venues such as:

♦ The Garage (20 Highbury Corner, N5, ☎ 020-7607 1818, 💻 www.meanfiddler.com) – famous live rock/indie venue.

♦ Scala (275 Pentonville Road, N1, ☎ 020-7833 2022, 💻 www.scala-london.co.uk) – alternative music venue.

♦ Union Chapel (Compton Ave, N1, ☎ 020-7226 3750, 💻 www.unionchapel.org.uk) – unique music venue in a working church.

Pubs

Islington's pubs range from late-licensed bars and gastropubs to traditional working men's boozers, with chains, cocktail bars and grubby dives in between. The trendier places tend to be located around central Islington and Clerkenwell, such as the Embassy Bar (119 Essex Road, N1, ☎ 020-7226 7901, 💻 www.embassybar.com), while some of Tufnell Park's more traditional locals are gradually being reinvented as gastropubs, including the Junction Tavern (101 Fortess Road, NW5, ☎ 020-7485 9400). For more choices, refer to a London guidebook such as Time Out's *Bars, Pubs and Clubs*.

Restaurants

Most areas are bursting with restaurants offering every type of food imaginable, with the exception of Upper Holloway, which has few. Well-known names such as Pizza Express and Ask! sit next to small independent eateries in central Islington, such as Sir Terence Conran's Almeida Restaurant and Bar (30 Almeida Street, N1, ☎ 020-7354 4777, 💻 www. conran-restaurants.co.uk). Camden Passage is noted for stylish restaurants. Further south, the restaurant that appeared in the film *Lock, Stock and Two Smoking Barrels*, Vic Naylor's Bar and Grill (38 St John Street, EC1, ☎ 020-7608 2181), is one of many places packed with after-work diners. Highbury and Holloway are bursting with ethnic restaurants such as Iznik (19 Highbury Park, N5, ☎ 020-7704 8099), serving fine African cuisine, and the Royal Cous-Cous (316 Holloway Road, N7, ☎ 020-7700 2188), a first-rate Moroccan restaurant.

Sports Facilities

As well as outdoor sports pitches in many of the borough's parks, there are seven council-funded leisure centres, in Archway, Finsbury, Highbury, Lower Holloway and St Luke's. The Aquaterra charity manages all seven and full details can be found at 💻 *www.islington.gov.uk/leisure/ Sports/170.asp*. Amenities include:

♦ Swimming pools at Archway, Caledonian Road, Ironmonger Row and Highbury (claimed to be one of London's best).

♦ A climbing wall and ice rink at the Sobell Leisure Centre in Lower Holloway.

♦ Two Astroturf sports pitches and tennis courts at the Islington Tennis Centre in Lower Holloway.

There are also branches of well-known health clubs and gyms, as well as two gay saunas:

Pacific 33 (33 Hornsey Road, N7, ☎ 020-7609 8011) and Pleasuredrome North (278 Caledonian Road, N1, ☎ 020-7607 0063). Premiership football club Arsenal is a major sports attraction. Its home is at the new Emirates Stadium in Ashburton Grove, N5, which has a capacity of over 60,000 (☎ 020-7704 4000, 🖥 www.arsenal.com) – tickets cost £33 to £66.

Green Spaces

Islington has fewer open spaces than any other London borough. Its largest park is the 29-acre (12-hectare) Highbury Fields (Highbury & Islington underground station), home to Highbury Pool, tennis courts and an award-winning adventure playground. Next door to Arsenal station is Gillespie Park, one of three nature reserves in the borough. Across in Lower Holloway there's Freightliners City Farm (Sheringham Road, N7,

☎ 020-7609 0467). For waterside walks, the Regent's Canal runs across the centre of the borough and the New River Walk at Canonbury Grove is a 3-mile trail that follows the line of the New River, a fresh water aqueduct built in 1612.

LOCAL INFORMATION

Regent's Canal (named after the Prince Regent) was designed by John Nash and opened in 1816, and is part of the Grand Union Canal that links London and Birmingham. The last horse-drawn commercial traffic was in 1956 – today the canal's towpath is a cycle route for commuters and a leisure area for walkers and boat trips on the canal.

Regent's Canal

Albert Memorial, Kensington Gardens, Westminster

Kensington & Chelsea

SW3, SW5, SW7, SW10, W8, W10, W11, W14 (part)

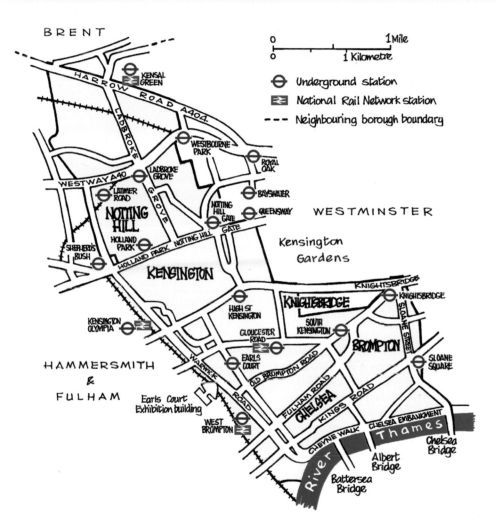

At a Glance

Best for: exclusivity, shopping, culture, entertainment, schools, public transport

Not so good for: affordable housing, traffic congestion, parking, crowds

Who lives there: the seriously wealthy, professionals, young couples/singles

Housing stock: period houses, mews cottages, period flat conversions

Housing costs: very expensive

General Information

Council Offices: The Town Hall, Hornton Street, W8 7NX (☎ 020-7937 5464)

CAA Assessment: (see ⌨ http://oneplace.direct.gov.uk > Search by area > London > Kensington & Chelsea)

Controlling Party: Conservative

Website: ⌨ www.rbkc.gov.uk

Council Tax 2010/11: £1,799 (Band G), £2,158 (Band H)

Main Areas/towns: Brompton, Chelsea, Earl's Court, Holland Park, Kensington, North Kensington, Notting Hill, South Kensington

Postcodes: SW3, SW5, SW7, SW10, W8, W10, W11, W14 (part)

Population & Ethnicity: 180,300, with around 20 per cent ethnic minorities, mostly Afro-Caribbean living in North Kensington and Notting Hill. There are large Chinese, French, Spanish and Italian communities, as well as transient populations of visitors, diplomats and international executives. The borough attracts the super-rich, politicians and members of the glitterati.

Unemployment: 6.9 per cent (London average 8.2 per cent)

Overview

Birthplace of the 'swinging sixties' and punk music, home to royalty, diplomats and film stars, and the setting for several films as well as the famous Notting Hill Carnival, Kensington & Chelsea is London's most desirable and affluent borough. Boasting several important museums, beautiful parks and fashionable shopping districts, the 'Royal Borough' (an honorary title granted in 1901 on the wishes of Queen Victoria after her death) is a magnet for tourists, particularly in summer.

Chelsea and Kensington are the most expensive areas of London and have always attracted the 'A-list' and wealthy foreigners. Notting Hill has become one of London's trendiest areas, with a bustling shopping district including Portobello Road Market. The borough isn't exclusively the preserve of the prosperous, however, and there's also deprivation, mainly concentrated around the council estates in North Kensington. But even there gentrification is beginning to take over, as the middle classes priced out of Notting Hill transform the area.

 FAMOUS RESIDENTS

Kensington – Famous Residents

Edward Elgar (1857-1934), the English romantic composer, lived for some years in Avonmore Road.

Mahatma Gandhi (1869-1948) lived in West Kensington for around a year when he was a law student at the Inner Temple (1888-1891).

Bram Stoker (1847-1912), the Irish writer and author of *Dracula*, lived at 18 St. Leonard's Terrace, SW3.

Development Plans

A major redevelopment of the Royal Hospital Chelsea is currently underway, and includes the now completed Margaret Thatcher Infirmary building (care home) which was opened in 2009; upgrading the Long Wards (sheltered accommodation) to meet modern standards,

City whiz kids and film stars with wallets large enough to afford the sky-high prices. The King's Road remains one of London's favourite shopping districts and the roads off it feature highly-prized small terraces, with larger homes near the Royal Hospital and redbrick mansion blocks around Sloane Square. Some of the most sought-after streets are towards the river.

The former Chelsea Art College now houses ultra-expensive flats, where a parking space alone costs £100,000. As an alternative, a houseboat on the river at Chelsea Wharf costs from £300,000-£500,000, plus mooring fees – from £20,000-£50,000, usually paid every fifteen years. Cheyne Walk (pronounced Chaine-ee) is one of London's best addresses and has always attracted the rich and famous.

which is due for completion in 2010; and the reorganisation of ancillary facilities to provide improved services to live-in pensioners. To fund the redevelopment, the Chelsea Pensioners' Appeal was launched in late 2003 to raise £35mn. The work is proving successful, with all planned improvements having being finished on schedule, to date.

Residential Areas

Over 70 per cent of the borough is a conservation area, with a plethora of beautiful Georgian and Victorian buildings, interspersed with modern developments. Over 80 per cent of properties are flats and it's the only borough where the number of conversions exceeds the number of purpose-built flats. Some 15 per cent of homes are terraced houses and just 2 per cent semi-detached or detached.

Brompton & South Kensington (SW5, SW7, SW10)

Dominated by the major museums in Exhibition Road (where a redevelopment will improve pedestrian walkways) and popular with the French community whose children attend the *Lycée Français*, this is a smart and respectable area. Many large houses have been converted into flats, although there are smaller terraces and attractive mews cottages north of the Fulham Road. The Boltons is a unique almond-shaped estate of Italianate, semi-detached villas built in the 1850s.

Chelsea (SW3, SW10)

Once an arty and bohemian quarter, Chelsea's comfortable squares are now home to bankers,

Earl's Court (SW5)

For years, many of the tall stucco houses provided cheap hotels and bedsits. Nowadays, the shabby facades have been smartened up and the apartments restored, and they're inhabited by young professionals. The area is particularly popular with the gay community. Away from the noisy Earl's Court Road are streets and squares of pleasant Victorian houses (around £1.25mn for three bedrooms), while larger properties can be found towards Kensington.

Holland Park & Kensington (W8)

The rich and the powerful live in the area's lovely tall houses and spacious apartments near the open spaces of Holland Park and Kensington Gardens. Favoured by a cosmopolitan mix of diplomats and wealthy executives, with a few royals in residence at Kensington Palace, these are among the best addresses in London, with excellent amenities on the doorstep in Kensington High Street and Notting Hill. Holland Park has some of the largest mansions in the borough, some converted into flats, plus several modern apartment blocks and townhouses. There's a buoyant rental market at the upper end of the scale.

Notting Hill & North Kensington (W10, W11)

Notting Hill was fashionable before the film of the same name, since when its popularity has soared, along with its property prices. Garden squares and wide streets lined with elegant, spacious houses surround Ladbroke Grove, while the area by Portland Road is almost village-like in character. Property is mixed (flats, grand villas and modest terraces) and so is the population, with media professionals, executives and celebrities all living there. Cosmopolitan 'North Ken' is more down-at-heel and is the cheapest neighbourhood, but even there prices can rise above £1.75mn for larger homes in 'better' roads. Housing associations own a lot of property and there are several high-rise council estates, including Trellick Tower, a 30-storey concrete eyesore containing spacious flats.

Property Costs

Property Prices

House prices in Kensington & Chelsea are among the highest in London, with a house in Holland Park easily costing £10-15mn and a three-bedroom Chelsea flat over £4mn. The table below shows average property prices in the borough:

Detached: £0 (no recent sales)
Semi-detached: £2,097,000
Terraced: £2,231,016
Flat: £741,192

Rental Costs

The table below shows average monthly rents in the borough:

House 5+ bed: £7,600
House 4/5 bed: £5,650
House 3/4 bed: £5,200
House 2/3 bed: £4,000
Flat 2 bed: £2,475
Flat 1 bed: £1,850

Crime

Kensington & Chelsea has the ninth-lowest overall crime rate in London, with the fourth-lowest rate of violent offences. A Controlled Drinking Zone has been introduced around Earl's Court to deter drinking on the street, while the crack cocaine houses that were appearing in North Kensington are gradually being eliminated by successful police campaigns.

The police station HQ is in Kensington (72-74 Earl's Court Road, W8, ☎ 0300-123 1212), with other stations in Chelsea and Notting Hill.

To compare crime rates throughout London, see the table in **Appendix D**.

Health

The residents of Kensington & Chelsea have the UK's highest life expectancy, at nearly 85 years for women and 80 for men. NHS services in the borough are provided by the Kensington and Chelsea Primary Care Trust. For a full list of doctors, dentists and clinics, visit 🖥 www.nhs.uk.

To see how the Primary Care Trust compares with others in London, see the table in **Appendix D**.

Doctors & Dentists

♦ There are 82 NHS GP surgeries in the borough, providing a range of clinics and health services.

♦ Kensington & Chelsea has 83 dental and orthodontic practices, around half of which accept new NHS patients.

Hospitals

♦ Chelsea & Westminster Hospital (369 Fulham Road, SW10, ☎ 020-8746 8000, 🖥 www.chelwest.nhs.uk); A&E.

♦ The Royal Brompton Hospital (Sydney Street, SW3, ☎ 020-7352 8121, 🖥 www.rbht.nhs.uk); heart and lung treatment.

♦ The Royal Marsden Hospital (Fulham Road, SW3, ☎ 020-7352 8171, 🖥 www royalmarsden.org); cancer care and treatment.

♦ St Charles Hospital (Exmoor Street, W10, ☎ 020-8969 2488); centre for health and care.

There are two NHS nursing homes: the Joan Bartlett in Kensington and the Princess Louise in Notting Hill.

Private Medical Facilities

♦ Courtfield Private Medical Centre (73 Courtfield Gardens, SW5, ☎ 020-8846 6093); private GP services.

FAMOUS RESIDENTS

Chelsea – Famous Residents

Isambard Kingdom Brunel (1806-1859), Britain's most celebrated civil engineer (98 Cheyne Walk, SW3).

Freddie Mercury (1946-1991), iconic lead singer with the band *Queen* **(1 Logan Place, W8) – the outer wall is covered in graffiti and messages from Queen fans from around the world.**

JMW Turner (1775-1851), celebrated English artist, died at 119 Cheyne Walk (SW3) on December 19th, 1851.

Oscar Wilde (1854-1900), Irish playwright, novelist and poet (34 Tite Street – 16 Tite Street in Wilde's lifetime).

♦ The Cromwell Hospital (Cromwell Road, SW5, ☎ 020-7460 2000, 🖳 www.cromwell-hospital. co.uk); private hospital to the rich and famous.

♦ The Florence Nightingale Clinic (1-5 Radnor Walk, SW3, ☎ 020-7349 3900); treatment for acute psychological and emotional problems.

To find a private GP you can also visit 🖳 www. privatehealth.co.uk.

Schools

Over half of the borough's children are educated privately and independent schools outnumber state schools. A large proportion of students learn English as an additional (second) language. In the 2009 school league tables, primary schools were placed second out of the 33 London boroughs (second out of 150 UK local authorities) and secondary schools third (third in the UK).

To compare schools throughout London, see the table in **Appendix D**.

Pre-school

The state sector has excellent facilities, with four state nursery schools, plus nursery classes attached to many primary schools. There are several private day nurseries and nursery schools, including one for French children, one for Spanish pupils and a nursery section at the Southbank International School.

State Schools

First schools: 26 primary schools, of which 14 are voluntary aided.

Secondary schools: Four comprehensive schools, three of which are voluntary aided. Two schools have sixth forms and three have specialist status. The top performer in 2009 was the Holland Park School at Campden Hill Road. The school is currently being totally rebuilt by the council, and is due for completion in 2013. A new Church of England Academy in Lots Road in Chelsea opened in 2009.

Special schools: Two special schools cater for students with physical disabilities and learning difficulties.

Private Schools

There are 39 private schools in the borough, including five for international students:

♦ The Hellenic College of London (Greek) in Chelsea;

♦ The Instituto Español Vicente Canada (Spanish) in Notting Hill;

♦ The Jamahiriy School in Chelsea;

♦ Lycée Français Charles de Gaulle (French) in South Kensington;

♦ The Southbank International School in Notting Hill.

In 2009, the top performer was the Lycée Français (where pupils gained some of the best GCSE and A level results in the country).

Further Education

♦ Kensington and Chelsea College in Chelsea (💻 www.kcc.ac.uk).

♦ St Charles Catholic Sixth Form College in North Kensington (💻 www.stcharles.ac.uk).

Higher Education

South Kensington is home to Imperial College London (💻 www.imperial.ac.uk), the Institute of Cancer Research (💻 www.icr.ac.uk) and the Royal College of Music (💻 www.rcm.ac.uk). The English National Ballet School is in Chelsea (💻 www.enbschool.org.uk).

Public Transport

Underground, train and bus services are extensive. A new station on the West London Line at Imperial Wharf welcomed its first passengers in September 2009 (see **Hammersmith & Fulham**). The station is situated between West Brompton and Clapham Junction stations (services are provided by London Overground).

Underground

The Central, Circle, District and Piccadilly lines serve all areas, although parts of Chelsea are a long walk from a station. Typical journey times are as follows:

♦ Earl's Court (Piccadilly line, zone 1) to Piccadilly Circus, 11 minutes.

♦ Notting Hill Gate (Central line, zone 1) to Oxford Circus, 8 minutes.

Rail

Kensington Olympia is served by two trans-London lines, the West London line from Willesden to Clapham Junction and the Southern Railways service from Watford to the south coast.

Buses

Bus connections to central London are excellent. Routes include the 19 and 22 from Chelsea, the 94 (Notting Hill to Oxford Circus) and the 74 (Earl's Court to Marble Arch). The number 11 travels the length of the King's Road and stops at all the main tourist sights en route to Liverpool Street.

Bus services have recently been improved in frequency and scope in response to the western extension of the London Congestion Charge Zone (see **Chapter 2**), which requires drivers of vehicles driving into the borough to pay a daily fee of £8.

The 148 (Notting Hill to Marble Arch) is a 24-hour service and night buses include the N11, N19 and N97.

River Transport

A commuter river service runs mornings and evenings between Chelsea Embankment (Cadogan Pier) and Blackfriars, Monday to Friday, with a journey time of 20 minutes.

Portobello Road, colourful houses

Airports

Below are approximate distances and journey times from Earl's Court to the five London international airports using public transport.

◆ **City** – 11 miles; 50 minutes via Bank.

◆ **Gatwick** – 24 miles; 40 minutes via Victoria.

◆ **Heathrow** – 11 miles; 30 minutes via Paddington or 45 minutes on the Piccadilly line.

◆ **Luton** – 27 miles; 60 minutes via Kings Cross.

◆ **Stansted** – 33 miles; 65 minutes via Tottenham Hale.

Roads

The M40 Westway and the A4 run east-west through the borough and can be slow during rush hours; the Cromwell Road section of the A4 is particularly congested. Traffic congestion is a problem on many other roads, including the King's Road, Kensington High Street, the Earl's Court one-way system and along Chelsea Embankment. The Congestion Charge Zone was extended to include most streets in the borough from 19th February 2007, although residents qualify for a 90 per cent discount.

Parking

Controlled Parking Zones are in operation almost everywhere. Additional restrictions apply around Earl's Court and spaces are scarce in many areas. A resident's parking permit costs from £66 to £104 per year, based on vehicle emissions or engine capacity, and entitles the holder to park in marked bays anywhere in the borough.

Waste & Recycling

Household rubbish and recyclable materials are collected two or three times a week. Recyclable materials include cans, cardboard, glass, paper (except telephone directories) and plastic bottles. Garden waste is also collected for composting and the council removes bulky items such as furniture for a fee. Other domestic waste can be taken to the civic amenity sites (recycling/waste) at Cringle Street in Battersea and Smugglers Way in Wandsworth.

Shopping

Kensington & Chelsea is famous for three major shopping areas, each with its own identity:

◆ Kensington High Street has a wide range of top fashion chains as well as the ubiquitous M&S. Kensington Church Street is renowned for antiques.

◆ The King's Road isn't as trend-setting as it once was, but it's still noted for its designer and up-market furniture shops, as well as the revamped Peter Jones (Sloane Square) department store. The Old Brompton and Fulham Roads also have interesting and exclusive shopping.

◆ Notting Hill's Portobello Road Market is world famous, and elsewhere shops range from designer boutiques to rare vinyl record shops.

LOCAL INFORMATION

Earls Court (est. 1937) and Olympia (1886) are London's premier exhibition centres, staging a range of consumer shows, including antiques, property, careers and numerous trade exhibitions. Major events include the Ideal Home Show (March), the London Book Fair (April), the Olympia International Art & Antiques Fair (June) and the France Show (January).

Shopping Centres

◆ Duke of York Square (off the King's Road, SW3) is a shopping complex featuring quality chains, shoe shops and independent boutiques. Kensington residents are benefitting from the giant Westfield shopping centre in the neighbouring borough of Hammersmith & Fulham, which opened in October 2008. It's the largest in-town shopping mall in Europe, twice the size of Brent Cross (see Brent) and around the same size as Bluewater in Kent, featuring over 250 shops, 40 cafés and restaurants, a state-of-the-art 14-screen Cinema de Lux, a health and beauty retreat, and a gymnasium.

Supermarkets

♦ Marks & Spencer 'Simply Food' stores in Brompton Road, Chelsea, Earls Court and Notting Hill Gate. A new outlet at the Westfield London shopping centre in Shepherd's Bush.

♦ Sainsbury's in Chelsea and Kensington, with local stores in Brompton, Earl's Court and South Kensington.

♦ Tesco in Kensington (open 24 hours) with Metro and Express stores in Brompton, Holland Park, Kensington, Notting Hill and South Kensington.

♦ Waitrose in Kensington, Chelsea and the Westfield London shopping centre in Shepherd's Bush.

Markets

♦ Antiquarius (131 King's Road, SW3) – indoor antiques market; Monday to Saturday.

♦ Portobello Road Market – one of the ten most visited tourist sites in London, it's several markets rolled into one: the antiques market (Saturday) and the flea market, a clothes section and a general food market (all open Monday to Sunday).

There are two farmers' markets in the borough: the Notting Hill Farmer's Market (Kensington Place, W8; Saturday 9am-1pm) and the new Bute Street farmers' market (Saturday 9am-1pm).

Entertainment

With three major museums and several small ones, cinemas, theatres and concert halls, there's plenty to see and do in the borough. The annual Notting Hill Carnival (August – see box) is a huge street festival that attracts hordes of visitors. If there aren't enough pubs and restaurants to suit you in Kensington & Chelsea, you're extremely hard to please!

Theatres

♦ Chelsea Centre Theatre (7 World's End Place, SW10, ☎ 020-7352 1967) – showcases new writing.

♦ The Gate Theatre (11 Pembridge Road, W11, ☎ 020-7229 0706, 🖥 www.gatetheatre.co.uk) – small theatre above the Prince Albert pub producing international works.

♦ Holland Park Theatre (Holland Park, W8, ☎ 020-7602 7856, 🖥 www.operahollandpark. com) – open-air theatre presenting opera programmes.

♦ Royal Court Theatre (Sloane Square, SW1, ☎ 020-7565 5000, 🖥 www.royalcourttheatre. com) – national theatre of new writing, with a second, smaller theatre upstairs.

LOCAL INFORMATION

Notting Hill Carnival

Held in August over two days, the Notting Hill Carnival (since 1965) is staged mainly by the local Caribbean population. It's the largest street festival in Europe (and second worldwide only to Rio's Carnival) and attracts some 2mn people.

Cinemas

As well as the cinemas listed below, Notting Hill Gate hosts the annual Portobello Film Festival (🖥 www.portobellofilmfestival.com), described by *Time Out* as 'London's largest film free-for-all'; the festival shows short films by new filmmakers.

♦ Ciné Lumière (Institut Français, 17 Queensbury Place, SW7, ☎ 020-7073 1350, 🖥 www.institut-francais.org.uk).

◆ Cineworld Fulham Road (142 Fulham Road, SW10, ☎ 0871-200 2000, 🖳 www.ugccinemas.co.uk).

◆ The Electric Cinema (191 Portobello Road, W11, ☎ 020-7908 9696, 🖳 www.the-electric.co.uk).

◆ The Gate Cinema (87 Notting Hill Gate, W11, ☎ 020-7727 4043, 🖳 www.gatecinema.co.uk).

◆ Notting Hill Coronet (103 Notting Hill Gate, W11, ☎ 020-7727 6705, 🖳 www.coronet.org).

◆ Odeon Kensington (263 Kensington High Street, W8, ☎ 0871-224 4007, 🖳 www.odeon.co.uk).

Museums & Galleries

Kensington is home to some of London's (and the world's) best museums, including the Natural History Museum (🖳 www.nhm.ac.uk), the Science Museum (🖳 www.sciencemuseum.org.uk) and the Victoria & Albert Museum (🖳 www.vam.ac.uk), which are situated in an area dubbed 'Albertopolis' in South Kensington. Nearby, the State Apartments and Court Dress Collection are open to the public in Kensington Palace (🖳 www.hrp.org.uk). Other attractions include:

◆ Carlyle's House (24 Cheyne Row, SW3, ☎ 020-7352 7087, 🖳 www.nationaltrust.org.uk) – former home of the Victorian writer and historian, Thomas Carlyle.

◆ Leighton House Museum (12 Holland Park Road, W14, ☎ 020-7602 3316) – studio-house built by the Victorian artist Frederic, Lord Leighton.

◆ Linley Sambourne House (18 Stafford Terrace, W8, ☎ as Leighton House) – former home of Punch cartoonist Edward Linley Sambourne.

◆ National Army Museum (Royal Hospital Road, SW3, ☎ 020-7730 0717, 🖳 www.national-army-museum.ac.uk) – history of the British Army.

◆ Royal College of Music Museum of Instruments (Prince Consort Road, SW7, ☎ 020-7591 4346, 🖳 www.rcm.ac.uk) – renowned collection of mainly European instruments.

◆ Royal Hospital Museum (Royal Hospital Road, SW3, ☎ 020-7881 5203, 🖳 www.chelsea-pensioners.org.uk) – history of army veterans known as 'Chelsea Pensioners'.

Libraries

There are six local authority libraries in the borough with one mobile service. The main library is Kensington Central Library (Phillimore Walk, W8, ☎ 020-7361 3010). None are open on Sundays.

Clubs

The borough is home to a wealth of clubs, including:

◆ 606 Club (90 Lots Road, SW10, ☎ 020-7352 5953, 🖳 www.606club.com) – one of the best live jazz clubs in Europe.

◆ Blag Club (Canalot Studios, 222 Kensal Road, W10, ☎ 020-8960 2732).

◆ Club 9 (9 Young Street, W8, ☎ 020-7937 9403).

◆ Ion Bar (161 Ladbroke Grove, W10, ☎ 020-8960 1702).

◆ Neighbourhood (12 Acklam Road, W10, ☎ 020-7524 7979, 🖳 www.meanfiddler.com).

◆ Notting Hill Arts Club (21 Notting Hill Gate, W11, ☎ 020-7460 4459, 🖳 www.nottinghillartsclub.com).

Live Music

As well as the major concert halls listed below, there's live opera in Holland Park (see **Green Spaces** below) and regular gigs are held in several of the borough's pubs.

◆ Cadogan Hall (5 Sloane Terrace, SW1, ☎ 020-7730 4500, 🖳 www.cadoganhall.com) – new 900-seat concert venue, formerly a Christian Scientist church.

◆ Earl's Court Exhibition Centre (Warwick Road, SW5, ☎ 020-7385 1200, 🖳 www.eco.co.uk) – London's largest concert venue, with a capacity for 20,000.

◆ The Royal Albert Hall (Kensington Gore, SW7, ☎ 020-7589 8212, 🖳 www.royalalberthall.com) – premier venue and home of the proms.

Pubs

There are plenty of pubs and bars to suit every taste, but it's a good idea to avoid the busy main roads and seek out back street gems, where a guidebook, such as Time Out's *Bars, Pubs and Clubs,* is helpful. Chelsea has its fair share of trendy establishments, many betraying an arty influence left over from its bohemian past, of which the Cross Keys is a fine example (1 Lawrence Street, SW3, ☎ 020-7349 9111). The gastropub is also much in evidence, including the Lots Road Pub & Dining Room (114 Lots Road, SW10, ☎ 020-7352 6645). Notting Hill has some highly fashionable new bars, particularly in the Westbourne Grove area, mixed with eccentric delights such as Beach Blanket Babylon (45 Ledbury Road, W11, ☎ 020-7229 2907) and the Lonsdale (44-48 Lonsdale Road, W11, ☎ 0871-075 7159).

In Kensington, the better pubs are off the tourist trail. The Windsor Castle (114 Campden Hill Road, W8, ☎ 020-7243 9551) is an unspoilt local with a wealthy clientele, while the Troubadour (265 Old Brompton Road, SW5, ☎ 020-7370 1434) is a delicatessen/café/bar with live music and a long history (Bob Dylan and John Lennon both played there in the '60s). Earl's Court has several gay-friendly bars, including the Coleherne (261 Old Brompton Road, SW5, ☎ 020-7244 5951).

Restaurants

The borough is overflowing with cafes and restaurants to suit every taste and wallet. For recommendations, see any London guidebook. There are lots of chains, particularly around Kensington High Street and the King's Road, but also some excellent independents. London's only three-starred Michelin restaurant is in Chelsea – the Gordon Ramsay (68 Royal Hospital Road, SW3, ☎ 020-7352 4441, www.gordonramsay.com) – while one of London's best Indian restaurants is Zaika in Kensington (1 Kensington High Street, W8, ☎ 020-7795 6533, 💻 www.zaika-restaurant.co.uk).

Brompton is where the beautiful and the wealthy go to be seen in numerous restaurants, such as Bibendum in the glorious Michelin building (81 Fulham Road, SW3, ☎ 020-7581 5817, 💻 www.bibendum.co.uk). Notting Hill's most expensive restaurants lie around Kensington Park Road, but the most interesting are closer to Westbourne Grove and include Ashbells, serving delightful South Carolinian food (29 All Saints Road, W11, ☎ 020-7221 8585) and Beach Blanket Babylon (45 Ledbury Road, W11, ☎ 020-7229 2907, 💻 www.beachblanket.co.uk), a seriously chic venue serving international food.

Sports Facilities

Sports facilities are limited in the borough, but there are two council-funded leisure centres:

◆ Chelsea Sports Centre – swimming pool, sports hall and a floodlit tarmac court.

◆ Kensington Leisure Centre – swimming pools, sports halls and floodlit Astroturf sports pitches.

The council maintains a purpose-built canoeing facility on the Grand Union Canal in Notting Hill and several sports can be played in the borough's parks – there's even a golf bunker in Holland Park. Branches of the main private gym chains are dotted throughout the borough and the Earl's Court Gym is a popular gay hangout. See 💻 www.thefitmap.co.uk/healthclubs to find your nearest gym.

Green Spaces

Open spaces include Kensington Gardens and Holland Park, as well as several smaller parks and 'garden squares' (the latter open only to residents). Kensington Gardens is a popular venue for sunbathing and picnics, and features the Princess Diana Memorial Playground. Holland Park is considered by many to be London's most romantic park and is the borough's largest open space, boasting numerous sports facilities, an open-air theatre, an ecology centre and an orangery.

There are attractive riverside walks and gardens around Albert and Battersea Bridges and the Chelsea Embankment, while the canal-side walk along the Grand Union has been planted with native shrubs and wild flowers. The Chelsea Flower Show (see box) takes place in the grounds of the Chelsea Royal Hospital, and nearby is the UK's second-oldest botanical garden (after Kew), the Chelsea Physic Garden.

LOCAL INFORMATION

Chelsea Flower Show

Organised by the Royal Horticultural Society, the Chelsea Flower Show (established 1862) is held annually over five days in May at the Chelsea Royal Hospital, SW3 (since 1913), home of the Chelsea pensioners. It's one of the world's most prestigious flower (or garden) shows, attracting over 150,000 visitors annually (limited by the 11-acre/4.5-hectare site), and one of the season's hottest tickets.

Kingston-upon-Thames

KT1, KT2, KT3, KT5, KT6 (part), KT9

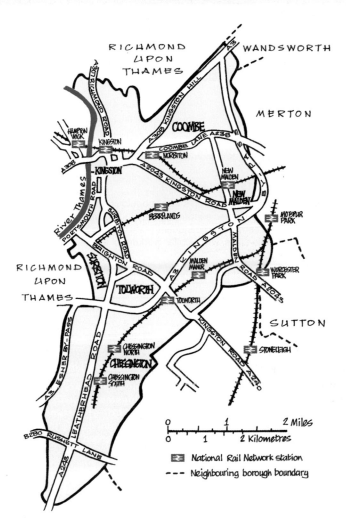

At a Glance

Best for: schools, public transport, shopping, low crime

Not so good for: no tube, traffic congestion, parking

Who lives there: middle-class families, young professionals, City commuters

Housing stock: period properties, high proportion of detached/semis, one-third flats

Housing costs: moderate

General Information

Council Offices: Guildhall, High Street, Kingston-upon-Thames, KT1 1EU, (☎ 020-8547 5757)

CAA Assessment: (see ⌨ http://oneplace.direct.gov.uk > Search by area > London > Kingston-upon-Thames)

Controlling Party: Liberal Democrat

Website: ⌨ www.kingston.gov.uk

Council Tax 2010/11: £2,770 (Band G), £3,324 (Band H)

Main Areas/towns: Chessington, Kingston-upon-Thames, New Malden, Surbiton, Tolworth

Postcodes: KT1, KT2, KT3, KT5, KT6 (part), KT9

Population & Ethnicity: 160,100 – London's least populous borough. Some 15 per cent of the population is from an ethnic minority, mostly Indian, with a sizeable Korean community in New Malden. There's a large student population in Kingston town. The borough is popular with middle-class, white-collar workers of all age groups, many of whom commute to central London.

Unemployment: 5.2 per cent (London average is 8.2 per cent)

Overview

With its southern border on the edge of green belt countryside, Kingston is more like a part of Surrey (which it used to be) than London. It's a popular commuter location, with some good schools, fast links to the centre of London and one of the best shopping districts outside central London. Kingston-upon-Thames is the borough's largest town. Once an attractive market town with a royal charter, and still boasting one of the best-preserved medieval street plans in the south-east, Kingston has enjoyed extensive redevelopment in recent years and today is a dynamic and modern town, with a host of recreational facilities.

To the south is Surbiton, a highly popular residential area with its own lively character, while to the east is New Malden, home to a large retail park off the A3 trunk road and streets of substantial but reasonably priced family properties. In the far south of the borough is Chessington, best known for its World of Adventures theme park, whose visitors clog the roads during the summer season.

LOCAL INFORMATION

Seven Anglo-Saxon kings were crowned at Kingston-upon-Thames between 800 and 979AD – the stone believed to have been used during the coronations is preserved in the marketplace.

Development Plans

After a postal ballot in the winter of 2007, Kingston became the UK's first Business Improvement District (BID), generating £4mn over five years through a 1 per cent supplement on the rateable value of properties, doubling the borough's current spending on town centre services. Business rate payers have voted to invest collectively in local improvements to enhance their trading environment. This idea has been promoted successfully in the US, but Kingston is the first council to try the scheme in the UK.

Residential Areas

Some 13 per cent of houses in Kingston are detached, 32 per cent are semi-detached, 21 per cent are terraced and 34 per cent are flats. Much of its housing was built in the inter-war period, although there are Victorian and Edwardian homes near the town centres, and several new developments around Kingston and Chessington.

Kingston-upon-Thames (KT1, KT2)

A self-contained town, with an attractive riverside location, Kingston is home to the borough's main shopping and commercial centre, as well as the best schools. In the centre, property consists largely of Victorian and Edwardian terraces, while apartments with a river view – some inter-war, some new – command premium prices (around £285,000 for two bedrooms). North Kingston has more semis built in the '20s and '30s. Families come here for the schools, while first-time buyers like the wide choice of flats. Coombe in the north-east is an expensive and up-market neighbourhood, with substantial detached houses with large gardens, including some individual '30s designs.

New Malden (KT3)

This is a large residential area with two railway stations and a busy, faintly shabby high street, as well as a sizeable retail park at Shannon's Corner on the eastern border with Merton. While Victorian terraces fill the roads off the high street, larger family homes line streets away from the centre. To the south are areas of semis and terraces, and there are plenty of flats that are popular with first-time buyers. A three-bedroom semi costs around £335,000. Old Malden and Motspur Park are quiet districts with a good supply of family houses.

New Malden is home to the largest expatriate community of South Koreans in the world.

Surbiton (KT6)

With a non-stop rail connection to central London (just 16 minutes), easy access to the A3 and a bustling shopping area, Surbiton is the quintessential commuter town. Much of the property is Victorian – houses and conversions – and there are some attractive modern apartments and retirement flats. Prices tend to be higher closer to the station. Away from the centre are substantial inter-war family houses – detached around Southborough in the south-west and semis in Berrylands to the east. Commuters, local families, young professionals and retirees all live in the area.

Tolworth & Chessington (KT6, KT9)

Divided by the A3, these are ordinary suburban towns dominated by mid-war semis and terraces, with modern infill developments here and there. On the plus side, there are no high-rise blocks and it's a short distance to the pleasant Surrey countryside. Council housing is concentrated around South Chessington, which is also the site of the theme park. Prices are among the lowest in

Houseboat at Kingston Bridge

the borough, attracting first-time buyers and local families.

Property Costs

Property Prices

The table below shows average property prices in the borough:

> Detached: £674,196
> Semi-detached: £359,589
> Terraced: £295,851
> Flat: £217,523

Rental Costs

The table below shows average monthly rents in the borough:

> House 5+ bed: £3,750
> House 4-5 bed: £2,450
> House 3-4 bed: £1,750
> House 2-3 bed: £1,500
> Flat 2-bed: £1,300
> Flat 1-bed: £950

Crime

Kingston is one of the safest London boroughs, with the lowest overall crime rate at the start of 2010, and the lowest rates for burglary and stolen cars. Much of the street crime in the borough involves teenagers and includes the theft of mobile phones and graffiti. An extensive network of CCTV cameras is helping reduce street crime and an anti-graffiti strategy has been developed.

The police station HQ is in Kingston (5 High Street, KT1, ☎ 0300-123 1212), with other stations in New Malden and Surbiton.

To compare crime rates throughout London, see the table in **Appendix D**.

Health

NHS services in the borough are provided by the Kingston Primary Care Trust. For a full list of doctors, dentists and clinics, visit 💻 www.nhs.uk.

To see how the Primary Care Trust compares with others in London, see the table in **Appendix D**.

Doctors & Dentists

♦ There are 51 NHS GP surgeries in the borough, providing a range of clinics and health services.

♦ Kingston has 36 dental and orthodontic practices, although few accept new NHS patients.

Hospitals

♦ Kingston Hospital (Galsworthy Road, KT2, ☎ 020-8546 7711, 💻 www.kingstonhospital. nhs.uk) – A&E.

♦ Surbiton Hospital (Ewell Road, KT6, ☎ 020-8399 7111) – out-patient clinics and rehabilitation care.

♦ Tolworth Hospital (Red Lion Road, KT6, ☎ 020-8390 0102) – out-patient clinics, rehabilitation and psychiatric care.

Private Medical Facilities

The New Victoria Hospital is in Coombe (184 Coombe Lane West, KT2, ☎ 020-8949 9000, 💻 www.newvictoria.co.uk). To find a private GP, visit 💻 www.privatehealth.co.uk.

Schools

Kingston has some excellent schools in both the state and private sectors, so the best can hand pick their pupils, many of whom travel from outside the borough. In the 2009 school league tables, primary schools were placed third out of the 33 London boroughs (fifth out of 150 UK local authorities) and secondary schools first (first in the UK).

To compare schools throughout London, see the table in **Appendix D**.

Pre-school

Nursery classes are attached to many of the borough's infant and primary schools, and there's one state nursery in Surbiton. There's a wide choice of privately-run nursery schools and playgroups.

State Schools

First schools: 34 primary schools, of which 14 are voluntary aided.

Secondary schools: Two selective schools and ten comprehensives. Three schools are voluntary aided, all have sixth forms and eight have specialist status. Tiffin (boys) and Tiffin Girls in Kingston are highly popular selective schools, where students achieve consistently high results. In 2009, the Tiffin School was among the top 200 for A level results, while Tiffin Girls was among the top UK schools for GCSE and A level results. The best performer among non-selective schools was the Holy Cross School at New Malden.

Special schools: Three special schools cater for students with physical disabilities and learning difficulties.

The Plough, Old Malden

Private Schools

There are four private schools catering for senior age pupils in Kingston, all of which are selective. The top performers in 2009 were Kingston Grammar (one of the top UK schools for GCSE results) and Surbiton High. The Marymount International School in Kingston town follows a syllabus based on American college and international baccalaureate curricula.

Further Education

♦ Hillcroft College in Surbiton (www.hillcroft. ac.uk) is a national residential college for women returning to education.

♦ Kingston College (www.kingston-college.co.uk).

Higher Education

♦ Kingston University (www.kingston.ac.uk) is located in the centre of Kingston town.

👤 FAMOUS RESIDENTS

Famous people associated with Kingston include Enid Blyton (author), Richard Briers (actor), Eric Clapton (rock musician), James Cracknell (Olympic rower), Lawrence Dallaglio (rugby player), Michael Frayn (playwright & novelist), John Galsworthy (writer), Simon May (musician & composer), Alec Stewart (cricketer) and Lynn Truss (author).

Public Transport

The underground network doesn't reach as far as Kingston – the nearest stations are in Richmond and Wimbledon, which are both a 15-minute bus ride from Kingston town. Rail connections are more extensive.

Rail

South West Trains provides frequent services to Waterloo on three branch lines in the borough and stop at ten stations. The fastest service is from Surbiton, where the non-stop service takes 16 minutes to Waterloo. Trains from Chessington South have a journey time of 40 minutes, while trains from Kingston take 30 minutes.

Buses

As with most outer London boroughs, bus routes stop short of central London, although there are good services to Hampton, Kew, Richmond and parts of Surrey. The 285 from Kingston and the X26 from New Malden go to Heathrow Airport. Local services are frequent and at Christmas there's a useful park-and-ride scheme from Chessington World of Adventures to Kingston town centre. Two night buses make the journey from the West End – N22 and N77 – while the N213 goes from Kingston to West Croydon.

River Transport

Scheduled river boats run daily from Kingston to Richmond or Hampton Court throughout the spring and summer.

Airports

Below are the approximate distances and journey times from Kingston to the five London airports using public transport.

♦ **City** – 17 miles; 85 minutes via Canary Wharf.

♦ **Gatwick** – 18 miles; 60 minutes via Clapham Junction.

♦ **Heathrow** – 8 miles; 85 minutes by 285 bus.

♦ **Luton** – 32 miles; 100 minutes via Kings Cross.

♦ **Stansted** – 41 miles; 120 minutes via Tottenham Hale.

Roads

There's easy access from most towns to the A3, which cuts across the middle of the borough and connects with the M25 at Cobham. Local roads around Kingston can be slow during rush hours and at weekends, when shoppers flood into the town from neighbouring areas. The main A243 through Chessington is often clogged during the morning run to work, as well as during the summer months when visitors descend on the theme park. The borough was named the Good Going Borough of the Year in 2005 for promoting car sharing and public transport as ways of reducing traffic congestion.

Parking

Only Kingston and Surbiton town centres and adjacent residential streets have Controlled Parking Zones, where parking costs £60 per year for a resident's permit. However, parking is often difficult in Kingston's shopping district, particularly at weekends (when it's virtually impossible unless you arrive early), despite the large number of car parks. The Christmas period is another problem time, although there's a park and ride bus from Chessington.

Waste & Recycling

Household rubbish is collected weekly. Recyclable materials, which include cans, glass, paper, plastic bottles, shoes and textiles, are collected fortnightly, although there are currently trial weekly collections from some council flats. The council also collects garden waste and bulky items such as furniture. The borough's amenity site (recycling/waste) is at Villiers Road in Kingston.

Shopping

Kingston town is a Mecca for shoppers, with shopping malls, pedestrianised shopping streets and outdoor markets. Branches of most leading chain stores are represented, as well as Bentalls and John Lewis department stores, a massive M&S (+food) and independent retailers. It's no surprise that Kingston is regularly listed in the top ten shopping destinations in the south-east.

Surbiton has a small shopping district for daily essentials, with one or two more unusual 'art' shops. New Malden has a tired-but-busy high street with small chains and charity shops, but it also has a branch of upmarket furniture retailer Ligne Roset. Chessington has small local parades of shops selling everyday groceries and there's an M&S food store at Tolworth.

Shopping Centres

♦ The Bentalls Shopping Centre (Clarence Street, KT1) – Bentalls department store and branches of leading chains, including Waterstones, HMV and the Disney Store.

♦ Crown Arcade (off Union Street, KT1) – small covered area with a few shops.

♦ Eden Walk Shopping Centre (off Eden Street, KT1) – chains including BHS, Habitat and Heal's.

♦ Shannon's Corner Retail Park (off the A3 at New Malden) has numerous out of town superstores such as Comet, DFS and MFI.

The Bentalls Shopping Centre

Supermarkets

♦ Asda on the London Road in Kingston.

♦ Marks & Spencer in Surbiton (Simply Food) and Tolworth.

♦ Sainsbury's in Kingston town centre, on the Richmond Road and in Surbiton.

♦ Tesco Superstore at Shannon's Corner (open 24 hours), plus an Express store in Tolworth.

♦ Waitrose in Kingston town centre (in John Lewis), New Malden and Surbiton.

Markets

♦ Kingston Market (Market Place, KT1; Monday-Saturday 9am-5pm) – fruit and veg, household goods and crafts.

♦ Fairfield Market (Wheatfield Way, KT1; Monday 8am-2pm) – general household goods.

Entertainment

The borough's main entertainment centre is Kingston town, where there's a brand new theatre, a 14-screen cinema in the Rotunda complex, art galleries and the local history museum. The town hosts annual literary and film festivals, and there are plenty of restaurants, bars and night-clubs. Elsewhere entertainment options are thin on the ground, although there are some decent restaurants in Surbiton and New Malden.

Theatres

♦ Rose Theatre or Rose of Kingston Theatre (26 High Street, KT1, ☎ 0871-230 1552, 💻 www.kingstontheatre.org) – a new 1,000-seat theatre, opened in 2008.

Cinemas

♦ Odeon Kingston (The Rotunda, Clarence Street, KT1, ☎ 0871-224 4007, 💻 www.odeon.co.uk).

Museums & Galleries

♦ Guildhall Art Gallery (The Guildhall, High Street, KT1, ☎ 020-8547 5757).

♦ Kingston Museum (Wheatfield Way, KT1, ☎ 020-8547 6460) – local history collection and art gallery.

LOCAL INFORMATION

One of the more unusual sights in Kingston is several disused red telephone boxes that have been tipped up to lean against one another (see photo) in an arrangement resembling dominoes. This sculpture by David Mach was commissioned in 1988, and is aptly titled 'Out of Order'.

♦ Stanley Picker Gallery (Kingston University, Middle Mill Island, Knights Park, KT1, ☎ 020-8417 4074, 💻 www.kingston.ac.uk/picker/gallery.htm) – broad programme of contemporary exhibitions.

♦ The Toilet Gallery (151 Clarence Street, KT1, ☎ 07881-832 291, 💻 www.toiletgallery.org) – converted public loo showcasing young artists' work.

Libraries

There are seven local authority libraries in the borough, with one mobile service. The main library is in Kingston (Fairfield Road, KT1, ☎ 020-8547 6400), closed on Sundays.

Clubs

♦ Bacchus (2 Union Street, KT1, ☎ 020-8546 7798, 💻 www.bacchuslatebar.co.uk).

♦ Bar Eivissa (48 High Street, KT1, ☎ 020-8408 4900, 💻 www.bar-eivissa.com).

- Isha Lounge Bar (43-51 Richmond Road, KT2, ☎ 020-8546 0099, 🖥 www.whenthemusicstops.com).

- McClusky's (4 Bishops Hall, KT1, ☎ 020-8541 1515, 🖥 www.mccluskys.com).

- Oceana (154 Clarence Street, KT1, ☎ 020-8547 2848, 🖥 www.oceanaclubs.com).

- Ram Jam Club (behind the Grey Horse Pub, see below).

- Reflex (184 London Road, KT2, ☎ 020-8549 9911).

- The Works (1 St James Road, KT1, ☎ 020-8541 4411, 🖥 www.workskingston.com).

There's also the Crack Comedy Club every Sunday evening at the Grey Horse Pub (see below).

Live Music

- Boaters Inn (Canbury Gardens, Lower Ham Road, KT2, ☎ 020-8541 4672) – Sunday jazz nights.

- The Fighting Cocks (56 Old London Road, KT, ☎ 020-8974 6469, 🖥 www.the-fighting-cocks.co.uk) – Kingston's only alternative music venue.

- The Grey Horse (46 Richmond Road, KT2, ☎ 020-8541 4328, 🖥 www.grey-horse.co.uk)

Saxon Coronation Stone, 10th Century

– live music, comedy and a night-club at the back.

- Kingston Parish Church (Market Square, KT1, ☎ 020-8546 5964) – regular classical concerts.

- The Peel (160 Cambridge Road, KT1, ☎ 020-8255 8104, 🖥 www.peelmuzik.com) – Kingston's largest live music venue.

Pubs

Kingston town is the best bet for pubs and bars, with plenty of choice in the town centre and a crop of new bars along the river joining the more traditional pubs there. The Boater's Inn (see above) is a popular pub along the towpath, while the more modern Gazebo (King's Passage, Thames Street, KT1, ☎ 020-8456 4495) is closer to the shops. For excellent beer there's the Wych Elm (93 Elm Road, KT2, ☎ 020-8546 3271), a friendly local and CAMRA award-winner.

Surbiton has a few lively places for a good night out, such as the Antelope (87 Maple Road, KT6, ☎ 020-8399 5029) and the Fox and Hounds (60 Portsmouth Road, KT6, ☎ 020-8390 3408), which are 'proper' pubs. Elsewhere pubs are fairly ordinary, although for a taste of the countryside there's the Star just over the border in Surrey (Kingston Road, KT22, ☎ 01372-842 416), an attractive pub with a beer garden and excellent food.

Restaurants

Kingston's restaurants have improved along with the new developments around the town centre and there's now a wide selection of eateries, with branches of chains such as Carluccio's, Pizza Express, TGI Fridays and Wagamama. Riverside restaurants are popular, including Riverside Vegetaria (64 High Street, KT1, ☎ 020-8456 7992) and Frere Jaques (10 Riverside Walk, KT1, ☎ 020-8546 1332, 🖥 www.frerejacques.co.uk).

Surbiton has enough restaurants to avoid the need for a trip into Kingston, such as the French Table (85 Maple Road, KT6, ☎ 020-8399 2365, 🖥 www.thefrenchtable.co.uk), with simple but beautifully prepared food, plus Chinese restaurant Yumcha (59 Brighton Road, KT6, ☎ 020-8399 5533, 🖥 www.yumchauk.com). New Malden boasts some interesting Korean restaurants, including Korea Garden (73 Kingston Road, KT3, ☎ 020-8336 1208) and MiGa, which serves Korean 'fusion' food (79 Kingston Road, KT3, ☎ 020-8942 1811), while Tolworth and Chessington are dominated by takeaways.

Sports Facilities

There are six council-funded sports centres in the borough, in Chessington, Kingston, New Malden and Tolworth. The sports facilities at Tiffin Girls' School in Kingston are also open to the public. Overall, facilities include:

- Swimming pools at Kingston and New Malden.
- Indoor sports halls at Chessington, Tolworth and the Tiffin Girls' School.
- All-weather athletics stadium and five-a-side pitches at the Kingsmeadow Centre in Kingston.
- Outdoor sports pitches at Tolworth and the Tiffin Girls' School.
- Kayaking, canoeing and dinghy sailing courses at the Albany Park Canoe and Sailing Centre in Kingston.

There are four golf courses in the borough and outdoor sports pitches are available in many of the borough's parks. The YMCA in Kingston offers a full range of dry sports facilities and was winner of the *Time Out* award for the best family facility in 2002. There's another YMCA gym in Surbiton. Branches of various health clubs and gyms can be found in Kingston town, including a David Lloyd centre, Esporta and Holmes Place. For the less sporty, there are tenpin bowling alleys in Kingston and Tolworth. Spectators may enjoy sporting events in neighbouring boroughs, including tennis at Wimbledon (see **Merton**), rugby in Twickenham (see **Richmond**) and horse racing at Sandown Park in Esher, Surrey.

Green Spaces

The main tracts of local open space are outside the borough, in Richmond Park and Wimbledon Common to the north, Bushy Park and Hampton Court to the west, and Horton Country Park to the south-east. Within Kingston town, Canbury Gardens is a leafy spacious park on the river, which hosts summer concerts on the bandstand. Fishponds Park is an attractive open space in Surbiton, which was formerly the garden of an 18th century Georgian house.

There are attractive walks and cycle routes to Hampton Court, Teddington and Richmond

along the Thames, and pleasant trails along the picturesque Hogsmill River, which joins the Thames in Kingston town.

LOCAL INFORMATION

The largest open space in the borough is Chessington World of Adventures (Leatherhead Road, KT9, ☎ 0870-444 7777, 🖳 www.chessington.com), which has a small children's zoo as well as the theme park attractions.

Lambeth

SE1 (part), SE11, SE21 (part), SE24 (part), SE27, SW2, SW4, SW8 (part), SW9, SW16 (part)

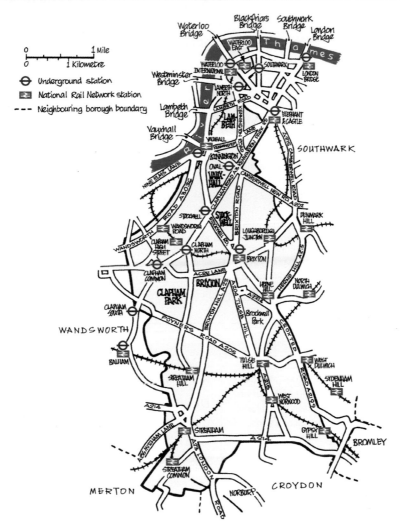

At a Glance

Best for: affordable properties, culture, entertainment, restaurants

Not so good for: deprivation, crime, traffic congestion, binge drinking

Who lives there: middle-class families, young professionals, first time buyers

Housing stock: mostly flats (over 70%, one-fifth conversions) and terraces (mostly Victorian)

Housing costs: average

General Information

Council Offices: Town Hall, Brixton Hill, SW2 1RW (☎ 020-7926 1000)

CAA Assessment: (see 🖵 http://oneplace.direct.gov.uk > Search by area > London Lambeth)

Controlling Party: Labour

Website: 🖵 www.lambeth.gov.uk

Council Tax 2010/11: £2,059 (Band G), £2,470 (Band H)

Main Areas/towns: Brixton, Clapham, Kennington, Streatham, Tulse Hill, Vauxhall, Waterloo, West Norwood

Postcodes: SE1 (part), SE11, SE21 (part), SE24 (part), SE27, SW2, SW4, SW8 (part), SW9, SW16 (part)

Population & Ethnicity: 274,500, with almost half aged between 20 and 35. Around 38 per cent have an ethnic minority background, mainly Afro-Caribbean around Brixton, with a growing Somali community in Stockwell and Streatham. The largest Portuguese community outside Portugal is also in Stockwell. The borough attracts young professionals, key workers and families.

Unemployment: 9.6 per cent (London average is 8.2 per cent)

Overview

Stretching from the South Bank arts complex on the banks of the Thames to the heart of suburban South London at Streatham, Lambeth is a diverse and fascinating borough. It encompasses some landmark tourist attractions but is also one of the most densely populated districts in the UK, where areas of severe deprivation sit alongside pockets of middle-class affluence. Dogged by racial tension in the past, today the borough embraces its multiculturalism, and regeneration programmes have improved many areas.

Each of the main areas has an individual character. The northern districts are the most commercial, with Waterloo station, the London Eye and a thriving arts and entertainment industry. Towards the centre of the borough are the famous Oval cricket ground, the buzzing club scene in Vauxhall and the contrasting towns of gentrified Clapham and street-wise Brixton, one of London's new trendy areas. In the south are the quieter residential districts of Streatham and West Norwood.

Development Plans

Current development and regeneration includes work in the Waterloo area and a scheme to improve the air quality in the borough's most polluted town centres, Brixton, Clapham, Stockwell and Streatham. There are proposals to transform and rehabilitate the pedestrian environments around the many railway viaducts from Vauxhall to Bermondsey, and a programme has been suggested for the reintroduction of two-way cycling on one-way streets. Plans for further road safety initiatives will continue the borough's good record on casualty reduction, particularly around schools.

The council is planning to improve leisure facilities in the north of the borough (possibly by building a leisure centre) and its master plan for the Streatham area is well advanced, including a state-of-the-art ice rink, swimming pool and leisure centre, all due to open in 2010.

Founder's Place charity is planning to redevelop land opposite St Thomas' Hospital to provide accommodation for key workers, a nursery, affordable housing and accommodation for the charity's long-term tenants.

 FAMOUS RESIDENTS

Famous people with Lambeth links include Jeffrey Archer (novelist), Elias Ashmole (alchemist, after whom the Ashmolean Museum in Oxford is named), William Blake (poet & artist), Charlie Chaplin (actor), David Bowie (singer), John & Henry Doulton (who started their famous Royal Doulton pottery factory in Lambeth), Ken Livingstone (former mayor of London), John Major (Prime Minister) and Sir Arthur Sullivan (composer).

Residential Areas

Around 71 per cent of Lambeth's properties are flats (22 per cent conversions), 22 per cent are terraces, 6 per cent are semi-detached houses and a mere 1 per cent are detached. The northern areas are predominantly Victorian, with a few new developments, while Clapham has some fine Georgian houses. Inter-war semis are found in Streatham in the south.

Brixton (SW2, SW9)

The unofficial capital of black culture in the UK and singled out for a visit from Nelson Mandela in 1996, Brixton has put the race riots of the '80s firmly in the past. Today the area is popular with young people who enjoy the energetic atmosphere and a nightlife that rocks until dawn. There's a good supply of affordable properties to rent and buy. Former council properties are good value for first-time buyers, with two-bedroom flats going for as little as £165,000. The most expensive period properties line the streets around Brixton Hill.

Clapham (SW4)

This established middle-class family neighbourhood has long been a favourite with those who want a home close to central London without the price tag of northern postcodes. In recent years, an influx of trendy young professionals, followed by new shops, bars and restaurants, has injected fresh life into the area. There's a good supply of Victorian terraces, Georgian villas and attractive mews cottages, plus new apartments and townhouses. Slightly grittier

Lambeth Bridge

North Clapham is good for first-time buyers, with new one-bedroom apartments costing £285,000.

Kennington, Vauxhall & Waterloo (SE1, SW8, SE11)

Away from the busy roads and railway lines that dominate Waterloo, this district becomes a sprawl of residential streets, favoured by MPs and young professionals who want easy access to Westminster. Kennington is forever associated with the Oval cricket ground, while Vauxhall is becoming known for its thriving gay and night-club scene. Property is varied, with mews cottages, period villas and council estates now joined by upmarket loft-style apartments in former industrial buildings. A charming oddity is Bonnington Square near the Oval, where 'eco-hippy' residents enjoy a community garden and hold annual street festivals.

Streatham (SW2, SW12, SW16)

More affordable than Clapham, leafy Streatham enjoys comprehensive entertainment and leisure facilities, and good links to central London. There's a stock of reasonably priced three- and four-bedroom houses (many with garages) and large conversion flats, with inter-war properties towards Streatham Vale. The downside is the lack of an underground station, which leads to busy and congested roads.

Tulse Hill & West Norwood (SW2, SE24, SE27)

Fine views and lower property prices than Brixton are the principal attractions of these areas. First-time buyers find plenty of opportunities to climb onto the property ladder, as do families trading up from smaller homes elsewhere. Tulse Hill has a large concentration of council property as well as some shabby-but-grand Victorian mansions, usually shared occupancy or converted into flats. West Norwood has a more varied property mix, with plenty of flats and small terraces, plus a few new developments.

Property Costs

Property Prices

There's a huge variation in prices, with Waterloo and Clapham the most expensive areas and West Norwood the cheapest. The table below shows average property prices in the borough:

Detached: £878,888
Semi-detached: £565,950
Terraced: £500,270
Flat: £278,320

Rental Costs

The table below shows average monthly rents in the borough:

House 5+ bed: £2,550
House 4-5 bed: £2,000
House 3-4 bed: £1,600
House 2-3 bed: £1,500
Flat 2-bed: £1,200
Flat 1-bed: £995

Crime

Lambeth currently has one the highest crime rates of all the London Boroughs, third behind Westminster, where figures are distorted by the influx of tourists, and Southwark. It has the highest rate for robbery and violent crimes, and drugs offences are also a major problem. Since 2003, a successful 'zero tolerance' policy has reduced street crime by over a third, and in 2009 the anti-fraud team secured the return of some £6mn to the council. Current priorities include tackling drugs and alcohol-related crimes.

The police station HQ is in Brixton (367 Brixton Road, SW9, ☎ 0300-123 1212), with other stations in Clapham (two), Gypsy Hill, Streatham and Vauxhall.

To compare crime rates throughout London, see the table in **Appendix D**.

Health

NHS services in the borough are provided by the Lambeth Primary Care Trust. For a full list of doctors, dentists and clinics, visit 🖥 www.nhs.uk.

To see how the Primary Care Trust compares with others in London, see the table in **Appendix D**.

Doctors & Dentists

♦ Lambeth has over 90 NHS GP surgeries, providing a range of clinics and health services.

◆ There are 39 dental and orthodontic practices in the borough, two-thirds of which accept new NHS patients.

Hospitals

◆ King's College Hospital (Denmark Hill, SE5, ☎ 020-3299 9000, 💻 www.kingsch.nhs.uk) – A&E in Ruskin Wing.

◆ Lambeth Hospital (108 Landor Road, SW9, ☎ 020-7411 6100, 💻 www.slam.nhs.uk) – mental health and substance abuse treatment.

◆ St Thomas' Hospital (Lambeth Palace Road, SE1, ☎ 020-7188 7188, 💻 www.gstt.nhs.uk) – A&E, minor injuries unit.

Private Medical Facilities

There are no private hospitals in Lambeth. The nearest is the Lister Hospital in Pimlico (see **Westminster**). To find a private GP, visit 💻 www.privatehealth.co.uk.

Schools

Educational results in Lambeth's primary schools are below the national average, but secondary school results have vastly improved. In the 2009 school league tables, primary schools were placed 26th out of the 33 London boroughs (110th out of 150 UK local authorities) and secondary schools were 15th (46th in the UK).

To compare schools throughout London, see the table in **Appendix D**.

Pre-school

There are five local authority nursery schools and one early years centre, plus nursery classes attached to many infant and primary schools. The private sector also offers a choice of pre-school provision.

State Schools

First schools: Lambeth has 61 primary schools, of which 21 are voluntary aided.

Secondary schools: There are 11 comprehensive schools, including one City Academy, in Clapham (Lambeth Academy). Five schools are voluntary aided, seven have sixth forms and nine have specialist status. The top performers in 2009 were La Retraite RC Girls' School in Atkins Road and the Bishop Thomas Grant Catholic Secondary School in Belltrees Grove. Dunraven School in Streatham and

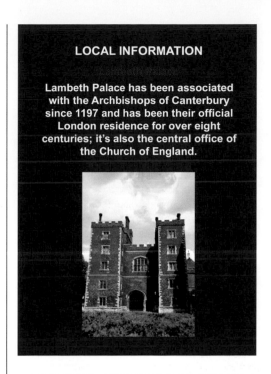

LOCAL INFORMATION

Lambeth Palace has been associated with the Archbishops of Canterbury since 1197 and has been their official London residence for over eight centuries; it's also the central office of the Church of England.

Stockwell Park School in Clapham Road also had excellent results.

Special schools: Five schools cater for students with physical disabilities and learning difficulties, plus the Larkhill Centre for Autism in Clapham.

Private Schools

There are five independent schools, most catering for junior pupils up to age 11. Streatham and Clapham High School is a selective school for girls aged 3-18 and the Schiller International School is for pupils aged 14-19 and follows an international curriculum. The Five Bridges Project is an independent school for behaviourally-disturbed students.

Further Education

◆ Lambeth College (💻 www.lambethcollege.ac.uk).

◆ Morley College (💻 www.morleycollege.ac.uk).

◆ North Lambeth Sixth Form Centre (a consortium sixth form for Charles Edward Brooke School, Archbishop Tenison's School and the London Nautical School).

◆ South Chelsea College (💻 www.southchelseacollege.co.uk).

Higher Education

♦ The City & Guilds of London Art School
(🖥 www.cityandguildsartschool.ac.uk) –
independent art college in Kennington.

♦ School of Computing & Business Studies in
Brixton (🖥 www.scbslondon.ac.uk).

Public Transport

Only the north and west of the borough are served by
the underground, although other areas can be reached
by rail. Buses are among the busiest in London.
Several river services run from Waterloo and the South
Bank complex to Westminster and Greenwich. The
new Cross River Tram Link, due for completion in
2011, will link Brixton and Waterloo with King's Cross,
Euston and Camden.

Underground

Brixton is the terminus of the busy Victoria line, which
also stops in Stockwell and Vauxhall. The Northern
line serves Clapham, Stockwell and the Oval, before
splitting into the Bank and Charing Cross branches.
Waterloo is a main underground hub, with connections
to the Bakerloo, Jubilee, Northern and Waterloo & City
lines. Typical journey times are as follows:

♦ Brixton (Victoria line, zone 2) to Oxford Circus, 14
minutes.

♦ Clapham Common (Northern line, zone 2) to Bank,
17 minutes.

Rail

Waterloo is a major terminus for national routes to the
south and west of the UK. Various overground services
stop at other stations in the borough:

Waterloo Train Station

♦ Southern trains runs extensive services from
Victoria to Clapham (10 minutes), Streatham
and Tulse Hill. There's an additional service
between Streatham Hill and Watford junction.

♦ South Eastern trains provide a fast service
from Victoria to Denmark Hill or Brixton in just
7 minutes.

♦ South West train services from Waterloo stop
at Vauxhall.

♦ The Thameslink service from Kings Cross and
the north stops at Loughborough Junction,
Tulse Hill, Herne Hill and Streatham on the
way to Wimbledon.

Buses

There are several routes into central London and
many local services between most areas within
the borough. Useful routes include the numbers 2
(to Victoria), 59 (to Euston), 88 (to Oxford Circus)
and the 133 (to Liverpool Street). The X68 runs
non-stop from west Norwood to Holborn. Night
buses include the N68, N133 and N159.

River Transport

River services operate from Waterloo Millennium
Pier to Embankment and Westminster in one
direction, and to Bankside, Tower Bridge and
Greenwich in the other. An additional service
travels between the Tate Britain and Tate Modern
galleries, stopping at Waterloo en route.

Airports

Below are the approximate distances and journey
times from Brixton to the five London airports
using public transport.

♦ **City** – 8 miles; 50 minutes via Canning Town.

♦ **Gatwick** – 14 miles; 55 minutes via Victoria.

♦ **Heathrow** – 21 miles; 62 minutes via
Paddington.

♦ **Luton** – 31 miles; 70 minutes via Thameslink.

♦ **Stansted** – 34 miles; 105 minutes via
Liverpool Street.

Roads

Roads are busy, particularly around Clapham
(where the A3 to Portsmouth meets the A205
South Circular) and Vauxhall, where the
Congestion Charge Zone begins at the A3204
Kennington Lane.

The A24 to Epsom begins at Clapham Common, while the A23 to Brighton runs through Brixton and Streatham, and can be clogged with traffic, despite being a red route in the towns.

Parking

Much of the borough is a Controlled Parking Zone, with the exception of Streatham and West Norwood. An annual resident's parking permit costs £190 inside the Congestion Charge Zone and £200 outside it.

Waste & Recycling

Household rubbish is collected weekly, as are recyclable materials, which include aerosols, glass, paper and cardboard, plastic bottles and tins. Garden waste can be recycled in special biodegradable bags. The council collects bulky items by arrangement. Domestic waste can also be taken to reuse and recycling centres at Cringle Dock, Battersea and Smugglers Way, Wandsworth. The centre at West Norwood is now only able to accept items for recycling, and no longer takes general household waste.

LOCAL INFORMATION

Royal Doulton

The pottery industry was developed in the Vauxhall area in the 17th and 18th centuries, when John Doulton had premises in Lambeth Walk. The company received its royal warrant from King Edward VII in 1901, when the name was changed to Royal Doulton. The Lambeth factory closed in 1956 due to new clean air regulations, when production was transferred to its factory in Burslem (Staffs) in the Potteries.

Shopping

Shopping in the borough is at its best for everyday essentials. Brixton has a busy shopping street with typical high street names (Argos and M&S among them) and many more unusual shops – some of London's best reggae stores are there, for example. There's also a number of bustling markets, selling everything from ethnic foods to wigs. Clapham High Street has a range of average shops with a growing number of speciality stores, such as a Kung Fu movie shop.

Streatham High Road is Europe's longest shopping street, with over 300 stores, a mix of small branches of high street favourites and locally-owned shops. At Waterloo, Gabriel's Wharf (between the South Bank complex and Blackfriars Bridge) has some interesting craft outlets and there's a daily book market by the National Film Theatre (see below). There are no covered shopping centres in the borough.

Supermarkets

♦ Marks & Spencer in Clapham and Waterloo Station (Simply Food).

♦ Sainsbury's in Brixton, Clapham, Herne Hill, Streatham Common and Vauxhall, with a local store in Streatham.

♦ Tesco in Brixton, Clapham and Streatham, with a Metro store in Kennington.

Markets

♦ Brixton Market (Atlantic Road, Brixton Station Road, Electric Avenue, Electric Road and Popes Road; Mon, Tue, Thu-Sat, 8am-6pm, Wed, 8am-3pm) – a huge, lively market selling ethnic foods, clothing and accessories, bric-a-brac, electrical goods and art.

♦ South Bank Book Market (Riverside Walk, SE1; daily) – over 100 tables selling thousands of second-hand books.

♦ West Norwood Farmers' Market (Norwood Road, SE27; first and third Saturdays in the month, 10am-12.30pm).

Entertainment

Lambeth is home to London's largest arts complex, the South Bank complex, comprising three concert halls, a theatre, a gallery and the National Film Theatre. As if that weren't enough, the Old and Young Vic theatres and several visitor attractions are in the area, while Clapham, Brixton and Streatham all have cinemas, theatres and plenty of pubs, bars and restaurants.

Theatres

♦ The Landor Theatre (70 Landor Road, SW9, ☎ 020-7737 7276, 🖳 www.landortheatre. co.uk) – intimate pub theatre presenting musicals.

- National Theatre (Upper Ground, SE1, ☎ 020-7452 3000, 💻 www.nationaltheatre.org.uk).

- The Old Vic (Waterloo Road, SE1, ☎ 0844-871 7628, 💻 www.oldvictheatre.com) – revitalised mainstream theatre.

- The Oval House Theatre (52 Kennington Oval, SE11, ☎ 020-7582 0080, 💻 www.ovalhouse. com) – lively theatre and arts centre.

- The Young Vic (66 The Cut, SE1, ☎ 020-7922 2922, 💻 www.youngvic.org).

Cinemas

- BFI London IMAX Cinema (1 Charlie Chaplin Walk, SE1, ☎ 0870-787 2525, 💻 www.bfi.org. uk/incinemas/imax) – 3D cinema.

- Clapham Picturehouse (76 Venn Street, SW4, ☎ 0870-755 0061, 💻 www.picturehouses.co.uk).

- BFI Southbank (South Bank Waterloo, Lambeth, SE1, ☎ 020-7928 3232, 💻 www.bfi.org.uk/ incinemas/nft) – London's premier art house cinema.

- Odeon Streatham (44 High Road, SW16, ☎ 0871-224 4007, 💻 www.odeon.co.uk).

- The Ritzy (Brixton Oval, Coldharbour Lane, SW2, ☎ 0871-704 2065, 💻 www. picturehouses.co.uk) – London's largest independent cinema.

Museums & Galleries

The main visitor attractions lie close to the Thames, including the London Eye (☎ 0871-781 3000, 💻 www. londoneye.com – see box), the London Aquarium (☎ 020-7967 8000, 💻 wwwlondonaquarium.co.uk) and the Hayward Art Gallery in the South Bank complex (☎ 020-7921 0813, 💻 www.hayward.org.uk). Other museums include:

Clapham Common panorama

- Black Cultural Archives and Museum (1 Othello Close, SE11, ☎ 020-7582 8516) – the history of London's black community.

- Brixton Windmill (Blenheim Gardens, SW2, ☎ 020-8683 9584, 💻 www.brixtonwindmill. org) – a Grade II listed windmill, currently being restored with Heritage Lottery funding and set in a small park, Windmill Gardens.

- Florence Nightingale Museum (St Thomas' Hospital, 2 Lambeth Palace Road, SE1, ☎ 020-7620 0374, 💻 www.florence-nightingale.co.uk) – exhibition about the famous nurse.

- Imperial War Museum (Lambeth Road, SE1, ☎ 020-7416 5000, 💻 www.iwm.org.uk) – history of war since WWI.

- Museum of Garden History (Lambeth Palace Road, SE1, ☎ 020-7401 8865, 💻 www. museumgardenhistory.org) – collection of garden tools and curiosities.

- National Museum of Type and Communication (100 Hackford Road, SW9, ☎ 020-7735 0055) – typographic collection, open by appointment.

Libraries

There are nine local authority libraries, with one mobile service. The main library is in Brixton (Brixton Oval, SW2, ☎ 020-7926 1056) and opens seven days a week, as does the library in Streatham. The Lambeth Archives are held at the Minet Library in Brixton. There's a specialist library at the Museum of Garden History (see above).

Clubs

The borough has a thriving nightlife, with Brixton, Clapham and Vauxhall increasingly 24-hour entertainment districts. There's a multitude of clubs to suit every taste and musical preference,

with the largest choice in Brixton and Clapham, while Vauxhall's clubs are carving a reputation for great gay nights. The choice in Streatham is more limited.

There are too many clubs to mention in this book, although a good starting point is the Myvillage website for Brixton and Clapham (💻 www.myvillage. co.uk). Some of the best include:

- ◆ The Clapham Grand (21 St John's Hill, SW11, ☎ 020-7223 6523).

- ◆ Crash (Arch 66, Goding Street, SE11, ☎ 020-7278 0995, 💻 www.crashlondon.co.uk).

- ◆ Jamm (261 Brixton Road, SW9, ☎ 020-7274 5537, 💻 www.brixtonjamm.org).

- ◆ Substation South (9 Brighton Terrace, SW9, ☎ 020-7737 2095).

For comedy there's the Brixton Comedy Club at The Dogstar (389, Coldharbour Lane, SW9, ☎ 020-7633 9539, 💻 www.brixtoncomedy.co.uk) and the Clapham Comedy Club at the Grey Goose (100 Clapham Park Road, SW4, ☎ 020-7720 8902), as well as regular comedy nights at several pubs.

Live Music

The South Bank's Royal Festival Hall, together with the smaller Queen Elizabeth Hall and Purcell Room, are among London's premier classical and avant-garde venues (☎ 0871-663 2500, 💻 www.rfh.org. uk). A large number of pubs have regular live music and two of London's favourite rock venues are in the borough:

- ◆ Carling Academy Brixton (211 Stockwell Road, SW9, ☎ 020-7960 4200, 💻 www.brixton-academy.co.uk).

- ◆ The Windmill (22 Blenheim Gardens, SW2, ☎ 020-8671 0700, 💻 www.windmillbrixton. co.uk).

LOCAL INFORMATION

Clapham Common is one of the largest open spaces in London, with 220 acres (89ha) of grassland, wooded areas, tree-lined paths and three ponds (see photo). Although half of the common's area is situated in Wandsworth, it's managed and maintained by Lambeth.

Pubs

Lively DJ bars, cocktail bars, slick gastropubs, traditional locals, chains – Lambeth has them all and more. Brixton and Clapham have the widest choices for pre-club drinking, and often a bar adjoins a club, with a restaurant on the side. The Bug Bar, in the crypt of St Matthews Church (Peace Garden, SW9, ☎ 020-7738 3184) is a popular haunt with Brixton's arty crowd, and the Fridge Bar, next to the club of the same name (1 Town Hall Parade, SW9, ☎ 020-7326 5100), is also popular.

Clapham has a number of interesting bars, including the unique SO.UK with its vast cocktail list (165 Clapham High Street, SW4, ☎ 020-7622 4004), while Streatham veers more towards the traditional pub, although for live jazz there's the Waterfront Bar (426 Streatham High Street, SW16, ☎ 020-8679 7180). Elsewhere, Kennington is known for Irish pubs and Stockwell for Portuguese bars, but Vauxhall is disappointing

and Waterloo has few salubrious drinking holes for a pre-theatre drink, with the exception of the Archduke (Concert Hall Approach, South Bank, SE1, ☎ 020-7928 9370).

Restaurants

Clapham is the best place for eating out, with some excellent and unusual European and ethnic restaurants, including award-winning Japanese cuisine at Tsunami (15 Voltaire Road, SW5, ☎ 020-7978 1610). Brixton has a large number of reasonably priced Caribbean, African and other ethnic stalwarts, while the choice in Streatham is improving. In northern parts of the borough, Meson Don Felipe is a reliable choice for excellent *tapas* near Waterloo Station (53 The Cut, SE1, ☎ 020-7928 3237) and Stockwell is becoming known for its Portuguese cuisine.

Sports Facilities

Lambeth has leisure centres in Brixton and Clapham, and a community sports centre in Brixton. Facilities include:

♦ Swimming pools in Brixton and Clapham, plus an outdoor pool at Brockwell Lido in Brockwell Park, which has recently enjoyed a facelift.

♦ Indoor sports halls in Brixton and Clapham.

♦ A climbing wall, squash courts and indoor cricket nets in Brixton.

♦ All-weather sports pitches at the Ferndale community sports centre in Brixton.

There are facilities for various outdoor sports, including basketball, bowls, cricket, football and tennis, in many Lambeth parks. Streatham Common provides bridle-paths for horse riding and there's also has an ice rink. For cricket fans there's the Oval cricket ground.

Green Spaces

Lambeth has 64 parks and open spaces. Kennington Park is popular and hosts various outdoor events during the summer, while Brockwell Park in Tulse Hill is one of London's finest and includes an 18th century walled garden and Brockwell Lido. Streatham Common is well tended and home to the Rookery, a terraced garden that has featured in several garden guides. By Vauxhall Cross is a city farm, a popular spot for families, which is also the site of a large tethered hot-air balloon from which visitors can enjoy

views of London sights. One of London's hidden treasures is West Norwood Cemetery, with ornate Victorian tombs and the final resting place of several famous people, including Mrs. Beeton and the founder of the Tate Gallery, Sir Henry Tate.

LOCAL INFORMATION

London Eye

Also known as the Millennium Wheel, the London Eye on the banks of the Thames is the tallest (443ft/135m) Ferris wheel in Europe and has become the most popular paid tourist attraction in the UK, enjoyed by over 3mn people a year.

Lewisham

SE4, SE6, SE8, SE12, SE13, SE14, SE23, SE26, BR1

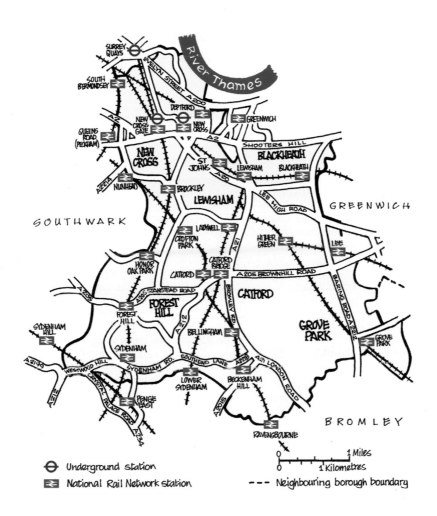

At a Glance

Best for: culture, shopping, entertainment, restaurants

Not so good for: few tube stations, deprivation, hospitals

Who lives there: young families, City commuters, young professionals, first-time buyers

Housing stock: mainly flats (over 50% – one-third conversions) and terraces (35%)

Housing costs: inexpensive

General Information

Council Offices: Town Hall, Catford, SE6 (☎ 020-8314 6000)

CAA Assessment: (see 🖳 http://oneplace.direct.gov.uk > Search by area > London Lewisham)

Controlling Party: Labour

Website: 🖳 www.lewisham.gov.uk

Council Tax 2010/11: £2,253 (Band G), £2,704 (Band H)

Main Areas/towns: Blackheath, Catford, Deptford, Lewisham, New Cross, Sydenham Hill

Postcodes: SE4, SE6, SE8, SE12, SE13, SE14, SE23, SE26, BR1

Population & Ethnicity: 261,600, with a high proportion aged under 40, many of whom rent shared accommodation. Around a third of residents are council tenants and some 35 per cent belong to an ethnic minority, with Afro-Caribbeans forming the largest group, particularly around Deptford and Lewisham. The borough is popular with white-collar families and an increasing numbers of City workers, attracted by improved transport links.

Unemployment: 8.7 per cent (London average is 8.2 per cent)

Overview

The arrival of the Docklands Light Railway (DLR) in 1999 put Lewisham back on the map. Lacking the historic attractions of its neighbours Southwark and Greenwich, parts of this once smart Victorian suburb had become neglected and down-at-heel. Rapid transport into the City has begun to change that, with the short stretch of Thames-side frontage at Deptford beginning to attract City workers and regeneration following in their wake. Although high unemployment and inner city deprivation have left their mark on the borough, there are pockets of affluence.

Blackheath, south-east of Deptford, is a popular middle-class village bordering Greenwich, with stylish shops and an attractive heath (which is the starting point of the London Marathon). Elsewhere, Victorian suburbia takes over in the south-west, encompassing the towns of New Cross, Lewisham and Sydenham Hill, before the borough's boundary at Crystal Palace (see **Bromley**). Catford lies in the centre of the borough and the areas south-east of there were mostly developed between 1920 and 1940.

LOCAL INFORMATION

The name Lewisham comes from old English, the first settlement is thought to have been founded by a pagan Jute, Leof, and it may have meant 'Leofsa's village'. During Saxon times it was called Levesham, 'the house among the meadows'; leswe, læs, læse, or læsew, in Saxon, signifies a meadow, and ham, a dwelling.

Development Plans

The Lewisham Gateway Scheme will provide 1,000 new homes and new shopping and environmental improvements. The town centre roundabout will be removed to make way for further land development, and a new road junction will be created near the railway line to improve the transport interchange in the area. The Lewisham Shopping Centre (formerly Riverdale) is being extended and refurbished, and the public areas renewed. There are also proposals for the redevelopment of sites at Lewis Grove and Engate Street, while there's planning consent for over 200 homes each at Venson and Thurston Road.

The East London tube line will re-open in June 2010 as part of the overground (run by London Overground) rail network. The line will run from Dalston Junction in the north to New Cross, Crystal Palace and West Croydon in the south.

Residential Areas

The borough has some large council estates in the north around Deptford and south of Catford, and many of their properties are now privately owned and represent good value. There are a lot of sizeable Victorian houses and terraces in western and central areas, while inter-war properties predominate in the south-east. Some 52 per cent of properties are flats (a third conversions), with 37 per cent terraced houses, 9 per cent semi-detached and just 2 per cent detached houses.

Blackheath (SE3)

Classy, genteel and a world apart from gritty Deptford, this is an attractive, genuine village, which started life as a smart Georgian suburb and continues to be highly popular today. The centre of the village is packed with trendy shops, restaurants and comfortable pubs, while the heath itself, windswept and undulating, is a favourite family haunt at weekends. Property isn't cheap and ranges from Regency villas to grand Victorian or Edwardian detached homes, with some now converted to flats. The most desirable properties overlook the heath.

Catford (SE6)

This multicultural area suffers from the A205 South Circular Road running through the centre, although there are good sports facilities and plenty of family housing. One of the most desirable areas is the quiet and respectable Corbett Estate to the south-east of the town centre. Built after WWI, it consists of high quality homes laid out in a rigid grid pattern, with no pub in sight. A double-fronted, five-bedroom villa there costs around £565,000.

To the south-west is the Bellingham Estate, with '20s cottage-style houses, while to the far south is Downham, featuring some of London's few surviving prefabricated bungalows dating from 1945. Forest Hill to the west offers a good choice of conversion flats which are ideal for first-time buyers.

Deptford (SE8, SE14)

There are two sides to Deptford: the river frontage (once Henry VIII's naval dockyard) now dominated by '60s tower blocks and where, until recently, no one wanted to live; and the town centre, scruffy in parts but full of character. There's a large stock of ex-council housing, which appeals to first-time buyers, as well as a few streets of Victorian terraces for young families, although it's the new developments that are attracting young professionals into the area.

Deptford Creek, to the east of the town centre, is the site of several developments of flats and houses, while along the Thames to the west at the Pepys Estate, a former council block has been revamped by a private developer (£465,000 for a two-bedroom penthouse). In between, redevelopment of the Convoy's Wharf site into a mixed-use quarter has recently been given the go-ahead. To the south of Deptford, around New Cross and Brockley, there's a good supply of Victorian houses, many ripe for refurbishment.

Students at Goldsmith's College provide a reliable source of tenants for rental properties.

Lewisham (SE13)

Another area to benefit from the arrival of the DLR (and in 2010 the East London line extension), busy Lewisham is popular with families who find larger houses for their money than in other local areas. Victorian terraces south and east of the centre give way to larger properties, some converted to flats, with the most favoured being up the hill towards Blackheath. The fairly dull town centre is currently having a £16mn facelift; new shared ownership developments have already been built, with more new homes planned. Ex-local authority houses remain affordable. Ladywell to the west and quiet Hither Green to the east offer a large stock of Victorian terraces and conversions.

Sydenham Hill (SE26)

This elegant area provides wonderful views over the city, while Sydenham Hill Nature Reserve is one of the loveliest spots in south London. Some large, expensive period homes appeal to comfortably-off residents, and there's a good supply of inter-war semis (around £475,000 for four bedrooms). Terraced cottages, conversion flats, council properties, modern townhouses and flats are all also available. Down the hill, traffic-

clogged Bell Green is little more than a home for a large Savacentre, although there are plans to turn the area into a retail park.

Property Costs

Property Prices

The table below shows average property prices in the borough:

Detached: £520,833
Semi-detached: £338,947
Terraced: £289,776
Flat: £185,593

Rental Costs

The table below shows average monthly rents in the borough:

House 5+ bed: £2,200
House 4- bed: £1,950
House 3- 4 bed: £1,500
House 2-3 bed: £1,300
Flat 2- bed: £1,050
Flat 1- bed: £950

Crime

Lewisham's crime rates are well above the London average, with those for violent crime and robbery being the highest, and rates for burglary and motor offences only a little lower. It also has the seventh-highest rate of drug offences in the capital. A priority is to tackle anti-social behaviour, with initiatives to make neighbourhoods safer and quickly remove abandoned cars and graffiti.

The police station HQ is in Lewisham (43, Lewisham High Street, SE13, ☎ 0300-123 1212), with other stations in Brockley, Catford, Deptford and Sydenham.

To compare crime rates throughout London, see the table in **Appendix D**.

Health

NHS services in the borough are provided by the Lewisham Primary Care Trust. For a full list of doctors, dentists and clinics, visit ▦ www.nhs.uk.

To see how the Primary Care Trust compares with others in London, see the table in **Appendix D**.

Doctors & Dentists

♦ There are 91 NHS GP surgeries in the borough, offering a range of clinics and health services.

♦ Lewisham has 63 dental and orthodontic practices, including four community dental practices that accept adults with special needs, elderly patients and vulnerable children. Around three-quarters of practices accept new NHS patients.

Hospitals

♦ Lewisham Hospital NHS Trust (Lewisham High Street, SE13, ☎ 020-8333 3000, 💻 www. lewisham.nhs.uk) – A&E, primary care suite for minor injuries.

♦ New Cross NHS Walk In Centre (Henderson House, 40 Goodwood Road, SE14, ☎ 020-7206 3100).

Private Medical Facilities

♦ Blackheath Hospital (40 Lee Terrace, SE3, ☎ 020-8318 7722, 💻 www.bmihealthcare. co.uk) – surgery and outpatient clinics, including minor injuries treatment. To find a private GP, visit 💻 www.privatehealth.co.uk.

Schools

Educational standards in Lewisham are mixed. In the 2009 school league tables, primary schools were placed 27th out of the 33 London boroughs (113th out of 150 UK local authorities) and secondary schools 25th (106th in the UK).

To compare schools throughout London, see the table in **Appendix D**.

Pre-school

There's a good choice of nursery schools and playgroups in all areas, including two council-assisted nurseries. Most primary schools have nursery classes.

State Schools

First schools: 67 primary schools, of which 20 are voluntary aided. In 2009, Brindishe Primary School in Lee Green was one of the top 229 schools in the UK for Key Stage 2 results.

Secondary schools: 11 comprehensive schools, five of which are voluntary aided. Six schools have specialist status and nine have sixth form facilities, seven of which are linked by two sixth form consortia. The top performers in 2009 were the Haberdashers' Aske's Hatcham College at New Cross and the Prendergast-Hilly Fields College in Adelaide Avenue.

Special schools: Six special schools cater for students with physical disabilities and learning difficulties.

Private Schools

There are eight private schools in the borough, with three catering for secondary age pupils. The top performers in 2009 were Sydenham High School at Westwood Hill, which also scored highly for added value, and St Dunstan's College in Catford.

Further Education

♦ Christ the King Sixth Form College in Lewisham (💻 www.ctksfc.ac.uk).

♦ Lewisham College (💻 www.lewisham.ac.uk).

Higher Education

♦ Goldsmith's College in New Cross (💻 www. goldsmiths.ac.uk) is a renowned creative university and part of the University of London.

♦ The Laban Centre in Deptford (💻 www.laban. org) is a contemporary dance conservatoire.

Public Transport

Currently overground rail lines provide the most far-reaching services in the borough and the DLR extends as far as Lewisham town. The East London tube line has been closed and will re-open in June 2010 as part of the overground (run by London Overground). The line will run from Dalston Junction in the north to New Cross, Crystal Palace and West Croydon in the south, and by February 2011 will be extended to Highbury & Islington. Bus services are good, with several routes into central London.

Underground

The East London Line was closed in December 2007 for a major extension of the line. It will become part of the overground rail network and is due to re-open in 2010.

FAMOUS RESIDENTS

Famous people associated with Lewisham include Kate Bush (singer), Jim Callaghan (politician & Prime Minister), W.G. Grace (Cricketer), Glenda Jackson (actress & politician), Jude Law (actor), C.S. Lewis (author), Sir Ernest Shackleton (Antarctic explorer), Terry Waite (humanitarian), Barnes Wallis (Engineer) and Ian Wright (ex-footballer and TV pundit).

Rail

◆ Southern trains provides services between London Bridge and stations to Sydenham, with a typical journey time of 16 minutes to Forest Hill.

◆ South eastern trains runs from Charing Cross and London Bridge to Deptford, New Cross, Lewisham, Blackheath and Hither Green (10 minutes to Lewisham). Another service runs between City Thameslink and Catford in 11 minutes.

Buses

Over 40 bus routes serve the borough, with frequent services to central London on several routes, including the number 21 (to Moorgate), 47 (to Liverpool Street) and 171 (to Waterloo). Other routes serve nearby boroughs, including Bexley, Bromley and Croydon. Night buses include the N47, N89 and N171.

River Transport

The nearest stops for river bus services are in Lambeth (Greenland Pier) and Greenwich, from where you can travel west to Westminster and east to Barrier Gardens.

Airports

Below are the approximate distances and journey times from Lewisham to the five London airports using public transport.

◆ **City** – 6 miles; 40 minutes via Canary Wharf.

◆ **Gatwick** – 22 miles; 45 minutes via London Bridge.

◆ **Heathrow** – 19 miles; 80 minutes via Victoria.

◆ **Luton** – 34 miles; 60 minutes via London Bridge.

◆ **Stansted** – 33 miles; 90 minutes via Liverpool Street.

Roads

Lewisham is a major transport hub and is criss-crossed by main roads, including the A2 and A20, which link central London with Kent and converge in the north of the borough; the A205 South Circular Road, which cuts across the south; and the A21, which splits it from north to south. The council has a well-established traffic calming (i.e. motorist infuriating) policy to reduce speeds and improve safety, and there are several 20mph zones.

Parking

There are Controlled Parking Zones in parts of Blackheath, Catford, Forest Hill, Grove Park, Hither Green and Lewisham, where a resident's parking permit costs £60 per year.

Waste & Recycling

Household waste is collected weekly, as are recyclable materials, including cans, glass, paper and cardboard, and plastic bottles. Garden waste is collected for a fee. In an effort to reduce fly tipping, the council provides a special collection for large items such as furniture. The borough's reuse and recycling centre is at Landmann Way in New Cross.

Shopping

In theory, Lewisham town is the best place for shopping, with a pedestrianised high street and a large shopping centre, although in practice, Deptford and Blackheath are more interesting. Deptford's bustling town centre has a renowned tri-weekly market and a wealth of small, independent specialist shops, and the high street was listed as the best in London for diversity in a 2005 *Yellow Pages* survey. Blackheath is the place to find stylish boutiques, organic food shops, bookshops and jewellers. Catford has a distinctive shopping centre, with a huge black cat clambering over the front of it, as well as useful markets. Elsewhere, local high streets and shopping parades provide daily essentials.

Shopping Centres

◆ Catford Shopping Centre (Winslade Way, SE6) – high street chains.

◆ Lewisham Shopping Centre (Molesworth Street, SE13) – chain stores and eateries.

Supermarkets

◆ Sainsbury's in Bell Green (open 24 hours), Deptford (Local), Forest Hill, Lee Green, Lewisham and New Cross.

◆ Tesco in Catford and Lewisham (open 24 hours).

Markets

◆ Catford Broadway Market (next to the Civic Centre; Monday, Thursday, Friday and Saturday 9am-5pm) – ethnic and household goods.

◆ Deptford Markets (High Street, Giffin Square and Douglas Way; Wednesday, Friday and Saturday 9am-4pm) – new and second-hand goods.

◆ Lewisham High Street Market (Monday to Saturday 9am-5pm,) – fruit and veg, flowers, and general goods (on Sunday).

◆ Blackheath Farmers' Market (Blackheath Railway Station car park, SE3; Sunday 10am-2pm).

Entertainment

With a high concentration of resident arts students and working artists, Lewisham is becoming known for quality arts events. Several festivals take place annually and public galleries and theatres present a diverse range of interesting programmes. On the downside, there's no mainstream cinema and only one museum. The widest choice of restaurants is in Deptford and Blackheath.

Theatres

◆ The Albany Theatre (Douglas Way, SE8, ☎ 020-8692 4446, 💻 www.thealbany.org.uk) – fringe theatre.

◆ Blackheath Halls (23 Lee Road, SE3, ☎ 020-8463 0100, 💻 www.blackheathhalls. com) – varied programme of theatre, dance and music.

◆ The Broadway Theatre (Catford Broadway, SE6, ☎ 020-8690 0002, 💻 www. broadwaytheatre.org.uk) – mainstream productions in an art deco environment.

◆ The Brockley Jack Theatre (410 Brockley Road, SE4, ☎ 020-8291 6354, 💻 www. brockleyjack.co.uk) – theatre, comedy, music and film events.

◆ The Laban Centre (Creekside, SE8, ☎ 020-8691 8600, 💻 www.laban.org) – new venue for dance, music and physical theatre.

Cinemas

◆ The Broadway Theatre in Catford and Blackheath Halls maintain regular screening programmes of art house and contemporary films. Blackheath Halls also manages a mobile film club in a 35-seat theatre truck. The nearest multiplex cinemas are in Greenwich and Peckham.

Museums & Galleries

The borough's only museum is the Horniman (100 London Road, SE23, ☎ 020-8699 1872, 💻 www.horniman.ac.uk – see box). There are several art galleries, including the Lewisham Arthouse (140 Lewisham Way, SE14, ☎ 020-8244 3168).

Libraries

There are 12 local authority libraries in the borough, with one mobile service. The main library is in Lewisham (199 Lewisham High Street, SE13, ☎ 020-8314 9800), which includes a reference collection and opens on Sundays.

Clubs

The best choice of night-clubs is around the New Cross area, where the large student population from Goldsmiths College and the Laban

Centre keeps bars and clubs busy. Favourites include:

♦ Le Fez (23 New Cross Road, SE14, ☎ 020-8694 9644).

♦ The Paradise Bar (460 New Cross Road, SE14, ☎ 020-8692 1530).

♦ Scenarios (178 New Cross Road, SE14, ☎ 020-7732 0777).

♦ The Venue (2a Clifton Rise, SE14, ☎ 020-8692 4077, 🖳 www.thevenuelondon.com).

Elsewhere, the Roebuck in Lewisham (25 Rennell Street, SE13, ☎ 020-8852 1705) has an intimate gay-friendly club, Voltz, in the basement. Comedy is a regular feature at the Broadway Theatre (see above), where many mainstream comedians cut their teeth (Ruby Wax and Jack Dee among them). There's also a well-known comedy club in Forest Hill at the Hob (7 Devonshire Road, SE23, ☎ 020-8855 0496, 🖳 www.edcomedy.com).

LOCAL INFORMATION

The Horniman Museum (Forest Hill) was founded by tea trader Frederick John Horniman in 1901 to house his fascinating collection of natural history, cultural artefacts and musical instruments – a total of 350,000 objects! Today it contains a Living Waters aquarium, a 16-acre (6.5-hectare) garden and a new eco-building, the Centre for Understanding the Environment.

Live Music

Concerts are on the menu at all the borough's theatres, including opera at Blackheath Halls. Goldsmiths College throws open its doors to the public for various performances, while the Venue night-club (see above) includes live music as part of its regular events. Several pubs have live gigs, including:

♦ The White Swan (13 Blackheath Road, SE10, ☎ 020-8694 6456).

♦ The Fox and Firkin (316, Lewisham High Street, SE13, ☎ 020-8690 8925).

♦ The Montague Arms (289, Queens Road, SE15, ☎ 020-7639 4923).

♦ The Amersham Arms (388, New Cross Road, SE14, ☎ 020-8692 2047).

Pubs

New Cross has a number of lively bars, including Goldsmiths Tavern (316 New Cross Road, SE14, ☎ 020-8692 7381). Blackheath village has a cluster of pubs tending towards the quaint, with the most popular overlooking the heath. The Hare & Billet (1a Elliot Cottages, Hare & Billet Road, SE3, ☎ 020-8852 2352) is a fine example of a friendly, traditional pub. Elsewhere, bland, ordinary boozers predominate, although there are some exceptions worth seeking out. These include the Rutland Arms in Catford (55 Perry Hill, SE6, ☎ 020-8291 9426), a lovely jazz bar and free house, and the Dulwich Wood House (39 Sydenham Hill, SE26, ☎ 020-8693 5666), which is a good traditional pub.

Restaurants

The cheaper restaurant and fast food chains crop up in all the borough's areas, such as McDonalds, Nando's and Pizza Hut. For the smartest restaurants, head to Blackheath, where there's a good choice of establishments serving all kinds of cuisine. Loco Locale (1 Lawn Terrace, Blackheath, SE3, ☎ 020-8850 0700) is a relaxed Italian, while the Laughing Buddha (41 Montpellier Vale, SE3, ☎ 020-8852 4161) is the longest-established and best-known Peking restaurant in the area.

Deptford's eateries are mostly cheap and cheerful (not a swanky gastropub in sight). A. J. Goddards (203 Deptford High Street, SE8, ☎ 020-8692 3601) is a traditional pie and mash licensed café, while the area's top eatery is the Last Lick (189 Deptford High Street, Deptford, SE8 3NT, ☎ 020-320 2340), which serves modern European food. Gracelands Palace in New Cross (881 Old Kent Road, SE15, ☎ 020-7639 3961) stands out as a fun-packed Chinese, and Thailand (15 Lewisham Way, SE14, ☎ 020-8691 4040) serves fine Thai food.

Sports Facilities

The borough has four swimming pools, located at the leisure centres in Deptford, Forest Hills, Lewisham and Sydenham, although Forest Hills is currently temporarily closed due to site improvements. Each centre also has a fitness suite. To the west of Lewisham town, the Ladywell Arena provides outdoor sports pitches and a running track. In addition, facilities are available for a range of sports in the borough's parks, including athletics, basketball, bowls, cricket, football, golf and tennis.

Other facilities include branches of Esporta Fitness Club and Fitness First, as well as the Sydenham Lawn Tennis and Croquet Club, with five all-weather tennis courts, two squash courts and a croquet lawn. For the less active, there's a tenpin bowling alley. The famous former greyhound racing stadium in Lewisham town has been demolished for redevelopment of the site.

Green Spaces

There are over 40 open spaces and parks in Lewisham, from Blackheath in the north to the fabulous Beckenham Place Park on the southern boundary. Blackheath, with its lovely views and four natural ponds, provides a natural habitat for insects such as the endangered stag beetle. Often windswept, it's a popular kite flying destination and in November hosts one of London's best free firework displays.

To the west, Deptford Park provides green relief in the middle of the borough's most densely built-up area, while Telegraph Hill Park in New Cross is named after the semaphore station that broadcast news across London of victory at the Battle of Waterloo. The most attractive open space is Sydenham Wells Park, which boasts fine water features and formal gardens, as well as sports facilities.

LOCAL INFORMATION

Beckenham Place Park is the largest park in Lewisham (237 acres/96ha) and an important wildlife habitat, with extensive ancient woodlands and some lovely walking trails. Tennis, football and golf can be played there, where the 18th century Mansion House (Grade II) houses the golf clubhouse.

Merton

SW19 (part), SW20, CR4, SM4

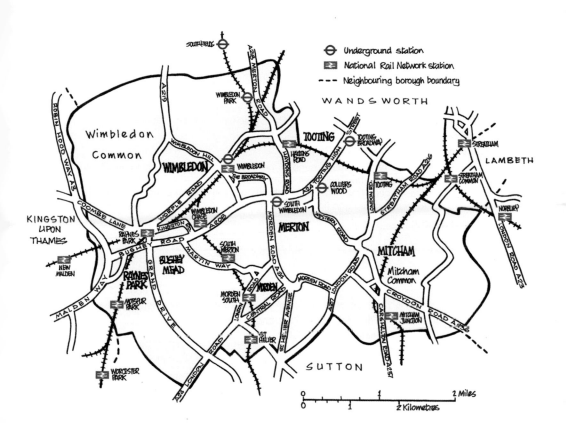

At a Glance

Best for: leisure, restaurants, sports facilities, open spaces, low crime

Not so good for: state schools, traffic congestion, culture. few tube stations

Who lives there: wealthy middle-class families, young professionals, commuters, first-time buyers

Housing stock: mostly terraces (50%) and flats (over one-third), Victorian & Edwardian period properties

Housing costs: affordable

General Information

Council Offices: Merton Civic Centre, London Road, Morden, SM4 5DX (☎ 020-8543 2222)

CAA Assessment: (see 🖳 http://oneplace.direct.gov.uk > Search by area > London Merton)

Controlling Party: no overall control

Website: 🖳 www.merton.gov.uk

Council Tax 2010/11: £2,355 (Band G), £2,826 (Band H)

Main Areas/towns: Colliers Wood, Merton Park, Mitcham, Morden, Raynes Park, Wimbledon

Postcodes: SW19 (part), SW20, CR4, SM4

Population & Ethnicity: 201,400. Around 25 per cent of residents belong to an ethnic minority, mostly Indian or Afro-Caribbean. Wimbledon attracts the well-heeled, the middle classes, celebrities (many actors live there) and young professionals, while other areas appeal to local families and first-time buyers.

Unemployment: 6.1 per cent (London average is 8.2 per cent)

Overview

Merton's most famous area is Wimbledon, home to the world's most prestigious Grand Slam tennis championship. For two weeks in June, the area's transformed from a smart and stylish neighbourhood perched on the edge of one of London's largest commons, to a gridlock of people and traffic. For the rest of the year, life in this prosperous Victorian suburb proceeds at a more measured pace, where residents enjoy a village-like atmosphere, decent schools and good shopping, all only 20 minutes from central London.

While Wimbledon and its surrounding districts provide some of the best addresses, the rest of the borough is less distinguished, dominated by streets of mediocre inter-war housing that followed the extension of the Northern line to Morden in the '20s. In parts grubby and unkempt, although with some attractive green spaces in the shape of Mitcham Common and Morden Hall Park, the borough's eastern and southern areas suffer from busy and congested roads, although public transport has been boosted in recent years by the Tramlink service between Croydon and Wimbledon.

LOCAL INFORMATION

The borough derives its name from the historic parish of Merton which was centred on the area now known as South Wimbledon. In a borough with a broad socio-economic range, between generally affluent Wimbledon and less affluent Mitcham, the name was seen as a compromise.

Residential Areas

Nearly half of all property consists of terraced houses, with 34 per cent flats, 13 per cent semi-detached houses and 4 per cent detached. Much of Wimbledon, South Wimbledon and Merton Park are Victorian, with later Edwardian property around Raynes Park. Inter-war homes predominate in Morden and Mitcham.

Colliers Wood, Mitcham & Morden (SW17, CR4, SM4)

Popular with families and first-time buyers who either cannot afford or don't want inner-city living, these areas offer densely packed streets of sensible if uninspiring semis, flats and modern developments, all priced lower than in Tooting or Clapham. Colliers Wood is marginally the most expensive, and has some period homes. It also has the best shopping, including an attractive craft 'village' at Merton Abbey Mills.

Morden has a large supply of good value small houses on the vast St Helier ex-council estate, shared with Sutton, which was originally built to house people bombed out of central London. It's also the location of the largest mosque in Europe, built on the site of an old dairy. Mitcham is the only major town in the borough without a tube station, although Tramlink (see **Chapter 2**) has improved public transport considerably. Faintly down-at-heel in places, it benefits from some attractive properties by the common and around the old cricket green in the centre.

Merton Park (SW19)

This is one of the earliest garden suburbs, created by John Innes (of compost fame) in the latter part of the 19th century. Quiet and leafy, there's a varied selection of Arts and Crafts-style homes, ranging from two-bedroom cottages to five-bedroom villas with large gardens. Like Hampstead Garden Suburb in North London (see **Barnet**), there are no pubs or shops in the area. There's always a high demand for properties, particularly from families priced out of Wimbledon.

Raynes Park (SW20)

At the bottom of Wimbledon Common and split by the railway line, Raynes Park has some lovely leafy streets lined with Edwardian terraces and semis, with larger homes in the south. Prices are highest close to the common, where two-bedroom flats sell for around £250,000. There are several developments of new flats and small houses. Roads in the south-west bordering the A3 feature retail parks and light industry.

Wimbledon (SW19)

Popular with celebrities, international executives and affluent families, Wimbledon Village is trendy,

expensive and exclusive. The village centre is packed with designer boutiques and cafes, and property ranges from large Edwardian detached houses overlooking the common (selling for £4mn or more) to two-bedroom cottages costing around £500,000. Canny residents make a tidy profit from renting their homes to tennis celebrities during June. Down the hill, Wimbledon Broadway is one of the busiest shopping districts in South London, as well as offering a host of recreational amenities. Popular with all ages (*Yellow Pages* recently identified Wimbledon as a good place for pensioners), families love the large Victorian semis, while younger commuters like the two-bedroom houses and modern apartment blocks that are within walking distance of the station.

Property Costs

Property Prices

Property prices vary widely, with the cheapest housing around Mitcham and Morden, and the most expensive in Wimbledon. The table below shows average property prices in the borough.

> Detached: £1,615,479
> Semi-detached: £499,916
> Terraced: £335,738
> Flat: £260,870

Rental Costs

The table below shows average monthly rents in the borough.

House 5+ bed: £2,600
House 4-5 bed: £2,450
House 3-4 bed: £1,900
House 2-3 bed: £1,500
Flat 2-bed: £1,150
Flat 1-bed: £975

Crime

Merton is one of the safest London boroughs, with the fourth-lowest overall crime rate and the third-lowest rate of theft from cars and drugs offences. Recent borough statistics show a marked reduction in motor vehicle crime. Successful crime reduction initiatives include more uniformed police and plain-clothes patrols on the streets.

The police station HQ is in Wimbledon (15 Queens Road, SW19, ☎ 0300-123 1212), with other stations in Mitcham and Morden.

To compare crime rates throughout London, see the table in **Appendix D**.

Health

NHS services in the borough are provided by the Sutton and Merton Primary Care Trust. For a full list of doctors, dentists and clinics, visit 💻 www.nhs.uk.

To see how the Primary Care Trust compares with others in London, see the table in **Appendix D**.

Doctors & Dentists

◆ There are 56 NHS GP surgeries, providing a range of clinics and health services.

◆ There are 42 dental and orthodontic practices, less than half of which accept new NHS patients.

Hospitals

Nelson Hospital (Kingston Road, SW20, ☎ 020-8296 2000, 💻 www.epsom-sthelier.nhs.uk) offers a range of outpatient clinics. The nearest hospitals with A&E facilities are Kingston Hospital (see **Kingston**), Mayday Hospital (see **Croydon**), St George's Hospital, which also has a walk-in centre (see **Wandsworth**), and St Helier Hospital (see **Sutton**).

Private Medical Facilities

◆ Parkside Hospital (53 Parkside, SW19, ☎ 020-8971 8000, 💻 www.parkside-hospital.co.uk) is a private hospital with a new oncology clinic on the same site. To find a private GP, visit 💻 www.privatehealth.co.uk.

Schools

Private schools in the borough are highly sought-after, while state schools gain mixed results, although they're steadily improving. In the 2009 school league tables, primary schools were placed 14th out of the 33 London boroughs (49th out of 150 UK local authorities) and secondary schools 23rd (95th in the UK).

To compare schools throughout London, see the table in **Appendix D**.

Pre-school

Merton boasts the best selection of nurseries, both state and private, in London, with nursery classes attached to every state primary school.

State Schools

Until 2003, Merton had a three-tier state system, although this has changed to the usual primary/secondary structure.

First schools: The borough has 43 primary schools, of which 11 are voluntary aided. The top primary school in 2009 was the Singlegate Primary School in Colliers Wood.

Secondary schools: There are six comprehensive schools, two of which are voluntary aided and one voluntary controlled. Two schools have sixth forms and three have specialist status. The top performer in 2009 was the Ursuline High School in Wimbledon.

Special schools: Three special schools cater for students with physical disabilities and learning difficulties.

Private Schools

Most private schools are in the Wimbledon area. Two cater for students aged up to 18, both of which are among the top schools in the country: Kings College School (boys) in Wimbledon Common and Wimbledon High School (girls). Wimbledon also has the Norwegian School of London, which caters for Norwegian-speaking students aged 11 to 16.

Further Education

◆ Merton College (💻 www.merton.ac.uk).

Higher Education

◆ Wimbledon School of Art (💻 www.wimbledon. ac.uk).

 FAMOUS RESIDENTS

Famous names associated with the borough include Richard Briers (actor), Eric Clapton (musician), Sandy Denny (singer), Robert Graves (poet), James Hunt (Formula 1 world champion), William Morris (artist & designer), Admiral Lord (Horatio) Nelson, Lord Baden-Powell (founder of the Boy Scouts), Oliver Reed (actor), Max Wall (actor & comedian) and William Wilberforce (anti-slavery campaigner).

Public Transport

Wimbledon has the best transport links in the borough, with underground, rail and tram links. Other parts of the borough have reasonable underground or rail connections, except for Mitcham which is poorly served, with no underground and a long walk from some areas to the railway station. However, Tramlink now provides a useful east-west service. Bus services are generally good, although there are no routes into central London.

A new rail station, Mitcham Eastfields, opened in June 2008, the first new station in a south London suburb since the Second World War.

Underground

The District line terminates at Wimbledon, while the Northern line serves Colliers Wood and South Wimbledon before terminating at Morden. Typical journey times are:

◆ Morden (Northern line, zone 4) to Waterloo, 30 minutes.

◆ Wimbledon (District line, zone 3) to Piccadilly Circus via Earl's Court, 35 minutes.

Rail

◆ South West trains provides services to Waterloo, stopping at Raynes Park and Wimbledon (journey time is 20 minutes).

◆ The Thameslink service stops at Mitcham Junction, Morden South, South Merton, Wimbledon Chase and Wimbledon, on the way to Blackfriars, King's Cross and the north.

Buses

As with most outer London boroughs, no buses serve central London, but several go to Wandsworth for connections to a variety of destinations. Local services are extensive, with many buses serving neighbouring boroughs. Useful routes include the number 118 (Morden to Brixton), 156 (Wimbledon to Clapham junction) and the 157 (Morden to Crystal Palace). The N57 and N155 night buses serve the borough.

Trams

Trams run every 10 minutes between Wimbledon and West Croydon. Stops include Merton Park and Mitcham, and the journey takes 25 minutes.

Airports

Below are the approximate distances and journey times from Wimbledon to the five London airports using public transport.

◆ **City** – 13 miles; 60 minutes via Canning Town.

◆ **Gatwick** – 18 miles; 50 minutes via Clapham Junction.

◆ **Heathrow** – 11 miles; 70 minutes via Paddington, or 75 minutes on the Piccadilly line from Earl's Court.

◆ **Luton** – 32 miles; 90 minutes using the Thameslink service.

◆ **Stansted** – 38 miles; 110 minutes via Liverpool Street.

Roads

The busy A3 skirts Merton's western border at Raynes Park, although traffic usually flows easily. Not so on the A24, which cuts through the borough on its way to Surrey and can be slow through Colliers Wood and even slower through Morden, with heavy local traffic and through traffic to Kingston or Sutton. Additional problems in Colliers Wood are caused by shoppers visiting the area's retail areas (see below). Heavy traffic through Wimbledon Broadway and Wimbledon Village are made worse by delivery lorries and buses, and traffic is chaotic during the Wimbledon tennis fortnight.

Parking

Controlled Parking Zones are in operation in Wimbledon Village and the Broadway, as well as in parts of Colliers Wood, Merton Park, Mitcham (around the tram stop), Morden and Raynes Park. The council is considering proposals to extend the CPZs in Raynes Park and around Wimbledon Common. A resident's parking permit costs £65 per year for one car, £110 per year for a second and £140 for a third.

Waste & Recycling

The council collects general household rubbish and recyclable materials (e.g. cans, cardboard, glass, paper and plastic bottles) on the same day each week. Garden waste is collected by arrangement, as are bulky items such as furniture and kitchen appliances. Merton's civic amenity site (recycling/waste) is in Morden, while there's a second site in Wimbledon for recyclable materials only.

LOCAL INFORMATION

The Bait´ul Futuh Mosque ('House of Victories') was opened in Morden in 2003 by the Ahmadiyya Muslim Community. It's the largest mosque in Western Europe, accommodating 10,000 people, and cost £5.5mn.

Shopping

Wimbledon has an attractive and up-market shopping centre (appropriately named 'Centre Court'), thriving shops along the high street and exclusive boutiques in the village. Elsewhere, shopping in Merton is a pretty unexciting experience, with the exception of Merton Abbey Mills, a craft 'village' and markets on the banks of the River Wandle near Colliers Wood underground station. Colliers Wood has two retail parks, while Morden and Mitcham offer a selection of local shops to meet day-to-day needs.

Shopping Centres

◆ Centre Court Shopping Centre (4 Queens Road, SW19) – over 60 chains, including M&S and Debenhams.

◆ The Priory Retail Park (131 High Street, SW19) – electrical goods and furniture chains, including PC World and Carphone Warehouse.

◆ Tandem Retail Centre (Christchurch, SW19) – chains such as Argos, Boots, Comet and Next.

Supermarkets

◆ Marks & Spencer in Wimbledon.

◆ Morrisons in Wimbledon.

◆ Sainsbury's in Colliers Wood and Wimbledon.

◆ Tesco Metro store in Wimbledon and Express stores in Colliers Wood and Wimbledon.

Markets

◆ Merton Abbey Mills (Watermill Way, SW19, ☎ 020-8542 5511) – clothing, fine foods, crafts and flowers; Saturday and Sunday 10am-5pm. Antiques; Thursday 7am-12pm.

◆ Wimbledon Stadium (Stadium car park, Plough Lane, SW19) – household goods and food; every Sunday until 3pm.

◆ Wimbledon Farmers' Market (Wimbledon Park First School, Havana Road, SW19) – Saturday 9am-1pm.

Entertainment

The majority of leisure amenities are concentrated around Wimbledon, where there are theatres, the borough's only cinema, several museums and a couple of night-clubs. Annual summer festivals include Abbeyfest at Merton Abbey Mills, the River Wandle festival along the riverside and the Wimbledon Arts festival in Cannizaro Park (see **Green Spaces** below). There are plenty of restaurants in the borough, with the widest choice in Wimbledon, the 'in' place to eat out.

Theatres

♦ Colour House Theatre (Merton Abbey Mills, Watermill Way, SW19, ☎ 020-8542 5111, 🖳 www.wheelhouse.org.uk) – weekend children's shows and regular blues nights.

♦ The New Wimbledon Theatre and Studio Theatre (The Broadway, SW19, ☎ 0844-871 7627, 🖳 www.ambassadortickets.com) – off-West End productions, with new drama at the smaller Studio.

♦ The Polka Children's Theatre (240 The Broadway, SW19, ☎ 020-8543 4888, 🖳 www.polkatheatre.com) – children's shows.

Cinemas

♦ Wimbledon Odeon (the Crescent, 39 The Broadway, SW19, 0871-22 44 007, 🖳 www.odeon.co.uk).

Museums & Galleries

As well as the museums listed below there are several private art galleries in Wimbledon.

♦ Canons House and Gardens (Madeira Road, CR4, ☎ 020-8545 3532) – Grade II listed building with a 16th century dovecote.

♦ Merton Priory (Merton Abbey, off Merantun Way, SW19, ☎ 020-8543 9608, 🖳 www.mertonpriory.org) – remains of the original priory.

♦ Southside House (3 Woodhayes Road, SW19, ☎ 020-8946 7643, 🖳 www.southsidehouse.com) – home of the Pennington family (still in use today) set in fascinating gardens.

♦ The Wandle Industrial Museum, Vestry Hall Annexe (London Road, CR4, ☎ 020-8648 0127, 🖳 www.wandle.org) – history of tobacco and textile industries.

♦ Wimbledon Lawn Tennis Museum (Centre Court, All England Lawn Tennis and Croquet Club, Church Road, SW19, ☎ 020-8944 1066, 🖳 www.wimbledon.org) – history of the sport (see also box).

♦ Wimbledon Society Museum of Local History (22 Ridgeway, SW19, ☎ 020-8296 9914, 🖳 www.wimbledonmuseum.org.uk) – local history collection.

♦ Wimbledon Windmill Museum (Wimbledon Common, SW19, ☎ 020-8947 2825) – impressively restored windmill.

Libraries

There are eight local authority libraries in the borough, with one mobile service. The largest, with a visitor information centre and gallery, is Wimbledon Library (35 Wimbledon Hill Road, SW19, ☎ 020-8274 5757). Aragon Library only opens on Tuesdays and Fridays. No libraries open on Sundays.

Clubs

♦ Bar China (Haydons Road, SW19, ☎ 020 8543 3111).

♦ The Crown (London Road, SM4, ☎ 020-8540 4481).

♦ Po Na Na, Wimbledon (The Broadway, SW19, ☎ 020-8540 1616).

♦ The Watershed (267 The Broadway, SW19, ☎ 020-8540 0080).

Regular comedy nights are held at Po Na Na, the Watershed and at GJ's Bar (62 High Street Colliers Wood, SW19, ☎ 0871-971 6963).

Live Music

Live music is presented at Po Na Na, the Watershed and GJ's Bar (see above). Some pubs also have regular gigs, including the Leather Bottle (277 Kingston Road, SW19, ☎ 020-8542 7490).

Pubs

There's a wide choice of pubs and bars in and around Wimbledon, including chains such as All Bar One in Wimbledon Village and JD Wetherspoon's Wibbas Down Inn off the Broadway. The quieter and more refined establishments tend to be in Wimbledon Village and by the Common. For a traditional pub atmosphere (warm, friendly and no background music), there's the Rose & Crown (55 High Street, SW19, ☎ 020-8947 4713), while the quaint Hand in Hand (6 Crooked Billet, SW19, ☎ 020-8946 5720) is a popular spot with New Zealanders. The Common Room (18 High Street, SW19, ☎ 020-8944 1909) is a favourite with young and old alike.

Livelier places are clustered around the Broadway. Bar Sia is a stylish bar in former Turkish baths (105 The Broadway, SW19, ☎ 020-8540 8339), while the Suburban Bar & Lounge (27 Hartfield Road, SW19, ☎ 020-8543 9788) is a cocktail bar. Down the road in Colliers Wood the best pub is the Sultan (78 Norman Road, SW19, ☎ 020-8542 4532), winner of many CAMRA awards. Elsewhere pubs are fairly ordinary, although the Cavern, a traditional pub in Raynes Park (100 Coombe Lane, SW20, ☎ 020-8946 7980) is popular, as is Irish pub Ganleys in Morden (43 London Road, SM4, ☎ 020-8685 0481).

Restaurants

The best place to eat out is Wimbledon, where many well-known chains, such as Café Rouge, Chiquita's, Jim Thompson's Flaming Wok and Pizza Express, sit alongside some interesting independents. The Light House (75 The Ridgeway, SW19, ☎ 020-8944 6338) serves excellent European food, while Walkabout (74 The Broadway, SW19, ☎ 020-8543 8624) is an Australian restaurant. Slightly further afield is SLURP (138 Merton Road, SW19, ☎ 020-8543 4141) for speedy and tasty Chinese and Japanese cuisine.

Zayka Indian Cuisine in Merton (281 Kingston Road, SW20, ☎ 020-8543 9484) is a friendly restaurant with good service, as is Le Bombayz (164 Kenley Road, SW19, ☎ 020-8545 0999). Colliers Wood has one or two nice eateries, of which Rehab Pizza is the best (186a High Street, SW19, ☎ 020-8543 5151), while Morden, which is something of a culinary desert, has a good Thai restaurant, Toa-Roong (20 Morden Court Parade, London Road, SM4, ☎ 020-8687 0182).

Sports Facilities

There are three indoor swimming pools, at Mitcham, Morden and Wimbledon, where there are also fitness suites. Wimbledon Park (opposite the All England Tennis Club) has facilities for a number of outdoor activities, including a sports stadium, an excellent synthetic athletics track, floodlit tennis courts, football pitches, putting and bowling greens, and a golf course. Sailing and canoeing take place on the lake. Other parks in the borough also have outdoor sports pitches and courts.

For indoor sports halls and classes, the YMCA Wimbledon (200 The Broadway, SW19, ☎ 020-8542 9055, 🖥 www.kymca.org.uk) offers a good range of facilities. There are also branches of many gym chains, including a David Lloyd Centre in Raynes Park. Wimbledon Common is a haven for horse riding, with extensive bridle-ways and two riding stables, and there's also an 18-hole golf course, with another on Mitcham Common. Naturally, the largest spectator sport is tennis at the All England Tennis Club (Church Road, SW19).

Green Spaces

There are some 60 parks and recreation grounds in Merton, including Wimbledon and Mitcham Commons, 13 of which are designated as local nature reserves. Wimbledon Common is an area of wild heathland, where the most prominent feature is the Wimbledon Windmill (see **Museums & Galleries** above). In the bottom south-east corner is Cannizaro Park, a lovely Grade II listed landscape with an Italian garden and an open air theatre. Wimbledon Park was landscaped by Capability Brown and today provides the borough's best outdoor sports facilities (see above), although it becomes a car park during the tennis championships. Not far away in South Wimbledon is a Grade II listed Victorian town garden at South Park Gardens.

South London's only working community farm is Deen City Farm at Merton Abbey, close to the River Wandle, where there are also attractive riverside walks. Ramblers are spoilt for choice with the commons and there are other walking trails that form part of the London Capital Ring (a series of footpaths around the capital); one extends from Streatham Common to Wimbledon Park, while another goes from Wimbledon Park to Richmond Bridge.

LOCAL INFORMATION

Wimbledon

Each year the All England Lawn Tennis Championship (founded in 1868), referred to simply as Wimbledon, is held over a fortnight at the end of June and beginning of July. It's one of the world's four tennis Grand Slam tournaments (along with the Australian, French and US Opens) and the largest sporting event in the UK, attracting over 200,000 visitors.

St. Pauls Cathedral, City of London

Newham

E6, E7, E12 (part), E13, E15, E16

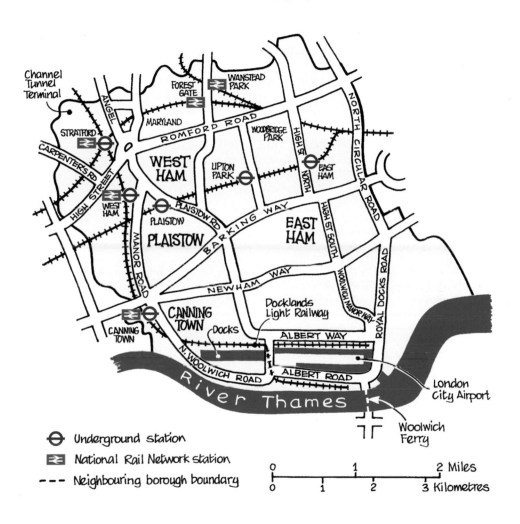

- ⊖ Underground station
- ⇄ National Rail Network station
- --- Neighbouring borough boundary

At a Glance

Best for: affordable housing, public transport, sports facilities

Not so good for: deprivation, crime, traffic congestion

Who lives there: working class families, singles, Asians, first-time buyers

Housing stock: mostly terraces (many Victorian) and flats/flat conversions, council housing

Housing costs: inexpensive

General Information

Council Offices: Newham Town Hall, Barking Road, East Ham, E6 2RP (☎ 020-8430 2000)

CAA Assessment: (see 💻 http://oneplace.direct.gov.uk > Search by area > London Newham)

Controlling Party: Labour

Website: 💻 www.newham.gov.uk

Council Tax 2010/11: £2,092 (Band G), £2,511 (Band H)

Main Areas/towns: Beckton, Canning Town, East Ham, Forest Gate, Plaistow, Silvertown, Stratford, West Ham

Postcodes: E6, E7, E12 (part), E13, E15, E16

Population & Ethnicity: 249,500, with one of the youngest populations in London – over 40 per cent of residents are aged under 25. It's a culturally diverse borough, with over 50 per cent of the population from an ethnic minority (largely Asian and African) and the second-highest percentage of Muslims in Britain (24 per cent). The majority of residents work in white-collar administrative jobs, many locally. Newcomers are increasingly attracted by the transport links, including young professionals and City commuters priced out of other areas.

Unemployment: 12.9 per cent (London average is 8.2 per cent)

Overview

Just 3mi (5km) from the City, Newham is one of London's fastest-changing boroughs. Although still among the most deprived areas in England, it's now the site of major regeneration schemes, home to the successful City Airport and soon to become a hub for international travel when the fast rail link to the continent from Stratford is completed. However, it's as the centre of the 2012 Olympic Games that Newham is attracting the world's attention. Two-thirds of the Olympic Park facilities will be in the borough, including an 80,000-seat stadium and the Aquatics Centre, both to be built at Stratford. After the games, these and the athletes' accommodation will be at the heart of a new urban development scheme, Stratford City, which will comprise new homes, offices, shops and leisure facilities.

Millions are also being pumped into other areas, including Canning Town and West Ham, which are already benefiting from the Olympics as buy-to-let investors snap up the relatively inexpensive housing. Newham is also the location of the world's largest flood barrier (across the River Thames), the ExCeL Exhibition Centre, the University of East London's Docklands Campus and the acclaimed Theatre Royal in Stratford. A new National Aquarium is planned at Silvertown. By the end of 2012, with new jobs, homes and businesses in place, Newham is likely to be one of London's most prosperous boroughs.

LOCAL INFORMATION

Newham is the most ethnically diverse district in the UK (or the world, according to Newham council), with no particular ethnic group dominating; 39 per cent of the population is white, 31 per cent Asian and 24 per cent black.

Development Plans

Newham is one of London's fastest-changing boroughs, where ambitious regeneration projects include the 2012 Olympics, the Thames Gateway, Stratford City, and Canning Town & Custom House.

London 2012 Olympic Games: Newham is one of the five boroughs that will host the 2012 Olympics, along with Greenwich, Hackney, Tower Hamlets and Waltham Forest. Stratford in Newham will be the site of a new 80,000-seat athletics stadium and many other sports venues in a 500-acre (200-ha) landscaped park – the largest urban park built in Europe for 150 years. The Olympics will speed up regeneration plans for the Lower Lea Valley and provide a lasting legacy of jobs and sporting and cultural facilities. A £100mn upgrade has begun to treble the capacity of Stratford Regional Station, which will be one of the main gateways for spectators travelling to the Olympic Park (Stratford International will be a Eurostar station with links to the continent). Newham council plans to redevelop 11 sites in the borough in time for the Olympics, at a cost of £800mn.

The Thames Gateway: Newham is a core part of the Thames Gateway, Europe's largest regeneration project, which extends from the Isle of Dogs (Tower Hamlets) to Southend in Essex and the Isle of Sheppey in Kent. Public funding is expected to reach £9bn between 2008 and 2011.

Stratford City: Redevelopment in Stratford is underway to create a new £4bn metropolitan centre in East London, which will house most of the Olympic athletes and provide homes for Newham residents after the Games. Stratford City's retail element alone, Westfield Stratford City (the same developer as the Shepherds Bush centre), will be similar in size to Bluewater (Kent) and include over 100 shops, three department stores, cafés, schools, hotels, parks and health centres, in addition to new homes.

Canning Town & Custom House: The Canning Town and Custom House Regeneration Project has been included in the Government's new mixed communities initiatives, which aim to create neighbourhoods with a balanced mix of owned and rented accommodation. Canning Town and Custom House is a highly accessible location and the £3.8bn project aims to transform the area physically, socially and economically, with almost 10,000 new homes and a revitalised town centre.

Transportation: Public transport in Newham is undergoing a major upgrade, with new or improved stations at Canning Town, West Ham and Stratford, where the Stratford International Eurostar station partially opened in 2009, although only for Southeastern services on High Speed 1. The borough will also benefit from improvements to the London Overground Line and the Crossrail scheme (see **Chapter 2**), both of which will provide rail connections to several stations in the borough. A new Stratford International DLR extension is set to open in 2010, with new stations planned for Star Lane, Abbey Road and Stratford High Street, in time for the 2012 Olympics.

Residential Areas

Architecturally the borough is undistinguished, with long rows of late Victorian terraces in most

areas and pockets of post-war council housing, particularly around Canning Town. The Royal Docks area and Beckton have seen large new developments in recent years, many alongside the river, with more to come. Newham has a high proportion of terraced houses (57 per cent), 39 per cent flats, 3 per cent semi-detached houses and just 1 per cent detached.

Canning Town & Silvertown (E16)

Traditionally working class, Canning Town is a dense and run-down urban area to the north of the Royal Docks. Badly bombed during World War II, this is largely an area of council estates and housing association property. The infamous Ronan Point tower block was finally demolished in the '80s and replaced by low-rise housing. A £1.7bn regeneration scheme involves demolishing 1,700 homes, building 8,000 new ones and revitalising the town centre. For now, privately owned property is a bargain.

Across the water of the former docks lies the thriving City Airport (which recently gained its own DLR station), the ExCeL exhibition centre, several hotels and a considerable number of modern homes, some council-owned and some privately-owned. Former warehouses are being revamped and there are attractive apartments overlooking the Thames Barrier. Prices are cheaper than Canary Wharf, starting at around £235,000 for a one-bedroom flat. Eventually the area will have 10,000 dwellings in new communities, complete with shops, businesses and leisure facilities.

East Ham & Beckton (E6)

Divided by the A13, these are contrasting districts. East Ham is older, home to a well-established Asian community, with streets of Victorian and standard '30s semis. Larger homes crop up towards Wallend and new flats and houses are being built. Beckton is part of the Docklands area, featuring modern housing estates of council and privately-owned two- and three-bedroom family houses, with new shopping and leisure facilities. A two-bedroom terraced house costs around £195,000. The DLR station area attracts young couples looking to commute into central London.

Forest Gate & Manor Park (E7, E12)

In the north of the borough, Forest Gate is one of the more expensive areas of Newham, with some attractive leafy streets and a good supply of Victorian and inter-war semis, some of which are quite large. The most sought-after houses are in a conservation area to the east of the station, where a detached six-bedroom house costs around £525,000. Properties overlooking the open space of Wanstead Flats are also desirable. The area is popular with families and the well-established multicultural community is reflected in the array of ethnic shops. Manor Park to the north-east has plenty of flats in converted houses and is a good hunting ground for first-time buyers.

Stratford (E15)

Olympics apart, it's the new international train station with its (eventual) links to the north of England, Scotland and Europe, plus the existing underground services, that have propelled Stratford from obscure deprivation to the up-and-coming centre of East London. New flats have been built and old buildings have been transformed into trendy lofts, attracting young commuters priced out of areas closer to the City. More building is to come in the shape of Stratford City, with plans for a new retail centre, homes and offices. Away from all this activity, Stratford features streets of small Victorian terraces and ex-council housing, with pockets of larger houses converted into flats and modern purpose-built apartment complexes. A two-bedroom terrace sells for around £245,000. Larger houses near West Ham Park are sought-after.

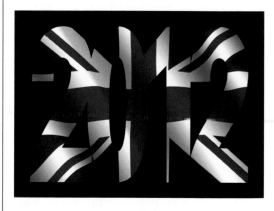

West Ham & Plaistow (E13)

Much like East Ham in character, with streets of small terraces, '60s and '70s council homes and some new estates of family houses, Plaistow also has several modern apartment blocks. Traditionally home to local families, predominantly

Asian, these areas are becoming increasingly popular with first-time buyers looking for an easy commute into central London via the underground.

Property Costs

Property Prices

The table below shows average property prices in the borough:

> Detached: £0 (no recent sales)
> Semi-detached: £241,250
> Terraced: £213,716
> Flat: £176,844

Rental Costs

The table below shows average monthly rents in the borough:

> House 5+ bed: £1,850
> House 4-5 bed: £1,350
> House 3-4 bed: £1,150
> House 2-3 bed: £975
> Flat 2-bed: £860
> Flat 1-bed: £700

Crime

Newham has the fifth-highest crime rate of London's boroughs, with the highest rates of theft from vehicles and of car theft. Plans are underway to reduce crime by around 25 per cent over the next three years by improving safety on the streets through 'Safer Neighbourhood' initiatives.

The police station HQ is in Forest Gate (350 Romford Road, E7, ☎ 0300-123 1212), with other stations in East Ham, North Woolwich, Plaistow and Stratford.

To compare crime rates throughout London, see the table in **Appendix D**.

Health

NHS services in the borough are provided by the Newham Primary Care Trust. For a full list of doctors, dentists and clinics, visit 🖥 www.nhs.uk.

To see how the Primary Care Trust compares with others in London, see the table in **Appendix D**.

Doctors & Dentists

♦ There are 70 NHS GP surgeries in the borough, providing a range of clinics and health services.

♦ Newham has 35 dental and orthodontic practices, most of which accept new NHS patients.

Hospitals

♦ East Ham Day Hospital (Shrewsbury Road, E7, ☎ 020-8586 5100) – mental health care.

♦ Newham Hospital (Glen Road, E13, ☎ 020-7476 4000, 🖥 www.newhamuniversityhospital. nhs.uk) – A&E; NHS walk-in centre.

Private Medical Facilities

There are no private hospitals in the borough. The nearest is the London Independent Hospital in Stepney Green (see **Tower Hamlets**). To find a private GP, visit 🖥 www. privatehealth.co.uk.

Schools

After some welcome improvements in recent years, educational standards in Newham have been slipping again, especially in primary schools. In the 2009 school league tables, primary schools were placed 30th out of the 33 London boroughs (140th out of 150 UK local authorities) and secondary schools 24th (105th in the UK). Newham has a high proportion of children with special needs.

To compare schools throughout London, see the table in **Appendix D**.

Pre-school

There are seven council-funded nursery schools and three nursery centres, with over 50 nursery classes attached to primary schools. In the private sector there are eight independent nursery schools and a choice of playgroups.

State Schools

First schools: There are 66 infant, junior and primary schools, of which ten are voluntary aided or controlled.

Secondary schools: The borough has 15 comprehensive schools, of which two are voluntary aided and nine have specialist status.

Only the two voluntary aided schools have sixth forms, with most pupils transferring to a further education college or sixth form institution at the age of 16 (see **Further Education** below). The best performers in 2009 were St Angela's Ursuline Convent School (Girls) and the St Bonaventure's RC School (Boys), both in Forest Gate.

Special schools: Two special schools cater for students with physical disabilities and learning difficulties.

LOCAL INFORMATION

According to a recent study carried out for a Channel 4 television programme, Newham was the third-worst place to live in the whole of the UK; the study took into account crime rates, school results, pollution, economic activity and property prices.

Private Schools

There are three private schools, with only one catering for secondary age pupils, the JMU Islamic Institute in Plaistow.

Further Education

♦ Newham College of Further Education (💻 www.newham.ac.uk).

♦ Newham Sixth Form Centre in Plaistow (💻 www.newvic.ac.uk).

Higher Education

The University of East London (💻 www.uel.ac.uk) has its main campus at Royal Albert Dock by Cyprus DLR station. The university has been rated as among the top ten modern universities for research by *The Guardian* newspaper.

Public Transport

The borough has good transport links, with underground, DLR, rail and bus services, as well as London City Airport, whose runway occupies a strip of land between Royal Albert Dock and King George V Dock. A Eurostar station in Stratford is due to open in 2010 and will provide direct connections to Europe, and will also eventually be part of the high-speed, trans-London Crossrail service.

Underground

The northern part of Newham is served by the Hammersmith & City and District lines, the southern part by the DLR and Jubilee line, as is Stratford, which is also on the Central line. A new extension to the DLR opened in December 2005, providing links to City Airport and North Woolwich. Typical journey times are as follows:

♦ London City Airport (DLR, zone 3) to Bank, 22 minutes.

♦ Plaistow (District Line, zone 3) to Victoria, 35 minutes.

♦ Stratford (Jubilee line, zone 3) to Waterloo, 23 minutes.

♦ Upton Park (Hammersmith & City line, zone 3) to Liverpool Street, 20 minutes.

Rail

Two overground lines run through Newham from east to west:

♦ 'One' railway services stop at Manor Park, Forest Gate, Maryland and Stratford en route to Liverpool Street (8 minutes from Stratford).

♦ First Great Western trains run to Fenchurch Street, stopping at West Ham only (9 minutes).

London Overground trains provide a third service, linking London City Airport with Richmond via Stratford and North London. In December 2006, the line between Stratford and North Woolwich was permanently closed to make way for a future DLR extension from Canning Town to Stratford International. This will take over the section of the line between Stratford and Canning Town, with other parts of the line earmarked for the future Crossrail development (see **Chapter 2**).

Buses

Local buses are frequent and there are plenty of services to central London and neighbouring boroughs, including routes 86 (to Romford), 25 (to Oxford Circus), 108 (to Lewisham) and 11 (to Aldgate). Night buses include routes N8, N15, and N86.

River Transport

The Woolwich Ferry for cars and foot passengers is a free service connecting North Woolwich to

Woolwich across the Thames, taking 15 minutes. The nearest river boat service is at Barrier Gardens, from where boats go to Westminster daily during the spring and summer.

Airports

Within the borough is London City Airport, built in 1987, which caters for ten million passengers annually, heading for destinations in the UK and Europe.

Below are the approximate distances and journey times from Stratford to the five London airports using public transport.

♦ **City** – 3 miles; 18 minutes using the DLR.

♦ **Gatwick** – 28 miles; 70 minutes via London Bridge.

♦ **Heathrow** – 22 miles; 70 minutes via Paddington.

♦ **Luton** – 30 miles; 60 minutes via Liverpool Street.

♦ **Stansted** – 27 miles; 60 minutes via Liverpool Street.

LOCAL INFORMATION

The Thames Barrier, the world's largest movable flood barrier, is located in the borough of Newham (at Woolwich Reach); costing over £400mn, it opened in 1984, since when it has been used over 100 times. See photo.

Roads

Newham's roads suffer from congestion throughout most of the day, with heavy traffic heading into the centre of London and Canary Wharf, much of it on the main A13, which cuts across the borough east to west. The A406 north circular road runs along the boundary with Barking & Dagenham in the east. In several residential areas 20mph zones have been introduced to reduce traffic speeds.

Parking

Controlled Parking Zones are in operation throughout much of the borough, particularly around the main town centres. A resident's parking permit is free of charge for the first vehicle, £30 for a second and £50 for a third and subsequent vehicles.

Waste & Recycling

General household rubbish is collected weekly, along with recyclable materials, which include cans, glass, paper and cardboard, and plastic bottles. Bulky items such as furniture and kitchen appliances are collected free-of-charge. The nearest civic amenity site (recycling/waste) is at Jenkins Lane in Barking.

Shopping

All the main areas have traditional high streets with all the usual shops providing daily essentials. The borough's main shopping district is in Stratford, where there's a covered centre and a selection of useful shops. A massive new shopping centre, Westfield Stratford City, is being built as part of the Stratford regeneration scheme, which will include 1.6mft² (150,000m²) of retail space, including three department stores.

Green Street is Upton Park's colourful shopping centre, with bustling ethnic shops selling saris, Indian embroidery, glittering fabrics and footwear, Asian jewellery and food. Three retail parks, at Gallions Reach and Beckton, provide DIY, furniture and other superstores.

Thames Barrier

Shopping Centres

Stratford Shopping Centre (The Broadway, E15) houses 60 shops, including branches of the cheaper fashion chains such as New Look.

Supermarkets

♦ Asda in Beckton.

♦ Morrisons in Stratford.

♦ Sainsbury's in Stratford and East Ham.

♦ Tesco in Beckton (open 24 hours), plus a Metro store in Upton Park (open 24 hours).

Markets

♦ East Ham Market Hall (High Street, E6) – fresh produce, ethnic foods, fashions and assorted household goods; daily.

♦ Queen's Market (Queen's Road, E13) – fresh foods, ethnic produce, fabrics, fashions and assorted household goods; Tuesday, Thursday to Saturday.

♦ The nearest Farmers Market is in Walthamstow (Town Square, off the High Street, E17); Sunday 10am-2pm.

🖤 FAMOUS RESIDENTS

Famous people associated with Newham include Honor Blackman (actress), Max Bygraves (singer), David Essex (singer & actor), Marty Feldman (comedian & actor), Elizabeth Fry (social reformer), Brian Forbes (actor), Stanley Holloway (actor), Vera Lynn (singer), Alexander McQueen (fashion designer), Anna Neagle (actress), Brian Poole (pop singer), Terry Spinks (boxer), Terence Stamp (actor) and Reg Varney (comedy actor).

Entertainment

Facilities include three cinemas, the acclaimed Theatre Royal in Stratford and a high-tech performing arts centre, Stratford Circus. Stratford also has the Discover Centre – an interactive 'story trail' space where children can invent and act out stories (1 Bridge Terrace, E15, ☎ 020-8536 5555, 🖳 www.discover.org.uk). By the Royal Docks, the ExCeL Exhibition Centre (One Western Gateway,

Royal Victoria Dock, E16, ☎ 020-7069 5000, 🖳 www.excel-london.co.uk) is a major draw, hosting the prestigious London International Boat Show among other events. There are a few night-clubs, plenty of pubs and numerous ethnic restaurants.

Theatres

♦ Brick Lane Music Hall (443 North Woolwich Road, E16, ☎ 020-751 6655, 🖳 www.bricklanemusichall.co.uk) – the last traditional music hall in the UK.

♦ Stratford Circus (Theatre Square, Stratford, E15, ☎ 020-8279 1000, 🖳 www.stratford-circus.com) – performing arts venue presenting an exciting programme of theatre, dance and live music.

♦ Theatre Royal Stratford East (Gerry Raffles Square, Newham, E15, ☎ 020-8279 1160, 🖳 www.stratfordeast.com) – premier theatre presenting a wide range of mainstream and fringe productions, including regular comedy nights.

Cinemas

♦ Boleyn Cinema (9 Barking Road, E6, ☎ 020-8471 4884).

♦ Newham Showcase Cinema (Jenkins Lane, IG11, ☎ 0871-220 1000, 🖳 www.showcasecinemas.co.uk).

♦ Stratford Picture House (Gerry Raffles Square, Salway Road, E15, ☎ 0870-755 0064, 🖳 www.picturehouses.co.uk).

Museums & Galleries

♦ Abbey Mills Pumping Station (Abbey Lane, E15, ☎ 020-7730 9472) – recently restored Victorian sewage station designed by Joseph Bazalgette and nicknamed 'The Cathedral of Sewage' because of its church-like shape.

♦ Newham Museum (Manor Park Library, Romford Road, E12, ☎ 020-8514 0274) – local history collection.

♦ North Woolwich Old Station Museum (Pier Road, E16, ☎ 020-7474 7244) – family-friendly museum with carriages, locomotives, a 1920s ticket office and other exhibits.

♦ West Ham United FC Museum (Boleyn Ground, E13, ☎ 020-8548 2700) – history of the club.

Libraries

There are 12 local authority libraries, with one mobile service. The largest is Stratford Library

(3 The Grove, Stratford E15, ☎ 020-8430 6886), which also houses the Newham Archives collection and is the only library in the borough to open on Sundays.

Clubs

There are a few clubs and DJ bars, mostly concentrated around Stratford:

◆ Club Afrique (145 Barking Road, E16, ☎ 020-7511 8494).

◆ EQ Club (East Cross Centre, Waterden Road, E15, ☎ 020-8525 8115).

◆ The Fox (108 The Grove, E15, ☎ 020-8221 0563).

◆ Newham Rex (361 Newham High Street, E15, ☎ 020-8215 6003).

◆ Zar Zars (405 High Street, E15, ☎ 020-8519 6449).

The Theatre Royal (see above) hosts a comedy club on Monday nights.

Live Music

The Rex and the Fox (see above) both host regular live gigs, while Stratford Circus (see above) has jazz nights. The Ruskin Arms in Manor Park (386 High Street North, E12, ☎ 020-8472 0377) is a well-known pub gig, which has presented some major acts in the past, including Iron Maiden, and was once the stomping ground of the Small Faces.

Pubs

The borough isn't known for quality pubs and the gastropub certainly hasn't made any inroads, although food is served in many establishments, such as the King Edward VII in Stratford (47 Broadway, E15, ☎ 020-8534 2313), which has an upstairs restaurant, and the Ruskin Arms (see above). The Victoria Pub & Kitchen (272 Victoria Dock Road, E16, ☎ 020-7474 0011) is an upmarket hostelry in Canning Town, which is noted for its friendly atmosphere and good food. There are several chain pubs – notably JD Wetherspoon – in most towns, including the Golden Grove (146

The Grove, E15, ☎ 020-8519 0750), one of the better examples. Pubs in the West Ham area are best avoided on match days, but are usually much quieter during the week.

Restaurants

Newham is hardly a gastronomic paradise, although there are plenty of cheap restaurants and takeaways in all areas. The range encompasses cheerful pie and mash cafes, a Pizza Express in Stratford, plus some upmarket Docklands restaurants with waterside views. Ethnic cuisine is something of a borough speciality, with fine examples of Bengali, Greek and Nigerian restaurants. Green Street in Upton Park is noted for authentic Asian food. Popular restaurants include:

◆ Nakhon Thai (Waterfront Studios, 1 Dock Road, Royal Victoria Docks, E16, ☎ 020-7474 5510).

◆ Nigeria Palace (247 Plashet Road, E13, ☎ 020-8552 8310).

◆ Thatched House (156 Leytonstone Road, E15, ☎ 020-8519 1970).

◆ Vijay's Chawalla (268-270 Green Street, E7, ☎ 020-8470 3535).

◆ Yi-Ban Chinese Restaurant (London Regatta Centre, Dockside Road, Royal Albert Dock, E16, ☎ 020-7473 6699).

Sports Facilities

There are four council-funded leisure centres, in East Ham, Plaistow and Stratford, which provide swimming pools and a range of fitness classes,

gym equipment and indoor sports facilities. There's also a climbing wall at the East Ham centre. The Terence MacMillan sports Stadium in Plaistow is a fully-equipped athletics venue, while there's the Ramgarhia Sikh Sports Centre in Forest Gate for outdoor sports pitches and indoor halls.

There are tennis courts and other sports pitches in many of the borough's parks, as well as over 60 football pitches at Wanstead Flats in the neighbouring borough of Redbridge, where there are also horse riding trails. Branches of well-known fitness centres include Esporta, Fitness first and Holmes Place. There's also ten-pin bowling at the Hollywood Bowl in Beckton and go-karting near the ExCeL centre. Newham is home to Premiership West Ham United Football

LOCAL INFORMATION

The Royal Docks area in Newham comprises three docks: the Royal Albert Dock, the Royal Victoria Dock and the King George V Dock, built between 1880 and 1921. The three docks collectively formed the largest enclosed docks in the world, with a water area of nearly 250 acres (over 100ha). Today the docks have been regenerated and are a popular watersports venue for sailing, rowing, kayaking and other activities.

Green Spaces

Only 10 per cent of Newham's land is devoted to open spaces, although the borough borders the expanses of Hackney Marshes and the Lea Valley to the west and Wanstead Flats and Epping Forest to the north-east. Newham's most popular space is East Ham's Central Park, a 25-acre (10-ha) Victorian park with formal rose gardens, a bowling green and rare tree species. During the summer the park hosts open air concerts and Newham's Town Show. A major makeover of the park has recently been announced.

East Ham has an important nature reserve in the churchyard of the ancient Norman church of St Mary Magdalene – nature trails teem with wildlife and there are permanent displays about wildlife, the wartime kitchen and Victorian school life. Another attraction is Newham City Farm, with various animals, horse rides and a study centre. The borough's newest green space is the 22-acre (9-ha) Thames Barrier Park, a quiet waterside area with lovely views and a fun fountain for children's summer splashing games.

Redbridge

E11 (part), E12 (part), E18, IG1, IG2, IG3, IG4, IG5, IG6, IG7, IG8, RM6 (part)

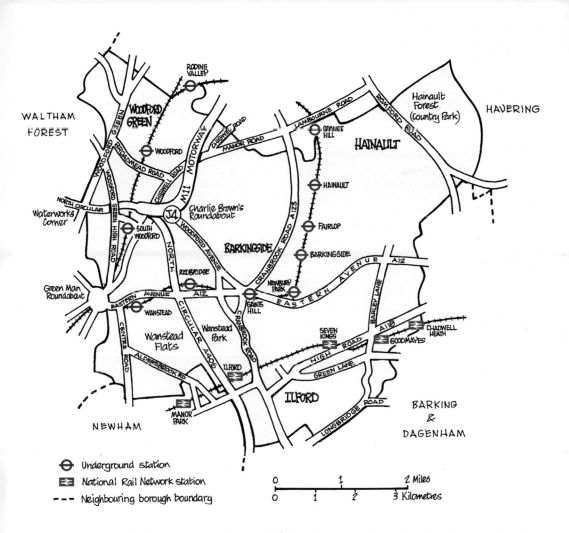

- ⊖ Underground station
- ⇄ National Rail Network station
- --- Neighbouring borough boundary

At a Glance

Best for: families, education, transport links, sports facilities, open spaces

Not so good for: parking, traffic congestion, culture

Who lives there: families, middle-class professionals, City commuters, first-time buyers

Housing stock: 40% terraces, remainder mostly semis and flats, lots of council housing

Housing costs: inexpensive

General Information

Council Offices: Town Hall, High Road, Ilford, IG1 1DD (☎ 020-8478 3020)

CAA Assessment: (see 💻 http://oneplace.direct.gov.uk > Search by area > London Redbridge)

Controlling Party: Conservative

Website: 💻 www.redbridge.gov.uk

Council Tax 2010/11: £2,342 (Band G), £2,811 (Band H)

Main Areas/towns: Clayhall, Gants Hill, Goodmayes, Hainault, Ilford, Seven Kings, Wanstead, Woodford

Postcodes: E11 (part), E12 (part), E18, IG1, IG2, IG3, IG4, IG5, IG6, IG7, IG8, RM6 (part)

Population & Ethnicity: 257,600, with a high proportion aged between 20 and 34. Around 37 per cent of residents belong to an ethnic minority, mostly Asian, and there's a significant Jewish community around Gants Hill. The borough is popular with families and commuters, and the population is fairly evenly split between well-off, middle-class professionals and lower paid local workers.

Unemployment: 8.2 per cent (London average is 8.2 per cent)

Overview

Leafy, pleasant and only and only 9mi (14km) from central London, much of Redbridge has an almost countryside feel, with a third of its land designated as green belt and its northern boundary fringed by Epping Forest. The borough is neither significantly deprived nor particularly affluent; its eastern areas are generally poorer than those in the north and west, which are home to the smart, wealthy middle-class suburbs of Wanstead and Woodford.

The main town is Ilford, well positioned to become an important centre in the Thames Gateway scheme and close to Stratford (see **Newham**) with its new international (Eurostar) rail terminal and the facilities being built for the 2012 Olympic Games. Ilford enjoys good transport links to central London and is on the planned east-west Crossrail route (see **Chapter 2**). The council has initiated an ambitious regeneration programme for the town, with improvements to the retail district and new housing already underway.

LOCAL INFORMATION

The name Redbridge comes from a bridge over the River Roding (demolished in 1921), which was made of red brick, unlike other bridges in the area which are made of white stone.

Development Plans

The council is involved in a number of major development projects, including Ilford Town Centre (Unity Square), Ilford Hill Development and Station Interchange, Gants Hill, Chadwell Heath (new homes supported by the arrival of Crossrail), Barkingside and Hainault. In 2006, the council secured a government grant of £6.6mn for physical regeneration of the borough's town centres.

The £100mn regeneration of Ilford town centre, known as 'Unity Square', will provide a new cultural focus for Ilford, based on a public square with retail and leisure facilities, new transport systems and over 500 new homes (including affordable housing for key workers). An integral part of the project will be the replacement of Ilford's Kenneth More Theatre with a modern 300-seat theatre, which will be integrated with the concert hall in the Grade II listed Town Hall. The project is scheduled for completion in 2012.

Residential Areas

The southern areas around Ilford, Goodmayes and Seven Kings feature mainly Victorian and Edwardian terraces, while larger properties from the same periods can be found in Wanstead and Woodford. Inter-war properties, mostly suburban semis, crop up around Gants Hill and Clayhall, with post-war council estates in the Hainault area. Overall, property consists of 6 per cent detached houses, 27 per cent semis and 40 per cent terraces, with the remaining 27 per cent flats (some conversions and some purpose-built)

Gants Hill & Clayhall (IG2, IG4, IG5)

Respectable and tidy, Gants Hill is popular with families and home to an established Jewish community. Inter-war semis predominate (the roads in the Commonwealth estate, which lies to the south-east of the station bordering lovely Valentine's Park, are named after cities of former British colonies), although some new flats have recently been built in the town centre on the site of an old cinema. Clayhall is more expensive, with larger homes and good local schools.

Seven Kings & Goodmayes (IG3)

Nowadays home to established Asian communities, Seven Kings was largely developed in the 19th century when the railway was being built. Roads are arranged in a grid pattern and lined with small period terraces, with the most desirable overlooking Seven Kings Park. Property prices are reasonable (around £235,000 for a two-bedroom house), making this a good area for first-time buyers. Goodmayes to the east is largely similar, with slightly larger houses. It also has the 'Bungalow Estate' near Goodmayes Park, an area of inter-war bungalows with gables and bay windows. Newham's Becontree council estate lies to the east.

Hainault (IG6, IG7)

Bordered by Hainault Forest Country Park and with its own underground station, much of Hainault consists of council housing originally constructed to re-house people from central London. Many of the three-bedroom houses are now privately owned and provide good accommodation for families. Larger houses lie to the west.

Ilford (IG1)

The borough's main shopping area, Ilford gave its name to one of the country's famous photographic film manufacturers. The town developed when the railway line reached the area in the 19th century and the densely-packed roads provide a good stock of small Victorian terraces. Decent transport connections make this a popular area for commuters and it's also favoured by many of London's taxi drivers (so no problem getting a cab locally). Larger period homes appear to the north of the town and new apartments are going up in the town centre.

Wanstead (E11)

This is a pleasant commuter suburb, with tree-lined streets, good schools and efficient public transport, together with the open spaces of Wanstead Park and Wanstead Flats. Properties are a mixture of handsome Victorian houses

Redbridge Town Hall

and later mid-war homes, with a good supply of purpose-built flats.

Woodford (E18, IG8, IG9)

On the edge of Epping Forest, Woodford consists of three areas: South Woodford, Woodford Green and Woodford Bridge. With two stations on the Central underground line, plus a mainline connection, the area attracts commuters as well as families drawn to the choice of good schools. This is the wealthiest area in the borough, with handsome Victorian and Edwardian houses, many detached, '30s family homes, flats in converted houses and modern apartment blocks. Prices are among the highest in Redbridge, with a typical four-bedroom '30s family home costing around £600,000. For an Edwardian mansion in The Drive, South Woodford's premier estate, you will need over £2mn.

Property Costs

Property Prices

The table below shows the average property prices in the borough:

```
Detached: £485,180
Semi-detached: £339,030
Terraced: £278,401
Flat: £187,079
```

Rental Costs

The table below shows average monthly rents in the borough:

```
House 5+ bed: £ 1,800
House 4-5 bed: £1,350
House 3-4 bed: £1,150
House 2-3 bed: £1,050
Flat 2-bed: £850
Flat 1-bed: £700
```

Crime

Redbridge is the 12th-safest London borough, with low crime rates for drugs offences and violence, average rates for burglary and above average levels of car theft, which are the fifth-worst in London. Current police initiatives include the use of CCTV surveillance in key areas to deter anti-social behaviour and street crime, while street wardens in the Hainault area maintain a visible presence to deter disorder and vandalism.

The police station HQ is in Ilford (270 High Road, IG1, ☎ 0300-123 1212), with other stations in Barkingside, Wanstead and Woodford.

To compare crime rates throughout London, see the table in **Appendix D**.

Health

NHS services in the borough are provided by the Redbridge Primary Care Trust. For a full list of doctors, dentists and clinics, visit ⌨ www.nhs.uk.

To see how the Primary Care Trust compares with others in London, refer to the table in **Appendix D**.

Doctors & Dentists

♦ There are 92 NHS GP surgeries in the borough, providing a range of clinics and health services.

♦ Redbridge has 78 dental and orthodontic practices, two-thirds of which accept new NHS patients.

Hospitals

♦ King George Hospital (Barley Lane, IG3, ☎ 020-8983 8000, ⌨ www.bhrhospitals.nhs. uk) – A&E; minor injuries unit.

♦ Tomswood Close (263 Tomswood Hill, IG6, ☎ 020-8539 5887, ⌨ as King George Hospital) – mental health care.

There's an NHS walk-in centre in central Ilford (201 Cranbrook Road, IG1, ☎ 020-8924 6633).

Private Medical Facilities

♦ BUPA Roding Hospital (Roding Lane South, IG4, ☎ 020-8551 1100, ⌨ www.bupahospitals. co.uk/roding). To find a private GP, visit ⌨ www.privatehealth.co.uk.

Schools

Educational standards are high, particularly at secondary level, with both independent and selective state schools among London's better performers. In the 2009 school league tables, primary schools were placed eighth out of the 33 London boroughs (29th out of 150 UK local

Cranbrook Primary School

13 have specialist status. The top performers in 2009 were Chadwell Heath Foundation School in Romford and the two grammar schools, Woodford County High and Ilford County High, all of which were among the top schools in the UK for GCSE results. Valentine's High School in Ilford was also commended for added value.

Special schools: Four special schools cater for students with physical disabilities and learning difficulties.

authorities) and secondary schools fourth (fifth in the UK).

To compare schools throughout London, see the table in **Appendix D**.

Pre-school

Nursery classes are attached to all of the borough's infant and primary schools. Provision is also good in the private sector, with several playgroups and nursery schools.

LOCAL INFORMATION

Ilford Photo

Ilford Photo, the eponymous photographic film and chemicals manufacturer specialising in the traditional world of silver halide black and white photography, was founded in Ilford in 1879 by Alfred H. Harman, a photographer from Peckham. The company went into receivership in 2004, but survived in a smaller form thanks to a management buyout.

State Schools

First schools: There are 52 infant, junior and primary schools, of which nine are voluntary aided, including two schools for Jewish children.

Secondary schools: Two selective grammar schools and 17 comprehensives, of which four are voluntary aided. All schools have sixth forms and

Private Schools

There are 11 private schools in Redbridge, with three catering for secondary-age pupils. The top performers in 2009 were Bancrofts School in Woodford Green, which is also one of the top UK schools for GCSE and A level results, and Park School for Girls in Ilford.

Further & Higher Education

♦ Redbridge College (💻 www.redbridge-college. ac.uk) offers a full range of courses leading to recognised qualifications, including degree courses.

Public Transport

Redbridge has a good underground service, although Ilford is only served by overground trains, which are restricted to southern areas. The overground stations will eventually become part of the Crossrail service, which is planned for 2017.

Underground

The Central line (which terminates at Epping in Essex) makes many stops in the borough, although the nearest station to Ilford is Barking. Stations on the Wanstead and Hainault branch terminate at Woodford. A typical journey from Woodford to Liverpool Street takes 20 minutes.

Rail

The 'one' railway provides a service from Liverpool Street through the southern part of the borough, stopping at Ilford, Seven Kings and Goodmayes (typical journey time is 15 minutes).

Barkingside Library

Trains pass through Stratford, which provide fast connections to Europe via the Eurostar station.

Buses

Local bus services are regular and frequent, with useful routes to neighbouring boroughs, including the number 123 (to Wood Green), 101 (to North Woolwich) and 147 (to Canning Town). Route 25 travels between Oxford Circus and Ilford. Redbridge is also served by the N8, N55 and N86 night buses.

Airports

Below are the approximate distances and journey times from Ilford to the five London airports using public transport.

♦ **City** – 5 miles; 30 minutes via Canary Wharf.

♦ **Gatwick** – 31 miles; 65 minutes via London Bridge.

♦ **Heathrow** – 24 miles; 65 minutes via Paddington.

♦ **Luton** – 29 miles; 65 minutes via Kings Cross.

♦ **Stansted** – 23 miles; 75 minutes via Liverpool Street.

Roads

The M11 (Redbridge's main escape route to the country) encroaches on the north-west corner of the borough, while the A12 cuts it in half from west to east. The A406 North Circular runs along the western boundary before separating Wanstead from Gants Hill and curving below Woodford Green. Both the A12 and A406 are prone to heavy rush-hour traffic.

Parking

Controlled Parking Zones operate in 12 districts – Barkingside, Chadwell Heath (shared with Newham), Gants Hill, Goodmayes, Hainault, Ilford, Newbury Park, Redbridge, Seven Kings, South Woodford, Wanstead and Woodford/ Woodford Green, although restrictions are for limited hours. An annual resident's parking permit costs £55.75, with a second permit £78 and all subsequent permits £100 per vehicle.

Waste & Recycling

General household rubbish is collected weekly, as are recyclable materials, which include cans, glass, paper and plastic bottles. Garden waste is collected free-of-charge during the spring and summer. The council collects bulky items such as furniture and kitchen appliances for a small fee. Rubbish and recyclable materials can also be taken to the borough's civic amenity site (recycling/waste) at Chigwell Road in Woodford Bridge.

Shopping

The borough's main shopping district is in Ilford, where there's a large shopping centre (The Exchange) and a pedestrianised high street. A large number of high street names can be found there, including BHS, M&S and Waterstones. The mile-long Ilford High Road also provides useful shopping. There are smaller shopping areas in Barkingside, Gants Hill, South Woodford, Wanstead and Woodford, where a mix of high street names and independent retailers provide daily essentials. There are also some interesting shops in Woodford Green.

Shopping Centres

♦ The Mall Ilford (formerly the Exchange Shopping Centre) – over 100 shops in a covered mall, with a range of high street names, including Debenhams, M&S and TK Maxx.

Supermarkets

♦ Sainsbury's in Barkingside, Ilford and South Woodford.

♦ Tesco in Barkingside, Goodmayes and Woodford Green (both open 24 hours), with an Express store in Gants Hill.

♦ Waitrose in South Woodford.

Markets

♦ Ilford Farmer's Market (Ilford High Road, IG1, near the Town Hall; 1st and 3rd Saturday of the month, 9am-2pm) – fresh produce and occasional French farm products.

Entertainment

Ilford is the main centre for entertainment, with one of the borough's only two cinemas, a theatre, museum and a choice of evening diversions. Concerts and other performances take place in various halls throughout the year. There are some good pubs and a selection of decent restaurants in the main towns. Annual arts events include a Dance Festival, which showcases professional and amateur talent in a range of shows, and a Literature Festival with workshops and readings.

FAMOUS RESIDENTS

Famous people with links to Redbridge include Clement Attlee (politician & first post-war Prime Minister), Sir Winston Churchill (statesman & wartime Prime Minister), Noel Edmonds (TV presenter), Sir Geoff Hurst (footballer), Bobby Moore (footballer), Sylvia Pankhurst (suffragette and pacifist campaigner), William Penn (Quaker and founder of the US state of Pennsylvania), Kathleen Raine (poet and writer) and Dame Maggie Smith (actress).

Theatres

♦ The Kenneth More Theatre (Oakfield Road, IG1, ☎ 020-8553 4466, 🖳 www.kmtheatre.co.uk) and the smaller Cowan Studio provide a forum for professional and amateur productions.

Cinemas

♦ Cineworld Cinema (92 Clements Road, IG1, ☎ 0871-220 8000, 🖳 www.cineworld.co.uk).

♦ Odeon South Woodford (60 High Road, E18, ☎ 0871-224 4007, 🖳 www.odeon.co.uk).

Museums & Galleries

♦ Redbridge Museum (Central Library, Clements Road, IG1, ☎ 020-8708 2317) contains a local history collection with interactive exhibits.

Libraries

There are ten local authority libraries in the borough, with one mobile service. The largest is the Central Library in Ilford (see **Museums & Galleries**, above), which includes a reference collection and local history archives. None of the libraries open on Sundays.

Clubs

Ilford has a choice of bustling clubs and DJ bars, with a couple of others slightly further afield:

♦ Blue Ice (Cranbrook Road, IG2, ☎ 020-8478 7645).

♦ Jumpin Jaks (240 High Road, IG1, ☎ 020-847 3128).

♦ Liquid Bar (333 High Road, IG1, ☎ 020-8220 2921).

♦ The Penthouse (197 High Road, IG1, ☎ 020-8478 5588).

♦ The Shannon Centre (14 Cameron Road, IG3, ☎ 020-8597 7014).

Live Music

The Kenneth More Theatre occasionally presents one-off concerts, often tribute bands. The other main live music venues are the Cauliflower in Seven Kings (553 High Road, IG1, ☎ 020-8553 2300) and the Valentine (27 Perth Road, IG2, ☎ 020-8554 6005). Various other pubs present live music from time to time.

LOCAL INFORMATION

The public house the 'Eva Hart' in Chadwell Heath is named after a resident who survived the sinking of the Titanic in 1912.

Pubs

Pubs and bars cater for all tastes, from chains to gastropubs and music bars. There's a reasonable choice in all areas, with a largely youthful clientele in Ilford. The most popular hostelries include:

♦ Bar Room Bar (33 High Street, E11, ☎ 020-8989 0552) – trendy and lively.

◆ The Eagle (73 Hollybush Hill, E11, ☎ 020-8989 7618) – a local landmark for generations, now reinvented as a Toby Carvery.

◆ The Hogshead (184 George Lane, E18, ☎ 020-8989 8542) – noisy gastropub.

◆ The Old Maypole (105 Fencepiece Road, IG6, ☎ 020-8502 7168) – friendly local.

Restaurants

Redbridge has all the usual choices of eateries. Popular chains include Pizza Express in Ilford and Woodford, Frankie & Benny's in Ilford and branches of Starbucks. The Exchange Centre in Ilford has a number of restaurants and cafés, and there are also plenty of fast food outlets and takeaways. South Woodford has some speciality restaurants, including:

◆ Ark Fish Restaurant (142 Hermon Hill, E18, ☎ 020-8989 5345).

◆ Jailhouse Rock (90 High Road, E18, ☎ 020-8518 8007).

◆ Yellow Book Californian Café (190 George Lane, E18, ☎ 020-8989 3999).

Ethnic restaurants are popular, with a predominance of Indian and Chinese in all areas, such as:

◆ Bhangra Beat (49 Chigwell Road, E18, ☎ 020-8989 8909).

◆ Durga Restaurant (173 Ilford Lane, IG1, ☎ 012-8478 3466).

◆ Mandarin Palace (559 Cranbrook Road, IG2, ☎ 020-8550 7661).

Sports Facilities

Two leisure centres (Fullwell Cross at Barkingside and Wanstead), one indoor swimming pool (at Barkingside), together with sports pitches and courts in the borough's parks, provide a range of sports facilities, including:

◆ an indoor public swimming pool;

◆ indoor sports halls;

◆ two synthetic athletics tracks;

◆ racket sports and basketball courts.

Wanstead Flats in the south of the borough provides over 100 sports pitches, for cricket, football, hockey and rugby, plus a floodlit artificial turf pitch. There are golf courses at Barkingside, Hainault, Ilford, Wanstead and Woodford, and facilities for watersports at Fairlop Waters, where there's a nationally-recognised centre for sailing, canoeing, windsurfing and powerboat training. Horse riding is also available there. There are a number of privately-run health centres, including a branch of Fitness First in Ilford.

Green Spaces

Called 'the leafy borough', Redbridge has two country parks, riverside trails, nature conservation areas, a watersports lake (Fairlop Waters) and is close to Epping Forest (see box). One of the most popular spaces is Hainault Forest Country Park, with a fishing lake, a rare breeds farm and many walks and bridle-paths. Another large open area is Roding Valley Park, which straddles the River Roding and is home to diverse wildlife and flowers. It's an ideal place for cycling, walking and angling.

The borough's formal parks include Valentine's Park in Gants Hill, the largest at 125 acres (50ha), with a listed mansion (currently empty and in need of restoration), a walled kitchen garden and a 17th century Rococo landscape. Residents can also take advantage of the Lea Valley Regional Park, a new 'countryside' area that stretches from the Docklands into Hertfordshire and Essex on both sides of the River Lea. The 100,000-acre (40,000-ha) area contains numerous leisure facilities, including country parks, heritage sites, nature reserves and walking trails.

LOCAL INFORMATION

Epping Forest

The northern fringe of Redbridge is fringed by Epping Forest, the largest public open space in the London area, at almost 6,000 acres (2,400ha), stretching 12mi (19km) from Manor Park in East London to just north of Epping in Essex. As well as being a popular area for recreation and enjoyment, it's also an important conservation area, with two-thirds being designated a Site of Special Scientific Interest and a Special Area of Conservation. It was entrusted to the care of the City of London by an Act of Parliament in 1878.

Richmond-upon-Thames

KT1 (part), KT8 (part), SW13, SW14, SW15 (part), TW1, TW2, TW10, TW11, TW12

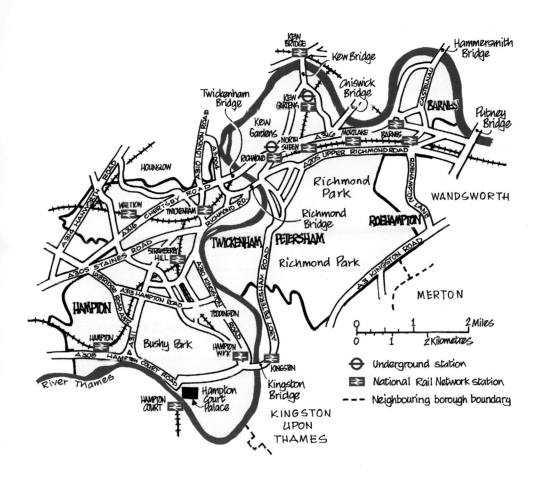

Underground station — ⊖

National Rail Network station — ⊒⊒

Neighbouring borough boundary — – – –

At a Glance

Best for: schools, transport links, shopping, leisure facilities, open spaces, restaurants

Not so good for: affordable housing, traffic congestion, airport noise, parking, tube

Who lives there: wealthy middle-class families, media stars, young professionals, City commuters

Housing stock: period properties, terraces, mansion blocks, modern apartments

Housing costs: expensive

General Information

Council Offices: Civic Centre, 44 York Street, Twickenham TW1 3BZ (☎ 020-8891 1411)

CAA Assessment: (see 🖥 http://oneplace.direct.gov.uk > Search by area > London Richmond-upon-Thames)

Controlling Party: Liberal Democrat

Website: 🖥 www.richmond.gov.uk

Council Tax 2010/11: £2,662 (Band G), £3,194 (Band H)

Main Areas/towns: Barnes, East Sheen, Ham, Hampton, Kew, Mortlake, Petersham, Richmond, St Margarets, Teddington, Twickenham, Whitton

Postcodes: KT1 (part), KT8 (part), SW13, SW14, SW15 (part), TW1, TW2, TW10, TW11, TW12

Population & Ethnicity: 180,100, with just 9 per cent belonging to an ethnic minority, mostly Asian. The borough is popular with affluent families and professional couples, including a large number of A-list celebrities.

Unemployment: 4.1 per cent (London average is 8.2 per cent)

Overview

Dominated by the River Thames and with 2,500 acres (1,000ha) of parks and gardens, Richmond is London's greenest borough. Its idyllic riverside landscape, from Richmond Hill to Petersham Meadows, has inspired generations of artists and writers, and has been protected by an Act of Parliament since 1902. Only 7mi (11km) from central London, Richmond is also one of the most expensive boroughs, populated by wealthy families, international executives and media stars, who enjoy the semi-rural location, good road and rail links, and excellent schools.

Each of the main areas sits on the river and has its own character. Pretty, village-like Barnes in the north; lively, elegant Richmond, with its bustling shopping district, in the centre, opposite historic Twickenham; and in the south, Hampton, with its famous royal palace. Not everything is perfect, however, and traffic congestion is chronic along the main roads (particularly around Hampton Court during rush hours), while northern parts of the borough suffer from the endless drone of aircraft landing at Heathrow.

LOCAL INFORMATION

Royal associations with Richmond abound and can be traced back some 900 years. It was the home of Edward III (1327-1377) and Henry V (1413-1422), both of whom had palaces by the river. Later, Henry VII, formerly the Duke of Richmond (Yorkshire), built Richmond Palace (completed in 1501), which was also home to Henry VIII until he moved to neighbouring Hampton Court Palace in around 1525.

Development Plans

The council plans to regenerate the Twickenham Riverside site bounded by Water Lane, Wharf Lane and the River Thames in the heart of

Twickenham, which was formerly occupied by a public swimming pool that closed in 1980. There are plans for the construction of a community River Centre at the south-east corner of the site, which will incorporate a boat house, learning centre, office space for voluntary organisations and a restaurant/café.

Residential Areas

Richmond has some of London's loveliest buildings, a high proportion of which are Victorian, with some fine Georgian properties in Richmond and Twickenham, and inter-war semis in Hampton and Whitton. Around 38 per cent of all properties are flats, 31 per cent terraces, 23 per cent semi-detached and 8 per cent detached houses.

Barnes (SW13)

Nestled in a curve of the Thames, Barnes is more like a traditional English village than a town in London. The lack of an underground station doesn't worry the residents, most of whom relish the semi-rural atmosphere (there's even a village duck pond). Five-bedroom villas sell for upwards of £1.65mn and there's a good supply of cheaper, smaller cottages and terraces, plus modern apartments along the river. North Barnes has some ex-council houses and mansion flats. Barnes appeals to wealthy families, including Swedes whose offspring attend the Swedish School there.

East Sheen, Mortlake & Kew (SW14, TW9)

These are pleasant residential areas, popular with families and professional couples. While Mortlake is best known as the end of the Oxford and Cambridge Boat Race, village-like Kew is famous for the Royal Botanical Gardens, which attract hordes of visitors annually. There's a good choice of housing in these areas, including large period semis, small cottages, terraces, '30s mansion blocks and a few new developments along the river. Ex-council property crops up towards Fulham cemetery and off Mortlake High Street. Generally, the higher-priced properties lie closer to the river near the open spaces of East Sheen Common, Richmond Park and Kew Gardens.

Ham & Petersham (TW10)

Enclosed by Richmond Park, Petersham Meadows and the grounds of Ham House, these remarkably unspoilt villages (complete with olde worlde pubs and a village pond) are cheaper than Richmond town. Petersham has a mixture of grand mansions, smaller cottages and 20th century detached houses (around £1.5mn-plus for five bedrooms), while Ham has a large council estate, Grade II listed Span-built properties from the '50s and a large development from the '60s. The only drawback of both areas is the lack of any kind of station, leading to heavy traffic during rush hours.

Richmond-upon-Thames (TW9, TW10)

Wealthy families and young professional couples flock to lively Richmond, which provides the borough's best shopping, entertainment and transport. Lovely old houses face the Green and line the riverside, smaller terraces occupy the town centre and '30s mansion blocks crop up along main roads. The most sought-after and expensive area is Richmond Hill, from the top of which residents can enjoy an Arcadian view. There's little new building in the town, although there are some modern apartments by the river and the park.

Twickenham, St Margarets & Whitton (TW1, TW2)

Just across the river from Richmond town, Twickenham has a useful shopping district, historic buildings, boatyards and pleasure boats along its waterfront, and a footbridge to tranquil Eel Pie Island, where the Rolling Stones once played regularly. The housing stock is a mix of some of the finest houses in London and ordinary suburbia. Four- and five-bedroom houses cost between £500,000 and £900,000. Smart new apartments sit by the river.

St Margarets is smaller, with similar housing, including an exclusive estate of large period houses backing onto private gardens. Strawberry Hill is a pleasant, village-like locality, sandwiched between Twickenham and Teddington. Cut off from Twickenham by the busy A316 (which leads to the M3) is Whitton, home of the rugby stadium and the cheapest part of the borough, with a large stock of inter-war houses of various sizes.

Teddington & The Hamptons (TW11, TW12)

Bordering Bushy Park, Teddington is a quiet residential area popular with airport workers and City types. Attractive waterfront estates appeal to young professional couples, while inland are streets of family-sized Victorian, inter-war and more modern homes. There's a large new development on the site of a former hospital and plenty of flats close to the station. The Hamptons, which includes Hampton Court Palace in the far south of the borough, is a mixed area, with mostly inter-war semis and terraces. Reservoirs dominate the riverside, although the council is planning regeneration schemes to improve the landscape.

Richmond Green

Property Costs

Property Prices

The table below shows average property prices in the borough:

Detached: £1,120,707

Semi-detached: £781,579

Terraced: £579,099

Flat: £322,818

Rental Costs

The table below shows average monthly rents in the borough:

House 5+ bed: £7,000

House 4-5 bed: £4,600

House 3-4 bed: £2,650

House 2-3 bed: £2,100

Flat 2-bed: £1,750

Flat 1-bed: £1,100

Crime

Richmond is London's second-safest borough, with a low overall crime rate and the lowest rates of violent and drugs-related offences.

CCTV cameras in town centres, stations and riverside spots help reduce street crime, while Safer Neighbourhood initiatives focus on anti-social behaviour and drug abuse. The council and police are currently waging war against graffiti.

The police station HQ is in Twickenham (41 London Road, TW1, ☎ 0300-123 1212), with other stations in Richmond and Teddington.

To compare crime rates throughout London, see the table in **Appendix D**.

Health

NHS services in the borough are provided by the Richmond and Twickenham Primary Care Trust. For a full list of doctors, dentists and clinics, visit 🖳 www.nhs.uk.

To see how the Primary Care Trust compares with others in London, see the table in **Appendix D**.

Doctors & Dentists

◆ There are 62 NHS GP surgeries in Richmond, providing a range of clinics and health services.

◆ The borough has 63 dental and orthodontic practices, few of which accept new NHS patients.

Hospitals

◆ Barnes Hospital (South Worpole Way, SW14, ☎ 020-8878 4981, 🖳 www.slwstg-tr.nhs.uk) – psychiatric care for the elderly.

◆ Teddington Memorial Hospital (Hampton Road, TW11, ☎ 020-8714 4000, 🖳 www.richmondandtwickenhampct.nhs.uk) – NHS walk-in centre.

The nearest A&E facilities are at Kingston Hospital (see **Kingston**) and the West Middlesex University Hospital in Isleworth (see **Hounslow**).

Private Medical Facilities

There are no private hospitals in the borough. The nearest is Parkside Hospital (see **Wimbledon**). To find a private GP, visit 🖳 www.privatehealth.co.uk.

Schools

Richmond's schools have generally high standards, particularly at primary level. In the 2009 school league tables, primary schools were ranked first out of the 33 London boroughs (also first out of all the 150 UK local authorities), while secondary schools were placed 13th out of the 33 London boroughs (33rd in the UK).

To compare schools throughout London, see the table in **Appendix D**.

Pre-school

Richmond borough provides limited nursery education in the state sector – less than half of the infant and primary schools have nursery classes and there's only one state nursery school. However, there's a wide choice of private nursery schools.

State Schools

First schools: There are 41 primary schools, of which 15 are voluntary aided.

Secondary schools: Richmond has eight comprehensive schools, one voluntary aided and six with specialist status. No schools have a sixth form; for 'A' levels, students move to one of Richmond's colleges (see below). The top performer in 2009 was the Waldegrave School in Twickenham.

Special schools: Two special schools cater for students with physical disabilities and learning difficulties.

Private Schools

There are nine private schools catering for senior age pupils, all selective, including the German School in Petersham and the Swedish School in Barnes, which teach the curricula of those countries. The Royal Ballet School is located in Richmond. In 2009, the Lady Eleanor Holles School in Hampton and St Catherine's School in Twickenham achieved some of the top GCSE and A level results in the UK.

Further Education

♦ Richmond Adult Community College (🖥 www. racc.ac.uk).

♦ Richmond-upon-Thames College (🖥 www. richmond-utcoll.ac.uk).

Higher Education

♦ St Mary's College, part of the University of Surrey, is in Strawberry Hill (🖥 www.smuc. ac.uk).

LOCAL INFORMATION

Hampton Court Palace

Hampton Court – one of England's great palaces – was built by Thomas (Cardinal) Wolsey (Archbishop of York and Chief Minister to Henry VIII) between 1515 and 1521. When Wolsey fell from favour, the palace was appropriated by Henry VIII and, along with St James's Place, is one of only two surviving palaces out of the 50 'built' by him. Today, the palace and gardens are a major tourist attraction and home to the annual Hampton Court Palace Festival and the Hampton Court Palace Flower Show.

Public Transport

The only underground station is in Richmond town, although services on the overground network are reasonable. There are no bus services into central London, but it's possible to get to Westminster by boat.

Underground

The District line stops at Kew Gardens and terminates at Richmond (both zone 4), with a typical journey time of 35 minutes to Piccadilly Circus via Earl's Court.

Rail

South West Trains runs services to Waterloo stopping at all towns in the borough except Ham and Petersham, where there's no station. The typical journey time from Richmond to Waterloo is 25 minutes. Richmond is also the last stop on the North London line to Gospel Oak, from where trains connect to North Woolwich and Barking.

Buses

No routes go directly to central London, although there are buses to Hammersmith (419), Wandsworth (485) and West Brompton (190) from Richmond. The best choice of buses is in Richmond. Local services are good and include buses to Kingston and Heathrow Airport. The borough is served by the N22 and N33 night buses from the West End.

River Transport

River ferries operate daily from Richmond to Kingston or Westminster during the spring and summer. Other services operate daily throughout the year between Marble Hill Park and Ham House, and between Hampton and East Molesey

Airports

Below are the approximate distances and journey times from Richmond to the five London airports using public transport.

♦ **City** – 16 miles; 65 minutes via Canning Town.

♦ **Gatwick** – 22 miles; 55 minutes via Clapham Junction.

♦ **Heathrow** – 7 miles; 65 minutes by bus, underground or rail via Paddington.

- ◆ **Luton** – 30 miles; 85 minutes via Clapham Junction.

- ◆ **Stansted** – 38 miles; 110 minutes via Tottenham Hale.

Roads

The A205 South Circular Road cuts across the north-east of the borough and the A316 (the extension of the M3) runs through the middle, intersecting with the South Circular at East Sheen, before crossing Chiswick Bridge. Both roads can be clogged during rush hour.

Richmond town has a tortuous one-way system that's often busy, while the main road through Petersham can be slow. Whitton is congested when matches are held at the rugby stadium.

Parking

Most of Barnes, Kew, Richmond and Twickenham are Controlled Parking Zones, with smaller zones in Hampton Court, Hampton Wick, St Margarets and Teddington. A resident's parking permit costs between £50 and £300 per year, depending on the area. Additional parking restrictions operate around Twickenham Rugby Stadium on event days. Parking is a particular problem in Richmond, even with a parking permit.

Waste & Recycling

General household rubbish is collected weekly, along with recyclable materials, which include glass, paper, textiles and tinfoil. Green garden waste is collected fortnightly. Residents can also sign up to have raw and cooked food waste collected. Bulky items such as furniture are collected for a fee. The borough's civic amenity site (recycling/waste) is in Townmead Road (off Mortlake Road, Kew) in Richmond.

Shopping

Richmond has the best choice of shops, with well-known chains in the main shopping streets, plus a wide selection of designer outlets, antique sellers and independent shops in cobbled lanes and alleyways. Twickenham's 17th century Church Street is excellent for unusual and designer goods, while the main shopping thoroughfare has a good mix of high street names. There are plenty of small, upmarket shops in East Sheen, Kew, Hampton Court and Teddington (where there's a branch of Liberty's), while the village-like high street in Barnes has jewellery shops, designer clothes and quality independent food shops. Elsewhere, local parades serve day-to-day needs.

Shopping Centres

Kew Retail Park (Bessant Drive, TW9) has branches of high street chains, including Gap, M&S, Mothercare, Next and TK Maxx.

Supermarkets

- ◆ Marks & Spencer in Teddington (Simply Food) and Twickenham (Simply Food).

- ◆ Sainsbury's in Hampton and Richmond.

- ◆ Tesco in Twickenham, with Metro stores in Richmond, Teddington and Whitton.

- ◆ Waitrose in East Sheen, Richmond and Twickenham.

Markets

- ◆ Country Markets selling home-made produce: Barnes (Rose House, 70 Barnes High Street, SW13) – Friday; Richmond (Vestry Hall, 21 Paradise Road, TW9) – Friday.

Hampton Court

◆ Farmers' Markets selling fresh produce are held at Barnes (Station Road, SW13), Richmond (Heron Square, TW9) and Twickenham (Holly Road car park, TW13) – all Saturday.

◆ Sheen Friday Market (Sheen lane Centre, SW14) – collectables, jewellery, bric-a-brac; first and third Friday of each month.

Crafts markets are held annually at Ham House (August bank holiday) and in Richmond (October). The annual Kew Fayre and Hampton Court's Country Affair feature stalls selling crafts, fashion, plants and food.

Entertainment

There are cinemas and theatres in Richmond town, and the borough hosts several annual arts festivals. Richmond and Twickenham have the largest choice of pubs and restaurants.

Theatres

◆ Richmond Theatre (The Green, TW9, ☎ 020-8940 0220, 🖳 www.richmondtheatre. net) – popular theatre for touring productions.

◆ The Orange Tree Theatre (1 Clarence Street, TW9, ☎ 020-8940 3633, 🖳 www. orangetreetheatre.co.uk) – London's only permanent theatre in the round.

◆ The Hampton Sport, Arts & Fitness Centre (Hanworth Road, TW12, ☎ 020-8941 4334) has a theatre space available for community use.

Cinemas

◆ Odeon Richmond (72 Hill Street, TW9, ☎ 0871-224 4007, 🖳 www.odeon.co.uk).

◆ Richmond Filmhouse (3 Water Lane, TW9, ☎ 0871-703 3992, 🖳 www.curzoncimemas.com).

Museums & Galleries

As well as the national treasures listed below, Richmond and Twickenham have local history museums. Twickenham Rugby Stadium has a museum dedicated to the sport, and the country's National Archives (including the Domesday Book) are in Kew. Other museums and galleries include:

◆ Ham House (Ham Street, TW10, ☎ 020-8940 1950, 🖳 www.nationaltrust.org) – 17th century house with rare furniture and textiles.

◆ Hampton Court Palace (East Molesey, KT8, ☎ 0844-482 7777, 🖳 www.hrp.org.uk) – famous royal palace.

◆ Marble Hill House (Richmond Road, TW1, ☎ 020-7973 3416, 🖳 www.english-heritage.org. uk) – magnificent Palladian villa.

◆ Orleans House Gallery (Riverside, TW1, ☎ 020-8831 6000) – public art gallery.

◆ Strawberry Hill House (St Mary's College, Waldegrave Road, TW1, ☎ 020-8240 4224) – Gothic former home of Horace Walpole.

Libraries

There are 15 local authority libraries in the borough, with one mobile service. The main library

Richmond Theatre

is in Richmond and has two sites – the lending library (Little Green, TW9, ☎ 020-8940 0981) and the reference library (Old Town Hall, Whittaker Avenue, TW9, ☎ 020-8940 5529). The libraries in East Sheen, Richmond and Teddington open on Sundays.

Clubs

The borough has only two night-clubs – Park Avenue Club in Richmond (1 Hill Rise, TW10, ☎ 020-8940 5283) and Piano Fantasy Lounge in Twickenham (57 King Street Parade, TW1, ☎ 020-8892 8899), although the central London club scene is within easy reach. For comedy there's the Bearcat Club at the Turk's Head pub (28 Winchester Road, TW1, ☎ 020-8892 1972, 💻 www.bearcatcomedy.co.uk).

Live Music

The Landmark Arts Centre (Teddington Lock, Ferry Road, TW11, ☎ 020-8977 7558, 💻 www. landmarkartscentre.org) presents a year-round programme of live music as well as exhibitions and other events in a former Gothic church. For large events, Twickenham Stadium is a popular venue. Richmond Theatre (see **Theatres**, above) also includes live music as part of its programme. In the summer, Marble Hill House (see above) hosts a series of highly popular open-air concerts. Otherwise, several pubs have regular live gigs, such as the Bull's Head in Barnes (373 Lonsdale Road, SW13, ☎ 020-8876 5241), which has a nightly jazz programme.

 FAMOUS RESIDENTS

A wealth of famous people have links with Richmond, including – to name but a few – David Attenborough (naturalist & film director), Sir Noel Coward (actor & playwright), Richard Dimbleby (broadcaster & journalist), Mick Jagger (rock singer), John Mills (actor), Alexander Pope (poet), Alfred Tennyson (poet), Tommy Steele (pop singer), JMW Turner (painter), Horace Walpole (writer) and Virginia Woolf (novelist).

Pubs

Charming riverside pubs can be found along the Thames. Some of the best include the Ship (10 Thames Bank, SW14, ☎ 020-8876 1439), the

historic Eel Pie (9 Church Street, TW1, ☎ 020-8891 1717), which serves excellent real ale, and the White Swan (Riverside, TW1, ☎ 020-8892 2166). The widest choice of drinking places is in Richmond, Twickenham and Teddington.

Chains are present but don't dominate and there are some olde worlde pubs in Barnes and Petersham. Some of the most popular establishments include the relaxed Sun Inn (7 Church Road, SW13, ☎ 020-8876 5256), the packed Cricketers (The Green, TW9, ☎ 020-8940 4372) and the New Inn (345 Petersham Road, TW10, ☎ 020-8940 9444). The gastropub is much in evidence in the borough, with one of the best being the Bridge Pub and Dining Rooms (204 Castelnau, SW13, ☎ 020-8563 9811), which was nominated for the *Evening Standard* Pub of the Year award in 2003.

Restaurants

Chains such as Ask! (Barnes), Pizza Express (Barnes, Kew, Richmond and Teddington), Bluebeckers (Hampton court), Smollensky's (Twickenham) and Wagamama (Richmond) are consistently popular, and there are some excellent independents in all areas serving food from around the globe. Several restaurants and cafes are recommended in the *Good Food Guide* or the *Michelin Guide*. Some of the best include:

♦ The Glasshouse (14 Station Parade, TW9, ☎ 020-8940 6777) – Michelin one-star establishment.

♦ McClements (2 Whitton Road, TW1, ☎ 020-8744 9610).

♦ The Restaurant at The Petersham (Petersham Hotel, Nightingale Lane, TW10, ☎ 020-8940 7471).

♦ RIVA (169 Church Road, SW13, ☎ 020-8748 0434).

Sports Facilities

There are six council-funded sports centres, in East Sheen, Hampton (two centres), Teddington (two centres) and Whitton, providing:

♦ Indoor swimming pools at Teddington and an outdoor pool at Hampton; and both indoor and outdoor pools at Spring Health Leisure Club at Richmond.

♦ Indoor sports halls and all-weather sports pitches at East Sheen, Hampton and Teddington.

Sports pitches and courts are available in several parks, including skateboarding and hockey in Bushy Park, and polo and horse riding in Richmond Park. There are golf courses in Richmond Park, Hampton Court Park, the Old Deer Park at Kew and Fulwell Park in Twickenham. Canoeing and rowing clubs practise on the Thames and there's a temporary ice rink at Hampton Court Palace in December and January.

Green Spaces

There are over 100 parks and open spaces in the borough and 21 miles of river frontage – five times more open space than any other London borough. Richmond's Royal Palace at Hampton Court provides 60 acres (24ha) of beautiful riverside gardens and includes one of the country's most famous hedge mazes. Along the river, the gardens at Richmond's historic houses – Ham, Marble Hill and Strawberry Hill – have delightful promenades, while in the north-west corner of the borough, Kew Gardens incorporates the famous Royal Botanical Gardens, with the world's largest plant collection. Next door is the Old Deer Park.

Richmond Park is the largest open space in London and home to a wide variety of wildlife, while Bushy Park is the second-largest of the royal parks and has its own distinct rural character, including herds of deer. The London Wetlands Centre in Barnes is an award-winning area that's a site of Special Scientific Interest, with important wildlife habitats. Petersham's meadows and pastures form part of the historic view from Richmond Hill and are soon to benefit from a government-funded project to improve the flood plain and maintain the area.

LOCAL INFORMATION

Kew Gardens

The Royal Botanic Gardens (usually referred to simply as Kew Gardens) originated in the exotic garden at Kew Park created by Lord Capel of Tewkesbury in the mid-18th century, adopted as a national botanical garden in 1840. The gardens, which welcome 1.5mn visitors annually, were designated a World Heritage Site by UNESCO in July 2003.

Kew Gardens

Southwark

SE1, SE5, SE15, SE16, SE17, SE21, SE22, SE24 (part)

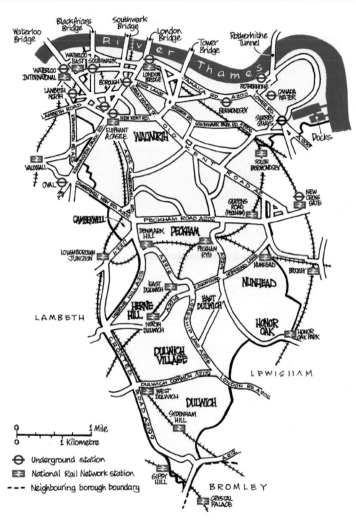

At a Glance

Best for: investment potential, leisure, culture, restaurants, sports facilities, nightlife

Not so good for: deprivation, crime, schools, traffic congestion, tube stations

Who lives there: working class families, ethnic minorities, singles, artists

Housing stock: council housing (double the London average), three-quarters flats and 20% terraces

Housing costs: relatively expensive

General Information

Council Offices: Town Hall, Peckham Road, SE5 (☎ 020-7525 5000)

CAA Assessment: (see 🖳 http://oneplace.direct.gov.uk > Search by area > London Southwark)

Controlling Party: Labour

Website: 🖳 www.southwark.gov.uk

Council Tax 2010/11: £2,037 (Band G), £2,444 (Band H)

Main Areas/towns: Bermondsey, The Borough, Camberwell, Dulwich, East Dulwich, Peckham, Walworth

Postcodes: SE1, SE5, SE15, SE16, SE17, SE21, SE22, SE24 (part)

Population & Ethnicity: 278,000, with a high proportion aged between 20 and 35. Over 35 per cent of the population belongs to an ethnic minority, principally Afro-Caribbean, and there's also a significant Turkish community. The majority of residents are local working class families, with wealthy middle-class residents around Dulwich. Young professionals are attracted to Thames-side areas.

Unemployment: 8.9 per cent (London average is 8.2 per cent)

Overview

Money has been pouring into this historic borough over the last few years, transforming areas where nobody wanted to go into fashionable urban territories. To the north is the capital's fastest-growing tourist area, along the banks of the River Thames, with landmark cultural sites such as the Tate Modern gallery and Shakespeare's Globe Theatre, not to mention the no-longer-wobbly Millennium Bridge and the London Eye. To the east are the former docklands of Bermondsey and Rotherhithe, where some 3,000 new homes have been carved out of former industrial areas and old warehouses. In the south is leafy and respectable Dulwich. Sandwiched in between are Camberwell and Peckham, where pockets of deprivation linger in the midst of massive regeneration programmes and trendy youth seek a slice of authentic London life.

 FAMOUS RESIDENTS

A wealth of famous people have links with Southwark, including – to name but a few – Edward Alleyn (actor & founder of Dulwich College), John Bacon (sculptor), Robert Browning (poet), Isambard Kingdom Brunel (engineer), Raymond Chandler (novelist), Geoffrey Chaucer (playwright), Charles Dickens (novelist), Jason Donovan (actor & pop star), Roy Jenkins (politician), Samuel Johnson (lexicographer & author), Florence Nightingale (nurse), John Ruskin (art critic, author & poet) and William Shakespeare (playwright).

Development Plans

Southwark is fast becoming one of London's most dynamic boroughs, with an abundance of areas due for regeneration and redevelopment, at a cost of some £4bn. One of the largest projects is the £1.5bn **Elephant & Castle** regeneration scheme, which is London's largest ever development by a single borough, covering 170 acres (69ha).

The development includes housing (including affordable housing), shops, a leisure centre, parks and gardens. The project was begun in 2007 and is expected to be completed around 2017.

The **Canada Water** regeneration programme will provide a major new centre for Rotherhithe, including 2,700 new homes (one-third affordable), new retail and office space, leisure facilities, a new library

City Hall & Tower Bridge

and a new civic square. The regeneration of **Bermondsey Spa** includes 15 separate sites, which will provide over 2,000 new homes, 40 per cent of which will be affordable. A planned development of **Bermondsey Square** will include a community-focused, 60-seat cinema, a boutique hotel, offices and retail units, residential properties (including affordable housing) and restaurants. There's also a huge ten-year redevelopment programme in **Peckham**, where the European Union has invested heavily, partly funding the futuristic, award-winning Peckham Library; plus a new town square and new housing to replace the North Peckham Estate. Eight key sites are earmarked for development, mainly housing, across Peckham.

There are a number of proposals to improve public transport in the borough, including a major extension of the East London tube line (closed in December 2007 for upgrading), which will become part of the overground rail network. The southern extension will link with existing overground lines to provide services to West Croydon (2010), with a further extension proposed from Surrey Quays via Peckham Rye to Clapham Junction. The existing London Overground line will be extended to the East London line in 2011.

There are a number of proposals for new tram lines which will take in Southwark, including the Cross River Tram, a light rail system expected to operate from King's Cross and Camden via Euston, Holborn and Waterloo to Peckham and Brixton; the scheme is still being planned and is expected to be in operation by 2016. Another proposal is the City Tram, a light rail system running from Battersea to Hackney via Vauxhall, Elephant & Castle, Borough High Street, Bishopsgate and Shoreditch.

Residential Areas

Just under half of Southwark's housing is council-owned (the London average is around 27 per cent), largely around Bermondsey, Camberwell and Peckham. There are new homes in the north-east, but much of the rest of Southwark is a mixture of period and inter-war properties. Some 76 per cent of homes are flats, with 19 per cent terraces, 4 per cent semi-detached and just 1 per cent detached.

Bermondsey, The Borough & Rotherhithe (SE1, SE16)

The arrival of the Jubilee underground line was the springboard for regeneration in these areas, together with the conversion of the Bankside Power Station into the Tate Modern. Lots of companies now have sparkling offices on the river, and Shad Thames, to the east of Tower Bridge, is a new trendy quarter with bars, restaurants, hi-tech work units and the Design Museum. Property-wise, there's a mix of shabby post-war council estates, housing association flats and smart conversions of old warehouses and factories.

Several new developments are appearing close to Borough Market, including shared ownership schemes and live/work units, with one-bedroom flats starting at around £275,000. Further east, Rotherhithe offers a curious landscape, with inter-war and '80s flats, plus swanky riverside apartments at Surrey Quays. Further inland are conventional family houses.

Walworth (SE1, SE17)

All roads lead to the Elephant & Castle, or at least they seem to, as this major junction (along with its notorious shopping centre) is the most distinctive feature of the area. All this will change over the next decade, with a £1.5bn regeneration programme set to improve the road layouts, provide new homes, shopping and leisure facilities, and remove the pink-clad shopping monstrosity for good. Housing is mixed, with council-owned low and high-rise blocks (many of which are due for redevelopment), streets of Victorian terraces and the occasional Georgian gem. The area is a good bet for first-time buyers and bargain hunters.

Camberwell (SE5)

Just up the road from fashionable Brixton, Camberwell is beginning to enjoy a similar rise in popularity, particularly among families looking to trade up. Green spaces, busy roads, high-rise council blocks and some attractive period homes all jostle for space, with the most sought-after period properties around Camberwell Grove. There's a good market for rental property, particularly among art and medical students attending the nearby teaching hospitals and art college.

Dulwich & East Dulwich (SE21, SE22, SE24)

Dulwich Village is quite unlike the rest of Southwark, with Mercedes-driving families, private schools and substantial detached properties interspersed with a few inter-war semis. Much of the area is controlled by a charitable foundation, which has kept developments at bay. Singles and couples prefer livelier East Dulwich, despite the lack of an underground station, attracted by the generous supply of Victorian terraces (around £425,000 for three bedrooms). New flats and townhouses near the golf course start at £185,000 for one bedroom and are proving a hit with first-time buyers and buy-to-let investors.

Peckham (SE15, SE22)

North Peckham is in the final phase of a £290mn regeneration programme – gone are many of the grim council blocks, replaced by low-level housing projects, and the local school has been transformed into a City Academy. To the south, Peckham Rye is rather different, with streets of Victorian terraces and some larger homes near

the pleasant park, while neighbouring Nunhead has a mixture of tidy terraces and modern homes. The whole area will be boosted further by the Cross Tram Link (see **Chapter 2**) and the redevelopment of the East London line.

Property Costs

Property Prices

Like many other inner city boroughs, Southwark has a huge range of property prices and rents. The table below shows the average property prices in the borough:

> Detached: £797,541
> Semi-detached: £565,913
> Terraced: £450,133
> Flat: £286,628

Rental Costs

The table below shows average monthly rents in the borough:

> House 5+ bed: £3,000
> House 4-5 bed: £2,600
> House 3-4 bed: £2,150
> House 2-3 bed: £1,750
> Flat 2-bed: £1,350
> Flat 1-bed: £1,150

Crime

Southwark's crime record has slightly improved in recent years, although it still has the second-highest overall crime rate in the capital, with the second-highest rate for violence and the third-highest for robbery; however, levels of car-theft and motor vehicle crime have dropped sharply. Currently the police and community safety teams are focusing on tackling drugs and hate crimes such as racist and homophobic incidents.

The police station HQ is in Southwark (323 Borough High Street, SE1, ☎ 0300-123 1212), with other stations in East Dulwich, Peckham, Rotherhithe and Walworth; and Camberwell police station, which is open on Wednesday and Friday from 1pm-5pm.

To compare crime rates throughout London, see the table in **Appendix D**.

Health

The Southwark Primary Care Trust provides NHS services in the borough. For a full list of doctors, dentists and clinics, visit ⌨ www.nhs.uk.

To see how the Primary Care Trust compares with others in London, see the table in **Appendix D**.

Doctors & Dentists

♦ There are 82 NHS GP surgeries in the borough, providing a range of clinics and health services.

♦ Southwark has 37 dental and orthodontic practices, around half of which accept new NHS patients.

Hospitals

♦ Guy's Hospital (St Thomas Street, SE1, ☎ 020-7188 7188, ⌨ www.guysandstthomas. nhs.uk) – A&E; minor injuries unit.

♦ King's College Hospital (Denmark Hill, SE5, ☎ 020-3299 9000, ⌨ www.kingsch.nhs.uk) – A&E.

♦ Maudsley Hospital (Denmark Hill, SE5, ☎ 020-3228 6000, ⌨ www.slam.nhs.uk) – mental health care.

Private Medical Facilities

The London Bridge Hospital (27 Tooley Street, SE1, ☎ 020-7407 3100, ⌨ www. londonbridgehospital.com) offers a range of facilities, including a private GP service. To find a private GP you can also visit ⌨ www. privatehealth.co.uk.

Schools

Educational standards in Southwark are generally well below average, although primary schools results have improved in recent years. A third of all pupils speak English as a second language. In the 2009 school league tables, primary schools were placed 19th out of the 33 London boroughs (84th out of 150 UK local authorities) and secondary schools 26th (112th in the UK).

To compare schools throughout London, see the table in **Appendix D**.

> **LOCAL INFORMATION**
>
> **Peckham, famous as the setting for TV's** *Only Fools and Horses*, **is of Saxon origin, the name meaning the village of the river Peck, a small stream that ran through the district until it was enclosed in 1823. It appears in the Domesday Book of 1086 as** *Pecheham*, **with assets of two hides (about the same as Del Boy in** *Only Fool and Horses***).**

Pre-school

There are five LEA-funded nursery schools, an Early Years Centre in Nunhead and nursery classes attached to many infant and primary schools. There's also a reasonable choice of playgroups and nursery schools in the private sector.

State Schools

Plans are underway to build a new all-age academy to replace the Joseph Lancaster Primary and the Geoffrey Chaucer Secondary schools in The Borough (an area of Southwark so-named since the 1550s).

First schools: There are 70 primary schools, of which 24 are voluntary aided.

Secondary schools: Southwark has seven comprehensive schools, including City Academies in Bermondsey and Peckham. Five schools are voluntary aided and four have sixth forms. The top

Southwark Bridge

performers in 2009 were St. Michael's RC School and the Harris Academy, both in Bermondsey.

Special schools: Nine special schools cater for students with physical disabilities and learning difficulties.

Private Schools

There are 14 private schools, including two specialist Christian schools: Chrysolyte in Bermondsey and Springfield in Peckham. The famous Dulwich College is also in Southwark. Five schools cater for secondary age pupils. The top performers in 2009 were the James Allen Girls School (JAGS) in East Dulwich and Alleyn's School in Dulwich, which both gained top exam results at GCSE or A level.

Further Education

♦ Southwark College in Waterloo (🖥 www. southwark.ac.uk). There are also a number of specialist FE organisations, including the Older Learning Project, the South London Science and Technology Centre (🖥 www. slstc.southwarklea.org.uk) and the Women's Training Workshop.

Higher Education

♦ Camberwell College of Arts (🖥 www. camberwell.arts.ac.uk) – part of the University of the Arts, London.

♦ London College of Communication (🖥 www. lcc.arts.ac.uk) – part of the University of the Arts, London.

♦ London South Bank University (🖥 www.lsbu. ac.uk).

Public Transport

Public transport is decent and most areas are only minutes away from the City by bus, rail or underground. The Cross River Tram will run from Peckham to Camden via Elephant & Castle and King's Cross, and is due for completion in 2016. Phase two of the East London underground line extension will link Surrey Quays to Clapham Junction via Peckham.

Underground

Only the northern areas are served by the tube. The Bakerloo line terminates at Elephant & Castle, which is also on the City branch of the Northern line; and the Jubilee line goes to Southwark, London Bridge and Bermondsey. The East London tube line is closed and will re-open in 2010 as part of the overground rail network. Typical journey times are as follows:

♦ Bermondsey (Jubilee line, zone 2) to Westminster, 8 minutes.

♦ Elephant & Castle (Bakerloo line, zone 1) to Oxford Circus, 12 minutes.

Rail

♦ Southern and South Eastern trains both run services from Blackfriars, London Bridge and Victoria into Bermondsey, Peckham and Dulwich. Journey time 11 minutes (Blackfriars to Peckham Rye).

♦ The Thameslink service from London Bridge goes to the south coast or King's Cross for the north (16 minutes from King's Cross to London Bridge).

Buses

Buses into central London are frequent, but are packed during rush hours and often slow, with a limited choice in Dulwich. Useful routes include the 148 (Camberwell to Shepherd's Bush), 185 (Dulwich to Victoria) and 188 (Elephant & Castle

Southwark Cathedral

to Holborn). Night buses include the N21, N35, N36, N63 and N68.

River Transport

Several commuter services stop at Bankside and London Bridge piers, serving Embankment and Westminster to the west, and St Katherine's and Greenwich to the east. An additional service travels between the Tate Britain and Tate Modern galleries.

Airports

Below are the approximate distances and journey times from Elephant & Castle to the five London airports using public transport.

♦ **City** – 7 miles; 30 minutes via Canning Town.

♦ **Gatwick** – 22 miles; 45 minutes via London Bridge.

♦ **Heathrow** – 16 miles; 45 minutes via Paddington.

♦ **Luton** – 31 miles; 50 minutes via Kings Cross.

♦ **Stansted** – 32 miles; 70 minutes via Liverpool Street.

Roads

Roads are continually congested and those in the heart of Camberwell are said to be the noisiest for miles around. Several major routes meet at the Elephant & Castle, including the A3 to the south coast and the A201 New Kent Road, which is the start of the Congestion Charge Zone. The A2 to Kent and the A100 to Tower Bridge begin at the Bricklayer's Arms Junction in Walworth, and the A205 South Circular Road cuts Dulwich village in half.

Parking

There are 18 Controlled Parking Zones in Southwark: in parts of North Bermondsey by the Thames, Camberwell, Herne Hill, Peckham, Rotherhithe and Walworth. The cost of a resident's annual parking permit is £99.30.

Waste & Recycling

Household waste is collected weekly, along with recyclable materials, which include cans, glass, paper and cardboard, and plastic bottles. Garden waste is collected (in certain areas) every two weeks and bulky items (such as kitchen appliances and furniture) are collected free of charge. Waste can also be taken to Southwark's reuse and recycle centre at the Manor Place depot off Walworth Road, SE17.

Shopping

Apart from the bijou designer shops and independent retailers at Shad Thames, Butler's Wharf and Hay's Galleria (see below), and the famous markets in the heart of The Borough, shopping in Southwark is a fairly ordinary experience. There's a large shopping centre at Surrey Quays, stocked with high street names, while Peckham's high street and markets score well for diversity and choice.

Neighbouring Nunhead has one of the best fishmongers (Sopers) in South London, while Camberwell has a small shopping district catering for daily essentials and multicultural goods. The shopping centre at Elephant & Castle is famously awful, although shops along the nearby Walworth Road include a small M&S and Argos (a new shopping centre is planned). Dulwich and East Dulwich are home to small independent retailers.

LOCAL INFORMATION

Borough Market is London's oldest food market and was established on the south bank of the Thames when the Romans built the first London Bridge. It has occupied its present site for 250 years and is one of the largest food markets in the world, selling a wide variety of foods.

Shopping Centres

♦ Aylesham Shopping Centre (Rye Lane, SE15) – Morrisons supermarket, Chinese food store and local shops.

♦ Butler's Wharf (Shad Thames, SE1) – specialist food outlets.

♦ Elephant & Castle Shopping Centre (SE1) – small chains, including Iceland and a Tesco Metro store.

♦ Hay's Galleria (London Bridge City, Tooley Street, SE1) – specialist clothing, jewellery and crafts.

♦ Oxo Tower (Bargehouse Street, South Bank, SE1) – designer shops.

- Surrey Quays Shopping Centre (Redriff Road, SE16) – nearly 100 high street names and independent shops.

Supermarkets

- Asda in Walworth (Old Kent Road).

- Marks & Spencer, London Bridge Station (Simply Food).

- Morrisons in Peckham.

- Sainsbury's in East Dulwich (open 24 hours) plus locals in Borough High Street and Herne Hill.

- Tesco in Walworth (off the Old Kent Road), Surrey Quays (open 24 hours), plus a Metro store in the Elephant & Castle Shopping Centre.

Markets

- Borough Market (Borough High Street, SE1) – wholesale fruit and vegetable market, often used as a film location; open to the public on Fridays and Saturdays.

- East Street and Westmoreland Road Markets (off the Walworth Road, SE17) – cut-price essentials, bric-a-brac; daily.

- Elephant & Castle Market (outside the shopping centre) – cheap household goods; Monday to Saturday, 7am-7pm.

- New Caledonian Antiques Market (Bermondsey Square, SE1) – London's largest antiques market; Friday.

- Peckham Markets (Choumert Road and Rye Lane, SE15) – fresh produce, ethnic foods and general household goods; Monday to Saturday.

- Peckham Farmers' Market (Peckham Square, SE15) – Sunday, 9.30am-1.30pm.

Entertainment

There's a host of visitor attractions in the heart of historic Southwark by the Thames, as well as several cinemas and theatres in other districts. In summer, the borough celebrates Latin American culture with Carnaval del Pueblo, the longest street festival in Europe, stretching from the Tate Modern to London Bridge. Dining out is particularly good at Butler's Wharf and Hay's Galleria, while Dulwich and East Dulwich have a variety of pleasant restaurants.

Theatres

- Blue Elephant Theatre (59a Bethwin Road, SE5, ☎ 020-7701 0100, 🖥 www. blueelephanttheatre.co.uk) – political theatrical programmes.

- The Globe Theatre (New Globe Walk, SE1, ☎ 020-7401 9919, 🖥 www.shakespeares-globe.org) – replica of the original Shakespearean open-air theatre (see box).

- Magic Eye Theatre (Havil Street, SE5, ☎ 020-7708 5401) – small theatre promoting work by local theatre companies and drama schools.

- Menier Chocolate Factory (51/53 Southwark Street, SE1, ☎ 020-7907 7060, 🖥 www. menierchocolatefactory.com) – arts complex with theatre in a former chocolate factory.

- Shunt Vaults (Joiner Street, SE1, ☎ 020-7378 7776, 🖥 www.nationaltheatre.org.uk) – award-winning theatre beneath London Bridge Station.

- Southwark Playhouse (62 Southwark Bridge Road, SE1, ☎ 020-7620 3494, 🖥 www. southwarkplayhouse.co.uk) – lively theatre with a diverse repertoire.

- Union Theatre (Union Street, SE1, ☎ 020-7201 9070, 🖥 www.uniontheatre.freeserve co.uk) – fringe theatre.

Cinemas

- Peckham Multiplex (95a Rye Lane, SE15, ☎ 0870-0429 399, 🖥 www.peckhamplex.com).

- UCI Cinema Surrey Quays (Redriff Road, SE16, ☎ 0871-224 4007, 🖥 www.uci.co.uk).

Museums & Galleries

National visitor attractions include the Imperial War Museum and HMS Belfast (🖥 www.iwm.org. uk), Tate Modern (🖥 www.tate.org.uk/modern)

and the London Dungeon (💻 www.thedungeons. com), although there are many other interesting exhibitions and galleries. For example, on the Thames there's the Golden Hinde (💻 www. goldenhinde.co.uk), a reconstruction of Sir Francis Drake's famous ship, while nearby there's a wine museum at Vinopolis, and a tea and coffee museum in Southwark Street. Other museums include:

♦ Britain at War Museum (64 Tooley Street SE1, ☎ 020-7403 3171, 💻 www.britainatwar.co.uk) – recreation of wartime Britain.

♦ The Design Museum (28 Shad Thames, Butler's Wharf, SE1, ☎ 020-7403 6933, 💻 www.designmuseum.org) – contemporary design.

♦ Fashion and Textile Museum (83 Bermondsey Street, SE1, ☎ 020-7407 8664, 💻 www.ftm. org) – contemporary fashion and textiles, founded by Zandra Rhodes.

For a full list of museums and galleries in the borough, visit 💻 www.southwark.gov.uk/ discoversouthwark.

LOCAL INFORMATION

The Globe Theatre was built in 1599 by Shakespeare's company, the Lord Chamberlain's Men, and was destroyed by fire in 1613. A modern reconstruction of the Globe, named 'Shakespeare's Globe', opened in 1997 and is sited just 750ft (230m) from the original theatre.

Libraries

There are 13 local authority libraries in the borough, with one mobile service. The busiest is the architecturally-stunning, award-winning Peckham Library (122 Peckham Hill Street, SE15, ☎ 020-7525 0200), which was designed to make people curious about what lies inside. Peckham Library and Southwark's two other main libraries, in Dulwich and Walworth Road, are open on Sundays.

Clubs

Most of Southwark's club scene is centred around London Bridge and Walworth, although there are a couple of venues in Camberwell and Peckham. The best known is the Ministry of Sound (103 Gaunt Street, SE1, ☎ 020-7378 6528, 💻 www. ministryofsound.com/home), while others include:

♦ The Arches (53 Southwark Street, SE1, ☎ 020-7403 4001).

♦ Ezekiel's (1a Rye Lane, SE15, ☎ 020-7732 9000).

♦ Funky Munky (25 Camberwell Church Street, SE5, 020-7277 1806).

Live Music

Venues such as the Southwark playhouse often stage musical events, while classical lovers will find that a number of churches present regular concerts, including Southwark Cathedral (Montague Close, SE1, ☎ 020-7367 6700, 💻 www.southwark.anglican.org/ cathedral) and St Giles in Camberwell (Camberwell Church Street, SE5, ☎ 020-7701 2462, 💻 www. stgilescamberwell.org.uk). Several bars and pubs host contemporary gigs, usually advertised in the local press.

Pubs

Pubs and bars in Southwark offer all the variety you'd expect from an inner London borough. Shad Thames, Butler's Wharf and Thames-side areas are the trendiest, but further east in Bermondsey and Rotherhithe, new gastro bars are appearing. You can choose between new bars such as Garrison (99 Bermondsey Street, SE1, ☎ 020-7089 9355) or more traditional tourist haunts such as the Mayflower (117 Rotherhithe Street, SE16, ☎ 020-7237 4088) or the 15th century Angel (101 Bermondsey Wall East, SE1, ☎ 020-7237 3608), which has trap doors leading down to the river that were allegedly used by smugglers.

Market Porter in the Borough masquerades as the Leaky Cauldron in the *Harry Potter* films (9 Stoney Street, SE1, ☎ 020-7407 2495), while the George Inn (Borough High Street, SE1, ☎ 020-7407 2056) is the only galleried pub left in London. Further south, Camberwell has a crop of interesting new bars, such as the Old Dispensary (325 Camberwell New Road, SE5, ☎ 020-7708 8831), and East Dulwich's Lordship Lane features several pleasant pubs and bars.

Restaurants

Southwark boasts several of London's most fashionable restaurants, including fine European cuisine at the Oxo Tower (Oxo Wharf Bridge, Barge House Street, SE1, ☎ 020-7803 3888) and the cluster of gastronomic delights Sir Terence Conran has installed at Butler's Wharf. Of these the most famous is Le Pont de la Tour (Butler's Wharf Building, 36d Shad Thames, SE1, ☎ 020-7403 8403), visited by the Blairs and the Clintons, while Horniman's (Hay's Galleria, Battlebridge Lane, SE1, ☎ 020-7407 1991) has excellent river views.

For traditional Southwark delicacies go to Manze's (87 Tower Bridge Road, SE1, ☎ 020-7407 2985), which reputedly serves the best pie and mash in London. Camberwell has reasonable ethnic restaurants, while fast food outlets predominate in Peckham. There are some pleasant eateries in East Dulwich, where Belair House in Dulwich's Belair Park is an expensive but genteel restaurant in a grand Georgian mansion (Gallery Road, SE21, ☎ 020-8299 9788).

Sports Facilities

As well as outdoor sports pitches in many of the borough's parks, Southwark has eight council-funded sports and leisure facilities, at Camberwell, Dulwich, Elephant & Castle, Peckham, Peckham Rye, Rotherhithe, Southwark and Surrey Docks. Facilities include:

◆ Three indoor swimming pools (for outdoor bathing there's Brockwell Lido in neighbouring Lambeth).

◆ Indoor sports halls and multi-use sports and games areas.

◆ Outdoor sports pitches and an athletics track at the Southwark Park Sports Centre.

◆ Watersports facilities, including sailing and windsurfing at Surrey Docks.

Gym facilities are available at most of the leisure centres and there are branches of popular fitness centres, including Fitness First and Holmes Place. Golf can be played in Dulwich and Peckham Rye, and there's horse-riding on Dulwich Common. For the less active, there's ten-pin bowling at the Mega Bowl in the Elephant & Castle Shopping Centre and at the Hollywood Bowl at the Mast Leisure Park (Teredo Street, SE16).

Green Spaces

Despite being an inner borough, around 25 per cent of Southwark's area is devoted to gardens and open spaces, a total of some 130. One of the largest is Burgess Park in Walworth, home to the unique Chumleigh Gardens (see box), planted to display flora from around the globe. Forming a backdrop to the Imperial War Museum is Geraldine Mary Harmsworth Park, with its Tibetan Garden of Contemplation and Peace, while a surprising find in Rotherhithe is Surrey Docks Farm, a miniature commercial farm complete with a blacksmith and dairy.

Dulwich Village has three large spaces: Belair Park, one of Southwark's loveliest; Dulwich Park, with its boating lake and duck pond; and the open space of Dulwich golf course, which borders Sydenham Hill Wood Nature Reserve. Over in East Dulwich, the London Wildlife Garden Centre is an award-winning park. The Edwardian park in Peckham Rye has recently being restored, while nearby Nunhead Cemetery, a Gothic masterpiece with some magnificent Victorian monuments, has been refurbished with Heritage Lottery funds.

LOCAL INFORMATION

Chumleigh Gardens

Chumleigh Gardens are one of London's most unusual parks, set in the grounds of Grade II-listed former almshouses on the edge of Burgess Park (Camberwell). Owned and managed by the borough of Southwark, the gardens capture the spirit of five distinct gardening styles: Islamic, English, African/Caribbean, Mediterranean and Oriental. There are also two ponds and a community gardening area, where local groups grow a variety of produce.

Sutton

CR0 (part), CR4, KT4 (part), SM1, SM2 (part), SM3, SM5 and SM6

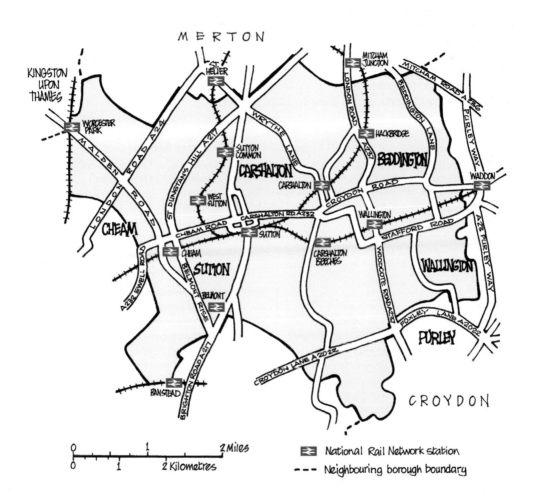

Map legend:
- National Rail Network station
- Neighbouring borough boundary

Scale:
0 — 1 — 2 Miles
0 — 1 — 2 Kilometres

At a Glance

Best for: schools, low crime, open spaces, culture, recycling

Not so good for: no tube, nightlife

Who lives there: middle-class families, professionals, commuters, first-time buyers

Housing stock: high proportion of inter-war detached houses and semis (40 per cent), remainder flats and terraces

Housing costs: inexpensive

General Information

Council Offices: Civic Offices, St Nicholas Way, SM1 1EA (☎ 020-8770 5000)

CAA Assessment: (see ▭ http://oneplace.direct.gov.uk > Search by area > London Sutton)

Controlling Party: Liberal Democrat

Website: ▭ www.sutton.gov.uk

Council Tax 2010/11: £2,418 (Band G), £2,901 (Band H)

Main Areas/towns: Beddington, Carshalton, Cheam, North Cheam, Rosehill, St Helier, Sutton, Wallington

Postcodes: CR0 (part), CR4, KT4 (part), SM1, SM2 (part), SM3, SM5 and SM6

Population & Ethnicity: 187,600, with just 10 per cent from an ethnic minority, mostly Asian and Afro-Caribbean. Like neighbouring Kingston, the borough is popular with middle-class, white-collar workers of all age groups.

Unemployment: 5.2 per cent (London average is 8.2 per cent)

Overview

More Surrey than London, Sutton is a well-established middle-class borough within easy commuting distance of the City. This is a pleasant, prosperous area, with a thriving local economy providing plenty of employment, and if the nightlife lacks the excitement of central London, there are compensations in the form of green belt countryside and some excellent state schools. Sutton also has a reputation for being the 'cleaner and greener' borough, with the best recycling rates in London, a community food growing project and the UK's first eco-friendly housing development, at Beddington. The official council cars even run on electricity!

Sutton itself is a typical urban town centre, with the borough's main shopping and entertainment facilities. There are also some village-like areas such as Carshalton, with its pond and the historic house of Honeywood, and the centre of Cheam, which has some beautiful 16th century buildings. The grandest area is Carshalton Beeches, home to stockbrokers and wealthy professionals.

LOCAL INFORMATION

Sutton was recorded as Sudtone in a charter of Chertsey Abbey, believed to have been drawn up in the late 7th century, when the Manor was granted to the Abbot of Chertsey (who held it until 1538) by Frithwald, Governor of Surrey. The Domesday Book of 1086 also refers to Sudtone, although some sources give the early name as Suthtone or Sudtana.

Development Plans

Despite its wealth and prosperous appearance, Sutton has pockets of deprivation. However, unlike many other boroughs, regeneration must be funded by the council, as the borough isn't eligible for neighbourhood renewal funding because it's one of London's least deprived.

The South Wandle Regeneration scheme, supported by the London boroughs of Sutton and Croydon, is now delivering regeneration projects in the area covering the Purley Way, the Croydon Airport Industrial estate, Valley Park and the Beddington Lane area of Sutton. The focus of the scheme is on the needs of the private sector, in particular manufacturing and retail, issues about the environment and transport, and concerns about skills, training and development.

Plans for a comprehensive regeneration of Kimpton Industrial Estate in Sutton are well advanced and include a Tesco store site, the former Sutton Sewage Works and the existing industrial estate. Plans include a state-of-the-art site for high-tech industrial units and a new access road from the A217, plus environmental improvements.

Residential Areas

Most of Sutton developed during the 20th century, so there's little in the way of Victorian suburbia, although there are pockets of period houses in northern parts and around Sutton town. The majority of homes are inter-war properties. The borough has a high proportion of detached houses (11 per cent), with 27 per cent semi-detached, 29 per cent terraced and 33 per cent flats, most of which are purpose-built and few have more than two bedrooms.

Beddington, Wallington & St Helier (CR0, SM4, SM5, SM6)

These are typical suburban towns, with a good supply of houses and flats in neat streets, punctuated by open spaces and busy main roads. Wallington developed around the railway and is more Victorian, with some grand detached houses, smaller semis and modern apartments near the useful high street. The last ten years have seen the redevelopment of the Roundshaw Estate, which has resulted in new homes, jobs, schools and public transport, all of which have contributed to creating a more sustainable community. At the heart of the Estate, a £6mn leisure, sport, library and recreational centre (the Phoenix Centre) was opened in autumn 2004, which turned one of the borough's worst estates into an area that's now popular with residents and has reduced crime. There's a council estate to the east at Roundshaw.

Beddington has a more diverse property mix and is cheaper. Built on the former sewage works, Beddington Zero Energy Development (BedZed) is the most interesting housing development of recent years; a scheme of innovative (and visually stunning) eco-friendly flats, houses and work units built by the Peabody Trust. To the north is St Helier,

a large council-built estate from the '20s and '30s, shared with Merton, which was laid out like a garden suburb with its own shops. Most of the properties are now privately owned.

Carshalton & Carshalton Beeches (SM5)

Carshalton is a quiet residential neighbourhood with a mixture of period and '30s semis providing good family accommodation. Although the high street is busy with traffic, it's attractive nonetheless, with its large pond and useful shops, together with a row of pretty 16th century cottages. Up the hill is the stockbroker country of Carshalton Beeches, where spacious and expensive houses are set in wide, tree-lined roads.

Cheam & North Cheam (SM1, SM2, SM3, KT4)

Cheam is an attractive area close to Nonsuch Park. In the centre are some historic 16th century buildings and small independent shops; property includes Victorian and Edwardian family houses, giving way to streets of '30s semis in North Cheam. A typical three-bedroom semi costs in the region of £300,000 and there's a healthy rental market. The most sought-after roads lie around South Cheam and Belmont, where larger properties of various styles and ages can be found.

Sutton (SM1, SM2)

By day the borough's main shopping and commercial district, in the evening a magnet for youths seeking a good time, Sutton is trying hard to create a vibrant image. To a certain extent it succeeds, with a range of leisure facilities making it a worthwhile alternative to central London for a mid-week night out. Popular with commuters and first-time buyers, property ranges from two- and three-bedroom Victorian cottages to '70s houses and modern apartments, while larger family-sized detached and semi-detached houses are also available. A two-bedroom flat costs around £160,000.

Property Costs

Property Prices

The table below shows average property prices in the borough.

Detached: £500,394

Semi-detached: £307,796

Terraced: £239,285

Flat: £162,212

Rental Costs

The table below shows average monthly rents in the borough.

House 5+ bed: £3,000

House 4-5 bed: £1,950

House 3-4 bed; £1,700

House 2-3 bed: £1,150

Flat 2-bed: £900

Flat 1-bed: £750

Crime

Sutton is one of the safest London boroughs, with the third-lowest overall crime rate and the second-lowest for burglary. The 'Safer Sutton Partnership', a collaboration between the council and the metropolitan police, focuses on reducing anti-social behaviour, particularly among young people in Sutton town centre, where disorderly conduct (usually fuelled by alcohol) is a problem.

The main police station is in Sutton (6 Carshalton Road West, SM1, ☎ 0300-123 1212), with other stations in Wallington and nearby Worcester Park in Surrey.

To compare crime rates throughout London, see the table in **Appendix D**.

Health

The Sutton Primary Care Trust provides NHS services in the borough.

For a full list of doctors, dentists and clinics, visit 🖥 www.nhs.uk.

To see how the Primary Care Trust compares with others in London, see the table in **Appendix D**.

Doctors & Dentists

♦ Sutton has 80 NHS GP surgeries providing a range of clinics and health services.

♦ There are 60 dental and orthodontic practices in the borough, less than half of which accept new NHS patients.

Hospitals

♦ Carshalton War Memorial Hospital (The Park, SM5, ☎ 020-8647 5534) – outpatient clinics and mental health care.

♦ Orchard Hill Hospital (Fountain Drive, SM5, ☎ 020-8770 8000, 🖥 www.suttonandmerton.nhs. uk) – care for the elderly.

♦ Royal Marsden Hospital (Downs Road, SM2, ☎ 020-8642 6011, 🖥 www.royalmarsden.nhs.uk) – cancer treatment.

♦ St Helier Hospital (Wrythe Lane, SM5, ☎ 020-8296 2000, 🖥 www.epsom-sthelier.nhs.uk) – A&E.

♦ Sutton Hospital (Cotswold Road, SM2, ☎ 020-8296 2000, 🖥 as St Helier) – care for people with learning disabilities.

Private Medical Facilities

♦ St Anthony's Hospital (North Cheam, SM3, ☎ 020-8337 6691, 🖥 www.stanthonys.org.uk) – surgery and outpatient clinics. To find a private GP, visit 🖥 www.privatehealth.co.uk.

Schools

Sutton has some of the best schools in London, particularly in the state sector, with five highly sought-after selective secondary schools. Many pupils at these schools travel from outside the borough. In the 2009 school league tables, primary schools were placed sixth out of the 33 London boroughs (17th out of 150 UK local authorities) and secondary schools second (second in the UK).

To compare schools throughout London, see the table in **Appendix D**.

Pre-school

Nursery classes are attached to all the borough's infant and primary schools and there are four state nurseries in Carshalton, Mitcham Junction, Sutton and Wallington. There's a wide choice of privately-run nursery schools and playgroups.

State Schools

First schools: There are 41 infant, junior and primary schools, of which nine are voluntary aided.

Secondary schools: Sutton has five selective schools and 14 comprehensives. Two schools are voluntary aided, all have sixth forms and ten have specialist status. The top performers in 2009 were the five selective schools, beating even the independent schools for GCSE results: Nonsuch High School for Girls (Cheam), Sutton Grammar School for Boys, Wallington County Grammar, Wallington High School for Girls and Wilson's School (Wallington). Three of these achieved some of the best GCSE and A level results in the UK. For budding tennis champions, Cheam High School has a full-time tennis and fitness programme (in conjunction with the Sutton Junior Tennis Centre), combined with an academic curriculum.

Special schools: Five special schools cater for students with physical disabilities and learning difficulties, and a further two units are attached to mainstream schools. There are also two private schools in Beddington (primary and secondary) for children with special educational needs.

Private Schools

There are nine private schools in the borough, with two catering for students aged up to 16 or 18: Stowford College in Sutton (7 to 16 years) and the selective Sutton High School (girls aged 4 to 18 years), which achieved excellent GCSE results in 2009.

Further & Higher Education

◆ Carshalton College (💻 www.carshalton.ac.uk) offers a range of further and higher education courses for students aged 16-plus.

◆ Sutton College of Learning for Adults (SCOLA, 💻 www.scola.ac.uk) is a specialist college for part-time adult education.

👤 FAMOUS RESIDENTS

Famous people with links to Sutton include Jeff Beck (musician), Noel Coward (actor & playwright), James Cracknell (Olympic rower), Quentin Crisp (writer), Sir John Major (Prime Minister), Sir Cliff Richard (singer), Sir Harry Secombe (comedian, actor & singer), Alec Stewart (cricketer), Graham Sutherland (author) and HG Wells (author).

Public Transport

Sutton is beyond the reach of the underground network (the nearest station is in Morden, 5mi/8km away), although there are extensive overground rail services. Buses serve the shopping centres of Kingston and Croydon but not central London.

Rail

◆ The Thameslink service to Blackfriars and King's Cross stops at most stations in the borough (typical journey time from Sutton, 45 minutes).

◆ Southern Trains services to London Bridge or Clapham Junction and Victoria stop at Belmont, Sutton and Carshalton (20 minutes from Sutton to Clapham Junction). Additional services from these stations go to Watford via west London.

◆ The nearest station to North Cheam is Worcester Park, which is on the South West Trains network to Waterloo (journey time 30 minutes).

Buses

Local bus services are reasonable in most areas, although more limited in North Cheam and not always frequent. Several services go to neighbouring boroughs and useful routes include the number 213 (to Kingston), 407 (to Croydon) and the 470 (to Colliers Wood in Merton). The X26 service

parking permit costs £40 a year for one car, £55 for a second, £80 for a third and £110 for a fourth vehicle. There are additional CPZs around Cheam station, to deter commuter parking, and around the Royal Marsden Hospital in Belmont. A Belmont resident pays £35 for the first permit, £50 for the second, £75 for a third and £100 for a fourth or subsequent permit, per year. There's also a CPZ scheme at Collingwood Estate, where the first permit is free and any others cost £5 each per year. In the Wellington Avenue CPZ, each permit costs £35.

to Heathrow Airport stops at several towns in the borough. No daytime buses serve central London, although the N44 night bus from Aldwych serves Sutton.

Trams

The Tramlink service between Croydon and Wimbledon stops at Beddington Lane, on the boundary with Merton.

Airports

Below are the approximate distances and journey times from Sutton to the five London airports using public transport.

- **City** – 15 miles; 70 minutes via Bank.
- **Gatwick** – 14 miles; 55 minutes via East Croydon.
- **Heathrow** – 13 miles; 80 minutes on the X26 bus, or 90 minutes on the Piccadilly line from Earl's Court.
- **Luton** – 36 miles; 90 minutes via Kings Cross.
- **Stansted** – 41 miles; 110 minutes via Liverpool Street.

Roads

Main roads through the borough include the A24 and A217, both running north-south, which provide access to the M25 and the motorway network. Traffic on these roads can be slow during rush hours. Sutton town centre has a one-way system that can be slow at peak periods and weekends.

Parking

Despite the high ratio of car ownership in the borough, parking is reasonably easy in most areas. There's a Controlled Parking Zone (CPZ) in Sutton town centre to deter shoppers from parking outside resident's homes. A resident's

Waste & Recycling

As befits the 'greener, cleaner borough', Sutton has an excellent recycling record, with the highest recycling rate in London. General household rubbish is collected fortnightly along with recyclable materials, which include cans, garden waste, glass, paper and cardboard, and plastic bottles. Other recyclable materials can be taken to 'bring banks' or the borough's re-use and recycling centre in Sutton (Kimpton Park Way). Householders are encouraged to donate unwanted items such as furniture, textiles and toys to charities. The council collects old fridges and freezers for a fee.

Shopping

The borough's main shopping centre is Sutton town, where there are two shopping centres and a pedestrianised shopping street with a range of high street names, including Boots, M&S and WH Smith. Consumer research is often carried out in the town to take advantage of shoppers' 'UK average' profile. Cheam and Carshalton have useful and attractive high streets with small shops catering for day-to-day needs. There are several antiques shops in Carshalton, while Wallington has a good selection of local shops, although elsewhere shopping is limited.

Shopping Centres

- St Nicholas Centre (St Nicholas Way, SM1) – high street chains, including Debenhams, HMV and Mothercare.
- Times Square (High Street, SM1) – high street chains, including BHS, Next and TK Maxx.

Supermarkets

◆ Asda in Sutton town centre.

◆ Morrisons in Sutton town centre.

◆ Sainsbury's in North Cheam and Wallington.

◆ Tesco in Sutton Common (open 24 hours).

◆ Waitrose in Worcester Park (Surrey).

Markets

◆ North East Surrey Farmers' Market (Old Town Hall, Woodcote Road, SM6) – fresh produce; second Saturday of each month.

◆ Sutton Market (High Street, SM1) – general goods; Tuesday and Saturday.

Entertainment

Sutton's recreational facilities are limited to one cinema, two theatres and a smattering of historic buildings. During the summer the borough is part of the River Wandle Festival, a programme of special events held along the river in Merton, Sutton and Wandsworth (☎ 0870-714 0750, 🖥 www.wandlevalleyfestival.org.uk). There are plenty of pubs and bars in Sutton town centre, while the best bets for dining out are Cheam and Carshalton.

Theatres

◆ The Secombe Theatre (42 Cheam Road, SM1, ☎ 020-8770 6990, 🖥 www.suttontheatres.co.uk) – mainstream productions and regular comedy nights.

◆ The Charles Cryer Studio Theatre (39 High Street, SM5, ☎ 020-8770 4950, 🖥 www.charlescryer.org.uk) – diverse programme.

Cinemas

◆ UCI Sutton (St Nicholas Way, SM1, ☎ 0871-224 4007, 🖥 www.uci.co.uk).

Museums & Galleries

◆ Carew Manor (Church Road, SM6, ☎ 020-8647 8349) – tours of the great hall, dovecote and orangerie wall at this former country house, now a school.

◆ The Carshalton House Water Tower (West Street, SM1, ☎ 020-8647 0984) – 18th century garden building, containing a cold bath lined with Delft tiles.

◆ Honeywood (Honeywood Walk, SM5, ☎ 020-8770 4297) – local heritage collection housed in a 17th century mansion.

◆ Little Holland House (40 Beeches Avenue, SM5, ☎ 020-8770 4781 – see info box) – Grade II listed interior in Arts and Crafts style.

◆ Nonsuch Mansion (Nonsuch Park, Ewell Road, SM3, ☎ 020-8393 4922, 🖥 www.nonsuch-mansion.co.uk) – tours of the kitchen areas and an exhibition of rare stained glass.

◆ The Oaks Bake House (The Oaks Park, SM5, ☎ see Honeywood, above) – original 19th century bread oven and fireplace.

◆ Whitehall (1 Malden Road, SM3, ☎ 020-8643 1236) – Tudor house set in a tranquil walled garden.

LOCAL INFORMATION

The former home of artist, designer and craftsman Frank Dickinson (1874-1961), Little Holland House has a Grade II* interior created entirely by Dickinson. It was inspired by the ideals of John Ruskin and William Morris, and contains Dickinson's paintings, hand-made furniture, furnishings, metalwork and friezes, in Arts and Crafts style.

Libraries

Sutton's award-winning library service is widely known for its excellence. There are nine local authority libraries, with one mobile service. The main library is in Sutton (St Nicholas Way, SM1, ☎ 020-8770 4700) and is open on Sunday afternoons, as is the new library at the Phoenix Centre at Roundshaw. Both libraries are self-service for borrowing and returning books. Beddington library is closed on Mondays, Wednesdays and Sundays.

Clubs

There are a few dance bars in Sutton town centre, usually packed with a young crowd, especially at weekends. Along the High Street, choices include Bar Room Bar (☎ 020-8770 0009) and Long Island Iced Tea (☎ 020-8642 4930), while in nearby Throwley Road there are the Chicago Rock Café (☎ 020-8643 2606) and Zoots Night Club (☎ 020-8770 0600).

Live Music

The main venues for live music are the Charles Cryer Studio and the Secombe Theatre (see **Theatres** above). The Studio hosts weekly jazz nights ('Carshalton Jazz') and regular 'Rockstock' evenings, where local bands have the opportunity to play before an audience. The Secombe theatre hosts the Sutton best band contest. Elsewhere a few pubs put on gigs, including the Butterchurn (Erskine Road, SM1, ☎ 020-8643 2205) and the Nightingale (53 Carshalton Road, SM1, ☎ 020-8241 2419).

Pubs

Sutton town centre has plenty of bars and pubs, particularly in and around the high street; elsewhere pubs are more traditional boozer rather than style bars or gastropubs. Cheam and Carshalton have a few attractive hostelries, such as Ye Olde Red Lion (17 Park Road, SM3, ☎ 020-8642 5108) and the Railway Tavern (47 North Street, SM5, ☎ 020-8669 8016).

Restaurants

Cheam and Carshalton are the best bet for eating out, with some pleasant independent restaurants serving food from various countries; Caffe la Fiamma (23 High Street, SM3, ☎ 020-8661 2200) and La Veranda (18 Benyon Road, SM5, ☎ 020-8647 4370) are good examples. Chains include El Torito (4 Ewell Road, SM3, ☎ 020-8661 2626). Restaurants in Sutton offer a fairly predictable experience, with the best choice along the High Street, including several ethnic restaurants as well as chains such as Garfunkels, Il Ponte and Pizza Express. There's also a tapas bar, Los Hermanos (29 High Street SM1, ☎ 020-8770 1707). Wallington has several restaurants along the Stafford Road, including a Pizza Express and the Brothers Bistro (80 Stafford Road, SM6, ☎ 020-8669 3032).

Sports Facilities

The Cheam Leisure Centre (North Cheam), the Phoenix Centre (Wallington) and the Westcroft Leisure Centre (Carshalton) provide a range of general-purpose sports facilities, including:

◆ Indoor sports halls.

◆ Fitness centres with gym equipment.

◆ Swimming pools and squash courts (Cheam and Westcroft).

In addition, the Sutton Arena in Carshalton is a large athletics centre with indoor and outdoor tracks, indoor sprint track and a field event hall.

The borough is also home to the country's first and only Junior Tennis Centre, in Sutton, which provides facilities for nurturing potential star players as well as offering opportunities for juniors and adults to fine-tune their tennis skills. The Oaks Sports Centre in Carshalton has two golf courses and a golf range open to the general public. Many sports can be played in the borough's parks, and Sutton's surrounding countryside is excellent for horse riding and walking. There are branches of leading fitness centres in Sutton and Cheam.

Green Spaces

Sutton is one of the greenest boroughs in London, with over 1,500 acres (600ha) of picturesque parks and open spaces. Carshalton has a number of parks, including Oaks Park (see box), the Grove and Carshalton Park. The River Wandle flows through the 14th century Grove Park, and from there you can follow the Wandle Trail to Wilderness Island, a small nature reserve. Carshalton Park is much larger and has an attractive 18th century grotto and ornamental lake. To the east, Beddington Park has mature trees and meadowland, while to the west is Cheam Park which merges with Nonsuch Park, originally designed as a hunting ground by Henry VIII.

LOCAL INFORMATION

Oaks Park

Oaks Park – after which the Epsom Oaks horse race was named and inaugurated in 1779, a year before the Derby Stakes was first run – in Carshalton is the largest in the borough and merges with the North Downs on the Surrey border. The Earl of Derby had the park landscaped in the 1770s in the manner of Capability Brown, and it has remained much the same ever since. It contains meadowland and woodland, has stunning views and is also home to a craft centre, wildlife sanctuary and an animal hospital.

Tower Hamlets

E1, E2, E3 (part), E14

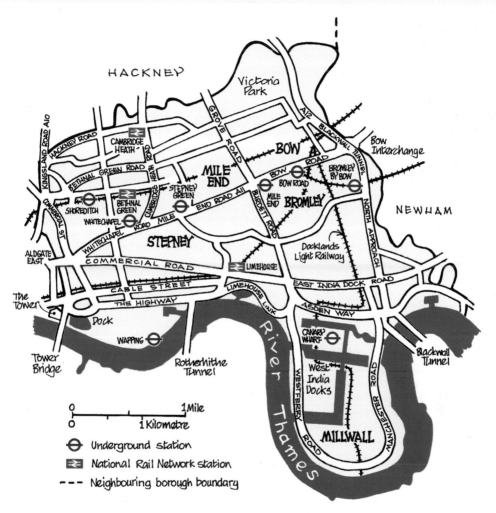

At a Glance

Best for: public transport, markets, culture, regeneration projects, high-rise flats

Not so good for: deprivation, parking, traffic congestion

Who lives there: working class families, young professionals, City workers, artists, large (45%) ethnic population

Housing stock: 85% flats, mostly new (including warehouse conversions), Georgian and Victorian terraces, council estates

Housing costs: above average

General Information

Council Offices: Town Hall, Mulberry Place, 5 Clove Crescent, E14 2BG (☎ 020-7364 5000)

CAA Assessment: (see 🖥 http://oneplace.direct.gov.uk > Search by area > London Tower Hamlets)

Controlling Party: Labour

Website: 🖥 www.towerhamlets.gov.uk

Council Tax 2010/11: £1,992 (Band G), £2,391 (Band H)

Main Areas/towns: Bethnal Green, Bow, Canary Wharf, Isle of Dogs, Limehouse, Poplar, Spitalfields, Stepney, Wapping, Whitechapel

Postcodes: E1, E2, E3 (part), E14

Population & Ethnicity: 220,500, with a high proportion aged between 20 and 35. Nearly 50 per cent of residents are from an ethnic minority, with over half from Bangladesh (mostly living around Stepney) and a significant Afro-Caribbean community in Poplar. Local East End families are increasingly joined by young professionals and City workers, drawn to the smart new communities in Docklands, Bethnal Green, Bow and Whitechapel.

Unemployment: 13.1 per cent (London average is 8.2 per cent)

Overview

Dominated by the gleaming, pyramid-topped tower (1 Canada Square) at Canary Wharf, Tower Hamlets is one of the fastest-changing boroughs in the capital. Heralded as one of the success stories of recent times, the transformation of Docklands from derelict warehouses to a thriving business centre kick-started a process of regeneration and renewal that will continue apace with the coming of the 2012 Olympic Games. More homes, jobs and leisure facilities, new bridges across the Thames and the expansion of the East London line are set to improve the remaining run down and deprived areas. Parts of the borough are also within the Thames Gateway housing scheme.

The River Thames defines the borough's southern boundary as it loops its way from Tower Bridge and Wapping, down past the Isle of Dogs and up to the Blackwall Tunnel. To the north lie the traditional East End areas of Spitalfields, Bethnal Green, Stepney and Bow. Multicultural, diverse and full of character, its working class roots increasingly overlaid by middle-class aspirations, Tower Hamlets looks set to become another of London's fashionable residential hotspots.

LOCAL INFORMATION

The borough gets its name from the Tower of London, built during the reign of William the Conqueror in the 11th century, and the small communities or hamlets that developed on the surrounding marshland. The Constable of the Tower of London had special jurisdiction over the area from the 16th century until 1889 and inhabitants of Tower Hamlets were originally required to provide yeomen for the Tower of London.

Development Plans

Tower Hamlets has some of the best and worst housing in the country – both in the public and private sectors – and is among the most deprived areas of the UK. There's been a lot of regeneration in the borough in the last few decades, particularly in the Isle of Dogs and Docklands (Canary Wharf), where there's a wealth of new housing developments. Current regeneration projects include the Crossways Estate in Bow and the Ocean Estate in Stepney, which are among the most deprived in London, ravaged by poverty, crime and drug use.

Tower Hamlets is one of the five host boroughs for the London 2012 Olympic and Paralympic Games. The men's and women's marathons and the Paralympic marathon will pass along Whitechapel Road, Mile End Road and Bow Road, while Victoria Park will be the main venue for the 50km walk, as well as hosting Olympic cultural events. The influence of the Games is being felt long before 2012 and includes thousands of new jobs, homes and improved public transport, as well as a new park and sports facilities.

The borough has also benefited from Transport for London funding to improve roads and public transport, town centres, pedestrian and cycling facilities, and travel plans to get children to and from school safely. New DLR stations have transformed public transport in recent years and Tower Hamlets will also benefit from the Crossrail project.

Residential Areas

While the Docklands district is packed with modern buildings and luxury warehouse conversions, the borough's northern areas offer the extremes of run down council blocks and modern apartments, with a wealth of Victorian terraces in between. Just 1 per cent of dwellings are detached or semi-detached houses; 14 per cent are terraces and a massive 85 per cent are flats, mostly purpose-built.

Bethnal Green (E2)

Close to the City (three minutes by tube to Liverpool Street) and trendy Shoreditch (see **Hackney**), Bethnal Green boasts lively markets, an interesting Museum of Childhood and a crop of good restaurants. Property consists of Victorian cottages and flats, loft-style conversions of former schools,

an increasing number of new apartments, plus some ugly council dwellings. The most popular and expensive homes overlook the Regent's Canal and Victoria Park, where a two-bedroom terrace costs around £500,000. The diverse population comprises local East Enders, City workers, first-time buyers, people priced out of Islington and Shoreditch, and refugees from around the world.

Bow (E3)

The area's slums have been demolished to make way for a mixture of loft apartments, new terraced houses and student homes. Bow Quarter is an imaginative conversion of an old match factory into 700 dwellings and two new developments, Bow Central and the Heart of Bow. Council towers are being refurbished and original period terraces remain popular. The area is set to benefit from the leisure facilities planned for the 2012 Olympic Games at Stratford in the east (see **Newham**).

Docklands (E14)

After a slow start, Docklands has taken off in the past decade, with banks, newspapers and legal practices just some of the businesses that have moved into the gleaming quayside towers of Canary Wharf (see below). Residential property includes warehouse conversions and smart waterside flats and houses, with penthouse apartments favoured by international celebrities. South of Canary Wharf, the Isle of Dogs features large areas of council-owned family houses, generally inland, with privately-owned flats and townhouses along the river. Not all property is new, with developments dating from the '70s and

'80s as well as traditional 19th century terraces, particularly around the Blackwall Tunnel. The Isle's infrastructure is finally improving, with new public transport, shops, schools and leisure facilities.

The 'U' bend in the River Thames borders the Isle of Dogs (the origin of the name is a mystery), which is famous as the site of Canary Wharf, home to the UK's tallest building (1 Canada Square – 771ft/235m). Also known as the Docklands, the area has undergone a massive redevelopment in the last few decades and now comprises a blend of restored warehouses and historic buildings, contemporary housing complexes and striking office developments.

Poplar (E14)

Originally industrial, Poplar is the poor relation to Docklands; dominated by council estates (many now being refurbished), close to the busy Blackwall Tunnel Approach Road and reliant on the DLR for public transport. However, as council homes are increasingly bought by their occupants they offer good value alternatives to the more upmarket properties in Docklands proper, and there are some interesting conversions of older buildings and a few new houses. Limehouse to the west has a stock of converted warehouses and the Limehouse Basin has been redeveloped as an attractive waterside residential area.

Spitalfields & Whitechapel (E1)

This cosmopolitan district is famous for bustling street markets and Asian food – some of the best Bangladeshi restaurants in London are in Brick Lane. Traditionally the centre of London's wholesale clothing industry, it's fast becoming an artists' quarter, with the renowned Whitechapel Art Gallery at its heart. Characterised by the narrow lanes and alleyways of Dickensian London, the area has a range of property, including ex-council flats, fine Georgian (some of the best in the country) and Victorian terraces (some Grade II listed), together with new apartments and live/work units. Part of the former wholesale fruit and vegetable market in Spitalfields is currently being redeveloped and the area is as popular with City workers and young professionals as it is with traditional East Enders.

Stepney & Wapping (E1)

Within walking distance of the City, these districts are popular with young professionals working in the City or Docklands. Stepney consists largely of two-bedroom Victorian terraces, council blocks and modern housing association homes. New mews developments and flats are also available, but the few 18th century houses rarely come onto the market. Waterside Wapping is the birthplace of Docklands regeneration, the first place to see former warehouses converted to desirable residences, with large tracts of stylish houses and flats dating from the mid-'80s onwards. Local authority and housing association complexes add to the mix. There's an attractive marina at St Katherine's Dock and a buzzing arts centre at Shadwell.

Property Costs

Property Prices

The table below shows average property prices in the borough:

Detached: £0 (no recent sales)
Semi-detached: £432,750
Terraced: £436,527
Flat: £343,930

Rental Costs

The table below shows average monthly rents in the borough:

House 5+ bed: £4,750
House 4-5 bed: £4,300
House 3-4 bed: £2,400
House 2-3 bed: £1,550
Flat 2-bed: £1,150
Flat 1-bed: £950

Crime

Overall, Tower Hamlets has slightly higher than average crime rates for inner London, with violent crime being much more common than burglary. Local police initiatives include high-visibility patrolling and automated number plate checks (where car licence plates are scanned to see if the drivers are wanted for crimes).

The police station HQ is in Bethnal Green (12 Victoria Park Square, E2, ☎ 0300-123 1212), with other stations in Bow, Brick Lane, Isle of Dogs, Limehouse and Poplar.

To compare crime rates throughout London, see the table in **Appendix D**.

Health

NHS services in the borough are provided by the Tower Hamlets Primary Care Trust. For a full list of doctors, dentists and clinics, visit 🖥 www.nhs.uk.

To see how the Primary Care Trust compares with others in London, see the table in **Appendix D**.

Doctors & Dentists

♦ There are 71 NHS GP surgeries in Tower Hamlets, providing a range of clinics and health services.

♦ The borough has 29 dental and orthodontic practices, around half of which accept new NHS patients.

Hospitals

♦ London Chest Hospital (Bonner Road, E2, ☎ 020-7377 7000, 🖥 www.bartsandthelondon.nhs.uk).

♦ Mile End Hospital (Bancroft Road, E1, ☎ 020-7377 7000) – community hospital.

♦ The Royal London Hospital (Whitechapel, E1, ☎ 020-7377 7000, 🖥 www.bartsandthelondon.nhs.uk) – A&E; NHS walk-in centre.

♦ St Andrew's Hospital (Devas Street, E3, ☎ 020-7476 4000, 🖥 www.newhamuniversityhospital.nhs.uk) – outpatient clinics.

Private Medical Facilities

♦ The London Independent Hospital (1 Beaumont Square, E1, ☎ 020-7780 2400, 🖥 www.bmihealthcare.co.uk). To find a private GP, visit 🖥 www.privatehealth.co.uk.

Schools

The borough offers excellent provision for the under-fives, but its secondary schools have variable standards. In the 2009 school league tables, primary schools were placed 18th out of the 33 London boroughs (76th out of 150 UK local authorities) and secondary schools 28th (114th in the UK).

To compare schools throughout London, see the table in **Appendix D**.

Pre-school

There are six LEA funded nursery schools, plus nursery classes attached to many of the borough's primary schools. There are also day nurseries, nursery schools and playgroups in the private sector.

State Schools

First schools: There are 69 primary schools, of which 18 are voluntary aided.

Secondary schools: The borough has 15 comprehensive schools, of which six are voluntary aided or controlled. Six schools have sixth forms and eight have specialist status. The best performing in 2009 was the Sir John Cass Foundation and Redcoat Church of England Secondary School in Stepney, which was also one of the top UK schools for added value.

Special schools: Six special schools cater for students with physical disabilities and learning difficulties.

Private Schools

There are 11 private schools in the borough, of which two are infant schools and five cater for secondary age pupils. Several schools cater for Muslim pupils. The best performing school in 2009 was the Madani Secondary School (girls) in Whitechapel.

Canary Wharf

Christ Church, Spitalfields

Further Education

◆ Tower Hamlets College (🖳 www.tower.ac.uk).

Higher Education

◆ London Metropolitan's University's North Campus is in the borough (🖳 www.londonmet. ac.uk).

◆ Queen Mary, University of London (🖳 www. qmul.ac.uk) has its main buildings in Mile End, with another campus in Whitechapel.

Public Transport

Tower Hamlets is well connected to the City and West End by underground, rail and bus links. The new Channel Tunnel rail link in nearby Stratford (see **Newham**) will give easy access to Europe and the planned extension to the East London line will provide an overground service from the borough to Hackney, New Cross, Crystal Palace and West Croydon by 2010. Eventually Crossrail will provide fast east-west links across London from Whitechapel and the Isle of Dogs.

Underground

No fewer than five underground lines run in various directions through Tower Hamlets –

Central, District, Hammersmith & City, Jubilee and the DLR. Typical journey times include:

◆ Bow Road (District line, zone 2) to Embankment, 22 minutes.

◆ Mile End (Central line, zone 2) to Bank, 10 minutes.

◆ Whitechapel (Hammersmith & City line, zone 2) to Liverpool Street, 5 minutes.

Rail

Overground services are better in the north of the borough than the south:

◆ 'One' trains from Bethnal Green reach Liverpool Street in 4 minutes. In the other direction trains go to East London and Essex, or Enfield, Chingford and Cambridge.

◆ c2c trains from Limehouse reach Fenchurch Street in 6 minutes, and travel to stations in East London, Essex and the east coast.

Buses

There are frequent bus services to the City and West End and to neighbouring boroughs. Useful services include the number 25 (to Oxford Circus), 100 (to Blackfriars), 205 (to Paddington) and the 395 (to Surrey Quays). Several routes provide a circular service around Tower Hamlets. Night buses include the N8, N15, N55, N106, N205 and N253.

River Transport

Commuter river services run mornings and evenings from Canary Wharf and St Katherine's piers to London Bridge and Savoy Pier, or to Greenwich. There's a daily shuttle service between the Hilton Hotel at Rotherhithe and Canary Wharf, a daily hop-on, hop-off service between St Katherine's Pier and Westminster, and additional services between Tower Bridge and Waterloo, Westminster, Embankment and Greenwich.

Airports

Below are the approximate distances and journey times from Bow to the five London airports using public transport.

◆ **City** – 4 miles; 29 minutes using the DLR.

◆ **Gatwick** – 26 miles; 70 minutes via London Bridge.

♦ **Heathrow** – 18 miles; 70 minutes via Paddington.

♦ **Luton** – 29 miles; 60 minutes via Farringdon.

♦ **Stansted** – 29 miles; 90 minutes via Liverpool Street.

Roads

The busy A11 and A13 cross the borough to connect with the A12 Blackwall Tunnel Approach Road in the east. Both roads can be heavily congested, while the tunnel, which crosses beneath the Thames to Greenwich, is notorious for problems. The Congestion Charge Zone starts at Whitechapel and the Tower of London. To reduce traffic problems, the council is actively promoting the use of car-sharing, cycling and public transport.

Parking

Tower Hamlets isn't a good place for car owners, with parking difficult in all areas, most of which are Controlled Parking Zones. The cost of a resident's annual parking permit depends on the vehicle's engine size/emissions: £40/150 for the first, £50/160 for the second and subsequent vehicles £190/300 each.

Waste & Recycling

Household rubbish is collected weekly and includes garden waste. Recyclable cans, glass and paper are collected from many homes. The council collects bulky items such as furniture and kitchen appliances by arrangement. The civic amenity site (recycling/waste) is at Northumberland Wharf near the Blackwall Tunnel.

Shopping

Tower Hamlets is unusual because its main shopping facilities are provided by numerous markets rather than major shopping centres. All the main areas have streets of useful shops catering for everyday needs, with some of the best in Bow and Bethnal Green. There are a large number of specialist shops, particularly in the Whitechapel area, selling a quirky mixture of fashions, vintage books and botanical remedies, among other items. Wapping and Canary Wharf both have extensive shopping facilities, largely catering for the working population, where shops range from chemists to boutiques.

Shopping Centres

♦ Cabot Place (E14) – five malls with shops selling a variety of goods. The Anchor Retail Park in Stepney Green has DIY, electrical goods and furniture superstores.

Supermarkets

♦ Asda on the Isle of Dogs.

♦ Marks & Spencer in Canary Wharf (Simply Food).

♦ Sainsbury's in Whitechapel.

♦ Tesco in Bromley-by-Bow (open 24 hours) with Metro stores in Bethnal Green and Canary Wharf.

♦ Waitrose in Canary Wharf.

Markets

Many of the borough's streets are crammed with colourful markets, of which the largest are listed below:

♦ Bethnal Green Road Market (E2) – general household goods; Monday to Saturday.

♦ Billingsgate Market (Trafalgar Way, E14) – wholesale fish market, although some traders will sell to individuals; Tuesday to Saturday.

♦ Brick Lane and Old Truman Brewery Markets (Brick Lane and nearby streets, E2) – fresh produce, household goods, vintage and designer fashions; Sunday.

♦ Columbia Road Flower Market (Columbia Road, E1) – famous for its flowers and plants; Sunday.

♦ Mile End Farmers' Market (Arts Pavilion at Mile End Park, E1) – 3rd Sunday monthly, 10am-2pm.

LOCAL INFORMATION

Petticoat Lane Market

Petticoat Lane Market is a fashion (particularly women's) and clothing market formally recognised until an Act of Parliament in 1936, although its long history as an informal market makes it one of the oldest surviving markets in Britain. Although open from Monday to Friday, the main day is Sunday (9am-2pm), when it extends over many of the surrounding streets with over 1,000 stalls.

◆ Petticoat Lane Market (Middlesex Street and surrounding lanes, E1 – see box) – famous fashion market; Monday to Friday and Sunday.

◆ Roman Road Market (E3) – cut price fashions; Tuesday, Thursday and Saturday.

◆ Spitalfields Market (Bushfield Street, E1) – arts and crafts, organic foods, furniture and fashions in a covered Victorian market hall; Monday to Friday and Sunday.

◆ Whitechapel Road Market (E1) – general household goods; Monday to Saturday.

Entertainment

Facilities have been improving in recent years, particularly in Docklands, which was originally bereft of leisure venues and now has a performing arts centre, the Space (see **Theatres**, below), and a multi-screen cinema. There's also a new arts centre in a former power station, the Wapping Project, as well as performance spaces for hire at Trinity Buoy Wharf (💻 www.trinitybuoywharf.com). Music venues and clubs are on the increase and there are some good restaurants, especially the ethnic restaurants around Spitalfields.

LOCAL INFORMATION

Tower of London

The Tower of London stands on the River Thames on the western boundary of the borough and was built by William the Conqueror in 1078. It's been used as a fortress, royal palace, zoo and a state prison (particularly for royal prisoners), and has also served as a place of execution and torture, an armoury, a treasury, a zoo, the Royal Mint, a public records office and an observatory; it has also been the home of the Crown Jewels since 1303.

Theatres

◆ The Emery Theatre (Annabel Close, E14, ☎ 020-7515 1177, 💻 www.emerytheatre. co.uk) – fringe theatre.

◆ Half Moon Young People's Theatre (43 White Horse Road, E1, ☎ 020-7265 8138, 💻 www. halfmoon.org.uk) – professional productions and participatory projects.

◆ The Octagon (1 Harbour Exchange Square, E14, ☎ 020-7410 0770) – independent theatre.

◆ The Space (269 Westferry Road, E14, ☎ 020-7515 7799, 💻 www.space.org.uk) – performances in a former church.

Cinemas

◆ Mile End Genesis Cinema (Mile End Road, E1, ☎ 020-7780 2000, 💻 www.genesiscinema.co.uk).

◆ UGC West India Quay (Hertsmere Road, E14, ☎ 0871-200 2000, 💻 www.ugccinemas.co.uk).

Museums & Galleries

As well as the Tower of London (Tower Hill, EC3, ☎ 0844-482 7777, 💻 www.hrp.org.uk/toweroflondon – see box), the borough is home to some fascinating museums and an astonishingly large number of galleries showcasing traditional and contemporary art. Attractions include:

◆ Museum in Docklands (No 1 Warehouse, West India Quay, Hertsmere Road, E14, ☎ 020-7001 9844, 💻 www.museumindocklands.org.uk) – local history collection.

◆ V & A Museum of Childhood (Cambridge Heath Road, E2, ☎ 020-7942 2000, 💻 www.vam.ac.uk/ moc) – one of the largest collections of toys in the UK.

◆ Ragged School Museum (46 Copperfield Road, E3, ☎ 020-8980 6405, 💻 www. raggedschoolmuseum.org.uk) – recreations of a Victorian classroom with artefacts from Dr. Barnardo's free ragged day schools.

◆ SS Robin (West India Quay, Herstmere Road, E14, ☎ 020-7538 0652, 💻 www.ssrobin.com) – the world's oldest complete steamship.

◆ Three Mills Island (Three Mill Lane, E3, ☎ 020-8980 4626, 💻 www.housemill.org.uk) – industrial artefacts housed in former mills.

◆ Wapping Project (Wapping Hydraulic Power Station, Wapping Wall, E1, ☎ 020-7680 2080, 💻 www.thewappingproject.com) – exhibits inspired by the building.

◆ Whitechapel Art Gallery (80 Whitechapel High Street, E1, ☎ 020-7522 7888) – leading contemporary art gallery.

Libraries

There are four local authority libraries and a mobile service in the borough. None open on Sundays. There are also several 'Ideas Stores' in local shopping districts that provide learning resources and lending services for books, DVDs and CDs. The largest libraries are Bancroft Library (277 Bancroft Road, E1, ☎ 020-7364 1289/90), which houses local history and Islamic collections, and Bethnal Green Library (Cambridge Heath Road, E2, ☎ 020-8980 3902/6274), housing the history and archive section. The Women's Library (Old Castle Street, E1, ☎ 020-7320 2222) is part of London Metropolitan University and provides an extensive women's history collection.

Clubs

There are many clubs in Tower Hamlets, including:

◆ Copyright Night-club (110 Pennington Street, E1, ☎ 0871-223-6923).

◆ 93 Feet East (150 Brick Lane, E1, ☎ 020-7247 3293).

◆ Purple 3E (562 Mile End Road, E3, ☎ 020-8980 6427).

◆ The Rhythm Factory (16-18, Whitechapel Road, E1, ☎ 020-7375 3774, 🖳 www.rhythmfactory.co.uk).

◆ The Vibe Bar (91 Brick Lane, E1, ☎ 020-7247 3479).

◆ The White Swan (556 Commercial Road, E1, ☎ 020-7780 9870).

For comedy, Lee Hurst's Backyard Comedy Club (231-237 Cambridge Heath Road, E2, ☎ 020-7739 3122, 🖳 www.leehurst.com) is the largest in the East End, and there's another venue, in the popular Jongleurs chain, Jongleurs Bow Wharf (221 Grove Road, E3, ☎ 020-8980 7874, 🖳 www.jongleurs.com/clubs/bow/intro.html).

Live Music

The London Arena (Limeharbour, E14, ☎ 020-7538 1212) and Cabot Hall (Cabot Place West, E14, ☎ 020-7418 2783) present regular concerts featuring national names, while the Rhythm Factory (see **Clubs** above) also has live music. Regular jazz sessions are held at Pizza Express in Docklands (Floor 2, Cabot Place, E14, ☎ 020-7513 0513), the Space (see **Theatres** above) and Spitz (Old Spitalfields Market, 109 Commercial Street, E1, ☎ 020-7392 9032).

Pubs

The borough's pubs range from old-fashioned boozers to modern bars and gastropubs. The most historic are in Wapping, where the Prospect of Whitby (57 Wapping Wall, E1, ☎ 020-7481 1095) claims to be the oldest on the Thames. In Limehouse, the Grapes (76 Narrow Street,

Waterside Wapping

E14, ☎ 020-7987 4396) is thought to be the pub described by Dickens in Our Mutual Friend. The majority of pubs and bars around Canary Wharf are strictly after-work watering holes and are closed at weekends. Whitechapel and Bethnal Green have a clutch of new bars, such as the trendy Napoleon (23 Wadeson Street, E2, ☎ 020-8983 7900), which has occasional cabaret evenings. Bow is another area where modern bars sit alongside traditional pubs.

Restaurants

For traditional East End grub you need look no further than Bethnal Green, where S&R Kelly (284 Bethnal Green Road, E2, ☎ 020-7739 8676) has been selling pie and mash since 1937. However, in these cosmopolitan times the curry has taken over as the borough's most popular cuisine, with some superb curry houses in Brick Lane (see 🖳 www.bricklanerestaurants.com for choices). American, Chinese, Mediterranean and Thai restaurants all crop up in the borough, while for something a little different there's Wapping Food at the Wapping Project (Wapping Hydraulic Power Station, E1, ☎ 020-7680 2080), a cafeteria-style eatery serving modern European dishes in stunning surroundings.

Sports Facilities

Seven council-funded leisure centres and an outdoor stadium provide ample sports facilities within the borough:

♦ Swimming pools in Bethnal Green, Docklands and Shadwell.

♦ Indoor sports halls and all-weather outdoor sports pitches in Poplar, Wapping and Whitechapel.

Mile End Stadium (Rhodeswell Road, E14, ☎ 020-8980 1885) has international-standard athletics facilities, with a running and sports track, indoor hall, all-weather Astroturf sports pitches, grass pitches, cricket green and tennis courts. The stadium will be used for training during the 2012 Olympics. The Docklands Sailing and Watersports Centre (235A, Westferry Road, E14, ☎ 020-7537 2626, 🖳 www.dswc. org) is London's premier venue for water-based activities and runs RYA-approved courses. Other sporting facilities include tennis courts and play areas in many parks, and there are a number

of private gyms. Mudchute Farm in Docklands offers horse riding.

Green Space

There are 122 parks and open spaces in Tower Hamlets, including the beautiful Victoria Park (see box), although many are small and do little to break up the urban sprawl. However, there's water in abundance, with docks and canals providing pleasant surroundings and areas for walking. Mile End Park, site of Mile End Stadium (see above), stretches from Limehouse to Victoria Park along the Regent's Canal. In Docklands, Island Gardens on the riverbank provides lovely views of Greenwich, plus access to the Greenwich Footway tunnel. The largest park there is Mudchute Park, which is home to the largest urban farm in Europe.

LOCAL INFORMATION

The largest space in the borough, Victoria Park was created in 1884; it has two lakes, ornamental gardens and a Chinese Pagoda, and is host to open-air concerts, festivals, fetes, rallies and meetings throughout the year. It also has tennis courts, a bowling green, a paddling pool, play areas for children and enclosures with deer.

Waltham Forest

E4, E10, E11 (part), E17

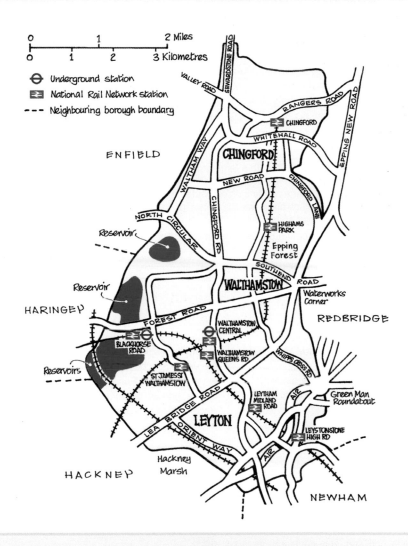

At a Glance

Best for: affordable housing, open spaces, sports facilities, restaurants

Not so good for: deprivation, schools, nightlife, culture. tube stations

Who lives there: working class families, commuters, first-time buyers, ethnic minorities

Housing stock: terraces (50%, many Victorian), flats (one third), semis

Housing costs: inexpensive

General Information

Council Offices: Town Hall, Forest Road, Walthamstow, E17 4JF (☎ 020-8496 3000)

CAA Assessment: (see 🖳 http://oneplace.direct.gov.uk > Search by area > London Waltham Forest)

Controlling Party: Labour

Website: 🖳 www.walthamforest.gov.uk

Council Tax 2010/11: £2,437 (Band G), £2,924 (Band H)

Main Areas/towns: Chingford, Leyton, Leytonstone, Walthamstow

Postcodes: E4, E10, E11 (part), E17

Population & Ethnicity: 223,200, with a large proportion aged under 35. Around a third of residents belong to an ethnic minority, mostly Pakistani and Afro-Caribbean. Local families have traditionally made up the bulk of residents, although first-time buyers, commuters and young families are increasingly moving in, attracted by good value housing and a sense of open space.

Unemployment: 10.7 per cent (London average is 8.2 per cent)

Overview

Situated on the north-east edge of London, between Epping Forest and the River Lea Valley, Waltham Forest offers plenty of green space, reasonable public transport and good schools. For the most part it's quintessential suburbia; neither affluent nor impoverished, neither trendy nor old-fashioned, but a pleasant, convenient – if unexciting – place to live. In the centre of the borough lies the town of Walthamstow, the administrative hub and shopping centre, currently undergoing major regeneration promising new jobs, offices, shops and homes. Just to the east of the town centre, Walthamstow 'village' has been voted the best urban village in London by *Time Out* magazine for its mixture of affordable housing, bars and restaurants, and its semi-rural feel. In the south are the largely working class areas of Leyton and Leytonstone, and to the north the smart suburb of Highams Park and the popular family town of Chingford.

Development Plans

Waltham Forest is one of five London boroughs which have been designated host boroughs for the 2012 Summer Olympics. The training facilities at the Waltham Forest Pool & Track will be used by Olympians to prepare for the Olympics, with the Velodrome being built in Leyton. The borough will also host the Paralympic Tennis and Archery events, and will be home to the wind turbine – the Angel of Leyton – providing power both during and after the Games.

LOCAL INFORMATION

Walthamstow is first recorded around 1075 as Wilcumestowe ('The Place of Welcome') and in the Domesday Book of 1086 as Wilcumestou. Until the 19th century it was largely rural, with a small village centre (now Walthamstow Village) and a number of large estates.

After 2012, Waltham Forest will have a state-of-the-art National Hockey Centre, tennis courts, and football and multi-sport facilities. The Velodrome sits only 50 metres over the border, therefore local people will be able to use the top cycling facilities at the sporting hub in the north of the Olympic Park. Residents will also have a 500-acre (200-ha) park on their doorstep, with a land bridge over the A406 joining the north of the Olympic Park to the rest of the Olympic Park.

The council is planning a number of regeneration projects, including Blackhorse Lane (station hub, waterfront and Sutherland Road areas, and the Forest Road access improvement scheme) and Walthamstow town centre. There are plans to build homes (including affordable housing) on the 8-acre (3.2-ha) Walthamstow Greyhound Racing Stadium site, which closed in 2008.

Residential Areas

Towns in the south and middle of the borough (Leyton, Leytonstone and Walthamstow) were largely developed during the 19th century housing boom that accompanied the building of the railways. Further north, '30s properties predominate around Chingford. Around half of the borough's properties are terraced houses, with 11 per cent semi-detached and just 2 per cent detached, the remainder being flats.

Chingford (E4)

This is the borough's wealthiest area, with a diverse population of commuters, self-made entrepreneurs, young families and retirees. North Chingford is characterised by tree-lined avenues of Victorian and Edwardian houses, mostly large, with the most sought-after properties near Epping Forest. South Chingford is less salubrious, with terraces and '30s semis providing affordable family accommodation close to Lea Valley Park. There are council properties at Chingford Hatch. To the south is Highams Park, with substantial period properties, some converted into flats, plus the usual '30s semis.

Leyton & Leytonstone (E10, E11)

As neighbouring Hackney becomes more expensive, so Leyton becomes more attractive to those looking for a reasonable amount of space for their money. The area's proximity to the site of the Olympic Park at Stratford is also likely to bring new opportunities for growth. Property consists largely of three-bedroom Victorian terraces, with a few council tower blocks in the town centre. Expect to pay between £250,000 and £300,000 for a three-bedroom house. The most sought-after roads are away from the main A12, which cuts through the middle of the area. Leytonstone to the north-east is slightly more expensive, particularly areas towards Bush Wood. There are proposals to redevelop the Whipps Cross University Hospital site to improve hospital facilities and provide accommodation for key workers and medical students.

Walthamstow (E17)

Multicultural and densely populated, Walthamstow offers streets of period terraces, ranging from small to medium sized. Good transport connections make this a popular commuter town and it's also a favourite with first-time buyers and families priced out of neighbouring areas. Restaurants and bars are improving, creating a livelier atmosphere. Upper Walthamstow has some larger detached houses (five bedrooms or more) as well as '30s semis. There are few new builds in the area and most that exist are owned by housing associations.

Property Costs

Property Prices

The table below shows average property prices in the borough:

Walthamstow Town Hall

Detached: £374,181

Semi-detached: £296,708

Terraced: £243,782

Flat: £167,977

Rental Costs

The table below shows average monthly rents in the borough:

House 5+ bed: £1,800

House 4-5 bed: £1,550

House 3-4 bed: £1,300

House 2-3 bed: £1,100

Flat 2-bed: £850

Flat 1-bed: £755

Crime

Waltham Forest's crime rates are slightly above the London average in all categories, particularly motor vehicle crime and robbery, although rates are generally reducing, helped by an increase in police visibility on the streets through the Street Warden and Safer Neighbourhood schemes. Current priorities include targeting violent crime and anti-social behaviour. An alcohol-restriction zone has been introduced in Leytonstone to deter drinking on the streets.

The police station HQ is in Chingford (King's Head Hill, E4, ☎ 0300-123 1212), with other stations in Leyton, Leytonstone and Walthamstow (three stations).

To compare crime rates throughout London, see the table in **Appendix D**.

Health

NHS services in the borough are provided by the Waltham Forest Primary Care Trust. For a full list of doctors, dentists and clinics, visit 🖥 www.nhs.uk.

To see how the Primary Care Trust compares with others in London, see the table in **Appendix D**.

Doctors & Dentists

♦ Waltham Forest has 55 NHS GP surgeries, providing a range of clinics and health services.

♦ The borough has 30 dental and orthodontic practices, around half of which accept new NHS patients.

Hospitals

♦ Nasebury Court Hospital (Nasebury Court, 2 Merriam Close, E4, ☎ 020-8531 0744) – mental health care.

♦ Whipps Cross University Hospital (Whipps Cross Road, E11, ☎ 020-8539 5522, 🖥 www.whipps.nhs.uk) – A&E.

Private Medical Facilities

There are no private hospitals in the borough. The nearest facilities are at the Holly House Hospital in Buckhurst Hill and the BUPA Roding Hospital in Redbridge. To find a private GP, visit 🖥 www.privatehealth.co.uk.

Schools

Educational standards in the borough are below the national average, although a few schools do particularly well. In the 2009 school league tables, primary schools were placed 29th out of the 33 London boroughs (117th out of 150 UK local authorities) and secondary schools 27th (111th in the UK).

To compare schools throughout London, see the table in **Appendix D**.

Pre-school

There are four LEA-funded nurseries, as well as nursery classes attached to infant and primary schools. Pre-school provision in the private sector is good, with a choice of nursery schools and playgroups.

State Schools

First schools: There are 54 infant, junior and primary schools, of which ten are voluntary aided or controlled.

Secondary schools: The borough has 15 comprehensive schools, of which two are voluntary aided. Three schools have sixth forms and seven have specialist status. The best performers in 2009 were Highams Park School and Walthamstow School for Girls, which is one of the top UK schools for added value.

Special schools: Five special schools cater for students with physical disabilities and learning difficulties.

connections and will provide fast connections to the continent when Stratford International station opens fully for Eurostar train services in 2010. Stratford will also be on the Crossrail cross-London line.

Underground

The Central line serves only Leyton and Leytonstone in the south, while the Victoria line stops at Blackhorse Lane in the west before terminating at Walthamstow. Chingford doesn't have an underground station – the nearest are Walthamstow Central and Woodford, both a couple of miles away. Typical journey times are as follows:

- Leyton (Central line, zone 3) to Bank, 15 minutes.
- Walthamstow Central (Victoria line, zone 3) to Kings Cross, 20 minutes.

Rail

Walthamstow, Highams Park and Chingford are on a branch line served by 'one' trains from Liverpool Street (typical journey time 20-30 minutes). The only other overground service in the borough is the North London line service from Leytonstone High Road to Gospel Oak and Barking, which isn't particularly useful to commuters. Residents from Leyton and Leytonstone are better off commuting on the underground or going to nearby Stratford, where there's a choice of rail connections.

Private Schools

Three private schools cater for pupils at secondary level:

- Bluecurve Learning in Chingford (non-selective).
- Forest School in Snaresbrook (selective and one of the top UK schools for GCSE results in 2009).
- Normanhurst School in Chingford (non-selective).

Further Education

- Leyton Sixth Form College (⌨ www.leyton.ac.uk).
- Sir George Monoux Sixth Form College (⌨ www.george-monoux.ac.uk).
- Waltham Forest College (⌨ www.waltham.ac.uk).

Higher Education

Waltham Forest College (see above) offers undergraduate courses in automotive engineering and IT internet technology.

Public Transport

Walthamstow has good underground and overground services into central London; the borough's other main areas have either service but not both. Local bus services are efficient and there's a route to central London, although it's slow. Nearby Stratford (see **Newham**) already provides access to a range of train

FAMOUS RESIDENTS

Famous people with links to Waltham Forest include David Bailey (fashion photographer), David Beckham (footballer), Fanny Cradock (TV cook), Benjamin Disraeli (Britain's only Jewish Prime Minister), Graham Gooch (cricketer), Alfred Hitchcock (film director & producer), Derek Jacobi (actor & director), William Morris (artist & writer), Ronnie O'Sullivan (snooker player) and Jonathan Ross (TV presenter).

Buses

Local bus services are extensive and several routes serve neighbouring boroughs, including towns on the other side of the River Lea. The number 48 from Walthamstow goes to London Bridge, although it's a slow journey. Other useful routes include the 69 (to City Airport), the 123 (to Wood Green), the 257 (to Stratford) and the 313 (to Potters Bar in Hertfordshire). Several night buses serve Waltham Forest, including the N8, N26, N38, N55 and N73.

Airports

Below are the approximate distances and journey times from Walthamstow Central to the five London airports using public transport:

♦ **City** – 7 miles; 45 minutes via Stratford.

♦ **Gatwick** – 31 miles; 70 minutes via Victoria.

♦ **Heathrow** – 21 miles; 60 minutes via Paddington.

♦ **Luton** – 26 miles; 55 minutes via Kings Cross.

♦ **Stansted** – 25 miles; 45 minutes via Tottenham Hale.

Roads

The A406 North Circular Road cuts across the centre of the borough and the A12 runs through the south-east corner. The A104 Lea Bridge Road runs out to Epping and into Hackney, and is often heavily congested. Junction 4 of the M11 is nearby, providing a fast route to central London (30 minutes) and to the M25, Stansted Airport and Cambridge.

Parking

Parking restrictions in the borough are designed to deter long term parking in shopping areas and around popular commuter stations. Controlled Parking Zones are in operation in Walthamstow's shopping areas, by the station and around the Greyhound Racing Stadium (which closed in 2008), as well as around Blackhorse Road, Leytonstone, Queens Road and St James Street stations. The cost of a resident's annual parking permit depends on engine size/emissions, and varies in different areas of the borough: £22.50/45/95 for a first vehicle, £42/90/170 for a second and £55/122/225 for a third and subsequent vehicles.

Waste & Recycling

General household rubbish is collected weekly, along with recyclable materials, which include batteries, cans, cardboard, engine oil, glass, newspapers and magazines, shoes, textiles and tinfoil. Bulky items such as furniture and kitchen appliances are collected by arrangement. Household rubbish and recyclable materials can also be taken to the main civic amenity site in Walthamstow or recycling centres in Chingford and Leyton.

Shopping

Walthamstow is the main shopping district, with a shopping mall, arcade, supermarkets and many high street names. There are a number of out-of-town superstores such as B&Q along the Lea Bridge Road. Shopping in Leyton and Leytonstone focuses on daily essentials, although there's a reasonable selection of chain stores in Chingford, together with a number of independent traders.

Shopping Centres

♦ The Mall (Selbourne Walk, Selbourne Road, E17) has over 40 well-known chain stores, including BHS, Dixons and HMV.

LOCAL INFORMATION

Walthamstow High Street is dominated by the market, which began in 1885 and occupies all but the last 100 metres of the street – it's reputed to be a mile long but in fact measures around one kilometre.

Supermarkets

♦ Asda in Leyton (open 24 hours) and Walthamstow.

♦ Morrisons in Chingford.

♦ Sainsbury's in Chingford (Hall Lane and Walthamstow Avenue) and Walthamstow.

♦ Tesco in Leyton and Leytonstone (open 24 hours).

Markets

♦ Walthamstow Market (High Street, E17 – see box) has over 450 stalls selling a huge range of goods, from fresh foods to designer clothing and antiques; open daily.

♦ Walthamstow Farmers' Market (Walthamstow High Street, E17) – Sunday 10am-2pm; fresh produce, honey, flowers and much more.

Entertainment

There's no cinema and only one theatre in the borough, although the Assembly Halls in Chingford and Walthamstow host regular events, ranging from ballroom dancing to cookery classes. There are art galleries in Aveling and Lloyd parks, and the annual Waltham Forest Mela takes place in Lloyd Park, providing family fun and Asian entertainment. Leyton's Coronation Gardens hosts the Leyton Carnival and an annual festival.

Theatres

♦ Waltham Forest Theatre (Lloyd Park, Forest Road, E17, ☎ 020-8527 8417) – community productions and other events.

Cinemas

The nearest cinemas are the Odeon South Woodford (see **Redbridge**) and the UCI complex at Pickett's Lock (see **Enfield**).

Museums & Galleries

♦ The Changing Room Gallery (Aveling Park, E17, ☎ 020-8496 3000) – multi-purpose visual arts and crafts centre, including a gallery and studio space for local artists.

♦ Vestry House Museum (Vestry Road, E17, ☎ 020-8509 1917 – see box) – various historical exhibitions plus local history collection.

♦ The William Morris Gallery (Lloyd Park, Forest Road, E17, ☎ 020-8527 3782) – gallery dedicated to the work of the Victorian designer.

LOCAL INFORMATION

Vestry House Museum (☎ 020-8496 4391, ☐ www.walthamforest.gov.uk/vestry-house-museum) is situated in the village of Church End in a two-storey building of brown stock brick constructed in 1730 by order of the Vestry (church council). It's been financed by the borough council since 1931 and is the borough's museum and local studies library and archive.

Libraries

There are 11 local authority libraries in the borough, with one mobile service. The largest and busiest is Walthamstow Library (High Street, E17, ☎ 020-8496 5132). Walthamstow and Leytonstone libraries open on Sundays between 12pm-4pm.

Clubs

♦ Zulus Bar in Leytonstone is the closest to a DJ bar in the area, attracting a predominantly young crowd (640 High Road, E11, ☎ 020-8558 9116).

Live Music

A variety of concerts and choral events takes place throughout the year in the historic Chingford Parish Church of St Peter and St Paul (The Green, E4, ☎ 020-8529 6092). For rock lovers, the borough's main venue is the Standard (1 Blackhorse Road, E17, ☎ 020-8503 2523, ☐ www.standardmusicvenue.co.uk) and occasional gigs are held in the Plough (173 Wood Street, E17, ☎ 020-8503 7419).

Pubs

There are plenty of pubs in all areas, with the largest choice in Walthamstow. The majority are fairly average, although there are some lovely traditional pubs in the 'village', including the Nag's Head (9 Orford Road, E17, ☎020-8520 9709) and the Village (31 Orford Road, E17, ☎ 020-8521 9982), which serves CAMRA-approved ales. The Queen's Arms (42 Orford Road, E17, ☎ 020-8520 6760) is a busy pub, with DJs and dancing at weekends. Chingford has a couple of pleasant places, such as the King's Head, an Ember Inns establishment (2B Kings Head Hill, E4, ☎ 020-8529 6283), popular if predictable, and Larkshall (205 Larkshall Road, E4, ☎ 020-8524 6026), which is a pretty country pub.

There's a limited selection of hostelries in Leyton. JD Wetherspoon's the Drum (557 Lea Bridge Road, E10, ☎ 020-8539 9845) has a good selection of real ales, and the William IV (816 High Road, E10, ☎ 020-8556 2460) is a decent boozer. Leytonstone has the friendly Alfred Hitchcock (147 Whipps Cross Road, E11, ☎ 020-8530 3724), close to Epping Forest, and the Bell (468 High Road, E11, ☎ 020-8518 7042), which is attractive and serves reasonable beer.

Restaurants

As with pubs, Walthamstow's village area has some of the nicest restaurants, mostly independents, such as the Village Kitchen (41 Orford Road, E17, ☎ 020-8509 2144) and Trattoria La Ruga (59 Orford Road, E17, ☎ 020-8520 5008). Chingford has a good choice of eateries, ranging from French cuisine at Godot Bistro (139 Station Road, E4, ☎ 020-8529 6235) to Chinese at the Royal Palace (140 Station Road, E4, ☎ 020-8524 7788). Leyton and Leytonstone have a limited selection, although the Singburi Royal Thai Café (593 High Road, E11, ☎ 020-8281 4082) is a no-frills café serving excellent food at a budget price.

Sports Facilities

Five council-funded leisure centres provide comprehensive sports facilities in Chingford, Leyton and Walthamstow. All five have swimming pools and there are squash courts at the Cathall Centre in Leyton, an all-weather sports pitch at the Kelmscott Centre in Walthamstow and a running track at Waltham Forest Pool & Track. Additional facilities include fitness centres and indoor sports halls, while a number of the borough's parks provide facilities for outdoor sports such as athletics, cricket, football, rugby and tennis.

The borough also has an ice rink in Leyton, a golf course in Chingford, a riding school at Leyton Marshes and branches of private gyms such as Fitness First and Holmes Place. The leisure facilities of the Lea Valley are within easy reach (see **Enfield**), as are those of Epping Forest.

Green Spaces

Waltham Forest is surrounded by protected areas of countryside such as Epping Forest, Lea Valley Park and Walthamstow Marshes. Within the borough itself there are over 400 acres (160ha) of parks and open spaces. Lloyd Park and Aveling Park in Walthamstow feature a wildfowl aviary, ornamental moat, formal gardens and a scented garden for the visually impaired. Greenway Avenue Wood, also in Walthamstow, is a nature reserve. Leyton's Coronation Gardens are traditional Victorian parkland, featuring ornamental gardens. Skeltons Lane Park, off Leyton High Road, is home to Brooks Farm, a popular city farm, and Langthorne Park has an amphitheatre and ecology area, as well as good sports facilities.

There's a variety of popular parks in Chingford, including Mansfield Park – boasting ornamental gardens and impressive views over the Lea Valley reservoirs – and Ridgeway Park, which has sports facilities and a model railway for family entertainment on Sundays. Ancient Ainslie Wood is a conservation area noted for its magnificent oaks and annual display of bluebells.

LOCAL INFORMATION

Waltham Forest is home to many musicians who have made it into the UK charts, including East 17 (later re-grouped as E-17), a pop boy band founded in 1992, which took its name from the postcode for Walthamstow. They achieved 18 Top 20 singles and four Top 10 albums, and were one of the most famous acts (along with Take That) in the UK in the early to mid '90s.

Wandsworth

SW8 (part), SW11, SW12, SW15 (part), SW17, SW18, SW19 (part)

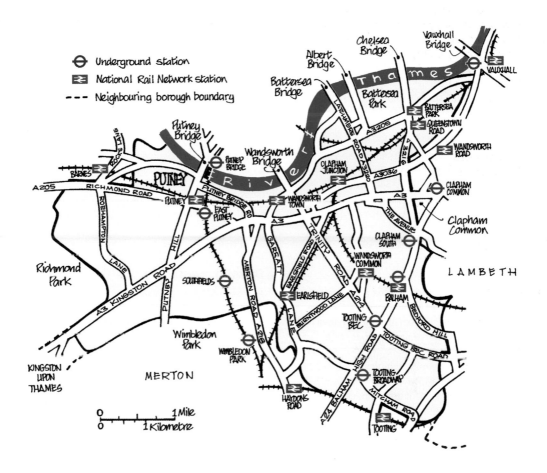

- ⊖ Underground station
- ⇄ National Rail Network station
- --- Neighbouring borough boundary

At a Glance

Best for: housing variety, schools, open spaces, low council tax, entertainment

Not so good for: traffic congestion, parking

Who lives there: wealthy middle-class families, professionals, City commuters, singles/students

Housing stock: 60% flats (many conversions), one-third terraces, period properties

Housing costs: expensive

General Information

Council Offices: Town Hall, Wandsworth High Street, SW18 2PU (☎ 020-8871 6000)

CAA Assessment: (see 🖥 http://oneplace.direct.gov.uk > Search by area > London Wandsworth)

Controlling Party: Conservative

Website: 🖥 www.wandsworth.gov.uk

Council Tax 2010/11: £1,136 (Band G), £1,364 (Band H)

Main Areas/towns: Balham, Battersea, Earlsfield, Putney, Roehampton, Southfields, Tooting, Wandsworth

Postcodes: SW8 (part), SW11, SW12, SW15 (part), SW17, SW18, SW19 (part)

Population & Ethnicity: 284,000, with the highest proportion of people aged between 20 and 35 of all London's boroughs. Around 23 per cent of residents belong to an ethnic minority, mainly Afro-Caribbean and Asian, with a large Polish community around Balham. The borough attracts middle-class professionals and families.

Unemployment: 5.9 per cent (London average is 8.2 per cent)

Overview

Wandsworth is the largest of the inner London boroughs and one of its most upwardly mobile. Since the '90s, large injections of cash have transformed former industrial stretches into desirable residential locations and revitalised shabby and dull areas. The professional middle classes have descended in droves. It's easy to see why, with plenty of green spaces, good schools and a wide range of property styles and sizes. The council has collected several charter marks for its services and council tax is one of the lowest in London. The main drawback is the lack of underground stations in some areas, which leads to heavy congestion on the roads.

LOCAL INFORMATION

The town of Wandsworth appears in the Domesday Book of 1086 as *Wandesorde* and *Wendelesorde*. It was held partly by William, son of Ansculf, and partly by St Wandrille's Abbey. Its Domesday assets were 12 hides.

Development Plans

A substantial area of Wandsworth is eligible for grants and loans under the Town Centre Improvement Scheme. The town of Wandsworth itself is thriving, with record levels of high quality investment in residential, leisure and retail facilities throughout the town centre. Current regeneration developments within the town centre include 127 to 129 Hardwicks Way; Young's Ram Brewery site, Wandsworth High Street and 20 to 30 Buckhold Road; Wandsworth Business Village, Broomhill Road; Wandsworth South Thames College; Wandsworth Riverside Quarter and Battersea Reach.

Proposals include a plan to build 831 flats on the Ram Brewery site in buildings ranging from two to forty-two storeys in height, plus a mixture of shops, bars, restaurants, offices and other commercial units, a riverside walk, pedestrian routes, public spaces and basement car parking. The Buckhold Road plan is for 216 flats in buildings ranging from five to sixteen storeys in height, plus a mixture of shops, community uses, offices, bars and restaurants, and underground parking.

There have been numerous plans to redevelop the landmark but ill-fated Battersea Power Station site (36 acres/15ha) since it closed in 1983. The building is now in a very poor state of repair due to almost 25 years of neglect and the cost alone of making the power station safe to develop now stands at £150mn! The latest plan includes apartments, shops, restaurants, bars, a hotel, cafés, museums and a major redevelopment of the surrounding site, including an 'eco-dome', which would all be open to the public and the development would be the greenest of its kind in Europe. If it receives planning approval, it's hoped that the scheme can be completed by 2014.

Residential Areas

Typically for an inner city borough, over 60 per cent of homes are flats (including many conversions), 30 per cent are terraced houses, 5 per cent are semi-detached and just 2 per cent are detached. Many buildings are Victorian and Edwardian, although there are increasing numbers of modern developments, particularly along the Thames. Ex-council housing represents good value in all areas.

Balham (SW12)

One of the smaller Wandsworth towns, Balham is popular with bankers, lawyers and other solid middle-class professionals seeking a spacious family home. There are also many smaller terraces and smart modern developments which appeal to younger residents. The most exclusive areas border Clapham (see **Lambeth**), Battersea and Wandsworth Common. Transport links are good for south London, with both underground and main line stations.

Battersea (SW8, SW11)

Home to a famous dog's home and the busiest railway junction (Clapham Junction) in the UK, not to mention a noisy heliport, modern Battersea is nonetheless a fashionable place to live. Luxury riverside flats, trendy loft-style spaces in former schools, elegant mansion blocks overlooking the beautiful park and streets of tidy Victorian terraces all appeal to professional couples and families seeking better value than they can find in neighbouring Clapham. A three-bedroom terrace costs in the region of £550,000.

Battersea is famous for the Battersea Dogs and Cats Home, which was established in Holloway in 1860 and moved to Battersea in 1871. It's the world's oldest and most famous animal home and is financed entirely by voluntary donations.

Putney & Roehampton (SW15)

Situated on the south bank of the Thames, pretty Putney boasts leafy streets, decent schools and is only a stone's throw from central

Battersea Power Station

London. Cheaper than Fulham, there's a good mix of period properties as well as several new developments on former industrial sites. The town is moving inexorably up market, attracting young professionals and wealthy young families. Roehampton is less fashionable due to its poor public transport and large number of council estates. However, many of the properties on these are now privately-owned, while the five high-rise blocks of the Alton Estate are Grade II listed. Some desirable and large period family homes overlook Putney Heath. There's a steady demand for rental properties from students at Roehampton University.

Southfields & Earlsfield (SW18)

Close to the borough boundary with Merton and divided by the River Wandle, these two small towns offer good schools, well equipped parks and plenty of three- and four-bedroom family homes. Southfields, once a working class enclave, underwent a transformation in the '90s, when house prices rose dramatically. It's more expensive than Earlsfield and has the advantage of an underground station. Earlsfield attracts young families due to its relative affordability in comparison to its neighbours.

Tooting (SW17)

The busiest of the borough's town centres (and once the setting for a '70s TV comedy), Tooting's colourful high street is lined with ethnic restaurants, which are a reminder of the cosmopolitan mix of residents there, including a large Asian community. Cheaper than Balham, with good public transport, property consists mainly of three-bedroom terraces and two-bedroom flats or maisonettes (costing from around £250,000), which are popular with singletons. The grandest neighbourhood, with some of the largest houses, is the Heaver Estate in Tooting Bec.

Wandsworth (SW11, SW18)

In the centre of the borough, carved up by busy roads and with no tube stations in sight, Wandsworth is home to Young's Brewery, a smart revamped shopping centre and over 2,000 new flats. While these attract a young professional crowd, Wandsworth's older properties, many substantial and with large gardens, are the most sought-after by families. The most popular locations are around Wandsworth Common.

Property Costs

Property Prices

The table below shows average property prices in the borough:

Detached: £1,688,270
Semi-detached: £1,051.042
Terraced: £629,110
Flat: £326,188

Rental Costs

The table below shows average monthly rents in the borough:

House 5+ bed: £3,700
House 4-5 bed: £2,750
House 3-4 bed: £1,750
House 2-3 bed: £1,500
Flat 2-bed: £1,200
Flat 1-bed: £1,000

Crime

Wandsworth's crime rates are below average for London in all categories except robbery and car crime, both of which are well above average. Specific initiatives to combat crime include more police patrols and Police Community Support Officers, which has resulted in a reduction in street crimes such as mugging and robbery. CCTV cameras in main town centres and at railway stations are further deterrents.

The police station HQ is in Battersea (112-118 Battersea Bridge Road, SW11, ☎ 0300-123 1212), with other stations at Lavender Hill, Tooting and Wandsworth, and a part-time sector office at Putney.

To compare crime rates throughout London, see the table in **Appendix D**.

Health

NHS services in the borough are provided by the Wandsworth Primary Care Trust. For a full list of doctors, dentists and clinics, visit 🖳 www.nhs.uk.

To see how the Primary Care Trust compares with others in London, see the table in **Appendix D**.

Doctors & Dentists

♦ There are 96 NHS GP surgeries in Wandsworth, providing a range of clinics and health services.

♦ The borough has 63 dental and orthodontic practices, around half of which accept new NHS patients.

Hospitals

♦ Bolingbroke Hospital (Bolingbroke Road, SW11, ☎ 020-7223 7411, 🖥 as St George's Hospital) – outpatient clinics and care for the elderly.

♦ Queen Mary's University Hospital (Roehampton Lane, SW15, ☎ 020-8789 6611) – minor injuries unit.

♦ St George's Hospital (Blackshaw Road, SW17, ☎ 020-8672 1255, 🖥 www.st-georges.org.uk) – A&E; NHS walk-in centre.

♦ Springfield University Hospital (61 Glenburnie Road, SW17, ☎ 020-8682 6000) – psychiatric care.

Private Medical Facilities

♦ MediClinic Putney (30a Putney Hill, SW15, ☎ 020-8785-7273, 🖥 www.mediclinic.co.uk) – private clinic.

♦ The Priory Hospital (Priory Lane, SW15, ☎ 020-8876 8261, 🖥 www.priorygroup.com) – rehabilitation (e.g. alcoholism, drug addiction) for the rich and famous.

♦ Putney Private Patients Partnership (327d Upper Richmond Road, SW15, ☎ 020-8788 4212) – private GP practice.

To find a private GP, visit 🖥 www.privatehealth.co.uk.

 FAMOUS RESIDENTS

Famous people – past and present – associated with Wandsworth include **Tony Blair (Prime Minister), Martin Bashir (journalist), Jack Dee (comedian), Daniel Defoe (author), David Lloyd George (Prime Minister), Keira Knightly (actress), Kevin Pietersen (cricketer), Gordon Ramsey (chef), Prunella Scales (actress), William Makepeace Thackeray (novelist) and Voltaire (French philosopher).**

Schools

Like Southwark, Wandsworth has a high proportion of schoolchildren for whom English is a second language. Nevertheless, exam results have improved considerably in recent years and some schools are among the most popular in London. In the 2009 school league tables, primary schools were placed seventh out of the 33 London boroughs (28th out of 150 UK local authorities) and secondary schools 18th (56th in the UK).

To compare schools throughout London, see the table in **Appendix D**.

Pre-school

There's a good choice of nursery schools and playgroups, including three state nursery schools. Most primary schools have nursery classes.

State Schools

First schools: There are 56 primary schools, of which 19 are voluntary aided. In 2009, Our Lady of Victories Catholic Primary School (Clarendon Drive, SW15) was one of the top UK schools for Key Stage 2 results.

Secondary schools: Wandsworth has ten comprehensive schools, four of which are voluntary aided. All but one school has a sixth form and six have specialist status. St Cecilia's in

Wandsworth is a relatively new Church of England school, that opened in 2003. The top performer in 2009 was the Graveney School in Tooting.

Special schools: Eight special schools cater for students with physical disabilities and learning difficulties, plus three units attached to mainstream schools.

Private Schools

There are several private schools in Wandsworth, most of which are selective. In 2009, Putney High School was among the best in the country for GCSE results.

Further Education

- South Thames College (🖥 www.south-thames.ac.uk).
- St Francis Xavier Sixth Form College (🖥 www.sfx.ac.uk).

Higher Education

- Roehampton University (🖥 www.roehampton.ac.uk).
- Royal Academy of Dance (🖥 www.rad.org.uk).
- Royal College of Art Sculpture School (🖥 www.rca.ac.uk).
- St George's, University of London (🖥 www.sgul.ac.uk) – medical school.

Public Transport

Like many areas of south London, there's a better service on the overground rail network than the tube, with parts of Putney and Roehampton a long walk from any kind of station. The bus service is good, although congestion leads to slow journeys. The commuter river bus to Blackfriars stops at Cadogan Pier, just across the river by Albert Bridge (see **Kensington & Chelsea**).

Underground

The District line slices north-south through the centre of the borough, but only stops at East Putney and Southfields. The Northern line cuts across the south-east corner to serve Balham and Tooting (which have the luxury of two stations each). Typical journey times are as follows:

- Southfields (District line, zone 3) to Piccadilly Circus via Earl's Court, 27 minutes.
- Tooting Bec (Northern line, zone 3) to Waterloo, 20 minutes.

Rail

Clapham Junction in Wandsworth is the UK's busiest railway station, providing links with the whole of the south of England and the north.

- South West trains provides services to the west and south from Waterloo, stopping in Battersea, Putney and Wandsworth (10 minutes from Waterloo to Clapham Junction).
- Southern trains run between Watford and the south-east, stopping at Clapham Junction and Balham.
- The West London line runs between Willesden and Clapham Junction (typical journey time 20 minutes).
- The Thameslink service stops at Tooting Junction, providing access to the north of England via King's Cross.

Buses

A large number of bus routes run to central London and neighbouring boroughs, including number 14 (to Putney Heath), 35 (to Clapham Junction), 77a (to Wandsworth) and 137 (to Battersea). In the south of the borough services tend to be more local, with routes to Kingston (57), Croydon (264) and Sutton (280). Night buses include the N10, N19, N22, N28, N35, N44 and the N155.

Airports

Below are the approximate distances and journey times from Clapham Junction to the five London airports using public transport.

- **City** – 10 miles; 50 minutes via Bank.
- **Gatwick** – 20 miles; 30 minutes via Victoria.
- **Heathrow** – 13 miles; 60 minutes via Paddington.
- **Luton** – 31 miles; 70 minutes via Kings Cross.
- **Stansted** – 35 miles; 95 minutes via Tottenham Hale.

Roads

Despite being red routes, the A3 and A205 South Circular Roads merge in an almost constant traffic jam in Wandsworth, while the A24 is busy along its entire length. One of the main railway lines cuts Balham in half, with only three bridges crossing it, leading to congestion in the town. Other bottlenecks include Putney and Battersea high streets. Crossing the Thames becomes difficult if any of the bridges are closed.

Parking

Parking is restricted in many areas and Controlled Parking Zones are in operation in all the borough's main towns. A resident's parking permit costs £95 per year.

Waste & Recycling

The council provides a weekly collection service for household rubbish and recyclable materials, which include aerosols, cans, glass, paper and cardboard, and plastic bottles. The council also collects bulky items such as kitchen appliances and furniture. Wandsworth has two civic amenity sites (recycling/waste), at Smugglers Way in Wandsworth and Cringle Street in Battersea.

Shopping

The borough's shopping areas are concentrated around the main town centres, with Battersea's shops centred near Clapham Junction station. Most towns have a range of high street chains, with M&S in both Putney and Tooting, but there are also some interesting independents, particularly along Northcote Road in Battersea and near Wandsworth Common.

LOCAL INFORMATION

Battersea Power Station

Battersea Power Station is one of London's most famous landmarks; designed by Sir Giles Gilbert Scott and built between 1929 and 1939, it's the largest brick building in Europe and an important heritage monument. The power station was closed in 1983, since when it has languished, disused and roofless, for 25 years. There have been many grandiose plans to redevelop the site – the latest as a mass entertainment and commercial complex with dedicated transport links – although to date all have come to nought.

Putney's high street is rated one of the top ten in the capital for its diversity, thanks to its mix of upmarket chains, specialist independents and a wide range of shops catering for children. Tooting has an unusual retail mix, with mainstream shops sitting side-by-side with colourful ethnic shops stocking everything from Indian sweets to saris.

Shopping Centres

- Exchange Shopping Centre (142 Putney High Street, SW15, ☎ 020-8780 1056) – chains, including Argos, Gap and Next.
- Southside Shopping Centre (Wandsworth High Street, SW18, ☎ 020-8870 2141) – revitalised centre with high street names, including H&M and Mothercare, plus a cinema and Virgin Active health club.
- StopShop 1-20 St John's Hill, SW11, ☎ 020-7924 3451) – high street chains and specialist shops.

Supermarkets

- Asda in Battersea and Roehampton Vale (on the A3).
- Marks & Spencer in Balham (Simply Food).
- Sainsbury's in Balham, Putney, Tooting and Wandsworth, with Locals in Battersea, Clapham Junction, Putney and Roehampton.
- Tesco Express in Balham, Battersea and Putney.
- Waitrose in Wandsworth (Southside Centre).

Markets

New Covent Garden Market in Battersea is a wholesale fruit and veg. market, and there are plenty of other street markets for retail shoppers, including:

◆ Balham Market (Hildreth Street, SW12) – Afro-Caribbean groceries, fruit and veg; Monday to Saturday, 7am-6.15pm.

◆ Battersea Market (High Street, SW11) – fruit and veg, bread and groceries; Monday-Saturday, 9.30am-4.30pm.

◆ Broadway & Tooting Markets (Upper Tooting Road, SW17) – two covered venues selling cheap Afro-Caribbean foods and crafts, Indian fabrics and assorted household goods; Monday to Saturday.

◆ Clapham Junction Antique Market (Northcote Road, SW11) – covered market; Monday to Saturday, 10am-6pm, Sundays 12pm-5pm, closed Bank Holidays.

◆ Nine Elms Market (inside New Covent Garden Market, SW8) – fashion, bric-a-brac, household goods and toys etc.; Monday-Saturday, 10am-8pm, Sunday, 11am-6pm.

◆ Northcote Road Market (north end of Northcote Road, SW11) – fruit and veg, arts and crafts; Monday to Saturday, 10am-6pm, Sunday 12pm-5pm.

◆ Putney Farmers' Market (Mission Hall Garden, Walkers Place, SW15) – Friday, 11am-3pm, Saturday, 10am-2pm.

Entertainment

The borough's entertainment options have improved considerably in recent years, with the addition of a 14-screen cinema at the Southside Shopping Centre In Wandsworth and smart new restaurants and bars in Battersea and Putney. A summer attraction is the River Wandle Valley Festival, a programme of special events held along the river in Merton, Sutton and Wandsworth (☎ 0870-714 0750, 🖳 www.wandlevalleyfestival. org.uk).

Theatres

◆ Battersea Arts Centre (Lavender Hill, SW11, ☎ 020-7223 6557, 🖳 www.bac.org.uk) – award-winning fringe theatre.

Putney Riverside Apartments

◆ Putney Arts Theatre (Ravenna Road, SW15, ☎ 020-8788 6943, 🖳 www.putneyartstheatre. org.uk) – amateur productions.

◆ Theatre 503 (The Latchmere Pub, 503 Battersea Park Road, SW11, ☎ 020-7978 7040) – intimate fringe venue with comedy nights.

Cinemas

◆ Cineworld (Southside Shopping Centre, Wandsworth High Street, SW10, ☎ 0871-200 2000, 🖳 www.cineworld.co.uk).

◆ Putney Odeon (26 Putney High Street, SW15, ☎ 0871-224 4007, 🖳 www.odeon.co.uk).

Museums & Galleries

◆ The De Morgan Centre (38 West Hill, SW18, ☎ 020-8871 1144, 🖳 www.demorgan.org.uk) – study of 19th century art and society.

◆ The New Wandsworth Museum (The Courthouse, 11 Garratt Lane, SW18, ☎ 020-8871 7074) – local history collection.

◆ The Pump House Gallery (Battersea Park, SW11, ☎ 020-7350 0523) – art gallery.

Libraries

There are 11 local authority libraries in the borough, with one mobile service. The largest is Battersea Library (265, Lavender Hill, SW11, ☎ 020-8871 7468), which houses reference, local history and Afro-Caribbean collections. Tooting Library (75 Mitcham Road, SW17, ☎ 020-8871 7175) has an Asian Community library. Five libraries open on Sundays: Balham, Battersea, Putney, Tooting and Wandsworth Town Library.

Clubs

There's a large number of clubs and pubs with club nights in the borough, including:

◆ The Clapham Grand (21-25 St John's Hill, SW11, ☎ 020-7223 6523).

◆ Fez Club (200 Upper Richmond Road, SW15, ☎ 020-8780 0123).

◆ Liquid Night-club (High Street, Wandsworth, SW18, ☎ 020-8871 3910).

◆ Tea Rooms des Artistes (697 Wandsworth Road, SW8, ☎ 020-7652 6526).

◆ Wessex House (1A St John's Hill, SW11, ☎ 020-7622 6818).

There are two comedy clubs:

◆ Banana Moon (The Bedford, 77 Bedford Hill, SW12, ☎ 020-8673 8904, ☐ www.bananacabaret.co.uk) – popular venue.

◆ Jongleurs @ Battersea (49 Lavender Hill Gardens, SW11, ☎ 0870-787 0707, ☐ www.jongleurs.com) – another venue for this London chain.

Comedy nights are also hosted at other venues, including the Half Moon and Jack Beard's (see below), the Castle in Tooting High Street and Theatre 503 (see above).

Live Music

The hugely popular Putney Music Festival is an annual attraction in March, organised to coincide with the Oxford and Cambridge Boat Race. Pubs, bars, restaurants and clubs in the area host three days of music.

Live music is performed in numerous pubs such as:

◆ The Balham Tup (21 Chestnut Grove, SW12, ☎ 020-8772 0546) – large pub with regular live music.

◆ The Bedford (see above, Banana Moon) – shabby but popular pub with live music and comedy in back rooms.

◆ Half Moon, Putney (93 Lower Richmond Road, SW15, ☎ 020-8780 9383) – popular gig throughout the year, plus comedy nights.

◆ Jack Beard's (76 Mitcham Road, SW17, ☎ 020-8767 8425) – regular live music and comedy nights.

◆ National Opera Studio (2 Chapel Yard, SW18, ☎ 020-8874 8811) – classical performances.

Pubs

Putney, Balham and Battersea offer the widest choice of pubs and bars, ranging from traditional to modern and including the inevitable chains: A Bar 2 Far, JJ Moons, O'Neill's and Pitcher & Piano are all present in the borough. Balham High Road bustles with lively establishments, many offering comedy and music as well as large TV screens, while Battersea Park Road is another hotspot.

Putney has some lovely riverside pubs and smart bars along the High Street, and for a taste of the country there's the Green Man by Putney Heath (Wildcroft Road, SW15, ☎ 020-8788 8096), which has a roaring fire in winter. Tooting isn't well endowed with good watering holes, but the slightly camp Trafalgar Arms (148 Tooting High Street, SW17, ☎ 020-8767 6059) remains popular. Wandsworth has a mixture of lively and stylish establishments such as the Hope (1 Bellevue Road, SW17, ☎ 020-8672 8717).

Restaurants

The restaurant scene in the borough has kept pace with gentrification and there's a far wider choice of trendy eateries than a few years ago. Restaurants known for their excellent food include Le Bouchon Bordelais in Battersea (5 Battersea Rise, SW11, ☎ 020-7738 0307), Lamberts in Balham (2 Station Parade, SW12, ☎ 020-8675 2233) and the Michelin one-starred Chez Bruce (2 Bellevue Road, SW17, ☎ 020-8672 0114). There are also some excellent ethnic restaurants in the borough, such as the classy Bombay Bicycle (95 Nightingale Lane, SW12, ☎ 020-8673 6217) and award-winning Eastern Empire in Balham (57 Bedford Hill, SW12, ☎ 020-8673 8843). However, the best are in Tooting, including south London's oldest south Indian restaurant, Sree Krishna, in the High Street (☎ 020-8672 4250).

Sports Facilities

Wandsworth has four council-funded leisure centres and two recreation centres. Facilities include:

- ◆ Swimming pools at Latchmere (Battersea), Putney and Tooting.
- ◆ Indoor sports halls at Battersea, Roehampton, Tooting and Wandsworth.
- ◆ Workout studios and gyms in Balham, Battersea, Putney and Tooting.
- ◆ Indoor cycling studios in Putney and Tooting.
- ◆ All-weather sports pitches at the Battersea Park Millennium Arena.

The borough is also home to one of London's most famous lidos, at Tooting Bec, the largest open-air pool in Europe. Many sports can be played in Wandsworth's parks, including golf – there's an 18-hole course in Roehampton and a 9-hole course with a driving range near Springfield Hospital in Wandsworth. Horse riding is possible on Putney Common and gyms and health clubs include branches of Cannons and Fitness First. Putney Bridge is the starting point for the annual Oxford and Cambridge Boat Race in March.

Green Spaces

Wandsworth boasts over 70 parks, commons and open spaces, which account for almost 20 per cent of its area – the largest proportion of any London borough. The most popular is Battersea Park (see box), a Grade II listed space, which was recently given an £11mn face-lift. Other popular spots are Tooting Common, the largest in the borough and site of the lido (see above), which has an unspoiled, natural character, and Wandsworth Common, home to a fishing lake. Putney Heath and Putney Common are informal areas of heathland.

LOCAL INFORMATION

Battersea Park

Battersea Park, opened in 1858, covers an area of 200 acres (80ha) on the south bank of the River Thames opposite Chelsea. It features riverside promenades, a boating lake, a formal flower garden and spectacular fountains, as well as a peace pagoda built by Japanese monks and nuns in 1985 as a memorial to Hiroshima. There's also a children's zoo in summer and the Pumphouse Gallery.

Chelsea Bridge

Westminster

NW1 (part), NW8, SW1, W1, W2, W9, WC2 (part)

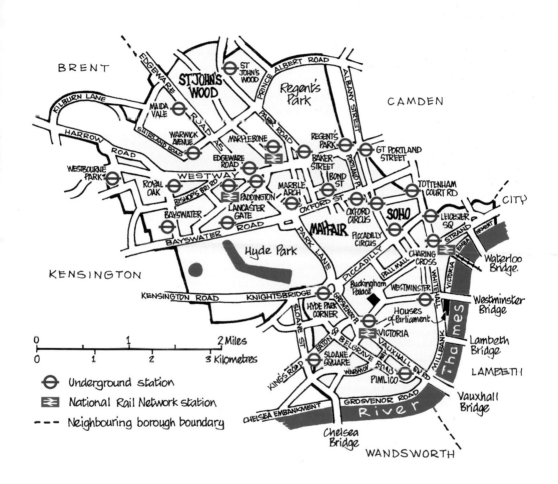

- ⊖ Underground station
- ⧰ National Rail Network station
- --- Neighbouring borough boundary

At a Glance

Best for: shopping, public transport, leisure, culture, restaurants, low council tax

Not so good for: affordable homes, traffic congestion, parking, crime

Who lives there: wealthy professionals, international businessmen, diplomats

Housing stock: 90% flats (one-third conversions), terraces/mews, period properties

Housing costs: very expensive

General Information

Council Offices: Victoria Street, SW1E 6QP (☎ 020-7641 6000)

CAA Assessment: (see 💻 http://oneplace.direct.gov.uk > Search by area > London Westminster)

Controlling Party: Conservative

Website: 💻 www.westminster.gov.uk

Council Tax 2010/11: £1,146 (Band G), £1,375 (Band H)

Main Areas/towns: Bayswater, Belgravia, Covent Garden, Knightsbridge, Maida Vale, Marylebone, Mayfair, Pimlico, Soho, St John's Wood, Westminster

Postcodes: NW1 (part), NW8, SW1, W1, W2, W9, WC2 (part)

Population & Ethnicity: 236,000, with the lowest proportion under 20 outside the City and a large number aged between 20 and 35. Around 25 per cent of the population are from Afro-Caribbean or South Asian backgrounds, and London's largest Chinese community is in Soho. There's a significant Jewish community in the north of the borough. Some of the UK's richest people have homes in the borough, as well as visiting international business people and diplomats.

Unemployment: 7.1 per cent (London average is 8.2 per cent)

Overview

To tourists, Westminster is the essence of London and is home to the monarchy and the seat of government, has most of the capital's famous sights on the doorstep, and the best entertainment and shopping in the country. Westminster takes in some of London's smartest areas, including Belgravia, Knightsbridge, Mayfair and St James. As a place to live it cannot be beaten for excitement and convenience, although not surprisingly the price is very high, with property in central areas among the most expensive in Europe.

Westminster also has its less salubrious aspects, with large numbers of homeless people, high crime, constant traffic noise, and, since July 2005, an underlying fear of terrorist attacks. However, regeneration schemes are improving some of the more deprived areas (such as those around Paddington) and the council's One City programme aims to increase safety and provide more affordable housing and better services for all local communities.

The City of Westminster is a borough with city status. The name was historically used to describe the area around Westminster Abbey, the West Minster or monastery church that gave the area its name. The term Westminster Village, sometimes used in the context of British politics, doesn't refer to a geographical area. It refers to people who're associated with the Palace of Westminster (Parliament), such as Members of Parliament and their staff, political journalists, spin doctors and others.

New Developments

A £25mn plan to redevelop the historic Marshall Street baths in Soho, which were closed in 1997, is in progress. The project will see the restoration of the baths as well as a wider development of the site, with a new purpose-built leisure centre, including the building of a gym and health suite, including dance and exercise studios. As part of the development, 52 new homes will be built, 15 of which will be affordable. When it opens (supposedly in 2010, although progress has been slow), Marshall Street will be the third new leisure facility in as many years in Westminster, on top of major refurbishments of five existing indoor and outdoor sites.

Westminster was recently allocated £3.7mn from the GLA for local transport improvements to make the borough safer, greener and more accessible. The funding includes £885,000 for the London Cycle Network to add more cycle lanes and better facilities for cyclists in Westminster, £375,000 for improvements at the junction of the Strand and Aldwych to improve bus services and journey times, and £15,000 for schools to encourage primary-school age children to walk to school. Westminster will benefit from both the Cross River Tram and Crossrail train projects (see **Chapter 2**), which are planned for completion in 2016 and 2017 respectively.

Residential Areas

Almost 90 per cent of properties are flats, with a third of those conversions of grand mansions. Houses (9 per cent terraced and 1 per cent each of detached and semi-detached) range from attractive mews cottages to imposing villas. The most expensive areas are Mayfair, Knightsbridge and Belgravia, while the cheapest are West Bayswater, West Kilburn and Paddington.

Belgravia & Knightsbridge (SW1)

These are among the capital's most exclusive districts, favoured by international diplomats and business people with pockets deep enough to pay the stratospheric prices. Grand mansions predominate, mostly now converted into luxurious flats, with attractive mews cottages behind the busy main streets. Much of the property is leasehold, with an enormous variation in length of lease, service charges and ground rent. Quiet Belgravia is dominated by foreign embassies, while Eaton and Chester Squares remain sought-after residential addresses among the elite. Bustling Knightsbridge, famed for its shops, has some new developments of smart apartments to add to the property mix (£400,000 or more for a studio), with more to come. Part of Knightsbridge is actually situated in the borough of Kensington & Chelsea, which leads to confusing residents' parking arrangements.

Maida Vale & Little Venice (NW8, W9)

These quiet and leafy residential areas are hugely popular, with a large supply of spacious period flats, as well as excellent access to major road and rail routes into and out of the West End. Entrepreneurs, bankers and celebrities choose to live in the area, and a strong demand for corporate lets keeps the rental market buoyant. The most desirable locations overlook the canal in Little Venice.

Marylebone & St John's Wood (W1, NW8)

Bounded by Regent's Park to the north and Oxford Street to the south, Marylebone is more central than Belgravia but not quite as expensive, largely because offices long ago colonised many of the buildings. House hunters have rediscovered the quiet pockets of stylish residences and it's increasingly fashionable, aided by the reinvention of Marylebone High Street as a bijou shopping district. Flats predominate, with a sprinkling of mews cottages. To the west is St John's Wood, home to many wealthy families. Property includes large period houses, inter-war mansion blocks, modern townhouses and luxury apartments complete with a concierge.

Mayfair & St James (W1)

Right in the heart of the capital, with the finest shops, restaurants and nightlife a walk away, these are among the premier addresses in the world. Property costs £millions and is scarce, although in recent years many fine buildings have reverted from offices to homes. Many residents are foreign business people. In Mayfair, housing

Little Venice

consists of Georgian and Victorian mansions, grand townhouses and luxury apartment blocks, while St James, home to members of the royal family, has a few grand flats, with the most desirable overlooking Green Park.

Paddington & Bayswater (W2, W9)

Regeneration has swept across Paddington Basin, transforming a derelict area by the canal and station into a Docklands-like commercial district, with shops, offices and new homes in striking tall buildings linked by walkways and bridges. Elsewhere, there are seedy areas full of cheap hotels and short term lets close to Paddington station, as well as leafy squares with highly desirable homes nearer to Hyde Park. Flats are common, while the few houses range from cottages to modern townhouses. Queensway provides the main shopping and restaurant quarter. Bayswater is truly cosmopolitan, with the fastest population turnover in London, and is becomingly more fashionable.

Pimlico & Westminster (SW1, W2)

Pimlico is central, quiet, has a riverside frontage and is popular with MPs – who like the proximity to the Houses of Parliament – and wealthy professionals. There's a good supply of flats (mostly conversions), as well as complete family houses and ex-council properties. Many of Westminster's buildings house government offices, although residential property includes mansion blocks, period townhouses and new apartments in former office blocks.

Soho & Covent Garden (W1, WC2)

A warren of narrow streets and alleyways, Soho is one of London's famous 'villages' with a strong local community (there's even a primary school there). Around 20 years ago Soho was a sleazy red light district, since when it's been reinvented as a lively cosmopolitan quarter. Some of this transformation is down to the buzzing new restaurants (China Town is also located there) and bars that are often open all night. Flats predominate, many of them above shops, although new apartments have been squeezed into corners. Covent Garden is more touristy, crammed with restaurants and bars and packed at weekends with shoppers. Space is at a premium, so property consists almost entirely of highly-priced apartments, largely populated by rich

wannabes. Ex-council properties around Tavistock Lane remain good value; Seven Dials is the most popular location and a roof garden or balcony is the most sought-after attribute.

Property Costs

Property Prices

The table below shows average property prices in the borough:

> Detached: £0 (no recent sales)
> Semi-detached: £2,265,681
> Terraced: £1,477,403
> Flat: £651,509

Rental Costs

The table below shows average monthly rents in the borough:

> House 5+ bed: £10,900
> House 4-5 bed: £8,450
> House 3-4 bed: £7,600
> House 2-3 bed: £6,500
> Flat 2-bed: £2,400
> Flat 1-bed: £1,950

Crime

Westminster has by far the highest overall crime rate in London, as well as the highest rates for robbery, violent crimes and drugs-related offences. However, the large number of tourists falling victim to petty crime distorts these figures. Westminster has average rates of theft from cars and a low rate of stolen cars. In an effort to reduce crime, there's a strong police presence on the streets, with CCTV cameras providing 24-hour surveillance of crime hotspots.

There are seven police stations: Belgravia, Charing Cross, Harrow Road, Marylebone, Paddington Green, St John's Wood and the West End, all of which are open 24 hours, except St John's Wood, which isn't open at weekends or on Bank Holidays. (All stations ☎ 0300-123 1212).

To compare crime rates throughout London, see the table in **Appendix D**.

Health

NHS services in the borough are provided by the Westminster Primary Care Trust. For a full list of doctors, dentists and clinics, visit 🖳 www.nhs.uk.

To see how the Primary Care Trust compares with others in London, see the table in **Appendix D**.

Doctors & Dentists

◆ There are 108 NHS GP surgeries in the borough, providing a range of clinics and health services.

◆ Westminster has 110 dental and orthodontic practices, fewer than half of which accept new NHS patients.

Hospitals

◆ Royal National Orthopaedic Hospital (45 Bolsover Street, W1, ☎ 020-8954 2300, 🖳 www.rnoh.nhs.uk).

◆ St Mary's Hospital (Praed Street, W2, ☎ 020-7886 6666, 🖳 www.st-marys.nhs.uk) A&E.

There's an NHS walk-in centre at the Soho Centre for Health and Care (1 Frith Street, W1, ☎ 020-7534 6500) and a minor injuries unit at the South Westminster Clinic (82 Vincent Square, SW1, ☎ 020-3315 5757). Additional A&E facilities are at the University College Hospital (off the Tottenham Court Road). Specialist hospitals include the Heart Hospital and the Western Eye Hospital, both in Marylebone.

Private Medical Facilities

There are many private doctors and hospitals in the borough, ranging from emergency GP services in Harley Street and Soho to acute hospitals such as the Portland or Lister. For your nearest facility, see 🖳 www.privatehealth. co.uk.

Schools

Educational standards are variable and there are more independent than state schools at secondary level. Over 120 languages are spoken by Westminster schoolchildren. In the 2009 school league tables, primary schools were placed 15th out of the 33 London boroughs (66th out of 150 UK local authorities) and secondary schools 16th (50th in the UK).

To compare schools throughout London, see the table in **Appendix D**.

Pre-school

There are four LEA-funded nursery schools and several nursery classes attached to primary schools, as well as plenty of independent nursery schools and playgroups.

State Schools

First schools: Westminster has 40 primary schools, of which 26 are voluntary aided. In 2009, the Hampden Gurney C of E Primary School in Marylebone and the St Joseph's RC Primary School in Maida Vale were two of the top UK schools for Key Stage 2 results.

Secondary schools: There are six comprehensive schools, five of which are voluntary aided. All six schools have sixth forms and four have specialist status. In 2009, the top performers by a large margin were the Grey Coat Hospital School (girls) and the St George RC School in Maida Vale.

Special schools: Two schools cater for students with physical disabilities and learning difficulties.

Private Schools

There are over 30 private schools in Westminster, including two international schools (the American School in London in St John's Wood and the

International Community School in Regent's Park), the Sylvia Young Theatre School in Marylebone and the prestigious Royal Ballet School in Covent Garden. Many schools are selective, with 12 catering for secondary age children. In 2009, the two Francis Holland Schools (girls) in Clarence Gate and Graham Terrace had some of the best GCSE results in the UK.

Further Education

♦ City of Westminster College (🖥 www.cwc.ac.uk).

♦ Westminster Adult Education Institute (🖥 www.waes.ac.uk).

♦ Westminster Kingsway college (🖥 www.westking.ac.uk).

Higher Education

As well as colleges of the University of London (🖥 www.lon.ac.uk) and medical schools attached to hospitals, Westminster has several other prestigious educational institutions:

♦ American InterContinental University (🖥 www.aiulondon.ac.uk).

♦ Courtauld Institute of Art (🖥 www.courtauld.ac.uk).

♦ London Business School (🖥 www.london.edu).

♦ London School of Economics and Political Science (🖥 www.lse.ac.uk).

♦ Royal Academy of Music (🖥 www.ram.ac.uk).

♦ University of the Arts London (🖥 www.arts.ac.uk).

♦ University of Westminster (🖥 www.westminster.ac.uk).

Public Transport

Getting around Westminster is easy thanks to the extensive underground network, several main line railway stations, plenty of buses and good river services – and it's also relatively easy to get around on foot. Westminster is scheduled to have two stations on the Crossrail route, at Paddington and Bond Street.

Underground

All underground lines stop at stations in Westminster and it's never more than a few minutes journey to most central destinations, although travelling to the City may require a change of line. Access to the Docklands Light Railway (DLR) is via the Central line at Bank. Typical journey times are as follows:

♦ Westminster (Jubilee line, zone 1) to Moorgate, 15 minutes via London Bridge.

♦ Oxford Circus (Bakerloo line, zone 1) to Paddington, 8 minutes.

Rail

Paddington, Charing Cross and Victoria stations provide routes out of London to the west and south. Marylebone station is served by Chiltern Railways with trains going to the north-west.

Buses

Buses are frequent and serve all areas, although they can be crowded and journeys slow due to heavy traffic. Open-top tourist buses are a useful way to see the sights. A large number of night buses from central areas serve the outer boroughs.

River Transport

Commuter river services run mornings and evenings, as follows:

♦ Embankment Pier to Blackfriars or Chelsea Harbour (Monday to Friday).

♦ Savoy Pier to Greenwich, via Blackfriars, London Bridge and Docklands (daily).

Additional services include Westminster to Hampton Court via Kew; Westminster or

Embankment to Greenwich via Waterloo, with some services going as far as Barrier Gardens; and a circular service between Westminster and St Katherine's Pier (Tower Bridge).

Airports

Below are the approximate distances and journey times from Oxford Circus to the five London airports using public transport.

- **City** – 9 miles; 40 minutes via Bank.
- **Gatwick** – 25 miles; 40 minutes via Victoria.
- **Heathrow** – 13 miles; 40 minutes via Paddington.
- **Luton** – 27 miles; 75 minutes via Kings Cross.
- **Stansted** – 31 miles; 62 minutes via Tottenham Hale.

Roads

The Congestion Charge Zone takes in all of W1, from the A40 in the north to the A4202 which runs along Hyde Park to the west and along the A202 down to the Thames. Despite this, traffic can still be slow-moving, particularly on roads heading out of London, which include the A302 around Hyde Park Corner, the A4 through Knightsbridge, the A5 and A41 through St John's Wood and the A40 through Marylebone. Other bottlenecks include Trafalgar Square and roads around Victoria Station.

Parking

Parking is a nightmare nearly everywhere and residents without garages (the majority) have to fight for parking spaces near their homes. Garages attract premium prices of up to £100,000 or more. Nearly all the borough is a Controlled Parking Zone, with the exception of Maida Vale and St John's Wood. The cost of an annual residents permit is £85/120 per vehicle, depending on engine size. Permits may be discounted for owners of environmentally friendly cars (under 1,200cc or powered by battery or liquid petroleum gas). Eco vehicles are free.

Waste & Recycling

General household rubbish is collected at least twice a week from most areas and more frequently from the West End. The council also collects recyclable materials, including cans, cardboard, glass, paper and plastic bottles. There's a free collection service for bulky items such as furniture and kitchen appliances. Residents can also dispose of rubbish, including garden waste, in local community skips or use civic amenity sites (recycling/waste) in Wandsworth.

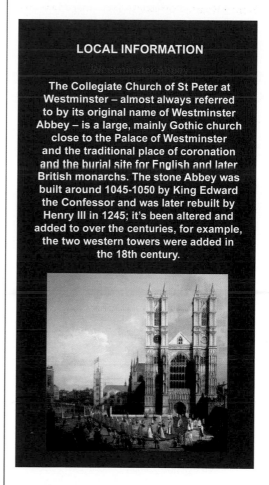

LOCAL INFORMATION

The Collegiate Church of St Peter at Westminster – almost always referred to by its original name of Westminster Abbey – is a large, mainly Gothic church close to the Palace of Westminster and the traditional place of coronation and the burial site for English and later British monarchs. The stone Abbey was built around 1045-1050 by King Edward the Confessor and was later rebuilt by Henry III in 1245; it's been altered and added to over the centuries, for example, the two western towers were added in the 18th century.

Shopping

Westminster's shopping facilities are legendary, with Knightsbridge, Covent Garden, Carnaby Street, Oxford Street, Bond Street and Regent Street all providing every kind of shop imaginable (and then some), including major branches of all the main chains, department stores and flagship designer shops. Other districts also provide interesting shops, such as Marylebone High Street, with delis and upmarket independent boutiques; Queensway, with a large shopping centre; and Soho, which has some unusual shops and a bustling street market.

FAMOUS RESIDENTS

Famous people associated with Westminster comprise a who's who of the rich and famous, including John Adams (second American President), Lord Byron (poet), Sir Winston Churchill (Prime Minister), Robert Clive (soldier & administrator), Sir Alexander Fleming (scientist), Hugh Grant (actor), George Frideric Handel (German-born composer), Jimi Hendrix (musician), Somerset Maugham (novelist), Sir Paul McCartney (musician), Kate Moss (model), Wolfgang Amadeus Mozart (Austrian composer), Vivien Leigh (actress) and Lord Tennyson (poet).

Shopping Centres

◆ Kingly Court (Carnaby Street, W1, 🖥 www.carnaby.co.uk) – three-storey warehouse of independent stores selling clothes and grown up toys.

◆ Plaza Shopping Centre (120 Oxford Street, W1, 🖥 www.plaza-oxfordst.com) – inexpensive boutiques and well-known chains.

◆ Thomas Neal Centre (29 Earlham Street, WC2, ☎ 020-7240 4741) – converted warehouse, with surfing, snowboarding and skateboarding paraphernalia.

◆ Whiteleys (151 Queensway, W2, 🖥 www.whiteleys.com) – grandest central London centre, with high street names and independent stores.

Supermarkets

◆ Marks & Spencer 'Simply Food' in Bond Street, Green Park, Marylebone Station, Paddington Station and Victoria Station (two branches).

◆ Sainsbury's in Mayfair, Pimlico, Tottenham Court Road and Victoria, with Local stores in Charing Cross, Marble Arch, Marylebone, Paddington, Victoria and Westbourne Grove.

◆ Tesco Metro stores in Covent Garden, Queensway, Regent Street, Soho, and Victoria.

◆ Waitrose in Belgravia and Marylebone.

Markets

◆ Berwick Street (Berwick Street, W1) – fruit and veg, fish, flowers and general household goods; Monday to Saturday, 9am-5pm.

◆ Charing Cross Collector's Fair (The Arches, end of Northumberland Avenue, WC2) – medals, coins, stamps, postcards, cigarette cards etc; Saturday, 8am-5pm.

◆ Covent Garden Market (The Piazza, WC2) – antiques on Monday; handcrafted goods; Monday to Saturday.

◆ Earlham Street Market (between Shaftesbury Avenue and Seven Dials, WC2) – clothes and exotic flowers; Monday to Saturday.

◆ Marylebone Farmers' Market (Cramer Street car park, W1) – Sunday 10am-2pm.

◆ Piccadilly Market (St James's Churchyard, W1) – arts and crafts; Wednesday to Saturday, 11am-6pm; antiques Tuesday, 10am-6pm.

◆ Pimlico Farmers' Market (Orange Square, SW1) – Saturday, 9am-1pm.

◆ Strutton Ground Market (south side of Victoria Street, SW1) – fruit and veg, flowers, DVDs and CDs, fashions; Monday to Friday, 8am-2.30pm.

◆ Tachbrook Street Market (between Warwick Way and Churton Street, SW1) – fruit and veg, flowers, bread, linens; Monday to Saturday, 8am-6pm.

Entertainment

Westminster is home to many important visitor attractions, art galleries, museums and concert halls – not to mention London's 'theatreland' in the West End and the cinema enthusiasts' 'Mecca' in Leicester Square. Almost every street in central areas features a pub or bar (often several) and Westminster is blessed with some of London's most exclusive dining establishments. It's beyond the scope of this book to list all the entertainment venues in the borough, but there are plenty of guidebooks available and the *Evening Standard* and *Time Out* magazine are good places to find information about what's on, when and where.

Theatres

Over 40 theatres are crammed into the West End, in an area loosely bounded by Oxford Street, Regent Street and the Strand. Beyond this area, Regent's Park is home to the famous Open-air Theatre (☎ 0844-826 4242, 🖥 http://openairtheatre.org), while the Canal Café Theatre in Little Venice (The Bridge House pub, Delamere Terrace, W2, ☎ 020-7289 6054, 🖥 www.canalcafetheatre.com) has an award-winning reputation for comedy and new writing. You can check what's on and buy your tickets online at 🖳 www.officiallondontheatre.co.uk.

Cinemas

Leicester Square houses the capital's largest cinemas, with others in nearby streets. Slightly further afield, there are cinemas at Baker Street, Covent Garden, Knightsbridge, Marble Arch and Whitley's Shopping Centre in Queensway. You can check what's on at 🖳 www.londonnet.co.uk/in/out/ent/cinema.html.

LOCAL INFORMATION

Palace of Westminster

The Palace of Westminster (see photo below), also known as the Houses of Parliament or Westminster Palace, is the seat of the UK government, who sit in the upper (the House of Lords) and lower (the House of Commons) Houses of Parliament. After a fire in 1834, the present Houses of Parliament were designed by Sir Charles Barry and his assistant Augustus Welby Pugin, who was responsible for the splendid Gothic interiors, and built over 30 years. The palace's layout is intricate and contains some 1,100 rooms, 100 staircases and 3mi (5km) of corridors.

Museums & Galleries

Some of London's most famous attractions are in Westminster, ranging from Buckingham Palace (parts of which are open to the public in summer), Westminster Abbey and the Houses of Parliament to Madame Tussaud's and the Planetarium. There are also many smaller, less well-known museums (some of which are fascinating), such as the Sherlock Holmes Museum in Baker Street, the Handel House and Faraday museum in Mayfair, while in St John's Wood there's the MCC Museum at the Lord's Cricket Ground. There are abundant art galleries, including the National and National Portrait Galleries in Trafalgar Square, Tate Britain on the Thames at Millbank, the Royal Academy of Arts and the ICA Gallery near Piccadilly. The Courtauld Institute of Art is at Somerset house in the Strand.

For addresses, contact details and opening times consult any London guidebook or visit 🖳 www.24hourmuseum.org.uk.

Libraries

There are 11 lending libraries in the borough, plus a mobile service. One of the largest is the Charing Cross library (4 Charing Cross Road, WC2, ☎ 020-7641 1300), which houses a Chinese collection. The Westminster Reference Library (35 St Martin's Street, WC2, ☎ 020-7641 1300) contains several specialist collections. Libraries in Charing Cross, Marylebone (two), Paddington, Pimlico and St John's Wood open on Sundays,

Houses of Parliament

as does the Little Venice Sports Centre Library. In addition to residents, Westminster's libraries are also open to visitors and those who work in the area.

Clubs

The club scene is varied and lively, and includes well-known venues such as Ghetto in Soho (🖳 www.ghetto-london.co.uk), Heaven near Charing Cross station (🖳 www.heaven-london.com), Pacha in Victoria (🖳 www.pachalondon.com) and Rouge in Charing Cross Road (🖳 www.rougeclublondon.com). *Time Out* and other listings magazines provide weekly club details. Top quality comedy clubs include:

◆ Amused Moose Soho (Moonlighting, 17 Greek Street, W1, ☎ 020-7287 3727, 🖳 www.amusedmoose.co.uk).

◆ The Comedy Store (1A Oxendon Street, SW1, ☎ 0844-847 1728 – ticket master, 🖳 www.thecomedystore.co.uk).

◆ Covent Garden Comedy Club (Villiers Street, WC2, ☎ 07960-071 340).

Live Music

Venues range from landmark concert halls such as the Wigmore Hall (36 Wigmore Street, W1, ☎ 020-7935 2141, 🖳 www.wigmore-hall.org.uk) to the legendary Ronnie Scott's Jazz Club (47 Frith Street, W1, ☎ 020-7439 0747, 🖳 www.ronniescotts.co.uk). Other popular venues include:

◆ The 100 Club (100 Oxford Street, W1, ☎ 020-7636 0933, 🖳 www.the100club.co.uk).

◆ Borderline (Orange Yard, Manette Street, W1, ☎ 020-7734 5547, 🖳 www.meanfiddler.com).

◆ Pizza Express (10 Dean Street, W1, ☎ 020-7437 9595, 🖳 www.pizzaexpresslive.co.uk).

Pubs

You never have to venture far to find somewhere for a drink, whether you favour traditional pubs, modern gastrobars, noisy music bars, cool places to-be-seen-in or intimate inns to hide in. Inevitably pubs and bars in the West End and Covent Garden tend to be packed with tourists, although it's possible to find quieter establishments hidden away in back streets around Soho and further afield in Bayswater,

Marylebone and Victoria. Belgravia and Mayfair pubs tend to be expensive, while there are some pleasant and quiet gems in Maida Vale, Little Venice and St John's Wood. A guidebook such as Time Out's *Bars, Pubs & Clubs* is useful.

Restaurants

Westminster's restaurants cater for every food preference and every price range. Whether you're seeking afternoon tea in one of London's top hotels, celebrity spotting at the Ivy in West Street or something in-between, there's a place for everyone. For lively eateries try Soho (for the best Chinese food in London) or Covent Garden (which is usually packed with tourists), seek out surprising gourmet establishments in Marylebone, or dine in luxury in Mayfair or Belgravia. A wealth of Westminster establishments is recommended in the *Good Food Guide* and the *Michelin Guide*.

Sports Facilities

Council-funded leisure centres in Marylebone, Pimlico, Queensway and West Kilburn provide four swimming pools, three indoor sports halls, squash courts and fitness centres. For outdoor sports, the Paddington Recreation Ground is well equipped, with 15 tennis courts, two all-weather sports pitches, cricket facilities and an athletics track. There are plenty of private gyms and fitness clubs in the borough.

Tennis courts are available in several parks, while Regent's Park offers one of the largest sports areas in the capital, with facilities for rugby, hockey, athletics, tennis, football and cricket, plus canoeing on the lake and a golf school. The expanse of Hyde Park (see box) has areas for rounders, rugby, tennis, football, rowing, cycling and horse riding, and the park is the starting point for regular mass roller skating events. It's also home to the popular Serpentine Lido for outdoor bathing. In the winter, there's a temporary outdoor ice rink at Somerset House, while for spectators there's cricket at the Lord's ground in St John's Wood.

Green Spaces

Westminster has 56 parks, gardens and open spaces, including four of London's royal parks – Green Park, Hyde Park (see box), St James's Park and Regent's Park. These offer some of the loveliest landscapes in the capital, although they're quite different in character. Green Park, with its mature trees and grassland, is a peaceful oasis, while St James's Park, the oldest, is surrounded by three palaces – Buckingham, St James's and Westminster (the Houses of Parliament) – and home to pelicans, rare breeds of wild duck and other bird life.

Regent's Park, designed by architect John Nash, has one of the largest sports areas (see above), a boating lake, an open-air theatre and London Zoo (☎ 020-7722 3333, 🖥 www.londonzoo.co.uk). Three areas in the borough have Green Flag (🖥 www.greenflagaward.org.uk) status: Paddington Recreation Ground, St John's Wood Church Grounds and Victoria Embankment Gardens.

LOCAL INFORMATION

Hyde Park is the largest open space in Westminster (350 acres/140ha) and London's most famous public park (since 1637), hosting many major events throughout the year, from demonstrations to concerts. Its many landmarks include Serpentine Lake (swimming and boating), Speakers' Corner and the Diana, Princess of Wales Memorial Fountain, which has become one of the capital's most popular attractions.

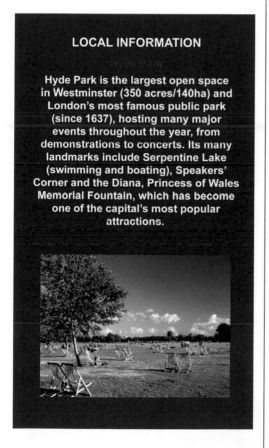

APPENDICES

APPENDIX A: USEFUL ADDRESSES

LONDON EMBASSIES & CONSULATES

A selection of foreign embassies and high commissions in London is listed below. A full list of embassies and consulates in London is published in *The Diplomatic List* (The Stationery Office) and available online from the Foreign & Commonwealth Office website (💻 www.fco.gov.uk – click on 'Find an embassy' under 'Travel & living abroad' and then 'Find a foreign embassy in the UK').

Antigua & Barbuda: 2nd Floor, 45 Crawford Place, W1H 4LP (☎ 020-7258 0070, 💻 www.antigua-barbuda.com).

Argentina: 65 Brook Street, Westminster, W1K 4AH (☎ 020-7318 1300, 💻 www.argentine-embassy-uk.org).

Australia: Australia House, Strand, WC2B 4LA (☎ 020-7379 4334, 💻 www.uk.embassy.gov.au).

Austria: 45 Princes Gate, SW7 2QA (☎ 020-7584 4411, 💻 www.bmeia.gv.at/en/embassy/london.html).

Bahamas: 10 Chesterfield Street, W1J 5JL (☎ 020-7408 4488).

Bangladesh: 28 Queen's Gate, SW7 5JA (☎ 020-7584 0081, 💻 www.bhclondon.org.uk).

Barbados: 1 Great Russell Street, WC1B 3ND (☎ 020-7631 4975).

Belgium: 17 Grosvenor Crescent, SW1X 7EE (☎ 020-7470 3700, 💻 www.diplomatie.be/london).

Belarus: 6 Kensington Court, W8 5DL (☎ 020-7937 3288, 💻 www.uk.belembassy.org).

Belize: 45 Crawford Place, W1H 4LP (☎ 020-7723 3603).

Bolivia: 106 Eaton Square, SW1W 9AD (☎ 020-7235 4248).

Bosnia & Herzegovina: 5-7 Lexham Gardens, W8 5JJ (☎ 020-7373 0867, 💻 http://bhembassy.co.uk).

Brazil: 32 Green Street, W1K 7AT (☎ 020-7399 9000, 💻 www.brazil.org.uk).

Brunei Darussalam: 19-20 Belgrave Square, SW1X 8PG (☎ 020-7581 0521).

Bulgaria: 186-188 Queen's Gate, SW7 5HL (☎ 020-7584 9400, 🖥 www.bulgarianembassy-london.org).

Cameroon: 84 Holland Park, W11 3SB (☎ 020-7727 0771).

Canada: Macdonald House, 1 Grosvenor Square, W1K 4AB (☎ 020-7258 6600, 🖥 www.canadainternational.gc.ca/united_kingdom-royaume_uni).

Chile: 12 Devonshire Street, W1G 7DS (☎ 020-7580 6392, 🖥 http://chileabroad.gov.cl/reino-unido).

China: 49-51 Portland Place, W1B 1JL (☎ 020-7299 4049, 🖥 www.chinese-embassy.org.uk/eng).

Colombia: 3 Hans Crescent, SW1X 0LN (☎ 020-7589 9177).

Croatia: 21 Conway Street, W1T 6BN (☎ 020-7387 2022, 🖥 http://uk.mvp.hr).

Cuba: 167 High Holborn, WC1 6PA (☎ 020-7240 2488, 🖥 www.cubaldn.com).

Cyprus: 93 Park Street, W1K 7ET (☎ 020-7499 8272).

Czech Republic: 26 Kensington Palace Gardens, W8 4QY (☎ 020-7243 1115, 🖥 www.mzv.cz/london).

Denmark: 55 Sloane Street, SW1X 9SR (☎ 020-7333 0200, 🖥 www.amblondon.um.dk/en).

Dominica: 1 Collingham Gardens, South Kensington, SW5 0HW (☎ 020-7370 5194/5).

Ecuador: Flat 3b, 3 Hans Crescent, SW1X 0LS (☎ 020-7584 2648/1376).

Egypt: 26 South St, Westminster, SW1X (☎ 020-7499 2401).

El Salvador: 39 Great Portland Street, W1N 7JZ (☎ 020-7436 8282).

Estonia: 16 Hyde Park Gate, SW7 5DG (☎ 020-7589 3428, 🖥 www.estonia.gov.uk).

Fiji: 34 Hyde Park Gate, SW7 5DN (☎ 020-7584 3661).

Finland: 38 Chesham Place, SW1X 8HW (☎ 020-7838 6200, 🖥 www.finemb.org.uk).

France: 58 Knightsbridge, SW1X 7JT (☎ 020-7201 1000, 🖥 www.ambafrance-uk.org).

The Gambia: 27 Elvaston Place, SW7 5NL (☎ 020-7823 9986).

Germany: 23 Belgrave Square, 1 Chesham Place, SW1X 8PZ (☎ 020 7824 1300, 🖥 www.london.diplo.de).

Ghana: 13 Belgrave Square, SW1X 8PN (☎ 020-7201 5900, 🖥 www.ghanahighcommissionuk.com).

Greece: 1A Holland Park, W11 3TP (☎ 020-7229 3850, 🖥 www.greekembassy.org.uk).

Grenada: The Chapel, Archel Road, West Kensington, W14 (☎ 020-7385 4415).

Guatemala: 13 Fawcett Street, SW10 9HN (☎ 020-7351 3042).

Guyana: 3 Palace Court, Bayswater Road, W2 4LP (☎ 020-7229 7684, 🖥 www.guyanahc.com).

Honduras: 115 Gloucester Place, W1U 6JT (☎ 020-7486 4880).

Hungary: 35 Eaton Place, SW1X 8BY (☎ 020-7201 3440, 💻 www.mfa.gov.hu/kulkepviselet/uk/hu).

Iceland: 2A Hans Street, SW1X 0JE (☎ 020-7259 3999, 💻 www.iceland.org/uk).

India: India House, Aldwych, WC2B 4NA (☎ 020-7836 8484, 💻 http://hcilondon.in).

Indonesia: 38 Grosvenor Square, W1K 2HW (☎ 020-7499 7661, 💻 www.indonesianembassy.org.uk).

Iran: 16 Prince's Gate, SW7 1PT (☎ 020-7225 3000, 💻 www.iran-embassy.org.uk).

Ireland: 17 Grosvenor Place, SW1X 7HR (☎ 020-7235 2171, 💻 www.embassyofireland.co.uk).

Israel: 2 Palace Green, W8 4QB (☎ 020-7957 9500, 💻 http://london.mfa.gov.il).

Italy: 14 Three Kings Yard, Davies Street, W1K 2EH (☎ 020-7312 2200, 💻 www.amblondra.esteri.it).

Jamaica: 1-2 Prince Consort Road, SW7 2BZ (☎ 020-7823 9911, 💻 http://jhcuk.org).

Japan: 101-104 Piccadilly, W1J 7JT (☎ 020-7465 6500, 💻 www.uk.emb-japan.go.jp).

Jordan: 6 Upper Phillimore Gardens, W8 7HA (☎ 020-7937 3685).

Kenya: 45 Portland Place, W1B 1AS (☎ 020-7636 2371, 💻 www.kenyahighcommission.net).

Korea (South): 60 Buckingham Gate, SW1E 6AJ (☎ 020-7227 5500, 💻 http://ukinkorea.fco.gov.uk).

Kuwait: 2 Albert Gate, SW1X 7JU (☎ 020-7590 3400).

Latvia: 40 Nottingham Place, W1U 5LY (☎ 020-7312 0040, 💻 www.london.mfa.gov.lv).

Lebanon: 21 Palace Gardens Mews, W8 4RA (☎ 020-7229 7265).

Lesotho: 7 Chesham Place, Belgravia, SW1X 8HN (☎ 020-7235 5686, 💻 www.lesotholondon.org.uk).

Lithuania: 84 Gloucester Place, W1U 6AU (☎ 020-7486 6401, 💻 http://uk.mfa.lt).

Luxembourg: 27 Wilton Crescent, SW1X 8SD (☎ 020-7235 6961, 💻 http://londres.mae.lu/en).

Macedonia: Suites 2.1 & 2.2, Buckingham Court, 75-83 Buckingham Gate, SW1E 6PE (☎ 020-7976 0535, 💻 www.macedonianembassy.org.uk).

Malawi: 33 Grosvenor Street, W1K 4QT (☎ 020-7491 4172).

Malaysia: 45-46 Belgrave Square, SW1X 8QT (☎ 020-7235 8033, 💻 www.jimlondon.net).

Malta: Malta House, 36-38 Piccadilly, W1V 0PQ (☎ 020-7292 4800, 💻 www.foreign.gov.mt).

Mauritius: 32-33 Elvaston Place, SW7 5NW (☎ 020-7581 0294).

Mexico: 16 St. George Street, Hanover Square, W1S 1LX (☎ 020-7499 8586, 💻 www. sre.gob.mx/reinounido).

Morocco: 49 Queen's Gate Gardens, SW7 5NE (☎ 020-7581 5001/4, 💻 www. moroccanembassylondon.org.uk/en).

Mozambique: 21 Fitzroy Square, W1T 6EL (☎ 020-7383 3800).

Namibia: 6 Chandos Street, W1G 9LU (☎ 020-7636 6244).

Nepal: 12A Kensington Palace Gardens, W8 4QU (☎ 020-7229 1594, 💻 www. nepembassy.org.uk).

Netherlands: 38 Hyde Park Gate, SW7 5DP (☎ 020-7590 3200, 💻 www.netherlands-embassy.org.uk/home).

New Zealand: New Zealand House, 80 Haymarket, SW1Y 4TQ (☎ 020-7930 8422, 💻 www.nzembassy.com/home.cfm?c=14).

Nigeria: Nigeria House, 9 Northumberland Avenue, WC2N 5BX (☎ 020-7839 1244, 💻 www.nhcuk.org).

Norway: 25 Belgrave Square, SW1X 8QD (☎ 020-7591 5500, 💻 www.norway.org.uk).

Oman: 167 Queen's Gate, SW7 5HE (☎ 020-7225 0001).

Pakistan: 34-36 Lowndes Square, SW1X 9JN (☎ 020-7664 9200, 💻 www.pakmission-uk.gov.pk).

Panama: 40 Hertford Street, W1J 7SH (☎ 020-7493 4646).

Papua New Guinea: 14 Waterloo Place, SW1Y 4AR (☎ 020-7930 0922, 💻 www. pnghighcomm.org.uk).

Paraguay: 344 High Street, Kensington, W14 8NS (☎ 020-7610 4180, 💻 www. paraguayembassy.co.uk).

Peru: 52 Sloane Street, SW1X 9SP (☎ 020-7235 1917, 💻 www.conperlondres.com).

Philippines: 9A Palace Green, W8 4QE (☎ 020-7937 1600, 💻 www.philemb.org.uk).

Poland: 47 Portland Place, W1B 1JH (☎ 0870-774 2700, 💻 www.londynkg. polemb.net).

Portugal: 11 Belgrave Square, SW1X 8PP (☎ 020-7235 5331).

Qatar: 1 South Audley Street, W1K 1NB (☎ 020-7493 2200).

Romania: Arundel House, 4 Palace Green, W8 4QD (☎ 020-7937 9666, 💻 http:// londra.mae.ro).

Russia: 6/7 Kensington Palace Gardens, W8 4QP (☎ 020-7229 3628, 💻 www.great-britain.mid.ru).

Saudi Arabia: 30 Charles Street, W1J 5DZ (☎ 020-7917 3000).

Serbia: 28, Belgrave Square, SW1X 8QB (☎ 020-7235 9049, 💻 www.serbianembassy. org.uk).

Sierra Leone: 41 Eagle St., Holborn, WC1R 4TL (☎ 020-7404 0140).

Singapore: 9 Wilton Crescent, SW1X 8SP (☎ 020-7235 8315, 🖥 www.mfa.gov.sg/london).

Slovak Republic: 25 Kensington Palace Gardens, W8 4QY (☎ 020-7313 6470, 🖥 www.slovakembassy.co.uk).

Slovenia: 10 Little College Street, SW1P 3SH (☎ 020-7222 5700).

South Africa: South Africa House, Trafalgar Square, WC2N 5DP (☎ 020-7451 7299, 🖥 www.southafricahouse.com).

Spain: 39 Chesham Place, SW1X 8SB (☎ 020-7235 5555, 🖥 www.maec.es/en).

Sri Lanka: 13 Hyde Park Gardens, W2 2LU (☎ 020-7262 1841, 🖥 www.slhclondon.org).

Swaziland: 20 Buckingham Gate, SW1E 6LB (☎ 020-7630 6611).

Sweden: 11 Montague Place, W1H 2AL (☎ 020-7917 6400, 🖥 www.swedenabroad.com/Start_20308.aspx).

Switzerland: 16-18 Montague Place, W1H 2BQ (☎ 020-7616 6000, 🖥 www.eda.admin.ch/london.html).

Syria: 8 Belgrave Square, SW1X 8PH (☎ 020-7245 9012, 🖥 http://syremb.com).

Tanzania: 3 Stratford Place, W1C 1AS (☎ 020-7569 1470, 🖥 www.tanzania-online.gov.uk).

Thailand: 29-30 Queen's Gate, SW7 5JB (☎ 020-7589 2944, 🖥 www.thaiembassyuk.org.uk).

Tonga: 36 Molyneux Street, W1H 5BQ (☎ 020-7724 5828).

Trinidad & Tobago: 42 Belgrave Square, SW1X 8NT (☎ 020-7245 9351).

Turkey: 43 Belgrave Square, SW1X 8PA (☎ 020-7393 0202, 🖥 www.turkishconsulate.org.uk).

Uganda: 58-59 Trafalgar Square, WC2N 5DX (☎ 020-7839 5783, 🖥 www.ugandahighcommission.co.uk).

Ukraine: 60 Holland Park, W11 3SJ (☎ 020-7727 6312, 🖥 www.mfa.gov.ua/uk/en).

United Arab Emirates: 30 Prince's Gate, SW7 1PT (☎ 020-7581 1281).

United States of America: 24 Grosvenor Square, W1A 1AE (☎ 020-7499 9000, 🖥 www.usembassy.org.uk).

Uruguay: 2nd Floor, 140 Brompton Road, SW3 1HY (☎ 020-7589 8835).

Venezuela: 1 Cromwell Road, SW7 2HW (☎ 020-7584 4206).

Zaire: 26 Chesham Place, SW1X 8HH (☎ 020-7235 6137).

Zambia: 2 Palace Gate, Kensington, W8 5NG (☎ 020-7589 6655).

Zimbabwe: Zimbabwe House, 429 Strand, WC2R 0JR (☎ 020-7836 7755).

Government Departments

Department for Business Enterprise and Regulatory Reform, 1 Victoria Street, SW1H 0ET (☎ 020-7215 5000, 🖳 www.dti.gov.uk).

Department for Culture, Media & Sport, 2-4 Cockspur Street, SW1Y 5DH (☎ 020-7211 6200, 🖳 www.culture.gov.uk).

Department for Children, Schools and Families, Sanctuary Buildings, Great Smith Street, SW1P 3BT and other addresses listed on website (☎ 0870-000 2288, 🖳 www.dfes.gov.uk).

Department for Environment, Food & Rural Affairs, Nobel House, 17 Smith Square, SW1P 3JR (☎ 020-7238 6951, 🖳 www.defra.gov.uk).

Department of Health, Richmond House, 79 Whitehall, SW1A 2NS (☎ 020-7210 4850, 🖳 www.dh.gov.uk).

Department for International Development, 1 Palace Street, SW1E 5HE (☎ 020-7023 0000, 🖳 www.dfid.gov.uk).

Department for Work and Pensions, Caxton House, Tothill Street, SW1H 9DA (☎ 020-7238 0800, 🖳 www.dwp.gov.uk).

Foreign & Commonwealth Office, King Charles Street, SW1A 2AH (☎ 020-7008 1500, 🖳 www.fco.gov.uk).

HM Revenue and Customs, Victoria Avenue, Southend-on-Sea, Essex SS99 1BD (☎ 0845-000 0200 🖳 www.hmrc.gov.uk).

Home Office, 2 Marsham Street, SW1P 4DF (☎ 020-7035 4848, 🖳 www.homeoffice.gov.uk).

Ministry of Defence, Main Building, Whitehall, SW1A 2HB (☎ 020-7218 9000, 🖳 www.mod.uk).

Tourist Information

English Tourist Board, Thames Tower, Black's Road, W6 9EL (☎ 020-8846 9000, 🖳 www.enjoyengland.com).

London Tourist Board, 2 More London Riverside, SE1 2RR (☎ 020-7234 5800, 🖳 www.visitlondon.com).

Visit Britain, Thames Tower, Black's Road, Hammersmith, W6 9EL (☎ 020-8846 9000, 🖳 www.visitbritain.com).

Transport & Travel

Association of British Travel Agents, 68-71 Newman Street, W1T 3AH (☎ 020-7637 2444, 💻 www.abta.co.uk).

Automobile Association (AA), Lambert House, Stockport Road, Cheadle SK8 2DY (☎ 0161-488 7544, 💻 www.theaa.com).

British Airports Authority (BAA), 130 Wilton Road, SW1V 1LQ (☎ 020-8745 9800, 💻 www.baa.co.uk).

National Express, 7 Triton Square, NW1 3HG (☎ 0845-130130, 💻 www.nationalexpress.com).

Royal Automobile Club (RAC), RAC House, 8 Surrey Street, Norwich, Norfolk NR1 3NG (☎ 01922-727 313, 💻 www.rac.co.uk).

Miscellaneous

British Council, 10 Spring Gardens, SW1A 2BN (☎ 0161-957 7755, 💻 www.britishcouncil.org).

BBC Television Centre, Wood Lane, W12 7RJ (☎ 0870-603 0304, 💻 www.bbc.co.uk).

Border and Immigration Agency, Lunar House, 40 Wellesley Road, Croydon CR9 2BY (☎ 0870-606 7766, 💻 www.bia.homeoffice.gov.uk).

British Telecom, 81 Newgate Street, EC1A 7AJ (☎ 020-7356 5000, 💻 www.bt.com).

Central Office of Information, Hercules Road, SE1 7DU (☎ 020-7928 5037, 💻 www.coi.gov.uk).

Confederation of British Industry (CBI), Centre Point, 103 New Oxford Street, WC1A 1DU (☎ 020-7379 7400, 💻 www.cbi.org.uk).

Driver & Vehicle Licensing Agency (DVLA), Swansea SA6 7JL (☎ 0870-240 0009, 💻 www.dvla.gov.uk).

The National Archives, Ruskin Avenue, Kew, Richmond, Surrey TW9 4DU (☎ 020-8876 3444, 💻 www.nationalarchives.gov.uk).

National Association of Citizens Advice Bureaux, Myddelton House, 115-123 Pentonville Road, N1 9LZ (☎ 020-7833 2181, 💻 www.citizensadvice.org.uk).

National Consumer Focus, 4th Floor Artillery House, Artillery Row , SW1P 1RT (☎ 020-7799 7900, 💻 www.consumerfocus.org.uk).

National Federation of Women's Institutes, 104 New Kings Road, SW6 4LY (☎ 020-7371 9300, 💻 www.womens-institute.co.uk).

Office of Fair Trading, Fleetbank House, 2-6 Salisbury Square, EC4Y 8JX (☎ 020-7211 8000, 🖳 www.oft.gov.uk).

Office for National Statistics, Room 1.015, Government Buildings, Cardiff Road, Newport, NP10 8XG (☎ 0845 601 3034, 🖳 www.statistics.gov.uk).

Which (Consumers' Association), Castlemead, Gascoyne Way, Hertford SG14 1LH (☎ 01992-822800, 🖳 www.which.co.uk).

APPENDIX B: FURTHER READING

BOOKS

The books listed below are just a selection of the hundreds written about London (and England). Some books may be out of print, but you should still be able to find a copy in a bookshop or on Amazon. The publication title is followed by the author's name (where applicable) and the publisher (in brackets).

Cycling & Walking

50 Walks in London, Deborah King (AA)

Adventure Walks for Families in and Around London, Beck Jones & Clare Lewis (Frances Lincoln)

American Walks in London, Richard Tames (Interlink Publishing)

Andrew Duncan's Favourite London Walks, Andrew Duncan (New Holland)

City Cycling, Richard Ballantine (Snowbooks)

In and Around London Pathfinder Guide (Jarrold/Ordnance Survey)

London Pub Walks, Bob Steel (CAMRA)

London Step by Step, Christopher Turner (Independent Traveller)

London's Waterside Walks, Brian Cookson (Mainstream)

Off-beat Walks in London, John Wittich & Ron Philips (Shire)

On your Bike, Guide to Cycling in London (London Cycling Campaign)

Secret London, Andrew Duncan (New Holland)

A Walk Through Charles Dickens' London, Paul Garner (Louis London Walks)

Walking London, Andrew Duncan (Globetrotter Walking Guides)

Walking Dickensian London, Richard Jones (New Holland)

History

The Blitz, Vince Cross (Scholastic)

Building London: The Making of a Modern Metropolis, Bruce Marshall (Mainstream)

Derelict London, Paul Talling (Random House)

Everybody's Historic London, Jonathan Kiek (Quiller Press)

Historic London: An Explorer's Companion, Stephen Inwood (Macmillan)

A History of London, Stephen Inwood (Macmillan)

I Never Knew That About London, Christopher Winn (Ebury)

The Little Book of London, David Long (History Press)

London in the Nineteenth Century: A Human Awful Wonder of God, Jerry White (Vintage)

London, Edward Rutherford (Arrow)

London in the Twentieth Century: A City and its People, Jerry White (Vintage)

London: A Life in Maps, Peter Whitfield (British Library)

London: The Biography, Peter Ackroyd (Vintage)

London: The Illustrated History, John Clark & Cathy Ross (Allen Lane)

London: A Social History, Roy Porter (Penguin)

London Lore: The Legends and Traditions of the World's Most Vibrant City, Steve Roud (Random House)

Lost London 1870-1945: English Heritage, Davies Philip (Transatlantic Press)

The Phoenix: St. Paul's Cathedral and The Men Who Made Modern London, Leo Hollis (Weidenfeld & Nicholson)

The Secret History of Georgian London: How the Wages of Sin Shaped the Capital, Dan Cruickshank (Random House)

Secret London – an Unusual Guide, Rachel Howard & Bill Nash (Jonglez)

Shadows Of The Workhouse: The Drama Of Life In Post-war London, Jennifer Worth (Weidenfeld & Nicolson)

Spectacular Vernacular: London's 100 Most Extraordinary Buildings, David Long (History Press)

St Pancras Station (Wonders of the World), Simon Bradley (Profile)

The Subterranean Railway: How the London Underground Was Built and How It Changed the City Forever, Christian Wolmar (Atlantic)

Thames: Sacred River, Peter Ackroyd (Chatto & Windus)

The 'Times' History of London, Hugh Clout (Times Books)

Tunnels, Towers and Temples: London's 100 Strangest Places, David Long (History Press)

Living & Working

Buying or Renting a Home in London, David Hampshire & Sue Harris (Survival Books)

Buying, Selling & Letting Property, David Hampshire (Survival Books)

Culture Wise England, David Hampshire & Liz Opalka (Survival Books)

Guide to Good Living in London (Francis Chichester)

Living and Working in Britain, David Hampshire (Survival Books)

London by London: The Insider's Guide, Graham Pond (Friday project)

The London Jobs Guide: All the Information You Need to Get the Right Job with the Least Stress, Tim Gough (Prentice Hall)

London Living, Lisa Lovatt-Smith & Paul Duncan (Weidenfeld)

London Schools Guide (Mitchell Beazley)

'Time Out' London for Londoners (Time Out)

Which London School, Derek Bingham (John Catt)

Miscellaneous

Access in London: A Guide for People Who Have Difficulty Getting Around, Gordon Couch, William Forrester and David McGaughay (Access Project)

The Art & Architecture of London, Anne Saunders (Phaidon)

The Bookshops of London, Matt Jackson (Mainstream)

Focus on London (Office for National Statistics); can be viewed on or downloaded from 🖥 www.statistics.gov.uk/london or purchased as a hard copy.

Gay London, Will McLoughlin (Ellipsis)

Guide to Ethnic London, Ian McAuley (Immel Publishing)

Hawke's Eye View: London, Jason Hawkes (AA Publishing)

Holistic London, Kate Brady (Brainwave)

The London Compendium: A Street-by-street Exploration of the Hidden Metropolis, Ed Glinert (Penguin)

The London Encyclopaedia, Christopher Hibbert & Others (Macmillan)

Shops and Services, Ismay Atkins (Time Out)

The Traditional Shops & Restaurants of London: A Guide to Century-old Establishments and New Classics, Eugenia Bell (Little Bookroom)

Pubs & Restaurants

Charles Campion's London Restaurant Guide, Charles Campion (Profile)

Harden's London Restaurants (Harden's)

London Restaurants 2010 (Zagat)

London Restaurants: The Rough Guide, Charles Campion (Rough Guides)

The Michelin Guide London (Michelin)

'Time Out' Bars, Pubs and Clubs Guide, Jan Fuscoe (Time Out)

'Time Out' Cheap Eats in London, Tom Lamont (Time Out)

'Time Out' London Eating and Drinking Guide 2010, Guy Diamod & Cath Philips (Time Out)

Tourist Guides

1000 Things to Do in London, Tom Lamont (Time Out)

Baedeker Guide: London (AA Publishing)

The Best of London, Andre Gayot (Gault Millau)

Blue Guide: London, Ylva French (A&C Black)

Essential London, Paul Murphy (AA Publishing)

Everyman Guide to London (Everyman)

Explorer London, Christopher Catling (AA Publishing)

Fodor's London (Fodor)

Fodor's Around London With Kids (Fodor)

In and Around London (Pitkin Unichrome)

Let's Go London (St Martin's Press)

London (Eyewitness Travel Guides), Michael Leapman (Dorling Kindersley)

Lonely Planet: London, Pat Yale (Lonely Planet)

Michelin Green Guide London (Michelin)

The National Geographic Traveller: London (National Geographic)

Rick Steves' London, Rick Steves & Gene Openshaw (John Muir)

The Rough Guide to London, Rob Humphreys (Rough Guides)

Time Out London Guide (Penguin)

PUBLICATIONS

The Big Issue, 1-5 Wandsworth Road, SW8 2LN (☎ 020-7526 3200, 🖳 www. bigissue.com). Weekly 'street' magazine.

Evening Standard, Associated Newspapers, Northcliffe House, 2 Derry Street, W8 5EE (☎ 020-3367 7000, 🖳 www.thisislondon.co.uk). London's evening newspaper.

The London Magazine, Flat 5, 11 Queen's Gate, London, SW7 5EL (☎ 020-7584 5977, 🖳 www.thelondonmagazine.net). Bi-monthly literature and arts magazine.

Loot, 3rd Floor, Acresfield, 8-10 Exchange Street, Manchester, M2 7HA (☎ 0871-222 5000, 🖳 www.loot.com). London edition (also Liverpool and Manchester editions) published on Wed, Fri and Sun. Good for buying/selling properties (and just about everything else) privately and property rentals in an around London.

London Gazette, PO Box 7923, SE1 5ZH (☎ 020-7394 4517, 🖳 www.london-gazette.co.uk). Official newspaper of record for London and the UK.

Metro London, Northcliffe House, 2 Derry Street, W8 5TT, SE16 7ND (☎ 020-7651 5200, 🖳 www.metro.co.uk). Free daily newspaper (Mondays to Fridays).

Time Out, Universal House, 251 Tottenham Court Road, W1T 7AB (☎ 0020-7813 3000, 🖳 www.timeout.com). Weekly (Thursdays) entertainment guide.

MAPS

A-Z Big Street Atlas of London (Geographers A-Z Map Co.)

Geographers' London Atlas (Geographers A-Z Map Co.)

Guy Fox London Children's Map, Kourtney Harper (Guy Fox)

Master Atlas of Greater London (Geographers A-Z Map Co.)

The Penguin London Map Guide, Michael Middleditch (Penguin)

London all-on-one (Quickmap)

London Tube and Walk, (Quickmap)

Mapping London: Making Sense of the City, Simon Foxell (Black Dog)

The Way Out Tube Map, Roger Collings (Drumhouse)

APPENDIX C: USEFUL WEBSITES

The following list of websites (by subject) is by no means definitive, but includes many sites that will be of help and interest to those planning to live or work in London.

Business

British Business (⌨ www.britishbusinesses.com). Online UK business directory.

Business Link London (⌨ www.bllondon.co.uk). Includes hot topics and the latest news, plus e-commerce and e-business pages with masses of links to other useful sites.

Business – Visit London (⌨ http://business.visitlondon.com). London's official convention bureau.

Home Business Network (⌨ www.homebusinessnetwork.co.uk). Website operated by Wordzone Ltd., who run the *Sunday Times* Enterprise Network (in the UK and Ireland) and the *Daily Telegraph* Business Club.

Londinium (⌨ www.londinium.com). London website directory.

Touch London (⌨ www.touchlondon.co.uk). London business directory.

Culture

British Museum (⌨ www.thebritishmuseum.org). Houses a vast collection of world art and artefacts.

Flavor Pill (⌨ http://flavorpill.com/london). Culture site that embraces the high-brow, the underground, the low-brow, and the mainstream, and everything in between.

Icons (⌨ www.icons.org.uk). A portrait of England.

London Culture (⌨ www.london-culture.co.uk). List of London culture sites.

Pearly Society (⌨ www.pearlysociety.co.uk). Dedicated to the community of (Cockney) pearly kings and queens.

Victoria & Albert Museum (⌨ www.vam.ac.uk). The website of one of England's most celebrated museums, established in 1857.

We are the English.com (⌨ www.wearetheenglish.co.uk/quotes.html). A celebration of English heritage.

Wikipedia (⌨ http://en.wikipedia.org/wiki/London). The London pages of the free online encyclopaedia.

Education

British Council (🖥 www.britishcouncil.org). The UK's international organisation for educational opportunities and cultural relations.

Department for Children, Schools and Families (🖥 www.dfes.gov.uk). The DCSF is responsible for improving the focus on all aspects of policy affecting children and young people, as part of the Government's aim to deliver educational excellence.

Education UK (🖥 www.educationuk.org). Everything foreign students need to know about education in the UK, from the British Council.

European Business School (🖥 www.ebslondon.ac.uk). The EBSL is a leading London business school and the UK's oldest and largest private business school.

English in Britain (🖥 www.englishinbritain.co.uk). Online database of over 1,600 British Council Accredited English language courses, at over 300 schools.

Learn English (🖥 www.learnenglish.org.uk). Learn English online with the help of this free website from the British Council.

London Business School (🖥 www.london.edu). website of the LBS, one of the leading business schools in the world.

Office for Standards in Education (🖥 www.ofsted.gov.uk). The government department responsible for inspecting and regulating education and schools in England.

Parental Help (🖥 www.parentscentre.gov.uk). A centre for parents and carers with a 'search for a school' facility.

Student Accommodation (🖥 www.accommodationforstudents.com). A search engine for students seeking accommodation in and around the UK's major cities.

Entertainment & Tourism

All in London (🖥 www.allinlondon.co.uk). A cult entertainment guide.

Beer in the Evening (🖥 www.beerintheevening.com/pubs). UK pub and bar guide.

British Hotel Reservation Centre (🖥 www.londonhotels.bhrc.co.uk). Has been operating hotel booking desks at London airports and railway stations since 1971.

Dirty Dirty Dancing (🖥 www.dirtydirtydancing.com). London hottest night spots.

Enjoy England (🖥 www.enjoyengland.com). The website of the English Tourist Board.

Go East London (🖥 www.goeastlondon.co.uk). Comprehensive tours of East London's most historic areas.

Itchy London (🖥 www.itchylondon.co.uk). Online version of the city guidebook, with reviews of bars, clubs and pubs and suggestions for places to go out.

Live in London (🖥 www.liveinlondon.net). Guide to Hotels, Restaurants, Bars, Clubs, Music, Venue, Theatres, Shopping, places to visit and much more. Also publishes a free magazine.

London (🖥 www.londonby.com or www.londonnet.co.uk). Two of the most comprehensive London websites for both residents and visitors.

London Eye (🖥 www.londoneye.com). Website of London's newest landmark (apart from the gherkin).

London Theatre Guide (🖥 www.londontheatre.co.uk). Dedicated guide to what's on at London theatres.

London Town (🖥 www.londontown.com). One of London's best general entertainment sites with an excellent hotel booking feature (and you don't pay up front!). Also contains articles and restaurant reviews, films and theatre shows, travel bookings and general information.

London Restaurants Guide (🖥 www.londonrestaurantsguide.com). One of London's best restaurant guides.

Mayfair (🖥 www.mayfair-london.co.uk). Interesting guide to London's most exclusive district.

Off to London (🖥 www.offtolondon.com). 'The travellers' guide to London'; one the better sites packed with information on where to stay, what to do, getting around, shopping, events and more in London.

Restaurant.co.uk (🖥 www.restaurants.co.uk). One of the UK's most comprehensive restaurant search portals.

Secret London Walks (🖥 www.secretlondonwalks.co.uk). Discover the hidden and 'secret' parts of London.

Talking Tours (🖥 www.talking-tours.co.uk). Offers you the opportunity to walk through time and explore London with a personal commentary that brings the sights and history of the city alive.

This is London (🖥 www.thisislondon.com). General information from the *Evening Standard* newspaper.

Toptable (🖥 www.toptable.co.uk). Online restaurant booking service, offering deals such as two-for-one offers and tables at hard-to-book London restaurants.

UK Travel (🖥 www.uktravel.com/london.asp). Comprehensive UK travel information.

Urban Path (🖥 www.urbanpath.com/london). Good general entertainment guide to London.

Virtual London (🖥 www.virtual-london.com). Guided tours of London attractions.

Visit London (🖥 www.visitlondon.co.uk). The official website of the London Tourist Board.

Welcome to London (⌨ www.welcometolondon.com). London's most widely read online visitor magazine.

Your London (⌨ www.yourlondon.gov.uk). Good general website for visitors and residents alike.

Estate & Letting Agents

Countrywide (⌨ www.countrywideplc.co.uk). The UK's most largest provider of estate agency and property related finance & professional services.

Estate Agent (⌨ www.estateagent.co.uk). Advertise your house for sale free.

Find a Property (⌨ www.findaproperty.com). Property for sale in London and surrounding counties; includes a list of London estate agencies;

Fish 4 Homes (⌨ www.fish4.co.uk/homes). Selection of properties and directory of estate agents around the UK.

Foxtons (⌨ www.foxtons.co.uk). London's largest chain of estate and letting agents.

Hamptons International (⌨ www.hamptons.co.uk). Specialises in the top end of the property market, i.e. all of central London!

Home Pages (⌨ www.homepages.co.uk). Sell your home for £50 plus VAT.

Homes Online (⌨ www.homes-on-line.com). Useful information about buying, selling, home improvements and financing a property.

Hot Property (⌨ www.hotproperty.co.uk). The Hot Property magazine website, featuring property in London and the south-east.

Houseweb (⌨ www.houseweb.co.uk). Independent property website that contains comprehensive advice and tips for the homebuyer.

New-Homes (⌨ www.new-homes.co.uk). Comprehensive database of new home developments throughout the UK.

Prime Location (⌨ www.primelocation.com). Consortium of estate agents advertising properties.

PropertyFinder.com (⌨ www.propertyfinder.com). Comprehensive property website.

Right Move (⌨ www.rightmove.co.uk). Claims to be 'the UK's number one property website'.

Smart New Homes (⌨ www.smartnewhomes.co.uk). Search for new homes.

Vebra (⌨ www.vebra.com). One of the UK's most visited property sites, run by a consortium of estate agents.

Finance, Mortgages & Property Buying

Charcol (⌨ www.charcol.co.uk). Mortgage broker.

Environment Agency (⌨ www.environment-agency.gov.uk). Check the occurrence of flooding and other natural hazards in an area.

Home Check (⌨ www.homecheck.co.uk). Local information about the risks of flooding, landslip, pollution, radon gas, landfill, waste sites, etc. Also provides general information about neighbourhoods.

Hometrack (⌨ www.hometrack.co.uk). Online property reports.

Money Extra (⌨ www.moneyextra.co.uk). Financial services, including the best mortgage deals.

Money Net (⌨ www.moneynet.co.uk). Financial services, including the best mortgage deals.

Money Quest (⌨ www.moneyquest.co.uk). Mortgage brokers.

Money Supermarket (⌨ www.moneysupermarket.com). General finance, including mortgages.

This is Money (⌨ www.thisismoney.co.uk). Data and statistics on money matters, as well as useful finance guides.

Up My Street (⌨ www.upmystreet.com). Information about neighbourhoods, including property prices, local services, schools, local government, etc.

Virgin Money (⌨ www.uk.virginmoney.com). The Virgin Group's financial services online.

What Mortgage (⌨ www.whatmortgage.co.uk). Mortgage information and comprehensive advice on buying a property.

Your Mortgage Magazine (⌨ www.yourmortgage.co.uk). A wealth of information about mortgages and all aspects of buying and selling property.

Government

10 Downing Street (⌨ www.number10.gov.uk). Official website of the British Prime Minister (but don't expect him to answer your emails).

Crime Reduction (⌨ www.crimereduction.homeoffice.gov.uk). A government site providing crime statistics and advice on avoiding and preventing crime.

Government (⌨ www.direct.gov.uk). Access to the 'good and the great', i.e. the UK's elected officials.

Government Gateway (⌨ www.gateway.gov.uk). Access to over 1,000 government websites. Government Gateway is a centralised registration service that enables you to sign up for online government services.

Greater London Authority (💻 www.london.gov.uk). The Mayor of London's website, with information on campaigns, London issues and forthcoming events.

London Boroughs (💻 www.london.gov.uk/london/links.jsp). Links to all London's borough websites.

Mayor Watch (💻 www.mayorwatch.co.uk). Check up on what Boris is up to.

National Health Service (💻 www.nhsdirect.nhs.uk). Gateway to government health information, services and assistance.

National Statistics (💻 www.statistics.gov.uk). The government agency that produces and disseminates social, health, economic, demographic, labour market and business statistics.

UK Government Guide (💻 www.ukgovernmentguide.co.uk). An easy way to access local UK government websites.

UK Parliament (💻 www.parliament.uk). Official parliament website.

UK Visas (💻 www.ukvisas.gov.uk). All you need to know about UK visas.

Webmesh (💻 www.webmesh.co.uk/government.htm). Links to government departments.

History

Derelict London (💻 www.derelictlondon.com). Paul Talling's collection of over 1,000 photos of the parts of the city that are coming apart at the seams.

East London History (💻 www.eastlondonhistory.com). Collection of stories about the East End, focusing on the people who lived there and influenced the area's history.

Greenwood (💻 http://users.bathspa.ac.uk/greenwood). An interactive map of London in 1827, drawn by Christopher and John Greenwood (website hosted by Bath Spa University).

History (💻 www.history.ac.uk/cmh/cmh.main.html). A comprehensive history of London, from markets to the city's epidemics.

London City Churches (💻 www.london-city-churches.org.uk). A guide to City churches, some of the finest ecclesiastical buildings in Europe.

London Remembers (💻 www.londonremembers.com). A record of all the memorials in London, from blue plaques to fountains.

Pepys Diary (💻 www.pepysdiary.com). A spoof Pepys diary created by Phil Gyford – fascinating and much more readable than the original.

Port Cities (💻 www.portcities.org.uk/london). A wealth of information covering all aspects of the capital's enduring relationship with its river.

Living & Working

Accommodation London (🖳 www.accommodationlondon.net). Help with finding a place to live in London, with text in English, French, Spanish, Italian and Swedish.

Get A Map (🖳 www.ordnancesurvey.co.uk/oswebsite/getamap/). Free downloadable Ordnance Survey neighbourhood maps.

Gumtree (🖳 www.gumtree.com/london /2553_1.html). Jobs from one of London's best community websites.

Jobcentre (🖳 www.jobcentreplus.gov.uk). The government website for job seekers, with advice on job hunting, training, recruitment and benefits.

Just London Jobs (🖳 www.justlondonjobs.co.uk). Links to jobs from London's top recruitment agencies.

Knowhere (🖳 www.knowhere.co.uk). An alternative look at over 2,000 UK towns.

London Jobs (🖳 www.londonjobs.co.uk). One of London's best jobs websites.

LondonNet (🖳 www.londonnet.co.uk). General information about all aspects of living and working in London.

My Village (🖳 www.myvillage.com). Community sites for London and 20 other cities.

Neighbourhood Statistics (🖳 http://neighbourhood.statistics.gov.uk). Contains a wide range of statistics for neighbourhoods in England and Wales.

Proviser (🖳 www.proviser.com). Local property prices and street maps for England and Wales.

Stuck in London (🖳 www.stuckinlondon.com). Website targeted at newcomers from the 'colonies' (Aussies, Kiwis, Canucks, Saffas and the odd Yank).

Student Accommodation (🖳 www.accommodationforstudents.com). A search engine for students seeking accommodation in London and other UK cities.

UK Visas (🖳 www.ukvisas.gov.uk). All you need to know about British visas.

Up My Street (🖳 www.upmystreet.co.uk). Information about neighbourhoods, including property prices, local services, schools, local government, etc.

Volunteering (🖳 www.volunteering.org.uk). A useful site for those looking for volunteering work, with helpful 'I want a volunteer' pages to help you find a job in London.

Work Gateways (🖳 www.workgateways.com). Organises work for visitors on temporary working visas.

See also **Property** below.

Media

BBC London (⌨ www.bbc.co.uk/london). Excellent, comprehensive website from one of Britain's great institutions – provides local news, sport, entertainment and debate.

British Papers (⌨ www.britishpapers.co.uk). Links to the websites of all British newspapers that are online.

Capital Radio (⌨ www.capitalfm.com). The website of London's leading commercial radio station.

Loot (⌨ www.loot.com). Log on to buy and sell virtually anything under one roof.

London Gazette (⌨ www.londongazette.co.uk). Official newspaper of record for London and the UK.

This is England (⌨ www.thisengland.co.uk). Website of *This is England* magazine.

Time Out (⌨ www.timeout.com). Website of London's iconic, best-selling entertainment guide.

The Times (⌨ www.timesonline.co.uk). One of the UK's oldest (est. 1785) and most famous newspapers.

What's On (⌨ www.whatsoninlondon.co.uk). Weekly entertainment guide.

Which? Magazine (⌨ www.which.net). Monthly consumer magazine, available on subscription.

Miscellaneous

Advice Guide (⌨ www.adviceguide.org.uk). Established by the Citizens Advice Bureau (CAB), with down-to-earth advice, including information about civil rights, benefits and the legal system.

BBC London Weather (⌨ www.bbc.co.uk/london/weather). Provides weather services and maps for temperature, wind, satellite, lighting, pressure and radar.

Britannia (⌨ www.britannia.com/history). The internet's most comprehensive information resource for the times, places, events and people of British history.

British Library (⌨ www.bl.uk). Search the BL catalogues, order items for research, view exhibitions, etc.

British Monarchy (⌨ www.royal.gov.uk). Official website of the British Monarchy.

Cockney Rhyming Slang (⌨ www.cockneyrhymingslang.co.uk). A cornucopia of East End vernacular – helpful in case someone asks if you "saw the wooden pews [news] last night." (See also **Appendix F**.)

Football Association (🖥 www.thefa.com). The Official Website of the England Team, The FA Cup and football (soccer) at all levels in England.

Ginger Beer (🖥 www.gingerbeer.co.uk). London's premier guide to London life for its lesbian community.

Hidden London (🖥 www.hidden-london.com). A website dedicated to the little-known corners of London.

London Architecture Diary (🖥 www.londonarchitecturediary.com). Everything you ever wanted to know about the changing face of London.

London Cycle Sport (🖥 www.londoncyclesport.com). online resource for anyone looking to take up cycling seriously, with a comprehensive guide to gear, upcoming events and race reports.

London Directory (🖥 www.londondirectory.co.uk). a directory of hundreds of London sites listed by subject.

London is Free (🖥 www.londonisfree.com). Not quite free, but there are many events and activities that cost nothing, listed here.

London Weather (🖥 http://uk.weather.com/weather/today-London-UKXX0085). Provides a ten-day summary forecast, with maps for shorter periods ahead.

Londonist (🖥 www.londonist.com). 'A website about London and everything that happens in it' – news and events, restaurants and bars, happenings and goings-on – looks at the more unusual aspects of London.

Medical Care (🖥 www.med4u.co.uk). The leading UK online medical service. Obtain health advice and a second opinion with ease.

Multimap & Streetmap (🖥 www.multimap.com and www.streetmap.co.uk). Invaluable resources for finding your way around if you haven't got an *A-Z*, where you can find any street or postcode in London.

Ordnance Survey (🖥 www.ordnancesurvey.co.uk). Downloadable maps.

Photograph London (🖥 www.photograph-london.com). Photographic view of London.

Premier League (🖥 www.premierleague.co.uk). Official website of England's top soccer league, with links to the websites of London's top clubs.

River Thames (🖥 www.riverthames.co.uk). The definitive guide to everything about the Thames, from sea to source.

Run Riot (🖥 www.run-riot.com). A rundown on London's alternative events, particular those involving the arts.

Untold London (🖥 www.untoldlondon.org.uk). Vast archive of material on the history of London's diverse ethnic and cultural communities.

Walk It (🖥 www.walkit.com/cities/london). A site that attempts to encourage more people to walk around London – the best way to see the city and often the quickest route from A to B.

Wild Web (⌨ www.wildweb.london.gov.uk). A website that aims to encourage people to make the most of London's wild places – exploring them and getting out and experiencing them first hand.

Moving Home

British Association of Removers (⌨ www.bar.co.uk). Association of removal companies offering a professional service, with a conciliation and arbitration service.

I am Moving (⌨ www.iammoving.com). Will inform companies on your behalf that you're moving.

The Move Channel (⌨ www.themovechannel.com). General property website containing everything you need to know about moving house.

Really Moving (⌨ www.reallymoving.com). Comprehensive information about property, including home-moving services and a property finder.

Professional Associations

Building Societies' Association (⌨ www.bsa.org.uk). Central representative body for building societies.

Council for Licensed Conveyancers (⌨ www.conveyancer.org.uk). Council for licensed conveyancers.

Council of Mortgage Lenders (⌨ www.cml.org.uk). Trade association for mortgage lenders.

Federation of Master Builders (⌨ www.fmb.org.uk). Includes a directory of members.

Land Registry (⌨ www1.landregistry.gov.uk). Practical information about registering land and land registry archives.

The Law Society (⌨ www.lawsociety.org.uk). Professional body for solicitors in England and Wales.

National Association of Estate Agents/NAEA (⌨ www.naea.co.uk). The main organisation for estate agents.

Ombudsman for Estate Agents (⌨ www.oea.co.uk). Independent arbitration for property buyers with complaints about registered estate agents.

Property

English Heritage (🖥 www.english-heritage.org.uk). The organisation responsible for protecting and promoting the historic environment, officially known as the Historic Buildings and Monuments Commission for England.

Into London (🖥 www.intolondon.com). London's longest-running website for flatsharers.

My Property Spy (🖥 www.mypropertyspy.co.uk). Property sale prices in London dating back to 2000 – find out what your neighbour's paid and what your house might be worth.

The Rat & Mouse (🖥 www.theratandmouse.co.uk). In the form of a blog, R&M sifts through the endless conflicting reports on the state of the London property market and attempts to make sense of them. Contains an archive by postcode so you can find out what people say about your street. (Rat and mouse = 'house' in rhyming Cockney slang – see **Appendix F**).

Property Snake (🖥 www.propertysnake.co.uk). See at a glance whether property prices are up or down in a particular area – and by how much.

Save Britain's Heritage (🖥 www.savebritainsheritage.org). Conservation of historic buildings.

Scoot (🖥 www.scoot.co.uk). Find essential services for homeowners.

Shopping & Services

Amazon (🖥 www.amazon.co.uk). The UK's largest online retailer.

Borough Market (🖥 www.boroughmarket.org.uk). London's oldest food market, established by the Romans and held on its present site for 250 years.

Consumers' Association (🖥 www.which.net). The UK's consumer champion, who publish the monthly *Which?* consumer magazine.

Ebay (🖥 www.ebay.co.uk). The UK version of the ubiquitous auction site.

Harrods (🖥 www.harrods.com). London's largest and most famous department store, where it's said you can buy anything.

John Lewis (🖥 www.johnlewis.com). The website of London's (and the UK's) favourite retailer.

London Rate (🖥 www.londonrate.com). Useful resource for Londoners containing a collection of service-industry contacts, which are rated and searchable with prices. Everything from babysitters to builders, computer experts to cleaners, and hairdressers to housekeepers.

Lynku (🖥 www.lynku.com). Designer fashion and furniture sales website for London, offering free weekly update emails and alerts on sales and promotions by category.

Price Runner (💻 www.pricerunner.co.uk). Compare the prices of a wide range of goods and services.

Shopping Net (💻 www.shopping.net). The UK's most comprehensive shopping website, which allows you to search thousands of websites for products and services at the best prices.

Street Sensation (💻 www.streetsensation.co.uk). A virtual tour of London's busiest shopping streets, with photos and links to over 3,500 shops, restaurants and bars.

Time Out (💻 www.timeout.com/london/shopping). London's premier magazine for residents and visitor's, containing a wealth of 'insider' shopping information.

Travel

At UK (💻 www.atuk.co.uk). The foremost UK travel search engine and directory.

British Airways (💻 www.britishairways.com). The website of Britain's largest airline.

Easyjet (💻 www.easyjet.co.uk). The UK's best budget airline.

National Express (💻 www.nationalexpress.com). The UK's largest scheduled coach travel company.

National Rail (💻 www.nationalrail.co.uk). For when you want to get out of London. Timetables, special offers and a journey planner for all the UK's railway services.

Public Transport Information (💻 www.pti.org.uk). Covers all travel by rail, air, coach, bus, ferry, metro and tram within the UK (including the Channel Islands, Isle of Man and Northern Ireland), and between the UK and Ireland.

Rail (💻 www.rail.co.uk). The best independent rail information, including timetables.

Transport For London (💻 www.tfl.gov.uk). Everything you need to know about London's public transport systems.

Travel Britain Guide (💻 www.travelbritain.com). Travel and Tourism Deals and Resources Pages for travel and entertainment resources in the UK.

Travel Line (💻 www.traveline.org.uk). The UK's premier website for impartial information on planning a journey by bus, coach or train.

Virgin Atlantic (💻 www.virgin-atlantic.com). The website of Britain's best airline.

APPENDIX D: WEIGHTS & MEASURES

Officially, the UK converted to the international metric system of measurement in 1995 and the use of imperial measures was due to end in 1999. However, many traders insisted on using Imperial measures and the EU finally gave up the battle to ban them in 2007, although products priced in Imperial weights and measures must legally also show their equivalent in metric. If you're confused, the conversion tables on the following pages will prove useful. Some comparisons shown are approximate, but close enough for most everyday uses. You can make conversions online using a variety of websites, e.g. 🖳 www.unit-conversion.info. For information about the metric system, see 🖳 www.metric.org.uk/home.htm.

Women's Clothes										
Continental	34	36	38	40	42	44	46	48	50	52
UK	8	10	12	14	16	18	20	22	24	26
US	6	8	10	12	14	16	18	20	22	24

Pullover's												
	Women's						**Men's**					
Continental	40	42	44	46	48	50	44	46	48	50	52	54
UK	34	36	38	40	42	44	34	36	38	40	42	44
US	34	36	38	40	42	44	sm	med		lar	xl	

Men's Shirts										
Continental	36	37	38	39	40	41	42	43	44	46
UK/US	14	14	15	15	16	16	17	17	18	-

Men's Underwear						
Continental	5	6	7	8	9	10
UK	34	36	38	40	42	44
US	sm	med		lar	xl	

NB: sm = small, med = medium, lar = large, xl = extra large

Children's Clothes						
Continental	92	104	116	128	140	152
UK	16/18	20/22	24/26	28/30	32/34	36/38
US	2	4	6	8	10	12

Children's Shoes	
Continental	18 19 20 21 22 23 24 25 26 27 28 29 30 31 32
UK/US	2 3 4 4 5 6 7 7 8 9 10 11 11 12 13
Continental	33 34 35 36 37 38
UK/US	1 2 2 3 4 5

Shoes (Women's & Men's)	
Continental	35 36 37 37 38 39 40 41 42 42 43 44
UK	2 3 3 4 4 5 6 7 7 8 9 9
US	4 5 5 6 6 7 8 9 9 10 10 11

Weight			
Imperial	**Metric**	**Metric**	**Imperial**
1oz	28.35g	1g	0.035oz
1lb*	454g	100g	3.5oz
1cwt	50.8kg	250g	9oz
1 ton	1,016kg	500g	18oz
2,205lb	1 tonne	1kg	2.2lb

Area			
British/US	**Metric**	**Metric**	**British/US**
1 sq. in	0.45 sq. cm	1 sq. cm	0.15 sq. in
1 sq. ft	0.09 sq. m	1 sq. m	10.76 sq. ft
1 sq. yd	0.84 sq. m	1 sq. m	1.2 sq. yds
1 acre	0.4 hectares	1 hectare	2.47 acres
1 sq. mile	2.56 sq. km	1 sq. km	0.39 sq. mile

Capacity			
Imperial	**Metric**	**Metric**	**Imperial**
1 UK pint	0.57 litre	1 litre	1.75 UK pints
1 US pint	0.47 litre	1 litre	2.13 US pints
1 UK gallon	4.54 litres	1 litre	0.22 UK gallon
1 US gallon	3.78 litres	1 litre	0.26 US gallon

NB: An American 'cup' = around 250ml or 0.25 litre.

Length			
British/US	**Metric**	**Metric**	**British/US**
1in	2.54cm	1cm	0.39in
1ft	30.48cm	1m	3ft 3.25in
1yd	91.44cm	1km	0.62mi
1mi	1.6km	8km	5mi

Temperature	
°Celsius	**°Fahrenheit**
0	32 (freezing point of water)
5	41
10	50
15	59
20	68
25	77
30	86
35	95
40	104
50	122

Temperature Conversion

Celsius to Fahrenheit: multiply by 9, divide by 5 and add 32. (For a quick and approximate conversion, double the Celsius temperature and add 30.)

Fahrenheit to Celsius: subtract 32, multiply by 5 and divide by 9. (For a quick and approximate conversion, subtract 30 from the Fahrenheit temperature and divide by 2.)

NB: The boiling point of water is 100°C / 212°F. Normal body temperature (if you're alive and well) is 37°C / 98.6°F.

Power			
Kilowatts	**Horsepower**	**Horsepower**	**Kilowatts**
1	1.34	1	0.75

Oven Temperature		
Gas	**Electric**	
	°F	**°C**
-	225–250	110–120
1	275	140
2	300	150
3	325	160
4	350	180
5	375	190
6	400	200
7	425	220
8	450	230
9	475	240

Air Pressure	
PSI	**Bar**
10	0.5
20	1.4
30	2
40	2.8

APPENDIX E: TABLES

Average House Prices March 2010 (£000)				
Borough	Flat	Terraced House	Semi-det House	Detached House
Barking & Dagenham	117,000	176,850	205,150	263,800
Barnet	273,650	332,500	454,150	822,000
Bexley	147,050	194,500	239,200	388,200
Brent	243,150	402,600	390,700	840,500
Bromley	186,950	262,200	323,700	636,600
Camden	471,700	988,550	1,566,800	2,521,900
City of London	472,550	n/a	n/a	n/a
Croydon	161,650	212,800	283,150	448,700
Ealing	228,200	358,500	418,400	823,600
Enfield	186,300	251,000	352,000	732,300
Greenwich	228,700	250,500	309,550	606,050
Hackney	269,600	470,200	511,750	n/a
Hammersmith & Fulham	372,900	883,000	1,443,800	901,660
Haringey	250,000	428,000	816,900	769,250
Harrow	200,850	280,750	331,950	597,450
Havering	155,850	202,800	250,600	395,300
Hillingdon	183,150	239,300	268,450	499,950
Hounslow	226,400	335,550	388,250	732,950
Islington	348,600	726,100	772,650	n/a
Kensington & Chelsea	741,200	2,231,000	2,097,000	n/a
Kingston upon Thames	217,500	295,850	359,600	674,200
Lambeth	278,300	500,250	565,950	878,900
Lewisham	185,600	289,800	338,950	520,850
Merton	260,850	335,750	499,950	1,615,500
Newham	176,850	213,750	241,250	n/a
Redbridge	187,100	278,400	339,050	485,200
Richmond upon Thames	322,800	579,100	781,600	1,120,700
Southwark	286,650	450,150	565,900	797,550
Sutton	162,200	239,300	307,800	500,400
Tower Hamlets	343,950	436,550	432,750	n/a
Waltham Forest	168,000	243,800	296,700	374,200
Wandsworth	326,200	629,100	1,051,050	1,688,250
Westminster	651,500	1,477,400	2,265,700	n/a

Average Rental Prices March 2010 (£ pcm)			
Borough	Flat 1-2 bed	House 2-3 bed	House 3-4 bed	House 5+ bed
Barking & Dagenham	800	900	1,000	1,750
Barnet	900	1,250	1,550	4,000
Bexley	750	900	1,300	2,000
Brent	1,500	2,500	3,600	3,200
Bromley	900	1,300	1,600	2,100
Camden	2,000	2,500	3,750	4,050
City of London	1,700	2,600	3,250	6,500
Croydon	850	1,100	1,600	2,300
Ealing	1,400	2,100	2,500	5,200
Enfield	800	1,150	1,400	2,900
Greenwich	1,150	1,400	1,750	2,600
Hackney	1,050	1,550	1,700	3,300
Hammersmith & Fulham	1,500	1,800	2,200	6,500
Haringey	1,500	2,900	3,900	5,850
Harrow	950	1,200	1,550	2,200
Havering	800	1,100	1,350	1,750
Hillingdon	950	1,350	1,550	2,500
Hounslow	950	1,250	1,350	2,400
Islington	1,500	2,700	3,100	7,600
Kensington & Chelsea	2,150	4,000	5,200	7,600
Kingston upon Thames	1,150	1,500	1,750	3,750
Lambeth	1,100	1,500	1,600	2,550
Lewisham	1,000	1,300	1,500	2,200
Merton	1,075	1,500	1,900	2,600
Newham	800	975	1,150	1,850
Redbridge	800	1,050	1,150	1,800
Richmond upon Thames	1,450	2,100	2,650	7,000
Southwark	1,250	1,750	2,150	3,000
Sutton	850	1,150	1,700	3,000
Tower Hamlets	1,050	1,550	2,400	4,750
Waltham Forest	800	1,100	1,300	1,800
Wandsworth	1,100	1,500	1,750	3,700
Westminster	2,200	6,500	7,600	10,900

Annual Crime Rates - Jan 2010				
Borough	Total Crimes	Violence	Burglary	Robbery	Motor Vehicle
Barking & Dagenham	20,086	5,326	2,486	824	2,610
Barnet	25,930	4,925	4,111	942	3,085
Bexley	15,577	3,773	2,068	316	2,103
Brent	28,622	6,993	3,666	1,827	3,070
Bromley	24,107	5,493	3,637	612	3,020
Camden	33,729	5,712	3,243	1,073	3,029
City of London*	n/a	n/a	n/a	n/a	n/a
Croydon	33,204	7,154	4,246	1,598	4,220
Ealing	33,129	7,828	2,855	1,335	4,954
Enfield	24,208	4,563	3,940	1,232	3,647
Greenwich	25,984	6,257	3,050	836	3,370
Hackney	28,957	6,614	2,675	1,014	3,012
Hammersmith & Fulham	22,841	4,772	1,914	678	2,931
Haringey	26,114	5,207	3,627	1,077	3,684
Harrow	15,224	3,425	2,303	464	1,989
Havering	17,135	3,378	2,721	345	2,048
Hillingdon	24,481	5,945	3,283	690	3,738
Hounslow	23,338	5,619	2,741	638	3,069
Islington	28,555	5,880	2,919	982	3,332
Kensington & Chelsea	20,748	2,965	1,613	546	2,098
Kingston upon Thames	11,164	2,268	1,215	271	893
Lambeth	35,110	7,831	3,836	2,306	3,259
Lewisham	29,473	7,847	3,053	1,253	3,101
Merton	14,692	3,470	1,875	550	1,702
Newham	33,318	7,276	3,482	2,099	5,620
Redbridge	23,837	4,215	3,380	928	3,980
Richmond upon Thames	11,612	2,157	1,666	225	1,456
Southwark	36,619	8,781	3,311	2,018	3,152
Sutton	12,938	2,684	1,465	338	2,016
Tower Hamlets	27,222	6,196	2,092	883	2,567
Waltham Forest	27,310	5,833	3,347	1,592	4,281
Wandsworth	25,441	5,288	3,031	1,283	3,370
Westminster	63,655	8,823	3,529	1,763	3,086

NB: The Met Police publish monthly and annual figures for each borough, except for the *City of London, which has it's own police force and website ⌨ www.cityoflondon.police.uk/citypolice.

School League Tables 2009

Borough	Percentage of pupils achieving Level 4 at KS2		Pupils achieving 5 or more GCSEs at grades A* to C
	English	Maths	%
England	80	79	49.8
Barking & Dagenham	79	79	45.1
Barnet	84	83	61.4
Bexley	83	79	57.3
Brent	80	78	57.1
Bromley	83	81	62.6
Camden	82	82	51.1
City of London	86	100	n/a
Croydon	81	79	51.9
Ealing	80	80	54.0
Enfield	79	78	50.4
Greenwich	78	79	43.4
Hackney	74	72	52.2
Hammersmith & Fulham	78	77	64.1
Haringey	76	75	45.7
Harrow	82	81	60.8
Havering	85	82	58.1
Hillingdon	81	79	52.0
Hounslow	81	80	56.6
Islington	79	79	45.0
Kensington & Chelsea	86	86	66.1
Kingston upon Thames	86	83	68.2
Lambeth	79	78	53.5
Lewisham	78	76	47.0
Merton	81	81	48.0
Newham	77	79	47.1
Redbridge	84	81	64.5
Richmond upon Thames	91	87	55.7
Southwark	80	79	46.0
Sutton	85	82	67.9
Tower Hamlets	80	81	45.8
Waltham Forest	77	79	46.0
Wandsworth	83	84	52.1
Westminster	82	79	52.8

Council Tax Rates (£) 2010/11		
Borough	**Band G**	**Band H**
Barking & Dagenham	2,210	2,652
Barnet	2,372	2,846
Bexley	2,397	2,877
Brent	2,281	2,738
Bromley	2,169	2,602
Camden	2,219	2,663
City of London	1,584	1,901
Croydon	2,433	2,920
Ealing	2,283	2,740
Enfield	2,350	2,820
Greenwich	2,151	2,581
Hackney	2,180	2,617
Hammersmith & Fulham	1,869	2,243
Haringey	2,490	2,988
Harrow	2,494	2,992
Havering	2,518	3,022
Hillingdon	2,371	2,846
Hounslow	2,334	2,801
Islington	2,119	2,543
Kensington & Chelsea	1,799	2,158
Kingston upon Thames	2,770	3,324
Lambeth	2,060	2,470
Lewisham	2,253	2,703
Merton	2,395	2,874
Newham	2,092	2,511
Redbridge	2,342	2,810
Richmond upon Thames	2,662	3,194
Southwark	2,037	2,444
Sutton	2,418	2,901
Tower Hamlets	1,992	2,390
Waltham Forest	2,437	2,924
Wandsworth	1,136	1,364
Westminster	1,146	1,375

Primary Healthcare Trust Ratings 2010				
Borough	**Weak**	**Fair**	**Good**	**Excellent**
Barking & Dagenham	♦			
Barnet			♦	
Bexley		♦		
Brent *		♦		
Bromley		♦		
Camden			♦	
City of London *		♦		
Croydon			♦	
Ealing		♦		
Enfield		♦		
Greenwich *			♦	
Hackney *		♦		
Hammersmith & Fulham		♦		
Haringey *		♦		
Harrow		♦		
Havering	♦			
Hillingdon		♦		
Hounslow		♦		
Islington			♦	
Kensington & Chelsea		♦		
Kingston upon Thames		♦		
Lambeth			♦	
Lewisham		♦		
Merton		♦		
Newham		♦		
Redbridge	♦			
Richmond upon Thames			♦	
Southwark			♦	
Sutton		♦		
Tower Hamlets	♦			
Waltham Forest		♦		
Wandsworth		♦		
Westminster		♦		

NB: Primary Healthcare Trusts marked with an asterisk (*) include teaching hospitals.

INDEX

INDEX OF PLACE NAMES

Survival Books

Essential reading for anyone planning to live, work, retire or buy a home abroad

Survival Books was established in 1987 and by the mid-'90s was the leading publisher of books for people planning to live, work, buy property or retire abroad.

From the outset, our philosophy has been to provide the most comprehensive and up-to-date information available. Our titles routinely contain up to twice as much information as other books and are updated frequently. All our books contain colour photographs and some are printed in two colours or full colour throughout. They also contain original cartoons, illustrations and maps.

Survival Books are written by people with first-hand experience of the countries and the people they describe, and therefore provide invaluable insights that cannot be obtained from official publications or websites, and information that is more reliable and objective than that provided by the majority of unofficial sites.

Survival Books are designed to be easy – and interesting – to read. They contain a comprehensive list of contents and index and extensive appendices, including useful addresses, further reading, useful websites and glossaries to help you obtain additional information as well as metric conversion tables and other useful reference material.

Our primary goal is to provide you with the essential information necessary for a trouble-free life or property purchase and to save you time, trouble and money.

We believe our books are the best – they are certainly the best-selling. But don't take our word for it – read what reviewers and readers have said about Survival Books at the front of this book.

Order your copies today by phone, fax, post or email from:
Survival Books, PO Box 3780, Yeovil, BA21 5WX, United Kingdom.
Tel: +44 (0)1935-700060, email: sales@survivalbooks.net,
Website: www.survivalbooks.net

Buying a Home Series

Buying a home abroad is not only a major financial transaction but also a potentially life-changing experience; it's therefore essential to get it right. Our Buying a Home guides are required reading for anyone planning to purchase property abroad and are packed with vital information to guide you through the property jungle and help you avoid disasters that can turn a dream home into a nightmare.

The purpose of our Buying a Home guides is to enable you to choose the most favourable location and the most appropriate property for your requirements, and to reduce your risk of making an expensive mistake by making informed decisions and calculated judgements rather than uneducated and hopeful guesses. Most importantly, they will help you save money and will repay your investment many times over.

Buying a Home guides are the most comprehensive and up-to-date source of information available about buying property abroad – whether you're seeking a detached house or an apartment, a holiday or a permanent home (or an investment property), these books will prove invaluable.

For a full list of our current titles, visit our website at www.survivalbooks.net

Living and Working Series

Our Living and Working guides are essential reading for anyone planning to spend a period abroad – whether it's an extended holiday or permanent migration – and are packed with priceless information designed to help you avoid costly mistakes and save both time and money.

Living and Working guides are the most comprehensive and up-to-date source of practical information available about everyday life abroad. They aren't, however, simply a catalogue of dry facts and figures, but are written in a highly readable style – entertaining, practical and occasionally humorous.

Our aim is to provide you with the comprehensive practical information necessary for a trouble-free life. You may have visited a country as a tourist, but living and working there is a different matter altogether; adjusting to a new environment and culture and making a home in any foreign country can be a traumatic and stressful experience. You need to adapt to new customs and traditions, discover the local way of doing things (such as finding a home, paying bills and obtaining insurance) and learn all over again how to overcome the everyday obstacles of life.

All these subjects and many, many more are covered in depth in our Living and Working guides – don't leave home without them.

The Expats' Best Friend!

Culture Wise Series

Our **Culture Wise** series of guides is essential reading for anyone who wants to understand how a country really 'works'. Whether you're planning to stay for a few days or a lifetime, these guides will help you quickly find your feet and settle into your new surroundings.
Culture Wise guides:

- Reduce the anxiety factor in adapting to a foreign culture
- Explain how to behave in everyday situations in order to avoid cultural and social gaffes
- Help you get along with your neighbours
- Make friends and establish lasting business relationships
- Enhance your understanding of a country and its people.

People often underestimate the extent of cultural isolation they can face abroad, particularly in a country with a different language. At first glance, many countries seem an 'easy' option, often with millions of visitors from all corners of the globe and well-established expatriate communities. But, sooner or later, newcomers find that most countries are indeed 'foreign' and many come unstuck as a result. **Culture Wise** guides will enable you to quickly adapt to the local way of life and feel at home, and – just as importantly – avoid the worst effects of culture shock.

Culture Wise – The Wise Way to Travel

The essential guides to Culture, Customs & Business Etiquette

Other Survival Books

The Best Places to Buy a Home in France/Spain: Unique guides to where to buy property in Spain and France, containing detailed regional profiles and market reports.

Buying, Selling and Letting Property: The best source of information about buying, selling and letting property in the UK.

Earning Money From Your French Home: Income from property in France, including short- and long-term letting.

Investing in Property Abroad: Everything you need to know and more about buying property abroad for investment and pleasure.

Life in the UK - Test & Study Guide: essential reading for anyone planning to take the 'Life in the UK' test in order to become a permanent resident (settled) in the UK.

Making a Living: Comprehensive guides to self-employment and starting a business in France and Spain.

Renovating & Maintaining Your French Home: The ultimate guide to renovating and maintaining your dream home in France.

Retiring in France/Spain: Everything a prospective retiree needs to know about the two most popular international retirement destinations.

Running Gîtes and B&Bs in France: An essential book for anyone planning to invest in a gîte or bed & breakfast business.

Rural Living in France: An invaluable book for anyone seekingthe 'good life', containing a wealth of practical information about all aspects of French country life.

Shooting Caterpillars in Spain: The hilarious and compelling story of two innocents abroad in the depths of Andalusia in thelate '80s.

For a full list of our current titles, visit our website at
www.survivalbooks.net

PHOTO

www.dreamstime.com

Pages 1 © Postnikov, 16 © Baloncici, 29 © Navarone, 30 © Oscar1319, 36 © Nicalfc, 41 © Kenny1, 44 © Nikonite, 49 © Pixelstate, 50 © Sampete, 55 © Socrates, 61 © Dana, 67 © Klikk, 68 © Socrates, 80 © Tadija, 83 © Kcphotos, 85 © Fazon1, 86 © Tupungato, 91 © Katseyephoto, 92 © Socrates, 94 © Arekmalang, 97 © Tonybaggett, 98 © Milogu, 100 © Grynka, 107 © Presian1801, 118 © Antoine2000, 120 © Demiurge, 125 © Finnegan, 127 © Monkeybusinessimages, 131 © Mirrormere, 133 © Arnphoto, 135 © Mrmessy2, 139 © Basphoto, 141 © Soundsnaps, 143 © Franckito, 146 © Dave_zilla, 149 © Davidmartyn, 152 © Synchronista, 155 © Tupungato, 159 © Davidmartyn, 161 © Tonybaggett, 162 © Rtimages, 163 © Fcarucci, 164 © Diliff, 166 © Wotan, 170 © Gstrange, 176 © Nsilcock, 183 © Elenarostunova, 187 © Presian1801, 189 © Kev303, 195 © Sampete, 197 © Patrickwang, 199 © Fintastique, 200 © Fintastique, 202 © Krustynutz, 216 © Donsimon, 218 © Jyothi, 225 © Marcpk, 227 © Tonybaggett, 230 © Oneworld-images, 254 © Mtoumbev, 261 © Antoine2000, 265 © Joegough, 271 © Leetorrens, 273 © Isselee, 275 © Elenarostunova, 276 © Royalblue, 279 © Grauzikas, 281 © Jank1000, 282 © Trombax, 284 © Pcutter, 286 © Elnur, 289 © Aworsdell, 299 © Aworsdell, 301 © Tonybaggett, 309 © Presian1801, 310 © Davidmartyn, 313 © Jaboardm, 315 © Hmproudlove, 316 © Lisasvara, 319 © Douglas_freer, 320 © Gumbao, 323 © Sampete, 325 © Sparkia, 329 © Jesse, 330 © Fintastique, 333 © Lanceb, 336 © Baloncici, 351 © Stfnsn, 357 © Garnham123, 359 © Internedko, 360 © Baloncici, 362 © Grieg & Stephenson,

CREDITS

367 © Teo73, 378 © Chrisharvey, 381 © Godrick, 385 © Mirrormere, 387 © Antoine2000, 393 © D50m10, 395 © 1000words, 396 © Miluxian, 398 © Scottyh, 400 © Danredrup, 405 © Markwr, 406 © Sampete, 411 © Mirohasch, 412 © Baralgin, 462 © Shazie28, 462 © Erickn, 463 © Nsilcock, 463 © Elkeflorida.

.com

© graham tomlin, 24 © Tim Jenner, 33 © Paul
k, 43 © EML, 47 © fred goldstein, 256 © Gabi
land, 263 © Michal Rosak, 296 © Salvador
pher Penler, 369 © Gelpi, 377 © Andresr, 409
Puchugin Dmitry, 463 © Zaporozhchenko Yury.

Birmingham City Council	C2 000 004 401020	Askev's	914.2104	AG
		Oct-2010	£15.95	ACOUK GREEN

2980029

LIVING & WORK

LONDC

What's it really like living and working in London? Not surpr
to life than bobbies, beefeaters and busbys! This book is guarₐ
introduction to the London way of life and, most importantly, it
and money. Regardless of whether you're planning to stay fₒ
indefinitely, *Living and Working in London* has been writte

PRINTED IN COLOUR!

Topics include:

- ♦ How to find a job with a good salary and conditions
- ♦ How to avoid and overcome problems on arrival
- ♦ How to find somewhere to live
- ♦ How to find the best schools
- ♦ How to obtain the best health treatment
- ♦ How to stretch your pounds further
- ♦ How to make the best use of public transport and much, much more.

Living and Working in London is the most comprehensive source of practical information available about everyday life in London. It's packed with over 350 pages of important and useful data, designed to help you avoid costly mistakes and save both time and money.

Buy your copy today at www.survivalbooks.net

Survival Books – The Expatriates' Best Friend